Stocks, Bonds, Bills, and Inflation

SBBI

2003 Yearbook
Market Results for 1926–2002

IbbotsonAssociates

Stocks, Bonds, Bills, and Inflation® 2003 Yearbook.

Stocks, Bonds, Bills, and Inflation® and SBBI® are registered trademarks of Ibbotson Associates.

Published by:

Ibbotson Associates
225 North Michigan Avenue, Suite 700
Chicago, Illinois 60601-7676
Telephone (312) 616-1620
Fax (312) 616-0404
www.ibbotson.com

ISBN 1-882864-16-6
ISSN 1047-2436

Additional copies of this Yearbook may be obtained for $110, plus shipping and handling, by calling or writing to the address above. Order forms are provided inside the back cover. Information about volume discounts, companion publications and consulting services may also be obtained. The data in this Yearbook are also available with our Analyst software, a Microsoft® Windows® application. Statistics and graphs can be quickly accessed over any subperiod. Updates can be obtained annually, semi-annually, quarterly or monthly. For more information about Analyst, call (800) 758-3557 or write to the address listed above.

Table of Contents

Most Commonly Used References

Graph/Table/Equation

List of Tables

(Text)

Chapter 8

Chapter 9

Chapter 10

Chapter 11

List of Graphs

(Text)

Chapter 9

Chapter 10

Chapter 11

List of Graphs
(Image)

Graph 1-1
The Decade: Wealth Indices of Investments in U.S. Stocks, Bonds, Bills, and Inflation (1992–2002). *Page 16.*

Graph 1-2
1993–2002 Annual and 2002 Monthly Total Returns: A Comparison of Large Company Stocks with Long-Term Government Bonds, and Small Company Stocks with Large Company Stocks. *Page 21.*

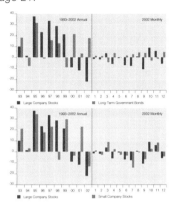

Graph 1-3
1993–2002 Annual and 2002 Monthly Total Returns: A Comparison of Long-Term Corporate Bonds with Long-Term Government Bonds, and Long-Term Government Bonds with Intermediate-Term Government Bonds. *Page 22.*

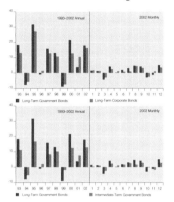

Graph 1-4
1993–2002 Annual and 2002 Monthly Total Returns: Treasury Bills, Inflation, and Real Riskless Rates of Return. *Page 23.*

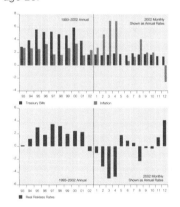

Table 2-1
Basic Series: Summary Statistics of Annual Total Returns. *Page 33.*

Series	Geometric Mean	Arithmetic Mean	Standard Deviation	Distribution
Large Company Stocks	10.2%	12.2%	20.5%	
Small Company Stocks	12.1	16.9	33.2	*
Long-Term Corporate Bonds	5.9	6.2	8.7	
Long-Term Government	5.5	5.8	9.4	
Intermediate-Term Government	5.4	5.6	5.8	
U.S. Treasury Bills	3.8	3.8	3.2	
Inflation	3.0	3.1	4.4	

–90%   0%   90%

*The 1933 Small Company Stocks Total Return was 142.9 percent.

Graph 2-1
Wealth Indices of Investments in the U.S. Capital Markets (1925–2002). *Page 28.*

Graph 3-1(a)
Large Company Stocks: Return Indices (1925–2002). *Page 54.*

Graph 3-1(b)
Large Company Stocks: Returns (1926–2002). *Page 54.*

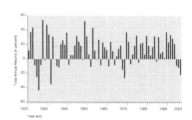

Graph 3-1(c)
Large Company Stocks: Yields (1926–2002). *Page 54.*

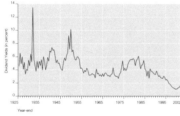

Graph 3-2(a)
Small Company Stocks: Return Index (1925–2002). *Page 56.*

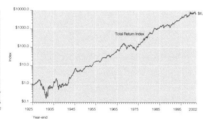

Graph 3-2(b)
Small Company Stocks: Returns (1926–2002). *Page 56.*

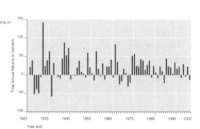

Graph 3-3(a)
Long-Term Corporate Bonds: Return Index (1925–2002). *Page 59.*

Graph 3-3(b)
Long-Term Corporate Bonds: Returns (1926–2002). *Page 59.*

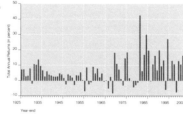

Graph 3-4(a)
Long-Term Government Bonds: Return Indices (1925–2002). *Page 60.*

Graph 3-4(b)
Long-Term Government Bonds: Returns (1926–2002). *Page 60.*

Graph 3-4(c)
Long-Term Government Bonds: Yields (1926–2002). *Page 60.*

Graph 3-5(a)
Intermediate-Term Government Bonds: Return Indices (1925–2002). *Page 62.*

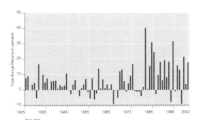

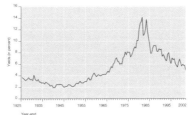

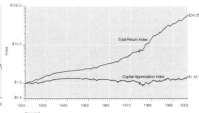

Graph 3-5(b)
Intermediate-Term Government Bonds: Returns (1926–2002). *Page 62.*

Graph 3-5(c)
Intermediate-Term Government Bonds: Yields (1926–2002). *Page 62.*

Graph 3-6(a)
U.S. Treasury Bills: Return Index (1925–2002). *Page 66.*

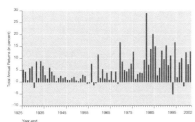

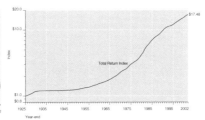

Graph 3-6(b)
U.S. Treasury Bills: Returns (1926–2002). *Page 66.*

Graph 3-7(a)
Inflation: Cumulative Index (1925–2002). *Page 68.*

Graph 3-7(b)
Inflation: Rates of Change (1926–2002). *Page 68.*

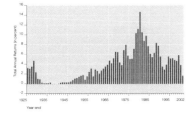

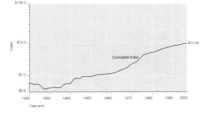

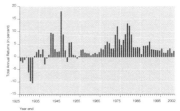

Graph 4-1
Equity Risk Premium Annual Returns (1926–2002). *Page 73.*

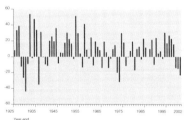

Graph 4-2
Small Stock Premium Annual Returns (1926–2002). *Page 74.*

Graph 4-3
Bond Default Premium Annual Returns (1926–2002). *Page 75.*

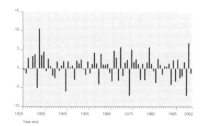

Graph 4-4
Bond Horizon Premium Annual Returns (1926–2002). *Page 77.*

Graph 4-5
Large Company Stocks: Real and Nominal Return Indices (1925–2002). *Page 78.*

Graph 4-6
Small Company Stocks: Real and Nominal Return Indices (1925–2002). *Page 80.*

Graph 4-7
Long-Term Corporate Bonds: Real and Nominal Return Indices (1925–2002). *Page 81.*

Graph 4-8
Long-Term Government Bonds: Real and Nominal Return Indices (1925–2002). *Page 83.*

Graph 4-9
Intermediate-Term Government Bonds: Real and Nominal Return Indices (1925–2002). *Page 84.*

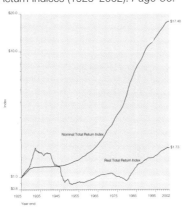
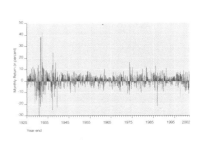
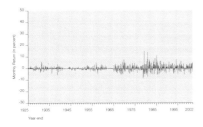

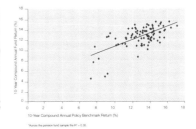

Graph 6-5a
Variation of Returns Across Funds
Explained by Asset Allocation.
Page 120.

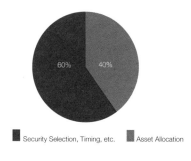

Graph 6-5b
Percentage of a Fund's Total Returns
Explained by Asset Allocation.
Page 120.

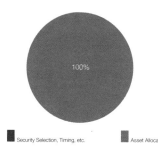

Graph 7-1
Size-Decile Portfolios of the NYSE/
AMEX/NASDAQ: Wealth Indices of
Investments in Mid-, Low-, Micro-, and
Total Capitalization Stocks (1925–2002).
Page 132.

Graph 7-2
Size-Decile Portfolios of the NYSE/
AMEX/NASDAQ: Security Market Line.
Page 136.

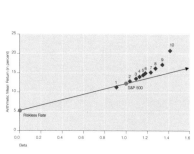

Graph 8-1
IA All Growth Stocks vs. IA All Value
Stocks (1967–2002). *Page 143.*

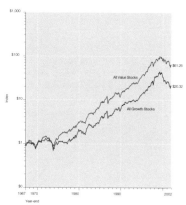

Graph 8-2
IA Large-cap Growth Stocks, IA Large-cap Value
Stocks, IA Mid-cap Growth Stocks, IA Mid-cap Value
Stocks, IA Small-cap Growth Stocks, IA Small-cap
Value Stocks, IA Micro-cap Growth Stocks, IA Micro-
cap Value Stocks (1967–2002). *Page 145.*

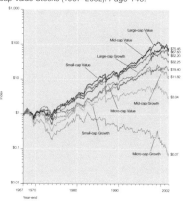

Graph 8-3
FF All Growth Stocks vs. FF All Value
Stocks (1927–2002). *Page 157.*

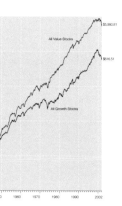

Graph 8-4
FF Small Value Stocks, FF Small Growth
Stocks, FF Large Value Stocks,
FF Large Growth Stocks (1927–2002).
Page 159.

Graph 9-1
Efficient Frontier: Large Company
Stocks, Long-Term Government Bonds,
and U.S. Treasury Bills. *Page 175.*

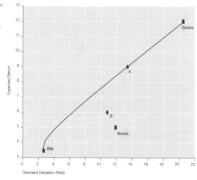

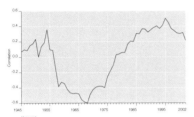

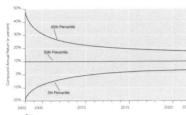

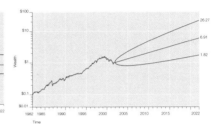

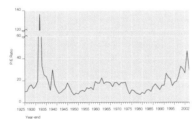

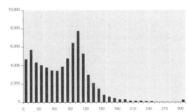

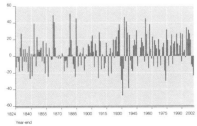

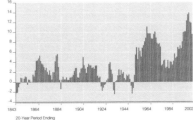

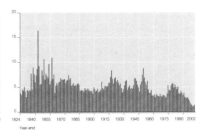

Graph 10-5
Large Company Stocks Annual Total Returns (1825–2002). *Page 200.*

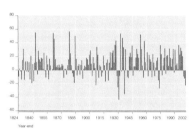

Graph 10-6
5-Year Rolling Standard Deviation for Large Company Stocks (1829–2002). *Page 201.*

Graph 10-7
Large Company Stocks (1824–2002). *Page 202.*

Graph 11-1
World Stock Market Capitalization (Year-End 2002). *Page 208.*

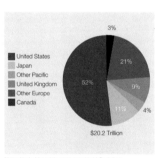

Graph 11-2
Global Investing (1969–2002). *Page 209.*

Graph 11-3
Total Return of U.S. Large Company Stocks and International Stocks: 10-Year Rolling Periods (1979–2002). *Page 210.*

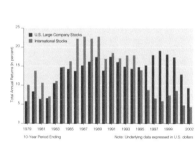

Graph 11-4
Best Performing Developed Stock Markets vs. U.S. Market (1993–2002). *Page 211.*

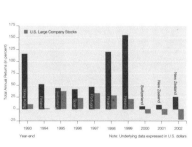

Graph 11-5
Benefits of Global Diversification (1969–2002). *Page 212.*

Graph 11-6
Rolling 60-Month Correlations: U.S. Large Company Stocks and International Stocks (1974–2002). *Page 213.*

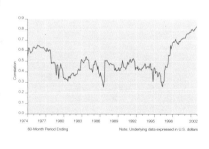

Graph 11-7
Efficient Frontier: U.S. Large Company
Stocks, Long-Term Government Bonds,
and International Stocks (1970–1985).
Page 214.

Graph 11-8
Efficient Frontier: U.S. Large Company
Stocks, Long-Term Government Bonds,
and International Stocks (1986–2002).
Page 215.

Graph 11-9
Global Stock Market Returns: Highest
and Lowest Historical Annual Returns
for Each Region (1970–2002).
Page 218.

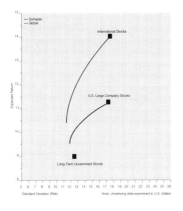

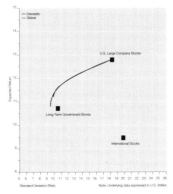

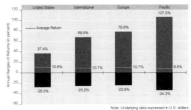

Acknowledgments

We thank, foremost, Roger G. Ibbotson, professor in the practice of finance at the Yale School of Management and chairman of Ibbotson Associates, for his contribution to this book. Professor Ibbotson and Rex A. Sinquefield, chairman of Dimensional Fund Advisors, Inc. (Santa Monica, CA), wrote the two journal articles and four books upon which this Yearbook is based and formulated much of the philosophy and methodology. Mr. Sinquefield also provides the small stock returns, as he has since 1982.

We thank others who contributed to this book. Rolf W. Banz provided the small stock returns for 1926–1981. Thomas S. Coleman (Greenwich, CT), Professor Lawrence Fisher of Rutgers University, and Roger Ibbotson constructed the model used to generate the intermediate-term government bond series for 1926–1933. The pioneering work of Professors Fisher and James H. Lorie of the University of Chicago inspired the original monograph. Stan V. Smith, President of the Corporate Financial Group, Ltd. and former Managing Director at Ibbotson Associates, originated the idea of the Yearbook and its companion update services. The Center for Research in Security Prices at the University of Chicago contributed the data and methodology for the returns on the NYSE by capitalization decile used in Chapter 7, Firm Size and Return. Ken French, of Dartmouth College, and Eugene Fama, of the University of Chicago, contributed the data and methodology for the returns on the growth and value portfolios. William N. Goetzmann and Liang Peng, both at the Yale School of Management, helped with the assembly of the New York Stock Exchange database for the period prior to 1926.

Design Staff

Scott Moore

Jim Hampton

Contributing Editors

Michael Barad

Edward Lopez

Anne Jablo

Devoki Dasgupta

Tara McDowell

Senior Editor

James Licato

Introduction

Who Should Read This Book

This book is a history of the returns on the capital markets in the United States from 1926 to the present. It is useful to a wide variety of readers. Foremost, anyone serious about investments or investing needs an appreciation of capital market history. Such an appreciation, which can be gained from this book, is equally valuable to the individual and institutional investor. For students at both the graduate and undergraduate levels, this book is both a source of ideas and a reference. Other intended readers include teachers of these students; practitioners and scholars in finance, economics, and business; portfolio strategists; and security analysts.

Chief financial officers and, in some cases, chief executive officers of corporations will find this book useful. More generally, persons concerned with history may find it valuable to study the detail of economic history as revealed in more than seven decades of capital market returns.

To these diverse readers, we provide two resources. One is the data. The other is a thinking person's guide to using historical data to understand the financial markets and make decisions. This historical record raises many questions. This book represents our way of appreciating the past—only one of the many possible ways—but one grounded in real theory. We provide a means for the reader to think about the past and the future of financial markets.

How to Read This Book

Intended Reader	Other Related Chapters	Chapters, Graphs, Tables, and Appendices
Persons Concerned with Data	Chapters 1, 2, 3, 10, and 11	Chapters 4, 7, and 8; Graphs 2-1, 10-7, and 11-2; Tables 2-1, 10-1, 10-2, 11-2, and 11-6; and Appendices A, B, and C
Financial Planners, Asset Allocators, and Investment Consultants	Chapters 1, 2, 8, 9, 10, and 11	Chapter 6; Graphs 2-1, 9-1, 10-7, and 11-2; and Tables 2-7, 6-6, 10-1,
Individual Investors	Chapters 1 and 2	Graph 2-1; and Table 2-1
Institutional Investors, Portfolio Managers, and Security Analysts	Chapters 1 through 11	Graphs 2-1, 10-7, and 11-2; Tables 2-7, 6-6, 7-1, 10-1, 10-2, 11-2, and 11-6
Students, Faculty, and Economists	Chapters 2, 5, 7, 8, 9, 10, and 11	Graphs 2-1, 10-7, and 11-2; Tables 6-6, 10-1, 10-2, 11-2, and 11-6
Brokers and Security Sales Representatives	Chapters 1 and 2	Graph 2-1; and Tables 2-1 and 2-5
Investment Bankers and Security Sales Representatives	Chapters 2, 7, 8, and 11	Table 2-1
Executives, Corporate Planners, Chief Financial Officers, Chief Executive Officers, and Treasurers	Chapters 1, 2, and 9	Chapters 1 and 2; and Graph 9-1
Pension Plan Sponsors	Chapters 1, 2, 6, and 9	Graph 2-1; and Tables 2-1 and 2-4

The Journal of Business published Roger G. Ibbotson and Rex A. Sinquefield's two companion papers on security returns in January 1976 and July 1976. In the first paper, the authors collected historical data on the returns from stocks, government and corporate bonds, U.S. Treasury bills, and consumer goods (inflation). To uncover the risk/return and the real/nominal relationship in the historical data, they presented a framework in which the return on an asset class is the sum of two or more elemental parts. These elements, such as real returns (returns in excess of inflation) and risk premia (for example, the net return from investing in large company stocks rather than bills), are referred to throughout the book as derived series.

In the second paper, the authors analyzed the time series behavior of the derived series and the information contained in the U.S. government bond yield curve to obtain inputs for a simulation model of future security price behavior. Using the methods developed in the two papers, they forecast security returns through the year 2000.

The response to these works showed that historical data are fascinating in their own right. Both total and component historical returns have a wide range of applications in investment management, corporate finance, academic research, and industry regulation. Subsequent work—the 1977, 1979, and 1982 Institute of Chartered Financial Analysts (ICFA) monographs; the 1989 Dow Jones-Irwin book; and Ibbotson Associates' 1983 through 2002 *Stocks, Bonds, Bills, and Inflation*™ *Yearbooks*—updated and further developed the historical data and forecasts. (All references to previous works used in the development of Stocks, Bonds, Bills, and Inflation [SBBI] data appear at the end of this introduction in the References section.)

In 1981, Ibbotson and Sinquefield began tracking a new asset class: small company stocks. This class consists of issues listed on the New York Stock Exchange (NYSE) that rank in the ninth and tenth (lowest) deciles when sorted by capitalization (price times number of shares outstanding), plus non-NYSE issues of comparable capitalization. This asset class has been of interest to researchers and investors because of its high long-term returns. Intermediate-term (five years to maturity) government bonds were added in 1988. Monthly and annual total returns, income returns, capital appreciation returns, and yields are presented.

The Stocks, Bonds, Bills, and Inflation 2003 Yearbook

In the present volume the historical data are updated. The motivations are: 1) to document this history of security market returns; 2) to uncover the relationships between the various asset class returns as revealed by the derived series: inflation, real interest rates, risk premia, and other premia; 3) to encourage deeper understanding of the underlying economic history through the graphic presentation of data; and 4) to answer questions most frequently asked by subscribers.

In keeping with the spirit of the previous work, the asset classes contained in this edition highlight the differences between targeted segments of the financial markets in the United States. Our intent is to show historical trade-offs between risk and return. International data was introduced in the 2002 edition.

In this book, the equity markets are segmented between large and small company stocks. Fixed income markets are segmented on two dimensions. Riskless U.S. government securities are differentiated by maturity or investment horizon. U.S. Treasury bills with approximately 30 days to maturity are used to describe the short end of the horizon; U.S. Treasury securities with approximately five years to maturity are used to describe the middle horizon segment; and U.S. Treasury securities with approximately 20 years to maturity are used to describe the long maturity end of the market. A corporate bond series with a long maturity is used to describe fixed income securities that contain risk of default.

Some indices of the stock and bond markets are broad, capturing most or all of the capitalization of the market. Our indices are intentionally narrow. The large company stock series captures the largest issues (those in the Standard & Poor's 500 Composite Index), while the small company stock series is composed of the smallest issues. By studying these polar cases, we identify the small stock premium (small minus large stock returns) and the premium of large stocks over bonds and bills. Neither series is intended to be representative of the entire stock market. Likewise, our long-term government bond and U.S. Treasury bill indices show the returns for the longest and shortest ends of the yield curve, rather than the return for the entire Treasury float. Readers and investors should understand that our bond indices do not, and are not intended to, describe the experience of the typical bond investor who is diversified across maturities; rather, we present returns on carefully focused segments of the market for U.S. Treasury securities.

Recent Changes and Additions

A significant addition to this Classic Edition is a revamped Chapter 8, "Growth and Value Investing." We have included expanded analysis of growth and value performance data, with a new construction methodology presented and discussed.

We are also pleased to add an overview of Monte Carlo simulation. We explore the technique itself and cover the various types and uses. This can be found in Chapter 9, "Using Historical Data in Forecasting and Optimization."

The SBBI Data Series

The series presented here are total returns, and where applicable or available, capital appreciation returns and income returns for:

SBBI Data Series	Series Construction	Index Components	Maturity Approximate
1. Large Company Stocks	S&P 500 Composite with dividends reinvested. (S&P 500, 1957–Present; S&P 90, 1926–1956)	Total Return Income Return Capital Appreciation Return	N/A
2. Small Company Stocks	Fifth capitalization quintile of stocks on the NYSE for 1926–1981. Performance of the Dimensional Fund Advisors (DFA) Small Company Fund 1982–March 2001. Performance of the DFA Micro Cap Fund April 2001-Present.	Total Return	N/A
3. Long-Term Corporate Bonds	Salomon Brothers Long-Term High Grade Corporate Bond Index	Total Return	20 Years
4. Long-Term Government Bonds	A One-Bond Portfolio	Total Return Income Return Capital Appreciation Return Yield	20 Years
5. Intermediate-Term Government Bonds	A One-Bond Portfolio	Total Return Income Return Capital Appreciation Return Yield	5 Years
6. U.S. Treasury Bills	A One-Bill Portfolio	Total Return	30 Days
7. Consumer Price Index	CPI—All Urban Consumers, not seasonally adjusted	Inflation Rate	N/A

References

1. Stocks, Bonds, Bills, and Inflation Yearbook, annual.

   1983, 1984, 1985, 1986, 1987, 1988, 1989, 1990, 1991, 1992, 1993, 1994, 1995, 1996, 1997, 1998, 1999, 2000, 2001, 2002.

   Ibbotson Associates, Chicago.

2. Banz, Rolf W.

   "The Relationship Between Return and Market Value of Common Stocks,"

   Journal of Financial Economics 9:3–18, 1981.

3. Brinson, Gary P., L. Randolph Hood, and Gilbert P. Beebower

   "Determinants of Portfolio Performance,"

   Financial Analysts Journal, July/August 1986.

4. Brinson, Gary P., Brian D. Singer, and Gilbert P. Beebower

   "Determinants of Portfolio Performance II,"

   Financial Analysts Journal, May/June 1991.

5. Coleman, Thomas S., Lawrence Fisher, and Roger G. Ibbotson

   Historical U.S. Treasury Yield Curves 1926–1992 with 1994 update,

   Ibbotson Associates, Chicago, 1994.

6. Coleman, Thomas S., Lawrence Fisher, and Roger G. Ibbotson

   U.S. Treasury Yield Curves 1926–1988,

   Moody's Investment Service, New York, 1990.

7. Cottle, Sidney, Roger F. Murray, and Frank E. Block

   "Graham and Dodd's Security Analysis,"

   Fifth Edition, McGraw-Hill, 1988.

8. Cowles, Alfred

   Common Stock Indices,

   Principia Press, Bloomington, 1939.

9. Goetzmann, William N., Roger G. Ibbotson, and Liang Peng

   "A New Historical Database for the NYSE 1815 to 1925: Performance and Predictability,"

   Journal of Financial Markets, December 2000.

10. Ibbotson, Roger G., and Rex A. Sinquefield

    Speech to the Center for Research in Security Prices, May 1974.

11. Ibbotson, Roger G., and Paul D. Kaplan

    "Does Asset Allocation Policy Explain 40, 90, or 100 Percent of Performance?,"

    Financial Analysts Journal, January/February 2000.

12. Ibbotson, Roger G., and Peng Chen

    "Stock Market Returns in the Long Run: Participating in the Real Economy."

    Financial Analysts Journal, January/February 2003.

13. Ibbotson, Roger G., and Rex A. Sinquefield (foreword by Jack L. Treynor)

    Stocks, Bonds, Bills, and Inflation: The Past (1926–1976) and the Future (1977–2000), 1977 ed.,

    Institute of Chartered Financial Analysts, Charlottesville, VA, 1977.

14. Ibbotson, Roger G., and Rex A. Sinquefield, (foreword by Laurence B. Siegel)

    Stocks, Bonds, Bills, and Inflation: The Past and the Future, 1982 ed.,

Institute of Chartered Financial Analysts, Charlottesville, VA, 1982.

15. **Ibbotson, Roger G., and Rex A. Sinquefield**

    Stocks, Bonds, Bills, and Inflation: Historical Returns (1926–1987), 1989 ed.,

    Dow-Jones Irwin, Homewood, IL, 1989.

16. **Ibbotson, Roger G., and Rex A. Sinquefield**

    Stocks, Bonds, Bills, and Inflation: Historical Returns (1926–1978),

    Institute of Chartered Financial Analysts, Charlottesville, VA, 1979.

17. **Ibbotson, Roger G., and Rex A. Sinquefield**

    "Stocks, Bonds, Bills, and Inflation: Year-By-Year Historical Returns (1926–1974),"

    The Journal of Business 49, No. 1 (January 1976), pp. 11–47.

18. **Ibbotson, Roger G., and Rex A. Sinquefield**

    "Stocks, Bonds, Bills, and Inflation: Simulations of the Future (1976–2000),"

    The Journal of Business 49, No. 3 (July 1976), pp. 313–338.

19. **Levy, Haim, and Deborah Gunthorpe**

    "Optimal Investment Proportions in Senior Securities and Equities Under Alternative Holding Periods,"

    Journal of Portfolio Management, Summer 1993, page 33.

20. **Lewis, Alan L., Sheen T. Kassouf, R. Dennis Brehm, and Jack Johnston**

    "The Ibbotson-Sinquefield Simulation Made Easy,"

    The Journal of Business 53, No. 2 (1980), pp. 205–214.

21. **Markowitz, Harry M.**

    Portfolio Selection: Efficient Diversification of Investments,

    John Wiley & Sons, New York, 1959.

22. **Nuttall, Jennifer A., and John Nuttall**

    "Asset Allocation Claims—Truth or Fiction?," (unpublished), 1998.

23. **Sharpe, William F.**

    "The Arithmetic of Active Management,"

    Financial Analysts Journal, January/February 1991.

24. **Stevens, Dale H., Ronald J. Surz, and Mark E. Wimer**

    "The Importance of Investment Policy,"

    The Journal of Investing, Winter 1999.

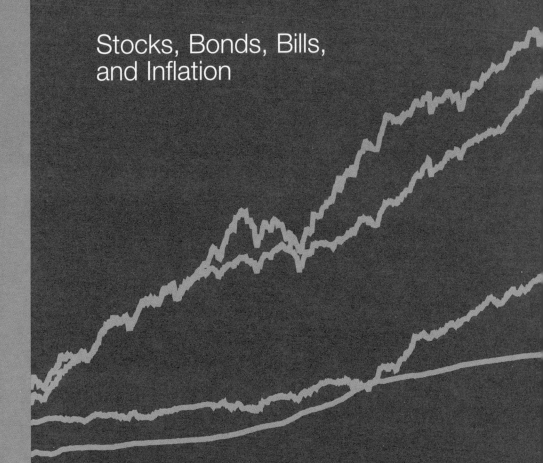

Stocks, Bonds, Bills, and Inflation

Chapters

IbbotsonAssociates

Chapter 1

Highlights of the 2002 Markets and the Past Decade

Events of 2002

The stock market in the year 2002 was marked with extreme volatility and produced returns well below historical averages. Both large and small company stocks posted negative returns for the year 2002, with small company stocks finishing the year ahead of large company stocks. This marked the third straight year of negative total returns for large company stocks after a nine-year period of positive total returns.

Bonds had a great year, producing returns well above their historical averages. Yields on all categories of bonds declined in 2002. The Federal Reserve lowered its fed funds rate on only one occasion during the past year. This important benchmark for borrowing, after the .50 percent reduction, ended the year at 1.25 percent. Last year, the Federal Reserve lowered the fed funds rate on 11 separate occasions. The rationale behind such drops is that lower interest rates should help improve the economy and corporate profits, both of which, in turn, should push stock prices higher. Large and small company stocks, however, stumbled throughout 2002.

Economic Growth

The Gross Domestic Product (GDP), a measure of the market value of all goods and services produced within the U.S., grew at a real (inflation-adjusted) rate of 2.4 percent for 2002. This rate of growth was higher than the revised growth rate for 2001 of 0.3 percent.

The U.S. civilian unemployment rate reached its highest level since August 1994 and barely budged since December 2001. From a rate of 5.8 percent at year-end 2001, unemployment rose to 6.0 percent by year-end 2002. The tightening of the job market did not appear to have a strong impact on wage inflation, with average hourly earnings up from the previous year.

War on Terror

Despite various war efforts throughout Afghanistan, signs indicate that the al Qaeda network has remained active and continues to operate. Authorities have connected the organization to a series of terrorist attacks—and foiled attempts—since the September 11 tragedy. President George Bush has stated on a number of occasions that he firmly believes al Qaeda will attack anywhere they can in an attempt to disrupt a civil society.

Homeland Security Bill

The Senate approved a bill that will create a Department of Homeland Security and President Bush subsequently signed the bill into law. The approval comes after months of debate between the Republican and Democratic parties. The Cabinet-level department is expected to be up and running within a year. The department's main function will be to protect the United States from all forms of terrorism and will employ about 170,000 federal workers from 22 agencies.

Iraqi Situation Intensifies

On November 13, Iraq accepted a new United Nations resolution that calls for the return of weapons inspectors to the country after nearly four years. Iraq hopes that its acceptance of the resolution will help to evade the lingering threat of war. The resolution permits inspectors to inspect anywhere at any time for weapons of mass destruction. Despite Iraq's continued reiteration that it has no weapons of mass destruction, the Bush administration argues against the declaration and states that it is full of holes.

WorldCom's Fall

WorldCom Inc. filed for Chapter 11 bankruptcy protection in July and acknowledged that it hid costs and inflated profits by more than $9 billion over four years. This has become one of the largest cases of accounting fraud in U.S. corporate history. The Securities and Exchange Commission has filed additional civil fraud charges against WorldCom, while stating that the company led investors astray for more years than it had previously revealed. The SEC said the fraud goes back to early 1999. WorldCom continues to claim that the scandal will not affect its service or its ability to emerge from Chapter 11.

Arthur Andersen Sentenced

Federal prosecutors charged Arthur Andersen with obstruction of a Securities and Exchange Commission investigation into Enron Corp.'s demise by its role in shredding tons of documents. The 89-year old accounting firm, once the fifth largest, has surrendered its licenses to practice accounting in every U.S. state, and a majority of its roughly 28,000 employees were left without jobs. Chicago-based Andersen was found guilty on June 16 of one count of obstruction linked to the destruction of Enron documents. The firm was subsequently fined $500,000 and sentenced to five years' probation. Federal criminal and civil investigations persist. Enron creditors and shareholders have sued Andersen, while its overseas partnerships settled with Enron shareholders for $60 million. The company plans to appeal its criminal conviction.

Enron Debacle

Enron has been accused by prosecutors and regulators of creating off-the-books partnerships along with employing aggressive accounting methods to conceal massive debt in an effort to inflate the firm's bottom line. Enron auditor Arthur Andersen was accused of destroying documents applicable to the investigation (see above). Former Enron Corp. Chief Financial Officer Andrew S. Fastow was indicted on 78 counts of federal fraud, conspiracy, and money laundering. Mr. Fastow pleaded not guilty to the 78-count indictment.

Sarbanes-Oxley Act

President Bush signed the Sarbanes-Oxley Act of 2002 into law on July 30, 2002, creating the most radical redesign of federal securities laws since the 1930s. Some of the key points of the act include a number of provisions pertaining to executive officers and directors of public companies. These include certification of financial reports by CEOs and CFOs, a ban on personal loans to executive officers and directors, accelerated reporting of trades by insiders, and more. Another key section of the act centers on public company disclosures and requires, among other things, that each company to disclose "on a rapid and current basis" additional information about the company's financial condition or operations as the SEC determines is necessary, useful to investors, or in the public interest. The SEC must also adopt rules that impose certain requirements on audit committees' functions and role. Each audit committee must be composed entirely of independent directors and will be responsible for the appointment, compensation, and oversight of the work of the auditor. Other aspects include criminal and civil penalties for securities violations, attorney obligation to report violations, personal loans to executives, and acceleration on insider reporting.

SEC Resignations

Securities and Exchange Commission Chairman Harvey Pitt quit, leaving a huge hole for President Bush to fill. The chairman failed to notify the White House or fellow commissioners that his choice to head a new accounting industry oversight board, William Webster, was himself under investigation in a corporate accounting mess. Robert Herdman, the Securities and Exchange Commission's chief accountant, resigned three days after Pitt announced his resignation. Herdman helped in Webster's selection. Webster said he intends to step aside as chairman prior to the board's first official meeting. Former investment banker William Donaldson was chosen by Bush as the new Securities and Exchange Commission Chairman.

Republicans Take Control of Congress

President George W. Bush and the Republican Party made history at the congressional midterm elections. The Republican Party seized control of the Senate and maintained its dominance in the House of Representatives. This marked the first time that a Republican president's party did not lose House seats in a midterm election. With the increase of Republicans in office, Bush should find it easier to push his own legislation through Congress.

Microsoft Antitrust Case

Microsoft Corp. emerged victorious in its long-running antitrust battle as U.S. District Court Judge Colleen Kollar-Kotelly approved nearly all elements of a proposed settlement reached by the Justice Department and nine states late last year. She also delivered a strict warning to Microsoft that it must follow the letter of the settlement. Microsoft founder Bill Gates said he was "personally committed" to abide by the agreement, which he called "a good compromise and good settlement." West Virginia has joined Massachusetts in an appeal of the U.S. District Court decision. Microsoft and the government settled the case late last year. Congress and competitors of Microsoft criticized the settlement citing its failure to restrain the company's power. The settlement included software-disclosure requirements, greater freedom for personal-computer makers to use rival software, and banned some forms of commercial retaliation by Microsoft.

Conseco Files for Bankruptcy

Conseco Inc. filed a voluntary petition for bankruptcy-court protection, becoming the third largest, in terms of assets, to do so behind WorldCom Inc. and Enron Corp. Also, the struggling company announced that it would sell the assets and operations of Conseco Finance Corp. to CFN Investment Holdings LLC. The proposed purchase price, which was agreed to in principle, would be equal to the outstanding amount of Conseco's secured debt as of the deal's close. The insurance operations of the firm were excluded from the proceedings and are expected to regain financial stability.

United Airlines Files for Bankruptcy

The parent company of United Airlines, UAL Corp., filed for bankruptcy in the U.S. Bankruptcy Court, becoming the largest U.S. airline to do so. The world's second-largest airline completed a financing package in advance of the filing under Chapter 11 of the Federal Bankruptcy Code. The package will ensure that the carrier can continue to fly as it restructures its operations in court. United currently operates 1,800 daily flights serving 117 cities in 26 countries. There are approximately 80,000 United employees. United had originally requested $1.8 billion in federal loan guarantees but was rejected.

Consumer Confidence Drops

Declining stock prices, fading job prospects, and the threat of war with Iraq have all taken a toll on consumer confidence. The widely followed and tracked index of consumer confidence plummeted to 79.6 in October, a 14.1-point plunge and the worst level since 1994. Surveys find Americans increasingly depressed and low-spirited about both the current economic situation and what the future may hold. The Consumer Confidence Survey is based on a representative sample of 5,000 U.S. households.

European Union Expansion

The European Union (EU) will add 10 new Central European countries to the current 15 nations, creating the world's largest trading bloc. The new countries are scheduled to join in May 2004. With a grouping of 445 million consumers, export and investment opportunities for companies outside Europe are likely to open. The North American Free Trade Agreement (Nafta), a bloc comprising the U.S., Canada, and Mexico, is home to 416 million people. The EU figures to surpass Nafta in terms of population after expanding, but the North American bloc will remain the richest. Total gross domestic product there stands at about $11.4 trillion compared to the $8.4 trillion of the EU after expansion.

Mergers and Acquisitions

Merger and acquisition activity in the United States for the year 2002 was less than last year's total in terms of value and number of deals, due mainly to the numerous accounting scandals, a struggling economy, poor earnings, and global uncertainty. Globally, the same results were encountered. Companies that did merge or acquire others have hopes for potential growth opportunities and possible market share gains. Other companies did so in an effort to sell assets in order to raise money or with a desire to return to their core business. All in all, the main goal is to become more competitive. The year ended with a few big deals giving dealmakers hope and optimism for a recovery in 2003.

The health care industry witnessed the proposed merger of Pfizer Inc. and Pharmacia Corp. Pfizer agreed to acquire Pharmacia in July in a deal valued then at about $60 billion. Pfizer, the world's largest drug company, would further distance itself from the rest of the industry with such an acquisition. The transaction would create a company with more than $40 billion in yearly sales. Industry analysts maintain that the product overlap between the two firms is minimal. Anthem Inc. acquired Trigon Healthcare Inc. for about $4 billion in cash and stock. The merger decisively positions Anthem as the fifth largest publicly traded health insurance company in the United States. Anthem will secure its first foothold in the southeastern U.S. by acquiring Richmond-based Trigon, as well as

Trigon's expertise and knowledge in selling specialty insurance products such as dental and life insurance plans.

The banking and financial services industry experienced the largest U.S. cross-border deal of the year and the largest financial merger since early last year. HSBC Holdings PLC, the world's second-largest banking company, agreed to purchase consumer lender Household International, Inc. for around $15 billion. Such a move is an unusual course of action for London-based HSBC, widely recognized as a frugal corporation and for its aversion to flashy deals. Household currently stands as one of the biggest U.S. lenders to individuals with poor credit history—a market where HSBC lacks experience. HSBC believes the deal will give the company nationwide presence in the United States along with 50 million new customers. Its earnings stream in the U.S., Europe, and Asia should be better balanced as a result. Credit Agricole offered to buy French rival Credit Lyonnais in a cash-and-stock deal valued at around $16.9 billion. The acquisition would create one of Europe's biggest financial institutions and would produce the largest bank in the euro zone, which consists of the 12 European countries that use the euro as a currency. The merged company will shift its main focus from investment banking to other areas such as higher-value-added retail banking, specialist financial services, and asset management. Citigroup Inc., in an attempt to enhance its branch-banking presence on the West Coast, acquired Golden State Bancorp of San Francisco in a deal estimated at around $5.8 billion in stock and cash. Golden State is the parent company of Cal Fed, the country's second-largest thrift behind Washington Mutual Inc. of Seattle. In addition to being the parent of Cal Fed, Golden State is also the parent of First Nationwide Mortgage, the nation's eighth-largest mortgage servicer. Manulife Financial Corp. launched a hostile attempt to acquire Canada Life Financial Corp. for around $4 billion in a cash and stock deal that would produce the fourth-largest insurance company in North America. The combined corporation would stand to have sizeable operations in Canada, the U.S., Asia, and Europe. Shareholders approved M&T Bank's purchase of Allfirst Financial, the American subsidiary of Allied Irish Banks PLC, for $3.1 billion in cash and stock. The move expands M&T's presence from upstate New York to rapid-growing Middle Atlantic states such as Maryland and Virginia. M&T will also benefit from Allfirst's profitable trust management business. The deal will place M&T as one of the 20 largest banks in the U.S., with $49 billion in total deposits.

The consumer products industry saw South African Breweries, a producer of malt beverages and soft drinks, acquire Miller Brewing Co. from Philip Morris Companies Inc., making it the world's second largest brewer and doubling its share of the global beer market. Competition in the U.S. beer market historically has been quite intense; thus a significant level of risk accompanies such an acquisition. The deal was estimated at around $5.6 billion. Cadbury Schweppes PLC announced an agreement to purchase Adams, a manufacturer of chewing gum and cough drops, from Pfizer Inc. for $4.2 billion in cash. Cadbury stated that the acquisition would make it the number one producer in the global confectionery market, slightly ahead of Mars Inc. and Nestle. The pact would also place Cadbury only behind Wm. Wrigley Jr. Co. in the chewing gum market. Coca-Cola Femsa SA de CV, Coke's largest Mexican bottler, agreed to acquire Panamerican Beverages Inc. for $2.72 billion, plus the assumption of $880 million of Panamerican debt. Once approved, the deal will create the world's second-largest Coca-Cola bottler, behind Coca-Cola Enterprises. Swiss food giant Nestle acquired Chef America Inc., a maker of hand-held pastry snacks, in a deal amounting to $2.6 billion.

Such an acquisition should enable the Swiss company to improve in lower-growth categories such as chocolate and coffee. The deal will also enable Nestle to become the clear leader in two of the three main frozen food categories in the United States. Nestle also merged its U.S. ice cream business with U.S. market leader Dreyer's Grand Ice Cream, Inc. in exchange for $2.4 billion in stock. The new combination will unite the Dreyer's brand with Nestle's Haagen-Dazs and compete closely with Anglo-Dutch group Unilever as the world's largest seller of ice cream by value of sales. H.J. Heinz Co. agreed to spin off and merge its U.S. and Canadian pet food, U.S. tuna and retail private label soup, and U.S. infant feeding businesses with Del Monte Foods Co. in a deal valued at $2.5 billion. Del Monte expects the deal to improve its ability to market its products to consumers due to an increased presence now in grocery stores. Diageo PLC announced that it will sell Burger King Corp., the nation's number two burger chain, to a group led by Texas Pacific Group for $1.5 billion, less than the $2.26 billion originally negotiated in July. Diageo plans to focus on its core liquor business and has been determined to sell or spin off Burger King for the past two years. As far as failed attempts go, Wm. Wrigley Jr. Co.'s effort to buy Hershey Food Corp. for more than $12.5 billion was aborted. The trust that controls Hershey decided to pull Hershey off of the selling block, mainly because of local opposition to the sale. This is just one prime example of how difficult it became to get deals negotiated and finalized this past year.

In other news, Northrop Grumann Corp. agreed to purchase rival TRW Inc. for around $6.7 billion. The combination of these two companies will create the nation's second-largest military/defense contractor, passing up Boeing Co. and leaving it behind only Lockheed Martin Corp. After the acquisition is completed, Northrop plans to sell TRW's automotive business to Blackstone Group for $4.13 billion in cash and equity. International Business Machines (IBM) acquired the consulting division of PricewaterhouseCoopers LLP in a $3.5 billion cash-and-stock deal. The combination will secure IBM Business Consulting Services as the world's largest consulting services organization, operating in more than 160 countries. IBM also agreed to acquire Rational Software Corp., a provider of tools and services for software development, for about $2.1 billion in cash. This marks IBM's largest software acquisition since it purchased Lotus Development in 1995 for $3.5 billion. It is said to fit in with IBM's approach of selling infrastructure software utilized by companies to run their computer operations.

IPOs Hit Two-Decade Low

2002 turned out to be yet another dismal year for initial public offerings. Both the number of companies and the equity capital raised were down compared to the prior year. The number of IPOs hit a two-decade low. Underwriters and analysts are hoping for better market conditions in the coming year to fuel the 2003 IPO market. In 1999 and 2000, new issues were numbering in the hundreds and investors were making a fortune. The last two years have proven to be quite the opposite. Many companies preparing for an initial public offering have simply decided to wait for a better market environment. The backlog of initial public offerings at the start of 2003 has stirred up cautious optimism. Only time will tell.

Results of 2002 Capital Markets

Large Company Stocks

The market for U.S. large company stocks is represented here by the total return on the S&P 500. (The total return includes reinvestment of dividends.) Large company stocks for the year produced a total return of –22.10 percent, which is substantially below the long-term average return (1926 to 2002) of 10.20 percent. Only four of the twelve months between January and December 2002 produced positive returns. The month of October produced the highest return at 8.80 percent while the month of September produced the lowest return at –10.87 percent. The year 2002 marked the third straight year of negative total returns after a five-year stretch (from 1995 to 1999) in which large company stocks produced returns that were substantially above the long-term average return.

Considering the relatively poor performance of the market this past year, an index of large company stock total returns, initialized at $1.00 on December 31, 1925, closed down versus the previous year. The index dropped to $1,775.34 by the end of 2002, compared with $2,279.13 a year earlier.

Small Company Stocks

Small company stocks outperformed the equities of larger companies for the fourth year in a row, with a total return of –13.28 percent. Five of the twelve months between January and December 2002 produced positive returns. The month of March produced the highest return at 8.84 percent while the month of July produced the lowest return at –14.48 percent. The small stock premium, or geometric difference of small over large stocks, was a positive 11.33 percent (versus 39.33 percent the previous year).

The cumulative wealth index, initialized at $1.00 at the end of 1925, closed well below the previous year. The index fell to $6,816.41 by the end of 2002, compared with $7,860.05 a year earlier.

Bond Yields Fall

Yields on all categories of bonds declined in 2002. Intermediate-term rates fell more than long-term rates. Intermediate-term bonds increased in value more than their long-term counterparts.

Long-Term Government Bonds

Long-term government bonds (with maturity near 20 years) returned 17.84 percent in 2002. This return was well above the 2001 annual return of 3.70 percent and ranks as the ninth highest annual total return since 1926. The yield on long-term government bonds was 4.84 percent compared to 5.75 percent at year-end 2001. The year-end 2002 yield was the lowest since 1966, which produced a year-end yield of 4.55 percent.

The wealth index of long-term government bonds, initialized at $1.00 at year-end 1925, grew to $59.70 by the end of December 2002. The capital appreciation index of long-term government bond returns closed at $1.04, which is substantially less than its all-time high of $1.43 reached in early 1946.

Graph 1-1

The Decade: Wealth Indices of Investments in U.S. Stocks, Bonds, Bills, and Inflation
Year-End 1992 = $1.00

from December 1992 to December 2002

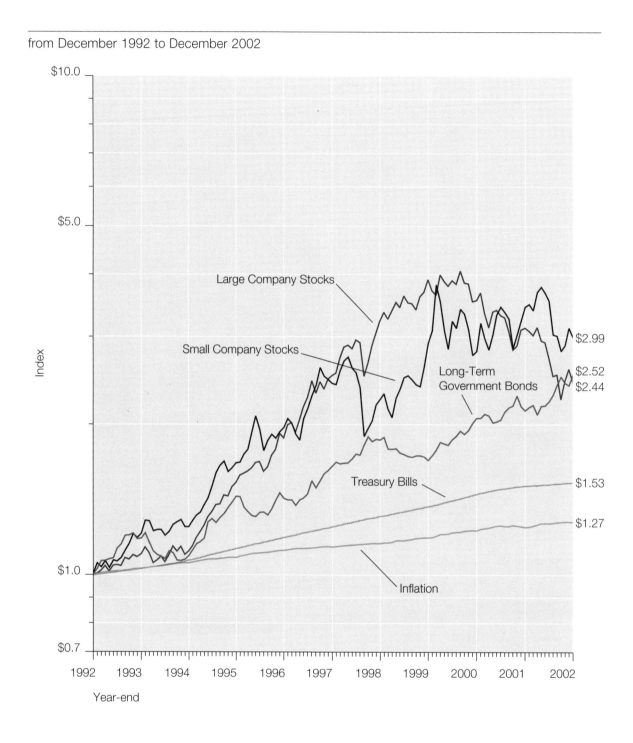

Year-end

Intermediate-Term Government Bonds

The total return on intermediate-term government bonds (with maturity 5 years) in 2002 was 12.93 percent. This return is much higher than the average return over the past 77 years of 5.44 percent. The highest year-end return was 29.10 achieved in 1982. The yield on intermediate-term government bonds was 2.61 percent compared to 4.42 percent at year-end 2001. The year-end 2002 yield was the lowest since 1954, which produced a year-end yield of 1.72 percent.

The wealth index of intermediate-term government bonds, initialized at $1.00 at year-end 1925, rose to $59.05 at the end of December 2002.

Long-Term Corporate Bonds

Long-term corporate bonds (with maturity near 20 years), as well as their government counterparts, experienced a great year, producing a year-end total return of 16.33 percent. Total returns were positive in ten of the twelve months during the year, with the highest being 4.52 percent, which was achieved in August.

The year-end bond default premium, or net return from investing in long-term corporate bonds rather than long-term government bonds of equal maturity, was –1.28 percent, compared to 6.70 percent in 2001. This is lower than that of its long-term (1926–2002) average of 0.42 percent. A dollar invested in long-term corporate bonds at year-end 1925, rose to $82.48 by the end of December 2002.

Treasury Bills

An investment in bills with approximately 30 days to maturity had a total return of 1.65 percent, well below its long-term average (1926–2002) of 3.79 percent. The cumulative index of Treasury bill total returns ended the year at $17.48, compared with $17.20 a year earlier. Because monthly Treasury bill returns are nearly always positive, each monthly index value typically sets a new all-time high.

Inflation

Consumer prices rose 2.38 percent in 2002, which is higher than the prior year but lower than the long-term historical average (1926–2002) of 3.05 percent. Inflation has remained below 5 percent for twenty of the last twenty-one years (inflation was above 5 percent in 1990).

A cumulative inflation index, initialized at $1.00 at year-end 1925, finished 2002 at $10.09, up from $9.86 at year-end 2001. That is, a "basket" of consumer goods and services that cost $1.00 in 1925 would cost $10.09 today. The two baskets are not identical, but are intended to be comparable.

A Graphic View of the Decade

The past decade, 1993–2002, has been characterized by a robust rate of increase in stock prices. The last three years, however, produced negative returns for large company stocks. Small company stocks posted a negative return in 2002. Both large and small company stocks produced a positive annual total return in seven of the past ten years.

Graph 1-1 shows the market results for the past decade—illustrating the growth of $1.00 invested on December 31, 1992 in stocks, bonds, and bills, along with an index of inflation. A review of the major themes of the past decade, as revealed in the capital markets, appears later in this chapter.

The Decade in Perspective

The great stock and bond market rise of the 1980s and 1990s was one of the most unusual in the history of the capital markets. In terms of the magnitude of the rise, these decades most closely resembled the 1920s and 1950s. These four decades accounted for a majority of the market's cumulative total return over the past 77 years. While the importance of a long-term view of investing is noted consistently in this book and elsewhere, the counterpart of this observation is: To achieve high returns on your investments, you only need to participate in the few periods of truly outstanding return. The bull markets of 1922 to mid-1929, 1949–1961 (roughly speaking, the Fifties), mid-1982 to mid-1987, and 1991–1999 were such periods. The 2000s have gotten off to a poor start for large company stocks—producing negative returns in 2000, 2001, and 2002. Small company stocks posted a negative return in 2000 as well as 2002. The bond market has performed quite well.

Table 1-1

Compound Annual Rates of Return by Decade (in percent)

	1920s*	1930s	1940s	1950s	1960s	1970s	1980s	1990s	2000s**	1993-02
Large Company	19.2	–0.1	9.2	19.4	7.8	5.9	17.5	18.2	–14.6	9.3
Small Company	–4.5	1.4	20.7	16.9	15.5	11.5	15.8	15.1	0.9	11.6
Long-Term Corporate	5.2	6.9	2.7	1.0	1.7	6.2	13.0	8.4	13.3	8.8
Long-Term Government	5.0	4.9	3.2	–0.1	1.4	5.5	12.6	8.8	14.1	9.7
Intermediate-Term Government	4.2	4.6	1.8	1.3	3.5	7.0	11.9	7.2	11.0	7.3
Treasury Bills	3.7	0.6	0.4	1.9	3.9	6.3	8.9	4.9	3.8	4.4
Inflation	–1.1	–2.0	5.4	2.2	2.5	7.4	5.1	2.9	2.4	2.5

*Based on the period 1926–1929.

**Based on the period 2000–2002.

Table 1-1 compares the returns by decade on all of the basic asset classes covered in this book. It is notable that either large company stocks or small company stocks were the best performing asset class in every full decade save one. In this table, the Twenties cover the period 1926–1929 and the 2000s cover the period 2000–2002.

It is interesting to place the decades of superior performance in historical context. The Twenties were preceded by mediocre returns and high inflation and were followed by the most devastating stock market crash and economic depression in American history. This sequence of events mitigated the impact of the Twenties bull market on investor wealth. Nevertheless, the stock market became a liquid secondary market in the Twenties, rendering that period important for reasons other than return. In contrast, the Fifties were preceded and followed by decades with roughly average equity returns. The Eighties were preceded by a decade of "stagflation" where modest stock price gains were seriously eroded by inflation and were followed by a period of stability in the Nineties.

The bond market performance of the Eighties and Nineties has no precedent. Bond yields, which had risen consistently since the 1940s, reached unprecedented levels in 1980–1981. (Other countries experiencing massive inflation have had correspondingly high interest rates.) Never before having had so far to fall, bond yields dropped further and faster than at any other time, producing what is indisputably the greatest bond bull market in history. Unfortunately, the boom came to an end in 1994. After falling to 21-year lows one year earlier, bond yields rose in 1994 to their highest level in over three years. Bond yields had mixed results in 2001, but fell in 2002.

The historical themes of the past decade, as they relate to the capital markets, can be summarized in three observations. First, the 17fi year period starting in mid-1982 and ending in 1999, comprised a rare span of time in which investors quickly accumulated wealth.

Second, the postwar aberration of ever-higher inflation rates ended with a dramatic disinflation in the early Eighties. In the Nineties, inflation remained low. However, the more deeply embedded aberration of consistently positive inflation rates—that is, ever-higher prices—has not ended. As this decade begins, inflation is below its long-term historical average.

Finally, participation in the returns of the capital markets reached levels not even approached in the Twenties, the Fifties, or the atypical boom period of 1967–1972. The vast size and importance of pension funds, as well as the rapidly increasing popularity of stock and bond mutual funds as a basic savings vehicle, have caused more individuals to experience the returns of the capital markets than ever before.

Graphic Depiction of Returns in the Decade

Graphs 1-2, 1-3, and 1-4 contain bar graphs of 1993–2002 annual and 2002 monthly total returns on the assets discussed above. The top part of Graph 1-2 compares large company stocks and long-term government bonds. The graph shows that while stocks have outperformed bonds during a majority of the years, bonds have out-performed stocks as of late. The bottom half of Graph 1-2 compares large company stocks and small company stocks, showing that neither consistently outperformed the other over the past decade.

The top part of Graph 1-3 compares corporate and government bonds of like maturity (approximately 20 years). Clearly, returns of corporate bonds did not always outperform government bonds over the past decade, contradicting their historical trend. The bottom part of Graph 1-3 compares long-term and intermediate-term government bonds. Intermediate-term bonds are less volatile; and, as usual, tended to return less than long-term bonds in rising markets.

Graph 1-4 displays bar graphs of the 1993–2002 annual and 2002 monthly Treasury bill returns, inflation rates, and real riskless rates of return. The top part of Graph 1-4 compares Treasury bills and inflation. The bottom part of Graph 1-4 shows month-by-month real riskless rates of return, defined as Treasury bill returns in excess of inflation.

Tables of Market Results for 1993–2002

The 1993–2002 annual and 2002 quarterly and monthly total returns on the seven basic asset classes studied in this book are presented in Table 1-2. Table 1-3 displays cumulative indices of the returns shown in Table 1-2, based on a starting value of $1.00 on December 31, 1925.

For the past decade, stocks have had unusually high returns, with the exception of the past three years for large company stocks and this past year for small company stocks. Bonds and Treasury bills produced returns that were well-above their long-term historical averages and inflation rates fell to levels below their 77-year average.

Graph 1-2

1993–2002 Annual and 2002 Monthly Total Returns

A Comparison of Large Company Stocks with Long-Term Government Bonds, and
Large Company Stocks with Small Company Stocks (in percent)

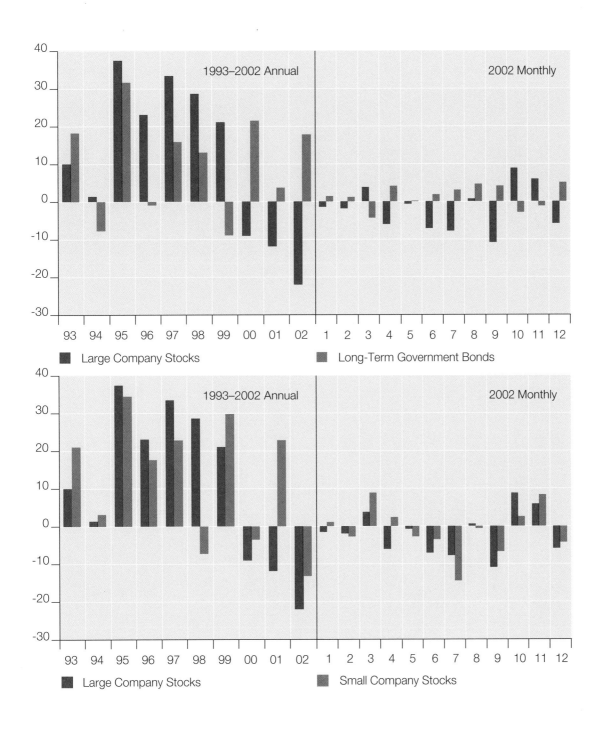

Graph 1-3

1993–2002 Annual and 2002 Monthly Total Returns

A Comparison of Long-Term Government Bonds with Long-Term Corporate Bonds, and Long-Term Government Bonds with Intermediate-Term Government Bonds (in percent)

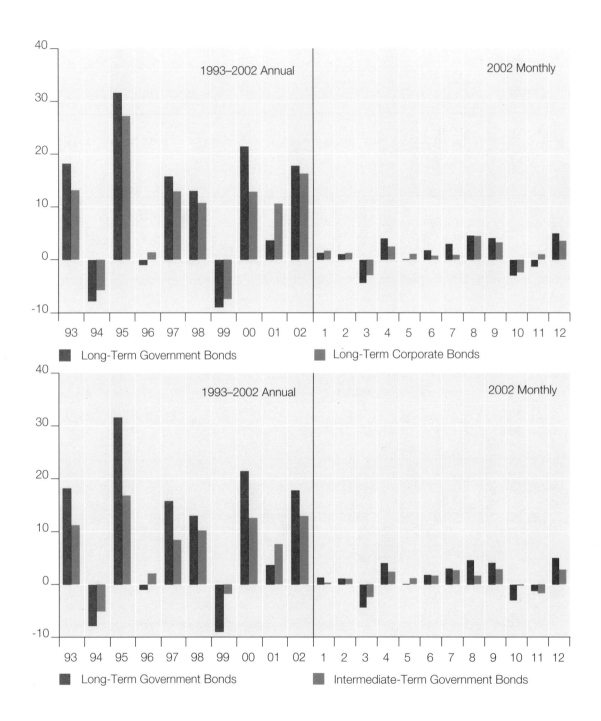

Graph 1-4

1993–2002 Annual and 2002 Monthly Total Returns

Treasury Bills, Inflation and Real Riskless Rates of Return (in percent)

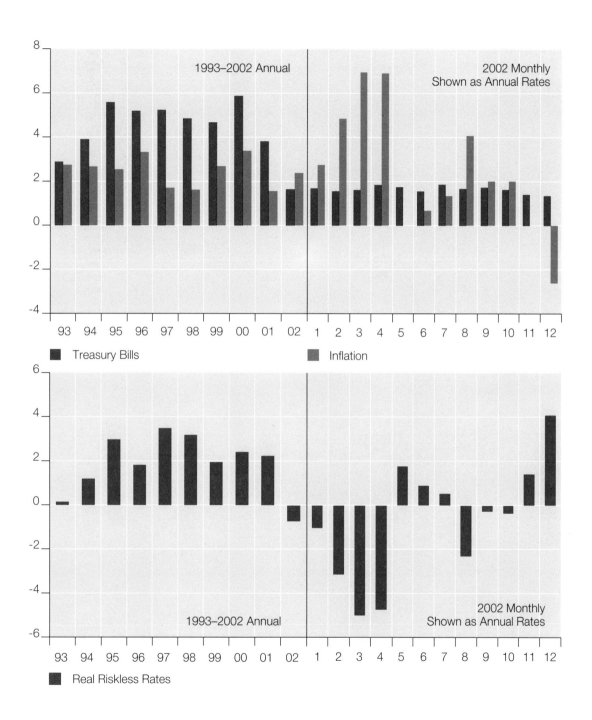

Table 1-2

1993–2002 Annual and 2002 Quarterly and Monthly Market Results
Returns on Stocks, Bonds, Bills, and Inflation (in percent)

Year	Large Company Stocks	Small Company Stocks	Long-Term Corporate Bonds	Long-Term Government Bonds	Intermediate Government Bonds	U.S. Treasury Bills	Inflation
1993–2002 Annual Returns							
1993	9.99	20.98	13.19	18.24	11.24	2.90	2.75
1994	1.31	3.11	−5.76	−7.77	−5.14	3.90	2.67
1995	37.43	34.46	27.20	31.67	16.80	5.60	2.54
1996	23.07	17.62	1.40	−0.93	2.10	5.21	3.32
1997	33.36	22.78	12.95	15.85	8.38	5.26	1.70
1998	28.58	−7.31	10.76	13.06	10.21	4.86	1.61
1999	21.04	29.79	−7.45	−8.96	−1.77	4.68	2.68
2000	−9.11	−3.59	12.87	21.48	12.59	5.89	3.39
2001	−11.88	22.77	10.65	3.70	7.62	3.83	1.55
2002	−22.10	−13.28	16.33	17.84	12.93	1.65	2.38
2002 Quarterly Returns							
I-02	0.28	6.99	0.04	−1.93	−1.01	0.40	1.19
II-02	−13.40	−3.91	4.45	6.20	5.34	0.43	0.62
III-02	−17.28	−20.7	8.98	12.30	7.44	0.44	0.61
IV-02	8.43	6.38	2.17	0.74	0.80	0.37	−0.06
2002 Monthly Returns							
12-01	0.88	6.72	−0.90	−1.83	−0.82	0.15	−0.39
01-02	−1.46	1.10	1.75	1.38	0.36	0.14	0.23
02-02	−1.93	−2.77	1.30	1.15	1.08	0.13	0.40
03-02	3.76	8.84	−2.95	−4.36	−2.42	0.13	0.56
04-02	−6.06	2.43	2.53	4.10	2.39	0.15	0.56
05-02	−0.74	−2.73	1.13	0.15	1.18	0.14	0.00
06-02	−7.12	−3.56	0.73	1.87	1.69	0.13	0.06
07-02	−7.80	−14.48	0.94	3.03	2.72	0.15	0.11
08-02	0.66	−0.57	4.52	4.64	1.67	0.14	0.33
09-02	−10.87	−6.74	3.30	4.17	2.88	0.14	0.17
10-02	8.80	2.57	−2.40	−2.94	−0.24	0.14	0.17
11-02	5.89	8.36	1.03	−1.22	−1.69	0.12	0.00
12-02	−5.88	−4.29	3.61	5.07	2.79	0.11	−0.22

Table 1-3

1993–2002 Annual and 2002 Monthly Market Results
Indices of Returns on Stocks, Bonds, Bills, and Inflation

Year-End 1925 = $1.00

Year	Large Company Stocks	Small Company Stocks	Long-Term Corporate Bonds	Long-Term Government Bonds	Intermediate Government Bonds	U.S. Treasury Bills	Inflation
1993–2002 Annual Indices							
1993	800.078	2757.147	40.336	28.034	32.516	11.728	8.133
1994	810.538	2842.773	38.012	25.856	30.843	12.186	8.351
1995	1113.918	3822.398	48.353	34.044	36.025	12.868	8.563
1996	1370.946	4495.993	49.031	33.727	36.782	13.538	8.847
1997	1828.326	5519.969	55.380	39.074	39.864	14.250	8.998
1998	2350.892	5116.648	61.339	44.178	43.933	14.942	9.143
1999	2845.629	6640.788	56.772	40.218	43.155	15.641	9.389
2000	2586.524	6402.228	64.077	48.856	48.589	16.563	9.707
2001	2279.127	7860.048	70.900	50.662	52.291	17.197	9.857
2002	1775.341	6816.409	82.480	59.699	59.054	17.480	10.091
2002 Monthly Indices							
12-01	2279.127	7860.048	70.900	50.662	52.291	17.197	9.857
01-02	2245.874	7946.508	72.139	51.361	52.477	17.221	9.879
02-02	2202.574	7726.390	73.080	51.951	53.043	17.243	9.919
03-02	2285.413	8409.403	70.925	49.686	51.761	17.266	9.974
04-02	2146.848	8613.752	72.720	51.721	52.997	17.293	10.030
05-02	2131.026	8378.596	73.542	51.798	53.621	17.318	10.030
06-02	1979.212	8080.318	74.079	52.769	54.526	17.340	10.036
07-02	1824.932	6910.288	74.772	54.368	56.007	17.367	10.047
08-02	1836.922	6870.899	78.152	56.888	56.942	17.391	10.080
09-02	1637.285	6407.801	80.729	59.258	58.583	17.416	10.097
10-02	1781.399	6572.481	78.794	57.517	58.442	17.440	10.114
11-02	1886.252	7121.941	79.605	56.817	57.451	17.460	10.114
12-02	1775.341	6816.409	82.480	59.699	59.054	17.480	10.091

Chapter 2
The Long Run Perspective

Motivation

A long view of capital market history, exemplified by the 77-year period (1926–2002) examined here, uncovers the basic relationships between risk and return among the different asset classes and between nominal and real (inflation-adjusted) returns. The goal of this study of asset returns is to provide a period long enough to include most or all of the major types of events that investors have experienced and may experience in the future. Such events include war and peace, growth and decline, bull and bear markets, inflation and deflation, and other less dramatic events that affect asset returns.

By studying the past, one can make inferences about the future. While the actual events that occurred during 1926–2002 will not be repeated, the event-types (not specific events) of that period can be expected to recur. It is sometimes said that only a few periods are unusual, such as the crash of 1929–1932 and World War II. This logic is suspicious because all periods are unusual. Two of the most unusual events of the century—the stock market crash of 1987 and the equally remarkable inflation of the 1970s and early 1980s—took place over the last three decades. From the perspective that historical event-types tend to repeat themselves, a 77-year examination of past capital market returns reveals a great deal about what may be expected in the future. [See Chapter 9.]

Historical Returns on Stocks, Bonds, Bills, and Inflation

Graph 2-1 graphically depicts the growth of $1.00 invested in large company stocks, small company stocks, long-term government bonds, Treasury bills, and a hypothetical asset returning the inflation rate over the period from the end of 1925 to the end of 2002. All results assume reinvestment of dividends on stocks or coupons on bonds and no taxes. Transaction costs are not included, except in the small stock index starting in 1982.

Each of the cumulative index values is initialized at $1.00 at year-end 1925. The graph vividly illustrates that large company stocks and small company stocks were the big winners over the entire 77-year period: investments of $1.00 in these assets would have grown to $1,775.34 and $6,816.41, respectively, by year-end 2002. This phenomenal growth was earned by taking substantial risk. In contrast, long-term government bonds (with an approximate 20-year maturity), which exposed the holder to much less risk, grew to only $59.70.

The lowest-risk strategy over the past 77 years (for those with short-term time horizons) was to buy U.S. Treasury bills. Since Treasury bills tended to track inflation, the resulting real (inflation-adjusted) returns were just above zero for the entire 1926–2002 period.

Graph 2-1

Wealth Indices of Investments in the U.S. Capital Markets
Year-End 1925 = $1.00

from 1925 to 2002

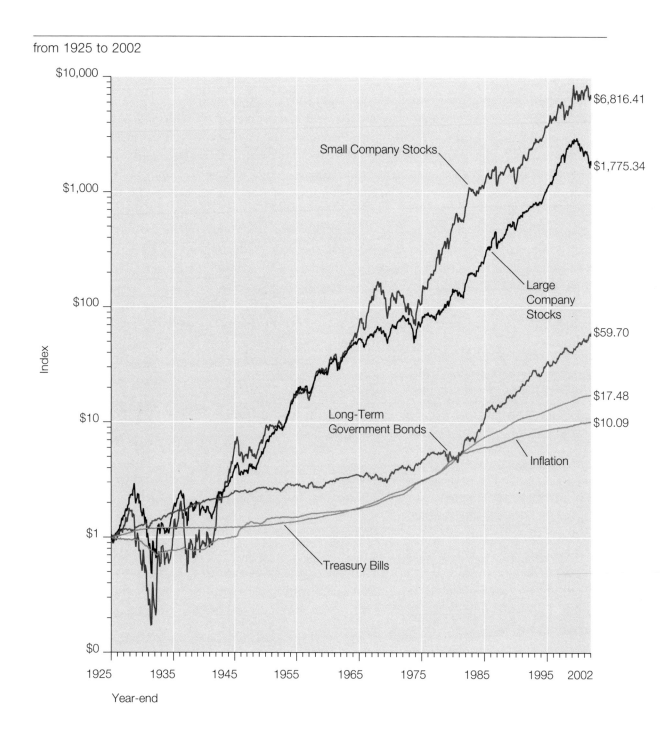

Year-end

Logarithmic Scale on the Index Graphs

A logarithmic scale is used on the vertical axis of our index graphs. The date appears on the horizontal axis.

A logarithmic scale allows for the direct comparison of the series' behavior at different points in time. Specifically, the use of a logarithmic scale allows the following interpretation of the data: the same vertical distance, no matter where it is measured on the graph, represents the same percentage change in the series. On the log scale shown below, a 50 percent gain from $10 to $15 occupies the same vertical distance as a 50 percent gain from $100 to $150. On the linear scale, the same percentage gains look different.

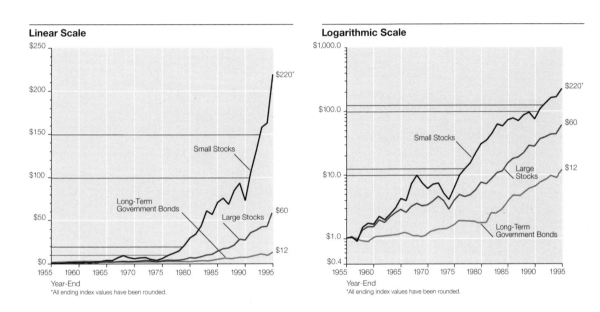

A logarithmic scale allows the viewer to compare investment performance across different time periods; thus the viewer can concentrate on rates of return, without worrying about the number of dollars invested at any given time. An additional benefit of the logarithmic scale is the way the scale spreads the action out over time. This allows the viewer to more carefully examine the fluctuations of the individual time series in different periods.

Large Company Stocks

As noted above, an index of S&P 500 total returns, initialized on December 31, 1925, at $1.00, closed 2002 at $1,775.34, a compound annual growth rate of 10.2 percent. The inflation-adjusted S&P 500 total return index closed 2002 at a level of $175.92.

Small Company Stocks

Over the long run, small stock returns surpassed the S&P 500, with the small stock total return index ending 2002 at a level of $6,816.41. This represents a compound annual growth rate of 12.1 percent, the highest rate among the asset classes studied here.

Long-Term Government Bonds

The long-term government bond total return index, constructed with an approximate 20-year maturity, closed 2002 at a level of $59.70 (based on year-end 1925 equaling $1.00). Based on the capital appreciation component alone, the $1.00 index rose to a level of $1.04, a 4 percent capital gain over the period 1926–2002. This indicates that more than all of the positive historical returns on long-term government bonds were due to income returns. The compound annual total return for long-term government bonds was 5.5 percent.

Intermediate-Term Government Bonds

One dollar invested in intermediate-term bonds at the end of 1925, with coupons reinvested, grew to $59.05 by year-end 2002. This compares with $59.70 for long-term government bonds. The compound annual total return for intermediate-term government bonds was 5.4 percent. Capital appreciation caused $1.00 to increase to $1.45 over the 77-year period, representing a compound annual growth rate of 0.5 percent.

Long-Term Corporate Bonds

Long-term corporate bonds outperformed both categories of government bonds with a compound annual total return of 5.9 percent. One dollar invested in the long-term corporate bond index at year-end 1925 was worth $82.48 by the end of 2002. This higher return reflected the risk premium that investors require for investing in corporate bonds, which are subject to the risk of default.

Treasury Bills

One dollar invested in Treasury bills at the end of 1925 was worth $17.48 by year-end 2002, with a compound annual growth rate of 3.8 percent. Treasury bill returns followed distinct patterns, described on the next page. Moreover, Treasury bills tended to track inflation; therefore, the average inflation-adjusted return on Treasury bills (or real riskless rate of return) was only 0.7 percent over the 77-year period. This real return also followed distinct patterns.

Patterns in Treasury Bill Returns

During the late 1920s and early 1930s, Treasury bill returns were just above zero. (These returns were observed during a largely deflationary period.) Beginning in late 1941, the yields on Treasury bills were pegged by the government at low rates while high inflation was experienced.

Treasury bills closely tracked inflation after March 1951, when Treasury bill yields were deregulated in the U.S. Treasury-Federal Reserve Accord. (Treasury bill returns after that date reflect free market rates.) This tracking relationship has weakened since 1973. From about 1974 to 1980, Treasury bill returns were consistently lower than inflation rates. Then, from about 1981 to 1986, Treasury bills outpaced inflation, yielding substantial positive real returns. Since 1987, real returns on Treasury bills have still been positive, with the exception of this past year.

Federal Reserve Operating Procedure Changes

The disparity between performance and volatility for the periods prior to and after October 1979 can be attributed to the Federal Reserve's new operating procedures. Prior to this date, the Fed used the federal funds rate as an operating target. Subsequently, the Fed de-emphasized this rate as an operating target and, instead, began to focus on the manipulation of the money supply (through non-borrowed reserves). As a result, the federal funds rate underwent much greater volatility, thereby bringing about greater volatility in Treasury returns.

In the fall of 1982, however, the Federal Reserve again changed the policy procedures regarding its monetary policy. The Fed abandoned its new monetary controls and returned to a strategy of preventing excessive volatility in interest rates. Volatility in Treasury bill returns from the fall of 1979 through the fall of 1982 was nearly 50 percent greater than that which has occurred since.

Inflation

The compound annual inflation rate over 1926–2002 was 3.0 percent. The inflation index, initiated at $1.00 at year-end 1925, grew to $10.09 by year-end 2002. The entire increase occurred during the postwar period. The years 1926–1933 were marked by deflation; inflation then raised consumer prices to their 1926 levels by the middle of 1945. After a brief postwar spurt of inflation, prices rose slowly over most of the 1950s and 1960s. Then, in the 1970s, inflation reached a pace unprecedented in peacetime, peaking at 13.3 percent in 1979. (On a month-by-month basis, the peak inflation rate was a breathtaking 24.0 percent, stated in annualized terms, in August 1973.) The 1980s saw a reversion to more moderate, though still substantial, inflation rates averaging about 5 percent. Inflation rates continued to decline in the 1990s with a compound annual rate of 2.9 percent.

Summary Statistics of Total Returns

Table 2-1 presents summary statistics of the annual total returns on each asset class over the entire 77-year period of 1926–2002. The data presented in these exhibits are described in detail in Chapters 3 and 6.

Note that in Table 2-1, the arithmetic mean returns are always higher than the geometric mean returns. (Where they appear the same, it is due to rounding.) The difference between these two means is related to the standard deviation, or variability, of the series. [See Chapter 6.]

The "skylines" or histograms to the right in Table 2-1 show the frequency distribution of returns on each asset class. The height of the common stock skyline in the range between +10 and +20 percent, for example, shows the number of years in 1926–2002 that large company stocks had a return in that range. The histograms are shown in 5 percent increments to fully display the spectrum of returns as seen over the last 77 years, especially in stocks.

Riskier assets, such as large company stocks and small company stocks, have low, spread-out skylines, reflecting the broad distribution of returns from very poor to very good. Less risky assets, such as bonds, have narrow skylines that resemble a single tall building, indicating the tightness of the distribution around the mean of the series. The histogram for Treasury bills is one-sided, lying almost entirely to the right of the vertical line representing a zero return; that is, Treasury bills rarely experienced negative returns on a yearly basis over the 1926–2002 period. The inflation skyline shows both positive and negative annual rates. Although a few deflationary months and quarters have occurred recently, the last negative annual inflation rate occurred in 1954.

The histograms in Tables 2-2 through 2-4 show the total return distributions on the basic series over the past 77 years. These histograms are useful in determining the years with similar returns.

Table 2-1

Basic Series: Summary Statistics of Annual Total Returns

from 1926 to 2002

Series	Geometric Mean	Arithmetic Mean	Standard Deviation	Distribution
Large Company Stocks	10.2%	12.2%	20.5%	
Small Company Stocks	12.1	16.9	33.2	
Long-Term Corporate Bonds	5.9	6.2	8.7	
Long-Term Government	5.5	5.8	9.4	
Intermediate-Term Government	5.4	5.6	5.8	
U.S. Treasury Bills	3.8	3.8	3.2	
Inflation	3.0	3.1	4.4	

−90%　　　0%　　　90%

*The 1933 Small Company Stocks Total Return was 142.9 percent.

Table 2-2

Histogram

Large Company Stock and Small Company Stock Total Returns (in percent)

from 1926 to 2002

Large Company Stocks

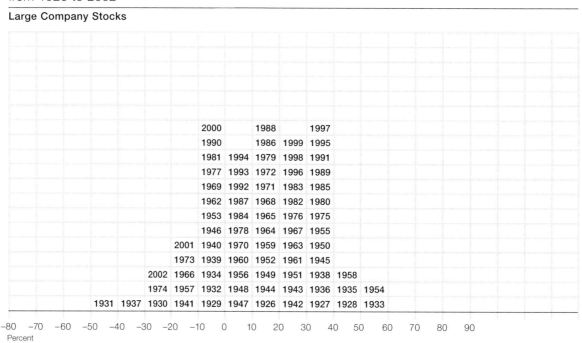

Small Company Stocks

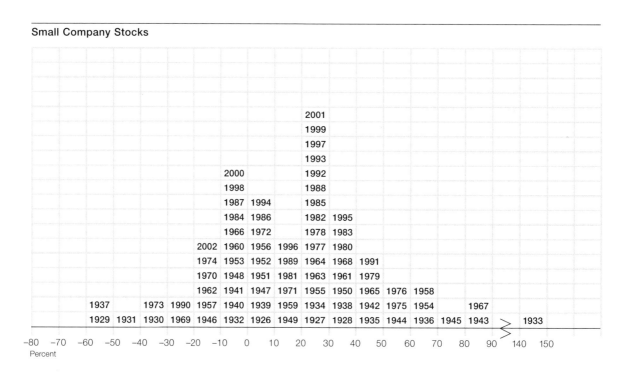

Table 2-3

Histogram

Long-Term Government Bond and Intermediate-Term Government Bond Total Returns (in percent)

from 1926 to 2002

Long-Term Government Bonds

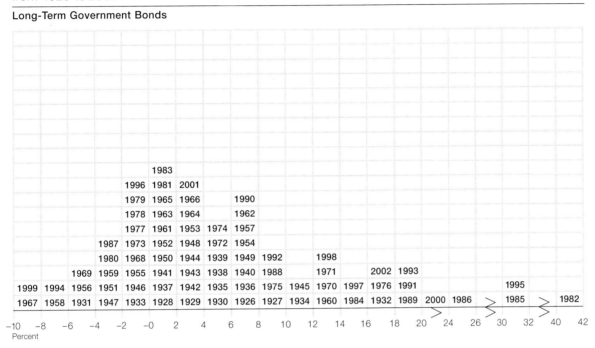

Intermediate-Term Government Bonds

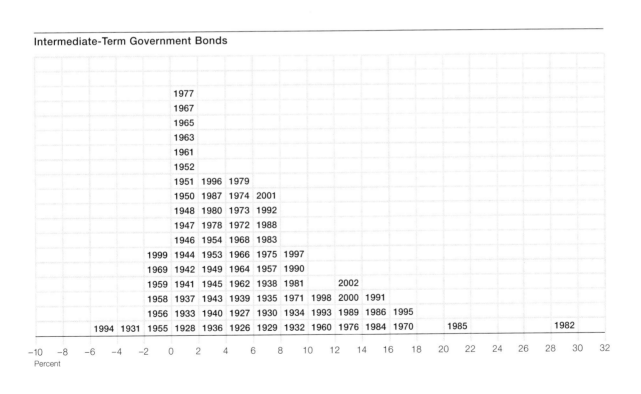

Table 2-4

Histogram

U.S. Treasury Bill Total Returns and Inflation (in percent)

from 1926 to 2002

U.S. Treasury Bills

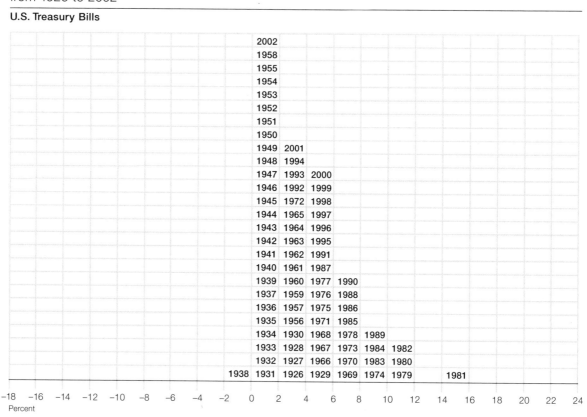

Inflation

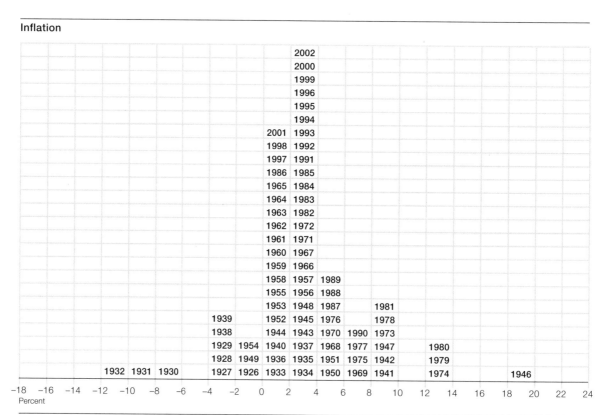

The stock histograms are shown in 10 percent increments while the bond, bill, and inflation histograms are in 2 percent increments. The increments are smaller for the assets with less widely distributed returns. Treasury bills are the most tightly clustered of any of the asset classes, confirming that this asset bears little risk; the annual return usually fell near zero.

Annual Total Returns

Table 2-5 shows annual total returns for the seven basic asset classes for the full 77-year time period. This table can be used to compare the performance of each asset class for the same annual period. Monthly total returns for large company stocks, small company stocks, long-term corporate bonds, long-term government bonds, intermediate-term government bonds, Treasury bills, and inflation rates are presented in Appendix A: Tables A-1, A-4, A-5, A-6, A-10, A-14, and A-15, respectively.

Capital Appreciation, Income, and Reinvestment Returns

Table 2-6 provides further detail on the returns of large company stocks, and long- and intermediate-term government bonds. Total annual returns are shown as the sum of three components: capital appreciation returns, income returns, and reinvestment returns. The capital appreciation and income components are explained in Chapter 3. The third component, reinvestment return, reflects monthly income reinvested in the total return index in subsequent months in the year. Thus, for a single month the reinvestment return is zero, but over a longer period of time it is nonzero. Since the returns in Table 2-6 are annual, reinvestment return is relevant.

The annual total return formed by compounding the monthly total returns does not equal the sum of the annual capital appreciation and income components; the difference is reinvestment return. A simple example illustrates this point. In 1995, an "up" year on a total return basis, the total annual return on large company stocks was 37.4 percent. The annual capital appreciation was 34.1 percent and the annual income return was 2.9 percent. These two components sum to 37.0 percent; the remaining 0.4 percent of the total 1995 return came from the reinvestment of dividends in the market. For more information on calculating annual total and income returns, see Chapter 5.

Monthly income and capital appreciation returns for large company stocks are presented in Appendix A: Tables A-2 and A-3, respectively. Monthly income and capital appreciation returns are presented for long-term government bonds in Appendix A: Tables A-7 and A-8; and for intermediate-term government bonds in Tables A-11 and A-12.

Table 2-5

Basic Series
Annual Total Returns (in percent)

from 1926 to 1970

Year	Large Company Stocks	Small Company Stocks	Long-Term Corporate Bonds	Long-Term Government Bonds	Intermediate-Term Government Bonds	U.S. Treasury Bills	Inflation
1926	11.62	0.28	7.37	7.77	5.38	3.27	−1.49
1927	37.49	22.10	7.44	8.93	4.52	3.12	−2.08
1928	43.61	39.69	2.84	0.10	0.92	3.56	−0.97
1929	−8.42	−51.36	3.27	3.42	6.01	4.75	0.20
1930	−24.90	−38.15	7.98	4.66	6.72	2.41	−6.03
1931	−43.34	−49.75	−1.85	−5.31	−2.32	1.07	−9.52
1932	−8.19	−5.39	10.82	16.84	8.81	0.96	−10.30
1933	53.99	142.87	10.38	−0.07	1.83	0.30	0.51
1934	−1.44	24.22	13.84	10.03	9.00	0.16	2.03
1935	47.67	40.19	9.61	4.98	7.01	0.17	2.99
1936	33.92	64.80	6.74	7.52	3.06	0.18	1.21
1937	−35.03	−58.01	2.75	0.23	1.56	0.31	3.10
1938	31.12	32.80	6.13	5.53	6.23	−0.02	−2.78
1939	−0.41	0.35	3.97	5.94	4.52	0.02	−0.48
1940	−9.78	−5.16	3.39	6.09	2.96	0.00	0.96
1941	−11.59	−9.00	2.73	0.93	0.50	0.06	9.72
1942	20.34	44.51	2.60	3.22	1.94	0.27	9.29
1943	25.90	88.37	2.83	2.08	2.81	0.35	3.16
1944	19.75	53.72	4.73	2.81	1.80	0.33	2.11
1945	36.44	73.61	4.08	10.73	2.22	0.33	2.25
1946	−8.07	−11.63	1.72	−0.10	1.00	0.35	18.16
1947	5.71	0.92	−2.34	−2.62	0.91	0.50	9.01
1948	5.50	−2.11	4.14	3.40	1.85	0.81	2.71
1949	18.79	19.75	3.31	6.45	2.32	1.10	−1.80
1950	31.71	38.75	2.12	0.06	0.70	1.20	5.79
1951	24.02	7.80	−2.69	−3.93	0.36	1.49	5.87
1952	18.37	3.03	3.52	1.16	1.63	1.66	0.88
1953	−0.99	−6.49	3.41	3.64	3.23	1.82	0.62
1954	52.62	60.58	5.39	7.19	2.68	0.86	−0.50
1955	31.56	20.44	0.48	−1.29	−0.65	1.57	0.37
1956	6.56	4.28	−6.81	−5.59	−0.42	2.46	2.86
1957	−10.78	−14.57	8.71	7.46	7.84	3.14	3.02
1958	43.36	64.89	−2.22	−6.09	−1.29	1.54	1.76
1959	11.96	16.40	−0.97	−2.26	−0.39	2.95	1.50
1960	0.47	−3.29	9.07	13.78	11.76	2.66	1.48
1961	26.89	32.09	4.82	0.97	1.85	2.13	0.67
1962	−8.73	−11.90	7.95	6.89	5.56	2.73	1.22
1963	22.80	23.57	2.19	1.21	1.64	3.12	1.65
1964	16.48	23.52	4.77	3.51	4.04	3.54	1.19
1965	12.45	41.75	−0.46	0.71	1.02	3.93	1.92
1966	−10.06	−7.01	0.20	3.65	4.69	4.76	3.35
1967	23.98	83.57	−4.95	−9.18	1.01	4.21	3.04
1968	11.06	35.97	2.57	−0.26	4.54	5.21	4.72
1969	−8.50	−25.05	−8.09	−5.07	−0.74	6.58	6.11
1970	4.01	−17.43	18.37	12.11	16.86	6.52	5.49

Table 2-5 (continued)

Basic Series
Annual Total Returns (in percent)

from 1971 to 2002

Year	Large Company Stocks	Small Company Stocks	Long-Term Corporate Bonds	Long-Term Government Bonds	Intermediate-Term Government Bonds	U.S. Treasury Bills	Inflation
1971	14.31	16.50	11.01	13.23	8.72	4.39	3.36
1972	18.98	4.43	7.26	5.69	5.16	3.84	3.41
1973	−14.66	−30.90	1.14	−1.11	4.61	6.93	8.80
1974	−26.47	−19.95	−3.06	4.35	5.69	8.00	12.20
1975	37.20	52.82	14.64	9.20	7.83	5.80	7.01
1976	23.84	57.38	18.65	16.75	12.87	5.08	4.81
1977	−7.18	25.38	1.71	−0.69	1.41	5.12	6.77
1978	6.56	23.46	−0.07	−1.18	3.49	7.18	9.03
1979	18.44	43.46	−4.18	−1.23	4.09	10.38	13.31
1980	32.42	39.88	−2.76	−3.95	3.91	11.24	12.40
1981	−4.91	13.88	−1.24	1.86	9.45	14.71	8.94
1982	21.41	28.01	42.56	40.36	29.10	10.54	3.87
1983	22.51	39.67	6.26	0.65	7.41	8.80	3.80
1984	6.27	−6.67	16.86	15.48	14.02	9.85	3.95
1985	32.16	24.66	30.09	30.97	20.33	7.72	3.77
1986	18.47	6.85	19.85	24.53	15.14	6.16	1.13
1987	5.23	−9.30	−0.27	−2.71	2.90	5.47	4.41
1988	16.81	22.87	10.70	9.67	6.10	6.35	4.42
1989	31.49	10.18	16.23	18.11	13.29	8.37	4.65
1990	−3.17	−21.56	6.78	6.18	9.73	7.81	6.11
1991	30.55	44.63	19.89	19.30	15.46	5.60	3.06
1992	7.67	23.35	9.39	8.05	7.19	3.51	2.90
1993	9.99	20.98	13.19	18.24	11.24	2.90	2.75
1994	1.31	3.11	−5.76	−7.77	−5.14	3.90	2.67
1995	37.43	34.46	27.20	31.67	16.80	5.60	2.54
1996	23.07	17.62	1.40	−0.93	2.10	5.21	3.32
1997	33.36	22.78	12.95	15.85	8.38	5.26	1.70
1998	28.58	−7.31	10.76	13.06	10.21	4.86	1.61
1999	21.04	29.79	−7.45	−8.96	−1.77	4.68	2.68
2000	−9.11	−3.59	12.87	21.48	12.59	5.89	3.39
2001	−11.88	22.77	10.65	3.70	7.62	3.83	1.55
2002	−22.10	−13.28	16.33	17.84	12.93	1.65	2.38

Table 2-6

Large Company Stocks, Long-Term Government Bonds, and Intermediate-Term Government Bonds

Annual Total, Income, Capital Appreciation, and Reinvestment Returns (in percent)

from 1926 to 1970

Year	Large Company Stocks				Long-Term Government Bonds					Intermediate-Term Government Bonds				
	Capital Apprec. Return	Income Return	Reinvest- ment Return	Total Return	Capital Apprec. Return	Income Return	Reinvest- ment Return	Total Return	Year- end Yield	Capital Apprec. Return	Income Return	Reinvest- ment Return	Total Return	Year- end Yield
1926	5.72	5.41	0.50	11.62	3.91	3.73	0.13	7.77	3.54	1.51	3.78	0.10	5.38	3.61
1927	30.91	5.71	0.87	37.49	5.40	3.41	0.12	8.93	3.16	0.96	3.49	0.07	4.52	3.40
1928	37.88	4.81	0.91	43.61	-3.12	3.22	0.01	0.10	3.40	-2.73	3.64	0.01	0.92	4.01
1929	-11.91	3.98	-0.49	-8.42	-0.20	3.47	0.15	3.42	3.40	1.77	4.07	0.18	6.01	3.62
1930	-28.48	4.57	-0.98	-24.90	1.28	3.32	0.05	4.66	3.30	3.30	3.30	0.11	6.72	2.91
1931	-47.07	5.35	-1.62	-43.34	-8.46	3.33	-0.17	-5.31	4.07	-5.40	3.16	-0.08	-2.32	4.12
1932	-15.15	6.16	0.80	-8.19	12.94	3.69	0.22	16.84	3.15	5.02	3.63	0.16	8.81	3.04
1933	46.59	6.39	1.01	53.99	-3.14	3.12	-0.05	-0.07	3.36	-0.99	2.83	-0.02	1.83	3.25
1934	-5.94	4.46	0.04	-1.44	6.76	3.18	0.09	10.03	2.93	5.97	2.93	0.09	9.00	2.49
1935	41.37	4.95	1.35	47.67	2.14	2.81	0.03	4.98	2.76	4.94	2.02	0.05	7.01	1.63
1936	27.92	5.36	0.64	33.92	4.64	2.77	0.10	7.52	2.55	1.60	1.44	0.02	3.06	1.29
1937	-38.59	4.66	-1.09	-35.03	-2.48	2.66	0.05	0.23	2.73	0.05	1.48	0.03	1.56	1.14
1938	25.21	4.83	1.07	31.12	2.83	2.64	0.06	5.53	2.52	4.37	1.82	0.04	6.23	1.52
1939	-5.45	4.69	0.35	-0.41	3.48	2.40	0.06	5.94	2.26	3.18	1.31	0.03	4.52	0.98
1940	-15.29	5.36	0.14	-9.78	3.77	2.23	0.09	6.09	1.94	2.04	0.90	0.02	2.96	0.57
1941	-17.86	6.71	-0.44	-11.59	-1.01	1.94	0.00	0.93	2.04	-0.17	0.67	0.00	0.50	0.82
1942	12.43	6.79	1.12	20.34	0.74	2.46	0.02	3.22	2.46	1.17	0.76	0.00	1.94	0.72
1943	19.45	6.24	0.21	25.90	-0.37	2.44	0.02	2.08	2.48	1.23	1.56	0.02	2.81	1.45
1944	13.80	5.48	0.47	19.75	0.32	2.46	0.03	2.81	2.46	0.35	1.44	0.01	1.80	1.40
1945	30.72	4.97	0.74	36.44	8.27	2.34	0.12	10.73	1.99	1.02	1.19	0.01	2.22	1.03
1946	-11.87	4.09	-0.29	-8.07	-2.15	2.04	0.01	-0.10	2.12	-0.08	1.08	0.00	1.00	1.12
1947	0.00	5.49	0.22	5.71	-4.70	2.13	-0.06	-2.62	2.43	-0.30	1.21	0.00	0.91	1.34
1948	-0.65	6.08	0.08	5.50	0.96	2.40	0.04	3.40	2.37	0.27	1.56	0.01	1.85	1.51
1949	10.26	7.50	1.03	18.79	4.15	2.25	0.06	6.45	2.09	0.95	1.36	0.01	2.32	1.23
1950	21.78	8.77	1.16	31.71	-2.06	2.12	0.00	0.06	2.24	-0.69	1.39	0.00	0.70	1.62
1951	16.46	6.91	0.65	24.02	-6.27	2.38	-0.04	-3.93	2.69	-1.63	1.98	0.01	0.36	2.17
1952	11.78	5.93	0.66	18.37	-1.48	2.66	-0.02	1.16	2.79	-0.57	2.19	0.01	1.63	2.35
1953	-6.62	5.46	0.18	-0.99	0.67	2.84	0.12	3.64	2.74	0.61	2.55	0.07	3.23	2.18
1954	45.02	6.21	1.39	52.62	4.35	2.79	0.05	7.19	2.72	1.08	1.60	0.01	2.68	1.72
1955	26.40	4.56	0.60	31.56	-4.07	2.75	0.03	-1.29	2.95	-3.10	2.45	0.00	-0.65	2.80
1956	2.62	3.83	0.11	6.56	-8.46	2.99	-0.12	-5.59	3.45	-3.45	3.05	-0.02	-0.42	3.63
1957	-14.31	3.84	-0.30	-10.78	3.82	3.44	0.20	7.46	3.23	4.05	3.59	0.20	7.84	2.84
1958	38.06	4.38	0.93	43.36	-9.23	3.27	-0.14	-6.09	3.82	-4.17	2.93	-0.05	-1.29	3.81
1959	8.48	3.31	0.16	11.96	-6.20	4.01	-0.07	-2.26	4.47	-4.56	4.18	-0.01	-0.39	4.98
1960	-2.97	3.26	0.19	0.47	9.29	4.26	0.23	13.78	3.80	7.42	4.15	0.19	11.76	3.31
1961	23.13	3.48	0.28	26.89	-2.86	3.83	0.00	0.97	4.15	-1.72	3.54	0.03	1.85	3.84
1962	-11.81	2.98	0.10	-8.73	2.78	4.00	0.11	6.89	3.95	1.73	3.73	0.10	5.56	3.50
1963	18.89	3.61	0.30	22.80	-2.70	3.89	0.02	1.21	4.17	-2.10	3.71	0.03	1.64	4.04
1964	12.97	3.33	0.18	16.48	-0.72	4.15	0.07	3.51	4.23	-0.03	4.00	0.07	4.04	4.03
1965	9.06	3.21	0.18	12.45	-3.45	4.19	-0.04	0.71	4.50	-3.10	4.15	-0.03	1.02	4.90
1966	-13.09	3.11	-0.08	-10.06	-1.06	4.49	0.22	3.65	4.55	-0.41	4.93	0.17	4.69	4.79
1967	20.09	3.64	0.25	23.98	-13.55	4.59	-0.23	-9.18	5.56	-3.85	4.88	-0.02	1.01	5.77
1968	7.66	3.18	0.22	11.06	-5.51	5.50	-0.25	-0.26	5.98	-0.99	5.49	0.03	4.54	5.96
1969	-11.42	3.04	-0.13	-8.50	-10.83	5.95	-0.19	-5.07	6.87	-7.27	6.65	-0.11	-0.74	8.29
1970	0.16	3.41	0.43	4.01	4.84	6.74	0.52	12.11	6.48	8.71	7.49	0.66	16.86	5.90

Table 2-6 (continued)

Large Company Stocks, Long-Term Government Bonds, and Intermediate-Term Government Bonds

Annual Total, Income, Capital Appreciation, and Reinvestment Returns (in percent)

from 1971 to 2002

Year	Large Company Stocks				Long-Term Government Bonds					Intermediate-Term Government Bonds				
	Capital Apprec. Return	Income Return	Reinvest- ment Return	Total Return	Capital Apprec. Return	Income Return	Reinvest- ment Return	Total Return	Year- end Yield	Capital Apprec. Return	Income Return	Reinvest- ment Return	Total Return	Year- end Yield
1971	10.79	3.33	0.19	14.31	6.61	6.32	0.31	13.23	5.97	2.72	5.75	0.25	8.72	5.25
1972	15.63	3.09	0.26	18.98	-0.35	5.87	0.17	5.69	5.99	-0.75	5.75	0.16	5.16	5.85
1973	-17.37	2.86	-0.16	-14.66	-7.70	6.51	0.08	-1.11	7.26	-2.19	6.58	0.22	4.61	6.79
1974	-29.72	3.69	-0.44	-26.47	-3.45	7.27	0.54	4.35	7.60	-1.99	7.24	0.44	5.69	7.12
1975	31.55	5.37	0.29	37.20	0.73	7.99	0.47	9.20	8.05	0.12	7.35	0.36	7.83	7.19
1976	19.15	4.38	0.31	23.84	8.07	7.89	0.80	16.75	7.21	5.25	7.10	0.51	12.87	6.00
1977	-11.50	4.31	0.01	-7.18	-7.86	7.14	0.04	-0.69	8.03	-5.15	6.49	0.06	1.41	7.51
1978	1.06	5.33	0.17	6.56	-9.05	7.90	-0.03	-1.18	8.98	-4.49	7.83	0.14	3.49	8.83
1979	12.31	5.71	0.42	18.44	-9.84	8.86	-0.25	-1.23	10.12	-5.07	9.04	0.12	4.09	10.33
1980	25.77	5.73	0.92	32.42	-14.00	9.97	0.08	-3.95	11.99	-6.81	10.55	0.17	3.91	12.45
1981	-9.72	4.89	-0.08	-4.91	-10.33	11.55	0.64	1.86	13.34	-4.55	12.97	1.03	9.45	13.96
1982	14.76	5.50	1.15	21.41	23.95	13.50	2.91	40.36	10.95	14.23	12.81	2.06	29.10	9.90
1983	17.27	5.00	0.24	22.51	-9.82	10.38	0.09	0.65	11.97	-3.30	10.35	0.35	7.41	11.41
1984	1.39	4.56	0.31	6.27	2.32	11.74	1.42	15.48	11.70	1.22	11.68	1.12	14.02	11.04
1985	26.34	5.10	0.72	32.16	17.84	11.25	1.88	30.97	9.56	9.01	10.29	1.04	20.33	8.55
1986	14.63	3.74	0.10	18.47	14.99	8.98	0.56	24.53	7.89	6.99	7.72	0.43	15.14	6.85
1987	2.03	3.64	-0.44	5.23	-10.69	7.92	0.06	-2.71	9.20	-4.75	7.47	0.19	2.90	8.32
1988	12.41	4.17	0.24	16.81	0.36	8.97	0.34	9.67	9.18	-2.26	8.24	0.13	6.10	9.17
1989	27.26	3.85	0.38	31.49	8.62	8.81	0.68	18.11	8.16	4.34	8.46	0.49	13.29	7.94
1990	-6.56	3.36	0.03	-3.17	-2.61	8.19	0.61	6.18	8.44	1.02	8.15	0.56	9.73	7.70
1991	26.31	3.82	0.42	30.55	10.10	8.22	0.98	19.30	7.30	7.36	7.43	0.67	15.46	5.97
1992	4.46	3.03	0.18	7.67	0.34	7.26	0.45	8.05	7.26	0.64	6.27	0.28	7.19	6.11
1993	7.06	2.83	0.11	9.99	10.71	7.17	0.35	18.24	6.54	5.56	5.53	0.15	11.24	5.22
1994	-1.54	2.82	0.03	1.31	-14.29	6.59	-0.07	-7.77	7.99	-11.14	6.07	-0.07	-5.14	7.80
1995	34.11	2.91	0.41	37.43	23.04	7.60	1.03	31.67	6.03	9.66	6.69	0.45	16.80	5.38
1996	20.26	2.54	0.27	23.07	-7.37	6.18	0.26	-0.93	6.73	-3.90	5.82	0.18	2.10	6.16
1997	31.01	2.11	0.25	33.36	8.51	6.64	0.71	15.85	6.02	1.94	6.14	0.30	8.38	5.73
1998	26.67	1.68	0.24	28.58	6.89	5.83	0.34	13.06	5.42	4.66	5.29	0.25	10.21	4.68
1999	19.53	1.36	0.15	21.04	-14.35	5.57	-0.19	-8.96	6.82	-7.06	5.30	-0.01	-1.77	6.45
2000	-10.14	1.10	-0.07	-9.11	14.36	6.50	0.62	21.48	5.58	5.94	6.19	0.46	12.59	5.07
2001	-13.04	1.18	-0.02	-11.88	-1.89	5.53	0.06	3.70	5.75	3.23	4.27	0.12	7.62	4.42
2002	-23.37	1.39	-0.12	-22.10	11.69	5.59	0.56	17.84	4.84	8.65	3.98	0.30	12.93	2.61

Rolling Period Returns

The highest and lowest returns on the basic series, expressed as annual rates, are shown for 1-, 5-, 10-, 15-, and 20-year holding periods in Table 2-7. This exhibit also shows the number of times that an asset had a positive return, and the number of times that an asset's return was the highest among all those studied. The number of times positive (or times highest) is compared to the total number of observations—that is, 77 annual, 73 overlapping 5-year, 68 overlapping 10-year, 63 overlapping 15-year, and 58 overlapping 20-year holding periods.

Tables 2-8, 2-9, 2-10, and 2-11 show the compound annual total returns for 5-, 10-, 15-, and 20-year holding periods. Often, these calculations are referred to as rolling period returns as they are obtained by rolling a data window of fixed length along each time series. They are useful for examining the behavior of returns for holding periods similar to those actually experienced by investors and show the effects of time diversification. Holding assets for long periods of time has the effect of lowering the risk of experiencing a loss in asset value.

Table 2-7

Basic Series
Maximum and Minimum Values of Returns for 1-, 5-, 10-, 15-, and 20-Year Holding Periods
(compound annual rates of return in percent)

Series

Annual Returns	Maximum Value Return and Year(s)		Minimum Value Return and Year(s)		Times Positive (out of 77 years)	Times Highest Returning Asset
Large Company Stocks	53.99	1933	−43.34	1931	54	16
Small Company Stocks	142.87	1933	−58.01	1937	53	33
Long-Term Corporate Bonds	42.56	1982	−8.09	1969	60	6
Long-Term Government Bonds	40.36	1982	−9.18	1967	56	8
Intermediate-Term Govt. Bonds	29.10	1982	−5.14	1994	69	2
U.S. Treasury Bills	14.71	1981	−0.02	1938	76	6
Inflation	18.16	1946	−10.30	1932	67	6

5-Year Rolling Period Returns	Maximum Value Return and Year(s)		Minimum Value Return and Year(s)		(out of 73 overlapping 5-year periods)	Times Highest Returning Asset
Large Company Stocks	28.55	1995–99	−12.47	1928–32	65	23
Small Company Stocks	45.90	1941–45	−27.54	1928–32	64	38
Long-Term Corporate Bonds	22.51	1982–86	−2.22	1965–69	70	7
Long-Term Government Bonds	21.62	1982–86	−2.14	1965–69	67	2
Intermediate-Term Govt. Bonds	16.98	1982–86	0.96	1955–59	73	2
U.S. Treasury Bills	11.12	1979–83	0.07	1938–42	73	0
Inflation	10.06	1977–81	−5.42	1928–32	66	1

10-Year Rolling Period Returns	Maximum Value Return and Year(s)		Minimum Value Return and Year(s)		(out of 68 overlapping 10-year periods)	Times Highest Returning Asset
Large Company Stocks	20.06	1949–58	−0.89	1929–38	66	20
Small Company Stocks	30.38	1975–84	−5.70	1929–38	66	38
Long-Term Corporate Bonds	16.32	1982–91	0.98	1947–56	68	6
Long-Term Government Bonds	15.56	1982–91	−0.07	1950–59	67	0
Intermediate-Term Govt. Bonds	13.13	1982–91	1.25	1947–56	68	2
U.S. Treasury Bills	9.17	1978–87	0.15	1933–42/1934–43	68	1
Inflation	8.67	1973–82	−2.57	1926–35	62	1

15-Year Rolling Period Returns	Maximum Value Return and Year(s)		Minimum Value Return and Year(s)		(out of 63 overlapping 15-year periods)	Times Highest Returning Asset
Large Company Stocks	18.93	1985–99	0.64	1929–43	63	14
Small Company Stocks	23.33	1975–89	−1.30	1927–41	60	45
Long-Term Corporate Bonds	13.66	1982–96	1.02	1955–69	63	4
Long-Term Government Bonds	13.53	1981–95	0.40	1955–69	63	0
Intermediate-Term Govt. Bonds	11.27	1981–95	1.45	1945–59	63	0
U.S. Treasury Bills	8.32	1977–91	0.22	1933–47	63	0
Inflation	7.30	1968–82	−1.59	1926–40	60	0

20-Year Rolling Period Returns	Maximum Value Return and Year(s)		Minimum Value Return and Year(s)		(out of 58 overlapping 20-year periods)	Times Highest Returning Asset
Large Company Stocks	17.87	1980–99	3.11	1929–48	58	8
Small Company Stocks	21.13	1942–61	5.74	1929–48	58	50
Long-Term Corporate Bonds	12.13	1982–01	1.34	1950–69	58	0
Long-Term Government Bonds	12.09	1982–01	0.69	1950–69	58	0
Intermediate-Term Govt. Bonds	9.97	1981–00	1.58	1940–59	58	0
U.S. Treasury Bills	7.72	1972–91	0.42	1931–50	58	0
Inflation	6.36	1966–85	0.07	1926–45	58	0

Table 2-8

Basic Series

Compound Annual Returns for 5-Year Holding Periods (percent per annum)

from 1926 to 1970

Period	Large Company Stocks	Small Company Stocks	Long-Term Corporate Bonds	Long-Term Government Bonds	Intermediate Government Bonds	U.S. Treasury Bills	Inflation
1926–1930	8.68	−12.44	5.76	4.93	4.69	3.42	−2.10
1927–1931	−5.10	−23.74	3.87	2.25	3.11	2.98	−3.75
1928–1932	−12.47	−27.54	4.52	3.69	3.95	2.54	−5.42
1929–1933	−11.24	−19.06	6.01	3.66	4.13	1.89	−5.14
1930–1934	−9.93	−2.37	8.09	4.95	4.71	0.98	−4.80
1931–1935	3.12	14.99	8.42	5.01	4.77	0.53	−3.04
1932–1936	22.47	45.83	10.26	7.71	5.90	0.35	−0.84
1933–1937	14.29	23.96	8.60	4.46	4.45	0.22	1.96
1934–1938	10.67	9.86	7.75	5.61	5.33	0.16	1.29
1935–1939	10.91	5.27	5.81	4.81	4.46	0.13	0.78
1936–1940	0.50	−2.64	4.59	5.03	3.65	0.10	0.38
1937–1941	−7.51	−13.55	3.79	3.71	3.13	0.08	2.02
1938–1942	4.62	10.70	3.76	4.32	3.21	0.07	3.21
1939–1943	3.77	18.71	3.10	3.63	2.54	0.14	4.44
1940–1944	7.67	29.28	3.25	3.01	2.00	0.20	4.98
1941–1945	16.96	45.90	3.39	3.90	1.85	0.27	5.25
1942–1946	17.87	45.05	3.19	3.69	1.95	0.33	6.82
1943–1947	14.86	35.00	2.17	2.49	1.75	0.37	6.77
1944–1948	10.87	18.43	2.43	2.75	1.55	0.47	6.67
1945–1949	10.69	12.66	2.15	3.46	1.66	0.62	5.84
1946–1950	9.91	7.72	1.76	1.39	1.36	0.79	6.57
1947–1951	16.70	12.09	0.87	0.60	1.23	1.02	4.25
1948–1952	19.37	12.55	2.05	1.37	1.37	1.25	2.65
1949–1953	17.86	11.53	1.91	1.41	1.64	1.45	2.23
1950–1954	23.92	18.27	2.31	1.55	1.72	1.41	2.50
1951–1955	23.89	14.97	1.98	1.28	1.44	1.48	1.43
1952–1956	20.18	14.21	1.10	0.93	1.28	1.67	0.84
1953–1957	13.58	10.01	2.10	2.15	2.49	1.97	1.27
1954–1958	22.31	23.22	0.96	0.16	1.58	1.91	1.49
1955–1959	14.96	15.54	−0.29	−1.67	0.96	2.33	1.90
1956–1960	8.92	10.58	1.36	1.16	3.37	2.55	2.12
1957–1961	12.79	15.93	3.77	2.53	3.83	2.48	1.68
1958–1962	13.31	16.65	3.63	2.42	3.39	2.40	1.33
1959–1963	9.85	10.11	4.55	3.97	4.00	2.72	1.30
1960–1964	10.73	11.43	5.73	5.17	4.91	2.83	1.24
1961–1965	13.25	20.28	3.82	2.63	2.81	3.09	1.33
1962–1966	5.72	12.13	2.88	3.17	3.38	3.61	1.86
1963–1967	12.39	29.86	0.30	−0.14	2.47	3.91	2.23
1964–1968	10.16	32.37	0.37	−0.43	3.04	4.33	2.84
1965–1969	4.96	19.78	−2.22	−2.14	2.08	4.93	3.82
1966–1970	3.34	7.51	1.23	−0.02	5.10	5.45	4.54
1967–1971	8.42	12.47	3.32	1.77	5.90	5.38	4.54
1968–1972	7.53	0.47	5.85	4.90	6.75	5.30	4.61
1969–1973	2.01	−12.25	5.55	4.72	6.77	5.65	5.41
1970–1974	−2.36	−11.09	6.68	6.72	8.11	5.93	6.60

Table 2-8 (continued)

Basic Series
Compound Annual Returns for 5-Year Holding Periods (percent per annum)

from 1971 to 2002

Period	Large Company Stocks	Small Company Stocks	Long-Term Corporate Bonds	Long-Term Government Bonds	Intermediate Government Bonds	U.S. Treasury Bills	Inflation
1971–1975	3.21	0.56	6.00	6.16	6.39	5.78	6.90
1972–1976	4.87	6.80	7.42	6.82	7.19	5.92	7.20
1973–1977	−0.21	10.77	6.29	5.50	6.41	6.18	7.89
1974–1978	4.32	24.41	6.03	5.48	6.18	6.23	7.94
1975–1979	14.76	39.80	5.78	4.33	5.86	6.69	8.15
1976–1980	13.95	37.35	2.36	1.68	5.08	7.77	9.21
1977–1981	8.08	28.75	−1.33	−1.05	4.44	9.67	10.06
1978–1982	14.05	29.28	5.57	6.03	9.60	10.78	9.46
1979–1983	17.27	32.51	6.87	6.42	10.42	11.12	8.39
1980–1984	14.76	21.59	11.20	9.80	12.45	11.01	6.53
1981–1985	14.71	18.82	17.86	16.83	15.80	10.30	4.85
1982–1986	19.87	17.32	22.51	21.62	16.98	8.60	3.30
1983–1987	16.49	9.51	14.06	13.02	11.79	7.59	3.41
1984–1988	15.38	6.74	15.00	14.98	11.52	7.10	3.53
1985–1989	20.40	10.34	14.88	15.50	11.38	6.81	3.67
1986–1990	13.14	0.58	10.43	10.75	9.34	6.83	4.13
1987–1991	15.36	6.86	10.44	9.81	9.40	6.71	4.52
1988–1992	15.89	13.63	12.50	12.14	10.30	6.31	4.22
1989–1993	14.50	13.28	13.00	13.84	11.35	5.61	3.89
1990–1994	8.69	11.79	8.36	8.34	7.46	4.73	3.49
1991–1995	16.57	24.51	12.22	13.10	8.81	4.29	2.79
1992–1996	15.20	19.47	8.52	8.98	6.17	4.22	2.84
1993–1997	20.24	19.35	9.22	10.51	6.40	4.57	2.60
1994–1998	24.06	13.16	8.74	9.52	6.20	4.96	2.37
1995–1999	28.55	18.49	8.35	9.24	6.95	5.12	2.37
1996–2000	18.35	10.87	5.79	7.49	6.17	5.18	2.54
1997–2001	10.70	11.82	7.66	8.48	7.29	4.90	2.18
1998–2002	−0.59	4.31	8.29	8.85	8.18	4.17	2.32

Table 2-9

Basic Series

Compound Annual Returns for 10-Year Holding Periods (percent per annum)

from 1926 to 1970

Period	Large Company Stocks	Small Company Stocks	Long-Term Corporate Bonds	Long-Term Government Bonds	Intermediate Government Bonds	U.S. Treasury Bills	Inflation
1926–1935	5.86	0.34	7.08	4.97	4.73	1.97	−2.57
1927–1936	7.81	5.45	7.02	4.95	4.50	1.66	−2.30
1928–1937	0.02	−5.22	6.54	4.08	4.20	1.37	−1.80
1929–1938	−0.89	−5.70	6.88	4.63	4.73	1.02	−1.98
1930–1939	−0.05	1.38	6.95	4.88	4.58	0.55	−2.05
1931–1940	1.80	5.81	6.49	5.02	4.21	0.32	−1.34
1932–1941	6.43	12.28	6.97	5.69	4.51	0.21	0.58
1933–1942	9.35	17.14	6.15	4.39	3.83	0.15	2.59
1934–1943	7.17	14.20	5.40	4.62	3.93	0.15	2.85
1935–1944	9.28	16.66	4.53	3.91	3.22	0.17	2.86
1936–1945	8.42	19.18	3.99	4.46	2.75	0.18	2.79
1937–1946	4.41	11.98	3.49	3.70	2.54	0.20	4.39
1938–1947	9.62	22.24	2.96	3.40	2.48	0.22	4.97
1939–1948	7.26	18.57	2.77	3.19	2.04	0.30	5.55
1940–1949	9.17	20.69	2.70	3.24	1.83	0.41	5.41
1941–1950	13.38	25.37	2.57	2.64	1.60	0.53	5.91
1942–1951	17.28	27.51	2.02	2.13	1.59	0.67	5.53
1943–1952	17.09	23.27	2.11	1.93	1.56	0.81	4.69
1944–1953	14.31	14.93	2.17	2.08	1.60	0.96	4.43
1945–1954	17.12	15.43	2.23	2.51	1.69	1.01	4.16
1946–1955	16.69	11.29	1.87	1.33	1.40	1.14	3.96
1947–1956	18.43	13.14	0.98	0.76	1.25	1.35	2.53
1948–1957	16.44	11.27	2.07	1.76	1.93	1.61	1.96
1949–1958	20.06	17.23	1.43	0.79	1.61	1.68	1.86
1950–1959	19.35	16.90	1.00	−0.07	1.34	1.87	2.20
1951–1960	16.16	12.75	1.67	1.22	2.40	2.01	1.77
1952–1961	16.43	15.07	2.43	1.73	2.55	2.08	1.26
1953–1962	13.44	13.28	2.86	2.29	2.94	2.19	1.30
1954–1963	15.91	16.48	2.74	2.05	2.78	2.31	1.40
1955–1964	12.82	13.47	2.68	1.69	2.92	2.58	1.57
1956–1965	11.06	15.33	2.58	1.89	3.09	2.82	1.73
1957–1966	9.20	14.02	3.33	2.85	3.60	3.05	1.77
1958–1967	12.85	23.08	1.95	1.13	2.93	3.15	1.78
1959–1968	10.00	20.73	2.44	1.75	3.52	3.52	2.07
1960–1969	7.81	15.53	1.68	1.45	3.48	3.88	2.52
1961–1970	8.18	13.72	2.51	1.30	3.95	4.26	2.92
1962–1971	7.06	12.30	3.10	2.47	4.63	4.49	3.19
1963–1972	9.93	14.22	3.04	2.35	4.59	4.60	3.41
1964–1973	6.00	7.77	2.93	2.11	4.89	4.98	4.12
1965–1974	1.24	3.20	2.13	2.20	5.05	5.43	5.20
1966–1975	3.27	3.98	3.59	3.03	5.74	5.62	5.71
1967–1976	6.63	9.60	5.35	4.26	6.54	5.65	5.86
1968–1977	3.59	5.50	6.07	5.20	6.58	5.74	6.24
1969–1978	3.16	4.48	5.79	5.10	6.47	5.94	6.67
1970–1979	5.86	11.49	6.23	5.52	6.98	6.31	7.37

Table 2-9 (continued)

Basic Series

Compound Annual Returns for 10-Year Holding Periods (percent per annum)

from 1971 to 2002

Period	Large Company Stocks	Small Company Stocks	Long-Term Corporate Bonds	Long-Term Government Bonds	Intermediate Government Bonds	U.S. Treasury Bills	Inflation
1971–1980	8.44	17.53	4.16	3.90	5.73	6.77	8.05
1972–1981	6.47	17.26	2.95	2.81	5.80	7.78	8.62
1973–1982	6.68	19.67	5.93	5.76	8.00	8.46	8.67
1974–1983	10.61	28.40	6.45	5.95	8.28	8.65	8.16
1975–1984	14.76	30.38	8.46	7.03	9.11	8.83	7.34
1976–1985	14.33	27.75	9.84	8.99	10.31	9.03	7.01
1977–1986	13.82	22.90	9.95	9.70	10.53	9.14	6.63
1978–1987	15.26	18.99	9.73	9.47	10.69	9.17	6.39
1979–1988	16.33	18.93	10.86	10.62	10.97	9.09	5.93
1980–1989	17.55	15.83	13.02	12.62	11.91	8.89	5.09
1981–1990	13.93	9.32	14.09	13.75	12.52	8.55	4.49
1982–1991	17.59	11.97	16.32	15.56	13.13	7.65	3.91
1983–1992	16.19	11.55	13.28	12.58	11.04	6.95	3.81
1984–1993	14.94	9.96	14.00	14.41	11.43	6.35	3.71
1985–1994	14.40	11.06	11.57	11.86	9.40	5.76	3.58
1986–1995	14.84	11.90	11.32	11.92	9.08	5.55	3.46
1987–1996	15.28	12.98	9.48	9.39	7.77	5.46	3.68
1988–1997	18.05	16.46	10.85	11.32	8.33	5.44	3.41
1989–1998	19.19	13.22	10.85	11.66	8.74	5.29	3.12
1990–1999	18.20	15.09	8.36	8.79	7.20	4.92	2.93
1991–2000	17.46	17.49	8.96	10.26	7.48	4.74	2.66
1992–2001	12.93	15.58	8.09	8.73	6.73	4.56	2.51
1993–2002	9.33	11.58	8.75	9.67	7.29	4.37	2.46

Table 2-10

Basic Series

Compound Annual Returns for 15-Year Holding Periods (percent per annum)

from 1926 to 1970

Period	Large Company Stocks	Small Company Stocks	Long-Term Corporate Bonds	Long-Term Government Bonds	Intermediate Government Bonds	U.S. Treasury Bills	Inflation
1926–1940	4.04	−0.66	6.24	4.99	4.37	1.34	−1.59
1927–1941	2.44	−1.30	5.93	4.53	4.04	1.13	−0.88
1928–1942	1.53	−0.19	5.60	4.16	3.87	0.94	−0.16
1929–1943	0.64	1.82	5.60	4.29	4.00	0.73	0.12
1930–1944	2.46	9.94	5.70	4.25	3.71	0.44	0.24
1931–1945	6.62	17.77	5.44	4.65	3.42	0.30	0.81
1932–1946	10.11	22.29	5.70	5.02	3.65	0.25	2.62
1933–1947	11.15	22.81	4.81	3.75	3.13	0.22	3.96
1934–1948	8.39	15.59	4.40	3.99	3.13	0.26	4.11
1935–1949	9.75	15.31	3.73	3.76	2.70	0.32	3.85
1936–1950	8.91	15.23	3.24	3.43	2.28	0.39	4.03
1937–1951	8.36	12.02	2.61	2.66	2.10	0.47	4.34
1938–1952	12.78	18.92	2.66	2.72	2.11	0.56	4.19
1939–1953	10.68	16.18	2.48	2.59	1.91	0.68	4.43
1940–1954	13.88	19.88	2.57	2.67	1.79	0.74	4.43
1941–1955	16.78	21.80	2.38	2.18	1.55	0.85	4.39
1942–1956	18.24	22.91	1.71	1.73	1.49	1.01	3.94
1943–1957	15.91	18.68	2.11	2.00	1.87	1.20	3.53
1944–1958	16.92	17.63	1.76	1.44	1.59	1.28	3.44
1945–1959	16.39	15.47	1.39	1.09	1.45	1.45	3.40
1946–1960	14.04	11.05	1.70	1.28	2.05	1.61	3.35
1947–1961	16.52	14.07	1.91	1.35	2.11	1.72	2.25
1948–1962	15.38	13.04	2.59	1.98	2.41	1.87	1.75
1949–1963	16.56	14.81	2.46	1.84	2.40	2.03	1.67
1950–1964	16.40	15.05	2.56	1.65	2.51	2.19	1.88
1951–1965	15.18	15.21	2.38	1.69	2.54	2.37	1.63
1952–1966	12.74	14.08	2.58	2.21	2.82	2.59	1.46
1953–1967	13.09	18.56	2.00	1.47	2.78	2.76	1.61
1954–1968	13.96	21.55	1.94	1.21	2.87	2.98	1.88
1955–1969	10.14	15.53	1.02	0.40	2.64	3.36	2.31
1956–1970	8.43	12.66	2.13	1.25	3.75	3.69	2.65
1957–1971	8.94	13.50	3.33	2.49	4.36	3.82	2.69
1958–1972	11.05	15.03	3.23	2.37	4.19	3.86	2.71
1959–1973	7.27	8.55	3.47	2.73	4.59	4.22	3.17
1960–1974	4.31	5.87	3.32	3.18	5.00	4.56	3.86
1961–1975	6.50	9.15	3.66	2.89	4.75	4.77	4.23
1962–1976	6.32	10.43	4.52	3.90	5.47	4.97	4.51
1963–1977	6.44	13.06	4.11	3.39	5.19	5.13	4.89
1964–1978	5.44	13.06	3.95	3.22	5.32	5.40	5.38
1965–1979	5.56	14.19	3.34	2.90	5.32	5.85	6.17
1966–1980	6.71	14.09	3.18	2.58	5.52	6.33	6.87
1967–1981	7.11	15.64	3.08	2.46	5.83	6.97	7.24
1968–1982	6.96	12.89	5.90	5.47	7.58	7.40	7.30
1969–1983	7.66	13.10	6.15	5.54	7.77	7.64	7.24
1970–1984	8.74	14.76	7.86	6.93	8.77	7.85	7.09

Table 2-10 (continued)

Basic Series
Compound Annual Returns for 15-Year Holding Periods (percent per annum)

from 1971 to 2002

Period	Large Company Stocks	Small Company Stocks	Long-Term Corporate Bonds	Long-Term Government Bonds	Intermediate Government Bonds	U.S. Treasury Bills	Inflation
1971–1985	10.50	17.96	8.54	8.04	8.99	7.93	6.97
1972–1986	10.76	17.28	9.10	8.73	9.40	8.06	6.82
1973–1987	9.86	16.18	8.57	8.13	9.25	8.17	6.89
1974–1988	12.18	20.73	9.23	8.88	9.35	8.13	6.59
1975–1989	16.61	23.33	10.56	9.78	9.86	8.15	6.10
1976–1990	13.93	17.96	10.03	9.58	9.99	8.29	6.04
1977–1991	14.33	17.30	10.11	9.73	10.15	8.32	5.92
1978–1992	15.47	17.17	10.65	10.35	10.56	8.21	5.66
1979–1993	15.72	17.01	11.57	11.68	11.09	7.92	5.24
1980–1994	14.52	14.47	11.45	11.17	10.41	7.48	4.55
1981–1995	14.80	14.17	13.46	13.53	11.27	7.11	3.92
1982–1996	16.79	14.41	13.66	13.32	10.76	6.50	3.55
1983–1997	17.52	14.09	11.91	11.88	9.47	6.15	3.41
1984–1998	17.90	11.02	12.22	12.75	9.66	5.89	3.26
1985–1999	18.93	13.49	10.49	10.98	8.58	5.55	3.17
1986–2000	16.00	11.56	9.45	10.43	8.10	5.43	3.15
1987–2001	13.73	12.60	8.87	9.09	7.61	5.27	3.18
1988–2002	11.48	12.26	9.99	10.49	8.28	5.01	3.04

Table 2-11

Basic Series
Compound Annual Returns for 20-Year Holding Periods (percent per annum)

from 1926 to 1970

Period	Large Company Stocks	Small Company Stocks	Long-Term Corporate Bonds	Long-Term Government Bonds	Intermediate Government Bonds	U.S. Treasury Bills	Inflation
1926–1945	7.13	9.36	5.52	4.72	3.73	1.07	0.07
1927–1946	6.10	8.67	5.24	4.32	3.51	0.93	0.99
1928–1947	4.71	7.64	4.74	3.74	3.33	0.80	1.53
1929–1948	3.11	5.74	4.80	3.91	3.38	0.66	1.72
1930–1949	4.46	10.61	4.80	4.06	3.20	0.48	1.61
1931–1950	7.43	15.17	4.51	3.82	2.90	0.42	2.22
1932–1951	11.72	19.65	4.47	3.90	3.04	0.44	3.02
1933–1952	13.15	20.16	4.11	3.15	2.69	0.48	3.63
1934–1953	10.68	14.56	3.77	3.34	2.76	0.55	3.64
1935–1954	13.13	16.04	3.37	3.20	2.45	0.59	3.51
1936–1955	12.48	15.17	2.92	2.89	2.07	0.66	3.37
1937–1956	11.20	12.56	2.23	2.22	1.90	0.77	3.46
1938–1957	12.98	16.63	2.52	2.58	2.20	0.91	3.45
1939–1958	13.48	17.90	2.10	1.98	1.83	0.99	3.69
1940–1959	14.15	18.78	1.85	1.57	1.58	1.14	3.79
1941–1960	14.76	18.89	2.12	1.93	2.00	1.27	3.82
1942–1961	16.86	21.13	2.22	1.93	2.07	1.37	3.37
1943–1962	15.25	18.17	2.48	2.11	2.25	1.50	2.98
1944–1963	15.11	15.70	2.45	2.06	2.19	1.63	2.90
1945–1964	14.95	14.44	2.45	2.10	2.30	1.79	2.86
1946–1965	13.84	13.29	2.23	1.61	2.24	1.97	2.84
1947–1966	13.72	13.58	2.15	1.80	2.42	2.19	2.15
1948–1967	14.63	17.03	2.01	1.45	2.43	2.38	1.87
1949–1968	14.92	18.97	1.93	1.26	2.56	2.60	1.96
1950–1969	13.43	16.21	1.34	0.69	2.41	2.87	2.36
1951–1970	12.10	13.23	2.09	1.26	3.17	3.13	2.35
1952–1971	11.65	13.67	2.77	2.10	3.58	3.28	2.22
1953–1972	11.67	13.75	2.95	2.32	3.76	3.39	2.35
1954–1973	10.85	12.04	2.83	2.08	3.83	3.64	2.75
1955–1974	6.87	8.21	2.41	1.94	3.98	4.00	3.37
1956–1975	7.10	9.51	3.08	2.46	4.41	4.21	3.70
1957–1976	7.91	11.78	4.34	3.55	5.06	4.34	3.80
1958–1977	8.12	13.95	3.99	3.15	4.74	4.44	3.98
1959–1978	6.53	12.31	4.10	3.41	4.99	4.72	4.34
1960–1979	6.83	13.49	3.93	3.46	5.22	5.09	4.92
1961–1980	8.31	15.61	3.34	2.59	4.84	5.51	5.46
1962–1981	6.76	14.75	3.03	2.64	5.21	6.12	5.87
1963–1982	8.30	16.92	4.47	4.04	6.28	6.51	6.01
1964–1983	8.28	17.63	4.68	4.01	6.57	6.80	6.12
1965–1984	7.79	16.00	5.25	4.58	7.06	7.12	6.26
1966–1985	8.66	15.25	6.67	5.97	8.00	7.31	6.36
1967–1986	10.17	16.06	7.63	6.94	8.52	7.38	6.24
1968–1987	9.27	12.04	7.88	7.31	8.62	7.44	6.31
1969–1988	9.54	11.47	8.30	7.82	8.70	7.50	6.30
1970–1989	11.55	13.64	9.58	9.01	9.42	7.59	6.22

Table 2-11 (continued)

Basic Series
Compound Annual Returns for 20-Year Holding Periods (percent per annum)

from 1971 to 2002

Period	Large Company Stocks	Small Company Stocks	Long-Term Corporate Bonds	Long-Term Government Bonds	Intermediate Government Bonds	U.S. Treasury Bills	Inflation
1971–1990	11.15	13.35	9.01	8.71	9.08	7.66	6.26
1972–1991	11.89	14.58	9.43	9.00	9.40	7.72	6.24
1973–1992	11.33	15.54	9.54	9.12	9.51	7.70	6.21
1974–1993	12.76	18.82	10.16	10.10	9.85	7.49	5.91
1975–1994	14.58	20.33	10.00	9.42	9.25	7.29	5.44
1976–1995	14.59	19.57	10.58	10.45	9.69	7.28	5.22
1977–1996	14.55	17.84	9.71	9.54	9.14	7.28	5.14
1978–1997	16.65	17.71	10.29	10.39	9.51	7.29	4.89
1979–1998	17.75	16.04	10.86	11.14	9.85	7.17	4.52
1980–1999	17.87	15.46	10.66	10.69	9.53	6.89	4.00
1981–2000	15.68	13.33	11.49	11.99	9.97	6.62	3.57
1982–2001	15.24	13.76	12.13	12.09	9.88	6.09	3.21
1983–2002	12.71	11.57	10.99	11.12	9.15	5.65	3.13

Chapter 3

Description of the Basic Series

This chapter presents the returns for the seven basic asset classes and describes the construction of these returns. More detail on the construction of some series can be found in the January 1976 *Journal of Business* article, referenced at the end of the Introduction. Annual total returns and capital appreciation returns for each asset class are formed by compounding the monthly returns that appear in Appendix A. Annual income returns are formed by summing the monthly income payments and dividing this sum by the beginning-of-year price. Returns are formed assuming no taxes or transaction costs, except for returns on small company stocks that show the performance of an actual, tax-exempt investment fund including transaction and management costs, starting in 1982.

Large Company Stocks

Overview

One dollar invested in large company stocks at year-end 1925, with dividends reinvested, grew to $1,775.34 by year-end 2002; this represents a compound annual growth rate of 10.2 percent. [See Graph 3-1.] Capital appreciation alone caused $1.00 to grow to $68.97 over the 77-year period, a compound annual growth rate of 5.7 percent. Annual total returns ranged from a high of 54.0 percent in 1933 to a low of –43.3 percent in 1931. The 77-year average annual dividend yield was 4.3 percent.

Total Returns

From September 1997 to the present, the large company stock total return is provided by Standard and Poor's, which calculates the total return based on the daily reinvestment of dividends on the ex-dividend date. Standard and Poor's uses closing pricing (usually from the New York Stock Exchange) in their calculation. From 1977 to August 1997, the total return was provided by the American National Bank and Trust Company of Chicago, which modified monthly income numbers provided by Wilshire Associates, Santa Monica, California. Dividends (measured as of the ex-dividend date) are accumulated over the month and invested on the last trading day of the month in the S&P 500 index at the day's closing level. Wilshire uses the last trading price of the day for the stocks, usually from the Pacific Stock Exchange. Prior to 1977, the total return for a given month was calculated by summing the capital appreciation return and the income return as described on the following pages.

The large company stock total return index is based upon the S&P Composite Index. This index is a readily available, carefully constructed, market-value-weighted benchmark of large company stock performance. Market-value-weighted means that the weight of each stock in the index, for a given month, is proportionate to its market capitalization (price times the number of shares outstanding) at the beginning of that month. Currently, the S&P Composite includes 500 of the largest stocks (in terms of stock market value) in the United States; prior to March 1957 it consisted of 90 of the largest stocks.

Graph 3-1

Large Company Stocks

Return Indices, Returns, and Dividend Yields

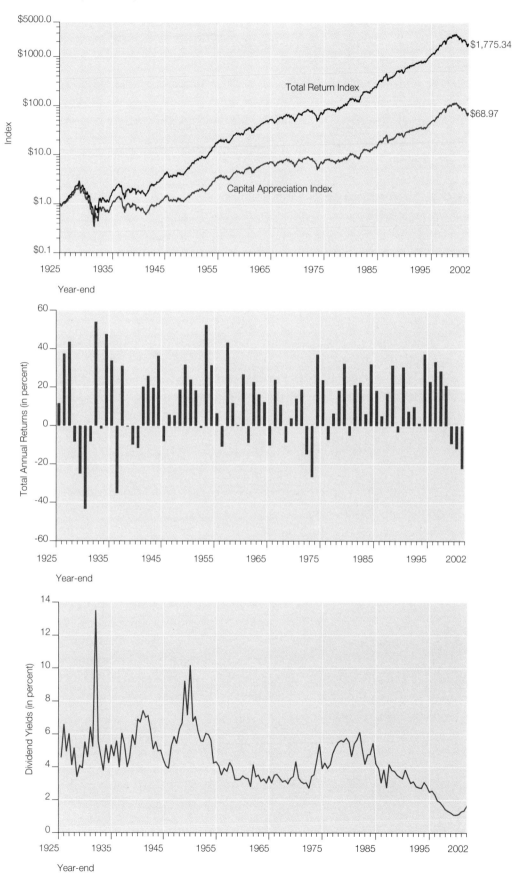

Capital Appreciation Return

The capital appreciation component of the large company stock total return is the change in the S&P 500-stock index (or 90-stock index) as reported in *The Wall Street Journal* for the period 1977–2002, and in Standard & Poor's *Trade and Securities Statistics* from 1926–1976.

Income Return

For 1977–2002, the income return was calculated as the difference between the total return and the capital appreciation return. For 1926–1976, quarterly dividends were extracted from rolling yearly dividends reported quarterly in S&P's *Trade and Securities Statistics,* then allocated to months within each quarter using proportions taken from the 1974 actual distribution of monthly dividends within quarters.

The dividend yields depicted in the bottom graph of Graph 3-1 were derived by annualizing the semiannual income return.

Small Company Stocks

Overview

One dollar invested in small company stocks at year-end 1925 grew to $6,816.41 by year-end 2002. [See Graph 3-2.] This represents a compound annual growth rate of 12.1 percent over the past 77 years. Total annual returns ranged from a high of 142.9 percent in 1933 to a low of –58.0 percent in 1937.

DFA Micro Cap Fund (April 2001–December 2002)

For April 2001 to December 2002, the small company stock return series is the total return achieved by the Dimensional Fund Advisors (DFA) Micro Cap Fund. In April 2001, DFA renamed their DFA Small Company 9/10 Fund (see below) to the DFA Micro Cap Fund and changed some of their criteria. The Micro Cap Fund's target universe includes those companies that have a market capitalization in the lowest 4 percent of the market universe. The market universe is defined as the aggregate of the New York Stock Exchange, American Stock Exchange, and NASDAQ National Market System. Currently companies with a market capitalization of approximately $483 million or less are eligible for purchase. The fund is designed to capture the returns and diversification benefits of a broad cross-section of U.S. small companies, on a market-cap weighted basis.

On a monthly basis, the market capitalization ranking of eligible stocks is examined to determine which issues are eligible for purchase or sale. Size ranges are based upon the aggregate capitalization of the market universe—NYSE, AMEX, NASDAQ NMS firms. A hold or buffer range is created for issues that migrate above the buy range. Issues that migrate above the hold range are sold and proceeds are invested into the portfolio. Sell candidates are determined based on market capitalization. Stocks become eligible for sale when they migrate above the 5th percentile of the market universe.

At year-end 2002, the DFA Micro Cap Fund contained approximately 3,000 stocks, with a weighted average market capitalization of $239 million. The unweighted average market

Graph 3-2

Small Company Stocks
Return Index and Returns

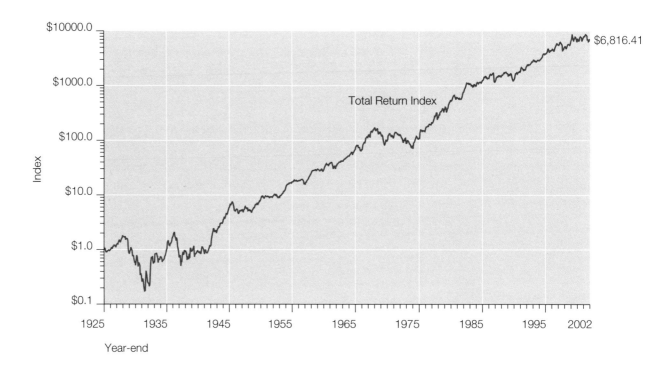

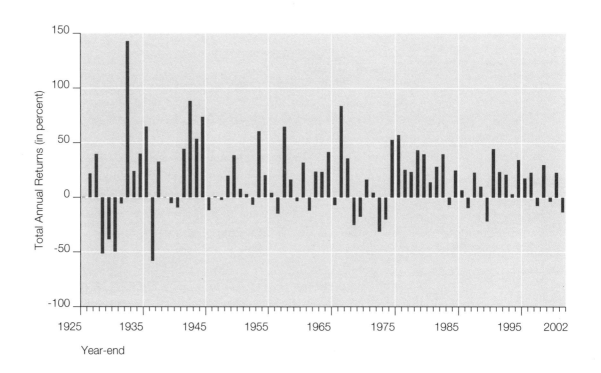

capitalization was $140 million, while the median was $74 million. See Table 7-5 for decile size, bounds, and composition.

DFA Small Company Fund (1982–March 2001)

For 1982–March 2001, the small company stock return series was the total return achieved by the Dimensional Fund Advisors (DFA) Small Company 9/10 (for ninth and tenth deciles) Fund. The fund was a market-value-weighted index of the ninth and tenth deciles of the New York Stock Exchange (NYSE), plus stocks listed on the American Stock Exchange (AMEX) and over-the-counter (OTC) with the same or less capitalization as the upper bound of the NYSE ninth decile. Since the lower bound of the tenth decile is near zero, stocks were not purchased if they were smaller than $10 million in market capitalization (although they were held if they fell below that level).

Stocks remained in the portfolio if they rose into the eighth NYSE decile, but they were sold when they rose into the seventh NYSE decile or higher. The returns for the DFA Small Company 9/10 Fund represent after-transaction-cost returns, while the returns for the other asset classes and for pre-1982 small company stocks are before-transaction-cost returns.

NYSE Fifth Quintile Returns (1926–1981)

The equities of smaller companies from 1926 to 1980 are represented by the historical series developed by Professor Rolf W. Banz (see reference section). This is composed of stocks making up the fifth quintile (i.e., the ninth and tenth deciles) of the New York Stock Exchange (NYSE); the stocks on the NYSE are ranked by capitalization (price times number of shares outstanding), and each decile contains an equal number of stocks at the beginning of each formation period. The ninth and tenth decile portfolio was first ranked and formed as of December 31, 1925. This portfolio was "held" for five years, with value-weighted portfolio returns computed monthly. Every five years the portfolio was rebalanced (i.e., all of the stocks on the NYSE were re-ranked, and a new portfolio of those falling in the ninth and tenth deciles was formed) as of December 31, 1930 and every five years thereafter through December 31, 1980. This method avoided survivorship bias by including the return after the delisting or failure of a stock in constructing the portfolio returns. (Survivorship bias is caused by studying only stocks that have survived events such as bankruptcy and acquisition.)

For 1981, Dimensional Fund Advisors, Inc. updated the returns using Professor Banz' methods. The data for 1981 are significant to only three decimal places (in decimal form) or one decimal place when returns are expressed in percent.

Long-Term Corporate Bonds

Overview

One dollar invested in long-term high-grade corporate bonds at the end of 1925 was worth $82.48 by year-end 2002. [See Graph 3-3.] The compound annual growth rate over the 77-year period was 5.9 percent. Total annual returns ranged from a high of 42.6 percent in 1982 to a low of –8.1 percent in 1969.

Total Returns

For 1969–2002, corporate bond total returns are represented by the Salomon Brothers Long-Term High-Grade Corporate Bond Index. Since most large corporate bond transactions take place over the counter, a major dealer is the natural source of these data. The index includes nearly all Aaa- and Aa-rated bonds. If a bond is downgraded during a particular month, its return for the month is included in the index before removing the bond from future portfolios.

Over 1926–1968 total returns were calculated by summing the capital appreciation returns and the income returns. For the period 1946–1968, Ibbotson and Sinquefield backdated the Salomon Brothers' index, using Salomon Brothers' monthly yield data with a methodology similar to that used by Salomon for 1969–2002. Capital appreciation returns were calculated from yields assuming (at the beginning of each monthly holding period) a 20-year maturity, a bond price equal to par, and a coupon equal to the beginning-of-period yield.

For the period 1926–1945, Standard & Poor's monthly High-Grade Corporate Composite yield data were used, assuming a 4 percent coupon and a 20-year maturity. The conventional present-value formula for bond price was used for the beginning and end-of-month prices. (This formula is presented in Ross, Stephen A., and Randolph W. Westerfield, *Corporate Finance*, Times Mirror/Mosby, St. Louis, 1990, p. 97 ["Level-Coupon Bonds"]). The monthly income return was assumed to be one-twelfth the coupon.

Long-Term Government Bonds

Overview

One dollar invested in long-term government bonds at year-end 1925, with coupons reinvested, grew to $59.70 by year-end 2002; this represents a compound annual growth rate of 5.5 percent. [See Graph 3-4.] Returns from the capital appreciation component alone caused $1.00 to increase to $1.04 over the 77-year period, representing a compound annual growth rate of 0.05 percent. Total annual returns ranged from a high of 40.4 percent in 1982 to a low of –9.2 percent in 1967.

Total Returns

The total returns on long-term government bonds from 1977 to 2002 are constructed with data from *The Wall Street Journal*. The bond used in 2002 is the 6.250 percent issue that matures on August 15, 2023. The data from 1926–1976 are obtained from the Government Bond File at the Center for Research in Security Prices (CRSP) at the University of Chicago Graduate School of Business. The bonds used to construct the index are shown in Table 3-1. To the greatest extent possible, a one-bond portfolio with a term of approximately 20 years and a reasonably current coupon—whose returns did not reflect potential tax benefits, impaired negotiability, or special redemption or call privileges—was used each year. Where "flower" bonds (tenderable to the Treasury at par in payment of estate taxes) had to be used, we chose the bond with the smallest potential tax benefit. Where callable bonds had to be used, the term of the bond was assumed to be a simple average of the maturity and first call dates minus the current date. The bond was "held" for the calendar year and returns were computed.

Graph 3-3

Long-Term Corporate Bonds
Return Index and Returns

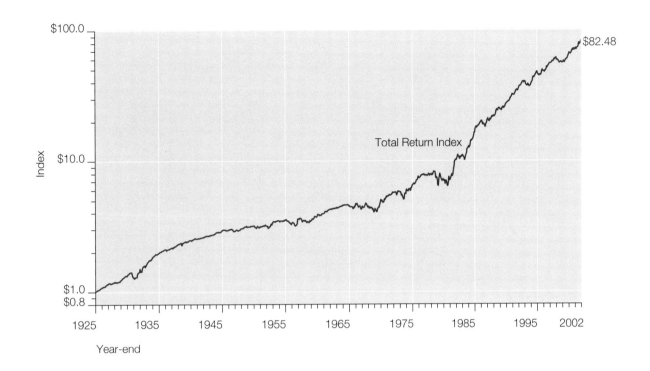

Year-end

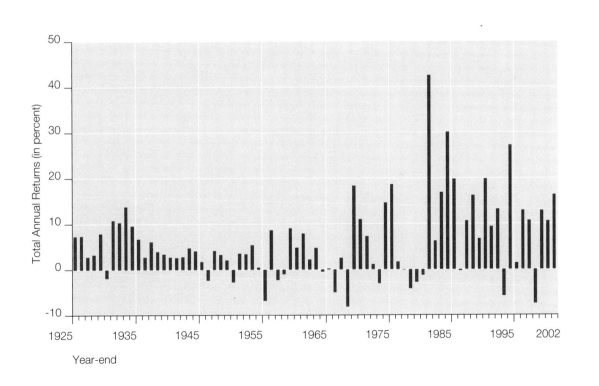

Year-end

Graph 3-4

Long-Term Government Bonds
Return Indices, Returns, and Yields

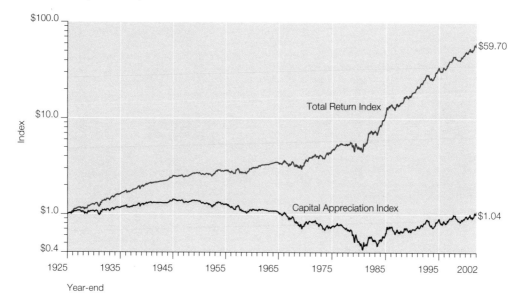

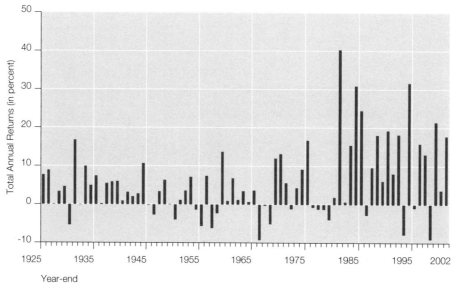

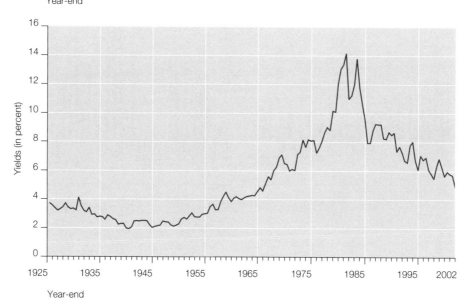

Total returns for 1977–2002 are calculated as the change in the flat or and-interest price.[1] The flat price is the average of the bond's bid and ask prices, plus the accrued coupon.[2] The accrued coupon is equal to zero on the day a coupon is paid, and increases over time until the next coupon payment according to this formula:

$$A = fC \qquad (1)$$

where,

A = accrued coupon;

C = semiannual coupon rate; and

$$f = \frac{\text{number of days since last coupon payment}}{\text{number of days from last coupon payment to next coupon payment}}$$

Income Return

For 1977–2002, the income return is calculated as the change in flat price plus any coupon actually paid from one period to the next, holding the yield constant over the period. As in the total return series, the exact number of days comprising the period is used. For 1926–1976, the income return for a given month is calculated as the total return minus the capital appreciation return.

Capital Appreciation or Return in Excess of Yield

For 1977–2002, capital appreciation is taken as the total return minus the income return for each month. For 1926–1976, the capital appreciation return (also known as the return in excess of yield) is obtained from the CRSP Government Bond File.

A bond's capital appreciation is defined as the total return minus the income return; that is, the return in excess of yield. This definition omits the capital gain or loss that comes from the movement of a bond's price toward par (in the absence of interest rate change) as it matures. Capital appreciation, as defined here, captures changes in bond prices caused by changes in the interest rate.

Yields

The yield on the long-term government bond series is defined as the internal rate of return that equates the bond's price (the average of bid and ask, plus the accrued coupon) with the stream of cash flows (coupons and principal) promised to the bondholder. The yields reported for 1977–2002 were calculated from *The Wall Street Journal* prices for the bonds listed in Table 3-1. For noncallable bonds, the maturity date is shown. For callable bonds, the first call date and the maturity dates are shown as in the following example: 10/15/47–52 refers to a bond that is first callable on 10/15/1947 and matures on 10/15/1952. Dates from 47–99 refer to 1947–1999; 00–16 refers to 2000–2016. For callable bonds trading below par, the yield to maturity is used; above par, the yield to call is used. The yields for 1926–1976 were obtained from the CRSP Government Bond File.

---

1 "Flat price" is used here to mean the unmodified economic value of the bond, i.e., the and-interest price, or quoted price plus accrued interest. In contrast, some sources use flat price to mean the quoted price.

2 For the purpose of calculating the return in months when a coupon payment is made, the change in the flat price includes the coupon.

Graph 3-5

Intermediate-Term Government Bonds
Return Indices, Returns, and Yields

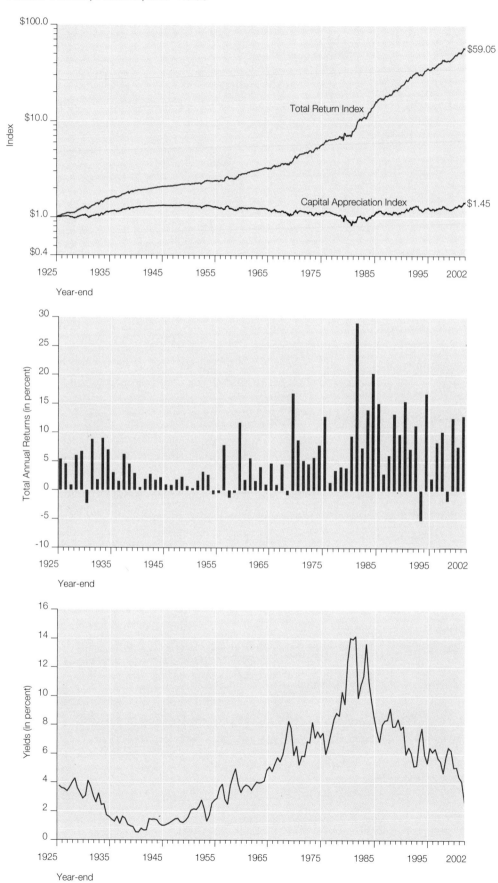

Intermediate-Term Government Bonds

Overview

One dollar invested in intermediate-term government bonds at year-end 1925, with coupons reinvested, grew to $59.05 by year-end 2002. [See Graph 3-5.] This represents a 77-year compound annual growth rate of 5.4 percent. Total annual returns ranged from a high of 29.1 percent in 1982 to a low of –5.1 percent in 1994.

Capital appreciation caused $1.00 to increase to $1.45 over the 77-year period, representing a compound annual growth rate of 0.5 percent. This increase was unexpected: Since yields rose on average over the period, capital appreciation on a hypothetical intermediate-term government bond portfolio with a constant five-year maturity should have been negative. An explanation of the positive average return is given at the end of this chapter.

Total Returns

Total returns of the intermediate-term government bonds for 1987–2002 are calculated from *The Wall Street Journal* prices, using the coupon accrual method described above for long-term government bonds. [See Equation (1).] The bond used in 2002 is the 6.125 percent issue maturing on August 15, 2007. Returns over 1934–1986 are obtained from the CRSP Government Bond File. The bonds used to construct the index over 1934–2002 are shown in Table 3-1.

As with long-term government bonds, one-bond portfolios are used to construct the intermediate-term government bond index. The bond chosen each year is the shortest noncallable bond with a maturity not less than five years, and it is "held" for the calendar year. Monthly returns are computed. (Bonds with impaired negotiability or special redemption privileges are omitted, as are partially or fully tax-exempt bonds starting with 1943.)

Over 1934–1942, almost all bonds with maturities near five years were partially or fully tax-exempt and selected using the rules described above. Personal tax rates were generally low in that period, so that yields on tax-exempt bonds were similar to yields on taxable bonds.

Over 1926–1933, there are few bonds suitable for construction of a series with a five-year maturity. For this period, five-year bond yield estimates are used. These estimates are obtained from Thomas S. Coleman, Lawrence Fisher, and Roger G. Ibbotson, *Historical U.S. Treasury Yield Curves: 1926–1992* with 1995 update (Ibbotson Associates, Chicago, 1995). The estimates reflect what a "pure play" five-year Treasury bond, selling at par and with no special redemption or call provisions, would have yielded had one existed. Estimates are for partially tax-exempt bonds for 1926–1932 and for fully tax-exempt bonds for 1933. Monthly yields are converted to monthly total returns by calculating the beginning and end-of-month flat prices for the hypothetical bonds. The bond is "bought" at the beginning of the month at par (i.e., the coupon equals the previous month-end yield), assuming a maturity of five years. It is "sold" at the end of the month, with the flat price calculated by discounting the coupons and principal at the end-of-month yield, assuming a maturity of 4 years and 11 months. The flat price is the price of the bond including coupon accruals, so that the change in flat price represents total return. Monthly income returns are assumed

Table 3-1

Long-Term and Intermediate-Term Government Bond Issues

Long-Term Government Bonds

Period Bond is Held in Index	Coupon (%)	Call/Maturity Date
1926–1931	4.25	10/15/47–52
1932–1935	3.00	9/15/51–55
1936–1941	2.875	3/15/55–60
1942–1953	2.50	9/15/67–72
1954–1958	3.25	6/15/78–83
1959–1960	4.00	2/15/80
1961–1965	4.25	5/15/75–85
1966–1972	4.25	8/15/87–92
1973–1974	6.75	2/15/93
1975–1976	8.50	5/15/94–99
1977–1980	7.875	2/15/95–00
1981	8.00	8/15/96–01
1982	13.375	8/15/01
1983	10.75	2/15/03
1984	11.875	11/15/03
1985	11.75	2/15/05–10
1986–1989	10.00	5/15/05–10
1990–1992	10.375	11/15/07–12
1993–1996	7.25	5/15/16
1997–1998	8.125	8/15/19
1999	8.125	8/15/21
2000	8.125	8/15/21
2001	8.125	8/15/21
2002	6.250	8/15/23

Intermediate-Term Government Bonds

Period Bond is Held in Index	Coupon (%)	Call/Maturity Date
1934–1936	3.25	8/01/41
1937	3.375	3/15/43
1938–1940	2.50	12/15/45
1941	3.00	1/01/46
1942	3.00	1/01/47
1943	1.75	6/15/48
1944–1945	2.00	3/15/50
1946	2.00	6/15/51
1947	2.00	3/15/52
1948	2.00	9/15/53
1949	2.50	3/15/54
1950	2.25	6/15/55
1951–1952	2.50	3/15/58
1953	2.375	6/15/58
1954	2.375	3/15/59
1955	2.125	11/15/60
1956	2.75	9/15/61
1957–1958	2.50	8/15/63
1959	3.00	2/15/64
1960	2.625	2/15/65

Intermediate-Term Government Bonds (continued)

Period Bond is Held in Index	Coupon (%)	Call/Maturity Date
1961	3.75	5/15/66
1962	3.625	11/15/67
1963	3.875	5/15/68
1964	4.00	2/15/69
1965	4.00	8/15/70
1966	4.00	8/15/71
1967	4.00	2/15/72
1968	4.00	8/15/73
1969	5.625	8/15/74
1970	5.75	2/15/75
1971	6.25	2/15/76
1972	1.50	10/01/76
1973	6.25	2/15/78
1974	6.25	8/15/79
1975	6.875	5/15/80
1976	7.00	2/15/81
1977	6.375	2/15/82
1978	8.00	2/15/83
1979	7.25	2/15/84
1980	8.00	2/15/85
1981	13.50	2/15/86
1982	9.00	2/15/87
1983	12.375	1/01/88
1984	14.625	1/15/89
1985	10.50	1/15/90
1986	11.75	1/15/91
1987	11.625	1/15/92
1988	8.75	1/15/93
1989	9.00	2/15/94
1990	8.625	10/15/95
1991–1992	7.875	7/15/96
1993	6.375	1/15/99
1994	5.50	4/15/00
1995	8.50	2/15/00
1996	7.75	2/15/01
1997	6.375	8/15/02
1998	5.75	8/15/03
1999	7.25	8/15/04
2000	6.50	8/15/05
2001	6.50	10/15/06
2002	6.125	8/15/07

to be equal to the previous end-of-month yield, stated in monthly terms. Monthly capital appreciation returns are formed as total returns minus income returns.

Income Return and Capital Appreciation

For the period 1987–2002, the income return is calculated according to the methodology stated under "Long-Term Government Bonds." Monthly capital appreciation (return in excess of yield) over this same period is the difference between total return and income return.

For 1934–1986, capital appreciation (return in excess of yield) is taken directly from the CRSP Government Bond File. The income return is calculated as the total return minus the capital appreciation return. Prior to 1934, the income and capital appreciation components of total return are generated from yield estimates as described earlier under Total Returns.

Yields

The yield on an intermediate-term government bond is the internal rate of return that equates the bond's price with the stream of cash flows (coupons and principal) promised to the bondholder. The yields reported for 1987–2002 are calculated from *The Wall Street Journal* bond prices listed in Table 3-1. For 1934–1986, yields were obtained from the CRSP Government Bond File. Yields for 1926–1933 are estimates from Coleman, Fisher, and Ibbotson, *Historical U.S. Treasury Yield Curves: 1926–1992* with 1995 update.

U.S. Treasury Bills

Overview

One dollar invested in U.S. Treasury bills at year-end 1925 grew to $17.48 by year-end 2002; this represents a compound annual growth rate of 3.8 percent. [See Graph 3-6.] Total annual returns ranged from a high of 14.7 percent in 1981 to a low of 0.0 percent for the period 1938 to 1940.

Total Returns

For the U.S. Treasury bill index, data from *The Wall Street Journal* are used for 1977–2002; the CRSP U.S. Government Bond File is the source until 1976. Each month a one-bill portfolio containing the shortest-term bill having not less than one month to maturity is constructed. (The bill's original term to maturity is not relevant.) To measure holding period returns for the one-bill portfolio, the bill is priced as of the last trading day of the previous month-end and as of the last trading day of the current month.

Graph 3-6

U.S. Treasury Bills
Return Index and Returns

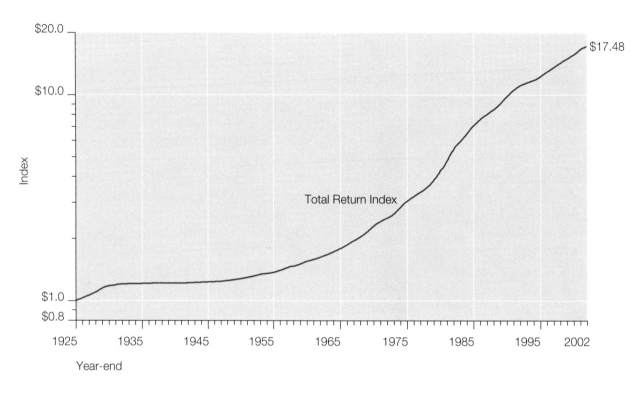

Year-end

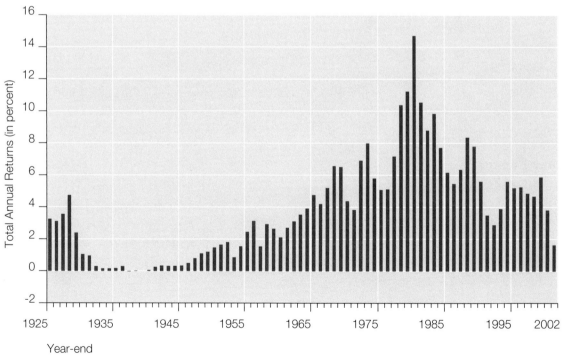

Year-end

The price of the bill **(P)** at each time **(t)** is given as:

$$P_t = \left[1 - \frac{rd}{360} \right]$$

(2)

where,

r = decimal yield (the average of bid and ask quotes) on the bill at time **t**; and,

d = number of days to maturity as of time **t**.

The total return on the bill is the month-end price divided by the previous month-end price, minus one.

Negative Returns on Treasury Bills

Monthly Treasury bill returns (as reported in Appendix A-14) were negative in February 1933, and in 12 months during the 1938–1941 period. Also, the annual Treasury bill return was negative for 1938. Since negative Treasury bill returns contradict logic, an explanation is in order.

Negative yields observed in the data do not imply that investors purchased Treasury bills with a guaranteed negative return. Rather, Treasury bills of that era were exempt from personal property taxes in some states, while cash was not. Further, for a bank to hold U.S. government deposits, Treasury securities were required as collateral. These circumstances created excessive demand for the security, and thus bills were sold at a premium. Given the low interest rates during the period, owners of the bills experienced negative returns.

Inflation

Overview

A basket of consumer goods purchased for $1.00 at year-end 1925 would cost $10.09 by year-end 2002. [See Graph 3-7.] Of course, the exact contents of the basket changed over time. This increase represents a compound annual rate of inflation of 3.0 percent over the past 77 years. Inflation rates ranged from a high of 18.2 percent in 1946 to a low of -10.3 percent in 1932.

Inflation

The Consumer Price Index for All Urban Consumers (CPI-U), not seasonally adjusted, is used to measure inflation, which is the rate of change of consumer goods prices. Unfortunately, the CPI is not measured over the same period as the other asset returns. All of the security returns are measured from one month-end to the next month-end. CPI commodity prices are collected during the month. Thus, measured inflation rates lag the other series by about one-half month. Prior to January 1978, the CPI (as compared with CPI-U) was used. For the period 1978 through 1987, the index uses the year 1967 in determining the items comprising the basket of goods. Following 1987, a three-year period, 1982 through 1984, was used to determine the items making up the basket of goods. All inflation measures are constructed by the U.S. Department of Labor, Bureau of Labor Statistics, Washington.

Graph 3-7

Inflation
Cumulative Index and Rates of Change

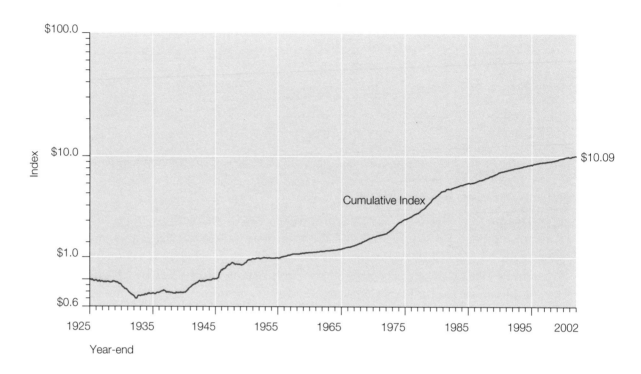

Year-end

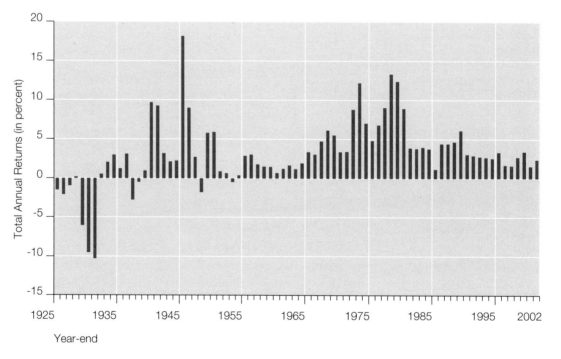

Year-end

Positive Capital Appreciation on Intermediate-Term Government Bonds

The capital appreciation component of intermediate-term government bond returns caused $1.00 invested at year-end 1925 to grow to $1.45 by the end of 2002, representing a compound annual rate of 0.5 percent. This is surprising because yields, on average, rose over the period.

An investor in a hypothetical five-year constant maturity portfolio, with continuous rebalancing, suffered a capital loss (that is, excluding coupon income) over 1926–2002. An investor who rebalanced yearly, choosing bonds according to the method set forth above, fared better. This investor would have earned the 0.5 percent per year capital gain recorded here.

This performance relates to the construction of the intermediate-term bond series. For 1926–1933, the one-bond portfolio was rebalanced monthly to maintain a constant maturity of five years. For the period 1934–2002, one bond (the shortest bond not less than five years to maturity) was chosen at the beginning of each year and priced monthly. New bonds were not picked each month to maintain a constant five years to maturity intrayear.

There are several possible reasons for the positive capital appreciation return. Chief among these reasons are convexity of the bond portfolio and the substitution of one bond for another at each year-end.

Convexity

Each year, we "bought" a bond with approximately five years to maturity and held it for one year. During this period, the market yield on the bond fluctuates. Because the duration of the bond shortens (the bond becomes less interest-rate sensitive) as yields rise and the duration lengthens as yields fall, more is gained from a fall in yield than is lost from a rise in yield. This characteristic of a bond is known as convexity.

For example, suppose an 8 percent coupon bond is bought at par at the beginning of a year; the yield fluctuates (but the portfolio is not rebalanced) during the year; and the bond is sold at par at the end of the year. The price of the bond at both the beginning and end of the year is $100; the change in bond price is zero. However, the fluctuations will have caused the gains during periods of falling yields to exceed the losses during periods of rising yields. Thus the total return for the year exceeds 8 percent. Since our measure of capital appreciation is the return in excess of yield, rather than the change in bond price, capital appreciation for this bond (as measured) will be greater than zero.

In 1992, the yield for intermediate-term government bonds started the year at 5.97 percent, rose, fell, and finally rose again to end at 6.11 percent, slightly higher than the starting point. In the absence of convexity, the capital appreciation return for 1992 would be negative. Because of the fluctuation of yields during the year, however, the capital appreciation return on the intermediate-term government bond index was positive 0.64 percent.

It should be noted that the return in excess of yield, or capital gain, from convexity is caused by holding, over the year, a bond whose yield at purchase is different than the current market yield. If the portfolio were rebalanced each time the data were sampled (in this case, monthly), by selling the old bond and buying a new five-year bond selling at par, the portfolio would have no convexity.

That is, over a period where yields ended where they started, the measured capital appreciation would be zero. However, this is neither a practical way to construct an index of actual bonds nor to manage a bond portfolio.

Bond Substitution

Another reason why the intermediate-term government bond series displays positive capital appreciation even though yields rose is the way in which bonds were removed from the portfolio and replaced with other bonds. In general, it was not possible to replace a bond "sold" by buying one with exactly the same yield. This produces a spurious change in the yield of the series—one that should not be associated with a capital gain or loss.

For example: Suppose a five-year bond yielding 8 percent is bought at par at the beginning of the year; at that time, four-year bonds yield 7 percent. Over the year, the yield curve rises in parallel by one percentage point so that when it comes time to sell the bond at year-end, it yields 8 percent and has four years to maturity. Therefore, at both the beginning and end of the year, the price of the bond is $100.

The proceeds from the sale are used to buy a new five-year bond yielding 9 percent. While the bond price change was zero over the year, the yield of the series has risen from 8 percent to 9 percent. Thus it is possible, because of the process of substituting one bond for another, for the yield series to contain a spurious rise that is not, and should not be expected to be, associated with a decline in the price of any particular bond. This phenomenon is likely to be the source of some of the positive capital appreciation in our intermediate-term government bond series.

Other Issues

While convexity and bond substitution may explain the anomaly of positive capital appreciation in a bond series with rising yields, there are other incomplete-market problems that may also help explain the capital gain. For example, intermediate-term government bonds were scarce in the 1930s and 1940s. As a result, the bonds chosen for this series occasionally had maturities longer than five years, ranging as high as eight years when bought. The 1930s and the first half of the 1940s were bullish for the bond market. Longer bonds included in this series had higher yields and substantially higher capital gain returns than bonds with exactly five years to maturity might have had if any existed. This upward bias is particularly noticeable in 1934, 1937, and 1938.

In addition, callable and fully or partially tax-exempt bonds were used when necessary to obtain a bond for some years. The conversion of the Treasury bond market from tax-exempt to taxable status produced a one-time upward jump in stated yields, but not a capital loss on any given bond. Therefore, part of the increase in stated yields over 1926–2002 was a tax effect that did not cause a capital loss on the intermediate-term bond index. Further, the callable bonds used in the early part of the period may have commanded a return premium for taking this extra risk.

Chapter 4
Description of the Derived Series

Historical data suggests that investors are rewarded for taking risks and that returns are related to inflation rates. The risk/return and the real/nominal relationships in the historical data are revealed by looking at the risk premium and inflation-adjusted series derived from the basic asset series. Monthly total returns for the four risk premia are presented in Appendix A: Tables A-16 through A-19. Monthly inflation-adjusted total returns for the six asset classes are presented in Appendix A: Tables A-20 through A-25.

Geometric Differences Used to Calculate Derived Series

Derived series are calculated as the geometric differences between two basic asset classes. Returns on basic series **A** and **B** and derived series **C** are related as follows:

$$(1+C) = \left[\frac{1+A}{1+B}\right] \tag{3}$$

where the series **A**, **B**, and **C** are in decimal form (i.e., 5 percent is indicated by 0.05). Thus **C** is given by:

$$C = \left[\frac{1+A}{1+B}\right] - 1 \approx A - B \tag{4}$$

As an example, suppose return **A** equals 15%, or 0.15; and return **B** is 5%, or 0.05. Then **C** equals (1.15 / 1.05) – 1 = 0.0952, or 9.52 percent. This result, while slightly different from the simple arithmetic difference of 10 percent, is conceptually the same.

Definitions of the Derived Series

From the seven basic asset classes—large company stocks, small company stocks, long-term corporate bonds, long-term government bonds, intermediate-term government bonds, U.S. Treasury bills, and consumer goods (inflation)—10 additional series are derived representing the component or elemental parts of the asset returns.

Two Categories of Derived Series

The 10 derived series are categorized as risk premia, or payoffs for taking various types of risk; and as inflation-adjusted asset returns. The risk premia series are the bond horizon premium, the bond default premium, the equity risk premium, and the small stock premium. The inflation-adjusted asset return series are constructed by geometrically subtracting inflation from each of the six asset total return series.

These 10 derived series are:

Series	Derivation
Risk Premia	
Equity Risk Premium	$\dfrac{(1 + \text{Large Stock TR})}{(1 + \text{Treasury Bill TR})} - 1$
Small Stock Premium	$\dfrac{(1 + \text{Small Stock TR})}{(1 + \text{Large Stock TR})} - 1$
Bond Default Premium	$\dfrac{(1 + \text{LT Corp Bond TR})}{(1 + \text{LT Govt Bond TR})} - 1$
Bond Horizon Premium	$\dfrac{(1 + \text{LT Govt Bond TR})}{(1 + \text{Treasury Bill TR})} - 1$
Inflation-Adjusted	
Large Company Stock Returns	$\dfrac{(1 + \text{Large Stock TR})}{(1 + \text{Inflation})} - 1$
Small Company Stock Returns	$\dfrac{(1 + \text{Small Stock TR})}{(1 + \text{Inflation})} - 1$
Corporate Bond Returns	$\dfrac{(1 + \text{Corp Bond TR})}{(1 + \text{Inflation})} - 1$
Long-Term Government Bond Returns	$\dfrac{(1 + \text{LT Govt Bond TR})}{(1 + \text{Inflation})} - 1$
Intermediate-Term Government Bond Returns	$\dfrac{(1 + \text{IT Govt Bond TR})}{(1 + \text{Inflation})} - 1$
Treasury Bill Returns (Real Riskless Rate of Returns)	$\dfrac{(1 + \text{Treasury Bill TR})}{(1 + \text{Inflation})} - 1$

TR = Total Return

Equity Risk Premium

Large company stock returns are composed of inflation, the real riskless rate, and the equity risk premium. The equity risk premium is the geometric difference between large company stock total returns and U.S. Treasury bill total returns.

Because large company stocks are not strictly comparable with bonds, horizon and default premia are not used to analyze the components of equity returns. (Large company stocks have characteristics that are analogous to horizon and default risk, but they are not equivalent.)

The monthly equity risk premium is given by:

$$\frac{(1 + \text{Large Stock TR})}{(1 + \text{Treasury Bill TR})} - 1 \qquad \text{\tiny (5)}$$

Graph 4-1 shows equity risk premium volatility over the last 77 years.

Graph 4-1

Equity Risk Premium Annual Returns
(in percent)

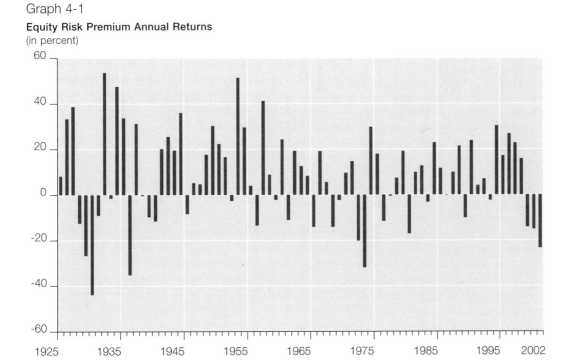

Year-end

Small Stock Premium

The small stock premium is the geometric difference between small company stock total returns and large company stock total returns. The monthly small stock premium is given by:

$$\frac{(1+\text{Small Stock TR})}{(1+\text{Large Stock TR})} - 1 \qquad _{(6)}$$

Graph 4-2 shows small stock premium volatility over the last 77 years.

Graph 4-2

Small Stock Premium Annual Returns
(in percent)

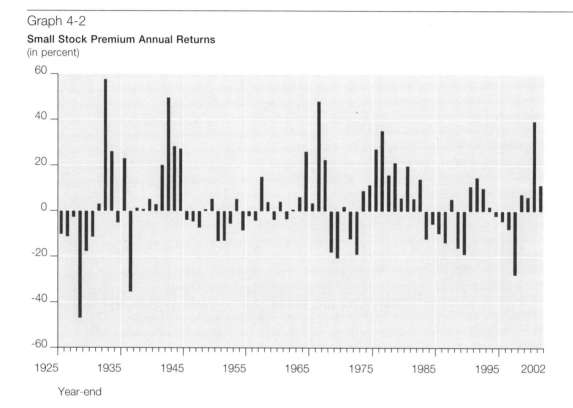

Year-end

Bond Default Premium

The bond default premium is defined as the net return from investing in long-term corporate bonds rather than long-term government bonds of equal maturity. Since there is a possibility of default on a corporate bond, bondholders receive a premium that reflects this possibility, in addition to inflation, the real riskless rate, and the horizon premium.

The monthly bond default premium is given by:

$$\frac{(1+\text{LT Corp Bond TR})}{(1+\text{LT Govt Bond TR})} - 1 \qquad _{(7)}$$

Components of the Default Premium

Bonds susceptible to default have higher returns (when they do not default) than riskless bonds. Default on a bond may be a small loss, such as a late or skipped interest payment; it may be a larger loss, such as the loss of any or all principal as well as interest. In any case, part of the default premium on a portfolio of bonds is consumed by the losses on those bonds that do default.

The remainder of the default premium—over and above the portion consumed by defaults—is a pure risk premium, which the investor demands and, over the long run, receives for taking the risk of default. The expected return on a corporate bond, or portfolio of corporate bonds, is less than the bond's yield. The portion of the yield that is expected to be consumed by defaults must be subtracted. The expected return on a corporate bond is equal to the expected return on a government bond of like maturity, plus the pure risk premium portion of the bond default premium.

Callability Risk is Captured in the Default Premium

Callability risk is the risk that a bond will be redeemed (at or near par) by its issuer before maturity, at a time when market interest rates are lower than the bond's coupon rate. The possibility of redemption is risky because it would prevent the bondholder of the redeemed issue from reinvesting the proceeds at the original (higher) interest rate. The bond default premium, as measured here, also inadvertently captures any premium investors may demand or receive for this risk.

Graph 4-3 shows bond default premium volatility over the last 77 years.

Graph 4-3

Bond Default Premium Annual Returns
(in percent)

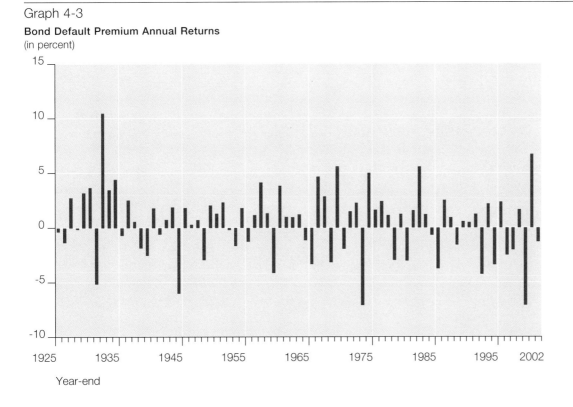

Year-end

Bond Horizon Premium

Long-term government bonds behave differently than short-term bills in that their prices (and hence returns) are more sensitive to interest rate fluctuations. The bond horizon premium is the premium investors demand for holding long-term bonds instead of U.S. Treasury bills.

The monthly bond horizon premium is given by:

$$\frac{\left(1 + \text{LT Govt Bond TR}\right)}{\left(1 + \text{Treasury Bill TR}\right)} - 1 \qquad (8)$$

Long-term rather than intermediate-term government bonds are used to derive the bond horizon premium so as to capture a "full unit" of price fluctuation risk. Intermediate-term government bonds may display a partial horizon premium, which is smaller than the difference between long-term bonds and short-term bills.

Does Maturity or Duration Determine the Bond Premium?

Duration is the present-value-weighted average time to receipt of cash flows (coupons and principal) from holding a bond, and can be calculated from the bond's yield, coupon rate, and term to maturity. The duration of a given bond determines the amount of return premium arising from differences in bond life. The bond horizon premium is also referred to as the "maturity premium," based on the observation that bonds with longer maturities command a return premium over shorter-maturity bonds. Duration, not term to maturity, however, is the bond characteristic that determines this return premium.

Why a "Horizon" Premium?

Investors often strive to match the duration of their bond holdings (cash inflows) with the estimated duration of their obligations or cash outflows. Consequently, investors with short time horizons regard long-duration bonds as risky (due to price fluctuation risk), and short-term bills as riskless. Conversely, investors with long time horizons regard short-term bills as risky (due to the uncertainty about the yield at which bills can be reinvested), and long-duration bonds as riskless or less risky.

Empirically, long-duration bonds bear higher yields and greater returns than short-term bills; that is, the yield curve slopes upward on average over time. This observation indicates that investors are more averse to the price fluctuation risk of long-duration bonds than to the reinvestment risk of bills.

Bond-duration risk is thus in the eye of the beholder, or bondholder. Therefore, rather than identifying the premium as a payoff for long-bond risk (which implies a judgment that short-horizon investors are "right" in their risk perceptions), it is better to go directly to the source of the return differential (the differing time horizons of investors) and use the label "horizon premium."

Graph 4-4 shows the bond horizon premium over the last 77 years.

Graph 4-4

Bond Horizon Premium Annual Returns
(in percent)

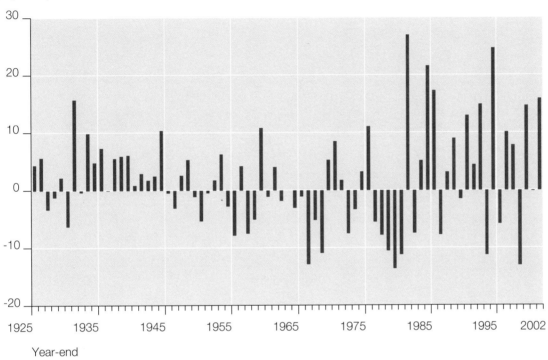

Year-end

Inflation-Adjusted Large Company Stock Returns

Overview

Large company stock total returns were 10.2 percent compounded annually over the period 1926–2002 in nominal terms. [See Graph 4-5.] In real (inflation-adjusted) terms, stocks provided a 6.9 percent compound annual return. Thus, a large company stock investor would have experienced a substantial increase in real wealth, or purchasing power, over the 77-year period.

Construction

The inflation-adjusted return is a geometric difference and is approximately equal to the arithmetic difference between the large company stock total return and the inflation rate. The monthly inflation-adjusted large company stock return is given by:

$$\frac{(1 + \text{Large Stock TR})}{(1 + \text{Inflation})} - 1 \qquad \text{(9)}$$

Graph 4-5

Large Company Stocks
Real and Nominal Return Indices

Year-End 1925 = $1.00

from 1925 to 2002

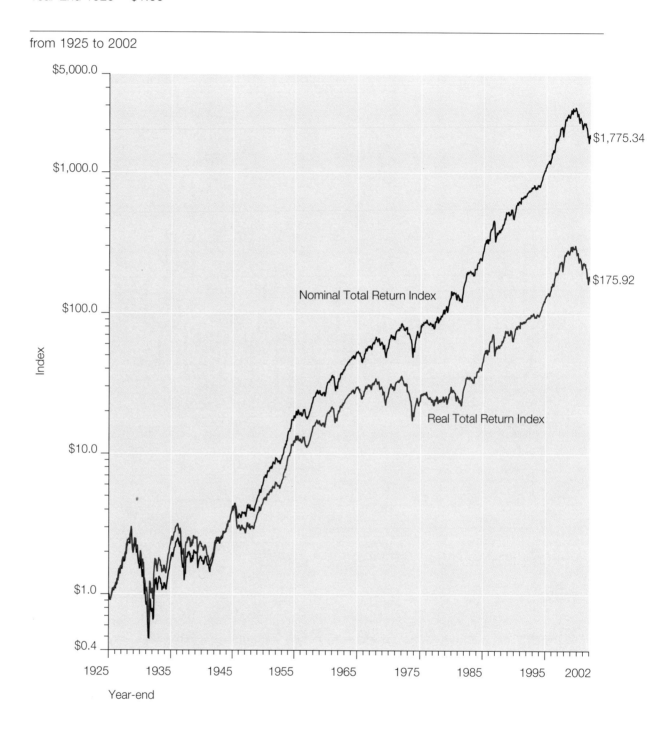

The inflation-adjusted large company stock return may also be expressed as the geometric sum of the real riskless rate and the equity risk premium:

$$[(1 + \text{Real Riskless Rate}) \times (1 + \text{Equity Risk Premium})] - 1 \qquad \text{(10)}$$

Inflation-Adjusted Small Company Stock Returns

Overview

Small company stock total returns were 12.1 percent compounded annually over the period 1926–2002 in nominal terms. [See Graph 4-6.] In real terms, small company stocks provided an 8.8 percent compound annual return. Thus, long-term a small company stock investor would have experienced a substantial increase in real wealth, or purchasing power, over the 77-year period.

Construction

The inflation-adjusted return is a geometric difference and is approximately equal to the arithmetic difference between the small company stock total return and the inflation rate. The monthly inflation-adjusted small company stock return is given by:

$$\frac{(1 + \text{Small Stock TR})}{(1 + \text{Inflation})} - 1 \qquad \text{(11)}$$

Inflation-Adjusted Long-Term Corporate Bond Returns

Overview

Corporate bonds returned 5.9 percent compounded annually over the period 1926–2002 in nominal terms, and a 2.8 percent compound annual return in real (inflation-adjusted) terms. [See Graph 4-7.] Thus, corporate bonds have outpaced inflation over the past 77 years.

Construction

The inflation-adjusted return is a geometric difference and is approximately equal to the arithmetic difference between the long-term corporate bond total return and the inflation rate. The monthly inflation-adjusted corporate bond total return is given by:

$$\frac{(1 + \text{Corp Bond TR})}{(1 + \text{Inflation})} - 1 \qquad \text{(12)}$$

Graph 4-6

Small Company Stocks
Real and Nominal Return Indices

Year-End 1925 = $1.00

from 1925 to 2002

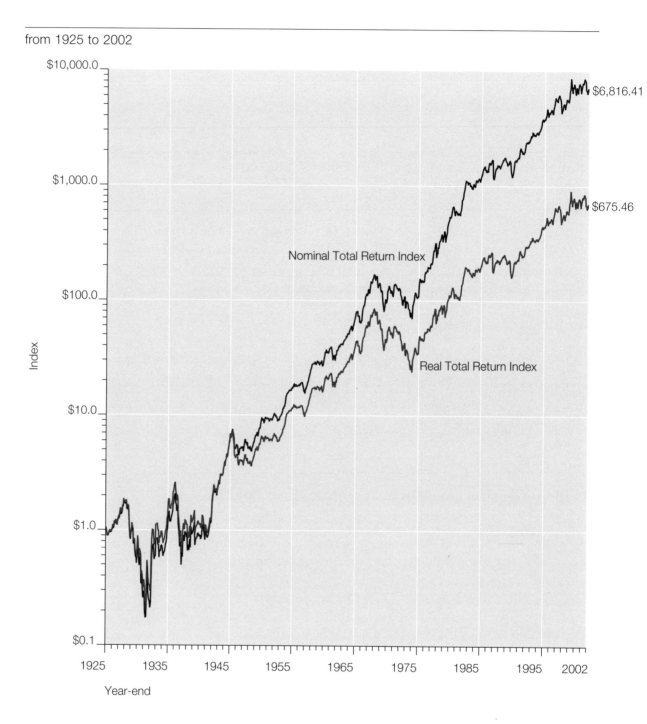

Graph 4-7

Long-Term Corporate Bonds
Real and Nominal Return Indices

Year-End 1925 = $1.00

from 1925 to 2002

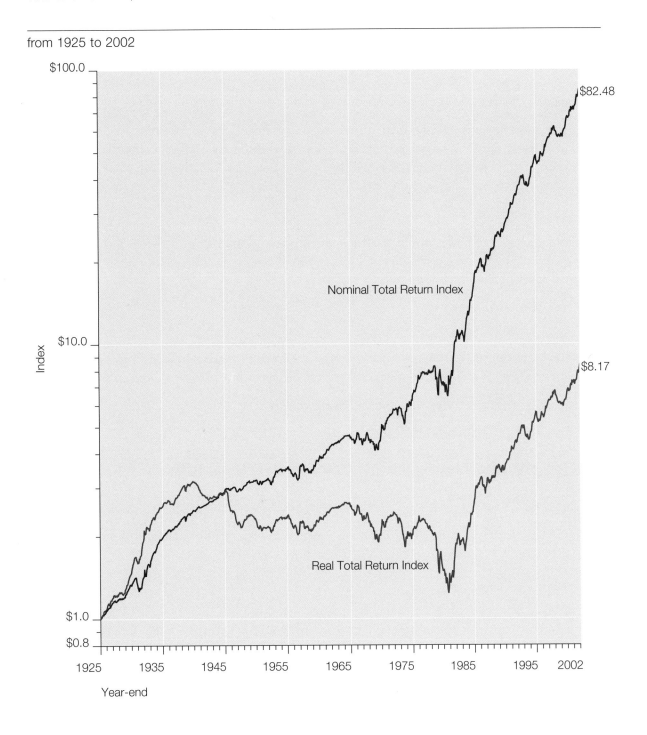

Index

Year-end

Inflation-Adjusted Long-Term Government Bond Returns

Overview

Long-term government bonds returned 5.5 percent compounded annually over the period 1926–2002 in nominal terms, and a 2.3 percent compound annual return in real (inflation-adjusted) terms. [See Graph 4-8.] Thus, long-term government bonds have outpaced inflation over the past 77 years despite falling bond prices over most of the period.

Construction

The inflation-adjusted return is a geometric difference and is approximately equal to the arithmetic difference between the long-term government bond total return and the inflation rate. The monthly inflation-adjusted long-term government bond total return is given by:

$$\frac{\left(1 + \text{LT Govt Bond TR}\right)}{\left(1 + \text{Inflation}\right)} - 1 \qquad (13)$$

Since government bond returns are composed of inflation, the real riskless rate, and the horizon premium, the inflation-adjusted government bond returns may also be expressed as:

$$\left[\left(1 + \text{Real Riskless Rate}\right) \times \left(1 + \text{Horizon Premium}\right)\right] - 1 \qquad (14)$$

Inflation-Adjusted Intermediate-Term Government Bond Returns

Overview

Intermediate-term government bonds returned 5.4 percent compounded annually in nominal terms, and 2.3 percent in real (inflation-adjusted) terms. [See Graph 4-9.]

Construction

The inflation-adjusted return is a geometric difference and is approximately equal to the arithmetic difference between the intermediate-term government bond total return and the inflation rate. The monthly inflation-adjusted intermediate-term government bond return is given by:

$$\frac{\left(1 + \text{IT Govt Bond TR}\right)}{\left(1 + \text{Inflation}\right)} - 1 \qquad (15)$$

Graph 4-8

Long-Term Government Bonds
Real and Nominal Return Indices

Year-End 1925 = $1.00

from 1925 to 2002

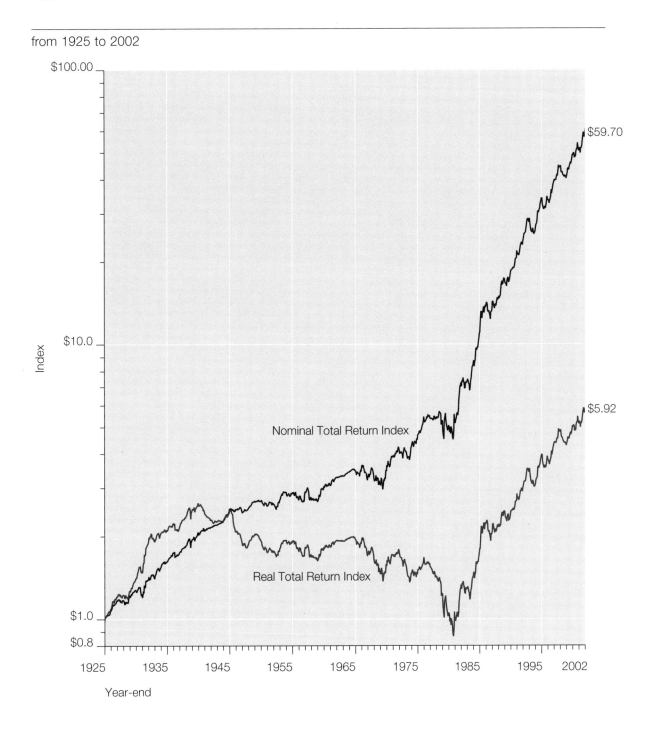

Year-end

Graph 4-9

Intermediate-Term Government Bonds
Real and Nominal Return Indices

Year-End 1925 = $1.00

from 1925 to 2002

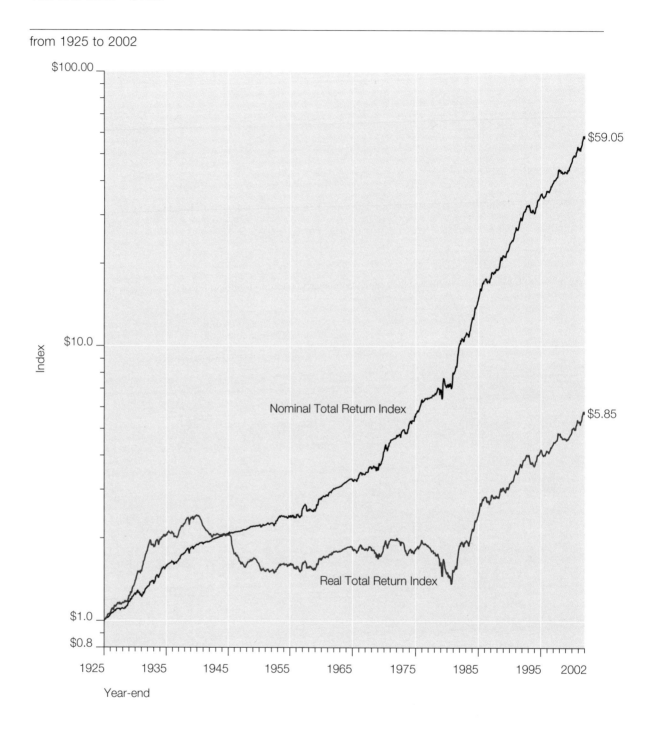

Inflation-Adjusted U.S. Treasury Bill Returns (Real Riskless Rates of Return)

Overview

Treasury bills returned 3.8 percent compounded annually over 1926–2002, in nominal terms, but only a 0.7 percent compound annual return in real (inflation-adjusted) terms. [See Graph 4-11.] Thus, an investor in Treasury bills would have barely beaten inflation over the 77-year period.

Construction

The real riskless rate of return is the difference in returns between riskless U.S. Treasury bills and inflation. This is given by:

$$\frac{\left(1 + \text{Treasury Bill TR}\right)}{\left(1 + \text{Inflation}\right)} - 1 \qquad (16)$$

Graph 4-10 shows the levels, volatility, and patterns of real interest rates over the last 77 years.

Graph 4-10

Annual Real Riskless Rates of Return
(in percent)

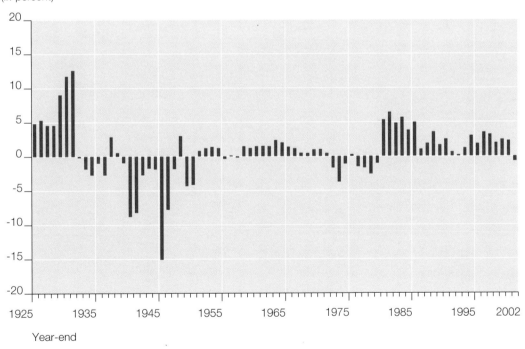

Year-end

Returns on the Derived Series

Annual returns for the 10 derived series are calculated from monthly returns in the same manner as the annual basic series. Table 4-1 presents annual returns for each of the 10 derived series. Four of the derived series are risk premia and six are inflation-adjusted total returns on asset classes.

Graph 4-11

U.S. Treasury Bills

Real and Nominal Return Indices

Year-End 1925 = $1.00

from 1925 to 2002

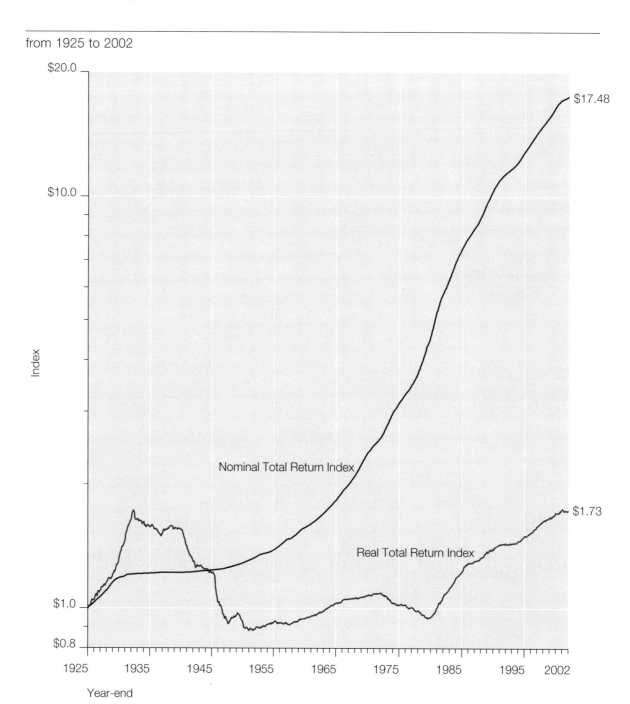

Table 4-1

Derived Series
Annual Returns (in percent)

from 1926 to 1970

Year	Equity Risk Premia	Small Stock Premia	Default Premia	Horizon Premia	Inflation-Adjusted					
					Large Company Stocks	Small Company Stocks	Long-Term Corp. Bonds	Long-Term Govt. Bonds	Intermed. Govt. Bonds	U.S. Treasury Bills
1926	8.09	−10.17	−0.37	4.36	13.31	1.79	9.00	9.40	6.97	4.83
1927	33.32	−11.19	−1.36	5.63	40.41	24.69	9.73	11.24	6.74	5.31
1928	38.67	−2.73	2.73	−3.34	45.01	41.06	3.84	1.08	1.90	4.57
1929	−12.57	−46.89	−0.14	−1.27	−8.59	−51.45	3.07	3.22	5.81	4.54
1930	−26.66	−17.64	3.17	2.20	−20.08	−34.18	14.90	11.38	13.56	8.98
1931	−43.94	−11.33	3.65	−6.31	−37.37	−44.46	8.48	4.66	7.96	11.71
1932	−9.07	3.05	−5.15	15.73	2.35	5.47	23.54	30.26	21.30	12.55
1933	53.53	57.72	10.46	−0.37	53.21	141.63	9.82	−0.58	1.31	−0.21
1934	−1.60	26.04	3.47	9.85	−3.40	21.75	11.58	7.84	6.83	−1.83
1935	47.42	−5.06	4.41	4.81	43.39	36.13	6.44	1.94	3.91	−2.73
1936	33.68	23.06	−0.72	7.32	32.32	62.83	5.47	6.23	1.83	−1.02
1937	−35.23	−35.37	2.51	−0.08	−36.98	−59.27	−0.35	−2.78	−1.50	−2.71
1938	31.14	1.28	0.57	5.55	34.87	36.59	9.16	8.55	9.27	2.84
1939	−0.43	0.76	−1.86	5.92	0.07	0.83	4.46	6.45	5.02	0.50
1940	−9.79	5.13	−2.54	6.08	−10.64	−6.05	2.41	5.08	1.99	−0.94
1941	−11.64	2.93	1.78	0.87	−19.42	−17.06	−6.37	−8.01	−8.40	−8.80
1942	20.02	20.08	−0.60	2.94	10.11	32.23	−6.12	−5.55	−6.73	−8.25
1943	25.46	49.62	0.73	1.73	22.04	82.60	−0.32	−1.04	−0.34	−2.73
1944	19.36	28.37	1.87	2.48	17.28	50.55	2.57	0.69	−0.31	−1.74
1945	35.99	27.25	−6.01	10.37	33.43	69.79	1.78	8.30	−0.03	−1.88
1946	−8.39	−3.87	1.83	−0.45	−22.20	−25.21	−13.91	−15.46	−14.52	−15.07
1947	5.18	−4.53	0.29	−3.11	−3.03	−7.42	−10.41	−10.67	−7.43	−7.80
1948	4.65	−7.22	0.71	2.57	2.72	−4.69	1.39	0.67	−0.84	−1.85
1949	17.50	0.80	−2.95	5.29	20.97	21.95	5.21	8.40	4.20	2.96
1950	30.16	5.34	2.05	−1.12	24.50	31.15	−3.47	−5.42	−4.81	−4.34
1951	22.19	−13.07	1.29	−5.34	17.14	1.82	−8.09	−9.26	−5.21	−4.14
1952	16.44	−12.96	2.33	−0.49	17.33	2.13	2.62	0.27	0.74	0.77
1953	−2.76	−5.55	−0.22	1.78	−1.60	−7.07	2.77	2.99	2.59	1.19
1954	51.32	5.21	−1.68	6.27	53.39	61.38	5.91	7.72	3.20	1.37
1955	29.52	−8.45	1.80	−2.82	31.07	19.99	0.10	−1.66	−1.02	1.19
1956	4.00	−2.13	−1.30	−7.85	3.59	1.38	−9.41	−8.21	−3.19	−0.39
1957	−13.50	−4.25	1.17	4.19	−13.40	−17.08	5.52	4.31	4.67	0.11
1958	41.19	15.01	4.13	−7.52	40.88	62.03	−3.91	−7.72	−3.00	−0.22
1959	8.75	3.97	1.32	−5.06	10.30	14.68	−2.43	−3.70	−1.86	1.43
1960	−2.14	−3.74	−4.14	10.83	−0.99	−4.70	7.48	12.12	10.13	1.17
1961	24.25	4.10	3.81	−1.13	26.04	31.21	4.12	0.30	1.17	1.44
1962	−11.16	−3.48	0.99	4.04	−9.83	−12.97	6.64	5.59	4.29	1.49
1963	19.09	0.62	0.97	−1.85	20.81	21.56	0.54	−0.43	−0.01	1.44
1964	12.50	6.04	1.22	−0.03	15.11	22.07	3.54	2.29	2.82	2.32
1965	8.20	26.06	−1.16	−3.10	10.33	39.08	−2.33	−1.19	−0.89	1.97
1966	−14.15	3.39	−3.33	−1.06	−12.98	−10.03	−3.06	0.29	1.29	1.36
1967	18.97	48.07	4.66	−12.85	20.32	78.15	−7.76	−11.86	−1.97	1.13
1968	5.57	22.43	2.84	−5.20	6.05	29.84	−2.05	−4.76	−0.18	0.46
1969	−14.16	−18.09	−3.18	−10.94	−13.77	−29.37	−13.38	−10.54	−6.45	0.45
1970	−2.36	−20.61	5.59	5.24	−1.41	−21.73	12.21	6.27	10.78	0.98

Table 4-1 (continued)

Derived Series

Annual Returns (in percent)

from 1971 to 2002

Year	Equity Risk Premia	Small Stock Premia	Default Premia	Horizon Premia	Inflation-Adjusted Large Company Stocks	Small Company Stocks	Long-Term Corp. Bonds	Long-Term Govt. Bonds	Intermed. Govt. Bonds	U.S. Treasury Bills
1971	9.51	1.91	−1.96	8.47	10.60	12.71	7.41	9.55	5.19	0.99
1972	14.58	−12.22	1.49	1.78	15.05	0.99	3.72	2.20	1.69	0.41
1973	−20.19	−19.03	2.27	−7.52	−21.56	−36.49	−7.04	−9.10	−3.85	−1.72
1974	−31.92	8.87	−7.11	−3.38	−34.46	−28.65	−13.60	−6.99	−5.80	−3.74
1975	29.68	11.38	4.99	3.21	28.21	42.80	7.13	2.04	0.76	−1.13
1976	17.85	27.08	1.62	11.11	18.16	50.15	13.20	11.40	7.69	0.26
1977	−11.70	35.08	2.41	−5.53	−13.07	17.43	−4.74	−6.99	−5.02	−1.55
1978	−0.58	15.86	1.12	−7.80	−2.26	13.24	−8.34	−9.36	−5.08	−1.69
1979	7.31	21.13	−2.98	−10.52	4.53	26.62	−15.43	−12.83	−8.13	−2.59
1980	19.04	5.63	1.24	−13.65	17.81	24.45	−13.48	−14.54	−7.55	−1.03
1981	−17.10	19.76	−3.04	−11.20	−12.71	4.53	−9.34	−6.50	0.47	5.30
1982	9.83	5.43	1.57	26.97	16.88	23.23	37.25	35.13	24.28	6.42
1983	12.61	14.00	5.57	−7.49	18.03	34.56	2.37	−3.03	3.48	4.82
1984	−3.26	−12.17	1.20	5.12	2.22	−10.22	12.42	11.08	9.68	5.67
1985	22.68	−5.67	−0.67	21.58	27.36	20.13	25.36	26.21	15.96	3.81
1986	11.59	−9.81	−3.76	17.30	17.15	5.66	18.51	23.14	13.85	4.98
1987	−0.22	−13.81	2.51	−7.76	0.79	−13.13	−4.48	−6.82	−1.44	1.01
1988	9.84	5.19	0.94	3.13	11.87	17.67	6.02	5.03	1.61	1.85
1989	21.33	−16.21	−1.59	8.99	25.65	5.29	11.07	12.87	8.26	3.56
1990	−10.19	−18.99	0.57	−1.51	−8.74	−26.08	0.64	0.07	3.42	1.61
1991	23.63	10.79	0.49	12.98	26.67	40.33	16.32	15.75	12.03	2.46
1992	4.02	14.56	1.24	4.39	4.64	19.87	6.31	5.01	4.17	0.59
1993	6.89	9.99	−4.28	14.91	7.05	17.74	10.16	15.08	8.26	0.14
1994	−2.50	1.78	2.18	−11.24	−1.33	0.42	−8.22	−10.17	−7.62	1.20
1995	30.15	−2.16	−3.39	24.69	34.03	31.13	24.06	28.41	13.91	2.98
1996	16.98	−4.43	2.35	−5.83	19.12	13.84	−1.86	−4.12	−1.18	1.82
1997	26.70	−7.94	−2.51	10.07	31.13	20.72	11.06	13.91	6.57	3.49
1998	22.63	−27.91	−2.04	7.83	26.54	−8.78	9.00	11.27	8.46	3.19
1999	15.63	7.22	1.67	−13.04	17.88	26.39	−9.87	−11.34	−4.34	1.95
2000	−14.16	6.07	−7.09	14.72	−12.08	−6.75	9.17	17.50	8.90	2.42
2001	−15.13	39.33	6.70	−0.13	−13.23	20.89	8.96	2.11	5.97	2.24
2002	−23.37	11.33	−1.28	15.93	−23.91	−15.29	13.63	15.10	10.31	−0.71

Chapter 5
Annual Returns and Indices

Returns and indices are used to measure the rewards investors earn for holding an asset class. Indices represent levels of wealth or prices, while returns represent changes in levels of wealth. Total returns for specific asset classes consist of component returns that are defined by the nature of the rewards being measured. For example: The total return on a security can be divided into income and capital appreciation components. The income return measures the cash income stream earned by holding the security, such as coupon interest or dividend payments. In contrast, the capital appreciation return results from a change in the price of the security. The method for computing a return varies with the nature of the payment (income or capital appreciation) and the time period of measure (monthly or annual frequency). Indices are computed by establishing a base period and base value and increasing that value by the successive returns. Indices are used to illustrate the cumulative growth of wealth from holding an asset class. This chapter describes the computation of the annual returns and indices.

Annual and Monthly Returns

Returns on the Basic Asset Classes

Annual total returns on each of the seven basic asset classes are presented in Table 2-5 in Chapter 2. The monthly total returns on the asset classes appear in Appendix A: Tables A-1, A-4, A-5, A-6, A-10, A-14, and A-15.

Calculating Annual Returns

Annual returns are formed by compounding the 12 monthly returns. Compounding, or linking, monthly returns is multiplying together the return relatives, or one plus the return, then subtracting one from the result. The equation is denoted as the geometric sum as follows:

$$r_{year} = [(1+r_{Jan})(1+r_{Feb})...(1+r_{Dec})]-1 \qquad (17)$$

where,

r_{year} = the compound total return for the year; and,

$r_{Jan}, r_{Feb}, ..., r_{Dec}$ = the returns for the 12 months of the year.

The compound return reflects the growth of funds invested in an asset. The following example illustrates the compounding method for a hypothetical year:

Month	Return (Percent)	Return (Decimal)	Return Relative
January	1%	0.01	1.01
February	6	0.06	1.06
March	2	0.02	1.02
April	1	0.01	1.01
May	−3	−0.03	0.97
June	2	0.02	1.02
July	−4	−0.04	0.96
August	−2	−0.02	0.98
September	3	0.03	1.03
October	−3	−0.03	0.97
November	2	0.02	1.02
December	1	0.01	1.01

The return for this hypothetical year is the geometric sum:

$$(1.01 \times 1.06 \times 1.02 \times 1.01 \times 0.97 \times 1.02 \times 0.96 \times 0.98 \times 1.03 \times 0.97 \times 1.02 \times 1.01) - 1 = 1.0567 - 1 = 0.0567$$

or a gain of 5.67 percent. Note that this is different than the simple addition result, $(1 + 6 + 2 + 1 - 3 + 2 - 4 - 2 + 3 - 3 + 2 + 1) = 6$ percent. One dollar invested in this hypothetical asset at the beginning of the year would have grown to slightly less than $1.06.

Calculation of Returns from Index Values

Equivalently, annual returns, r_t, can be formed by dividing index values according to:

$$r_t = \left[\frac{V_t}{V_{t-1}} \right] - 1 \tag{18}$$

where,

r_t = the annual return in period t;

V_t = the index value as of year-end t; and,

V_{t-1} = the index value as of the previous year-end, $t - 1$.

The construction of index values is discussed later in this chapter.

Calculation of Annual Income Returns

The conversion of monthly income returns to annual income returns is calculated by adding all the cash flows (income payments) for the period, then dividing the sum by the beginning period price:

$$r_I = \frac{(I_{Jan} + I_{Feb} + \ldots + I_{Dec})}{P_0}$$

(19)

where,

r_I	= the income return for the year;
$I_{Jan}, I_{Feb}, \ldots, I_{Dec}$	= the income payments for the 12 months of the year; and,
P_0	= the price of the security at the beginning of the year.

The following example illustrates the method for a hypothetical year:

Month	Beginning of Month Price	Income Return (Decimal)	Income Payment
January	$100	0.006	$0.60
February	102	0.004	0.41
March	105	0.002	0.21
April	101	0.001	0.10
May	99	0.005	0.50
June	103	0.004	0.41
July	105	0.003	0.32
August	103	0.002	0.21
September	105	0.003	0.32
October	103	0.004	0.41
November	106	0.001	0.11
December	105	0.002	0.21

Sum the income payments (not the returns), and divide by the price at the beginning of the year:

(0.60 + 0.41 + 0.21 + 0.10 + 0.50 + 0.41 + 0.32 + 0.21 + 0.32 + 0.41 + 0.11 + 0.21)/100 = 0.0381

or an annual income return of 3.81 percent.

Annual income and capital appreciation returns do not sum to the annual total return. The difference may be viewed as a reinvestment return, which is the return from investing income from a given month into the same asset class in subsequent months within the year.

Index Values

Index values, or indices, represent the cumulative effect of returns on a dollar invested. For example: One dollar invested in large company stocks (with dividends reinvested) as of December 31, 1925 grew to $1.12 by December 1926, reflecting the 12 percent total return in 1926. [See Table 5-1.] Over the year 1927, the $1.12 grew to $1.53 by December, reflecting the 37.5 percent total return for that year. By the end of 2002, the $1.00 invested at year-end 1925 grew to $1,775.34. Such growth reveals the power of compounding (reinvesting) one's investment returns.

Year-end indices of total returns for all seven basic asset classes are displayed in Table 5-1. This table also shows indices of capital appreciation for large company stocks as well as long- and intermediate-term government bonds. Indices of the inflation-adjusted return series are presented in Table 5-2. Monthly indices of total returns and, where applicable, capital appreciation returns on the basic asset classes are presented in Appendix B: Tables B-1 through B-10.

Graphs of index values, such as Graph 2-1 "Wealth Indices of Investments in the U.S. Capital Markets," depict the growth of wealth. The vertical scale is logarithmic so that equal distances represent equal percentage changes anywhere along the axis.

The inflation-adjusted indices in Table 5-2 are notable in that they show the growth of each asset class in constant dollars, or (synonymously) in real terms. Thus an investor in large company stocks, with dividends reinvested, would have multiplied his or her wealth in real terms, or purchasing power, by a factor of 175.9 between the end of 1925 and the end of 2002.

Calculation of Index Values

It is possible to mathematically describe the nature of the indices in Tables 5-1 and 5-2 precisely. At the end of each month, a cumulative wealth index (V_n) for each of the monthly return series (basic and derived) is formed. This index is initialized as of December 1925 at $1.00 (represented by $V_0 = 1.00$). This index is formed for month **n** by taking the product of one plus the returns each period, as in the following manner:

$$V_n = V_0 \left[\prod_{t=1}^{n} (1 + r_t) \right]$$

(20)

where,

V_n = the index value at end of period **n**;

V_0 = the initial index value at time **0**; and,

r_t = the return in period **t**.

Using Index Values for Performance Measurement

Index values can be used to determine whether an investment portfolio accumulated more wealth for the investor over a period of time than another portfolio, or whether the investment performed as well as an industry benchmark. In the following example, which produced more wealth—the "investor portfolio" or a hypothetical S&P 500 index fund returning exactly the S&P total return? Each index measures total return and assumes monthly reinvestment of dividends.

	Investor Portfolio	S&P 500
January 1990	−5.35%	−6.71%
February 1990	0.65	1.29
March 1990	0.23	2.63
Accumulated wealth of $1	$0.955	$0.970

Taking December 1989 as the base period, and using the computation method described above, the S&P 500 outperformed the investor portfolio.

Computing Returns for Non-Calendar Periods

Index values are also useful for computing returns for non-calendar time periods. To compute the capital appreciation return for long-term government bonds from the end of June 1987 through the end of June 1988, divide the index value in June 1988, 0.661, by the index value in June 1987, 0.683, and subtract 1. [Refer to Table B-6 in Appendix B.]

This yields: $(0.661/ 0.683) - 1 = -0.0322$, or −3.22 percent.

Table 5-1

Basic Series
Indices of Year-End Cumulative Wealth

Year-End 1925 = $1.00

from 1925 to 1970

Year	Large Stocks Total Returns	Large Stocks Capital Apprec	Small Stocks Total Returns	Long-Term Corp Bonds Total Returns	Long-Term Government Bonds Total Returns	Long-Term Government Bonds Capital Apprec	Intermediate-Term Government Bonds Total Returns	Intermediate-Term Government Bonds Capital Apprec	U.S. T-Bills Total Returns	Inflation
1925	1.000	1.000	1.000	1.000	1.000	1.000	1.000	1.000	1.000	1.000
1926	1.116	1.057	1.003	1.074	1.078	1.039	1.054	1.015	1.033	0.985
1927	1.535	1.384	1.224	1.154	1.174	1.095	1.101	1.025	1.065	0.965
1928	2.204	1.908	1.710	1.186	1.175	1.061	1.112	0.997	1.103	0.955
1929	2.018	1.681	0.832	1.225	1.215	1.059	1.178	1.014	1.155	0.957
1930	1.516	1.202	0.515	1.323	1.272	1.072	1.258	1.048	1.183	0.899
1931	0.859	0.636	0.259	1.299	1.204	0.982	1.228	0.991	1.196	0.814
1932	0.789	0.540	0.245	1.439	1.407	1.109	1.337	1.041	1.207	0.730
1933	1.214	0.792	0.594	1.588	1.406	1.074	1.361	1.031	1.211	0.734
1934	1.197	0.745	0.738	1.808	1.547	1.146	1.483	1.092	1.213	0.749
1935	1.767	1.053	1.035	1.982	1.624	1.171	1.587	1.146	1.215	0.771
1936	2.367	1.346	1.705	2.116	1.746	1.225	1.636	1.165	1.217	0.780
1937	1.538	0.827	0.716	2.174	1.750	1.195	1.661	1.165	1.221	0.804
1938	2.016	1.035	0.951	2.307	1.847	1.229	1.765	1.216	1.221	0.782
1939	2.008	0.979	0.954	2.399	1.957	1.272	1.845	1.255	1.221	0.778
1940	1.812	0.829	0.905	2.480	2.076	1.319	1.899	1.280	1.221	0.786
1941	1.602	0.681	0.823	2.548	2.096	1.306	1.909	1.278	1.222	0.862
1942	1.927	0.766	1.190	2.614	2.163	1.316	1.946	1.293	1.225	0.942
1943	2.427	0.915	2.242	2.688	2.208	1.311	2.000	1.309	1.229	0.972
1944	2.906	1.041	3.446	2.815	2.270	1.315	2.036	1.314	1.233	0.993
1945	3.965	1.361	5.983	2.930	2.514	1.424	2.082	1.327	1.237	1.015
1946	3.645	1.199	5.287	2.980	2.511	1.393	2.102	1.326	1.242	1.199
1947	3.853	1.199	5.335	2.911	2.445	1.328	2.122	1.322	1.248	1.307
1948	4.065	1.191	5.223	3.031	2.529	1.341	2.161	1.326	1.258	1.343
1949	4.829	1.313	6.254	3.132	2.692	1.396	2.211	1.338	1.272	1.318
1950	6.360	1.600	8.677	3.198	2.693	1.367	2.227	1.329	1.287	1.395
1951	7.888	1.863	9.355	3.112	2.587	1.282	2.235	1.307	1.306	1.477
1952	9.336	2.082	9.638	3.221	2.617	1.263	2.271	1.300	1.328	1.490
1953	9.244	1.944	9.013	3.331	2.713	1.271	2.345	1.308	1.352	1.499
1954	14.108	2.820	14.473	3.511	2.907	1.326	2.407	1.322	1.364	1.492
1955	18.561	3.564	17.431	3.527	2.870	1.272	2.392	1.281	1.385	1.497
1956	19.778	3.658	18.177	3.287	2.710	1.165	2.382	1.237	1.419	1.540
1957	17.646	3.134	15.529	3.573	2.912	1.209	2.568	1.287	1.464	1.587
1958	25.298	4.327	25.605	3.494	2.734	1.098	2.535	1.233	1.486	1.615
1959	28.322	4.694	29.804	3.460	2.673	1.030	2.525	1.177	1.530	1.639
1960	28.455	4.554	28.823	3.774	3.041	1.125	2.822	1.264	1.571	1.663
1961	36.106	5.607	38.072	3.956	3.070	1.093	2.874	1.243	1.604	1.674
1962	32.954	4.945	33.540	4.270	3.282	1.124	3.034	1.264	1.648	1.695
1963	40.469	5.879	41.444	4.364	3.322	1.093	3.084	1.237	1.700	1.723
1964	47.139	6.642	51.193	4.572	3.438	1.085	3.209	1.237	1.760	1.743
1965	53.008	7.244	72.567	4.552	3.462	1.048	3.242	1.199	1.829	1.777
1966	47.674	6.295	67.479	4.560	3.589	1.037	3.394	1.194	1.916	1.836
1967	59.104	7.560	123.870	4.335	3.259	0.896	3.428	1.148	1.997	1.892
1968	65.642	8.139	168.429	4.446	3.251	0.847	3.583	1.136	2.101	1.981
1969	60.059	7.210	126.233	4.086	3.086	0.755	3.557	1.054	2.239	2.102
1970	62.465	7.222	104.226	4.837	3.460	0.792	4.156	1.145	2.385	2.218

Table 5-1 (continued)

Basic Series
Indices of Year-End Cumulative Wealth

Year-End 1925 = $1.00

from 1971 to 2002

Year	Large Stocks Total Returns	Large Stocks Capital Apprec	Small Stocks Total Returns	Long-Term Corp Bonds Total Returns	Long-Term Government Bonds Total Returns	Long-Term Government Bonds Capital Apprec	Intermediate-Term Government Bonds Total Returns	Intermediate-Term Government Bonds Capital Apprec	U.S. T-Bills Total Returns	Inflation
1971	71.406	8.001	121.423	5.370	3.917	0.844	4.519	1.177	2.490	2.292
1972	84.956	9.252	126.807	5.760	4.140	0.841	4.752	1.168	2.585	2.371
1973	72.500	7.645	87.618	5.825	4.094	0.777	4.971	1.142	2.764	2.579
1974	53.311	5.373	70.142	5.647	4.272	0.750	5.254	1.120	2.986	2.894
1975	73.144	7.068	107.189	6.474	4.665	0.755	5.665	1.121	3.159	3.097
1976	90.584	8.422	168.691	7.681	5.447	0.816	6.394	1.180	3.319	3.246
1977	84.077	7.453	211.500	7.813	5.410	0.752	6.484	1.119	3.489	3.466
1978	89.592	7.532	261.120	7.807	5.346	0.684	6.710	1.069	3.740	3.778
1979	106.113	8.459	374.614	7.481	5.280	0.617	6.985	1.015	4.128	4.281
1980	140.514	10.639	523.992	7.274	5.071	0.530	7.258	0.946	4.592	4.812
1981	133.616	9.605	596.717	7.185	5.166	0.476	7.944	0.903	5.267	5.242
1982	162.223	11.023	763.829	10.242	7.251	0.589	10.256	1.031	5.822	5.445
1983	198.745	12.926	1066.828	10.883	7.298	0.532	11.015	0.997	6.335	5.652
1984	211.199	13.106	995.680	12.718	8.427	0.544	12.560	1.009	6.959	5.875
1985	279.117	16.559	1241.234	16.546	11.037	0.641	15.113	1.100	7.496	6.097
1986	330.671	18.981	1326.275	19.829	13.745	0.737	17.401	1.177	7.958	6.166
1987	347.967	19.366	1202.966	19.776	13.372	0.658	17.906	1.121	8.393	6.438
1988	406.458	21.769	1478.135	21.893	14.665	0.661	18.999	1.096	8.926	6.722
1989	534.455	27.703	1628.590	25.447	17.322	0.718	21.524	1.143	9.673	7.034
1990	517.499	25.886	1277.449	27.173	18.392	0.699	23.618	1.155	10.429	7.464
1991	675.592	32.695	1847.629	32.577	21.942	0.769	27.270	1.240	11.012	7.693
1992	727.412	34.155	2279.039	35.637	23.709	0.772	29.230	1.248	11.398	7.916
1993	800.078	36.565	2757.147	40.336	28.034	0.855	32.516	1.317	11.728	8.133
1994	810.538	36.002	2842.773	38.012	25.856	0.733	30.843	1.170	12.186	8.351
1995	1113.918	48.282	3822.398	48.353	34.044	0.901	36.025	1.283	12.868	8.563
1996	1370.946	58.066	4495.993	49.031	33.727	0.835	36.782	1.233	13.538	8.847
1997	1828.326	76.071	5519.969	55.380	39.074	0.906	39.864	1.257	14.250	8.998
1998	2350.892	96.359	5116.648	61.339	44.178	0.968	43.933	1.316	14.942	9.143
1999	2845.629	115.174	6640.788	56.772	40.218	0.829	43.155	1.223	15.641	9.389
2000	2586.524	103.496	6402.228	64.077	48.856	0.949	48.589	1.296	16.563	9.707
2001	2279.127	89.997	7860.048	70.900	50.662	0.931	52.291	1.338	17.197	9.857
2002	1775.341	68.969	6816.409	82.480	59.699	1.039	59.054	1.453	17.480	10.091

Table 5-2

Inflation-Adjusted Series
Indices of Year-End Cumulative Wealth

Year-End 1925 = $1.00

from 1925 to 1970

	Inflation-Adjusted					
	Large Company Stocks	Small Company Stocks	Long-Term Corporate Bonds	Long-Term Government Bonds	Intermediate Government Bonds	U.S. Treasury Bills
1925	1.000	1.000	1.000	1.000	1.000	1.000
1926	1.133	1.018	1.090	1.094	1.070	1.048
1927	1.591	1.269	1.196	1.217	1.142	1.104
1928	2.307	1.790	1.242	1.230	1.164	1.154
1929	2.109	0.869	1.280	1.270	1.231	1.207
1930	1.685	0.572	1.471	1.414	1.398	1.315
1931	1.056	0.318	1.596	1.480	1.509	1.469
1932	1.080	0.335	1.971	1.928	1.831	1.654
1933	1.655	0.810	2.165	1.917	1.855	1.650
1934	1.599	0.986	2.415	2.067	1.982	1.620
1935	2.292	1.342	2.571	2.107	2.059	1.576
1936	3.033	2.185	2.712	2.238	2.097	1.560
1937	1.912	0.890	2.702	2.176	2.065	1.517
1938	2.578	1.216	2.950	2.362	2.257	1.561
1939	2.580	1.226	3.082	2.514	2.370	1.568
1940	2.305	1.152	3.156	2.642	2.417	1.554
1941	1.858	0.955	2.955	2.430	2.214	1.417
1942	2.046	1.263	2.774	2.295	2.065	1.300
1943	2.496	2.306	2.765	2.271	2.058	1.264
1944	2.928	3.472	2.836	2.287	2.052	1.242
1945	3.907	5.895	2.887	2.477	2.051	1.219
1946	3.039	4.409	2.485	2.094	1.753	1.035
1947	2.947	4.081	2.227	1.871	1.623	0.955
1948	3.027	3.890	2.258	1.883	1.609	0.937
1949	3.662	4.744	2.375	2.042	1.677	0.965
1950	4.560	6.221	2.293	1.931	1.596	0.923
1951	5.341	6.335	2.107	1.752	1.513	0.885
1952	6.267	6.469	2.162	1.757	1.524	0.891
1953	6.166	6.012	2.222	1.809	1.564	0.902
1954	9.458	9.703	2.354	1.949	1.614	0.914
1955	12.397	11.642	2.356	1.917	1.597	0.925
1956	12.843	11.803	2.134	1.759	1.547	0.922
1957	11.122	9.788	2.252	1.835	1.619	0.923
1958	15.669	15.859	2.164	1.694	1.570	0.921
1959	17.283	18.187	2.112	1.631	1.541	0.934
1960	17.111	17.333	2.270	1.829	1.697	0.945
1961	21.567	22.741	2.363	1.834	1.717	0.958
1962	19.447	19.792	2.520	1.937	1.791	0.973
1963	23.494	24.060	2.534	1.928	1.790	0.987
1964	27.044	29.370	2.623	1.972	1.841	1.010
1965	29.838	40.848	2.562	1.949	1.825	1.029
1966	25.964	36.751	2.484	1.955	1.848	1.043
1967	31.239	65.471	2.291	1.723	1.812	1.055
1968	33.129	85.005	2.244	1.641	1.808	1.060
1969	28.567	60.042	1.944	1.468	1.692	1.065
1970	28.164	46.993	2.181	1.560	1.874	1.075

Table 5-2 (continued)

Inflation-Adjusted Series

Indices of Year-End Cumulative Wealth

Year-End 1925 = $1.00

from 1971 to 2002

	Inflation-Adjusted					
	Large Company Stocks	Small Company Stocks	Long-Term Corporate Bonds	Long-Term Government Bonds	Intermediate Government Bonds	U.S. Treasury Bills
1971	31.149	52.968	2.343	1.709	1.971	1.086
1972	35.837	53.492	2.430	1.746	2.005	1.091
1973	28.110	33.971	2.259	1.587	1.927	1.072
1974	18.422	24.238	1.951	1.476	1.815	1.032
1975	23.619	34.612	2.091	1.506	1.829	1.020
1976	27.908	51.971	2.366	1.678	1.970	1.023
1977	24.260	61.029	2.254	1.561	1.871	1.007
1978	23.712	69.108	2.066	1.415	1.776	0.990
1979	24.786	87.502	1.747	1.233	1.632	0.964
1980	29.201	108.894	1.512	1.054	1.508	0.954
1981	25.489	113.831	1.371	0.985	1.515	1.005
1982	29.792	140.278	1.881	1.332	1.884	1.069
1983	35.165	188.759	1.926	1.291	1.949	1.121
1984	35.947	169.470	2.165	1.434	2.138	1.184
1985	45.781	203.588	2.714	1.810	2.479	1.230
1986	53.631	215.106	3.216	2.229	2.822	1.291
1987	54.053	186.867	3.072	2.077	2.782	1.304
1988	60.466	219.893	3.257	2.182	2.826	1.328
1989	75.977	231.516	3.617	2.462	3.060	1.375
1990	69.333	171.148	3.641	2.464	3.164	1.397
1991	87.822	240.179	4.235	2.852	3.545	1.431
1992	91.893	287.908	4.502	2.995	3.693	1.440
1993	98.369	338.990	4.959	3.447	3.998	1.442
1994	97.059	340.412	4.552	3.096	3.693	1.459
1995	130.085	446.387	5.647	3.976	4.207	1.503
1996	154.953	508.167	5.542	3.812	4.157	1.530
1997	203.190	613.460	6.155	4.342	4.430	1.584
1998	257.121	559.616	6.709	4.832	4.805	1.634
1999	303.094	707.326	6.047	4.284	4.597	1.666
2000	266.472	659.577	6.601	5.033	5.006	1.706
2001	231.215	797.393	7.193	5.140	5.305	1.745
2002	175.925	675.462	8.173	5.916	5.852	1.732

Chapter 6
Statistical Analysis of Returns

Statistical analysis of historical asset returns can reveal the growth rate of wealth invested in an asset or portfolio, the riskiness or volatility of asset classes, the comovement of assets, and the random or cyclical behavior of asset returns. This chapter focuses on arithmetic and geometric mean returns, standard deviations, and serial and cross-correlation coefficients, and discusses the use of each statistic to characterize the various asset classes by growth rate, variability, and safety.

Calculating Arithmetic Mean Returns

The arithmetic mean of a series is the simple average of the elements in the series. The arithmetic mean return equation is:

$$r_A = \frac{1}{n} \sum_{t=1}^{n} r_t \qquad (21)$$

where,

r_A = the arithmetic mean return;

r_t = the series return in period **t**, that is, from time **t − 1** to time **t**; and,

n = the inclusive number of periods.

Calculating Geometric Mean Returns

The geometric mean of a return series over a period is the compound rate of return over the period. The geometric mean return equation is:

$$r_G = \left[\prod_{t=1}^{n} \left(1 + r_t\right) \right]^{\frac{1}{n}} - 1 \qquad (22)$$

where,

r_G = the geometric mean return;

r_t = the series return in period **t**; and,

n = the inclusive number of periods.

The geometric mean return can be restated using beginning and ending period index values. The equation is:

$$r_G = \left[\frac{V_n}{V_0} \right]^{\frac{1}{n}} - 1 \qquad (23)$$

where,

r_G = the geometric mean return;

V_n = the ending period index value at time **n**;

V_0 = the initial index value at time **0**; and,

n = the inclusive number of periods.

The annualized geometric mean return over any period of months can also be computed by expressing **n** as a fraction. For example: starting at the beginning of 1996 to the end of May 1996 is equivalent to five-twelfths of a year, or 0.4167. **V**$_n$ would be the index value at the end of May 1996, **V**$_0$ would be the index value at the beginning of 1996, and **n** would be 0.4167.

Geometric Mean Versus Arithmetic Mean

A simple example illustrates the difference between geometric and arithmetic means. Suppose $1.00 was invested in a large company stock portfolio that experiences successive annual returns of +50 percent and –50 percent. At the end of the first year, the portfolio is worth $1.50. At the end of the second year, the portfolio is worth $0.75. The annual arithmetic mean is 0.0 percent, whereas the annual geometric mean is –13.4 percent. Both are calculated as follows:

$$r_A = \frac{1}{2}(0.50 - 0.50) = 0.0, \text{ and}$$

$$r_G = \left[\frac{0.75}{1.00}\right]^{\frac{1}{2}} - 1 = -0.134$$

The geometric mean is backward-looking, measuring the change in wealth over more than one period. On the other hand, the arithmetic mean better represents a typical performance over single periods and serves as the correct rate for forecasting, discounting, and estimating the cost of capital. [See Chapter 9.]

In general, the geometric mean for any time period is less than or equal to the arithmetic mean. The two means are equal only for a return series that is constant (i.e., the same return in every period). For a non-constant series, the difference between the two is positively related to the variability or standard deviation of the returns. For example, in Table 6-7, the difference between the arithmetic and geometric mean is much larger for risky large company stocks than it is for nearly riskless Treasury bills.

The arithmetic mean is the rate of return which, when compounded over multiple periods, gives the mean of the probability distribution of ending wealth values. (A simple example given below shows that this is true.) This makes the arithmetic mean return appropriate for forecasting, discounting, and computing the cost of capital. The discount rate that equates expected (mean) future values with the present value of an investment is that investment's cost of capital. The logic of using the discount rate as the cost of capital is reinforced by noting that investors will discount their expected (mean) ending wealth values from an investment back to the present using the arithmetic mean, for the reason given above. They will, therefore, require such an expected (mean) return prospectively (that is, in the present looking toward the future) to commit their capital to the investment.

For example, assume a stock has an expected return of +10 percent in each year and a standard deviation of 20 percent. Assume further that only two outcomes are possible each year— +30 percent and –10 percent (that is, the mean plus or minus one standard deviation), and that these outcomes are equally likely. (The arithmetic mean of these returns is 10 percent, and the geometric mean is 8.2 percent.) Then the growth of wealth over a two-year period occurs as follows:

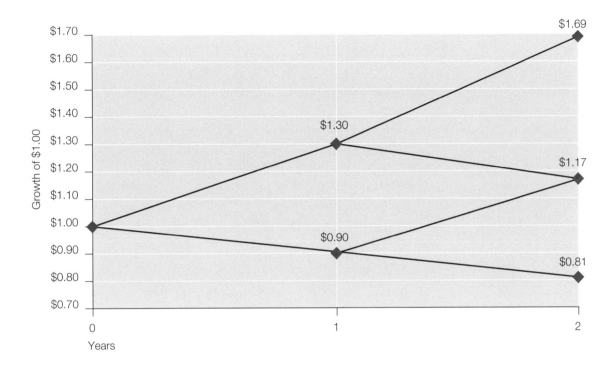

Note that the median (middle outcome) and mode (most common outcome) are given by the geometric mean, 8.2 percent, which compounds up to 17 percent over a two-year period (hence a terminal wealth of $1.17). However, the expected value, or probability-weighted average of all possible outcomes, is equal to:

$$
\begin{array}{r}
(.25 \times 1.69) = 0.4225 \\
+\ (.50 \times 1.17) = 0.5850 \\
+\ (.25 \times 0.81) = 0.2025 \\
\hline
\textbf{Total} \qquad \textbf{1.2100}
\end{array}
$$

Now, the rate that must be compounded up to achieve a terminal wealth of $1.21 after 2 years is 10 percent; that is, the expected value of the terminal wealth is given by compounding up the arithmetic, not the geometric mean. Since the arithmetic mean equates the expected future value with the present value, it is the discount rate.

Stated another way, the arithmetic mean is correct because an investment with uncertain returns will have a higher expected ending wealth value than an investment that earns, with certainty, its compound or geometric rate of return every year. In the above example, compounding at the rate of 8.2 percent for two years yields a terminal wealth of $1.17, based on $1.00 invested. But holding the uncertain investment, with a possibility of high returns (two +30 percent years in a row) as well as low returns (two –10 percent years in a row), yields a higher expected terminal wealth, $1.21. In other words, more money is gained by higher-than-expected returns than is lost by lower-than-expected returns. Therefore, in the investment markets, where returns are described by a probability distribution, the arithmetic mean is the measure that accounts for uncertainty, and is the appropriate one for estimating discount rates and the cost of capital.

Calculating Standard Deviations

The standard deviation of a series is a measure of the extent to which observations in the series differ from the arithmetic mean of the series. For a series of asset returns, the standard deviation is a measure of the volatility, or risk, of the asset. The standard deviation is a measure of the variation around an average or mean.

In a normally distributed series, about two-thirds of the observations lie within one standard deviation of the arithmetic mean; about 95 percent of the observations lie within two standard deviations; and more than 99 percent lie within three standard deviations.

For example, the standard deviation for large company stocks over the period 1926–2002 was 20.5 percent with an annual arithmetic mean of 12.2 percent. Therefore, roughly two-thirds of the observations have annual returns between –8.3 percent and 32.7 percent (12.2 ± 20.5); approximately 95 percent of the observations are between –28.8 percent and 53.2 percent (12.2 ± 41.0).

The equation for the standard deviation of a series of returns (σ_r) is:

$$\sigma_r = \sqrt{\frac{1}{n-1}\sum_{t=1}^{n}\left(r_t - r_A\right)^2} \qquad (24)$$

where,

r_t = the return in period **t**;

r_A = the arithmetic mean of the return series **r**; and,

n = the number of periods.

The scaling of the standard deviation depends on the frequency of the data; therefore, a series of monthly returns produces a monthly standard deviation. For example, using the monthly returns for the hypothetical year on page 90, a monthly standard deviation of 2.94 percent is calculated following equation (24):

$$[\tfrac{1}{12-1}((0.01 - 0.005)^2 + (0.06 - 0.005)^2 + (0.02 - 0.005)^2 + (0.01 - 0.005)^2$$
$$+ (-0.03 - 0.005)^2 + (0.02 - 0.005)^2 + (-0.04 - 0.005)^2 + (0.02 - 0.005)^2$$
$$+ (0.03 - 0.005)^2 + (-0.03 - 0.005)^2 + (0.02 - 0.005)^2 + (0.01 - 0.005)^2)]^{\frac{1}{2}} = 0.0294$$

It is sometimes useful to express the standard deviation of the series in another time scale. To calculate the annualized monthly standard deviations (σ_n), one uses equation (25).[1]

$$\sigma_n = \sqrt{\left[\sigma_1^2 + (1+\mu_1)^2\right]^n - (1+\mu_1)^{2n}} \qquad \text{(25)}$$

where,

n = the number of periods per year, e.g. 12 for monthly, 4 for quarterly, etc.;

σ_1 = the monthly standard deviation; and,

μ_1 = the monthly arithmetic mean.

Applying this formula to the prior monthly standard deviation of 2.94 percent results in an annualized monthly standard deviation of 10.78 percent. The annualized monthly standard deviation is calculated with equation (25) as follows:

$$\sqrt{\left[0.0294^2 + (1+0.005)^2\right]^{12} - (1+0.005)^{2(12)}} = 0.1078$$

This equation is the exact form of the common approximation:

$$\sigma_n \approx \sqrt{n}\,\sigma_1$$

The approximation treats an annual return as if it were the sum of 12 independent monthly returns, whereas equation (25) treats an annual return as the compound return of 12 independent monthly returns. [See Equation (17)]. While the approximation can be used for "back of the envelope" calculations, the exact formula should be used in applications of quantitative analysis. Forming inputs for mean-variance optimization, is one such example. Note that both the exact formula and the approximation assume that there is no monthly autocorrelation.

---

1 The equation appears in Haim Levy and Deborah Gunthorpe, "Optimal Investment Proportions in Senior Securities and Equities Under Alternative Holding Periods," *Journal of Portfolio Management*, Summer 1993, page 33.

Graph 6-1

Month-by-Month Returns on Stocks and Bonds
Large Company Stocks and Long-Term Government Bonds

from 1926 to 2002
Large Company Stocks

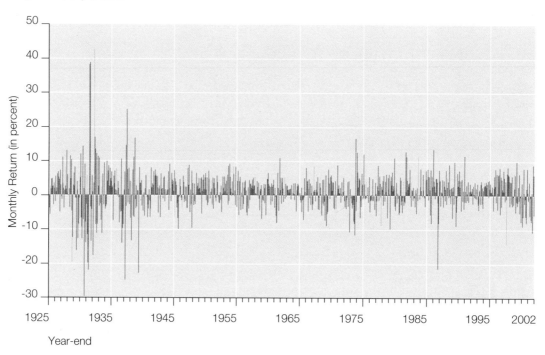

Year-end

Long-Term Government Bonds

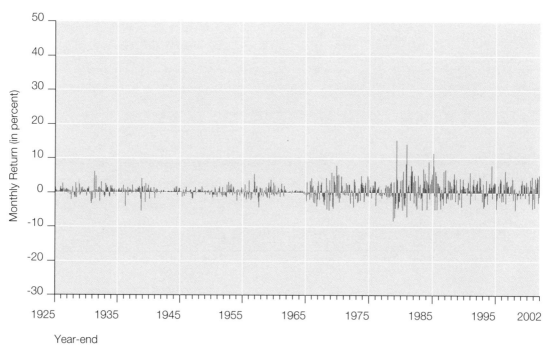

Year-end

Volatility of the Markets

The volatility of stocks and long-term government bonds is shown by the bar graphs of monthly returns in Graph 6-1. The stock market was tremendously volatile in the first few years studied; this period was marked by the 1920s boom, the crash of 1929–1932, and the Great Depression years. The market settled after World War II and provided more stable returns in the postwar period. In the 1970s and 1980s, stock market volatility increased, but not to the extreme levels of the 1920s and 1930s, with the exception of October 1987. In the 1990s, volatility was moderate.

Bonds present a mirror image. Long-term government bonds were extremely stable in the 1920s and remained so through the crisis years of the 1930s, providing shelter from the storms of the stock markets. Starting in the late 1960s and early 1970s, however, bond volatility soared; in the 1973–1974 stock market decline, bonds did not provide the shelter they once did. Bond pessimism (i.e., high yields) peaked in 1981 and subsequent returns were sharply positive. While the astronomical interest rates of the 1979–1981 period have passed, the volatility of the bond market remains higher.

Changes in the Risk of Assets Over Time

Table 6-1
Annualized Monthly Standard Deviations by Decade

	1920s*	1930s	1940s	1950s	1960s	1970s	1980s	1990s	2000s**	1993–2002
Large Company	23.9%	41.6%	17.5%	14.1%	13.1%	17.1%	19.4%	15.8%	16.7	17.1
Small Company	24.7	78.6	34.5	14.4	21.5	30.8	22.5	20.2	31.4	24.2
Long-Term Corp	1.8	5.3	1.8	4.4	4.9	8.7	14.1	6.9	7.5	7.3
Long-Term Govt	4.1	5.3	2.8	4.6	6.0	8.7	16.0	8.9	9.9	9.3
Inter-Term Govt	1.7	3.3	1.2	2.9	3.3	5.2	8.8	4.6	5.1	4.7
Treasury Bills	0.3	0.2	0.1	0.2	0.4	0.6	0.9	0.4	0.6	0.4
Inflation	2.0	2.5	3.1	1.2	0.7	1.2	1.3	0.7	1.0	0.7

*Based on the period 1926–1929.

**Based on the period 2000–2002.

Another time series property of great interest is change in volatility or riskiness over time. Such change is indicated by the standard deviation of the series over different subperiods. Table 6-1 shows the annualized monthly standard deviations of the basic data series by decade beginning in 1926 and illustrates differences and changes in return volatility. In this table, the '20s cover the period 1926–1929 and the 2000s cover the period 2000–2002. Equity returns have been the most volatile of the basic series, with volatility peaking in the 1930s due to the instability of the market following the 1929 market crash. The significant bond yield fluctuations of the '80s caused the fixed income series' volatility to soar compared to prior decades.

The standard deviation of a series for a particular year is the standard deviation of the 12 monthly returns for that year (around that year's arithmetic mean). This monthly estimate is then annualized according to equation (25). Table 6-2 displays the annualized standard deviation of the monthly returns on each of the basic and derived series from 1926 to 2002. The estimates in this table and in Table 6-1 are not strictly comparable to Table 2-1 and Table 6-7 and 6-8, where the 77-year period standard deviation of annual returns (around the 77-year annual arithmetic mean) was reported. The arithmetic mean drifts for a series that does not follow a random pattern. A series with a drifting mean will have much higher deviations around its long-term mean than it has around the mean during a particular calendar year.

As shown in Table 6-2, large company stocks and equity risk premia have virtually the same annualized monthly standard deviations because there is very little deviation in the U.S. Treasury bill series. These two series also have much higher variability in the pre-World War II period than in the postwar period. On the other hand, the various bond series (long- and intermediate-term government bonds, long-term corporate bonds, horizon premia, and default premia) were quite volatile in the Great Depression.

The series with drifting means (U.S. Treasury bills, inflation rates, and inflation-adjusted U.S. Treasury bills) all tend to have very low annualized monthly standard deviations, since these series are quite predictable from month to month. As seen in Tables 6-7 and 6-8, however, there is much less predictability for these series over the long term. Since it is difficult to forecast the direction and magnitude of the drift in the long-term mean, these series have higher standard deviations over the long term in comparison to their annualized monthly standard deviations.

Correlation Coefficients: Serial and Cross-Correlations

The behavior of an asset return series over time reveals its predictability. For example, a series may be random or unpredictable; or it may be subject to trends, cycles, or other patterns, making the series predictable to some degree. The serial correlation coefficient of a series determines its predictability given knowledge of the last observation. The cross-correlation coefficient (often shortened to "correlation") between two series determines the predictability of one series, conditional on knowledge of the other.

Serial Correlations

The serial correlation, also known as the first-order autocorrelation, of a return series describes the extent to which the return in one period is related to the return in the next period. A return series with a high (near one) serial correlation is very predictable from one period to the next, while one with a low (near zero) serial correlation is random and unpredictable.

The serial correlation of a series is closely approximated by the equation for the cross-correlation between two series, which is given in equation (26). The data, however, are the series and its "lagged" self. For example, the lagged series is the series of one-period-old returns:

Year	Return Series (X)	Lagged Return Series (Y)
1	0.10	undefined
2	−0.10	0.10
3	0.15	−0.10
4	0.00	0.15

Table 6-2

Basic and Derived Series
Annualized Monthly Standard Deviations (in percent)

from 1926 to 1970

	Basic Series							Derived Series				
Year	Large Company Stocks	Small Company Stocks	Long-Term Corporate Bonds	Long-Term Govt Bonds	Intermediate-Term Govt Bonds	U.S. Treasury Bills	Inflation	Equity Risk Premia	Small Stock Premia	Bond Default Premia	Bond Horizon Premia	Inflation-Adjusted T-Bills
1926	13.10	16.89	0.96	1.88	1.02	0.32	2.03	12.73	9.74	1.63	1.68	2.06
1927	17.90	21.19	1.49	2.88	1.05	0.11	2.78	17.35	11.13	2.90	2.76	3.03
1928	24.62	28.68	1.87	3.21	1.27	0.32	1.72	23.65	14.48	2.74	3.06	1.84
1929	30.55	18.35	2.42	6.56	2.82	0.21	1.62	29.16	7.76	6.79	6.20	1.62
1930	21.19	25.55	2.38	2.34	2.43	0.30	2.03	20.65	11.68	2.45	2.12	2.31
1931	30.04	45.35	5.91	5.24	3.72	0.16	1.35	29.72	27.44	5.25	5.18	1.75
1932	83.36	147.23	7.71	9.50	2.94	0.29	1.74	82.72	41.92	12.69	9.35	2.40
1933	99.82	286.56	11.74	5.11	3.70	0.10	4.24	99.27	72.06	7.67	5.06	4.15
1934	22.64	73.85	3.10	4.50	4.07	0.04	2.03	22.59	42.03	2.52	4.46	1.94
1935	23.73	36.09	2.53	2.88	2.78	0.01	2.18	23.69	15.08	1.36	2.88	2.05
1936	19.06	66.23	1.18	2.25	1.27	0.02	1.55	19.02	37.72	1.78	2.25	1.51
1937	16.33	21.81	1.99	5.04	2.44	0.05	1.74	16.28	16.46	3.93	5.01	1.63
1938	58.87	114.31	2.38	2.35	2.48	0.07	1.78	58.85	30.94	1.89	2.31	1.89
1939	31.09	95.06	5.36	8.59	5.06	0.02	2.26	31.07	43.55	8.40	8.59	2.24
1940	25.56	46.88	2.02	5.20	3.25	0.02	1.09	25.55	25.68	3.92	5.19	1.07
1941	12.95	29.10	1.67	3.71	1.50	0.03	2.30	12.92	20.75	3.59	3.70	1.90
1942	17.67	37.55	0.73	1.42	0.79	0.03	1.39	17.60	25.78	1.16	1.42	1.17
1943	19.59	71.56	0.90	0.65	0.51	0.01	2.35	19.53	33.94	0.58	0.65	2.21
1944	9.30	28.75	1.34	0.37	0.29	0.01	0.97	9.27	15.14	1.11	0.37	0.94
1945	17.64	37.50	1.42	2.97	0.50	0.01	1.32	17.59	16.92	1.92	2.96	1.26
1946	17.72	27.25	2.15	2.73	0.94	0.00	6.65	17.65	12.20	1.74	2.72	4.66
1947	10.15	18.24	2.13	2.86	0.52	0.07	3.34	10.09	10.58	3.26	2.90	2.79
1948	21.49	24.11	2.20	1.95	0.59	0.07	2.90	21.30	6.44	1.92	1.96	2.73
1949	12.02	18.75	2.17	1.83	0.47	0.02	1.63	11.89	6.72	2.44	1.80	1.71
1950	13.99	20.58	1.07	1.45	0.34	0.03	1.81	13.83	8.82	1.35	1.44	1.62
1951	15.04	16.02	3.92	3.03	1.91	0.05	1.79	14.80	6.12	2.67	2.95	1.63
1952	13.32	9.66	2.85	3.24	1.32	0.08	1.15	13.11	3.78	3.82	3.23	1.14
1953	9.32	10.90	5.53	5.16	3.26	0.11	1.01	9.21	8.74	3.50	5.07	0.95
1954	19.27	20.02	2.35	3.47	1.93	0.06	0.74	19.08	10.08	2.32	3.42	0.77
1955	16.11	7.70	2.17	3.60	1.65	0.14	0.67	15.91	8.83	2.36	3.47	0.71
1956	15.86	8.39	3.00	4.28	2.64	0.10	1.08	15.50	7.87	2.60	4.15	1.00
1957	11.48	10.42	9.40	8.26	5.57	0.07	0.66	11.13	9.98	5.48	8.00	0.65
1958	8.74	15.44	4.56	6.29	4.50	0.27	0.90	8.47	7.99	3.73	6.16	0.88
1959	8.91	10.34	3.91	3.25	2.72	0.18	0.65	8.67	7.31	3.35	3.18	0.59
1960	13.63	13.37	3.93	6.45	4.99	0.27	0.71	13.36	7.07	3.85	6.22	0.80
1961	11.16	19.02	3.63	3.55	1.57	0.07	0.51	10.94	7.72	3.93	3.51	0.50
1962	18.97	21.58	2.27	3.70	2.15	0.08	0.67	18.46	8.38	2.17	3.63	0.70
1963	11.91	13.47	1.25	0.72	0.60	0.08	0.55	11.54	7.26	1.28	0.72	0.55
1964	4.63	7.05	1.46	0.91	0.78	0.06	0.41	4.47	3.78	1.84	0.87	0.38
1965	9.56	20.55	1.96	1.51	1.83	0.08	0.67	9.26	11.19	1.09	1.47	0.64
1966	9.96	17.80	4.80	8.08	4.13	0.11	0.71	9.50	13.76	5.39	7.66	0.73
1967	14.89	36.96	7.33	6.58	3.81	0.16	0.44	14.24	17.30	5.14	6.27	0.54
1968	14.49	28.29	7.39	7.93	3.50	0.09	0.42	13.76	16.40	3.57	7.52	0.40
1969	12.10	18.71	6.93	9.95	5.54	0.22	0.62	11.35	9.73	7.39	9.34	0.63
1970	21.60	27.68	11.28	15.07	7.05	0.22	0.44	20.33	13.19	9.22	14.11	0.47

Table 6-2 (continued)

Basic and Derived Series
Annualized Monthly Standard Deviations (in percent)

from 1971 to 2002

Year	Basic Series							Derived Series				
	Large Company Stocks	Small Company Stocks	Long-Term Corporate Bonds	Long-Term Govt Bonds	Intermediate-Term Govt Bonds	U.S. Treasury Bills	Inflation	Equity Risk Premia	Small Stock Premia	Bond Default Premia	Bond Horizon Premia	Inflation-Adjusted T-Bills
1971	15.64	29.73	11.12	10.67	6.98	0.19	0.57	14.97	14.61	6.12	10.15	0.63
1972	7.80	16.60	3.21	5.85	1.97	0.17	0.41	7.51	11.39	3.97	5.61	0.42
1973	12.15	21.94	7.57	8.38	4.99	0.37	1.53	11.27	14.21	5.12	7.71	1.34
1974	18.74	20.15	11.45	8.64	5.73	0.36	0.91	17.52	22.03	5.76	8.05	0.89
1975	24.38	46.28	11.49	9.13	5.68	0.21	0.78	23.00	19.98	4.43	8.55	0.77
1976	16.89	50.83	5.21	5.43	4.24	0.13	0.48	16.00	27.53	1.55	5.15	0.45
1977	8.97	17.05	4.57	5.69	2.73	0.19	0.77	8.49	13.33	1.56	5.41	0.85
1978	17.92	42.56	4.45	4.45	2.07	0.36	0.67	16.75	26.56	1.66	4.21	0.78
1979	15.79	34.71	10.43	10.81	7.31	0.29	0.53	14.28	15.64	2.16	9.77	0.60
1980	24.19	39.80	20.12	21.16	16.77	0.98	1.45	22.26	14.54	4.57	18.60	1.18
1981	12.44	21.37	20.21	23.25	11.84	0.51	1.15	10.85	16.03	5.23	20.23	1.00
1982	23.38	21.97	17.80	14.40	8.91	0.78	1.64	21.57	7.84	5.37	13.37	1.42
1983	12.02	21.83	10.86	11.43	5.72	0.18	0.73	11.13	14.33	3.98	10.52	0.67
1984	15.00	14.57	12.97	13.34	7.17	0.34	0.61	13.63	4.37	1.92	11.97	0.61
1985	15.85	18.10	13.28	15.78	6.69	0.18	0.33	14.66	6.42	2.56	14.56	0.35
1986	21.39	15.49	9.71	21.58	6.53	0.20	1.03	20.12	6.61	9.54	20.26	1.17
1987	34.04	34.45	9.67	10.09	4.93	0.23	0.68	32.38	11.21	3.03	9.49	0.64
1988	11.69	16.08	9.10	11.03	5.00	0.36	0.57	11.07	11.14	2.45	10.45	0.64
1989	16.03	11.65	7.13	9.53	6.07	0.23	0.63	14.80	6.87	2.36	8.73	0.67
1990	18.25	16.85	7.55	9.89	4.75	0.18	1.16	16.92	6.83	2.67	9.18	1.16
1991	20.49	22.50	5.08	7.33	3.49	0.17	0.54	19.40	9.75	2.13	6.99	0.51
1992	7.91	21.58	5.77	7.62	5.83	0.14	0.54	7.68	19.95	2.32	7.38	0.53
1993	6.69	11.43	5.53	8.38	4.44	0.05	0.57	6.52	8.37	2.38	8.15	0.57
1994	10.74	10.38	6.70	8.12	4.50	0.24	0.47	10.31	6.35	2.27	7.77	0.62
1995	6.95	12.65	7.37	9.70	3.94	0.13	0.60	6.63	8.39	1.88	9.11	0.64
1996	13.29	21.06	7.62	9.33	3.89	0.09	0.61	12.67	15.16	2.14	8.87	0.62
1997	21.08	22.13	8.00	10.44	4.10	0.13	0.53	19.99	16.40	2.30	9.91	0.60
1998	27.90	25.76	5.91	7.70	4.63	0.16	0.30	26.69	6.81	4.35	7.24	0.31
1999	15.78	26.31	4.57	5.25	3.44	0.10	0.77	15.02	19.21	1.91	5.00	0.77
2000	16.02	40.42	5.88	6.92	3.43	0.17	1.00	15.14	44.92	4.10	6.58	1.07
2001	18.15	34.55	8.17	9.69	5.00	0.39	1.25	17.52	21.21	6.02	9.31	0.99
2002	16.90	20.14	8.82	12.36	6.77	0.04	0.83	16.64	18.02	4.50	12.15	0.79

Cross-Correlations

The cross-correlation between two series measures the extent to which they are linearly related.[2] The correlation coefficient measures the sensitivity of returns on one asset class or portfolio to the returns of another. The correlation equation between return series **X** and **Y** is:

$$\rho_{X,Y} = \left[\frac{Cov(X,Y)}{\sigma_X \sigma_Y} \right]$$

(26)

where,

$Cov(X,Y)$ = the covariance of **X** and **Y**, defined below;

σ_X = the standard deviation of **X**; and,

σ_Y = the standard deviation of **Y**.

The covariance equation is:

$$Cov(X,Y) = \frac{1}{n-1} \sum_{t=1}^{n} \left(r_{X,t} - r_{X,A} \right)\left(r_{Y,t} - r_{Y,A} \right)$$

(27)

where,

$r_{X,t}$ = the return for series **X** in period **t**;

$r_{Y,t}$ = the return for series **Y** in period **t**;

$r_{X,A}$ = the arithmetic mean of series **X**;

$r_{Y,A}$ = the arithmetic mean of series **Y**; and,

n = the number of periods.

Correlations of the Basic Series

Table 6-3 presents the annual cross-correlations and serial correlations for the seven basic series. Long-term government and long-term corporate bond returns are highly correlated with each other but negatively correlated with inflation. Since the inflation was largely unanticipated, it had a negative effect on fixed income securities. In addition, U.S. Treasury bills and inflation are reasonably highly correlated, a result of the post-1951 "tracking" described in Chapter 2. Lastly, both the U.S. Treasury bills and inflation series display high serial correlations.

2 Two series can be related in a non-linear way and have a correlation coefficient of zero. An example is the function $y = x^2$, for which $\rho_{X,Y} = 0$.

Table 6-3

Basic Series

Serial and Cross Correlations of Historical Annual Returns from 1926 to 2002

Series	Large Company Stocks	Small Company Stocks	Long-Term Corp Bonds	Long-Term Govt Bonds	Intermediate Govt Bonds	U.S. Treasury Bills	Inflation
Large Company Stocks	1.00						
Small Company Stocks	0.78	1.00					
Long-Term Corporate Bonds	0.19	0.08	1.00				
Long-Term Govt Bonds	0.13	−0.01	0.93	1.00			
Intermediate-Term Govt Bonds	0.05	−0.06	0.91	0.91	1.00		
U.S. Treasury Bills	−0.02	−0.09	0.20	0.23	0.47	1.00	
Inflation	−0.02	0.05	−0.15	−0.14	0.01	0.41	1.00
Serial Correlations*	0.05	0.07	0.08	−0.07	0.15	0.91	0.65

*The standard error for all estimates is 0.12

Correlations of the Derived Series

The annual cross-correlations and serial correlations for the four risk premium series and inflation are presented in Table 6-4. Notice that inflation is negatively correlated with the horizon premium. Increasing inflation causes long-term bond yields to rise and prices to fall; therefore, a negative horizon premium is observed in times of rising inflation.

Table 6-4

Risk Premia and Inflation

Serial and Cross Correlations of Historical Annual Returns from 1926 to 2002

Series	Equity Risk Premia	Small Stock Premia	Default Premia	Horizon Premia	Inflation
Equity Risk Premia	1.00				
Small Stock Premia	0.27	1.00			
Default Premia	0.17	0.18	1.00		
Horizon Premia	0.14	−0.07	−0.36	1.00	
Inflation	−0.08	0.12	−0.01	−0.29	1.00
Serial Correlations*	0.05	0.37	−0.34	−0.12	0.65

*The standard error for all estimates is 0.12

Table 6-5 presents annual cross-correlations and serial correlations for the inflation-adjusted asset return series. It is interesting to observe how the relationship between the asset returns are substantially different when these returns are expressed in inflation-adjusted terms (as compared with nominal terms). In general, the cross-correlations between asset classes are higher when one accounts for inflation (i.e., subtracts inflation from the nominal returns).

Table 6-5

Inflation-Adjusted Series
Serial and Cross Correlations of Historical Annual Returns from 1926 to 2002

Series	Large Company Stocks	Small Company Stocks	Long-Term Corp Bonds	Long-Term Govt Bonds	Inter-mediate Govt Bonds	T-Bills (Real Interest Rates)	Inflation
	Inflation-Adjusted						
Inflation-Adjusted Large Company Stocks	1.00						
Inflation-Adjusted Small Company Stocks	0.78	1.00					
Inflation-Adjusted Long-Term Corporate Bonds	0.26	0.11	1.00				
Inflation-Adjusted Long-Term Govt Bonds	0.21	0.03	0.95	1.00			
Inflation-Adjusted Intermd-Term Govt Bonds	0.15	−0.02	0.95	0.94	1.00		
Inflation-Adjusted T-Bills (Real Interest Rates)	0.12	−0.06	0.58	0.57	0.72	1.00	
Inflation	−0.21	−0.08	−0.56	−0.52	−0.61	−0.74	1.00
Serial Correlations*	0.04	0.04	0.19	0.03	0.23	0.67	0.65

*The standard error for all estimates is 0.12

Serial Correlation in the Derived Series: Trends or Random Behavior?

The risk/return relationships in the historical data are represented in the equity risk premia, the small stock premia, the bond horizon premia, and the bond default premia. The real/nominal historical relationships are represented in the inflation rates and the real interest rates. The objective is to uncover whether each series is random or is subject to any trends, cycles, or other patterns.

The one-year serial correlation coefficients measure the degree of correlation between returns from each year and the previous year for the same series. Highly positive (near 1) serial correlations indicate trends, while highly negative (near −1) serial correlations indicate cycles. There is strong evidence that both inflation rates and real riskless rates follow trends. Serial correlations near zero suggest no patterns (i.e., random behavior); equity risk premia and bond horizon premia are random variables. Small stock premia and bond default premia fall into a middle range where it cannot be determined that they either follow a trend or behave randomly, although the serial correlation of annual small stock premia is high enough to suggest a trend.

Each of the component series' serial correlations can be interpreted as following a random pattern, trend or uncertain path, as given in Table 6-6.

Table 6-6

Interpretation of the Annual Serial Correlations

Series	Serial Correlation	Interpretation
Equity Risk Premia	.05	Random
Small Stock Premia	.37	Likely Trend
Bond Default Premia	−.34	Possible Cycle
Bond Horizon Premia	−.12	Random
Inflation Rates	.65	Trend
Real Interest Rates	.67	Trend

Summary Statistics for Basic and Inflation-Adjusted Series

Table 6-7 presents summary statistics of annual total returns, and where applicable, income and capital appreciation, for each asset class. The summary statistics presented here are arithmetic mean, geometric mean, standard deviation, and serial correlation. Table 6-8 presents summary statistics for the six inflation-adjusted total return series.

Table 6-7

Total Returns, Income Returns, and Capital Appreciation of the Basic Asset Classes
Summary Statistics of Annual Returns from 1926 to 2002

Series	Geometric Mean	Arithmetic Mean	Standard Deviation	Serial Correlation
Large Company Stocks				
Total Returns	10.2%	12.2%	20.5%	0.05
Income	4.3	4.3	1.5	0.88
Capital Appreciation	5.7	7.6	19.8	0.05
Small Company Stocks (Total Returns)	12.1	16.9	33.2	0.07
Long-Term Corporate Bonds (Total Returns)	5.9	6.2	8.7	0.08
Long-Term Government Bonds				
Total Returns	5.5	5.8	9.4	−0.07
Income	5.2	5.2	2.8	0.96
Capital Appreciation	0.1	0.4	8.2	−0.22
Intermediate-Term Government Bonds				
Total Returns	5.4	5.6	5.8	0.15
Income	4.8	4.8	3.0	0.96
Capital Appreciation	0.5	0.6	4.5	−0.20
Treasury Bills (Total Returns)	3.8	3.8	3.2	0.91
Inflation	3.0	3.1	4.4	0.65

Total return is equal to the sum of three component returns; income return, capital appreciation return, and reinvestment return. Annual reinvestment returns for select asset classes are provided in Table 2-6.

Highlights of the Summary Statistics

Table 6-7 shows that over 1926–2002 small company stocks were the riskiest asset class with a standard deviation of 33.2 percent, but provide the greatest rewards to long-term investors, with an arithmetic mean annual return of 16.9 percent. The geometric mean of the small stock series is 12.1 percent. Large company stocks, long-term government bonds, long-term corporate bonds, and intermediate-term government bonds are progressively less risky, and have correspondingly lower average returns. Treasury bills were nearly riskless and had the lowest return. In general, risk is rewarded by a higher return over the long term.

Inflation-adjusted basic series summary statistics are presented in Table 6-8. Note that the real rate of interest is close to zero (0.7 percent) on average. For the 77-year period, the geometric and arithmetic means are lower by the amount of inflation than those of the nominal series.

The standard deviations of large company stock and small company stock returns remain approximately the same after adjusting for inflation, while inflation-adjusted bonds and bills are more volatile (i.e., have higher standard deviations).

Table 6-8

Inflation-Adjusted Series
Summary Statistics of Annual Returns from 1926 to 2002

Series	Geometric Mean	Arithmetic Mean	Standard Deviation	Serial Correlation
Inflation-Adjusted Large Company Stocks	6.9%	9.0%	20.6%	0.04
Inflation-Adjusted Small Company Stocks	8.8	13.5	32.6	0.04
Inflation-Adjusted Long-Term Corporate Bonds	2.8	3.2	9.9	0.19
Inflation-Adjusted Long-Term Government Bonds	2.3	2.9	10.6	0.03
Inflation-Adjusted Intermediate-Term Government Bonds	2.3	2.6	7.0	0.23
Inflation-Adjusted U.S. T-Bills (Real Riskless Rates of Returns)	0.7	0.8	4.0	0.67

Rolling Period Standard Deviations

Rolling period standard deviations are obtained by rolling a view window of fixed length along each time series and computing the standard deviation for the asset class for each window of time. They are useful for examining the volatility or riskiness of returns for holding periods similar to those actually experienced by investors. Graph 6-2 graphically depicts the volatility. Monthly data are used to maximize the number of data points included in the standard deviation computation.

The upper graph places the 60-month rolling standard deviation for large company stocks, small company stocks, and long-term government bonds on the same scale. It is interesting to see the relatively high standard deviation for small company stocks and large company stocks in the 1930s, with an apparent lessening of volatility for 60-month holding periods during the 1980s. Note also how the standard deviation for long-term government bonds reaches the level of both common stock asset classes during part of the 1980s.

The lower graph places the 60-month rolling standard deviation for long- and intermediate-term government bonds, and Treasury bills on the same scale.

Graph 6-2

Rolling 60-Month Standard Deviation
Small Company Stocks, Large Company Stocks, Long-Term Government Bonds,
Intermediate Bonds, and Treasury Bills

from January 1926–December 1930 to January 1998–December 2002

Small Company Stocks, Large Company Stocks, Long-Term Government Bonds

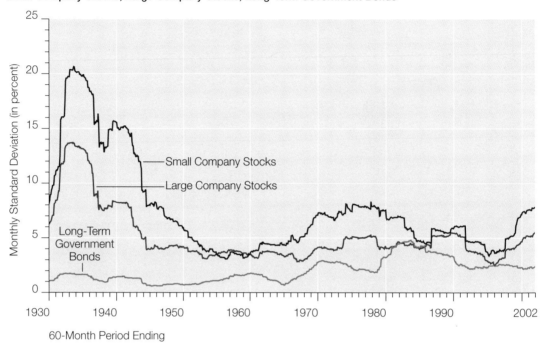

Long-Term Government Bonds, Intermediate-Term Government Bonds, Treasury Bills

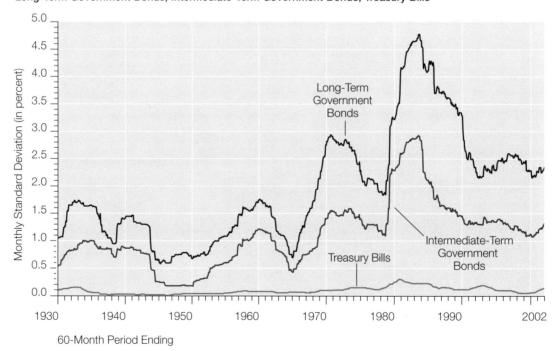

Graph 6-3

Rolling 60-Month Correlations

Large Company Stocks, Long-Term Government Bonds, Treasury Bills, and Inflation

from January 1926–December 1930 to January 1998–December 2002

Large Company Stocks and Long-Term Government Bonds

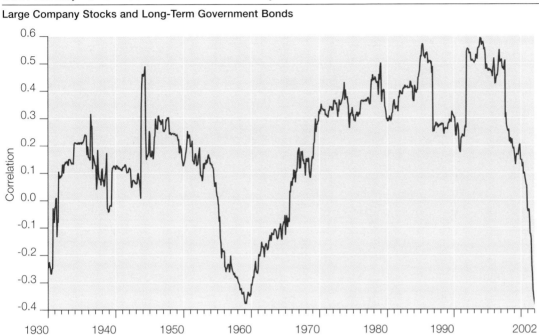

60-Month Period Ending

Treasury Bills and Inflation

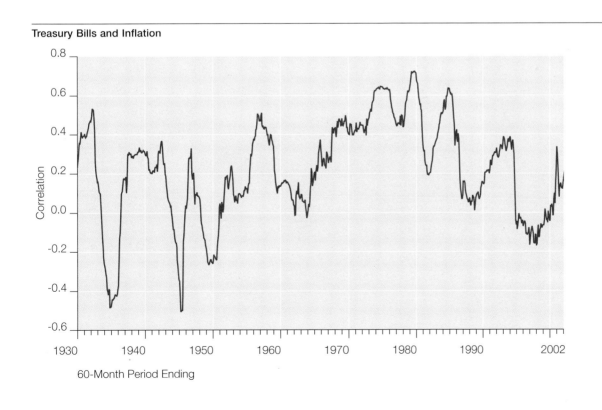

60-Month Period Ending

Rolling Period Correlations

Rolling period correlations are obtained by moving a view window of fixed length along time series for two asset classes and computing the cross-correlation between the two asset classes for each window of time. They are useful for examining how asset class returns vary together for holding periods similar to those actually experienced by investors. Monthly data are used to maximize the number of data points included in the correlation computation.

Graph 6-3 shows cross correlations between two asset classes for five year (60 months of monthly data) holding periods. The first rolling period covered is January 1926-December 1930 so the graphs begin at December 1930. The top graph shows the volatility of the correlations between large company stocks and long-term government bonds. There are wide fluctuations between strong positive and strong negative correlations over the past 77 years.

The lower graph shows the correlation between Treasury bills and inflation. These asset classes also show wide fluctuations in correlation over the past 77 years.

The True Impact of Asset Allocation on Returns

Universal Misunderstanding

How important is asset allocation policy and what type of impact does it have on fund returns? This is a frequently asked question throughout the financial world, with the answer depending on how you ask the question and what you are trying to explain. Financial professionals generally assert that asset allocation is the most important determinant of returns, accounting for more than 90 percent of fund performance. This assertion stems from the well-known studies by Brinson, Hood, and Beebower[3] which state, "...investment policy dominates investment strategy (market timing and security selection), explaining on average 93.6 percent of the variation in total plan return." Specific claims to the above statement vary, but if you are trying to explain the variability of returns over time, asset allocation is of prime importance.

However, a great deal of confusion in both the academic and financial community has arisen, and the results of the Brinson studies are attributed to questions that the studies never intended to

---

3 "Determinants of Portfolio Performance," Gary P. Brinson, L. Randolph Hood, and Gilbert P. Beebower, *Financial Analysts Journal*, July/August 1986.

"Determinants of Portfolio Performance II," Gary P. Brinson, Brian D. Singer, and Gilbert P. Beebower, *Financial Analysts Journal*, May/June 1991.

answer. A survey by Nuttall & Nuttall[4] reveals that out of fifty writers who quoted Brinson et al., only one quoted them correctly. Thirty-seven writers misinterpreted Brinson's work as an answer to the question, "What percent of total return is explained by asset allocation policy?" while five writers misconstrued the Brinson conclusion as an answer to the question, "What is the impact of choosing one asset allocation over another?"

This section is based upon the work by Roger G. Ibbotson and Paul D. Kaplan.[5] The goal of the study is to clear up this universal misinterpretation and explain the link between asset allocation and investment returns.

The Brinson Studies

According to the well-known studies by Brinson, Hood, and Beebower, more than 90 percent of the variability of a portfolio's performance over time is due to asset allocation. In other words, Brinson is measuring the relationship between the movement of a portfolio and the movement of the overall stock market. They find that more than 90 percent of a portfolio's movement from quarter to quarter is due to market movement of the asset classes in which the portfolio is invested.

Thus, while the Brinson studies state that more than 90 percent of the variability of a portfolio's performance over time is due to asset allocation, they are frequently misinterpreted and the results are attributed to questions that the studies never intended to answer. Two prime examples being:

- "When choosing between two different asset allocations, how much of a difference does it really make if I choose one over the other?"

- "What portion of my total return is due to asset allocation?"

Data Analysis Framework

To answer the above questions, as well as to confirm the Brinson result, ten years of monthly returns on 94 balanced mutual funds and five years of quarterly returns on 58 pension funds were analyzed. The 94 funds represent all of the balanced funds in the Morningstar universe that had at least ten years of data ending March 31, 1998. The data collected consist of the total return for each fund for each period of time—either monthly or quarterly.

For the mutual funds, the policy weights were determined by using returns-based style analysis over the entire 120-month period.

4 "Asset Allocation Claims—Truth or Fiction?," Jennifer A. Nuttall and John Nuttall (unpublished), 1998.

5 "Does Asset Allocation Policy Explain 40, 90, or 100 Percent of Performance?," Roger G. Ibbotson and Paul D. Kaplan, *Financial Analysts Journal*, January/February 2000.

Dale Stevens[6] provided the same type of analysis on quarterly returns of 58 pension funds over a five-year period 1993–1997. However, rather than using estimated policy weights and the same asset class benchmarks for all funds, the actual policy weights and asset class benchmarks of the pension funds were used. In each quarter, the policy weights are known in advance of the realized returns.

Questions and Answers

"How much of the movement in a fund's returns over time is explained by its asset allocation policy?"

The Brinson studies from 1986 and 1991 answer the above question. To confirm the results of the Brinson study, each fund's total returns is regressed against its policy returns with the R-squared value being reported for each fund.

Our results confirm the Brinson result that approximately 90 percent of the variability of a fund's return across time is explained by asset allocation. However, almost any stock market performance index would explain a high percentage of the time series variation. As Table 6-9 shows, even the S&P 500 index explains about 80 percent of the average fund's performance, almost as high as the fund's specific asset allocation policy benchmark. This is because all benchmarks and funds rise in a bull market and fall in a bear market.

Table 6-9

Asset Allocation Policy or Market Participation?
Time-Series R²s Compared to:

	Benchmark	
	S&P 500	Fund Policy
Mean	75.2%	81.4%
Median	81.9%	87.6%

"When choosing between two different asset allocations, how much of a difference does it really make if I choose one over the other?"

To answer the above question, each fund's return must be compared to the other in order to determine how much of the return variation across funds is explained by the funds' asset allocation variations. A cross-sectional regression of entire-period compound annual total returns on entire-period compound annual policy returns was performed. The R-squared statistic gives us the percentage of the variation explained.

6 "The Importance of Investment Policy," Dale H. Stevens, Ronald J. Surz, and Mark E. Wimer, *The Journal of Investing*, Winter 1999.

For the mutual fund sample, 40 percent of the return difference from one fund to another was explained by asset allocation, while for pension funds the result was 35 percent. Graph 6-4 shows the plot of the 10-year compound annual total returns against the 10-year compound annual policy returns for the mutual fund sample. For example, if one portfolio returns 5 percent more than the other, then on average, about 2 percent of the difference (40 percent of 5 percent) is attributable to the different asset allocations. The remaining 3 percent difference (60 percent of 5 percent) is explained by other factors such as asset class timing, security selection, and fees.

Graph 6-4

10-Year Compound Annual Return Across Mutual Funds*

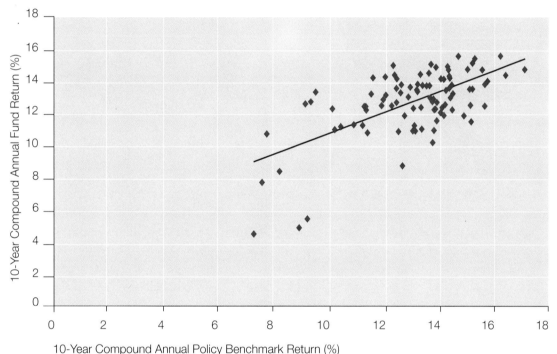

*Across the pension fund sample the $R^2 = 0.35$.

Graph 6-5

Variation of Returns Across Funds Explained by Asset Allocation

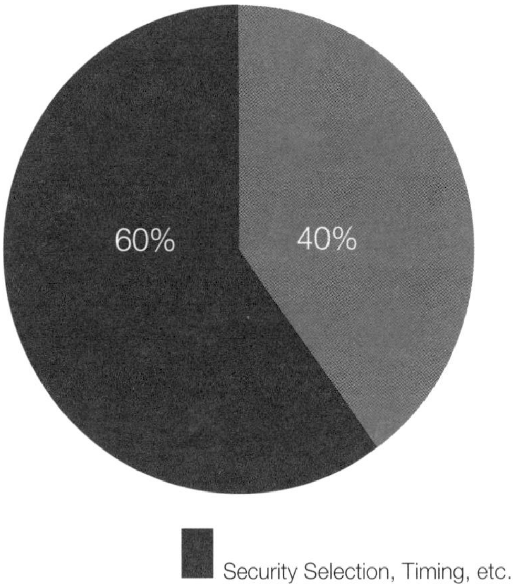

Percentage of a Fund's Total Return Explained by Asset Allocation

60% 40%

100%

■ Security Selection, Timing, etc.   ■ Asset Allocation

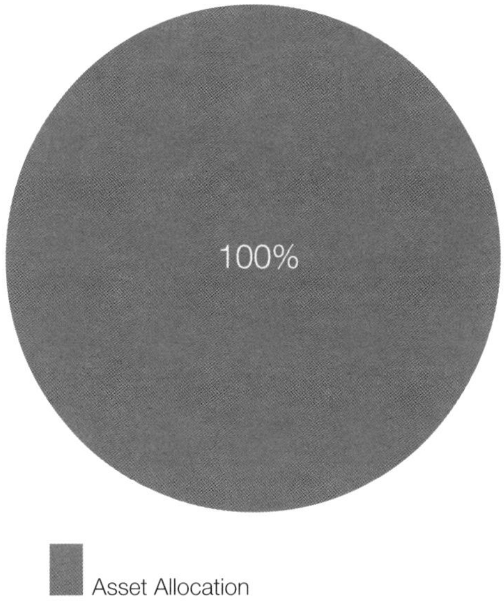

"What portion of my total return is due to asset allocation?"

To answer the above question, the percent of fund return explained by asset allocation was calculated for each fund as the ratio of compound annual policy return divided by the compound annual total return. In other words, we create a portfolio of benchmark asset classes that matches a balanced fund's asset allocation policy and then divide the return of the benchmark portfolio by the fund's return. This ratio of compound returns serves as a performance measure. A fund that has stayed exactly at its asset allocation mix and has invested passively will have a ratio of 1.0 or 100 percent. A fund that has outperformed its asset allocation will have a ratio of less than one, while a fund that has underperformed its asset allocation policy will have a ratio of greater than one.

$$\% \text{ of Return due to Policy} = \frac{\text{Policy Return}}{\text{Total Return}}$$

We find that, on average, the policy benchmarks perform as well as the actual portfolios producing a ratio of 1.0, or 100 percent. It is safe to say that, on average, the pension funds and balanced mutual funds are not adding value above their asset allocation policy due to their combination of timing, security selection, management fees, and expenses. Thus, about 100 percent of the total return is explained by asset allocation policy.

The above results were anticipated by William Sharpe.[7] Sharpe pointed out that since the aggregation of all investors is the market, the average performance before costs of all investors must equal the performance of the market. This implies that, on average, nearly 100 percent of the level of a fund's total return should be expected from asset allocation. Our results confirm such a prediction.

In summary, much of the recent controversy over the importance of asset allocation is due to the misinterpretation of the Brinson studies. These studies successfully provided an answer to one question, but never intended to address the two questions discussed in the above study. While the Brinson studies show that more than 90 percent of the variability of a portfolio's performance over time is due to asset allocation, through careful analysis, we have also come to the conclusion that asset allocation explains about 40 percent of the variation of returns across funds and about 100 percent of a fund's total return.

---

7 "The Arithmetic of Active Management," William F. Sharpe, *Financial Analysts Journal*, January/February 1991.

Chapter 7
Firm Size and Return

The Firm Size Phenomenon

One of the most remarkable discoveries of modern finance is the finding of a relationship between firm size and return.[1] On average, small companies have higher returns than large ones. Earlier chapters document this phenomenon for the smallest stocks on the New York Stock Exchange (NYSE). The relationship between firm size and return cuts across the entire size spectrum; it is not restricted to the smallest stocks. In this chapter, the returns across the entire range of firm size are examined.

Construction of the Decile Portfolios

The portfolios used in this chapter are those created by the Center for Research in Security Prices (CRSP) at the University of Chicago's Graduate School of Business. CRSP has refined the methodology of creating size-based portfolios and has applied this methodology to the entire universe of NYSE/AMEX/NASDAQ-listed securities going back to 1926.

In 1993, CRSP changed the method used to construct these portfolios, thereby causing the return and index values in Table 7-2 and 7-3 to be significantly different from those reported in previous editions of the *Yearbook*. Previously, some eligible companies had been excluded or delayed from inclusion when the portfolios were reformed at the end of each calendar quarter. Also, while in prior editions of the *Yearbook* we used NYSE-listed securities only in the composition of size decile portfolios, starting with the 2001 edition we use the entire population of NYSE, AMEX, and NASDAQ-listed securities for use in the firm size chapter.

The New York Stock Exchange universe is restricted by excluding closed-end mutual funds, preferred stocks, real estate investment trusts, foreign stocks, American Depository Receipts, unit investment trusts, and Americus Trusts. All companies on the NYSE are ranked by the combined market capitalization of all their eligible equity securities. The companies are then split into 10 equally populated groups or deciles. Eligible companies traded on the American Stock Exchange (AMEX) and the Nasdaq National Market (NASDAQ) are then assigned to the appropriate deciles according to their capitalization in relation to the NYSE breakpoints. The portfolios are rebalanced using closing prices for the last trading day of March, June, September, and December. Securities added during the quarter are assigned to the appropriate portfolio when two consecutive month-end prices are available. For securities that become delisted, when the last NYSE price is a month-end price, that month's return is included in the portfolio's quarterly return. When a month-end NYSE price is missing, the month-end value is derived from merger terms, quotations on regional exchanges, and other sources. If a month-end value is not available, the last available daily price is used.

Base security returns are monthly holding period returns. All distributions are added to the month-end prices. Appropriate adjustments are made to prices to account for stock splits and dividends. The return on a portfolio for one month is calculated as the weighted average of the returns for the individual stocks in the portfolio. Annual portfolio returns are calculated by compounding the monthly portfolio returns.

---

1 Rolf W. Banz was the first to document this phenomenon. See Banz, Rolf W., "The Relationship Between Returns and Market Value of Common Stocks," *Journal of Financial Economics*, Volume 9 (1981), pp. 3–18.

Aspects of the Firm Size Effect

The firm size phenomenon is remarkable in several ways. First, the greater risk of small stocks does not, in the context of the Capital Asset Pricing Model, fully account for their higher returns over the long term. In the CAPM, only systematic or beta risk is rewarded. Small company stocks have had returns in excess of those implied by the betas of small stocks. Secondly, the calendar annual return differences between small and large companies are serially correlated. This suggests that past annual returns may be of some value in predicting future annual returns. Such serial correlation, or autocorrelation, is practically unknown in the market for large stocks and in most other capital markets.

In addition, the firm size effect is seasonal. For example, small company stocks outperformed large company stocks in the month of January in a large majority of the years. Again, such predictability is surprising and suspicious in the light of modern capital market theory. These three aspects of the firm size effect (long-term returns in excess of risk, serial correlation and seasonality) will be analyzed after the data are presented.

Table 7-1
Size-Decile Portfolios of the NYSE/AMEX/NASDAQ
Summary Statistics of Annual Returns

from 1926 to 2002

Decile	Geometric Mean	Arithmetic Mean	Standard Deviation	Serial Correlation
1-Largest	9.4%	11.2%	19.44%	0.11
2	10.5	12.9	22.13	0.05
3	10.9	13.5	24.02	−0.01
4	11.0	14.0	26.26	0.00
5	11.1	14.5	27.06	0.00
6	11.3	14.9	28.11	0.06
7	11.1	15.2	30.33	0.02
8	11.3	16.2	34.03	0.06
9	11.5	17.1	36.90	0.07
10-Smallest	13.1	20.8	45.37	0.17
Mid-Cap 3–5	11.0	13.8	25.08	−0.01
Low-Cap 6–8	11.2	15.2	29.86	0.05
Micro-Cap 9–10	12.1	18.2	39.32	0.10
NYSE/AMEX/NASDAQ Total Value Weighted Index	9.8	11.8	20.48	0.05

Results are for quarterly re-ranking for the deciles. The small company stock summary statistics presented in earlier chapters comprise a re-ranking of the portfolios every five years prior to 1982.

Presentation of the Decile Data

Summary statistics of annual returns of the 10 deciles over 1926–2002 are presented in Table 7-1. Note from this exhibit that the average return tends to increase as one moves from the largest decile to the smallest. (Because securities are ranked quarterly, returns on the ninth and tenth deciles are different than those suggested by the small company stock index presented in earlier chapters. A detailed methodology for the small company stock index is included in Chapter 3.) The total risk, or standard deviation of annual returns, also increases with decreasing firm size. The serial correlations of returns are near zero for all but the smallest two deciles.

Table 7-2 gives the year-by-year history of the returns for the different size categories. Table 7-3 shows the growth of $1.00 invested in each of the categories as of year-end 1925.

The sheer magnitude of the size effect in some years is noteworthy. While the largest stocks actually declined in 2001, the smallest stocks rose more than 30 percent. A more extreme case occurred in the depression-recovery year of 1933, when the difference between the first and tenth decile returns was far more substantial. The divergence in the performance of small and large company stocks is a common occurrence.

In Table 7-4, the decile returns and index values of the NYSE/AMEX/NASDAQ population are broken down into mid-cap, low-cap, and micro-cap stocks. Mid-cap stocks are defined here as the aggregate of deciles 3–5. Based on the most recent data (Table 7-5), companies within this mid-cap range have market capitalizations at or below $5,012,705,000, but greater than $1,143,845,000. Low-cap stocks include deciles 6–8, and currently include all companies in the NYSE/AMEX/NAS-DAQ with market capitalizations at or below $1,143,845,000 but greater than $314,042,000. Micro-cap stocks include deciles 9–10, and include companies with market capitalizations at or below $314,042,000. The returns and index values of the entire NYSE/AMEX/NASDAQ population are also included. All returns presented are value-weighted based on the market capitalizations of the deciles contained in each sub-group. Graph 7-1 graphically depicts the growth of $1.00 invested in each of these capitalization groups.

Table 7-2

Size-Decile Portfolios of the NYSE/AMEX/NASDAQ
Year-by-Year Returns

from 1926 to 1970

	Decile 1	Decile 2	Decile 3	Decile 4	Decile 5	Decile 6	Decile 7	Decile 8	Decile 9	Decile 10
1926	0.1438	0.0545	0.0355	0.0085	0.0033	0.0335	−0.0250	−0.0932	−0.0997	−0.0605
1927	0.3400	0.2957	0.3116	0.4134	0.3467	0.2312	0.3025	0.2553	0.3190	0.3126
1928	0.3889	0.3777	0.3982	0.3736	0.4965	0.2809	0.3530	0.3212	0.3740	0.6974
1929	−0.1056	−0.0793	−0.2569	−0.3177	−0.2448	−0.4044	−0.3769	−0.4082	−0.4993	−0.5359
1930	−0.2422	−0.3747	−0.3465	−0.3418	−0.3627	−0.3781	−0.3661	−0.4951	−0.4570	−0.4567
1931	−0.4215	−0.5011	−0.4600	−0.4569	−0.4865	−0.5102	−0.4787	−0.4907	−0.4908	−0.5010
1932	−0.1197	−0.0078	−0.0185	−0.1333	−0.1144	0.0660	−0.1648	0.0129	−0.0029	0.3843
1933	0.4661	0.7467	1.0331	1.1220	0.9497	1.0972	1.1784	1.5880	1.7361	2.2160
1934	0.0223	0.0569	0.0894	0.1782	0.0753	0.2185	0.1480	0.2776	0.2253	0.3185
1935	0.4078	0.5846	0.3689	0.3702	0.6401	0.5537	0.6466	0.6423	0.6201	0.8212
1936	0.2961	0.3553	0.2857	0.4341	0.4612	0.4999	0.5213	0.4931	0.8344	0.8600
1937	−0.3185	−0.3662	−0.3801	−0.4352	−0.4867	−0.4763	−0.4918	−0.5275	−0.5165	−0.5562
1938	0.2507	0.3455	0.3534	0.3387	0.5054	0.4339	0.3505	0.4541	0.3040	0.0900
1939	0.0472	−0.0346	−0.0253	0.0025	0.0146	0.0386	0.0770	−0.0426	−0.0627	0.1908
1940	−0.0709	−0.0906	−0.0873	−0.0388	−0.0113	−0.0607	−0.0617	−0.0583	−0.0446	−0.3104
1941	−0.1065	−0.0650	−0.0614	−0.0973	−0.1207	−0.1024	−0.0915	−0.0933	−0.1226	−0.1684
1942	0.1308	0.2419	0.1969	0.2056	0.2117	0.2466	0.2892	0.3063	0.4322	0.7740
1943	0.2353	0.3465	0.3449	0.3967	0.4822	0.4254	0.7373	0.7034	0.8559	1.4216
1944	0.1696	0.2627	0.2381	0.3261	0.3951	0.4469	0.3730	0.4935	0.5675	0.6994
1945	0.2914	0.4890	0.5354	0.6345	0.5455	0.6075	0.6412	0.6954	0.7647	0.9507
1946	−0.0448	−0.0459	−0.0748	−0.1312	−0.0974	−0.0669	−0.1563	−0.1463	−0.0995	−0.1837
1947	0.0559	0.0064	−0.0009	0.0188	0.0343	−0.0339	−0.0226	−0.0291	−0.0342	−0.0246
1948	0.0370	0.0057	0.0208	−0.0188	−0.0145	−0.0370	−0.0294	−0.0725	−0.0670	−0.0522
1949	0.1870	0.2517	0.2628	0.1999	0.1872	0.2309	0.2202	0.1615	0.1992	0.2485
1950	0.2864	0.2851	0.2643	0.3172	0.3700	0.3451	0.3700	0.4076	0.4037	0.5571
1951	0.2147	0.2256	0.2187	0.1687	0.1446	0.1414	0.1801	0.1515	0.1128	0.0584
1952	0.1429	0.1303	0.1168	0.1240	0.1108	0.1022	0.0984	0.0839	0.0865	0.0180
1953	0.0110	0.0157	0.0016	−0.0203	−0.0258	−0.0081	−0.0251	−0.0780	−0.0437	−0.0841
1954	0.4844	0.4844	0.5839	0.5101	0.5793	0.5945	0.5725	0.5341	0.6359	0.6853
1955	0.2838	0.1873	0.1893	0.1897	0.1819	0.2304	0.1794	0.2076	0.1972	0.2648
1956	0.0779	0.1160	0.0782	0.0869	0.0845	0.0590	0.0854	0.0478	0.0589	−0.0149
1957	−0.0955	−0.0883	−0.1342	−0.1105	−0.1347	−0.1831	−0.1725	−0.1824	−0.1448	−0.1618
1958	0.4078	0.4959	0.5432	0.5889	0.5616	0.5627	0.6697	0.6648	0.7102	0.6963
1959	0.1322	0.0967	0.1297	0.1505	0.1885	0.1483	0.2103	0.1719	0.1927	0.1552
1960	−0.0007	0.0558	0.0455	0.0085	−0.0115	−0.0147	−0.0552	−0.0428	−0.0377	−0.0824
1961	0.2699	0.2690	0.2919	0.2955	0.2878	0.2733	0.3034	0.3416	0.2988	0.3183
1962	−0.0887	−0.0961	−0.1192	−0.1230	−0.1669	−0.1752	−0.1672	−0.1467	−0.1673	−0.1423
1963	0.2247	0.2101	0.1695	0.1682	0.1303	0.1848	0.1762	0.1893	0.1335	0.1094
1964	0.1596	0.1448	0.1992	0.1667	0.1662	0.1642	0.1580	0.1707	0.1590	0.2091
1965	0.0894	0.1909	0.2470	0.2395	0.3106	0.3862	0.3348	0.3180	0.3223	0.4303
1966	−0.1033	−0.0528	−0.0516	−0.0601	−0.0685	−0.0525	−0.0935	−0.0883	−0.0577	−0.1007
1967	0.2191	0.2126	0.3148	0.4513	0.5212	0.5202	0.6546	0.8094	0.9028	1.1453
1968	0.0760	0.1664	0.1974	0.1912	0.2694	0.3103	0.2693	0.4044	0.3717	0.6122
1969	−0.0592	−0.1305	−0.1145	−0.1710	−0.1727	−0.1943	−0.2453	−0.2449	−0.3196	−0.3282
1970	0.0226	0.0240	0.0273	−0.0619	−0.0634	−0.0611	−0.0948	−0.1611	−0.1490	−0.1783

Source: Center for Research in Security Prices, University of Chicago.

Table 7-2 (continued)

Size-Decile Portfolios of the NYSE/AMEX/NASDAQ
Year-by-Year Returns

from 1971 to 2002

	Decile 1	Decile 2	Decile 3	Decile 4	Decile 5	Decile 6	Decile 7	Decile 8	Decile 9	Decile 10
1971	0.1494	0.1329	0.1927	0.2494	0.1896	0.2248	0.2075	0.1810	0.1718	0.1864
1972	0.2225	0.1274	0.0921	0.0906	0.0906	0.0629	0.0646	0.0266	−0.0167	−0.0026
1973	−0.1277	−0.2268	−0.2404	−0.2605	−0.3311	−0.3186	−0.3728	−0.3534	−0.3893	−0.4192
1974	−0.2807	−0.2450	−0.2383	−0.2814	−0.2359	−0.2781	−0.2734	−0.2608	−0.2984	−0.2895
1975	0.3155	0.4676	0.5287	0.6431	0.5752	0.5689	0.6335	0.6793	0.6626	0.7256
1976	0.2079	0.3012	0.3835	0.4034	0.4557	0.4627	0.5059	0.5631	0.5317	0.5575
1977	−0.0873	−0.0380	0.0105	0.0486	0.1071	0.1527	0.1825	0.2098	0.2073	0.2322
1978	0.0635	0.0240	0.1146	0.0945	0.1185	0.1592	0.1677	0.1713	0.1538	0.2825
1979	0.1575	0.2856	0.3103	0.3707	0.3660	0.4620	0.4200	0.4433	0.4625	0.4234
1980	0.3246	0.3428	0.3149	0.3177	0.3184	0.3126	0.3683	0.3264	0.3883	0.3029
1981	−0.0832	0.0102	0.0274	0.0427	0.0485	0.0793	−0.0129	0.0123	0.0775	0.0794
1982	0.1942	0.1721	0.2077	0.2640	0.3099	0.2857	0.2943	0.2915	0.2730	0.2802
1983	0.2062	0.1686	0.2654	0.2644	0.2605	0.2606	0.2692	0.3667	0.3137	0.3737
1984	0.0831	0.0762	0.0259	−0.0441	−0.0250	0.0242	−0.0437	−0.0752	−0.0871	−0.1947
1985	0.3137	0.3767	0.2925	0.3379	0.3098	0.3095	0.3265	0.3654	0.3094	0.2570
1986	0.1789	0.1799	0.1649	0.1792	0.1436	0.0879	0.1249	0.0392	0.0564	0.0030
1987	0.0503	0.0072	0.0396	0.0174	−0.0424	−0.0519	−0.0838	−0.0811	−0.1277	−0.1486
1988	0.1486	0.1982	0.2126	0.2247	0.2138	0.2342	0.2393	0.2857	0.2272	0.2082
1989	0.3295	0.3008	0.2629	0.2308	0.2423	0.2107	0.1763	0.1773	0.1064	0.0555
1990	−0.0088	−0.0853	−0.1015	−0.0875	−0.1409	−0.1849	−0.1532	−0.1981	−0.2449	−0.3131
1991	0.3039	0.3467	0.4134	0.3877	0.4847	0.5351	0.4329	0.4768	0.5082	0.4829
1992	0.0474	0.1560	0.1404	0.1290	0.2558	0.1898	0.1895	0.1344	0.2431	0.3360
1993	0.0729	0.1321	0.1609	0.1615	0.1676	0.1699	0.1868	0.1850	0.1685	0.2568
1994	0.0181	−0.0190	−0.0389	-0.0150	−0.0212	0.0081	−0.0271	−0.0260	−0.0324	−0.0290
1995	0.3938	0.3535	0.3524	0.3286	0.3256	0.2751	0.3203	0.2994	0.3546	0.3005
1996	0.2375	0.1943	0.1743	0.1827	0.1443	0.1708	0.1923	0.1790	0.2066	0.1686
1997	0.3487	0.3027	0.2472	0.2600	0.1603	0.2825	0.3079	0.2464	0.2576	0.2199
1998	0.3520	0.1256	0.0777	0.0780	0.0032	0.0087	−0.0036	0.0047	−0.0470	−0.1138
1999	0.2466	0.2018	0.3483	0.2998	0.2613	0.3419	0.2735	0.3753	0.3549	0.2798
2000	-0.1378	−0.0048	−0.0580	−0.0989	−0.0762	−0.1029	−0.1048	−0.1235	−0.1342	−0.1345
2001	−0.1524	−0.0855	−0.0483	−0.0056	−0.0259	0.0972	0.1070	0.2212	0.3133	0.3685
2002	−0.2243	−0.1755	−0.1954	−0.1728	−0.1777	−0.2169	−0.2272	−0.1964	−0.1889	−0.0602

Source: Center for Research in Security Prices, University of Chicago.

Table 7-3

Size-Decile Portfolios of the NYSE/AMEX/NASDAQ
Year-End Index Values

from 1925 to 1970

	Decile 1	Decile 2	Decile 3	Decile 4	Decile 5	Decile 6	Decile 7	Decile 8	Decile 9	Decile 10
1925	1.000	1.000	1.000	1.000	1.000	1.000	1.000	1.000	1.000	1.000
1926	1.144	1.055	1.036	1.008	1.003	1.033	0.975	0.907	0.900	0.940
1927	1.533	1.366	1.358	1.425	1.351	1.272	1.270	1.138	1.187	1.233
1928	2.129	1.882	1.899	1.958	2.022	1.630	1.718	1.504	1.632	2.093
1929	1.904	1.733	1.411	1.336	1.527	0.971	1.071	0.890	0.817	0.972
1930	1.443	1.084	0.922	0.879	0.973	0.604	0.679	0.449	0.444	0.528
1931	0.835	0.541	0.498	0.478	0.500	0.296	0.354	0.229	0.226	0.263
1932	0.735	0.536	0.489	0.414	0.443	0.315	0.295	0.232	0.225	0.365
1933	1.077	0.937	0.994	0.878	0.863	0.661	0.644	0.600	0.616	1.173
1934	1.101	0.990	1.083	1.035	0.928	0.805	0.739	0.766	0.755	1.546
1935	1.551	1.569	1.482	1.418	1.522	1.251	1.217	1.259	1.223	2.816
1936	2.010	2.127	1.905	2.034	2.223	1.877	1.851	1.879	2.244	5.237
1937	1.370	1.348	1.181	1.149	1.141	0.983	0.941	0.888	1.085	2.324
1938	1.713	1.814	1.598	1.538	1.718	1.409	1.270	1.291	1.415	2.533
1939	1.794	1.751	1.558	1.542	1.743	1.464	1.368	1.236	1.326	3.017
1940	1.667	1.593	1.422	1.482	1.723	1.375	1.284	1.164	1.267	2.081
1941	1.489	1.489	1.335	1.338	1.515	1.234	1.166	1.056	1.112	1.730
1942	1.684	1.849	1.597	1.613	1.836	1.538	1.503	1.379	1.592	3.069
1943	2.080	2.490	2.148	2.252	2.722	2.193	2.612	2.349	2.955	7.432
1944	2.433	3.144	2.660	2.987	3.797	3.173	3.586	3.508	4.632	12.631
1945	3.142	4.681	4.084	4.882	5.868	5.100	5.885	5.947	8.174	24.638
1946	3.001	4.466	3.778	4.241	5.297	4.759	4.965	5.077	7.361	20.112
1947	3.169	4.495	3.775	4.321	5.478	4.597	4.853	4.930	7.110	19.619
1948	3.286	4.521	3.853	4.240	5.399	4.427	4.711	4.572	6.633	18.594
1949	3.901	5.659	4.866	5.087	6.410	5.449	5.748	5.311	7.954	23.214
1950	5.018	7.272	6.152	6.701	8.781	7.330	7.874	7.476	11.165	36.145
1951	6.095	8.913	7.497	7.832	10.051	8.366	9.292	8.608	12.425	38.255
1952	6.966	10.074	8.373	8.804	11.165	9.221	10.207	9.330	13.500	38.944
1953	7.042	10.232	8.386	8.625	10.876	9.147	9.951	8.602	12.909	35.669
1954	10.454	15.189	13.283	13.025	17.177	14.584	15.647	13.197	21.118	60.112
1955	13.421	18.034	15.798	15.496	20.301	17.944	18.455	15.937	25.283	76.032
1956	14.466	20.125	17.034	16.843	22.016	19.002	20.030	16.698	26.772	74.902
1957	13.085	18.349	14.748	14.982	19.051	15.524	16.575	13.653	22.895	62.781
1958	18.421	27.448	22.760	23.804	29.749	24.258	27.675	22.730	39.154	106.497
1959	20.857	30.103	25.712	27.386	35.356	27.856	33.494	26.637	46.700	123.020
1960	20.842	31.783	26.881	27.618	34.951	27.446	31.645	25.497	44.941	112.881
1961	26.467	40.332	34.728	35.778	45.011	34.947	41.245	34.206	58.368	148.816
1962	24.119	36.454	30.588	31.378	37.499	28.824	34.349	29.187	48.604	127.645
1963	29.538	44.112	35.772	36.655	42.384	34.151	40.401	34.712	55.095	141.604
1964	34.253	50.501	42.898	42.765	49.427	39.758	46.783	40.636	63.857	171.215
1965	37.317	60.141	53.493	53.007	64.777	55.112	62.444	53.557	84.437	244.894
1966	33.463	56.965	50.732	49.819	60.337	52.218	56.608	48.829	79.567	220.233
1967	40.794	69.073	66.705	72.302	91.784	79.381	93.664	88.348	151.404	472.464
1968	43.894	80.570	79.871	86.124	116.514	104.010	118.886	124.073	207.681	761.708
1969	41.294	70.057	70.729	71.395	96.388	83.803	89.723	93.693	141.312	511.685
1970	42.226	71.738	72.662	66.979	90.275	78.679	81.219	78.603	120.257	420.444

Source: Center for Research in Security Prices, University of Chicago.

Table 7-3 (continued)

Size-Decile Portfolios of the NYSE/AMEX/NASDAQ
Year-End Index Values

from 1971 to 2002

	Decile 1	Decile 2	Decile 3	Decile 4	Decile 5	Decile 6	Decile 7	Decile 8	Decile 9	Decile 10
1971	48.537	81.270	86.665	83.685	107.390	96.362	98.073	92.829	140.914	498.824
1972	59.337	91.625	94.645	91.268	117.120	102.424	104.410	95.302	138.564	497.520
1973	51.758	70.844	71.897	67.490	78.338	69.795	65.483	61.625	84.628	288.961
1974	37.231	53.484	54.766	48.497	59.858	50.383	47.583	45.552	59.374	205.292
1975	48.978	78.491	83.720	79.684	94.290	79.047	77.728	76.497	98.716	354.258
1976	59.160	102.132	115.824	111.829	137.253	115.624	117.054	119.576	151.200	551.751
1977	53.997	98.247	117.045	117.263	151.947	133.280	138.421	144.659	182.549	679.889
1978	57.428	100.606	130.453	128.342	169.958	154.497	161.629	169.444	210.625	871.937
1979	66.474	129.338	170.926	175.920	232.156	225.868	229.516	244.557	308.043	1241.082
1980	88.053	173.673	224.747	231.812	306.074	296.474	314.050	324.373	427.640	1616.997
1981	80.728	175.439	230.905	241.719	320.919	319.983	310.010	328.375	460.799	1745.417
1982	96.403	205.634	278.866	305.522	420.372	411.413	401.261	424.081	586.581	2234.566
1983	116.280	240.295	352.885	386.308	529.865	518.636	509.268	579.610	770.600	3069.655
1984	125.941	258.613	362.033	369.290	516.637	531.161	487.001	536.034	703.508	2471.916
1985	165.453	356.045	467.935	494.090	676.703	695.572	645.998	731.893	921.192	3107.246
1986	195.053	420.084	545.111	582.618	773.872	756.695	726.686	760.613	973.138	3116.514
1987	204.868	423.106	566.675	592.756	741.061	717.385	665.804	698.923	848.820	2653.462
1988	235.305	506.965	687.138	725.938	899.523	885.380	825.156	898.605	1041.658	3205.930
1989	312.845	659.451	867.801	893.478	1117.473	1071.944	970.640	1057.890	1152.443	3383.967
1990	310.084	603.191	779.688	815.344	960.010	873.692	821.978	848.340	870.224	2324.431
1991	404.318	812.329	1102.019	1131.462	1425.316	1341.236	1177.832	1252.847	1312.442	3446.873
1992	423.502	939.017	1256.697	1277.411	1789.895	1595.753	1401.036	1421.276	1631.554	4604.946
1993	454.381	1063.070	1458.917	1483.731	2089.826	1866.910	1662.800	1684.143	1906.416	5787.612
1994	462.602	1042.853	1402.123	1461.440	2045.598	1882.089	1617.718	1640.422	1844.648	5619.862
1995	644.781	1411.521	1896.182	1941.733	2711.603	2399.841	2135.813	2131.529	2498.851	7308.439
1996	797.900	1685.732	2226.610	2296.566	3102.876	2809.629	2546.603	2513.097	3015.023	8540.425
1997	1076.121	2196.035	2777.105	2893.615	3600.219	3603.476	3330.752	3132.286	3791.573	10418.327
1998	1454.916	2471.765	2993.019	3119.393	3611.883	3634.855	3318.872	3146.969	3613.303	9233.229
1999	1813.679	2970.540	4035.600	4054.696	4555.559	4877.780	4226.687	4328.157	4895.504	11816.938
2000	1563.712	2956.305	3801.696	3653.741	4208.470	4375.991	3783.809	3793.646	4238.405	10227.184
2001	1325.387	2703.564	3618.221	3633.293	4099.628	4801.540	4188.851	4632.707	5566.292	13996.104
2002	1028.076	2229.178	2911.130	3005.403	3371.192	3759.889	3237.121	3722.671	4514.758	13153.104

Source: Center for Research in Security Prices, University of Chicago.

Table 7-4

Size-Decile Portfolios of the NYSE/AMEX/NASDAQ

Mid-, Low-, Micro-, and Total Capitalization Returns and Index Values

from 1926 to 1965

	Total Return				Index Value			
Year	Mid-Cap Stocks	Low-Cap Stocks	Micro-Cap Stocks	Total Value Weighted NYSE/ AMEX/ NASDAQ	Mid-Cap Stocks	Low-Cap Stocks	Micro-Cap Stocks	Total Value Weighted NYSE/ AMEX/ NASDAQ
1925					1.000	1.000	1.000	1.000
1926	0.0217	−0.0129	−0.0891	0.0952	1.022	0.987	0.911	1.095
1927	0.3471	0.2591	0.3151	0.3301	1.376	1.243	1.198	1.457
1928	0.4100	0.3121	0.4502	0.3872	1.941	1.631	1.737	2.021
1929	−0.2714	−0.3967	−0.5081	−0.1452	1.414	0.984	0.854	1.728
1930	−0.3476	−0.3979	−0.4569	−0.2827	0.922	0.592	0.464	1.239
1931	−0.4637	−0.4968	−0.4960	−0.4392	0.495	0.298	0.234	0.695
1932	−0.0679	−0.0223	0.0908	−0.0975	0.461	0.291	0.255	0.627
1933	1.0415	1.2177	1.8718	0.5759	0.941	0.646	0.733	0.988
1934	0.1137	0.2056	0.2513	0.0435	1.048	0.779	0.917	1.031
1935	0.4145	0.6020	0.6754	0.4398	1.483	1.248	1.536	1.485
1936	0.3641	0.5064	0.8447	0.3226	2.023	1.880	2.834	1.964
1937	−0.4194	−0.4916	−0.5271	−0.3463	1.174	0.956	1.340	1.284
1938	0.3773	0.4110	0.2466	0.2824	1.617	1.349	1.670	1.646
1939	−0.0085	0.0350	−0.0015	0.0283	1.604	1.396	1.668	1.693
1940	−0.0574	−0.0605	−0.1213	−0.0717	1.512	1.312	1.466	1.571
1941	−0.0844	−0.0968	−0.1322	−0.0986	1.384	1.185	1.272	1.416
1942	0.2023	0.2715	0.5101	0.1591	1.664	1.506	1.921	1.642
1943	0.3869	0.5799	0.9979	0.2836	2.308	2.380	3.837	2.107
1944	0.2961	0.4325	0.6053	0.2131	2.991	3.409	6.159	2.556
1945	0.5678	0.6386	0.8224	0.3798	4.690	5.586	11.225	3.527
1946	−0.0975	−0.1154	−0.1280	−0.0592	4.233	4.941	9.789	3.319
1947	0.0127	−0.0293	−0.0309	0.0356	4.286	4.797	9.487	3.437
1948	0.0008	−0.0428	−0.0615	0.0217	4.290	4.592	8.903	3.511
1949	0.2272	0.2117	0.2156	0.2034	5.264	5.564	10.822	4.226
1950	0.3026	0.3675	0.4548	0.2945	6.857	7.608	15.744	5.470
1951	0.1870	0.1562	0.0941	0.2075	8.140	8.797	17.225	6.605
1952	0.1179	0.0970	0.0636	0.1342	9.100	9.650	18.321	7.492
1953	−0.0106	−0.0288	−0.0568	0.0059	9.003	9.372	17.281	7.536
1954	0.5607	0.5749	0.6513	0.5009	14.051	14.759	28.536	11.310
1955	0.1876	0.2093	0.2184	0.2521	16.687	17.848	34.767	14.161
1956	0.0822	0.0649	0.0353	0.0824	18.058	19.007	35.993	15.329
1957	−0.1270	−0.1796	−0.1503	−0.1027	15.765	15.592	30.582	13.754
1958	0.5607	0.6177	0.7058	0.4500	24.604	25.224	52.168	19.943
1959	0.1477	0.1729	0.1811	0.1315	28.239	29.586	61.618	22.566
1960	0.0227	−0.0337	−0.0511	0.0084	28.879	28.588	58.467	22.756
1961	0.2922	0.2972	0.3048	0.2743	37.318	37.085	76.285	28.999
1962	−0.1301	−0.1673	−0.1619	−0.1021	32.463	30.882	63.936	26.039
1963	0.1614	0.1835	0.1209	0.2093	37.703	36.550	71.666	31.489
1964	0.1832	0.1632	0.1861	0.1616	44.608	42.513	85.003	36.577
1965	0.2571	0.3525	0.3800	0.1442	56.076	57.497	117.306	41.853

Source: Center for Research in Security Prices, University of Chicago.

Table 7-4 (continued)

Size-Decile Portfolios of the NYSE/AMEX/NASDAQ
Mid-, Low-, Micro-, and Total Capitalization Returns and Index Values

from 1966 to 2002

	Total Return				Index Value			
Year	Mid-Cap Stocks	Low-Cap Stocks	Micro-Cap Stocks	Total Value Weighted NYSE/ AMEX/ NASDAQ	Mid-Cap Stocks	Low-Cap Stocks	Micro-Cap Stocks	Total Value Weighted NYSE/ AMEX/ NASDAQ
1966	−0.0577	−0.0740	−0.0819	−0.0871	52.841	53.240	107.698	38.209
1967	0.3985	0.6338	1.0339	0.2872	73.896	86.982	219.044	49.181
1968	0.2115	0.3213	0.5011	0.1421	89.522	114.926	328.804	56.168
1969	−0.1454	−0.2243	−0.3247	−0.1096	76.508	89.154	222.029	50.013
1970	−0.0206	−0.0984	−0.1664	0.0004	74.929	80.381	185.076	50.034
1971	0.2090	0.2070	0.1807	0.1618	90.592	97.021	218.526	58.131
1972	0.0913	0.0548	−0.0094	0.1693	98.864	102.342	216.469	67.971
1973	−0.2651	−0.3442	−0.4068	−0.1816	72.658	67.115	128.419	55.626
1974	−0.2506	−0.2724	−0.2930	−0.2716	54.451	48.833	90.798	40.519
1975	0.5701	0.6160	0.6977	0.3867	85.495	78.915	154.150	56.189
1976	0.4035	0.4999	0.5454	0.2673	119.994	118.364	238.228	71.208
1977	0.0405	0.1746	0.2202	−0.0421	124.855	139.028	290.678	68.208
1978	0.1093	0.1654	0.2209	0.0749	138.507	162.016	354.881	73.315
1979	0.3397	0.4455	0.4429	0.2298	185.554	234.187	512.048	90.163
1980	0.3169	0.3328	0.3476	0.3269	244.347	312.118	690.034	119.634
1981	0.0367	0.0343	0.0775	−0.0369	253.323	322.819	743.521	115.219
1982	0.2466	0.2901	0.2764	0.2086	315.800	416.482	948.998	139.252
1983	0.2640	0.2867	0.3434	0.2198	399.173	535.892	1274.876	169.864
1984	−0.0088	−0.0233	−0.1386	0.0448	395.648	523.401	1098.123	177.482
1985	0.3115	0.3287	0.2837	0.3217	518.892	695.430	1409.624	234.581
1986	0.1646	0.0879	0.0312	0.1612	604.296	756.592	1453.620	272.405
1987	0.0122	−0.0686	−0.1386	0.0171	611.680	704.659	1252.184	277.069
1988	0.2170	0.2477	0.2173	0.1803	744.415	879.200	1524.330	327.017
1989	0.2479	0.1912	0.0821	0.2886	928.945	1047.291	1649.405	421.383
1990	−0.1053	−0.1779	−0.2741	−0.0596	831.105	860.989	1197.247	396.286
1991	0.4193	0.4861	0.5024	0.3467	1179.600	1279.504	1798.770	533.696
1992	0.1620	0.1754	0.2761	0.0980	1370.639	1503.947	2295.406	585.988
1993	0.1635	0.1801	0.2028	0.1113	1594.713	1774.806	2760.917	651.215
1994	−0.0274	−0.0127	−0.0320	−0.0005	1551.094	1752.230	2672.698	650.862
1995	0.3389	0.2961	0.3330	0.3679	2076.827	2271.068	3562.598	890.301
1996	0.1700	0.1800	0.1909	0.2134	2429.860	2679.887	4242.775	1080.276
1997	0.2317	0.2792	0.2405	0.3139	2992.860	3428.237	5263.232	1419.402
1998	0.0612	0.0040	−0.0791	0.2433	3175.939	3442.009	4846.972	1764.713
1999	0.3160	0.3281	0.3224	0.2544	4179.535	4571.183	6409.700	2213.603
2000	−0.0745	−0.1076	−0.1331	−0.1156	3868.340	4079.535	5556.506	1957.702
2001	−0.0319	0.1300	0.3394	−0.1112	3744.998	4609.926	7442.235	1740.014
2002	−0.1847	−0.2158	−0.1411	−0.2116	3053.410	3615.034	6391.777	1371.884

Source: Center for Research in Security Prices, University of Chicago.

Graph 7-1

Size-Decile Portfolios of the NYSE/AMEX/NASDAQ: Wealth Indices of Investments in Mid-, Low-, Micro-, and Total Capitalization Stocks
Year-End 1925 = $1.00

from 1925 to 2002

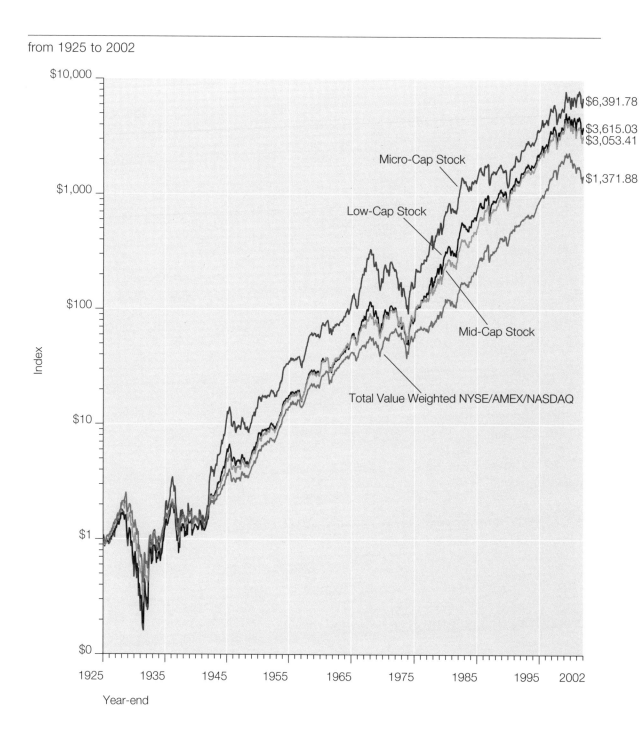

Size of the Deciles

Table 7-5 reveals that most of the market value of the stocks listed on the NYSE/AMEX/NASDAQ is represented by the top three deciles. Approximately two-thirds of the value is represented by the first decile, which currently consists of 168 stocks. The smallest decile represents less than one percent of the market value of the NYSE/AMEX/NASDAQ. The data in the second column of Table 7-5 are averages across all 77 years. Of course, the proportions represented by the various deciles vary from year to year.

In columns three and four are the number of companies and market capitalization. These present a snapshot of the structure of the deciles near the end of 2002.

The lower portion of Table 7-5 shows the largest firm in each decile and its market capitalization.

Table 7-5
Size-Decile Portfolios of the NYSE/AMEX/NASDAQ:
Bounds, Size, and Composition

from 1926 to 2002

Decile	Historical Average Percentage of Total Capitalization	Recent Number of Companies	Recent Decile Market Capitalization (in thousands)	Recent Percentage of Total Capitalization
1-Largest	63.27%	168	$6,099,523,614	66.27%
2	14.01%	182	1,174,194,524	12.76%
3	7.60%	197	584,693,698	6.35%
4	4.75%	200	344,651,829	3.74%
5	3.25%	244	282,490,634	3.07%
6	2.37%	268	206,453,954	2.24%
7	1.72%	347	175,969,268	1.91%
8	1.27%	427	136,629,517	1.48%
9	0.97%	703	117,578,857	1.28%
10-Smallest	0.79%	1994	81,984,379	0.89%
Mid-Cap 3–5	15.59%	641	1,211,836,161	13.17%
Low-Cap 6–8	5.36%	1042	519,052,738	5.64%
Micro-Cap 9–10	1.76%	2697	199,563,236	2.17%

Source: Center for Research in Security Prices, University of Chicago.

Historical average percentage of total capitalization shows the average, over the last 77 years, of the decile market values as a percentage of the total NYSE/AMEX/NASDAQ calculated each month. Number of companies in deciles, recent market capitalization of deciles and recent percentage of total capitalization are as of September 30, 2002.

Decile	Recent Market Capitalization (in thousands)	Company Name
1-Largest	$293,137,304	Microsoft Corp.
2	11,628,735	KeyCorp New
3	5,012,705	Rockwell Collins Inc.
4	2,680,573	Diebold Inc.
5	1,691,210	Smucker JM Co.
6	1,143,845	CEC Entertainment Inc.
7	791,336	Playtex Products Inc.
8	521,298	Buckle Inc.
9	314,042	Guess? Inc.
10-Smallest	141,459	NYMAGIC Inc.

Source: Center for Research in Security Prices, University of Chicago.

Market capitalization and name of largest company in each decile as of September 30, 2002.

Long-Term Returns in Excess of Risk

The Capital Asset Pricing Model (CAPM) does not fully account for the higher returns of small company stocks. Table 7-6 shows the returns in excess of risk over the past 77 years for each decile of the NYSE/AMEX/NASDAQ.

The CAPM can be expressed as follows:

$$k_s = r_f + (\beta_s \times ERP) \qquad (28)$$

where,

k_s = the expected return for company **s**;

r_f = the expected return of the riskless asset;

β_s = the beta of the stock of company **s**; and,

ERP = the expected equity risk premium, or the amount by which investors expect the future return on equities to exceed that on the riskless asset.

The amount of an asset's systematic risk is measured by its beta. A beta greater than 1 indicates that the security is riskier than the market, and according to the CAPM equation, investors are compensated for taking on this additional risk. However, based on historical return data on the NYSE/AMEX/NASDAQ decile portfolios, the smaller deciles have had returns that are not fully explainable by the CAPM. This return in excess of CAPM, grows larger as one moves from the largest companies in decile 1 to the smallest in decile 10. The excess return is especially pronounced for micro-cap stocks (deciles 9–10). This size related phenomenon has prompted a revision to the CAPM, which includes the addition of a size premium.

The CAPM is used here to calculate the CAPM return in excess of the riskless rate and to compare this estimate to historical performance. According to the CAPM, the return on a security should consist of the riskless rate, plus an additional return to compensate for the risk of the security. Table 7-6 uses the 77-year arithmetic mean income return component of 20-year government bonds as the historical riskless rate. (However, it is appropriate to match the maturity, or duration, of the riskless asset with the investment horizon.) This CAPM return in excess of the riskless rate is β (beta) multiplied by the realized equity risk premium. The realized equity risk premium is the return that compensates investors for taking on risk equal to the risk of the market as a whole (estimated by the 77-year arithmetic mean return on large company stocks, 12.20 percent, less the historical riskless rate, 5.23 percent). The difference between the excess return predicted by the CAPM and the realized excess return is the size premium, or return in excess of CAPM.

This phenomenon can also be viewed graphically, as depicted in the Graph 7-2. The security market line is based on the pure CAPM without adjusting for the size premium. Based on the risk (or beta) of a security, the expected return should fluctuate along the security market line. However, the expected returns for the smaller deciles of the NYSE/AMEX/NASDAQ lie above the line, indicating that these deciles have had returns in excess of their risk.

Table 7-6
Size-Decile Portfolios of the NYSE/AMEX/NASDAQ:
Long-Term Returns in Excess of CAPM

from 1926 to 2002

Decile	Beta*	Arithmetic Mean Return	Actual Return in Excess of Riskless Rate**	CAPM Return in Excess of Riskless Rate**	Size Premium (Return in Excess of CAPM)
1	0.91%	11.25%	6.01%	6.34%	−0.32%
2	1.03	12.86%	7.63%	7.21%	0.42%
3	1.09	13.51%	8.28%	7.62%	0.66%
4	1.13	14.03%	8.80%	7.85%	0.95%
5	1.16	14.48%	9.25%	8.08%	1.16%
6	1.18	14.93%	9.70%	8.22%	1.48%
7	1.23	15.16%	9.92%	8.58%	1.35%
8	1.27	16.17%	10.94%	8.88%	2.06%
9	1.34	17.12%	11.89%	9.33%	2.56%
10	1.41	20.75%	15.52%	9.85%	5.67%
Mid-Cap, 3–5	1.11	13.82%	8.59%	7.77%	0.82%
Low-Cap, 6–8	1.22	15.23%	9.99%	8.47%	1.52%
Micro-Cap, 9–10	1.35	18.20%	12.96%	9.44%	3.53%

*Betas are estimated from monthly returns in excess of the 30-day U.S. Treasury bill total return, January 1926–December 2002.

**Historical riskless rate measured by the 77-year arithmetic mean income return component of 20-year government bonds (5.23).

Graph 7-2
Size-Decile Portfolios of the NYSE/AMEX/NASDAQ:
Security Market Line

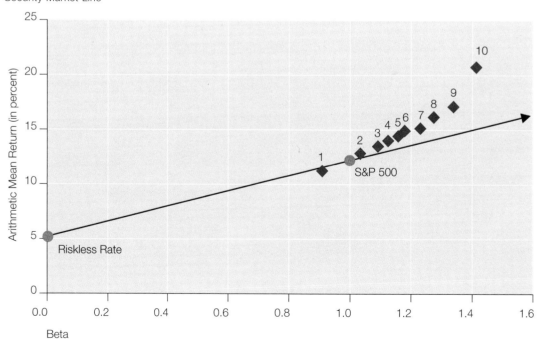

Serial Correlation in Small Company Stock Returns

The serial correlation, or first-order autocorrelation, of returns on large capitalization stocks is near zero. [See Table 7-1.] If stock returns are serially correlated, then one can gain some information about future performance based on past returns. For the smallest deciles of stocks, the serial correlation is near or above 0.1. This observation bears further examination.

Table 7-7

Size-Decile Portfolios of the NYSE/ AMEX/NASDAQ:

Serial Correlations of Annual Returns in Excess of Decile 1 Returns

1926–2002

Decile	Serial Correlations of Annual Returns in Excess of Decile 1 Return
Decile 2	0.23
Decile 3	0.29
Decile 4	0.23
Decile 5	0.26
Decile 6	0.35
Decile 7	0.28
Decile 8	0.34
Decile 9	0.32
Decile 10	0.40

To remove the randomizing effect of the market as a whole, the returns for decile 1 are geometrically subtracted from the returns for deciles 2 through 10. The result illustrates that these series differences exhibit greater serial correlation than the decile series themselves. Table 7-7 above presents the serial correlations of the excess returns for deciles 2 through 10. These serial correlations suggest some predictability of smaller company excess returns. However, caution is necessary. The serial correlation of small company excess returns for non-calendar years (February through January, etc.) do not always confirm the results shown here for calendar (January through December) years. The results for the non-calendar years (not shown in this book) suggest that predicting small company excess returns may not be easy.

Seasonality

Unlike the returns on large company stocks, the returns on small company stocks appear to be seasonal. In January, small company stocks often outperform larger stocks by amounts far greater than in any other month.

Table 7-8 shows the returns of capitalization deciles 2 through 10 in excess of the return on decile 1. This table segregates excess returns into months. For each decile and for each month, the exhibit shows both the average excess return as well as the number of times the excess return is positive. These two statistics measure the seasonality of the excess return in different ways. The average excess return illustrates the size of the effect, while the number of positive excess returns shows the reliability of the effect.

Virtually all of the small stock effect occurs in January. The excess outcomes of the other months are on net, mostly negative for small company stocks. Excess returns in January relate to size in a precisely rank-ordered fashion. This "January effect" seems to pervade all size groups.

Table 7-8
Size-Decile Portfolios of the NYSE/AMEX/NASDAQ:
Returns in Excess of Decile 1 (in percent)
from 1926 to 2002

First row: average excess return in percent
Second row: number of times excess return was positive (in 77 years)

Decile	Jan	Feb	Mar	Apr	May	Jun	Jul	Aug	Sep	Oct	Nov	Dec	Total (Jan–Dec)
2	0.84%	0.48%	−0.07%	−0.32%	0.02%	−0.11%	−0.06%	0.23%	0.04%	−0.29%	0.08%	0.38%	1.27%
	56	49	34	28	36	38	35	44	41	35	40	41	
3	1.18%	0.33%	0.01%	−0.08%	−0.27%	−0.18%	−0.02%	0.37%	−0.07%	−0.40%	0.50%	0.32%	1.75%
	58	50	37	30	32	33	38	46	41	32	42	46	
4	1.36%	0.59%	−0.12%	−0.20%	−0.02%	−0.09%	−0.06%	0.31%	0.10%	−0.82%	0.31%	0.52%	1.98%
	55	50	37	34	37	35	35	47	39	26	44	45	
5	2.23%	0.58%	−0.13%	−0.30%	−0.27%	−0.06%	−0.08%	0.30%	0.11%	−0.86%	0.31%	0.35%	2.29%
	57	47	35	30	31	34	37	44	40	29	43	41	
6	2.64%	0.56%	−0.26%	−0.13%	0.12%	−0.20%	−0.11%	0.54%	0.17%	−1.28%	0.18%	0.26%	2.69%
	58	49	39	32	35	34	40	44	41	29	40	41	
7	3.26%	0.68%	−0.24%	−0.12%	−0.01%	−0.39%	−0.12%	0.19%	0.26%	−1.08%	0.11%	0.04%	2.62%
	60	51	39	36	32	31	34	35	42	29	39	37	
8	4.50%	0.79%	−0.46%	−0.42%	0.33%	−0.51%	0.03%	0.03%	0.08%	−1.15%	0.17%	−0.30%	3.39%
	59	47	34	32	29	33	34	35	40	30	34	34	
9	5.99%	1.03%	−0.21%	−0.25%	0.13%	−0.49%	−0.02%	0.12%	−0.09%	−1.34%	0.06%	−1.07%	4.10%
	62	44	38	31	30	30	33	39	35	27	32	32	
10	9.35%	1.08%	−0.86%	0.08%	0.40%	−0.81%	0.47%	−0.13%	0.56%	−1.48%	−0.49%	−1.80%	7.10%
	70	41	33	35	33	29	35	28	39	26	29	27	

Chapter 8
Growth and Value Investing

Discussion of Style Investing

The concept of equity investment style has come into being over the past thirty years or so. Investment style can broadly be defined as common types of characteristics that groups of stocks or portfolios share. Probably the first discussion and consideration of style related to large company versus small company investing, and even this distinction was not too prominent until the 1960s. Now, styles of investing are broken down into more detail and used for performance measurement, asset allocation, and other purposes. Mutual funds and other investment portfolios are often measured against broad growth or value benchmarks. In some cases, investment manager-specific style benchmarks are constructed to separate pure stock selection ability from style effects.

Most investors agree on the broad definitions of growth and value, but when it comes to specific definitions, there are many ways of defining a growth stock and a value stock. In fact, a value investor may hold a stock that fits his or her definition of value, while a growth investor may hold the same stock because it fits his or her definition of growth. In general, growth stocks have high relative growth rates of earnings, sales, or return on equity. Growth stocks usually have relatively high price-to-earnings and price-to-book ratios. Value stocks will generally have lower price-to-earnings and price-to-book values, and often have higher dividend yields. Value stocks are often turn-around opportunities, companies that have had disappointing news, or companies with low growth prospects. Value investors generally believe that a value stock has been unfairly beaten down by the market, making the stock sell below its "intrinsic" value. Therefore, they buy the stock with the hope that the market will realize its full value and bid the price up to its fair value.

Different Ways of Measuring Growth and Value

In order to objectively measure the performance of value and growth stocks, several different data providers have constructed value and growth indices. Each index provider uses a different methodology to draw the line between growth and value, but all of the methodologies rely on some combination of accounting data, analyst growth estimates, and market capitalization. Three of the more prominent growth/value index providers are S&P/BARRA, Russell, and Wilshire.

S&P/BARRA starts with the universe of all companies in the S&P 500™ for their large-cap series. Companies are ranked by price-to-book, and the growth/value breakpoint is set where the total market capitalization of the growth and value indices are equal. Low price-to-book stocks are put in the value index, and high price-to-book stocks are put in the growth index. A price-to-book value calculation is employed, whereby the market capitalization of an index (S&P 500, S&P SmallCap 400, S&P SmallCap 600) is divided equally between growth and value. The indices are rebalanced twice a year. The large-cap style indices are available from January 1975, the mid-cap indices are available from June 1991, and small-cap indices are available from January 1994.

Russell also has large-, mid-, and small-cap style indices. To determine growth or value, each company is first ranked by a composite score of price-to-book and Institutional Brokers' Estimate System (IBES) forecast long-term growth mean. Using this score and a proprietary algorithm, 70 percent of companies are classified as all value or all growth, and 30 percent are weighted proportionately to both value and growth. Russell style indices are available starting in January 1979.

Wilshire defines growth and value by looking at two factors: price-to-book and projected price-to-earnings ratio. Wilshire style indices are available starting in January 1978.

It is evident that the prominent index providers use different measures to determine value and growth, and use different techniques for constructing portfolios. None of these three providers have growth and value indices going back before 1975. Growth and value stocks were certainly around before then, but much of the accounting data is not readily available today. However, Eugene Fama and Ken French constructed growth and value data from both Compustat and hand-collected data for the early years of the series. The Fama-French series use book-to-market to define value and growth. In addition to the Fama-French series, Ibbotson Associates, with the help of the Center for Research in Security Prices at the University of Chicago (CRSP), developed a set of growth and value indices dating back to 1968. This chapter places a heavy emphasis on the Ibbotson data but will also present the Fama-French data to some degree. A detailed description of both construction methodologies follows.

Growth and Value Index Construction Methodology

As discussed earlier, most growth and value indices go only as far back as the mid-1970s. However, both the Fama-French indices as well as the Ibbotson series date back even further.

Fama-French Methodology

Fama-French use all stocks traded on the New York Stock Exchange (NYSE) to set both growth/value and small/large breakpoints. They then apply these breakpoints to all stocks traded on NYSE, AMEX, and NASDAQ to construct each index.

The market capitalization breakpoint between small and large stocks is set as the median market capitalization of NYSE stocks. This breakpoint is then applied to all stocks traded on NYSE, AMEX, and NASDAQ.

To define value and growth, Fama-French use the book value of equity (BE) divided by market capitalization (ME), which is the inverse of how much investors are willing to pay for a dollar of book value. Value companies will have a high book-to-market ratio, while growth companies will have a low book-to-market ratio. Fama-French used Compustat as their data source to calculate book value from 1963 forward, and hand-collected data for 1928 to 1962.

Book value was calculated as follows:

$$BV = SE + DT + ITC - PS \qquad \text{(29)}$$

where,

BV	=	Fama-French book value;
SE	=	book value of stockholders' equity;
DT	=	balance sheet deferred taxes;
ITC	=	investment tax credit (if available); and,

PS = book value of preferred stock. Depending on availability, either redemption, liquidation, or par value (in that order) is used to estimate book value of preferred stock.

Stocks are put into three groups based on book-to-market: low, medium, or high. The definition of low, medium, and high is based on the breakpoints for the bottom 30 percent, middle 40 percent, and top 30 percent of the value of book-to-market for NYSE stocks. These breakpoints are then applied to all NYSE, AMEX, and NASDAQ stocks. For the growth/value analysis shown in this chapter, only the low and high portfolios are used. The medium portfolios, which are blends of growth and value, are not shown.

Firms with negative book values are not used when calculating the book-to-market breakpoints or when calculating size-specific book-to-market breakpoints. Also, only firms with ordinary common equity (as classified by CRSP) are included in the portfolios. This excludes ADRs, REITs, and unit trusts.

The four size-specific style indices used in this chapter are small value, small growth, large value, and large growth. These portfolios are defined as the intersections of the two size groups and the low and high book-to-market groups. An all-capitalization value index called "all value" is created by taking the market-cap weighted return of small value and large value, and the same procedure is used to calculate an all-capitalization growth index called "all growth."

Ibbotson Associates Methodology

Ibbotson Associates developed the methodology to construct the style indices, and then contracted CRSP to fill in the back history of asset class returns. The screening process starts each period by trimming the CRSP database of NYSE, AMEX, and NASDAQ securities to eliminate American Depository Receipts (ADRs) and companies without ordinary common equity. Firms with negative or missing market values of equity and firms missing book values are eliminated. Every company used in the analysis must have a market value of equity, a book-to-market (B/M) ratio, and market returns in order to make it through the screening process and into the data sets created therein.

Four portfolios were formed based on size at the end of June of each year by sorting the NYSE universe by June-end market capitalization into large-cap, mid-cap, small-cap, and micro-cap size groupings. These size portfolios were defined by selecting the top 20 percent (deciles 1-2) by number of companies for large-cap, the next 30 percent (deciles 3-5) for mid-cap, the next 30 percent (deciles 6-8) for small-cap, and the smallest 20 percent (deciles 9-10) for micro-cap. Once the breakpoints were established, similar-sized AMEX and NASDAQ companies were assigned to the corresponding portfolios.

The companies in each of the four size portfolios were ranked by book-to-market, and created a growth (low B/M) and value (high B/M) portfolio within each size grouping where the total market capitalization of the growth and value indices are equal within each portfolio.

Once the large-, mid-, small-, and micro-cap growth and value portfolios were constructed, the last step was to create asset class returns. Portfolios were formed at June-end of each year, and value-weighted monthly returns were calculated from July to the following June. Lagged market values were used so that the returns for each month are weighted by the market values of the previous month.

Using the resulting data sets, it was determined that 1968 was the most appropriate starting date for asset class analysis. The Ibbotson style indices were actually created going back to 1963, but 1968 was the year in which the series covered a significant portion of the market.

In addition to the size-based portfolios, an all-capitalization index called "IA all value" was created using the lagged market capitalization-weighted returns of the large-, mid-, small-, and micro-cap value series. The same procedure was used to create an "IA all growth" series from the four growth asset classes.

Ibbotson Growth and Value Series

The following commentary and corresponding data make use of the Ibbotson growth and value data series.

Historical Returns on Growth and Value

Graph 8-1 depicts the growth of $1.00 invested in IA all growth and IA all value stocks from the end of 1967 to the end of December 2002. The chart shows that over the long term value stocks have well outperformed growth stocks. An investment of $1.00 in value stocks at year-end 1967 would have returned $61.26 by the end of December 2002, a compound return of 12.5 percent. The same investment in growth stocks would have returned $20.32 to an investor, a compound return of 9.0 percent.

Graph 8-1

IA All Growth Stocks vs. IA All Value Stocks
Year-End 1967 = $1.00

from 1967 to 2002

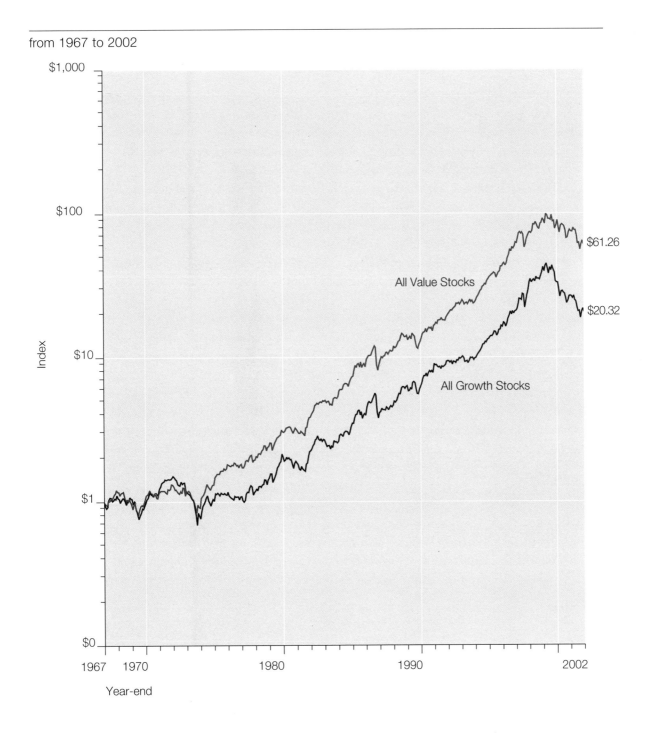

Year-end

Graph 8-2 depicts the growth of $1.00 invested in IA large-cap value, large-cap growth, mid-cap value, mid-cap growth, small-cap value, small-cap growth, micro-cap value, and micro-cap growth from the end of 1967 to the end of December 2002. The top three performers during this time period were small-cap value, large-cap value, and mid-cap value. Large-cap growth was the best-performing growth series, followed in order of performance by micro-cap value, mid-cap growth, small-cap growth, and micro-cap growth. Over time, a consistent pattern of value outperforming growth emerges within each of the size groupings.

As seen in Graph 8-2, micro-cap growth is literally off the chart. The poor performance of this asset class bears further analysis. One possible explanation for the poor performance of the Ibbotson micro-cap growth index is simply a lack of data in the early years of the analysis. While market capitalization coverage of the style indices is high from 1968 to present, the number of companies covered isn't as comprehensive. Many of the companies that are not included in the analysis are smaller companies for which Compustat book value data is not available. This may also be why many other data vendors have chosen not to present micro-cap style indices.

Another possible reason why the micro-cap growth data has such poor performance has to do with the upward movement of successful micro-cap companies into higher capitalization benchmarks. To understand micro-cap style performance, it is necessary to first understand the difference between growth and value stocks. In general, growth stocks usually have relatively high growth rates of earnings, sales, or return on equity. They typically have high price-to-earnings and market-to-book ratios. The opposite is true for value companies, which usually have lower price-to-earnings and market-to-book ratios, along with higher dividend yields. Value stocks are often turnaround opportunities, companies with disappointing news, or companies with low growth prospects. An investor putting money into a micro-cap growth company is paying relatively more per unit of earnings and book value based on the expectation that there is higher potential for greater gains down the road. While the performance of the many micro-cap companies that fail is included in the micro-cap growth index, those that hit their high potential tend to grow out of micro-cap and into a larger index. A micro-cap stock could move into small-, mid-, and eventually large-cap in very little time. For this reason, the companies that fail seem to stay very small and the companies that hit it big tend to grow out of the coverage of the micro-cap index. This may explain why the micro-cap growth index has such poor performance.

Graph 8-2

**IA Large-cap Growth Stocks, IA Large-cap Value Stocks, IA Mid-cap Growth Stocks,
IA Mid-cap Value Stocks, IA Small-cap Growth Stocks, IA Small-cap Value Stocks,
IA Micro-cap Growth Stocks, IA Micro-cap Value Stocks**
Year-End 1967 = $1.00

from 1967 to 2002

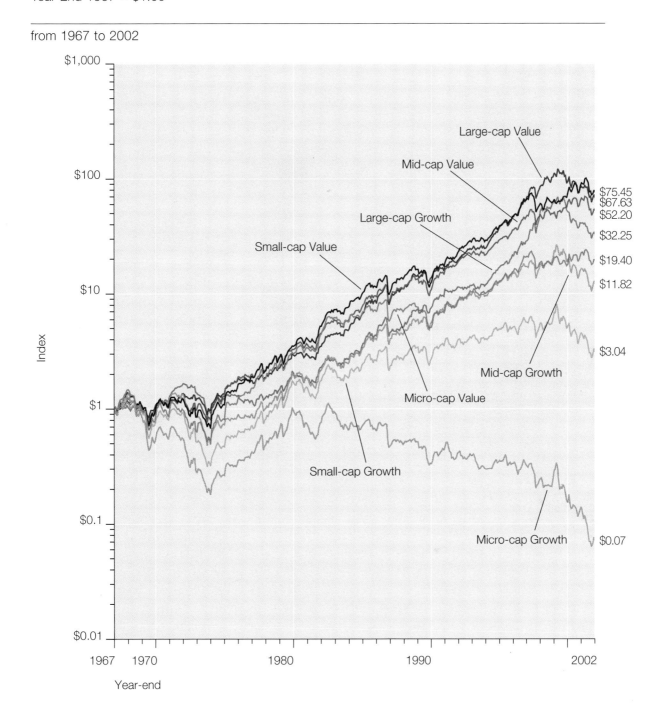

Summary Statistics for Growth and Value Series

Table 8-1 shows summary statistics of annual total returns for all of the Ibbotson growth and value series. The summary statistics presented are geometric mean, arithmetic mean, and standard deviation.

Value significantly outperformed growth across the market capitalization spectrum. In addition to outperforming their growth counterparts, value series did so with lower volatility. The traditional risk-return tradeoff does not seem to hold with regard to the split between growth and value. The value series are offering more return and less risk.

Table 8-1

Total Returns and Standard Deviation of Value and Growth
Summary Statistics of Annual Returns

from 1968 to 2002

Series	Geometric Mean (%)	Arithmetic Mean (%)	Standard Deviation (%)
IA Large-cap Growth Stocks	10.4	12.8	23.6
IA Large-cap Value Stocks	12.8	14.4	19.3
IA Mid-cap Growth Stocks	7.3	9.6	21.5
IA Mid-cap Value Stocks	12.0	13.7	20.1
IA Small-cap Growth Stocks	3.2	6.1	24.1
IA Small-cap Value Stocks	13.1	15.4	22.6
IA Micro-cap Growth Stocks	−7.3	−3.1	28.1
IA Micro-cap Value Stocks	8.8	11.8	25.2
IA All Growth Stocks	9.0	11.2	21.8
IA All Value Stocks	12.5	14.1	18.9

Returns by Decade

Table 8-2 shows the compound returns by decade for the growth and value series. Value stocks outperformed growth stocks during the 1970s and 1980s. The 1990s proved to be a little different with large-cap growth and mid-cap growth performing better than their value counterparts. However, small-cap value and micro-cap value continued to outperform their growth counterparts. Value stocks have outperformed growth stocks during the last ten years–1993 to 2002.

Table 8-2
Compound Annual Rates of Return by Decade

	1960s*	1970s	1980s	1990s	2000s**	1993-02
IA Large-cap Growth Stocks	3.2%	3.4%	17.4%	24.5%	−21.2%	10.9%
IA Large-cap Value Stocks	−1.6	8.9	20.4	22.6	−15.5	13.0
IA Mid-cap Growth Stocks	0.8	2.9	16.1	14.8	−20.9	2.9
IA Mid-cap Value Stocks	−2.4	11.5	16.9	14.4	0.5	10.5
IA Small-cap Growth Stocks	−1.4	2.0	11.2	7.3	−23.9	−2.8
IA Small-cap Value Stocks	2.5	10.4	19.2	15.0	4.7	12.3
IA Micro-cap Growth Stocks	−8.2	−2.2	−2.6	−5.5	−37.8	−16.4
IA Micro-cap Value Stocks	−2.2	10.0	11.9	10.5	−2.1	8.2
IA All Growth Stocks	2.1	3.4	15.9	20.9	−21.7	8.0
IA All Value Stocks	−1.5	9.7	19.3	20.6	−12.9	12.0

*Based on the period 1968–1969
**Based on the period 2000–2002

Monthly Standard Deviations

Table 8-3 shows the annualized monthly standard deviations of the growth and value data series by decade beginning in 1968 and illustrates the differences and changes in return volatility. In this table, the 1960s cover the period 1968 to 1969 and the 2000s cover the period 2000 to 2002. Value stocks across the various size groupings were less risky investments versus growth stocks in the 1980s and 1990s based on standard deviation. Micro-cap growth stocks had a lower standard deviation than micro-cap value stocks during the 1970s while all other value stocks performed with less or equal risk than their growth counterparts.

Table 8-3
Annualized Monthly Standard Deviations by Decade

	1960s*	1970s	1980s	1990s	2000s**	1993-02
IA Large-cap Growth Stocks	16.3%	19.4%	21.9%	21.7%	18.2%	22.5%
IA Large-cap Value Stocks	12.7	16.8	21.4	19.5	24.2	23.3
IA Mid-cap Growth Stocks	19.8	23.3	25.0	20.9	26.0	23.9
IA Mid-cap Value Stocks	16.9	23.3	19.5	17.8	24.0	19.3
IA Small-cap Growth Stocks	24.6	26.7	25.9	22.8	28.3	25.8
IA Small-cap Value Stocks	18.7	26.2	21.3	19.3	24.8	20.5
IA Micro-cap Growth Stocks	27.9	28.0	22.9	20.9	24.3	23.3
IA Micro-cap Value Stocks	21.7	31.2	21.1	18.5	24.2	19.9
IA All Growth Stocks	17.2	19.8	22.5	20.6	19.0	21.6
IA All Value Stocks	13.7	18.2	20.4	18.6	23.5	21.8

*Based on the period 1968–1969
**Based on the period 2000–2002

Presentation of the Annual Data

Table 8-4 shows year-by-year total annual returns from 1968 to 2002. This table compares the performance of large-cap growth, large-cap value, mid-cap growth, mid-cap value, small-cap growth, small-cap value, micro-cap growth, micro-cap value, all growth and all value. Table 8-5 shows the growth of $1.00 invested in each of the categories at year-end 1967.

In addition to the large differences in annual returns between large and small stocks noted in Table 7-2 of this book, there are large differences between growth and value as seen in Table 8-4. In 1998, for instance, all growth stocks returned 58.5 percent while all value stocks returned 16.2 percent. However, we know from the long-term analysis of value versus growth that value outperformed growth a majority of the time. Recent years where this occurred are 1992 to 1997, as well as 2000 to 2002.

Table 8-4

Growth and Value Series
Year-by-Year Returns

from 1968 to 2002

	IA Large-cap Growth Stocks	IA Large-cap Value Stocks	IA Mid-cap Growth Stocks	IA Mid-cap Value Stocks	IA Small-cap Growth Stocks
1968	0.0215	0.1431	0.1103	0.2157	0.2574
1969	0.0427	−0.1523	−0.0841	−0.2156	−0.2273
1970	−0.0332	0.1156	−0.0492	0.0600	−0.1930
1971	0.2490	0.0852	0.2938	0.1084	0.1518
1972	0.2928	0.1608	0.0707	0.0887	0.0252
1973	−0.1741	−0.0941	−0.3526	−0.1804	−0.4470
1974	−0.3327	−0.2100	−0.3892	−0.2019	−0.3807
1975	0.3039	0.3956	0.3755	0.6175	0.4788
1976	0.1106	0.3553	0.2350	0.4777	0.3734
1977	−0.1133	−0.0350	−0.0009	0.0491	0.1121
1978	0.0736	0.0565	0.1216	0.0919	0.1451
1979	0.1729	0.2102	0.3415	0.2961	0.4374
1980	0.3912	0.2969	0.4640	0.1584	0.4373
1981	−0.1077	−0.0033	−0.0520	0.0983	−0.1001
1982	0.2556	0.1914	0.1631	0.2606	0.1585
1983	0.1600	0.2738	0.2365	0.2929	0.2089
1984	0.0270	0.1062	−0.0565	0.0276	−0.1043
1985	0.3462	0.3822	0.3354	0.3297	0.3046
1986	0.1566	0.2042	0.1585	0.1653	0.0426
1987	0.0816	0.0630	0.0256	−0.0234	−0.0884
1988	0.1255	0.2685	0.1322	0.2301	0.1701
1989	0.4139	0.3169	0.3171	0.1968	0.2331
1990	0.0300	−0.0532	−0.0601	−0.1860	−0.2016
1991	0.4523	0.2427	0.4216	0.4706	0.4046
1992	0.0375	0.1643	0.1062	0.1964	0.0510
1993	0.0345	0.2419	0.1385	0.1758	0.0609
1994	0.0131	0.0069	−0.0474	−0.0356	−0.0513
1995	0.4120	0.5186	0.3023	0.3501	0.2201
1996	0.2549	0.2257	0.1933	0.2166	0.0413
1997	0.3566	0.5038	0.1451	0.3348	0.0967
1998	0.8051	0.2242	0.0494	0.0166	−0.0179
1999	0.2657	0.3084	0.3231	0.0565	0.2458
2000	−0.2218	−0.1531	−0.1655	0.2193	−0.2402
2001	−0.2010	−0.0999	−0.1693	0.0759	−0.1274
2002	−0.2126	−0.2081	−0.2855	−0.2260	−0.3364

Table 8-4 (continued)

Growth and Value Series
Year-by-Year Returns

from 1968 to 2002

	IA Small-cap Value Stocks	IA Micro-cap Growth Stocks	IA Micro-cap Value Stocks	IA All Growth Stocks	IA All Value Stocks
1968	0.3787	0.3530	0.4735	0.0601	0.1755
1969	−0.2387	−0.3766	−0.3514	−0.0162	−0.1751
1970	−0.0473	−0.3496	−0.1016	−0.0548	0.0913
1971	0.1560	0.1227	0.1341	0.2474	0.0940
1972	0.0396	−0.1065	−0.0009	0.2257	0.1387
1973	−0.2902	−0.4967	−0.3556	−0.2259	−0.1213
1974	−0.2090	−0.3519	−0.2195	−0.3469	−0.2109
1975	0.6048	0.4725	0.6527	0.3279	0.4424
1976	0.5158	0.3554	0.5449	0.1537	0.3902
1977	0.1692	0.1846	0.2201	−0.0701	0.0009
1978	0.1197	0.1530	0.2084	0.0909	0.0730
1979	0.3103	0.3738	0.3459	0.2328	0.2393
1980	0.2402	0.4254	0.2114	0.4110	0.2614
1981	0.1600	−0.2363	0.1270	−0.1004	0.0341
1982	0.2898	0.0510	0.3176	0.2201	0.2177
1983	0.3937	0.1952	0.3899	0.1806	0.2933
1984	0.0691	−0.2784	−0.0735	−0.0189	0.0783
1985	0.3268	0.0988	0.2211	0.3293	0.3594
1986	0.0888	−0.1188	−0.0034	0.1363	0.1779
1987	−0.0789	−0.2551	−0.1382	0.0436	0.0264
1988	0.3332	0.0528	0.1908	0.1281	0.2631
1989	0.1768	0.0231	0.0645	0.3657	0.2738
1990	−0.2223	−0.3495	−0.3310	−0.0161	−0.0988
1991	0.4695	0.3785	0.4046	0.4416	0.2995
1992	0.2684	−0.0895	0.2327	0.0478	0.1794
1993	0.2532	−0.0587	0.1766	0.0542	0.2279
1994	−0.0110	−0.2407	−0.0320	−0.0127	−0.0040
1995	0.3377	0.1883	0.2804	0.3681	0.4638
1996	0.2176	−0.0598	0.2215	0.2169	0.2231
1997	0.4125	−0.0489	0.3354	0.2859	0.4648
1998	−0.0993	−0.2303	−0.1193	0.5847	0.1615
1999	0.0868	0.1893	0.1155	0.2700	0.2618
2000	0.1613	−0.4748	−0.1301	−0.2202	−0.1097
2001	0.1994	−0.0867	0.2640	−0.1929	−0.0643
2002	−0.1763	−0.4987	−0.1462	−0.2380	−0.2074

Table 8-5

Growth and Value Series
Year-End Index Values

from 1967 to 2002

	IA Large-cap Growth Stocks	IA Large-cap Value Stocks	IA Mid-cap Growth Stocks	IA Mid-cap Value Stocks	IA Small-cap Growth Stocks
1967	1.000	1.000	1.000	1.000	1.000
1968	1.022	1.143	1.110	1.216	1.257
1969	1.065	0.969	1.017	0.954	0.972
1970	1.030	1.081	0.967	1.011	0.784
1971	1.286	1.173	1.251	1.120	0.903
1972	1.663	1.362	1.339	1.220	0.926
1973	1.373	1.234	0.867	1.000	0.512
1974	0.916	0.975	0.530	0.798	0.317
1975	1.195	1.360	0.728	1.291	0.469
1976	1.327	1.843	0.900	1.907	0.644
1977	1.177	1.779	0.899	2.001	0.716
1978	1.263	1.879	1.008	2.185	0.820
1979	1.482	2.274	1.352	2.832	1.179
1980	2.061	2.950	1.980	3.280	1.694
1981	1.839	2.940	1.877	3.603	1.525
1982	2.309	3.503	2.183	4.542	1.766
1983	2.679	4.462	2.699	5.872	2.135
1984	2.751	4.936	2.547	6.034	1.912
1985	3.704	6.823	3.401	8.024	2.495
1986	4.284	8.215	3.940	9.350	2.601
1987	4.633	8.733	4.041	9.132	2.371
1988	5.215	11.078	4.575	11.234	2.775
1989	7.374	14.588	6.025	13.444	3.421
1990	7.595	13.812	5.663	10.943	2.731
1991	11.030	17.164	8.051	16.093	3.837
1992	11.444	19.984	8.906	19.254	4.032
1993	11.839	24.818	10.139	22.640	4.278
1994	11.995	24.990	9.658	21.835	4.058
1995	16.936	37.950	12.578	29.479	4.951
1996	21.254	46.514	15.009	35.863	5.156
1997	28.833	69.950	17.187	47.870	5.654
1998	52.047	85.633	18.036	48.667	5.553
1999	65.873	112.042	23.864	51.417	6.918
2000	51.260	94.889	19.913	62.692	5.256
2001	40.958	85.406	16.542	67.448	4.587
2002	32.249	67.632	11.819	52.205	3.044

Table 8-5 (continued)

Growth and Value Series
Year-End Index Values

from 1967 to 2002

	IA Small-cap Value Stocks	IA Micro-cap Growth Stocks	IA Micro-cap Value Stocks	IA All Growth Stocks	IA All Value Stocks
1967	1.000	1.000	1.000	1.000	1.000
1968	1.379	1.353	1.473	1.060	1.176
1969	1.050	0.843	0.956	1.043	0.970
1970	1.000	0.549	0.859	0.986	1.058
1971	1.156	0.616	0.974	1.230	1.158
1972	1.202	0.550	0.973	1.507	1.318
1973	0.853	0.277	0.627	1.167	1.158
1974	0.675	0.180	0.489	0.762	0.914
1975	1.083	0.264	0.809	1.012	1.318
1976	1.641	0.358	1.249	1.167	1.833
1977	1.919	0.424	1.524	1.086	1.834
1978	2.149	0.489	1.842	1.184	1.968
1979	2.816	0.672	2.479	1.460	2.439
1980	3.492	0.958	3.003	2.060	3.077
1981	4.051	0.732	3.384	1.853	3.182
1982	5.225	0.769	4.459	2.261	3.875
1983	7.282	0.919	6.198	2.669	5.011
1984	7.785	0.663	5.742	2.619	5.404
1985	10.329	0.729	7.012	3.481	7.346
1986	11.246	0.642	6.988	3.956	8.653
1987	10.359	0.478	6.022	4.128	8.882
1988	13.811	0.504	7.171	4.657	11.218
1989	16.253	0.515	7.633	6.360	14.289
1990	12.640	0.335	5.106	6.257	12.877
1991	18.574	0.462	7.173	9.021	16.734
1992	23.560	0.421	8.842	9.452	19.737
1993	29.525	0.396	10.404	9.964	24.235
1994	29.200	0.301	10.071	9.838	24.139
1995	39.062	0.357	12.895	13.459	35.334
1996	47.562	0.336	15.750	16.377	43.216
1997	67.178	0.320	21.034	21.060	63.304
1998	60.508	0.246	18.524	33.373	73.528
1999	65.760	0.293	20.664	42.384	92.778
2000	76.368	0.154	17.975	33.049	82.598
2001	91.595	0.140	22.722	26.673	77.288
2002	75.448	0.070	19.400	20.324	61.260

Table 8-6 shows the monthly-annualized standard deviations of the growth and value series.

Table 8-6

Growth and Value Series
Annualized Monthly Standard Deviations (in percent)

from 1968 to 2002

	IA Large-cap Growth Stocks	IA Large-cap Value Stocks	IA Mid-cap Growth Stocks	IA Mid-cap Value Stocks	IA Small-cap Growth Stocks
1968	19.3	11.8	22.1	16.9	29.9
1969	13.5	12.1	18.1	14.6	19.2
1970	20.1	23.6	27.3	28.7	32.2
1971	16.8	14.0	20.8	20.7	23.7
1972	8.0	12.7	11.5	12.3	11.3
1973	10.8	15.5	21.9	20.3	22.5
1974	24.6	16.8	18.8	18.0	14.8
1975	27.8	22.8	29.8	45.2	35.3
1976	16.8	16.3	18.5	26.5	26.8
1977	11.1	8.4	11.7	11.0	12.6
1978	21.3	15.7	27.5	22.0	34.1
1979	15.9	15.3	25.5	24.2	31.2
1980	28.9	23.2	39.7	20.7	42.9
1981	15.2	10.7	18.9	15.3	19.0
1982	25.2	22.2	30.1	26.3	29.3
1983	13.9	13.2	18.8	11.7	21.8
1984	15.9	15.9	19.0	16.5	18.4
1985	19.9	18.6	21.9	16.1	25.2
1986	23.2	28.7	22.1	19.5	20.4
1987	38.7	38.8	41.3	32.0	42.0
1988	12.3	14.9	15.5	14.0	18.0
1989	19.3	18.2	17.4	13.4	14.1
1990	21.9	20.2	24.8	20.1	24.2
1991	27.9	20.3	26.1	26.0	24.3
1992	9.0	12.4	12.2	9.9	18.5
1993	10.1	8.0	14.0	9.1	14.9
1994	11.9	12.0	12.0	10.5	13.6
1995	7.5	11.3	13.9	8.2	15.5
1996	15.2	16.7	18.3	12.8	21.4
1997	25.4	24.2	19.1	17.1	26.9
1998	59.6	33.8	33.5	26.6	33.6
1999	19.7	23.7	27.6	18.4	29.4
2000	21.9	26.7	30.4	27.7	34.8
2001	17.8	28.0	28.6	25.1	32.3
2002	16.1	20.0	21.5	19.8	20.4

Table 8-6 (continued)

Growth and Value Series
Annualized Monthly Standard Deviations (in percent)

from 1968 to 2002

	IA Small-cap Value Stocks	IA Micro-cap Growth Stocks	IA Micro-cap Value Stocks	IA All Growth Stocks	IA All Value Stocks
1968	19.7	36.5	23.5	20.2	12.6
1969	13.9	18.5	13.8	14.8	12.6
1970	30.1	28.7	29.2	22.0	24.3
1971	25.8	28.4	32.3	17.9	15.8
1972	14.7	14.9	18.8	7.6	12.3
1973	20.0	21.3	19.5	12.4	16.3
1974	18.6	16.1	25.6	22.2	16.3
1975	51.4	36.8	67.3	27.5	27.1
1976	32.5	28.8	43.4	17.3	19.0
1977	11.3	13.2	13.5	11.1	8.9
1978	26.5	38.8	34.9	23.2	17.9
1979	26.4	31.8	27.3	19.2	18.0
1980	28.7	49.7	30.7	32.2	22.1
1981	17.2	17.4	17.5	15.8	12.0
1982	24.9	27.4	23.9	26.4	22.7
1983	14.3	26.1	19.8	15.0	12.0
1984	15.6	14.3	12.6	16.6	15.6
1985	17.2	19.6	19.3	20.3	17.3
1986	16.5	13.4	13.3	22.1	24.7
1987	34.7	30.8	34.8	38.9	36.6
1988	16.9	12.7	16.1	12.4	14.2
1989	13.3	9.5	10.0	17.5	16.0
1990	18.6	15.1	12.3	22.3	19.5
1991	25.2	22.9	24.9	26.7	21.3
1992	15.6	21.9	22.4	9.6	10.9
1993	11.4	13.9	11.7	10.7	8.1
1994	10.3	10.6	10.3	11.6	11.1
1995	13.2	13.2	10.0	8.6	10.2
1996	13.9	18.3	13.8	14.8	15.3
1997	20.4	23.5	20.5	21.8	21.8
1998	25.0	25.1	22.6	51.3	31.5
1999	21.4	36.6	21.7	19.6	21.6
2000	19.3	22.9	12.2	22.3	25.5
2001	33.1	32.4	41.8	19.4	27.7
2002	21.5	19.1	20.0	16.7	19.6

Correlation of Growth and Value Series

Table 8-7 presents the annual cross-correlations and serial correlations for the growth and value series. Both large-cap value and large-cap growth are perfectly positively correlated to all value and all growth, respectively. Mid-cap value stocks posted the only negative serial correlation out of the different size groupings.

Table 8-7
Growth and Value Series
Serial and Cross Correlations of Historical Annual Returns
from 1968 to 2002

Series	IA All Growth Stocks	IA All Value Stocks	IA Large-cap Growth Stocks	IA Large-cap Value Stocks	IA Mid-cap Growth Stocks	IA Mid-cap Value Stocks	IA Small-cap Growth Stocks	IA Small-cap Value Stocks	IA Micro-cap Growth Stocks	IA Micro-cap Value Stocks
IA All Growth Stocks	1.00									
IA All Value Stocks	0.80	1.00								
IA Large-cap Growth Stocks	0.98	0.72	1.00							
IA Large-cap Value Stocks	0.83	0.99	0.77	1.00						
IA Mid-cap Growth Stocks	0.87	0.85	0.76	0.83	1.00					
IA Mid-cap Value Stocks	0.60	0.87	0.49	0.78	0.76	1.00				
IA Small-cap Growth Stocks	0.77	0.84	0.64	0.78	0.94	0.82	1.00			
IA Small-cap Value Stocks	0.51	0.82	0.38	0.72	0.73	0.95	0.83	1.00		
IA Micro-cap Growth Stocks	0.64	0.75	0.49	0.67	0.85	0.76	0.96	0.81	1.00	
IA Micro-cap Value Stocks	0.49	0.77	0.34	0.66	0.70	0.88	0.84	0.95	0.87	1.00
Serial Correlations*	0.13	0.05	0.18	0.10	0.08	−0.04	0.08	0.01	0.01	0.04

*The standard error for all estimates is 0.12

Fama-French Growth and Value Series

The following commentary and corresponding data make use of the Fama-French growth and value data series.

Historical Returns on Growth and Value

Using the Fama-French series, Graph 8-3 depicts the growth of $1.00 invested in FF all growth and FF all value stocks from the end of 1927 to the end of 2002. All results assume reinvestment of dividends and exclude transaction costs. The chart shows that the return of value stocks was much greater than that of growth stocks over the 75-year period. Value stocks grew to $5,990.81 as opposed to $616.51 for growth stocks. The extra return from value stocks was accompanied by higher volatility, as the annual standard deviation of growth and value stocks were 20.5 percent and 28.1 percent, respectively.

Graph 8-3

FF All Growth Stocks vs. FF All Value Stocks

Year-End 1927 = $1.00

from 1927 to 2002

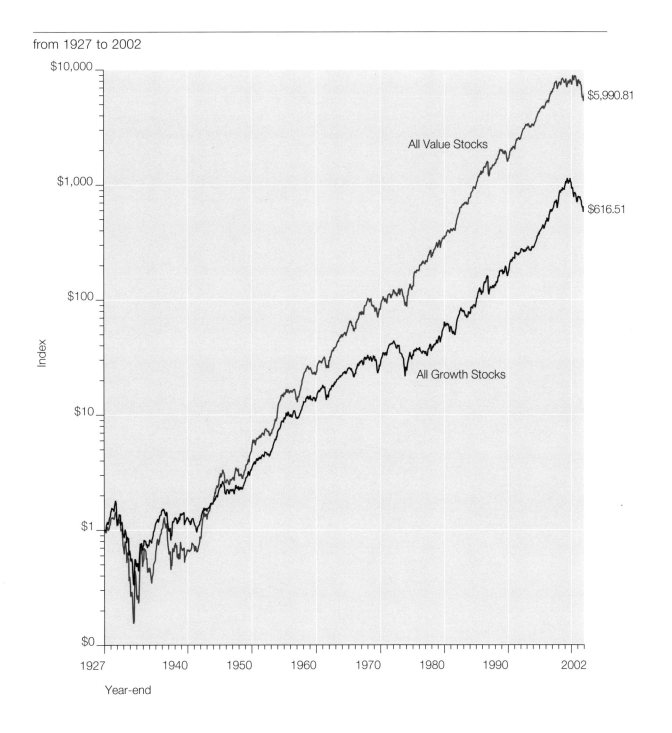

Year-end

Graph 8-4 breaks down the growth of $1.00 chart into FF small growth, small value, large growth, and large value stocks from the end of 1927 to the end of 2002. The top two performers during this time period were small value and large value stocks followed by large growth and small growth stocks. Over the period from 1928 to 2002, small value stocks outperformed all other stock series in the graph. One dollar invested in small value stocks at the end of 1927 grew to $19,650.24 by year-end 2002.

Graph 8-4

**FF Small Value Stocks, FF Small Growth Stocks, FF Large Value Stocks,
FF Large Growth Stocks**
Year-End 1927 = $1.00

from 1927 to 2002

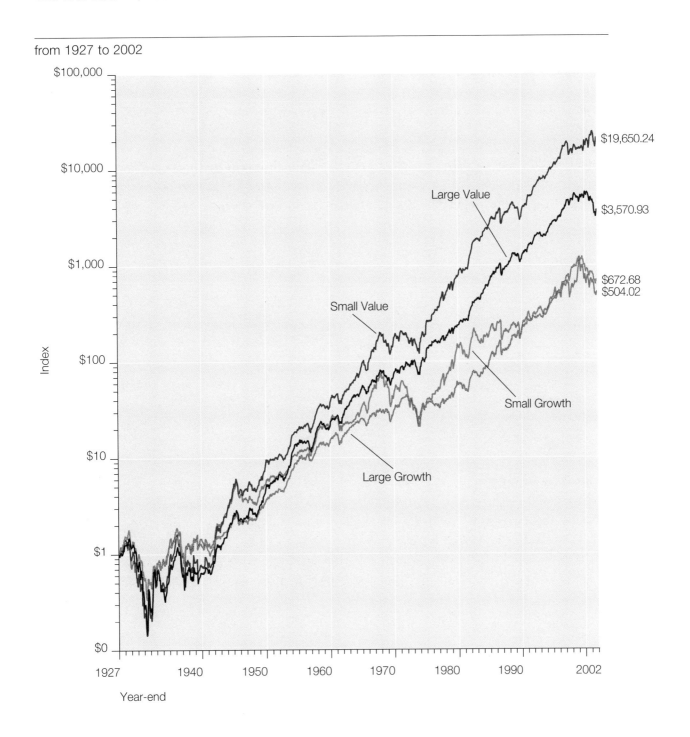

Summary Statistics for Growth and Value Series

Table 8-8 shows summary statistics of annual total returns for all of the Fama-French growth and value series. The summary statistics presented are geometric mean, arithmetic mean, and standard deviation.

Value significantly outperformed growth across the market capitalization spectrum. In the large capitalization arena, the extra return of value over growth was at the expense of increased risk, as the standard deviation of large value was 27.7 percent versus 20.3 percent for large growth. Among the small cap series, small value significantly outperformed small growth and did so with lower volatility (32.1 percent versus 33.2 percent).

Table 8-8

Total Returns and Standard Deviation of Value and Growth
Summary Statistics of Annual Returns

from 1928 to 2002

Series	Geometric Mean (%)	Arithmetic Mean (%)	Standard Deviation (%)
FF Large Growth Stocks	9.1	11.0	20.3
FF Large Value Stocks	11.5	15.0	27.7
FF Small Growth Stocks	8.7	13.2	33.2
FF Small Value Stocks	14.1	18.6	32.1
FF All Growth Stocks	8.9	10.9	20.5
FF All Value Stocks	12.3	15.8	28.1

Returns by Decade

Table 8-9 shows the compound returns by decade for the growth and value series. It is notable that all value stocks outperformed all growth stocks in every full decade except the 1930s and the 1990s. Small value stocks beat small growth stocks in all decades except the 1930s. It is also interesting to note that in any decade small value stocks were never the worst performing among all six stock series. In this table, the 1920s cover the period 1928 to 1929 and the 2000s cover the period 2000 to 2002.

Table 8-9

Compound Annual Rates of Return by Decade

	1920s*	1930s	1940s	1950s	1960s	1970s	1980s	1990s	2000s**	1993-02
FF Large Growth Stocks	8.0%	1.9%	7.3%	17.9%	8.0%	3.6%	15.5%	19.9%	−16.9%	8.6%
FF Large Value Stocks	8.5	−5.8	17.1	22.0	11.1	12.0	20.7	14.4	−11.4	7.1
FF Small Growth Stocks	−15.8	7.4	11.3	18.0	9.8	5.3	9.9	14.3	−18.3	4.7
FF Small Value Stocks	−6.5	−0.5	21.2	20.3	15.2	15.5	20.9	14.8	5.9	12.4
FF All Growth Stocks	7.5	1.9	7.3	17.9	8.0	3.8	14.7	19.4	−17.0	8.3
FF All Value Stocks	5.6	−4.6	17.9	21.8	12.3	13.9	20.8	14.4	−8.3	8.1

*Based on the period 1928–1929

**Based on the period 2000–2002

Presentation of the Annual Data

Table 8-10 shows year-by-year total annual returns from 1928 to 2002. This table compares the performance of large growth, large value, small growth, small value, all growth and all value stocks. Table 8-11 shows the growth of $1.00 invested in each of the categories at year-end 1927.

Table 8-10

Growth and Value Series
Year-by-Year Returns

from 1928 to 1970

	FF Large Growth Stocks	FF Large Value Stocks	FF Small Growth Stocks	FF Small Value Stocks	FF All Growth Stocks	FF All Value Stocks
1928	0.4586	0.2358	0.3123	0.3978	0.4552	0.2639
1929	−0.2005	−0.0467	−0.4597	−0.3743	−0.2056	−0.1183
1930	−0.2549	−0.4372	−0.3520	−0.4706	−0.2560	−0.4447
1931	−0.3577	−0.5870	−0.4160	−0.5219	−0.3580	−0.5710
1932	−0.0719	−0.0743	−0.0192	−0.0118	−0.0714	−0.0545
1933	0.4443	1.1550	1.5809	1.1808	0.4492	1.2009
1934	0.1043	−0.1979	0.3326	0.0821	0.1057	−0.1551
1935	0.4181	0.4881	0.4270	0.5118	0.4184	0.4843
1936	0.2544	0.4958	0.3307	0.7432	0.2564	0.5217
1937	−0.3322	−0.3960	−0.4629	−0.5034	−0.3353	−0.4069
1938	0.3255	0.2596	0.4188	0.2634	0.3270	0.2497
1939	0.0801	−0.1263	0.1086	−0.0242	0.0806	−0.1120
1940	−0.0924	−0.0179	−0.0076	−0.0935	−0.0915	−0.0315
1941	−0.1231	−0.0118	−0.1705	−0.0406	−0.1237	−0.0216
1942	0.1323	0.3362	0.1762	0.3534	0.1328	0.3369
1943	0.2142	0.4217	0.4564	0.9202	0.2168	0.5262
1944	0.1597	0.4200	0.3985	0.4907	0.1642	0.4302
1945	0.3084	0.4825	0.6242	0.7562	0.3176	0.5165
1946	−0.0669	−0.0746	−0.1273	−0.0694	−0.0702	−0.0725
1947	0.0326	0.0837	−0.0832	0.0546	0.0275	0.0806
1948	0.0347	0.0509	−0.0758	−0.0288	0.0303	0.0411
1949	0.2268	0.1852	0.2320	0.2155	0.2260	0.1871
1950	0.2421	0.5536	0.3077	0.5191	0.2436	0.5478
1951	0.1970	0.1375	0.1662	0.1169	0.1963	0.1335
1952	0.1314	0.2024	0.0560	0.0833	0.1299	0.1798
1953	0.0220	−0.0772	0.0059	−0.0665	0.0219	−0.0762
1954	0.5018	0.7734	0.4268	0.6424	0.5008	0.7462
1955	0.3013	0.2991	0.1777	0.2394	0.2995	0.2892
1956	0.0665	0.0478	0.0585	0.0748	0.0665	0.0549
1957	−0.0890	−0.2283	−0.1436	−0.1536	−0.0896	−0.2079
1958	0.4078	0.7458	0.7694	0.6820	0.4112	0.7285
1959	0.1317	0.1479	0.1988	0.1860	0.1325	0.1570
1960	−0.0268	−0.0702	−0.0103	−0.0576	−0.0266	−0.0657
1961	0.2600	0.2526	0.2119	0.3110	0.2593	0.2650
1962	−0.1051	−0.0153	−0.2092	−0.0883	−0.1068	−0.0304
1963	0.2106	0.3497	0.0822	0.2720	0.2079	0.3328
1964	0.1499	0.1984	0.1086	0.2265	0.1491	0.2053
1965	0.1358	0.2533	0.3512	0.4148	0.1407	0.2929
1966	−0.1092	−0.0902	−0.0556	−0.0760	−0.1080	−0.0804
1967	0.2985	0.3136	0.7942	0.6565	0.3144	0.3882
1968	0.0408	0.2363	0.2950	0.4515	0.0556	0.2827
1969	0.0302	−0.1666	−0.2452	−0.2577	0.0042	−0.1793
1970	−0.0545	0.1122	−0.2098	0.0627	−0.0677	0.1087

Source: Eugene Fama and Ken French

Table 8-10 (continued)

Growth and Value Series
Year-by-Year Returns

from 1971 to 2002

	FF Large Growth Stocks	FF Large Value Stocks	FF Small Growth Stocks	FF Small Value Stocks	FF All Growth Stocks	FF All Value Stocks
1971	0.2299	0.1240	0.2195	0.1572	0.2308	0.1239
1972	0.2186	0.1805	−0.0067	0.0806	0.2086	0.1762
1973	−0.2106	−0.0022	−0.4284	−0.2584	−0.2181	−0.0493
1974	−0.2972	−0.2546	−0.3264	−0.1788	−0.2979	−0.2424
1975	0.3383	0.5079	0.5880	0.5776	0.3466	0.5105
1976	0.1745	0.4650	0.3690	0.5779	0.1815	0.5120
1977	−0.0943	0.0131	0.1919	0.2422	−0.0809	0.0979
1978	0.0730	0.0360	0.1679	0.2177	0.0780	0.1052
1979	0.1817	0.2210	0.5006	0.3822	0.2105	0.2563
1980	0.3265	0.1515	0.5300	0.2242	0.3473	0.1609
1981	−0.0757	0.1441	−0.1203	0.1780	−0.0812	0.1495
1982	0.1987	0.2735	0.1993	0.4083	0.1996	0.2914
1983	0.1519	0.2745	0.2127	0.4796	0.1609	0.2998
1984	−0.0059	0.1765	−0.1441	0.0768	−0.0298	0.1651
1985	0.3351	0.3315	0.2836	0.3032	0.3276	0.3290
1986	0.1396	0.2171	0.0152	0.1326	0.1224	0.2092
1987	0.0763	−0.0228	−0.1314	−0.0626	0.0499	−0.0276
1988	0.1183	0.2514	0.1379	0.2955	0.1204	0.2539
1989	0.3690	0.3122	0.1870	0.1535	0.3479	0.2942
1990	0.0060	−0.1347	−0.1868	−0.2361	−0.0109	−0.1503
1991	0.4316	0.2677	0.5379	0.4078	0.4391	0.2884
1992	0.0683	0.2205	0.0471	0.3551	0.0677	0.2425
1993	0.0252	0.1972	0.1240	0.2823	0.0337	0.2124
1994	0.0201	−0.0591	−0.0392	0.0282	0.0137	−0.0466
1995	0.3726	0.3760	0.3559	0.2872	0.3709	0.3583
1996	0.2080	0.1340	0.1322	0.2145	0.2013	0.1487
1997	0.3165	0.3103	0.1526	0.3894	0.3031	0.3291
1998	0.3491	0.1820	0.0127	−0.0863	0.3311	0.1207
1999	0.2931	0.0539	0.5044	0.0386	0.2981	0.0540
2000	−0.1318	0.0055	−0.2120	−0.0320	−0.1340	−0.0016
2001	−0.1576	−0.0145	0.0049	0.4072	−0.1530	0.0586
2002	−0.2151	−0.2991	−0.3103	−0.1287	−0.2192	−0.2703

Source: Eugene Fama and Ken French

Table 8-11

Growth and Value Series
Year-End Index Values

from 1927 to 1970

	FF Large Growth Stocks	FF Large Value Stocks	FF Small Growth Stocks	FF Small Value Stocks	FF All Growth Stocks	FF All Value Stocks
1927	1.000	1.000	1.000	1.000	1.000	1.000
1928	1.459	1.236	1.312	1.398	1.455	1.264
1929	1.166	1.178	0.709	0.875	1.156	1.114
1930	0.869	0.663	0.459	0.463	0.860	0.619
1931	0.558	0.274	0.268	0.221	0.552	0.266
1932	0.518	0.254	0.263	0.219	0.513	0.251
1933	0.748	0.546	0.679	0.477	0.743	0.552
1934	0.826	0.438	0.905	0.516	0.822	0.467
1935	1.172	0.652	1.292	0.781	1.165	0.693
1936	1.470	0.975	1.719	1.361	1.464	1.054
1937	0.982	0.589	0.923	0.676	0.973	0.625
1938	1.301	0.742	1.310	0.854	1.292	0.781
1939	1.405	0.648	1.452	0.833	1.396	0.694
1940	1.275	0.637	1.441	0.755	1.268	0.672
1941	1.118	0.629	1.195	0.725	1.111	0.657
1942	1.266	0.841	1.406	0.981	1.259	0.879
1943	1.537	1.195	2.047	1.883	1.532	1.341
1944	1.783	1.697	2.863	2.807	1.783	1.919
1945	2.333	2.516	4.651	4.929	2.349	2.910
1946	2.177	2.328	4.059	4.587	2.184	2.699
1947	2.248	2.523	3.721	4.837	2.244	2.916
1948	2.326	2.652	3.439	4.698	2.312	3.036
1949	2.853	3.143	4.237	5.710	2.835	3.604
1950	3.544	4.883	5.541	8.674	3.525	5.578
1951	4.242	5.554	6.462	9.687	4.217	6.323
1952	4.800	6.678	6.823	10.495	4.765	7.460
1953	4.905	6.163	6.863	9.797	4.869	6.892
1954	7.366	10.929	9.793	16.091	7.308	12.034
1955	9.586	14.198	11.533	19.942	9.497	15.515
1956	10.224	14.876	12.207	21.433	10.129	16.367
1957	9.314	11.481	10.454	18.141	9.221	12.964
1958	13.112	20.043	18.497	30.514	13.013	22.408
1959	14.840	23.007	22.175	36.190	14.737	25.926
1960	14.443	21.392	21.947	34.105	14.345	24.221
1961	18.198	26.796	26.598	44.712	18.065	30.639
1962	16.285	26.386	21.033	40.765	16.135	29.707
1963	19.715	35.612	22.762	51.853	19.490	39.594
1964	22.670	42.676	25.235	63.599	22.396	47.721
1965	25.749	53.487	34.098	89.982	25.547	61.698
1966	22.937	48.664	32.201	83.147	22.788	56.740
1967	29.783	63.926	57.775	137.734	29.953	78.768
1968	30.998	79.032	74.821	199.918	31.617	101.034
1969	31.935	65.864	56.472	148.397	31.749	82.918
1970	30.194	73.252	44.623	157.703	29.599	91.930

Source: Eugene Fama and Ken French

Table 8-11 (continued)

Growth and Value Series
Year-End Index Values

from 1971 to 2002

	FF Large Growth Stocks	FF Large Value Stocks	FF Small Growth Stocks	FF Small Value Stocks	FF All Growth Stocks	FF All Value Stocks
1971	37.136	82.335	54.417	182.493	36.430	103.324
1972	45.254	97.198	54.054	197.203	44.028	121.533
1973	35.722	96.982	30.898	146.237	34.426	115.547
1974	25.107	72.288	20.812	120.085	24.170	87.539
1975	33.600	109.000	33.051	189.443	32.547	132.224
1976	39.462	159.685	45.246	298.914	38.456	199.917
1977	35.743	161.769	53.929	371.317	35.345	219.491
1978	38.351	167.585	62.982	452.167	38.104	242.576
1979	45.319	204.628	94.513	624.992	46.123	304.742
1980	60.116	235.623	144.605	765.118	62.141	353.780
1981	55.565	269.584	127.203	901.287	57.098	406.684
1982	66.606	343.318	152.555	1269.260	68.497	525.207
1983	76.726	437.548	184.999	1877.996	79.518	682.644
1984	76.273	514.764	158.342	2022.319	77.147	795.360
1985	101.830	685.409	203.253	2635.406	102.421	1057.033
1986	116.042	834.205	206.335	2984.921	114.958	1278.135
1987	124.898	815.147	179.213	2798.133	120.700	1242.901
1988	139.676	1020.062	203.933	3624.846	135.233	1558.521
1989	191.223	1338.508	242.071	4181.265	182.282	2016.962
1990	192.373	1158.225	196.857	3193.873	180.303	1713.901
1991	275.410	1468.307	302.756	4496.213	259.468	2208.258
1992	294.234	1792.001	317.030	6092.924	277.043	2743.840
1993	301.635	2145.445	356.350	7813.238	286.377	3326.538
1994	307.702	2018.606	342.398	8033.436	290.297	3171.451
1995	422.348	2777.624	464.268	10340.493	397.958	4307.633
1996	510.208	3149.852	525.637	12558.299	478.050	4948.048
1997	671.697	4127.288	605.845	17448.659	622.947	6576.494
1998	906.193	4878.387	613.514	15942.539	829.175	7370.404
1999	1171.797	5141.323	922.948	16557.203	1076.322	7768.151
2000	1017.382	5169.570	727.306	16027.071	932.127	7755.385
2001	857.013	5094.555	730.838	22552.869	789.540	8210.236
2002	672.685	3570.933	504.022	19650.241	616.510	5990.810

Source: Eugene Fama and Ken French

Table 8-12 shows the monthly-annualized standard deviations of the growth and value series. As show in Table 8-12, small value and small growth have the highest monthly-annualized standard deviations. These two series along with the other four all experience extreme volatility during the depression years of 1932 and 1933. These data series also exhibit a higher variability in the pre-World War II period than in the postwar period.

Table 8-12

Growth and Value Series
Annualized Monthly Standard Deviations (in percent)

from 1928 to 1970

	FF Large Growth Stocks	FF Large Value Stocks	FF Small Growth Stocks	FF Small Value Stocks	FF All Growth Stocks	FF All Value Stocks
1928	24.19	20.62	22.98	27.65	24.01	21.38
1929	30.98	18.17	16.29	18.10	30.64	17.76
1930	21.59	15.62	23.78	21.81	21.61	16.42
1931	30.48	35.89	27.65	38.46	30.46	35.89
1932	61.31	193.57	98.03	224.98	61.41	191.95
1933	71.14	241.57	276.25	305.89	71.60	258.27
1934	22.14	38.96	50.61	66.84	22.32	42.39
1935	17.51	50.87	30.92	50.07	17.58	48.62
1936	15.03	32.10	34.37	55.48	15.15	34.07
1937	14.05	22.71	18.60	21.12	14.15	22.41
1938	53.30	76.54	84.16	81.40	53.72	76.31
1939	26.35	58.10	63.99	86.22	26.73	61.98
1940	22.64	31.17	33.02	35.59	22.78	31.91
1941	12.03	15.79	15.24	27.21	12.05	17.09
1942	15.75	27.36	16.54	31.88	15.65	27.72
1943	15.27	32.36	32.32	69.28	15.43	38.64
1944	8.28	17.08	14.03	24.95	8.35	18.00
1945	15.23	24.68	23.90	35.21	15.36	25.82
1946	17.61	19.84	23.08	27.24	17.85	20.65
1947	10.72	13.69	13.61	16.36	10.80	13.76
1948	20.26	25.64	16.95	24.05	20.10	25.39
1949	11.64	16.61	18.37	20.29	11.79	16.92
1950	14.45	24.35	16.82	30.46	14.40	25.26
1951	13.84	21.36	13.78	21.26	13.80	21.25
1952	12.29	17.11	9.36	10.88	12.20	15.79
1953	9.44	10.97	8.21	9.93	9.39	10.56
1954	17.79	34.73	13.48	24.38	17.64	31.89
1955	14.82	17.28	9.71	8.70	14.70	14.75
1956	15.16	16.32	9.27	8.25	15.05	14.15
1957	13.39	10.49	11.35	11.16	13.34	10.54
1958	8.49	21.52	17.40	17.01	8.48	20.11
1959	10.51	10.68	11.16	10.09	10.48	10.29
1960	14.48	11.12	15.35	10.78	14.47	10.75
1961	9.98	15.44	18.91	19.29	10.08	15.69
1962	20.15	19.81	23.10	21.58	20.18	20.04
1963	11.59	16.13	12.47	16.07	11.58	15.78
1964	4.25	12.02	5.48	9.48	4.24	11.19
1965	9.39	12.95	20.14	20.24	9.54	14.11
1966	10.01	12.92	18.85	17.86	10.11	13.92
1967	15.87	19.91	32.01	33.31	16.14	22.29
1968	17.03	18.52	30.33	23.77	17.44	19.31
1969	14.00	11.64	18.99	14.78	14.50	11.92
1970	21.06	23.06	30.52	26.84	21.60	23.25

Table 8-12 (continued)

Growth and Value Series
Annualized Monthly Standard Deviations (in percent)

from 1971 to 2002

	FF Large Growth Stocks	FF Large Value Stocks	FF Small Growth Stocks	FF Small Value Stocks	FF All Growth Stocks	FF All Value Stocks
1971	17.47	20.34	26.60	27.93	17.89	21.29
1972	6.60	17.17	13.93	15.97	6.77	16.64
1973	12.47	17.96	23.50	17.71	13.14	17.81
1974	22.80	12.02	18.67	20.07	22.57	13.16
1975	25.30	36.04	44.86	51.12	25.61	38.83
1976	15.71	29.41	25.76	43.39	15.89	34.76
1977	10.17	10.17	14.04	12.69	10.31	10.69
1978	21.27	16.12	39.13	30.94	22.38	19.65
1979	16.66	19.11	33.08	28.26	17.96	20.78
1980	25.20	21.58	48.16	30.45	27.21	22.88
1981	14.95	10.27	20.26	16.16	15.30	11.04
1982	25.44	20.82	29.96	20.66	25.89	20.40
1983	13.29	11.62	26.19	15.34	14.44	11.21
1984	15.82	16.31	17.37	14.23	16.05	15.98
1985	19.97	13.80	25.25	14.19	20.62	13.59
1986	21.60	20.77	18.59	15.25	21.04	19.97
1987	37.89	26.01	38.80	33.67	37.94	26.65
1988	12.01	11.34	16.66	13.66	12.01	11.17
1989	17.99	12.82	12.34	12.23	16.97	12.40
1990	21.58	15.95	22.43	14.47	21.55	15.60
1991	25.72	18.91	28.74	22.62	25.74	19.08
1992	9.25	12.93	19.25	18.66	9.53	13.13
1993	9.53	8.86	14.48	9.76	9.70	8.60
1994	11.01	10.00	13.28	9.99	11.12	9.55
1995	7.44	10.47	17.21	10.99	7.83	9.98
1996	14.26	10.08	26.80	12.00	14.66	9.96
1997	22.93	15.32	29.63	18.32	22.52	15.15
1998	31.80	20.35	37.11	22.43	31.98	20.74
1999	19.80	17.78	39.29	20.00	20.01	17.07
2000	18.70	21.74	44.34	11.80	18.91	17.48
2001	18.83	23.46	39.34	58.26	19.25	28.41
2002	15.23	20.36	17.44	31.51	15.16	21.56

Correlation of Growth and Value Series

Table 8-13 presents the annual cross-correlations and serial correlations for the growth and value series. It is interesting to note that both large value and large growth are perfect positively correlated to all value and all growth, respectively. Likewise, both small value and small growth are highly correlated to all value and all growth, respectively.

Table 8-13

Growth and Value Series
Serial and Cross Correlations of Historical Annual Returns
from 1928 to 2002

Series	FF All Value Stocks	FF All Growth Stocks	FF Large Value Stocks	FF Large Growth Stocks	FF Small Value Stocks	FF Small Growth Stocks	U.S. Treasury Bills	Inflation
FF All Value Stocks	1.00							
FF All Growth Stocks	0.80	1.00						
FF Large Value Stocks	0.99	0.81	1.00					
FF Large Growth Stocks	0.80	1.00	0.81	1.00				
FF Small Value Stocks	0.93	0.74	0.90	0.73	1.00			
FF Small Growth Stocks	0.84	0.82	0.81	0.80	0.87	1.00		
U.S. Treasury Bills	−0.04	−0.02	−0.04	−0.02	−0.06	−0.11	1.00	
Inflation	0.06	−0.03	0.06	−0.03	0.06	−0.01	0.41	1.00
Serial Correlations*	−0.04	0.03	−0.06	0.04	0.06	0.05	0.91	0.64

*The standard error for all estimates is 0.12

Conclusion

What can explain this value effect? Readers of Graham and Dodd's Security Analysis,[1] first published in 1934, would say that the outperformance of value stocks is due to the market coming to realize the full value of a company's securities that were once undervalued. The Graham and Dodd approach to security analysis is to do an independent valuation of a company using accounting data and common market multiples, then look at the stock price to see if the stock is under- or overvalued. Several academic studies have shown that the market overreacts to bad news and underreacts to good news. This would lead us to conclude that there is more room for value stocks (which are more likely to have reported bad news) to improve and outperform growth stocks, which already have high expectations built into them.

Possibly a larger question is what does the future hold as far as growth and value investing goes? Advocates of growth investing would argue that technology- and innovation-oriented companies will continue to dominate as the Internet changes the way the world communicates and does business. Stalwarts of value investing would argue that there are still companies and industries that continue to be ignored and represent long-term investment bargains. Only time will tell.

1 Cottle, Sidney, Murray, Roger F., and Block, Frank E. "Graham and Dodd's Security Analysis," Fifth Edition, McGraw-Hill, 1988.

Chapter 9

Using Historical Data in Forecasting and Optimization

Probabilistic Forecasts

When forecasting the return on an asset or a portfolio, investors are (or should be) interested in the entire probability distribution of future outcomes, not just the mean or "point estimate." An example of a point estimate forecast is that large company stocks will have a return of 13 percent in 2003. It is more helpful to know the uncertainty surrounding this point estimate than to know the point estimate itself. One measure of uncertainty is standard deviation. The large company stock return forecast can be expressed as 13 percent representing the mean with 20 percent representing the standard deviation.

If the returns on large company stocks are normally distributed, the mean (expected return) and the standard deviation provide enough information to forecast the likelihood of any return. Suppose one wants to ascertain the likelihood that large company stocks will have a return of –25 percent or lower in 2003. Given the above example, a return of –25 percent is $[13 - (-25)]/20 = 1.9$ standard deviations below the mean. The likelihood of an observation 1.9 or more standard deviations below the mean is 2.9 percent. (This can be looked up in any statistics textbook, in the table showing values of the cumulative probability function for a normal distribution.) Thus, the likelihood that the stock market will fall by 25 percent or more in 2003 is 2.9 percent. This is valuable information, both to the investor who believes that stocks are a sure thing and to the investor who is certain that they will crash tomorrow.

In fact, the historical returns of large company stocks are not exactly normally distributed, and a slightly different method needs to be used to make probabilistic forecasts. The actual model used to forecast the distribution of stock returns is described later in this chapter.

Some people are wary of probabilistic forecasts because they seem too wide to be useful, or because they lack punch. (The most widely quoted forecasters, after all, make very specific predictions.) However, the forecast of a probability distribution actually reveals much more than the point estimate. The point estimate reflects what statisticians call an "expected value"—but one does not actually expect this particular outcome to happen. The actual return will likely be higher or lower than the point estimate. By knowing the extent to which actual returns are likely to deviate from the point estimate, the investor can assess the risk of every asset, and thus compare investment opportunities in terms of their risks as well as their expected returns. As Harry Markowitz showed nearly a half-century ago in his Nobel Prize-winning work on portfolio theory, investors care about avoiding risk as well as seeking return. Probabilistic forecasts enable investors to quantify these concepts.

The Lognormal Distribution

In the lognormal model, the natural logarithms of asset return relatives are assumed to be normally distributed. (A return relative is one plus the return. That is, if an asset has a return of 15 percent in a given period, its return relative is 1.15.)

The lognormal distribution is skewed to the right. That is, the expected value, or mean, is greater than the median. Furthermore, if return relatives are lognormally distributed, returns cannot fall below negative 100 percent. These properties of the lognormal distribution make it a more accurate characterization of the behavior of market returns than does the normal distribution.

In all normal distributions, moreover, the probability of an observation falling below the mean by as much as one standard deviation equals the probability of falling above the mean by as much as one standard deviation; both probabilities are about 34 percent. In a lognormal distribution, these probabilities differ and depend on the parameters of the distribution.

Forecasting Wealth Values and Rates of Return

Using the lognormal model, it is fairly simple to form probabilistic forecasts of both compound rates of return and ending period wealth values. Wealth at time **n** (assuming reinvestment of all income and no taxes) is:

$$W_n = W_0 (1 + r_1)(1 + r_2)...(1 + r_n) \tag{30}$$

where,

W_n	= the wealth value at time **n**;
W_0	= the initial investment at time **0**; and,
r_1, r_2, etc.	= the total returns on the portfolio for the rebalancing period ending at times 1, 2, and so forth.

The compound rate of return or geometric mean return over the same period, r_G, is:

$$r_G = \left(\frac{W_n}{W_0}\right)^{\frac{1}{n}} - 1 \tag{31}$$

where,

r_G	= the geometric mean return;
W_n	= the ending period wealth value at time **n**;
W_0	= the initial wealth value at time **0**; and,
n	= the inclusive number of periods.

By assuming that all of the **(1 + r_n)**s are lognormally distributed with the same expected value and standard deviation and are all statistically independent of each other, it follows that W_n and **(1 + r_G)** are lognormally distributed. In fact, even if the **(1 + r_n)**s are not themselves lognormally distributed but are independent and identically distributed, W_n and **(1 + r_G)** are approximately lognormal for large enough values of **n**. This "central-limit theorem" means that the lognormal model can be useful in long-term forecasting even if short-term returns are not well described by a lognormal distribution.

Calculating Parameters of the Lognormal Model

To use the lognormal model, we must first calculate the expected value and standard deviation of the natural logarithm of the return relative of the portfolio. These parameters, denoted **m** and **s** respectively, can be calculated from the expected return (μ) and standard deviation (σ) of the portfolio as follows:

$$m = \ln(1 + \mu) - \left(\frac{s^2}{2}\right) \tag{32}$$

$$s = \sqrt{\ln\left[1+\left(\frac{\sigma}{1+\mu}\right)^2\right]}$$ (33)

where,

ln = the natural logarithm function.

To calculate a particular percentile of wealth or return for a given time horizon, the only remaining parameter needed is the z-score of the percentile. The z-score of a percentile ranking is that percentile ranking expressed as the number of standard deviations that it is above or below the mean of a normal distribution. For example, the z-score of the 95th percentile is 1.645 because in a normal distribution, the 95th percentile is 1.645 standard deviations above the 50th percentile or median, which is also the mean. Z-scores can be obtained from a table of cumulative values of the standard normal distribution or from software that produces such values.

Given the logarithmic parameters of a portfolio (**m** and **s**), a time horizon (**n**), and the z-score of a percentile (**z**), the percentile in question in terms of cumulative wealth at the end of the time horizon (**W$_n$**) is:

$$e^{\left(mn+zs\sqrt{n}\right)}$$ (34)

Similarly, the percentile in question in terms of the compound rate of return for the period (**r$_G$**) is:

$$e^{\left(m+z\frac{s}{\sqrt{n}}\right)}-1$$ (35)

Mean-Variance Optimization

One important application of the probability forecasts of asset returns is mean-variance optimization. Optimization is the process of identifying portfolios that have the highest possible expected return for a given level of risk, or the lowest possible risk for a given expected return. Such a portfolio is considered "efficient," and the locus of all efficient portfolios is called the efficient frontier. An efficient frontier constructed from large company stocks, long-term government bonds, and Treasury bills is shown in Graph 9-1. All investors should hold portfolios that are efficient with respect to the assets in their opportunity set.

The most widely accepted framework for optimization is Markowitz or mean-variance optimization (MVO), which makes the following assumptions: 1) the forecast mean, or expected return, describes the attribute that investors consider to be desirable about an asset; 2) the risk of the asset is measured by its expected standard deviation of returns; and 3) the interaction between one asset and another is captured by the expected correlation coefficient of the two assets' returns. MVO thus requires forecasts of the return and standard deviation of each asset, and the correlation of each asset with every other asset.[1]

In the 1950s, Harry Markowitz developed both the concept of the efficient frontier and the mathematical means of constructing it (mean-variance optimization)[2]. Currently, there are a number of commercially available mean-variance optimization software packages, including Ibbotson Associates' *Portfolio Strategist*® and *EnCorr Optimizer.*™ [3]

Estimating the Means, Standard Deviations, and Correlations of Asset Returns

To simulate future probability distributions of asset and portfolio returns, one typically estimates parameters of the historical return data. The parameters that are required to simulate returns on an asset are its mean and standard deviation. To simulate returns on portfolios of assets, one must also estimate the correlation of each asset in the portfolio with every other asset. Thus, the parameters required to conduct a simulation are the same as those required as inputs into a mean-variance optimization.[4]

To illustrate how to estimate the parameters of asset class returns relevant to optimization and forecasting, we construct an example using large company stocks, long-term government bonds, and Treasury bills. The techniques used to estimate these parameters are described below. They are the same techniques as those used in Ibbotson Associates' *EnCorr InputsGenerator*™ software product.

Means, or Expected Returns

The mean return (forecast mean, or expected return) on an asset is the probability-weighted average of all possible returns on the asset over a future period. Estimates of expected returns are based on models of asset returns. While many models of asset returns incorporate estimates of GNP, the money supply, and other macroeconomic variables, the model employed in this chapter does not. This is because we assume (for the present purpose) that asset markets are informationally efficient, with all relevant and available information fully incorporated in asset prices. If this assumption holds, investor expectations (forecasts) can be discerned from market-observable data. Such forecasts are not attempts to outguess, or beat, the market. They are attempts to discern the market's expectations, i.e., to read what the market itself is forecasting.

For some assets, expected returns can be estimated using current market data alone. For example, the yield on a riskless bond is an estimate of its expected return. For other assets, current data are not sufficient. Stocks, for example, have no exact analogue to the yield on a bond. In such cases, we use the statistical time series properties of historical data in forming the estimates.

1 The standard deviation is the square root of the variance; hence the term "mean-variance" in describing this form of the optimization problem.
2 Markowitz, Harry M., Portfolio Selection: Efficient Diversification of Investments, New York: John Wiley & Sons, 1959.
3 For additional information regarding Portfolio Strategist and EnCorr software, refer to the Product Information page at the back of this book.
4 It is also possible to conduct a simulation using entire data sets, that is, without estimating the statistical parameters of the data sets. Typically, in such a nonparametric simulation, the frequency of an event occurring in the simulated history is equal to the frequency of the event occurring in the actual history used to construct the data set.

Graph 9-1

Efficient Frontier
Large Company Stocks, Long-Term Government Bonds, and U.S. Treasury Bills

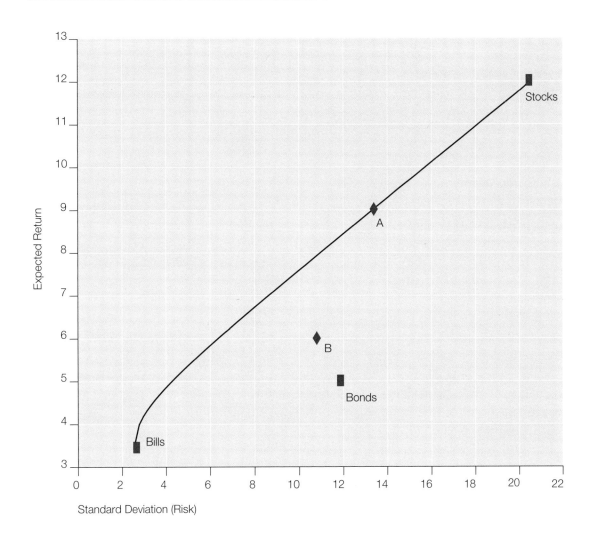

To know which data to use in estimating expected returns, we need to know the rebalancing frequency of the portfolios and the planning horizon. In our example, we will assume an annual rebalancing frequency and a twenty-year planning horizon. The rebalancing frequency gives the time units in which returns are measured.

With a twenty-year planning horizon, the relevant riskless rate is the yield on a twenty-year coupon bond. At the end of 2002, the yield on a twenty-year coupon bond was 4.8 percent. This riskless rate is the baseline, from which the expected return on every other asset class is derived by adding or subtracting risk premia.

Large Company Stocks

The expected return on large company stocks is the riskless rate, plus the expected risk premium of large company stocks over bonds that are riskless over the planning horizon. With a twenty-year planning horizon, this risk premium is 7.0 percent, shown as the long-horizon expected equity risk premium in Table 9-1. Hence, the expected return on large company stocks is 4.8 (the riskless rate) plus 7.0 (the risk premium) for a total of 11.8 percent (due to rounding).

Bonds and Bills

For default-free bonds with a maturity equal to the planning horizon, the expected return is the yield on the bond; that is, the expected return is the riskless rate of 4.8 percent. For bonds with other maturities, the expected bond horizon premium should be added to the riskless rate (for longer maturities) or subtracted from the riskless rate (for shorter maturities). Since expected capital gains on a bond are zero, the expected horizon premium is estimated by the historical average difference of the income returns on the bonds.[5]

For Treasury bills, the expected return over a given time horizon is equal to the expected return on a Treasury bond of a similar horizon, less the expected horizon premium of bonds over bills. This premium is estimated by the historical average of the difference of the income return on bonds and the return on bills. From Table 9-1, this is 1.5 percent. Subtracting this from the riskless rate gives us an expected return on bills of 3.3 percent. Of course, this forecast typically differs from the current yield on a Treasury bill, since a portfolio of Treasury bills is rolled over (the proceeds of maturing bills are invested in new bills, at yields not yet known) during the time horizon described.

5 The expected capital gain on a par bond is self-evidently zero. For a zero-coupon (or other discount) bond, investors expect the price to rise as the bond ages, but the expected portion of this price increase should not be considered a capital gain. It is a form of income return.

Standard Deviations

Standard deviations are estimated from historical data as described in Chapter 6. Since there is no evidence of a major change in the variability of returns on large company stocks, we use the entire period 1926–2002 to estimate the standard deviation of these asset classes. For bonds and bills, we use the period 1970–2002. The use of this more recent period reflects the fact that the volatility of bonds has increased over time.

Table 9-1

Building Blocks for Expected Return Construction

	Value (in percent)
Yields (Riskless Rates)[1]	
Long-Term (20-year) U.S. Treasury Coupon Bond Yield	4.8
Intermediate-Term (5-year) U.S. Treasury Coupon Note Yield	2.6
Short-Term (30-day) U.S. Treasury Bill Yield	1.2
Fixed Income Risk Premia[2]	
Expected default premium: *long-term corporate bond total returns minus long-term government bond total returns*	0.1
Expected long-term horizon premium: *long-term government bond income returns minus U.S. Treasury bill total returns**	1.5
Expected intermediate-term horizon premium: *intermediate-term government bond income returns minus U.S. Treasury bill total returns**	1.1
Equity Risk Premia[3]	
Long-horizon expected equity risk premium: *large company stock total returns minus long-term government bond income returns*	7.0
Intermediate-horizon expected equity risk premium: *large company stock total returns minus intermediate-term government bond income returns*	7.4
Short-horizon expected equity risk premium: *large company stock total returns minus U.S. Treasury bill total returns**	8.4
Small Stock Premium: *small company stock total return minus large company stock total return*	4.7

[1] As of December 31, 2002. Maturities are approximate.

[2] Expected risk premia for fixed income are based on the differences of historical arithmetic mean returns from 1970–2002.

[3] Expected risk premia for equities are based on the differences of historical arithmetic mean returns from 1926–2002.

*For U.S. Treasury bills, the income return and total return are the same.

Correlations

Correlations between the asset classes are estimated from historical data as described in Chapter 6. Correlation coefficients for stocks, bonds, and bills are derived from 1970–2002. Correlations between major asset classes change over time. Graph 9-2 shows the historical correlation of annual returns on large company stocks and intermediate term bonds over 20 year rolling periods from 1926–1945 through 1983–2002.

Generating Probabilistic Forecasts

For large company stocks in Table 9-2, the logarithmic parameters are calculated to be m = 0.0969 and s = 0.1815 based on equations (32) and (33). The z-scores of the 95th, 50th, and 5th percentile are 1.645, 0, and −1.645, respectively. Using these parameters, we can calculate the 95th, 50th, and 5th percentiles of cumulative wealth and compound returns over various time horizons using equations (34) and (35). Graph 9-3 shows percentiles of compound returns over the entire range of one to twenty year horizons in graphical form. This type of graph is sometimes called a "trumpet" graph because the high and low percentile curves taken together make the shape of a trumpet. The "mouthpiece" of the trumpet is on the right side of the graph because for long time horizons, all percentiles converge to the median (50th percentile).

Table 9-2

Optimization Inputs: Year-End 2002 Large Company Stocks, Long-Term Government Bonds, and U.S. Treasury Bills (in percent)

	Expected Return	Standard Deviation	Correlation with		
			Stocks	Bonds	Bills
Stocks	12.0	20.5	1.00		
Bonds	5.0	11.8	0.30	1.00	
Bills	3.5	2.7	0.09	−0.02	1.00

Graph 9-4 is a graph showing percentiles of cumulative wealth over the entire range of zero to twenty year time horizons, along with the back history of the portfolio's performance. The past and forecasted (future) values on the graph are connected by setting the wealth index to $1.00 at the end of 2002. The past index values show how much wealth one would have had to hold in large company stocks to have $1.00 at the end of 2002; the percentiles of future value show the probability distribution of future growth of $1.00 invested in large company stocks. This type of graph is sometimes called a "tulip" graph because of its overall shape.

Table 9-3 shows (in the top panel) the probability distribution of compound annual returns on large company stocks over the next 20 years. The top line shows the 95th percentile or optimistic case, the middle line the 50th percentile or median case, and the bottom line the 5th percentile or pessimistic case. The bottom panel shows the same projections, redrawn as cumulative values of $1.00 invested at the beginning of the period simulated. Simulations such as these are used for asset allocation, funding of liabilities, and other portfolio management-related applications; Ibbotson Associates' *Portfolio Strategist* and *EnCorr Optimizer* can produce these forecasts.

Graph 9-2

Twenty Year Rolling Period Correlations of Annual Returns
Large Company Stocks and Intermediate-Term Government Bonds

from 1926–1945 through 1983–2002

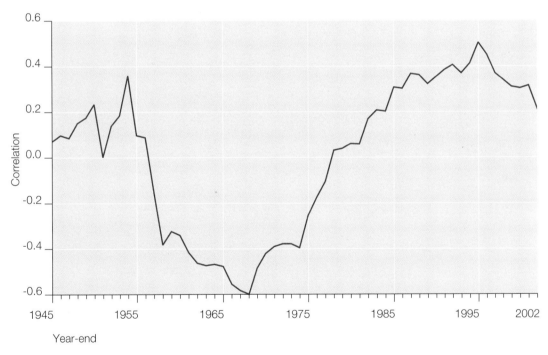

Graph 9-3

Forecast Total Return Distribution
100 Percent Large Stocks

from 2003 to 2022

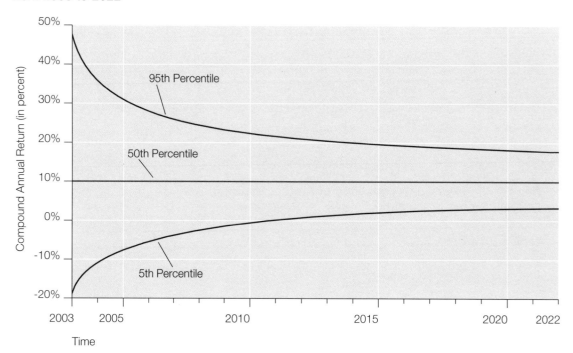

Table 9-3

**Forecast Distributions of Compound Annual Returns
and End of Period Wealth**

Large Company Stocks: Year-End 2002

| Percentile | Compound Annual Return (in percent) | | | | |
	2003	2004	2007	2012	2022
95th	48.47	36.04	25.88	21.05	17.75
90th	38.99	29.84	22.22	18.56	16.03
75th	24.49	20.11	16.35	14.50	13.21
50th	10.15	10.15	10.15	10.15	10.15
25th	−2.54	1.02	4.28	5.97	7.18
10th	−12.71	−6.55	−0.73	2.34	4.57
5th	−18.28	−10.81	−3.62	0.23	3.04

| Percentile | End of Period Wealth ($1 Invested on 12/31/02) | | | | |
	2003	2004	2007	2012	2022
95th	1.48	1.85	3.16	6.76	26.27
90th	1.39	1.69	2.73	5.49	19.56
75th	1.24	1.44	2.13	3.87	11.95
50th	1.10	1.21	1.62	2.63	6.91
25th	0.97	1.02	1.23	1.79	4.00
10th	0.87	0.87	0.96	1.26	2.44
5th	0.82	0.80	0.83	1.02	1.82

Constructing Efficient Portfolios

A mean-variance optimizer uses the complete set of optimizer inputs (the expected return and standard deviation of each asset class and the correlation of returns for each pair of asset classes) to generate an efficient frontier. The efficient frontier shown in Graph 9-1 was generated from the inputs described above and summarized in Table 9-2. Each point on the frontier represents a portfolio mix that is mean-variance efficient. The point labeled A represents a portfolio that contains 65 percent in large company stocks, and 35 percent in Treasury bills. (Recall that other asset classes were not considered in this example.) From the location of point A on the grid, we can find its expected return (9.02 percent) and standard deviation (13.44 percent).

Graph 9-4

Forecast Distribution of Wealth Index Value
100 Percent Large Stocks

from 2003 to 2022

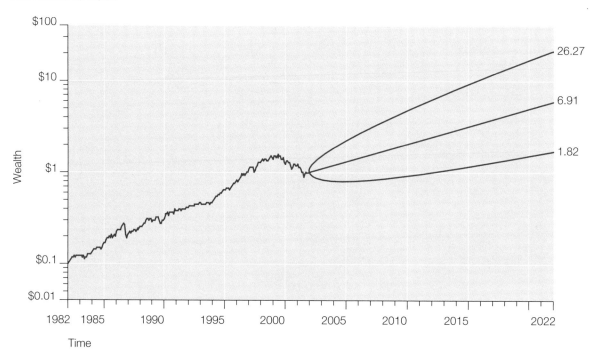

Using Inputs to Form Other Portfolios

Given a complete set of inputs, the expected return and standard deviation of any portfolio (efficient or other) of the asset classes can be calculated. The expected return of a portfolio is the weighted average of the expected returns of the asset classes:

$$r_p = \sum_{i=1}^{n} x_i r_i$$

(36)

where,

r_p = the expected return of the portfolio p;

n = the number of asset classes;

x_i = the portfolio weight of asset class i, scaled such that

$$\sum_{i=1}^{n} x_i = 1 \text{; and,}$$

r_i = the expected return of asset class i.

The point labeled B in Graph 9-1 represents a portfolio that contains 15 percent in large company stocks (asset class 1), 80 percent in long-term bonds (asset class 2), and 5 percent in Treasury bills (asset class 3). Applying the above formula to this portfolio using the inputs in Table 9-2, we calculate the expected return to be 6.0 percent as follows:

$$(0.15 \times 0.120) + (0.80 \times 0.050) + (0.05 \times 0.035) = 0.060$$

The standard deviation of the portfolio depends not only on the standard deviations of the asset classes, but on all of the correlations as well. It is given by:

$$\sigma_p = \sqrt{\sum_{i=1}^{n} \sum_{j=1}^{n} x_i x_j \sigma_i \sigma_j \rho_{ij}}$$

(37)

where,

σ_p = the standard deviation of the portfolio;

x_i and x_j = the portfolio weights of asset classes i and j;

σ_i and σ_j = the standard deviations of returns on asset classes i and j; and,

ρ_{ij} = the correlation between returns on asset classes i and j.

Note that ρ_{ii} equals one and that ρ_{ij} is equal to ρ_{ji}.

The standard deviation for point B in Graph 9-1 (containing three asset classes) would be calculated as follows:

	Stocks (asset class 1)	Bonds (asset class 2)	Bills (asset class 3)
Stocks	$x_1^2\,\sigma_1^2\,\rho_{1,1} =$ $(0.15)^2(0.205)^2(1) =$ 0.00095	$x_1\,x_2\,\sigma_1\,\sigma_2\,\rho_{1,2} =$ $(0.15)(0.8)(0.205)(0.118)(0.30)=$ 0.00087	$x_1\,x_3\,\sigma_1\,\sigma_3\,\rho_{1,3} =$ $(0.15)(0.05)(0.205)(0.027)(0.09) =$ 0.00000
Bonds	$x_1\,x_2\,\sigma_1\,\sigma_2\,\rho_{1,2} =$ $(0.15)(0.8)(0.205)(0.118)(0.30) =$ 0.00087	$x_2^2\,\sigma_2^2\,\rho_{2,2} =$ $(0.8)^2(0.118)^2(1)=$ 0.00891	$x_2\,x_3\,\sigma_2\,\sigma_3\,\rho_{2,3} =$ $(0.8)(0.05)(0.118)(0.027)(-0.02) =$ 0.00000
Bills	$x_1\,x_3\,\sigma_1\,\sigma_3\,\rho_{1,3} =$ $(0.15)(0.05)(0.205)(0.027)(0.09) =$ 0.00000	$x_2\,x_3\,\sigma_2\,\sigma_3\,\rho_{2,3} =$ $(0.8)(0.05)(0.118)(0.027)(-0.02) =$ 0.00000	$x_3^2\,\sigma_3^2\,\rho_{3,3} =$ $(0.05)^2(0.027)^2(1) =$ 0.00000

By summing these terms and taking the square root of the total, the result is a standard deviation of 10.8 percent.

Monte Carlo Simulation

Meeting Today's Challenges

Comprehending and communicating various types of risk is one of the most challenging tasks facing advisors before, during, and after the planning process. With the number of complicated products growing and investors' level of sophistication increasing, advisors confront difficult questions each day in understanding and conveying risk effectively.

What is Simulation and Why?

Real-life investing decisions involve all sorts of aspects, ranging from saving, to spending, to tax issues, and more. When all of these complexities need to be considered, a technique called Monte Carlo simulation can be useful. The process starts with a set of assumptions about the estimated mean, standard deviation, and correlations for a set of asset classes or investments. These assumptions are used to randomly generate hundreds of possible future return scenarios—similar to drawing numbers out of a hat. These returns can then be used in conjunction with a client's year-by-year cash flows, taxes, asset allocation, and financial product selections. A large number of possible "financial lives" for the client are produced. These "financial lives" can be used to answer a number of questions pertaining to the risk of the client's investment decisions. For example, how many times out of all of these lives did the client reach their goal versus running out of money? Used in this fashion, Monte Carlo techniques can calculate and display risk in a personalized way that is easy for investors to understand.

The most crucial factor in simulation-based techniques is the generation of the future return scenarios. There are quite a few ways to generate simulations, some better than others. Certain methods use only historical data. Other techniques just take into account the mean and standard deviation of the assets involved, while ignoring the correlations. In other words, the value of the Monte Carlo-based tool is only as good as the quality and richness of the return scenarios it generates.

Types of Monte Carlo Simulation

Non-Parametric

This method of Monte Carlo simulation uses purely historical data. The easiest way to describe this is to use this book as an example. Imagine if you were to take a page in this book that shows the annual returns for all of the asset classes (Appendix A) and create pieces of paper so that each piece has one year's numbers on it for all of the asset classes considered. The pieces are subsequently put into a hat. One of the pieces is drawn out of the hat, the numbers on the piece are written down, the piece is dropped back into the hat, and the process is repeated for as many years in the future as you want forecasted. Obviously, this method is very simple and takes no real thinking on the part of the user. The biggest problem here is that this technique only provides a limited amount of information because only what has happened in the past can be drawn out of the hat.

Parametric

This simulation method is based on the mean, standard deviation, and correlations for the assets being forecast. These are the parameters that give this method its name. Once these parameters are set, a computer program is used to generate random samples from the bell curve that these parameters define. This provides a much richer set of results, since the program can draw from any number under the curve, not just numbers that have occurred in the past.

Economic Modeling

This is the most complex method because it involves modeling the movements of the yield curve through time and then layering on various equity and fixed income risk premia to derive returns. It is the most realistic simulation method, but unfortunately cannot be easily customized by each user.

There is one point to remember when contemplating and choosing among the various simulation-based products. The quality of the forecast is directly related to the quality of the technique and inputs used.

All of the previous tables and graphs presented in this chapter were prepared using Ibbotson Associates' *Portfolio Strategist* and *EnCorr*™ suite of asset allocation software and data products. Using these tools, similar analyses can be performed for a wide variety of asset classes, historical time periods, percentiles, and planning horizons. Additionally, Ibbotson Associates offers returns based style analysis products to aid in the evaluation of mutual funds for use in implementing an optimal asset mix. These products include *EnCorr Attribution*™ and *Ibbotson Fund Strategist*® software.

The Debate over Future Stock Market Returns

The impressive performance of the stock market over the last two decades and the resultant increase in investor expectations have spurred numerous articles that call attention to the historical market return and caution investors about their overly optimistic expectations. The articles point to the return of the stock market over the past three years which was well below its historical average, while the bond market, on the contrary, has performed quite well. In fact, many studies are predicting stock returns that are much lower when compared to the historical average. A few even predict that stocks won't outperform bonds in the future.

Approaches to Calculating the Equity Risk Premium

The expected return on stocks over bonds, the equity risk premium, has been estimated by a number of authors who have utilized a variety of different approaches. Such studies can be categorized into four groups based on the approaches they have taken. The first group of studies derive the equity risk premium from historical returns between stocks and bonds. Supply side models, using fundamental information such as earnings, dividends, or overall productivity, are used by the second group to measure the expected equity risk premium. A third group adopts demand side models that derive the expected returns of equities through the payoff demanded by equity investors for bearing the additional risk. The opinions of financial professionals through broad surveys are relied upon by the fourth and final group.

This section is based upon the work by Roger G. Ibbotson and Peng Chen, who combined the first and second approaches to arrive at their forecast of the equity risk premium.[6] By proposing a new supply side methodology, the Ibbotson-Chen study challenges current arguments that future returns on stocks over bonds will be negative or close to zero. The results affirm the relationship between the stock market and the overall economy.

Supply Model

Long-term expected equity returns can be forecasted by the use of supply side models. The supply of stock market returns is generated by the productivity of the corporations in the real economy. Investors should not expect a much higher or lower return than that produced by the companies in the real economy. Thus, over the long run, equity return should be close to the long-run supply estimate.

Earnings, dividends, and capital gains are supplied by corporate productivity. Graph 9-5 illustrates that earnings and dividends have historically grown in tandem with the overall economy (GDP per capita). However, GDP per capita did not outpace the stock market. This is primarily because the P/E ratio increased 2.72 times during the same period. So, assuming that the economy will continue to grow, all three should continue to grow as well.

---

6 "Stock Market Returns in the Long Run: Participating in the Real Economy," Roger G. Ibbotson and Peng Chen, *Financial Analysts Journal*, January/February 2003.

Two main components make up the supply of equity returns: current returns in the form of dividends and long-term productivity growth in the form of capital gains. Two supply side models, the earnings model and the dividends model, are discussed in this section. The components of the two models are analyzed and those that are tied to the supply of equity returns are identified. Lastly, the long-term sustainable return based on historical information of the supply components is estimated.

Graph 9-5

Capital Gains, GDP Per Capita, Earnings, and Dividends
Year-End 1925 = $1.00

from 1925 to 2002

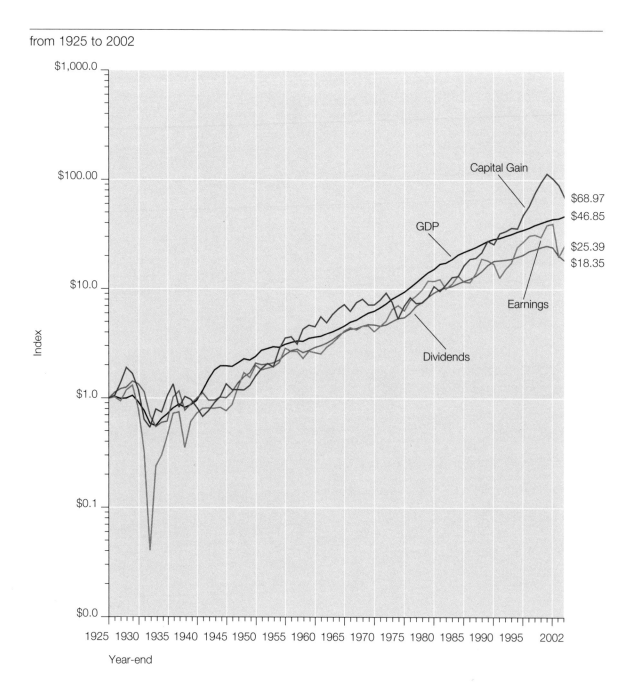

Forward-Looking Earnings Model

The earnings model breaks the historical equity return into four pieces, with only three historically being supplied by companies: inflation, income return, and growth in real earnings per share. The growth in the P/E ratio, the fourth piece, is a reflection of investors' changing prediction of future earnings growth. The past supply of corporate growth is forecasted to continue; however, a change in investors' predictions is not. P/E rose dramatically over the past 20 years because people believed that corporate earnings were going to grow faster in the future. This growth in P/E drove a small portion of the rise in equity returns over the last 20 years. Graph 9-6 illustrates the price to earnings ratio from 1926 to 2002. The P/E ratio was 10.22 at the beginning of 1926 and ended the year 2002 at 27.76—an average increase of 1.31 percent per year. The highest P/E was 136.50 recorded in 1932, while the lowest was 7.07 recorded in 1948.

Graph 9-6

Large Company Stocks
P/E Ratio

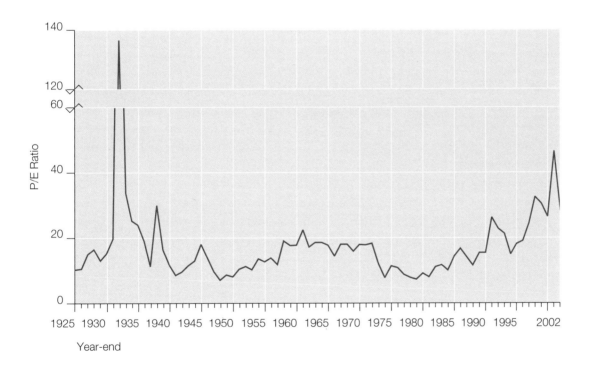

Year-end

The historical P/E growth factor of 1.31 percent per year is subtracted from the forecast, because it is not believed that P/E will continue to increase in the future. The market serves as the cue. The current P/E ratio is the market's best guess for the future of corporate earnings and there is no reason to believe, at this time, that the market will change its mind.

Thus, the supply of equity return only includes inflation, the growth in real earnings per share, and income return. The forward-looking earnings model calculates the long-term supply of U.S. equity returns to be 8.84 percent. The equity risk premium, based on the supply side earnings model, is calculated to be 3.41 percent.

Forward-Looking Dividends Model

Other academics also use a similar method to forecast stock over bond returns. However, historical equity returns are broken down using different factors. The dividend model decomposes the average historical equity return into factors that include inflation, the growth in real dividend, and the dividend yield. The forward-looking dividend model assumes that the expected equity return equals the dividend yield plus the expected dividend growth rate. This contrasts with the earnings model mentioned earlier which assumes expected equity return equals the dividend yield plus the expected corporate earnings growth rate. The dividend model combines the current dividend yield of 1.39 percent rather than the historical dividend yield of 4.33 percent. The historical dividend growth rate used was 0.78 percent. Consequently, the estimate of the supply of equity returns is reduced to 5.24 percent (similar to bonds), with the equity risk premium estimated to be 0.04 percent.

Problems with the Dividends Model

Both the earnings model and the dividends model break down historical equity returns into factors that represent corporate productivity. While historical earnings growth is used in the earnings model, the dividends model uses historical dividend growth to reflect growth in productivity. However, historical dividend growth underestimates growth in productivity because of the trend away from paying dividends. Lower payout ratios and lower dividend yields do not mean lower productivity or reduced return to investors.[7] Dividend growth has declined over the years due to share buybacks, changes in investor preference, corporate merger and acquisition activity, and corporate reinvestment—not due to reduced corporate productivity.[8]

Another problem with the dividends model is that it adds the current dividend yield with the historical dividend growth rate to arrive at a forecast. This is incorrect because of the relationship between the dividend yield and the dividend growth rate. With the dividend yield and payout ratio at all-time historical lows, that means companies are reinvesting more earnings. More earnings leads to more dividend growth which, in turn, leads to a higher dividend yield—not the low current yield we have today. Thus, a correct forecast would have to add current dividend yield with the current dividend growth rate or historical dividend yield with the historical dividend growth rate.

One final problem with the dividends model is related to the current P/E ratio (27.76). It is approximately twice as high as the historical average (13.98). The current high P/E ratio implies higher than average future growth relative to the past. This expected higher growth is not reflected in the dividends model forecast.

7 "Dividend Policy, Growth and the Valuation of Shares," Merton Miller and Franco Modigliani, *Journal of Business*, October 1961.
8 "The Personal-Tax Advantages of Equity," Richard C. Green and Burton Hollifield, Working Paper, January 2001.

Preferred Model

Despite the record earnings growth in the 1990s, the dividend yield and the payout ratio declined sharply, which renders dividends alone a poor measure for corporate profitability and future earnings growth. Historical growth in corporate earnings, however, has been in line with the growth of overall economic productivity. Therefore, earnings growth is a superior predictor of corporate profitability and future earnings growth, making the earnings model a better forecasting method than the dividends model.

Long-Term Market Predictions

Ibbotson and Chen believe that stocks will continue to provide significant returns over the long run, averaging around 8.8 percent per year, assuming historical inflation rates. The equity risk premium, based on the supply side earnings model, is calculated to be 3.41 percent.

In the future Ibbotson and Chen also predict increased earnings growth that will offset lower dividend yields. The fact that earnings will grow as dividend payouts shrink is in line with Miller and Modigliani Theory.

The forecasts for the market are in line with both the historical supply measures of public corporations (i.e. earnings) and overall economic productivity (GDP per capita).

Chapter 10
Stock Market Returns from 1815 to 1925

Introduction

Studies on the long-horizon predictability of stock returns, by necessity, require a database of return information that dates as far back as possible. Ibbotson Associates is the leading producer and supplier of a broad set of historical returns on asset classes dating back to 1926. Researchers interested in the dynamics of the U.S. capital markets over earlier decades have had to rely upon indices of uneven quality. Roger Ibbotson and William N. Goetzmann, professors of finance, and Liang Peng, a Ph.D. candidate in finance, all at Yale School of Management, have assembled a New York Stock Exchange database for the period prior to 1926. This chapter covers the sources and construction of this database extending back to 1815.

We firmly believe that a 1926 starting date was approximately when quality financial data became available. However, the hope is that the new data will allow modern researchers of pre-1926 stock returns, along with future researchers, to test a broad range of hypotheses about the U.S. capital markets as well as open up new areas for more accurate analysis.

Data Sources and Collection Methods

Share Price Collection

End-of-month equity prices for companies listed on the New York Stock Exchange (NYSE) were hand-collected from three different sources published over the period January 1815 to December 1870. For the time period 1871 through 1925, end-of-month NYSE stock prices were collected from the major New York newspapers.

The New York Shipping List, later called *The New York Shipping and Commercial,* served as the "official" source for NYSE share price collection up until the early 1850s. In the mid-1850s, *The New York Shipping List* reported prices for fewer and fewer stocks. This led to the collection of price quotes from *The New York Herald* and *The New York Times.* While neither claimed to be the official list for the NYSE, the number of securities quoted by each far exceeded the number quoted by *The New York Shipping List.*

It is important to note that in instances where no transaction took place in December, the latest bid and ask prices were averaged to obtain a year-end price. In total, at least two prices from 664 companies were collected. From a low number of eight firms in 1815, the number of firms in the index reached a high point in May of 1883 with 114 listed firms.

One interesting observation was the fact that share prices for much of the period of analysis remained around 100. Graph 10-1 illustrates this point. The graph shows that the typical price of a share of stock was around 100. The distribution of stock prices is significantly skewed to the left with only a few trading above 200. Such a distribution suggests that management maintained a ceiling on stock prices by paying out most of earnings as dividends. No reports of stock splits over the period of data were discovered.

Graph 10-1

Distribution of Raw Stock Prices
from 1815 to 1925

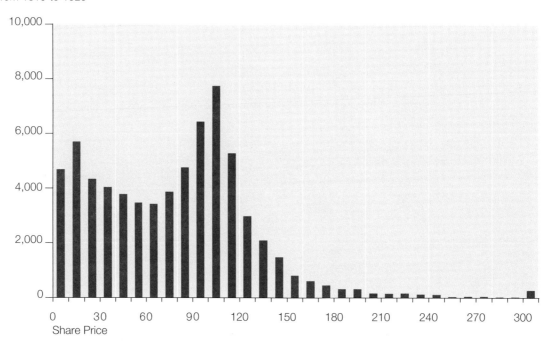

Dividend Collection

Dividend data was collected for the period 1825–1870 by identifying the semi-annual dividend announcements for equity securities as reported in *The New York Commercial*, *The Banker's Magazine*, *The New York Times*, and *The New York Herald*. From 1871 to 1925, aggregate dividend data from the Alfred Cowles[1] series was used. Whether or not the above publications reported dividends for all NYSE stocks is unknown. As a result, there is no way of knowing whether missing dividends meant that they were not paid or possibly not reported. Dividend records were collected for more than 500 stocks in the sample, and most stocks paid dividends semiannually.

In order to estimate the income return for each year, two approaches were implemented. The first approach, the low dividend return estimate, consisted of the summation of all of the dividends paid in a given year by firms whose prices were observed in the preceding year. This number is then divided by the sum of the last available preceding year prices for those firms. The second approach, the high dividend return estimate, focused solely on firms that paid regular dividends and for which price data was collected. The sample is restricted to firms that have two years of dividend payments (four semiannual dividends) and for which there was a price observation. Using the second approach, dividend yields tend to be quite high by modern standards.

---

1 Cowles, Alfred. (1939). *Common Stock Indices*. Principia Press, Bloomington.

It is important to note that when both a high and a low income return series were present, the average was computed. This holds true for the summary statistics table in this chapter as well as the graphs/tables presented throughout. Also, due to missing income return data for the year 1868, an average of the previous forty-three years was computed and used.

Price Index Estimation

Index Calculation Concerns

When attempting to construct an index without having market capitalization data readily available, one is left with one of two options: an equal-weighted index or a price-weighted index. One key concern with an equal-weighted index is the effect of a bid-ask bounce. Take for example an illiquid stock that trades at either $1.00 or $2.00 per share. When it rises in price from $1.00 to $2.00, it goes up by 100 percent. When it decreases in price from $2.00 to $1.00, it drops by 50 percent. Equally weighting these returns can produce a substantial upward bias. This led us to the construction of a price-weighted index.

Calculation of the Price-Weighted Index

The procedure used for calculating the price-weighted index is rather simple. For each month, returns are calculated for all stocks that trade in two consecutive periods. These returns are weighted by the price at the beginning of the two periods.

The return of the price-weighted index closely approximates the return to a "buy and hold" portfolio over the period. Buy and hold portfolios are not sensitive to bid-ask bounce bias. We believe that the price-weighted index does a fairly good job of avoiding such an upward bias.

It was found that companies were rather concentrated into specific industries. In 1815, the index was about evenly split between banks and insurance companies. Banks, transportation firms (primarily canals and railroads), and insurance companies made up the index by the 1850s. By the end of the sample period, the index was dominated by transport companies and other industrials.

A Look at the Historical Results

It is important to note that there are a few missing months of data that create gaps in the analysis. The NYSE was closed from July 1914 to December 1914 due to World War I. This is obviously an institutional gap. There are additional gaps. The number of available security records was quite lower after 1871. A change in the range of coverage by the financial press is the likely culprit for this. Missing data for the late 1860s quite possibly can be due to the Civil War because the NYSE was definitely open at that time. Further data collection efforts hopefully will allow these missing records to be filled in.

Table 10-1 illustrates summary statistics of annual returns of large company stocks for three different time periods. Note that the three different periods cover the pre-1926 data, the familiar 1926 to 2002 time period, and a combination of the two.

Table 10-1

Large Company Stocks
Summary Statistics of Annual Returns
from 1825 to 1925

	Geometric Mean	Arithmetic Mean	Standard Deviation
Total Return	7.3%	8.4%	16.3%
Income Return	5.9%	5.9%	1.9%
Capital Appreciation	1.3%	2.5%	16.1%

from 1926 to 2002

	Geometric Mean	Arithmetic Mean	Standard Deviation
Total Return	10.2%	12.2%	20.5%
Income Return	4.3%	4.3%	1.5%
Capital Appreciation	5.7%	7.6%	19.8%

from 1825 to 2002

	Geometric Mean	Arithmetic Mean	Standard Deviation
Total Return	8.5%	10.1%	18.3%
Income Return	5.2%	5.2%	1.9%
Capital Appreciation	3.2%	4.7%	17.9%

Price Returns

It is interesting to note that the price-weighted index in Table 10-1 has an annual geometric capital appreciation return from 1825 through 1925 of 1.3 percent. This number is significantly lower when compared to the 5.7 percent annual capital appreciation return experienced by large company stocks over the period 1926 through 2002. This once again alludes to the suggestion that dividend policies have evolved over the past two centuries, and that management of old most likely paid out earnings and kept their stock prices lower. In today's financial world, capital appreciation is accepted as a substitute for dividend payments.

Graph 10-2 shows the annual capital appreciation returns for the period 1825 to 2002. The rise in capital appreciation returns over the years is more evident when viewing returns on a twenty-year rolling period basis, as Graph 10-3 demonstrates.

Graph 10-2

Large Company Stocks Annual Capital Appreciation Returns (in percent)
from 1825 to 2002

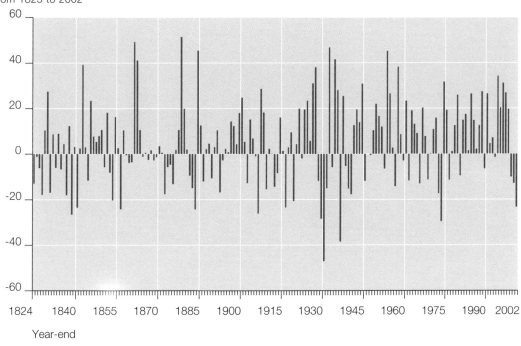

Year-end

Graph 10-3

20-Year Rolling Capital Appreciation Returns for Large Company Stocks (in percent)
from 1844 to 2002

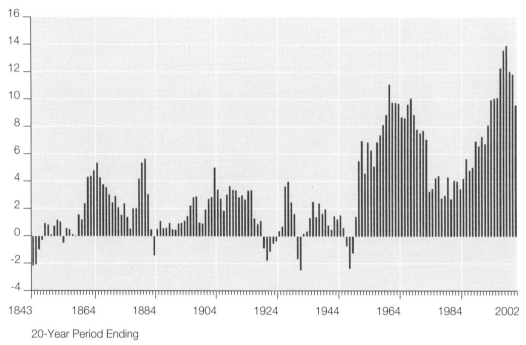

20-Year Period Ending

Income Returns

Table 10-1 also illustrates the summary statistics for the annual income return series. The higher income return of 5.9 percent in the earlier period, and the fact the many stocks traded near par, once again suggest that most companies paid out a large share of their profits rather than retaining them.

Graph 10-4 shows the annual income returns for the period 1825 to 2002. In fact, when looking at the time distribution of dividend changes over the new time period, dividend decreases were only slightly less common than increases, suggesting that managers may have been less averse to cutting dividends than they are today. Perhaps in the pre-income tax environment of the nineteenth century, investors had a preference for income returns, as opposed to capital appreciation.

Graph 10-4

Large Company Stocks Annual Income Returns (in percent)
from 1825 to 2002

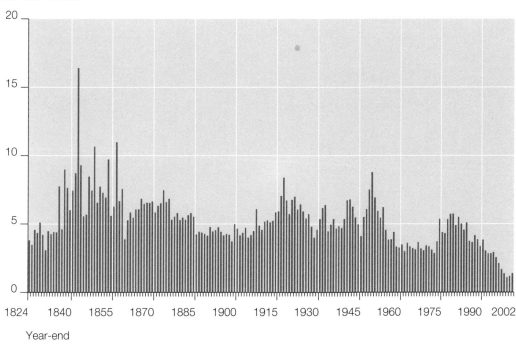

Year-end

Total Returns

Looking once again at the summary statistics in Table 10-1, it is interesting to notice that the annual geometric total return for large company stocks from 1825 to 1925 was 7.3 percent. This is quite low when compared to the 10.2 percent annual geometric total return of the commonly used 1926 to 2002 time period. For the entire period, the total return seems to fall somewhere in between.

Graph 10-5 illustrates the annual total returns for the period 1825 to 2002.

Graph 10-5

Large Company Stocks Annual Total Returns (in percent)
from 1825 to 2002

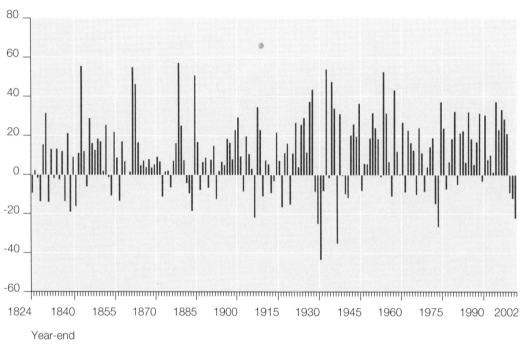

Year-end

The standard deviation of returns is also slightly lower for the 1825 to 1925 time period (16.3 percent) versus the time period of 1926 to 2002 (20.5 percent). Graph 10-6 illustrates a five-year rolling period standard deviation for the period 1825–2002.

Graph 10-6

5-Year Rolling Standard Deviation for Large Company Stocks (in percent)
from 1829 to 2002

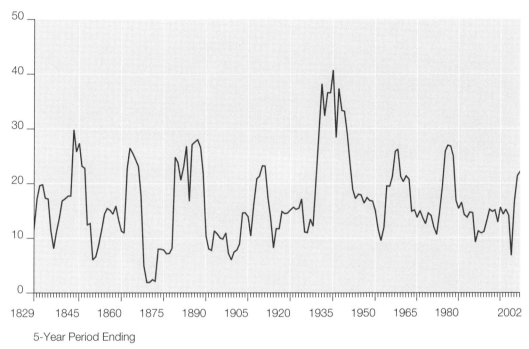

5-Year Period Ending

How much would a dollar be worth today if invested around the beginning of the New York Stock Exchange? Graph 10-7 depicts the growth of $1.00 invested in large company stocks over the period from the end of 1824 to the end of 2002.

Graph 10-7

Large Company Stocks
Year-End 1824 = $1.00

from 1824 to 2002

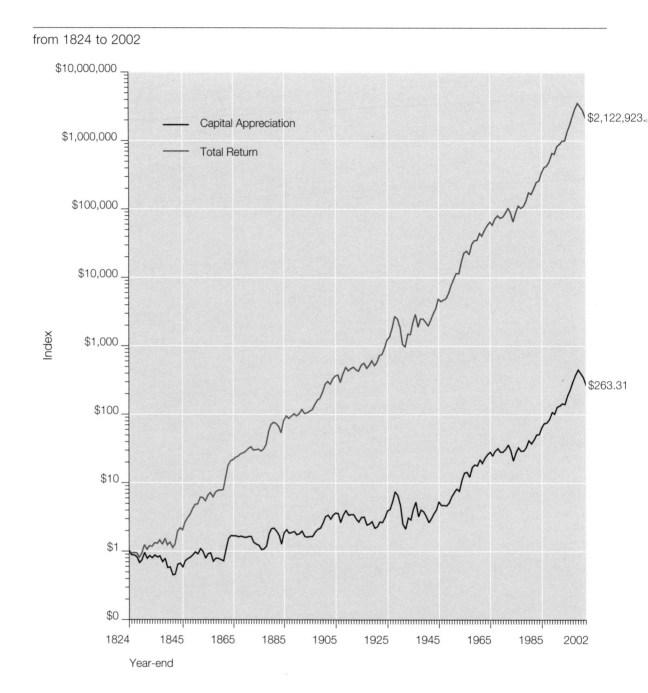

Table 10-2 shows year-by-year capital appreciation, average income, and total returns from 1815 to 1925 of large company stocks. Table 10-3 shows the growth of a dollar invested in large company stocks over the period from the end of 1824 to the end of 2002.

Conclusion

Data collection efforts over the past eleven years have yielded a comprehensive database of New York Stock Exchange security prices for nearly the entire history of the NYSE. The goal of the study is to assemble an NYSE database for the period prior to 1926. The 1926 starting date was approximately when high-quality financial data became available. However, with a pre-1926 database assembled, researchers can expand their analysis back to the early 1800s. It is our hope that the long time series outlined in this chapter will lead to a better understanding of how the New York Stock Exchange evolved from an emerging market at the turn of the eighteenth century to the largest capital market in the world today.

Table 10-2

Large Company Stocks
Annual Capital Appreciation, Income, and Total Returns (in percent)

from 1815 to 1925

Year	Cap App	Average Income Return	Total Return	Year	Cap App	Average Income Return	Total Return	Year	Cap App	Average Income Return	Total Return
1815	−6.65	—	—	1852	18.07	7.30	25.38	1889	4.49	4.28	8.77
1816	−1.93	—	—	1853	−8.15	6.94	−1.20	1890	−10.72	4.14	−6.59
1817	19.43	—	—	1854	−20.34	9.71	−10.63	1891	2.95	4.78	7.74
1818	−3.76	—	—	1855	16.26	5.60	21.86	1892	10.35	4.44	14.79
1819	−8.82	—	—	1856	2.49	6.28	8.77	1893	−16.86	4.54	−12.33
1820	9.59	—	—	1857	−24.22	10.99	−13.23	1894	−2.82	4.76	1.94
1821	3.34	—	—	1858	10.38	6.68	17.07	1895	2.14	4.42	6.56
1822	−12.85	—	—	1859	−0.62	7.56	6.94	1896	0.69	4.17	4.86
1823	5.29	—	—	1860	−3.93	3.88	−0.06	1897	14.15	4.27	18.41
1824	3.70	—	—	1861	−3.73	5.27	1.54	1898	12.17	4.21	16.38
1825	−12.99	3.81	−9.18	1862	49.15	5.85	55.00	1899	4.17	3.72	7.89
1826	−1.22	3.48	2.27	1863	40.95	5.46	46.41	1900	17.99	4.98	22.97
1827	−6.24	4.57	−1.67	1864	10.53	6.07	16.61	1901	24.60	4.66	29.26
1828	−17.95	4.34	−13.61	1865	−1.33	6.08	4.75	1902	5.29	4.15	9.44
1829	10.33	5.10	15.43	1866	0.46	6.85	7.31	1903	−12.88	4.35	−8.53
1830	27.31	4.20	31.51	1867	−2.61	6.48	3.87	1904	14.94	4.72	19.66
1831	−17.05	3.07	−13.98	1868	1.52	6.56	8.08	1905	6.67	4.00	10.67
1832	8.60	4.48	13.08	1869	−2.85	6.53	3.67	1906	−1.09	4.19	3.10
1833	−6.09	4.24	−1.85	1870	−1.44	6.66	5.22	1907	−26.26	4.47	−21.79
1834	8.84	4.40	13.24	1871	3.34	5.86	9.20	1908	28.47	6.09	34.56
1835	−6.74	4.38	−2.36	1872	0.50	6.33	6.83	1909	18.12	4.87	22.99
1836	4.33	7.76	12.09	1873	−17.70	6.51	−11.19	1910	−15.50	4.56	−10.94
1837	−18.02	4.60	−13.43	1874	−5.77	7.47	1.70	1911	2.17	5.19	7.37
1838	12.20	8.99	21.19	1875	−4.72	6.61	1.89	1912	0.03	5.27	5.30
1839	−26.62	7.64	−18.97	1876	−13.31	6.86	−6.45	1913	−14.44	5.12	−9.32
1840	3.01	6.03	9.04	1877	1.74	5.31	7.05	1914	−8.47	5.22	−3.25
1841	−23.52	7.46	−16.06	1878	10.50	5.54	16.04	1915	15.88	5.85	21.73
1842	2.34	8.71	11.05	1879	51.31	5.80	57.10	1916	1.29	5.91	7.19
1843	39.16	16.40	55.56	1880	19.83	5.28	25.12	1917	−23.48	7.04	−16.44
1844	2.81	9.29	12.11	1881	1.88	5.48	7.36	1918	2.88	8.38	11.27
1845	−11.61	5.56	−6.05	1882	−9.54	5.32	−4.22	1919	9.38	6.71	16.09
1846	23.21	5.70	28.91	1883	−15.04	5.65	−9.39	1920	−20.74	5.72	−15.02
1847	7.65	8.48	16.13	1884	−24.28	5.81	−18.47	1921	4.26	6.75	11.02
1848	5.28	7.45	12.72	1885	45.32	5.53	50.85	1922	19.74	6.98	26.72
1849	7.80	10.64	18.44	1886	12.46	4.23	16.69	1923	−2.13	6.04	3.90
1850	10.48	6.57	17.05	1887	−12.13	4.43	−7.70	1924	19.34	6.43	25.77
1851	−5.78	7.74	1.95	1888	2.09	4.36	6.45	1925	23.22	5.91	29.12

Table 10-3

Large Company Stocks
Annual Capital Appreciation and Total Return Index Values

from 1824 to 1943

Year	Cap App	Total Return	Year	Cap App	Total Return	Year	Cap App	Total Return
1824	1.00	1.00	1864	1.65	20.48	1904	3.32	322.65
1825	0.87	0.91	1865	1.63	21.45	1905	3.54	357.07
1826	0.86	0.93	1866	1.64	23.02	1906	3.51	368.14
1827	0.81	0.91	1867	1.59	23.91	1907	2.58	287.92
1828	0.66	0.79	1868	1.62	25.84	1908	3.32	387.42
1829	0.73	0.91	1869	1.57	26.79	1909	3.92	476.49
1830	0.93	1.20	1870	1.55	28.19	1910	3.31	424.37
1831	0.77	1.03	1871	1.60	30.78	1911	3.39	455.63
1832	0.84	1.16	1872	1.61	32.89	1912	3.39	479.76
1833	0.79	1.14	1873	1.32	29.21	1913	2.90	435.04
1834	0.86	1.29	1874	1.25	29.70	1914	2.65	420.90
1835	0.80	1.26	1875	1.19	30.26	1915	3.07	512.38
1836	0.83	1.42	1876	1.03	28.31	1916	3.11	549.24
1837	0.68	1.23	1877	1.05	30.31	1917	2.38	458.96
1838	0.77	1.49	1878	1.16	35.17	1918	2.45	510.66
1839	0.56	1.20	1879	1.75	55.25	1919	2.68	592.84
1840	0.58	1.31	1880	2.10	69.13	1920	2.13	503.78
1841	0.44	1.10	1881	2.14	74.22	1921	2.22	559.27
1842	0.45	1.22	1882	1.93	71.09	1922	2.65	708.68
1843	0.63	1.90	1883	1.64	64.41	1923	2.60	736.34
1844	0.65	2.14	1884	1.24	52.51	1924	3.10	926.09
1845	0.57	2.01	1885	1.81	79.21	1925	3.82	1195.79
1846	0.71	2.59	1886	2.03	92.44	1926	4.04	1334.79
1847	0.76	3.00	1887	1.79	85.32	1927	5.28	1835.18
1848	0.80	3.39	1888	1.82	90.83	1928	7.29	2635.47
1849	0.86	4.01	1889	1.91	98.79	1929	6.42	2413.68
1850	0.95	4.69	1890	1.70	92.28	1930	4.59	1812.75
1851	0.90	4.78	1891	1.75	99.42	1931	2.43	1027.17
1852	1.06	6.00	1892	1.93	114.12	1932	2.06	943.01
1853	0.97	5.93	1893	1.61	100.06	1933	3.02	1452.15
1854	0.78	5.30	1894	1.56	102.00	1934	2.84	1431.20
1855	0.90	6.45	1895	1.60	108.69	1935	4.02	2113.43
1856	0.92	7.02	1896	1.61	113.97	1936	5.14	2830.34
1857	0.70	6.09	1897	1.83	134.96	1937	3.16	1838.97
1858	0.77	7.13	1898	2.06	157.07	1938	3.95	2411.28
1859	0.77	7.63	1899	2.14	169.45	1939	3.74	2401.38
1860	0.74	7.62	1900	2.53	208.38	1940	3.17	2166.42
1861	0.71	7.74	1901	3.15	269.34	1941	2.60	1915.29
1862	1.06	12.00	1902	3.32	294.77	1942	2.92	2304.86
1863	1.49	17.56	1903	2.89	269.63	1943	3.49	2901.81

Table 10-3 (continued)

Large Company Stocks
Annual Capital Appreciation and Total Return Index Values

from 1944 to 2002

Year	Cap App	Total Return	Year	Cap App	Total Return	Year	Cap App	Total Return
1944	3.97	3474.99	1964	25.36	56367.95	1984	50.04	252548.89
1945	5.19	4741.14	1965	27.66	63386.32	1985	63.22	333763.56
1946	4.58	4358.47	1966	24.03	57007.57	1986	72.47	395411.36
1947	4.58	4607.25	1967	28.86	70675.53	1987	73.94	416094.53
1948	4.55	4860.71	1968	31.08	78493.24	1988	83.11	486037.11
1949	5.01	5774.16	1969	27.53	71817.70	1989	105.76	639094.09
1950	6.11	7605.31	1970	27.57	74695.15	1990	98.83	618817.55
1951	7.11	9431.84	1971	30.55	85386.04	1991	124.82	807863.22
1952	7.95	11164.23	1972	35.32	101588.98	1992	130.40	869827.94
1953	7.42	11053.79	1973	29.19	86694.82	1993	139.60	956722.01
1954	10.77	16870.70	1974	20.51	63748.52	1994	137.45	969229.24
1955	13.61	22195.54	1975	26.98	87464.94	1995	184.33	1332006.90
1956	13.96	23650.66	1976	32.15	108319.39	1996	221.69	1639356.83
1957	11.97	21100.53	1977	28.45	100537.72	1997	290.43	2186285.62
1958	16.52	30250.48	1978	28.76	107133.20	1998	367.88	2811163.21
1959	17.92	33866.95	1979	32.30	126888.02	1999	439.71	3402761.27
1960	17.39	34025.99	1980	40.62	168024.36	2000	395.13	3092926.24
1961	21.41	43175.07	1981	36.67	159776.38	2001	343.59	2725344.33
1962	18.88	39406.53	1982	42.08	193983.54	2002	263.31	2122923.32
1963	22.45	48391.69	1983	49.35	237656.61			

Chapter 11

International Equity Investing

Discussion of International Investing

With the disappearance of trade barriers and the opening of foreign markets, the level of global business has increased considerably. Communism and other systems have essentially been discredited, leading to increasingly open markets in nations around the world. Investing internationally literally offers a world of opportunity. The opportunities available today are growing rapidly, encouraged by open markets and the accelerating economies of many nations. The evidence in favor of taking a global approach to investing, and the possible rewards an investor can reap, is plentiful. However, significant risks are present as well—risks that apply strictly to the international marketplace. In this chapter, we consider both the rewards and the risks associated with international investments.

Construction of the International Indices

Our analysis of international investing uses the indices created by Morgan Stanley Capital International, Inc. (MSCI®). The MSCI indices are designed to measure the performance of the developed and emerging stock markets of such countries and regions as the United States, Europe, Canada, Australasia, and the Far East, and that of industry groups. MSCI indices are designed to reflect the performance of the entire range of stocks available to investors in each local market.

From January 1970 to October 2001, inclusion in the MSCI indices was based upon market capitalization. Stocks chosen for the indices were required to have a target market representation of 60 percent of total market capitalization. MSCI has recently decided to enhance its index construction methodology by free float-adjusting constituents' index weights and increasing the target market representation. Target market representation will be increased from 60 percent of total market capitalization to 85 percent of free float-adjusted market capitalization within each industry group, within each country. MSCI defines the free float of a security as the proportion of shares outstanding that is deemed to be available for purchase in the public equity markets by international investors. Implementation of the abovementioned changes was scheduled to take place in two separate phases, with the first phase being implemented as of the close of November 30, 2001 and the second as of the close of May 31, 2002.

The international stock series presented throughout this chapter is represented by the MSCI EAFE® (Europe, Australasia, Far East) index. The MSCI EAFE index consists of 21 developed equity markets outside of North America.

Benefits of Investing Internationally

The arguments for adding international investments to an investment portfolio can be rather powerful. Examples include participation in roughly half of the world's investable assets, growth potential, diversification, and the improvement of the risk/reward trade-off.

Investment Opportunities

An investor who chooses to ignore investment opportunities outside of the United States is missing out on roughly half of the investable developed stock market opportunities in the world. Graph 11-1 presents the relative size of international and domestic markets as of year-end 2002. The international markets represented in the graph constitute countries having developed economies. In 2002, the total developed world stock market capitalization was \$20.2 trillion, with \$9.8 trillion representing international stock market capitalization.[1]

Graph 11-1

World Stock Market Capitalization
Year-End 2002

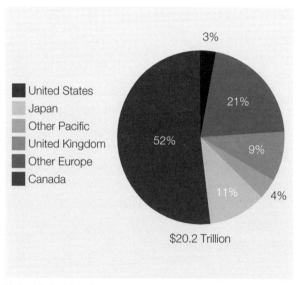

Note: Underlying data expressed in U.S. dollars

The domestic (U.S.) stock market continues to embody the majority of the world stock market capitalization. If an investor chooses to exclude international investments from his or her portfolio, however, almost half of the world's investable assets are being ignored.

Many of the possible investment choices available to you outside the United States are with companies you already know and whose products you may in fact be using on a daily basis. From the car you drive to the technology you use, many of these products are produced by companies that call other countries home. Some examples include: Daimler Chrysler (Germany), Toyota (Japan), Nokia (Finland), and Samsung (Korea). If an investor were to limit the scope of his or her investments strictly to the U.S., many countries that are home to world class industries would be excluded. Switzerland has a major presence in the pharmaceutical industry, Germany in the automotive industry, and Japan in the consumer electronics industry. Globalization has helped to increase brand awareness with investors across the world. When looking at the names listed above, international investing suddenly seems a little less foreign.

1 World Market Capitalization by County— Morgan Stanley Capital International Blue Book℠.

Growth Potential

As markets have grown and international companies have thrived, the performance of many international stock markets has been impressive. Graph 11-2 depicts the growth of $1.00 invested in international stocks as well as U.S. large company stocks, long-term government bonds, Treasury bills, and a hypothetical asset returning the inflation rate over the period from the end of 1969 to the end of 2002. Of the asset classes shown, U.S. large company stocks accumulated the highest ending wealth by year-end 2002. Notice, however, that the international stock index line was above that of large company stocks for much of the 33-year time period. The recent strong performance of U.S. large company stocks compared to international stocks produced higher accumulated wealth at the end of the 33-year period.

Graph 11-2

Global Investing
Year-End 1969 = $1.00

from 1969 to 2002

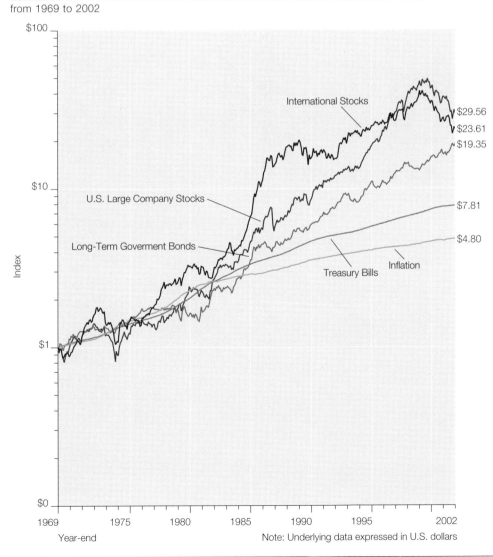

The analysis of longer holding periods indicates that international stocks have exceeded domestic stocks. Graph 11-3 compares the performance of international and U.S. large company stocks over rolling 10-year holding periods from 1970 through 2002. International stocks outperformed their domestic counterparts in 16 out of the 24 ten-year holding periods shown. Once again, the recent impressive performance of U.S. large company stocks is evident.

Graph 11-3

Total Return of U.S. Large Company Stocks and International Stocks
10-Year Rolling Periods

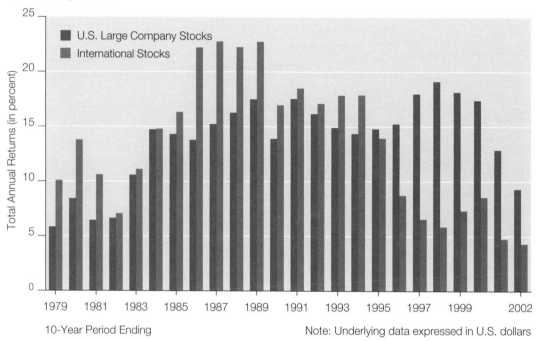

10-Year Period Ending

Note: Underlying data expressed in U.S. dollars

Diversification

Diversification can be another important benefit of international investing. By spreading risks among foreign and U.S. stocks, investors can potentially lower overall investment risk and/or improve investment returns. Fluctuations may occur at different times for different markets, and if growth is slow in one country, international investing provides a means of seeking healthier prospects elsewhere. Investing abroad may help an investor balance such fluctuations. Since it is almost impossible to forecast which markets will be top performers in any given year, it can be very valuable to be invested in a portfolio diversified across several countries.

Graph 11-4 presents the best-performing developed stock markets worldwide compared to the U.S. market over the past 10 years. The graph clearly indicates that by taking advantage of opportunities abroad, one may experience higher returns than by investing solely in the U.S. market.

Graph 11-4

Best Performing Developed Stock Markets vs. U.S. Market

from 1993 to 2002

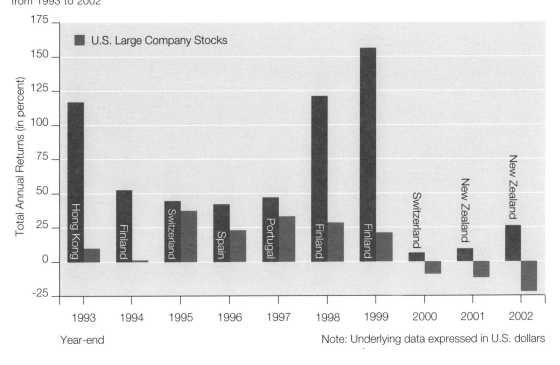

Year-end

Note: Underlying data expressed in U.S. dollars

Graph 11-5 depicts the growth of $1.00 invested in U.S. large company stocks, European, and Pacific stocks as well as a global portfolio that represents an equally weighted mix of the afore-mentioned stocks. Notice that the global portfolio outperformed the U.S., European, and Pacific stock indices at the end of the 33-year period. The global portfolio benefited from the long-term growth of the Pacific region, but with considerably less volatility.

The cross-correlation coefficient between two series, covered in Chapter 6, measures the extent to which they are linearly related. The correlation coefficient measures the sensitivity of returns on one asset class or portfolio to the returns of another.

Graph 11-5

Benefits of Global Diversification
Year-End 1969 = $1,000.00

from 1969 to 2002

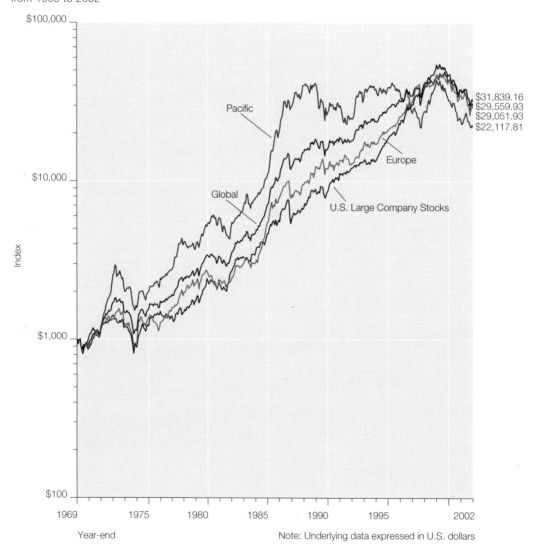

Graph 11-6 examines a 60-month rolling period correlation between international and U.S. large company stocks. This graph illustrates the recent rise in cross-correlation between the two, suggesting that the benefit of diversification has suffered in recent years. The maximum benefit to an investor would have come in the 60-month period ending July 1987, where the cross-correlation was 0.26. The least amount of diversification benefit would have come in the recent 60-month period ending December 2002, where the cross-correlation was 0.83. The monthly average over the entire time horizon has been 0.54.

Graph 11-6

Rolling 60-Month Correlations
U.S Large Company Stocks and International Stocks

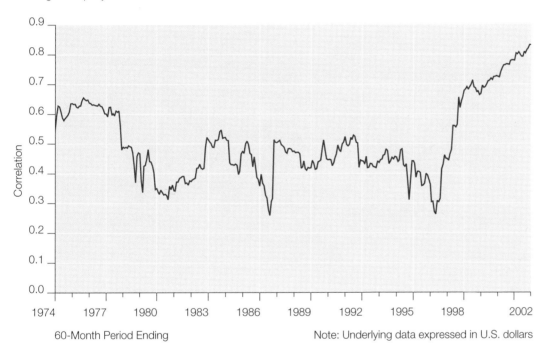

60-Month Period Ending   Note: Underlying data expressed in U.S. dollars

Expanding the Efficient Range

Expanding a set of domestic portfolios to include securities from specific countries and regions can possibly improve the risk/return trade-off of investment opportunities. How would an efficient frontier be affected by such an expansion?

Graph 11-7 shows two efficient frontiers—one constructed entirely of domestic portfolios and the other constructed of global portfolios for the period 1970 to 1985. The comparison of the two efficient frontiers in this image makes a strong case for global diversification. An investor could have achieved higher returns at given levels of risk by expanding the set of domestic portfolios to include international stocks.

Graph 11-7

Efficient Frontier
U.S. Large Company Stocks, Long-Term Government Bonds, and International Stocks
from 1970 to 1985

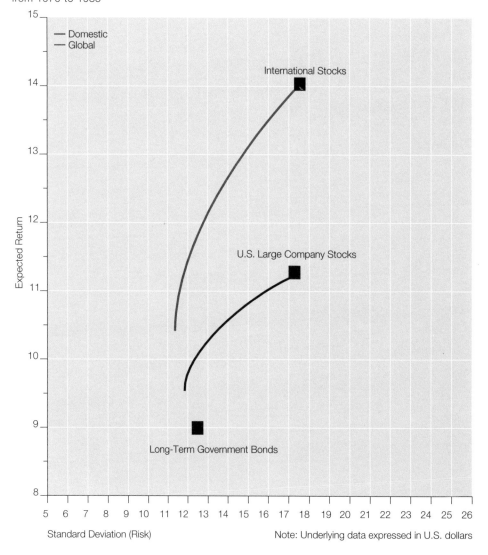

The time horizon is changed to cover the period 1986 to 2002 to construct the two efficient frontiers found in Graph 11-8. The comparison of the two efficient frontiers in this image makes somewhat of a weak case for global diversification. This can be attributed to the recent impressive performance of U.S. large company stocks. Although the diversification benefit and the risk/return trade-off have suffered of late, recent trends may not be indicative of future performance.

Graph 11-8

Efficient Frontier

U.S. Large Company Stocks, Long-Term Government Bonds, and International Stocks

from 1986 to 2002

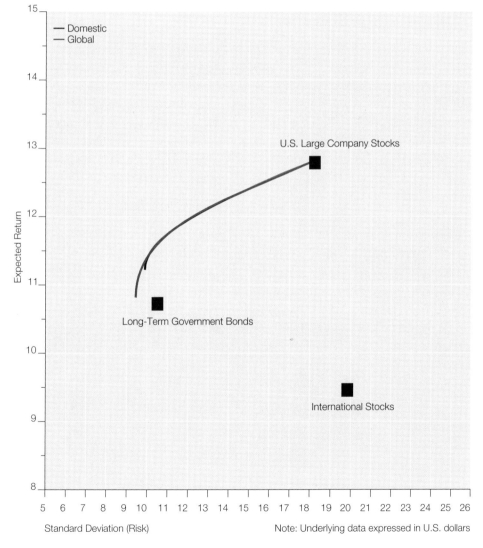

Risk Associated with International Investing

In addition to the potential rewards offered through international investing, significant risks apply as well. An investor assumes risk when investing in any type of stock. International investing, however, encompasses special risks—risks that should be carefully evaluated. Examples include currency risk, political and economic risk, liquidity risk, company information and accounting standards, market risk, and perhaps higher expenses.

Currency Risk

The risk of losing money when gains and losses are exchanged from foreign currencies into U.S. dollars is called currency risk. Exchange rates need to be considered with international stocks, and an investor should weigh the exchange rate risk (currency risk) in relation to the return benefit. Foreign exchange rates are continually fluctuating with changes in the supply and demand of each country's currency. Thus, returns realized by local investors are often quite different from the returns that U.S. investors attained—even though they are invested in the same security.

An investor purchases and trades foreign securities in the foreign country's local currency. When these securities are purchased by a U.S. investor, the investor's U.S. dollars must be converted to the foreign currency. When it is time to sell the securities or receive dividends, the currency is converted back to U.S. dollars. Movements in the foreign currency in relation to the U.S. dollar change the value of the foreign investment for the U.S. investor. Thus, a strengthening dollar diminishes the value of foreign assets owned by U.S. investors, while a weakening dollar increases the value of the foreign investment owned by U.S. investors.

Table 11-1 illustrates the impact of currency conversion. In 1999, Canadian stocks provided a local investor a return of 45.88 percent. The Canadian dollar appreciated relative to the U.S. dollar, translating into more dollars and a higher return for a U.S. investor (54.58 percent). The same holds true for Japanese stocks in 1999. On the other hand, in 2000, Canadian stocks provided a local investor a return of 9.34 percent. This time the Canadian dollar depreciated relative to the U.S. dollar, translating into fewer dollars and a lower return for a U.S. investor (5.35%). The strength of the U.S. dollar relative to the other currencies caused the return to U.S. investors to be less than the return to local investors.

Table 11-1

Impact of Currency Conversion

Company	Year	Return to Local Investors (%)	Return to U.S. Investors (%)	Currency Impact (%)
Canada	1999	45.88	54.58	8.70
Japan	1999	46.79	63.08	16.29
Canada	2000	9.34	5.35	−3.99
Japan	2000	−19.74	−28.32	−8.58

Political/Economic Risk

Governmental and political environments abroad can be quite unstable at times. Political events pose a considerable hazard to the stability of returns from foreign markets. In emerging markets, macro-economic conditions remain exceptionally volatile and political risk is a fact of life. U.S. investors could be affected by economic policy changes such as currency controls, changes in taxation, restrictive trade policies, or seizure of foreigners' assets. Political instability and economic risk can lead to greater volatility, which can negatively affect investment markets/values.

Liquidity Risk

Liquidity risk refers to the potential that an asset will be difficult to buy or sell quickly and in large volume without substantially affecting the asset's price. Shares in large blue-chip stocks such as General Electric are liquid because they are actively traded and, therefore, the stock price will not be dramatically moved by a few buy or sell orders.

International markets, however, normally have much lower daily trading volumes when compared to the stock exchanges of the United States. Thus, a few large orders can have the potential to move the price of a security up or down rather sharply. This would go almost unnoticed in a large, established market. Also, a number of developing countries allow foreigners to buy only limited quantities of specified classes of shares.

Company Information/Accounting Standards

The type of information provided to investors from foreign companies often differs from the information U.S. public companies supply. Financial information concerning specific foreign companies can be much more difficult to obtain, since accounting and financial disclosure practices can vary widely from U.S. standards. Moreover, once the information is obtained, it may not be in English.

Market Risk

Just as U.S. stock prices fluctuate from one period to the next, prices of foreign stocks are subject to significant gains and declines. However, past returns from international stocks have fluctuated even more so than the returns of U.S. stocks. Annual ranges of returns provide an indication of the historical volatility (risk) experienced by investments in various markets.

Graph 11-9 illustrates the range of annual returns for domestic and international composites, as well as the Europe and Pacific regional composites, over the period 1970 through 2002. All three international composites exhibit more volatility when compared to the domestic composite. However, when one compares the compounded average return of each composite over the same period, the numbers seem to be more in line with one another. International investments have the potential for significant short-term declines; however, a long-term approach to investing may help reduce the pain of volatility. Investors should plan on holding international stock investments for much longer time periods to reap the potential rewards.

Graph 11-9

Global Stock Market Returns

Highest and Lowest Historical Annual Returns for Each Region

from 1970 to 2002

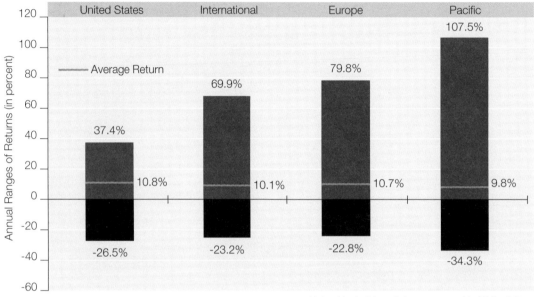

Note: Underlying data expressed in U.S. dollars

Expenses

Lastly, for the reasons stated earlier, investments in foreign securities generally have higher associated expenses compared to investments in domestic securities, including transaction costs as well as sales charges. All of these expenses work to reduce the investor's return on the foreign security.

The risks associated with international investing should be carefully examined by an investor interested in or already partaking in the international marketplace. While the potential rewards of investing internationally are quite clear, an investor should weigh those along with the added risks.

Summary Statistics for International and Domestic Series

Table 11-2 shows summary statistics of annual total returns for various international regions and composites. The summary statistics presented are geometric mean, arithmetic mean, and standard deviation.

Over the period 1970 to 2002, the Pacific regional composite was the riskiest, with a standard deviation of 33.2 percent. The geometric mean of the Pacific regional composite was 9.8 percent, similar to EAFE and the World composite, which were considerably less risky. The United States recorded the highest geometric mean with the lowest risk of the series in the table.

Table 11-2

Summary Statistics of Annual Returns (in percent)

from 1970 to 2002

Series	Geometric Mean	Arithmetic Mean	Standard Deviation
Canada	8.8	10.3	18.8
Europe	10.7	12.6	21.4
Pacific	9.8	14.2	33.2
EAFE (Europe, Australasia, Far East)	10.1	12.2	22.6
World	9.8	11.2	17.6
United States	10.8	12.2	17.5

Note: Underlying data expressed in U.S. dollars

Table 11-3 shows the compound returns by decade for the various international regions and composites. The Pacific regional composite provided the highest compound annual rate of return in the first two decades but performed rather poorly in the 1990s as well as in the last two time periods. The 1990s were a good time period in which to be a domestic investor, with a compound annual rate of return of 18.2 percent.

Table 11-3

Compound Annual Rates of Return by Decade (in percent)

	1970s	1980s	1990s	2000s*	1993-02
Canada	11.0	11.6	9.9	−9.7	8.1
Europe	8.6	18.5	14.5	−15.4	8.3
Pacific	14.8	26.4	0.5	−20.3	−1.2
EAFE (Europe, Australasia, Far East)	10.1	22.8	7.3	−17.0	4.3
World	7.0	19.9	12.0	−16.4	6.7
United States	5.9	17.5	18.2	−14.6	9.3

*Based on the period 2000–2002.
Note: Underlying data expressed in U.S. dollars

Table 11-4 shows the annualized monthly standard deviations by decade for the various international regions and composites. The World composite was the least risky asset in the first three decades as well as during the time period of 1993 to 2002. The Pacific regional composite was, quite the opposite, the riskiest asset in the 1970s, 1980s, and 1990s.

Table 11-4

Annualized Monthly Standard Deviation by Decade (in percent)

	1970s	1980s	1990s	2000s*	1993-02
Canada	20.7	24.7	18.7	21.9	21.9
Europe	18.6	21.5	16.8	16.2	16.9
Pacific	22.1	26.6	24.8	14.2	20.5
EAFE (Europe, Australasia, Far East)	17.4	21.6	18.7	14.0	16.4
World	15.1	17.6	15.7	14.7	15.7
United States	17.1	19.4	15.8	16.7	17.1

*Based on the period 2000–2002.
Note: Underlying data expressed in U.S. dollars

Table 11-5 presents annual cross-correlations and serial correlations from 1970 to 2002 for the six basic series and inflation as well as international stocks. International stocks, when compared to U.S. large company stocks, provided a higher cross-correlation than when compared to U.S. small company stocks. The serial correlation of international stocks suggests no pattern, and the return from period to period can best be interpreted as random or unpredictable.

Table 11-5

Basic Series and International Stocks
Serial and Cross-Correlations of Historical Annual Returns
from 1970 to 2002

Series	International Stocks	Large Company Stocks	Small Company Stocks	Long-Term Corp Bonds	Long-Term Govt Bonds	Intermediate Govt Bonds	U.S Treasury Bills	Inflation
International Stocks	1.00	0.58	0.38	0.11	0.11	−0.01	−0.04	−0.17
Large Company Stocks	0.58	1.00	0.65	0.35	0.30	0.22	0.09	−0.21
Small Company Stocks	0.38	0.65	1.00	0.16	0.09	0.04	0.08	0.03
Long-Term Corp Bonds	0.11	0.35	0.16	1.00	0.95	0.93	−0.04	−0.47
Long-Term Govt Bonds	0.11	0.30	0.09	0.95	1.00	0.93	−0.02	−0.42
Intermediate Govt Bonds	−0.01	0.22	0.04	0.93	0.93	1.00	0.21	−0.26
Treasury Bills	−0.04	0.09	0.08	−0.04	−0.02	0.21	1.00	0.62
Inflation	−0.17	−0.21	0.03	−0.47	−0.42	−0.26	0.62	1.00
Serial Correlations	0.20	0.12	0.15	−0.11	−0.25	−0.12	0.76	0.73

Note: Underlying data expressed in U.S. dollars

Conclusion

International investments are no different than any other investment when it comes to information gathering. Investors interested in or already taking part in the international marketplace should learn as much as possible about the corresponding risks and rewards. International investments are not for everyone, and the most appropriate mix for an individual investor depends on his or her risk tolerance, investment goals, time horizon, and financial resources.

Table 11-6

U.S. Large Company Stocks, International Stocks, Pacific Stocks, and Europe Stocks
Annual Total Returns (in percent)

from 1970 to 2002

Year	U.S. Large Company Stocks	International Stocks	Pacific Stocks	Europe Stocks
1970	4.01	-10.51	-11.99	-9.35
1971	14.31	31.21	38.75	28.04
1972	18.96	37.60	107.55	15.62
1973	-14.66	-14.17	-20.95	-7.73
1974	-26.47	-22.15	-20.94	-22.78
1975	37.20	37.10	26.73	43.90
1976	23.84	3.74	21.64	-6.37
1977	-7.18	19.42	13.69	23.92
1978	6.56	34.30	48.77	24.30
1979	18.44	6.18	-3.48	14.67
1980	32.42	24.43	36.38	14.53
1981	-4.91	-1.03	8.31	-10.45
1982	21.41	-0.86	-6.26	5.69
1983	22.51	24.61	26.42	22.38
1984	6.27	7.86	13.48	1.26
1985	32.16	56.72	39.39	79.79
1986	18.47	69.94	93.82	44.46
1987	5.23	24.93	39.85	4.10
1988	16.81	28.59	35.19	16.35
1989	31.49	10.80	2.68	29.06
1990	-3.17	-23.19	-34.29	-3.37
1991	30.55	12.49	11.54	13.66
1992	7.67	-11.85	-18.20	-4.25
1993	9.99	32.94	35.97	29.79
1994	1.31	8.06	13.03	2.66
1995	37.43	11.55	2.99	22.13
1996	23.07	6.36	-8.40	21.57
1997	33.36	2.06	-25.34	24.20
1998	28.58	20.33	2.69	28.91
1999	21.04	27.30	57.96	16.23
2000	-9.11	-13.96	-25.64	-8.14
2001	-11.88	-21.21	-25.22	-19.64
2002	-22.10	-15.66	-9.01	-18.09

Note: Underlying data expressed in U.S. dollars

Stocks, Bonds, Bills, and Inflation

0.0478	0.0013	−0.0103	0.0096	0.0424
−0.0071	−0.0176	0.0020	0.0571	0.0382
−0.0501	0.0034	0.0540	0.0204	0.0052
0.0589	−0.0275	0.0851	−0.0167	0.0909
0.0197	0.0098	−0.0030	0.0396	0.0055
−0.0328	−0.0440	0.0066	−0.0050	0.0370
0.0449	0.0176	0.0501	0.0270	0.0284

Appendix A

0.0209	−0.0046	−0.0607	−0.0811	−0.0803
−0.0022	0.0535	−0.0097	0.0339	−0.0046
0.0162	0.0178	0.0195	−0.0118	0.0301
−0.0133	0.0356	−0.0030	−0.0473	0.0147
0.0334	0.0289	−0.0031	0.0106	0.1245
−0.0120	−0.0725	−0.0053	0.0494	0.0095
0.0190	0.0468	−0.0070	0.0342	−0.0276
0.0105	−0.0172	0.0164	0.0400	0.0876

IbbotsonAssociates

Appendix A

Monthly Returns on Basic and Derived Series

Table A-1

Large Company Stocks: Total Returns

from January 1926 to December 1970

Year	Jan	Feb	Mar	Apr	May	Jun	Jul	Aug	Sep	Oct	Nov	Dec	Year	Jan-De
1926	0.0000	−0.0385	−0.0575	0.0253	0.0179	0.0457	0.0479	0.0248	0.0252	−0.0284	0.0347	0.0196	1926	0.116
1927	−0.0193	0.0537	0.0087	0.0201	0.0607	−0.0067	0.0670	0.0515	0.0450	−0.0502	0.0721	0.0279	1927	0.374
1928	−0.0040	−0.0125	0.1101	0.0345	0.0197	−0.0385	0.0141	0.0803	0.0259	0.0168	0.1292	0.0049	1928	0.436
1929	0.0583	−0.0019	−0.0012	0.0176	−0.0362	0.1140	0.0471	0.1028	−0.0476	−0.1973	−0.1246	0.0282	1929	−0.084
1930	0.0639	0.0259	0.0812	−0.0080	−0.0096	−0.1625	0.0386	0.0141	−0.1282	−0.0855	−0.0089	−0.0706	1930	−0.249
1931	0.0502	0.1193	−0.0675	−0.0935	−0.1279	0.1421	−0.0722	0.0182	−0.2973	0.0896	−0.0798	−0.1400	1931	−0.433
1932	−0.0271	0.0570	−0.1158	−0.1997	−0.2196	−0.0022	0.3815	0.3869	−0.0346	−0.1349	−0.0417	0.0565	1932	−0.081
1933	0.0087	−0.1772	0.0353	0.4256	0.1683	0.1338	−0.0862	0.1206	−0.1118	−0.0855	0.1127	0.0253	1933	0.539
1934	0.1069	−0.0322	0.0000	−0.0251	−0.0736	0.0229	−0.1132	0.0611	−0.0033	−0.0286	0.0942	−0.0010	1934	−0.014
1935	−0.0411	−0.0341	−0.0286	0.0980	0.0409	0.0699	0.0850	0.0280	0.0256	0.0777	0.0474	0.0394	1935	0.476
1936	0.0670	0.0224	0.0268	−0.0751	0.0545	0.0333	0.0701	0.0151	0.0031	0.0775	0.0134	−0.0029	1936	0.339
1937	0.0390	0.0191	−0.0077	−0.0809	−0.0024	−0.0504	0.1045	−0.0483	−0.1403	−0.0981	−0.0866	−0.0459	1937	−0.350
1938	0.0152	0.0674	−0.2487	0.1447	−0.0330	0.2503	0.0744	−0.0226	0.0166	0.0776	−0.0273	0.0401	1938	0.311
1939	−0.0674	0.0390	−0.1339	−0.0027	0.0733	−0.0612	0.1105	−0.0648	0.1673	−0.0123	−0.0398	0.0270	1939	−0.004
1940	−0.0336	0.0133	0.0124	−0.0024	−0.2289	0.0809	0.0341	0.0350	0.0123	0.0422	−0.0316	0.0009	1940	−0.097
1941	−0.0463	−0.0060	0.0071	−0.0612	0.0183	0.0578	0.0579	0.0010	−0.0068	−0.0657	−0.0284	−0.0407	1941	−0.115
1942	0.0161	−0.0159	−0.0652	−0.0399	0.0796	0.0221	0.0337	0.0164	0.0290	0.0678	−0.0021	0.0549	1942	0.203
1943	0.0737	0.0583	0.0545	0.0035	0.0552	0.0223	−0.0526	0.0171	0.0263	−0.0108	−0.0654	0.0617	1943	0.259
1944	0.0171	0.0042	0.0195	−0.0100	0.0505	0.0543	−0.0193	0.0157	−0.0008	0.0023	0.0133	0.0374	1944	0.197
1945	0.0158	0.0683	−0.0441	0.0902	0.0195	−0.0007	−0.0180	0.0641	0.0438	0.0322	0.0396	0.0116	1945	0.364
1946	0.0714	−0.0641	0.0480	0.0393	0.0288	−0.0370	−0.0239	−0.0674	−0.0997	−0.0060	−0.0027	0.0457	1946	−0.080
1947	0.0255	−0.0077	−0.0149	−0.0363	0.0014	0.0554	0.0381	−0.0203	−0.0111	0.0238	−0.0175	0.0233	1947	0.057
1948	−0.0379	−0.0388	0.0793	0.0292	0.0879	0.0054	−0.0508	0.0158	−0.0276	0.0710	−0.0961	0.0346	1948	0.055
1949	0.0039	−0.0296	0.0328	−0.0179	−0.0258	0.0014	0.0650	0.0219	0.0263	0.0340	0.0175	0.0486	1949	0.187
1950	0.0197	0.0199	0.0070	0.0486	0.0509	−0.0548	0.0119	0.0443	0.0592	0.0093	0.0169	0.0513	1950	0.317
1951	0.0637	0.0157	−0.0156	0.0509	−0.0299	−0.0228	0.0711	0.0478	0.0013	−0.0103	0.0096	0.0424	1951	0.240
1952	0.0181	−0.0282	0.0503	−0.0402	0.0343	0.0490	0.0196	−0.0071	−0.0176	0.0020	0.0571	0.0382	1952	0.183
1953	−0.0049	−0.0106	−0.0212	−0.0237	0.0077	−0.0134	0.0273	−0.0501	0.0034	0.0540	0.0204	0.0052	1953	−0.009
1954	0.0536	0.0111	0.0325	0.0516	0.0418	0.0031	0.0589	−0.0275	0.0851	−0.0167	0.0909	0.0534	1954	0.526
1955	0.0197	0.0098	−0.0030	0.0396	0.0055	0.0841	0.0622	−0.0025	0.0130	−0.0284	0.0827	0.0015	1955	0.315
1956	−0.0347	0.0413	0.0710	−0.0004	−0.0593	0.0409	0.0530	−0.0328	−0.0440	0.0066	−0.0050	0.0370	1956	0.065
1957	−0.0401	−0.0264	0.0215	0.0388	0.0437	0.0004	0.0131	−0.0505	−0.0602	−0.0302	0.0231	−0.0395	1957	−0.107
1958	0.0445	−0.0141	0.0328	0.0337	0.0212	0.0279	0.0449	0.0176	0.0501	0.0270	0.0284	0.0535	1958	0.433
1959	0.0053	0.0049	0.0020	0.0402	0.0240	−0.0022	0.0363	−0.0102	−0.0443	0.0128	0.0186	0.0292	1959	0.119
1960	−0.0700	0.0147	−0.0123	−0.0161	0.0326	0.0211	−0.0234	0.0317	−0.0590	−0.0007	0.0465	0.0479	1960	0.004
1961	0.0645	0.0319	0.0270	0.0051	0.0239	−0.0275	0.0342	0.0243	−0.0184	0.0298	0.0447	0.0046	1961	0.268
1962	−0.0366	0.0209	−0.0046	−0.0607	−0.0811	−0.0803	0.0652	0.0208	−0.0465	0.0064	0.1086	0.0153	1962	−0.087
1963	0.0506	−0.0239	0.0370	0.0500	0.0193	−0.0188	−0.0022	0.0535	−0.0097	0.0339	−0.0046	0.0262	1963	0.228
1964	0.0283	0.0147	0.0165	0.0075	0.0162	0.0178	0.0195	−0.0118	0.0301	0.0096	0.0005	0.0056	1964	0.164
1965	0.0345	0.0031	−0.0133	0.0356	−0.0030	−0.0473	0.0147	0.0272	0.0334	0.0289	−0.0031	0.0106	1965	0.124
1966	0.0062	−0.0131	−0.0205	0.0220	−0.0492	−0.0146	−0.0120	−0.0725	−0.0053	0.0494	0.0095	0.0002	1966	−0.100
1967	0.0798	0.0072	0.0409	0.0437	−0.0477	0.0190	0.0468	−0.0070	0.0342	−0.0276	0.0065	0.0278	1967	0.239
1968	−0.0425	−0.0261	0.0110	0.0834	0.0161	0.0105	−0.0172	0.0164	0.0400	0.0087	0.0531	−0.0402	1968	0.110
1969	−0.0068	−0.0426	0.0359	0.0229	0.0026	−0.0542	−0.0587	0.0454	−0.0236	0.0459	−0.0297	−0.0177	1969	−0.0850
1970	−0.0743	0.0586	0.0030	−0.0889	−0.0547	−0.0482	0.0752	0.0509	0.0347	−0.0097	0.0536	0.0584	1970	0.040

* Compound annual return

Table A-1 (continued)

Large Company Stocks: Total Returns

from January 1971 to December 2002

Year	Jan	Feb	Mar	Apr	May	Jun	Jul	Aug	Sep	Oct	Nov	Dec	Year	Jan-Dec*
1971	0.0419	0.0141	0.0382	0.0377	−0.0367	0.0021	−0.0399	0.0412	−0.0056	−0.0404	0.0027	0.0877	1971	0.1431
1972	0.0194	0.0299	0.0072	0.0057	0.0219	−0.0205	0.0036	0.0391	−0.0036	0.0107	0.0505	0.0131	1972	0.1898
1973	−0.0159	−0.0333	−0.0002	−0.0395	−0.0139	−0.0051	0.0394	−0.0318	0.0415	0.0003	−0.1082	0.0183	1973	−0.1466
1974	−0.0085	0.0019	−0.0217	−0.0373	−0.0272	−0.0128	−0.0759	−0.0828	−0.1170	0.1657	−0.0448	−0.0177	1974	−0.2647
1975	0.1251	0.0674	0.0237	0.0493	0.0509	0.0462	−0.0659	−0.0144	−0.0328	0.0637	0.0313	−0.0096	1975	0.3720
1976	0.1199	−0.0058	0.0326	−0.0099	−0.0073	0.0427	−0.0068	0.0014	0.0247	−0.0206	−0.0009	0.0540	1976	0.2384
1977	−0.0489	−0.0151	−0.0119	0.0014	−0.0150	0.0475	−0.0151	−0.0133	0.0000	−0.0415	0.0370	0.0048	1977	−0.0718
1978	−0.0596	−0.0161	0.0276	0.0870	0.0136	−0.0152	0.0560	0.0340	−0.0048	−0.0891	0.0260	0.0172	1978	0.0656
1979	0.0421	−0.0284	0.0575	0.0036	−0.0168	0.0410	0.0110	0.0611	0.0025	−0.0656	0.0514	0.0192	1979	0.1844
1980	0.0610	0.0031	−0.0987	0.0429	0.0562	0.0296	0.0676	0.0131	0.0281	0.0187	0.1095	−0.0315	1980	0.3242
1981	−0.0438	0.0208	0.0380	−0.0213	0.0062	−0.0080	0.0007	−0.0554	−0.0502	0.0528	0.0441	−0.0265	1981	−0.0491
1982	−0.0163	−0.0512	−0.0060	0.0414	−0.0288	−0.0174	−0.0215	0.1267	0.0110	0.1126	0.0438	0.0173	1982	0.2141
1983	0.0348	0.0260	0.0365	0.0758	−0.0052	0.0382	−0.0313	0.0170	0.0136	−0.0134	0.0233	−0.0061	1983	0.2251
1984	−0.0065	−0.0328	0.0171	0.0069	−0.0534	0.0221	−0.0143	0.1125	0.0002	0.0026	−0.0101	0.0253	1984	0.0627
1985	0.0768	0.0137	0.0018	−0.0032	0.0615	0.0159	−0.0026	−0.0061	−0.0321	0.0447	0.0716	0.0467	1985	0.3216
1986	0.0044	0.0761	0.0554	−0.0124	0.0549	0.0166	−0.0569	0.0748	−0.0822	0.0556	0.0256	−0.0264	1986	0.1847
1987	0.1343	0.0413	0.0272	−0.0088	0.0103	0.0499	0.0498	0.0385	−0.0220	−0.2152	−0.0819	0.0738	1987	0.0523
1988	0.0427	0.0470	−0.0302	0.0108	0.0078	0.0464	−0.0040	−0.0331	0.0424	0.0273	−0.0142	0.0181	1988	0.1681
1989	0.0723	−0.0249	0.0236	0.0516	0.0402	−0.0054	0.0898	0.0193	−0.0039	−0.0233	0.0208	0.0236	1989	0.3149
1990	−0.0671	0.0129	0.0263	−0.0247	0.0975	−0.0070	−0.0032	−0.0903	−0.0492	−0.0037	0.0644	0.0274	1990	−0.0317
1991	0.0442	0.0716	0.0238	0.0028	0.0428	−0.0457	0.0468	0.0235	−0.0164	0.0134	−0.0404	0.1143	1991	0.3055
1992	−0.0186	0.0128	−0.0196	0.0291	0.0054	−0.0145	0.0403	−0.0202	0.0115	0.0036	0.0337	0.0131	1992	0.0767
1993	0.0073	0.0135	0.0215	−0.0245	0.0270	0.0033	−0.0047	0.0381	−0.0074	0.0203	−0.0094	0.0123	1993	0.0999
1994	0.0335	−0.0270	−0.0435	0.0130	0.0163	−0.0247	0.0331	0.0407	−0.0241	0.0229	−0.0367	0.0146	1994	0.0131
1995	0.0260	0.0388	0.0296	0.0291	0.0395	0.0235	0.0333	0.0027	0.0419	−0.0035	0.0440	0.0185	1995	0.3743
1996	0.0344	0.0096	0.0096	0.0147	0.0258	0.0041	−0.0445	0.0212	0.0562	0.0274	0.0759	−0.0196	1996	0.2307
1997	0.0621	0.0081	−0.0416	0.0597	0.0614	0.0446	0.0794	−0.0556	0.0548	−0.0334	0.0463	0.0172	1997	0.3336
1998	0.0111	0.0721	0.0512	0.0101	−0.0172	0.0406	−0.0107	−0.1446	0.0641	0.0813	0.0606	0.0576	1998	0.2858
1999	0.0418	−0.0311	0.0400	0.0387	−0.0236	0.0555	−0.0312	−0.0050	−0.0274	0.0633	0.0203	0.0589	1999	0.2104
2000	−0.0502	−0.0189	0.0978	−0.0301	−0.0205	0.0246	−0.0156	0.0621	−0.0528	−0.0042	−0.0788	0.0049	2000	−0.0911
2001	0.0355	−0.0912	−0.0634	0.0777	0.0067	−0.0243	−0.0098	−0.0626	−0.0808	0.0191	0.0767	0.0088	2001	−0.1188
2002	−0.0146	−0.0193	0.0376	−0.0606	−0.0074	−0.0712	−0.0780	0.0066	−0.1087	0.0880	0.0589	−0.0588	2002	−0.2210

*Compound annual return

Table A-2

Large Company Stocks: Income Returns

from January 1926 to December 1970

Year	Jan	Feb	Mar	Apr	May	Jun	Jul	Aug	Sep	Oct	Nov	Dec	Year	Jan–Dec
1926	0.0016	0.0055	0.0016	0.0026	0.0102	0.0025	0.0024	0.0078	0.0023	0.0030	0.0123	0.0030	1926	0.0541
1927	0.0015	0.0061	0.0022	0.0029	0.0085	0.0027	0.0020	0.0070	0.0018	0.0029	0.0105	0.0029	1927	0.0571
1928	0.0011	0.0051	0.0017	0.0021	0.0071	0.0020	0.0016	0.0062	0.0019	0.0023	0.0092	0.0021	1928	0.0481
1929	0.0012	0.0039	0.0012	0.0016	0.0066	0.0016	0.0014	0.0048	0.0013	0.0020	0.0091	0.0029	1929	0.0398
1930	0.0014	0.0044	0.0013	0.0016	0.0068	0.0020	0.0020	0.0066	0.0019	0.0032	0.0130	0.0036	1930	0.0457
1931	0.0013	0.0050	0.0017	0.0024	0.0093	0.0031	0.0020	0.0087	0.0022	0.0051	0.0180	0.0053	1931	0.0538
1932	0.0012	0.0063	0.0024	0.0027	0.0137	0.0067	0.0045	0.0115	0.0024	0.0037	0.0172	0.0046	1932	0.0616
1933	0.0015	0.0072	0.0018	0.0034	0.0096	0.0021	0.0018	0.0060	0.0018	0.0031	0.0100	0.0030	1933	0.0639
1934	0.0010	0.0045	0.0009	0.0019	0.0076	0.0021	0.0020	0.0069	0.0022	0.0033	0.0114	0.0031	1934	0.0446
1935	0.0011	0.0055	0.0023	0.0024	0.0086	0.0021	0.0020	0.0063	0.0018	0.0026	0.0080	0.0023	1935	0.0498
1936	0.0015	0.0056	0.0014	0.0020	0.0087	0.0028	0.0020	0.0063	0.0019	0.0025	0.0093	0.0029	1936	0.0536
1937	0.0012	0.0045	0.0017	0.0022	0.0079	0.0025	0.0019	0.0071	0.0019	0.0036	0.0146	0.0045	1937	0.0466
1938	0.0019	0.0065	0.0018	0.0035	0.0113	0.0032	0.0017	0.0048	0.0017	0.0016	0.0061	0.0024	1938	0.0483
1939	0.0015	0.0065	0.0016	0.0027	0.0110	0.0026	0.0018	0.0066	0.0027	0.0023	0.0094	0.0033	1939	0.0469
1940	0.0016	0.0066	0.0025	0.0024	0.0107	0.0043	0.0030	0.0087	0.0028	0.0028	0.0108	0.0038	1940	0.0536
1941	0.0019	0.0089	0.0030	0.0040	0.0140	0.0043	0.0030	0.0096	0.0029	0.0029	0.0137	0.0044	1941	0.0671
1942	0.0023	0.0091	0.0023	0.0037	0.0157	0.0037	0.0024	0.0093	0.0023	0.0034	0.0117	0.0032	1942	0.0679
1943	0.0020	0.0076	0.0018	0.0026	0.0104	0.0025	0.0016	0.0068	0.0025	0.0025	0.0101	0.0027	1943	0.0624
1944	0.0017	0.0068	0.0025	0.0025	0.0101	0.0032	0.0015	0.0071	0.0023	0.0023	0.0094	0.0023	1944	0.0548
1945	0.0015	0.0067	0.0021	0.0022	0.0081	0.0027	0.0020	0.0061	0.0019	0.0019	0.0072	0.0017	1945	0.0497
1946	0.0017	0.0054	0.0017	0.0017	0.0064	0.0021	0.0016	0.0056	0.0018	0.0020	0.0088	0.0027	1946	0.0409
1947	0.0020	0.0070	0.0019	0.0026	0.0103	0.0028	0.0020	0.0076	0.0026	0.0026	0.0110	0.0027	1947	0.0549
1948	0.0020	0.0082	0.0021	0.0027	0.0097	0.0024	0.0024	0.0082	0.0025	0.0032	0.0121	0.0041	1948	0.0608
1949	0.0026	0.0099	0.0027	0.0033	0.0115	0.0035	0.0028	0.0100	0.0026	0.0045	0.0162	0.0050	1949	0.0750
1950	0.0024	0.0100	0.0029	0.0035	0.0116	0.0032	0.0034	0.0118	0.0033	0.0051	0.0179	0.0051	1950	0.0877
1951	0.0025	0.0092	0.0028	0.0028	0.0107	0.0033	0.0024	0.0085	0.0021	0.0034	0.0122	0.0035	1951	0.0691
1952	0.0025	0.0083	0.0026	0.0029	0.0111	0.0029	0.0020	0.0075	0.0020	0.0029	0.0106	0.0027	1952	0.0593
1953	0.0023	0.0076	0.0023	0.0028	0.0110	0.0029	0.0021	0.0077	0.0021	0.0030	0.0114	0.0032	1953	0.0546
1954	0.0024	0.0084	0.0023	0.0026	0.0088	0.0024	0.0017	0.0065	0.0020	0.0028	0.0101	0.0026	1954	0.0621
1955	0.0017	0.0063	0.0019	0.0019	0.0068	0.0018	0.0015	0.0053	0.0016	0.0021	0.0078	0.0022	1955	0.0456
1956	0.0018	0.0066	0.0018	0.0017	0.0064	0.0018	0.0015	0.0053	0.0015	0.0015	0.0059	0.0018	1956	0.0383
1957	0.0017	0.0063	0.0018	0.0018	0.0068	0.0017	0.0017	0.0056	0.0018	0.0019	0.0071	0.0019	1957	0.0384
1958	0.0017	0.0065	0.0020	0.0019	0.0062	0.0018	0.0018	0.0057	0.0017	0.0016	0.0060	0.0015	1958	0.0438
1959	0.0014	0.0051	0.0014	0.0014	0.0050	0.0014	0.0014	0.0048	0.0013	0.0016	0.0054	0.0015	1959	0.0331
1960	0.0015	0.0056	0.0016	0.0014	0.0057	0.0016	0.0014	0.0056	0.0014	0.0017	0.0062	0.0016	1960	0.0326
1961	0.0014	0.0050	0.0014	0.0012	0.0047	0.0014	0.0014	0.0046	0.0013	0.0015	0.0054	0.0014	1961	0.0348
1962	0.0013	0.0046	0.0013	0.0013	0.0049	0.0015	0.0016	0.0055	0.0017	0.0020	0.0071	0.0018	1962	0.0298
1963	0.0014	0.0050	0.0016	0.0015	0.0050	0.0014	0.0013	0.0048	0.0014	0.0017	0.0059	0.0018	1963	0.0361
1964	0.0013	0.0048	0.0013	0.0014	0.0048	0.0014	0.0012	0.0044	0.0013	0.0015	0.0057	0.0017	1964	0.0333
1965	0.0013	0.0046	0.0013	0.0014	0.0047	0.0014	0.0013	0.0047	0.0014	0.0016	0.0056	0.0016	1965	0.0321
1966	0.0013	0.0047	0.0013	0.0015	0.0049	0.0015	0.0014	0.0053	0.0017	0.0018	0.0064	0.0017	1966	0.0311
1967	0.0016	0.0052	0.0015	0.0014	0.0048	0.0015	0.0014	0.0047	0.0014	0.0014	0.0054	0.0015	1967	0.0364
1968	0.0013	0.0051	0.0016	0.0014	0.0049	0.0014	0.0013	0.0049	0.0014	0.0015	0.0051	0.0014	1968	0.0318
1969	0.0013	0.0048	0.0014	0.0014	0.0048	0.0014	0.0014	0.0053	0.0015	0.0016	0.0056	0.0016	1969	0.0304
1970	0.0015	0.0059	0.0016	0.0016	0.0063	0.0018	0.0019	0.0064	0.0017	0.0017	0.0061	0.0016	1970	0.0341

* Compound annual return

Table A-2 (continued)

Large Company Stocks: Income Returns

From January 1971 to December 2002

Year	Jan	Feb	Mar	Apr	May	Jun	Jul	Aug	Sep	Oct	Nov	Dec	Year	Jan–Dec*
1971	0.0014	0.0050	0.0014	0.0014	0.0048	0.0014	0.0014	0.0051	0.0014	0.0014	0.0052	0.0015	1971	0.0333
1972	0.0013	0.0046	0.0013	0.0013	0.0046	0.0013	0.0013	0.0047	0.0013	0.0014	0.0048	0.0013	1972	0.0309
1973	0.0012	0.0042	0.0013	0.0013	0.0050	0.0014	0.0014	0.0049	0.0014	0.0016	0.0056	0.0018	1973	0.0286
1974	0.0015	0.0055	0.0016	0.0017	0.0063	0.0018	0.0019	0.0074	0.0024	0.0027	0.0084	0.0024	1974	0.0369
1975	0.0023	0.0075	0.0020	0.0020	0.0068	0.0019	0.0018	0.0066	0.0018	0.0020	0.0066	0.0019	1975	0.0537
1976	0.0016	0.0056	0.0019	0.0011	0.0071	0.0018	0.0012	0.0065	0.0020	0.0017	0.0069	0.0015	1976	0.0438
1977	0.0016	0.0065	0.0021	0.0012	0.0086	0.0021	0.0011	0.0078	0.0025	0.0019	0.0100	0.0020	1977	0.0431
1978	0.0019	0.0086	0.0027	0.0016	0.0094	0.0023	0.0020	0.0081	0.0024	0.0025	0.0093	0.0023	1978	0.0533
1979	0.0024	0.0081	0.0024	0.0020	0.0095	0.0023	0.0022	0.0080	0.0025	0.0030	0.0088	0.0024	1979	0.0571
1980	0.0034	0.0075	0.0031	0.0018	0.0096	0.0026	0.0026	0.0073	0.0029	0.0026	0.0072	0.0024	1980	0.0573
1981	0.0019	0.0075	0.0020	0.0022	0.0079	0.0021	0.0032	0.0066	0.0036	0.0036	0.0075	0.0036	1981	0.0489
1982	0.0012	0.0093	0.0042	0.0014	0.0104	0.0029	0.0015	0.0107	0.0034	0.0022	0.0077	0.0021	1982	0.0550
1983	0.0017	0.0070	0.0034	0.0009	0.0071	0.0030	0.0017	0.0057	0.0034	0.0018	0.0059	0.0027	1983	0.0500
1984	0.0027	0.0061	0.0036	0.0014	0.0060	0.0046	0.0022	0.0062	0.0037	0.0027	0.0050	0.0029	1984	0.0456
1985	0.0027	0.0051	0.0047	0.0014	0.0074	0.0038	0.0022	0.0059	0.0026	0.0022	0.0065	0.0016	1985	0.0510
1986	0.0020	0.0046	0.0026	0.0017	0.0047	0.0025	0.0018	0.0036	0.0032	0.0009	0.0041	0.0019	1986	0.0374
1987	0.0025	0.0044	0.0008	0.0027	0.0043	0.0020	0.0016	0.0035	0.0022	0.0024	0.0034	0.0009	1987	0.0364
1988	0.0023	0.0052	0.0031	0.0014	0.0046	0.0031	0.0014	0.0055	0.0027	0.0013	0.0047	0.0034	1988	0.0417
1989	0.0012	0.0040	0.0028	0.0015	0.0051	0.0025	0.0014	0.0038	0.0026	0.0019	0.0043	0.0022	1989	0.0385
1990	0.0017	0.0044	0.0020	0.0022	0.0055	0.0019	0.0020	0.0040	0.0020	0.0030	0.0045	0.0026	1990	0.0336
1991	0.0027	0.0043	0.0016	0.0025	0.0042	0.0022	0.0019	0.0039	0.0027	0.0015	0.0035	0.0027	1991	0.0382
1992	0.0013	0.0032	0.0022	0.0012	0.0044	0.0028	0.0009	0.0038	0.0024	0.0015	0.0034	0.0030	1992	0.0303
1993	0.0003	0.0030	0.0028	0.0009	0.0043	0.0025	0.0006	0.0037	0.0026	0.0009	0.0035	0.0022	1993	0.0283
1994	0.0010	0.0030	0.0022	0.0015	0.0039	0.0021	0.0016	0.0031	0.0028	0.0020	0.0028	0.0023	1994	0.0282
1995	0.0017	0.0027	0.0023	0.0011	0.0032	0.0022	0.0015	0.0030	0.0018	0.0015	0.0030	0.0011	1995	0.0291
1996	0.0018	0.0027	0.0017	0.0013	0.0029	0.0018	0.0012	0.0024	0.0020	0.0013	0.0025	0.0019	1996	0.0254
1997	0.0008	0.0022	0.0010	0.0013	0.0028	0.0011	0.0013	0.0018	0.0016	0.0011	0.0017	0.0014	1997	0.0211
1998	0.0009	0.0017	0.0013	0.0010	0.0016	0.0012	0.0010	0.0012	0.0017	0.0010	0.0015	0.0012	1998	0.0168
1999	0.0008	0.0012	0.0012	0.0008	0.0014	0.0011	0.0008	0.0013	0.0011	0.0007	0.0013	0.0011	1999	0.0136
2000	0.0007	0.0012	0.0011	0.0007	0.0014	0.0007	0.0007	0.0014	0.0007	0.0007	0.0012	0.0008	2000	0.0110
2001	0.0008	0.0011	0.0009	0.0009	0.0016	0.0007	0.0009	0.0015	0.0010	0.0010	0.0015	0.0012	2001	0.0118
2002	0.0010	0.0015	0.0009	0.0008	0.0017	0.0012	0.0011	0.0017	0.0013	0.0016	0.0018	0.0015	2002	0.0139

*Compound annual return

Table A-3

Large Company Stocks: Capital Appreciation Returns

from January 1926 to December 1970

Year	Jan	Feb	Mar	Apr	May	Jun	Jul	Aug	Sep	Oct	Nov	Dec	Year	Jan–Dec
1926	−0.0016	−0.0440	−0.0591	0.0227	0.0077	0.0432	0.0455	0.0171	0.0229	−0.0313	0.0223	0.0166	1926	0.0572
1927	−0.0208	0.0477	0.0065	0.0172	0.0522	−0.0094	0.0650	0.0445	0.0432	−0.0531	0.0616	0.0250	1927	0.3091
1928	−0.0051	−0.0176	0.1083	0.0324	0.0127	−0.0405	0.0125	0.0741	0.0240	0.0145	0.1199	0.0029	1928	0.3788
1929	0.0571	−0.0058	−0.0023	0.0161	−0.0428	0.1124	0.0456	0.0980	−0.0489	−0.1993	−0.1337	0.0253	1929	−0.1191
1930	0.0625	0.0215	0.0799	−0.0095	−0.0165	−0.1646	0.0367	0.0075	−0.1301	−0.0888	−0.0218	−0.0742	1930	−0.2848
1931	0.0489	0.1144	−0.0692	−0.0959	−0.1372	0.1390	−0.0742	0.0095	−0.2994	0.0844	−0.0978	−0.1453	1931	−0.4707
1932	−0.0283	0.0507	−0.1182	−0.2025	−0.2333	−0.0089	0.3770	0.3754	−0.0369	−0.1386	−0.0589	0.0519	1932	−0.1515
1933	0.0073	−0.1844	0.0336	0.4222	0.1587	0.1317	−0.0880	0.1146	−0.1136	−0.0885	0.1027	0.0223	1933	0.4659
1934	0.1059	−0.0367	−0.0009	−0.0270	−0.0813	0.0208	−0.1152	0.0541	−0.0055	−0.0319	0.0829	−0.0042	1934	−0.0594
1935	−0.0421	−0.0396	−0.0309	0.0956	0.0323	0.0679	0.0831	0.0217	0.0239	0.0751	0.0393	0.0371	1935	0.4137
1936	0.0655	0.0168	0.0254	−0.0771	0.0458	0.0306	0.0681	0.0088	0.0013	0.0750	0.0041	−0.0058	1936	0.2792
1937	0.0378	0.0146	−0.0094	−0.0831	−0.0103	−0.0529	0.1026	−0.0554	−0.1421	−0.1017	−0.1011	−0.0504	1937	−0.3859
1938	0.0133	0.0608	−0.2504	0.1412	−0.0443	0.2470	0.0727	−0.0274	0.0149	0.0760	−0.0334	0.0377	1938	0.2521
1939	−0.0689	0.0325	−0.1354	−0.0055	0.0623	−0.0638	0.1087	−0.0714	0.1646	−0.0146	−0.0491	0.0238	1939	−0.0545
1940	−0.0352	0.0066	0.0099	−0.0049	−0.2395	0.0766	0.0311	0.0262	0.0095	0.0394	−0.0424	−0.0028	1940	−0.1529
1941	−0.0482	−0.0149	0.0040	−0.0653	0.0043	0.0535	0.0548	−0.0087	−0.0097	−0.0686	−0.0421	−0.0451	1941	−0.1786
1942	0.0138	−0.0250	−0.0675	−0.0437	0.0640	0.0184	0.0313	0.0070	0.0267	0.0644	−0.0138	0.0517	1942	0.1243
1943	0.0716	0.0506	0.0527	0.0009	0.0449	0.0198	−0.0543	0.0103	0.0237	−0.0132	−0.0755	0.0590	1943	0.1945
1944	0.0154	−0.0025	0.0169	−0.0125	0.0404	0.0510	−0.0208	0.0087	−0.0031	0.0000	0.0039	0.0351	1944	0.1380
1945	0.0143	0.0616	−0.0462	0.0880	0.0115	−0.0033	−0.0201	0.0580	0.0419	0.0303	0.0324	0.0099	1945	0.3072
1946	0.0697	−0.0695	0.0463	0.0376	0.0224	−0.0391	−0.0255	−0.0729	−0.1015	−0.0080	−0.0115	0.0429	1946	−0.1187
1947	0.0235	−0.0147	−0.0169	−0.0389	−0.0089	0.0526	0.0362	−0.0279	−0.0137	0.0212	−0.0285	0.0207	1947	0.0000
1948	−0.0399	−0.0470	0.0771	0.0265	0.0782	0.0030	−0.0532	0.0076	−0.0301	0.0678	−0.1082	0.0305	1948	−0.0065
1949	0.0013	−0.0394	0.0301	−0.0212	−0.0373	−0.0021	0.0621	0.0120	0.0237	0.0295	0.0012	0.0436	1949	0.1026
1950	0.0173	0.0100	0.0041	0.0451	0.0393	−0.0580	0.0085	0.0325	0.0559	0.0041	−0.0010	0.0461	1950	0.2178
1951	0.0612	0.0065	−0.0183	0.0481	−0.0406	−0.0260	0.0687	0.0393	−0.0009	−0.0138	−0.0026	0.0389	1951	0.1646
1952	0.0156	−0.0365	0.0477	−0.0431	0.0232	0.0461	0.0176	−0.0146	−0.0196	−0.0008	0.0465	0.0355	1952	0.1178
1953	−0.0072	−0.0182	−0.0236	−0.0265	−0.0032	−0.0163	0.0253	−0.0578	0.0013	0.0510	0.0090	0.0020	1953	−0.0662
1954	0.0512	0.0027	0.0302	0.0490	0.0329	0.0007	0.0572	−0.0340	0.0831	−0.0195	0.0808	0.0508	1954	0.4502
1955	0.0181	0.0035	−0.0049	0.0377	−0.0013	0.0823	0.0607	−0.0078	0.0113	−0.0305	0.0749	−0.0007	1955	0.2640
1956	−0.0365	0.0347	0.0693	−0.0021	−0.0657	0.0392	0.0515	−0.0381	−0.0455	0.0051	−0.0110	0.0353	1956	0.0262
1957	−0.0418	−0.0326	0.0196	0.0370	0.0369	−0.0013	0.0114	−0.0561	−0.0619	−0.0321	0.0161	−0.0415	1957	−0.1431
1958	0.0428	−0.0206	0.0309	0.0318	0.0150	0.0261	0.0431	0.0119	0.0484	0.0254	0.0224	0.0520	1958	0.3806
1959	0.0038	−0.0002	0.0005	0.0388	0.0189	−0.0036	0.0349	−0.0150	−0.0456	0.0113	0.0132	0.0276	1959	0.0848
1960	−0.0715	0.0092	−0.0139	−0.0175	0.0269	0.0195	−0.0248	0.0261	−0.0604	−0.0024	0.0403	0.0463	1960	−0.0297
1961	0.0632	0.0269	0.0255	0.0038	0.0191	−0.0288	0.0328	0.0196	−0.0197	0.0283	0.0393	0.0032	1961	0.2313
1962	−0.0379	0.0163	−0.0059	−0.0620	−0.0860	−0.0818	0.0636	0.0153	−0.0482	0.0044	0.1016	0.0135	1962	−0.1181
1963	0.0491	−0.0289	0.0355	0.0485	0.0143	−0.0202	−0.0035	0.0487	−0.0110	0.0322	−0.0105	0.0244	1963	0.1889
1964	0.0269	0.0099	0.0152	0.0061	0.0115	0.0164	0.0182	−0.0162	0.0287	0.0081	−0.0052	0.0039	1964	0.1297
1965	0.0332	−0.0015	−0.0145	0.0342	−0.0077	−0.0486	0.0134	0.0225	0.0320	0.0273	−0.0088	0.0090	1965	0.0906
1966	0.0049	−0.0179	−0.0218	0.0205	−0.0541	−0.0161	−0.0135	−0.0778	−0.0070	0.0475	0.0031	−0.0015	1966	−0.1309
1967	0.0782	0.0020	0.0394	0.0422	−0.0524	0.0175	0.0453	−0.0117	0.0328	−0.0291	0.0011	0.0263	1967	0.2009
1968	−0.0438	−0.0312	0.0094	0.0819	0.0112	0.0091	−0.0185	0.0115	0.0385	0.0072	0.0480	−0.0416	1968	0.0766
1969	−0.0082	−0.0474	0.0344	0.0215	−0.0022	−0.0556	−0.0602	0.0401	−0.0250	0.0442	−0.0353	−0.0193	1969	−0.1142
1970	−0.0759	0.0527	0.0015	−0.0905	−0.0610	−0.0500	0.0733	0.0445	0.0330	−0.0114	0.0474	0.0568	1970	0.0016

* Compound annual return

Table A-3 (continued)

Large Company Stocks: Capital Appreciation Returns

from January 1971 to December 2002

Year	Jan	Feb	Mar	Apr	May	Jun	Jul	Aug	Sep	Oct	Nov	Dec	Year	Jan–Dec*
1971	0.0405	0.0091	0.0368	0.0363	−0.0416	0.0007	−0.0413	0.0361	−0.0070	−0.0418	−0.0025	0.0862	1971	0.1079
1972	0.0181	0.0253	0.0059	0.0044	0.0173	−0.0218	0.0023	0.0345	−0.0049	0.0093	0.0456	0.0118	1972	0.1563
1973	−0.0171	−0.0375	−0.0014	−0.0408	−0.0189	−0.0066	0.0380	−0.0367	0.0401	−0.0013	−0.1139	0.0166	1973	−0.1737
1974	−0.0100	−0.0036	−0.0233	−0.0391	−0.0336	−0.0147	−0.0778	−0.0903	−0.1193	0.1630	−0.0532	−0.0202	1974	−0.2972
1975	0.1228	0.0599	0.0217	0.0473	0.0441	0.0443	−0.0677	−0.0211	−0.0346	0.0616	0.0247	−0.0115	1975	0.3155
1976	0.1183	−0.0114	0.0307	−0.0110	−0.0144	0.0409	−0.0081	−0.0051	0.0226	−0.0222	−0.0078	0.0525	1976	0.1915
1977	−0.0505	−0.0217	−0.0140	0.0002	−0.0236	0.0454	−0.0162	−0.0210	−0.0025	−0.0434	0.0270	0.0028	1977	−0.1150
1978	−0.0615	−0.0248	0.0249	0.0854	0.0042	−0.0176	0.0539	0.0259	−0.0073	−0.0916	0.0166	0.0149	1978	0.0106
1979	0.0397	−0.0365	0.0551	0.0017	−0.0263	0.0387	0.0088	0.0531	0.0000	−0.0686	0.0426	0.0168	1979	0.1231
1980	0.0576	−0.0044	−0.1018	0.0411	0.0466	0.0270	0.0650	0.0058	0.0252	0.0160	0.1023	−0.0339	1980	0.2577
1981	−0.0457	0.0133	0.0360	−0.0235	−0.0017	−0.0101	−0.0025	−0.0620	−0.0538	0.0492	0.0366	−0.0301	1981	−0.0972
1982	−0.0175	−0.0605	−0.0102	0.0400	−0.0392	−0.0203	−0.0230	0.1160	0.0076	0.1104	0.0361	0.0152	1982	0.1476
1983	0.0331	0.0190	0.0331	0.0749	−0.0123	0.0352	−0.0330	0.0113	0.0102	−0.0152	0.0174	−0.0088	1983	0.1727
1984	−0.0092	−0.0389	0.0135	0.0055	−0.0594	0.0175	−0.0165	0.1063	−0.0035	−0.0001	−0.0151	0.0224	1984	0.0139
1985	0.0741	0.0086	−0.0029	−0.0046	0.0541	0.0121	−0.0048	−0.0120	−0.0347	0.0425	0.0651	0.0451	1985	0.2634
1986	0.0024	0.0715	0.0528	−0.0141	0.0502	0.0141	−0.0587	0.0712	−0.0854	0.0547	0.0215	−0.0283	1986	0.1463
1987	0.1318	0.0369	0.0264	−0.0115	0.0060	0.0479	0.0482	0.0350	−0.0242	−0.2176	−0.0853	0.0729	1987	0.0203
1988	0.0404	0.0418	−0.0333	0.0094	0.0032	0.0433	−0.0054	−0.0386	0.0397	0.0260	−0.0189	0.0147	1988	0.1241
1989	0.0711	−0.0289	0.0208	0.0501	0.0351	−0.0079	0.0884	0.0155	−0.0065	−0.0252	0.0165	0.0214	1989	0.2726
1990	−0.0688	0.0085	0.0243	−0.0269	0.0920	−0.0089	−0.0052	−0.0943	−0.0512	−0.0067	0.0599	0.0248	1990	−0.0656
1991	0.0415	0.0673	0.0222	0.0003	0.0386	−0.0479	0.0449	0.0196	−0.0191	0.0119	−0.0439	0.1116	1991	0.2631
1992	−0.0199	0.0096	−0.0218	0.0279	0.0010	−0.0174	0.0394	−0.0240	0.0091	0.0021	0.0303	0.0101	1992	0.0446
1993	0.0070	0.0105	0.0187	−0.0254	0.0227	0.0008	−0.0053	0.0344	−0.0100	0.0194	−0.0129	0.0101	1993	0.0706
1994	0.0325	−0.0300	−0.0457	0.0115	0.0124	−0.0268	0.0315	0.0376	−0.0269	0.0209	−0.0395	0.0123	1994	−0.0154
1995	0.0243	0.0361	0.0273	0.0280	0.0363	0.0213	0.0318	−0.0003	0.0401	−0.0050	0.0410	0.0174	1995	0.3411
1996	0.0326	0.0069	0.0079	0.0134	0.0229	0.0023	−0.0457	0.0188	0.0542	0.0261	0.0734	−0.0215	1996	0.2026
1997	0.0613	0.0059	−0.0426	0.0584	0.0586	0.0435	0.0781	−0.0574	0.0532	−0.0345	0.0446	0.0157	1997	0.3101
1998	0.0102	0.0704	0.0499	0.0091	−0.0188	0.0394	−0.0116	−0.1458	0.0624	0.0803	0.0591	0.0564	1998	0.2667
1999	0.0410	−0.0323	0.0388	0.0379	−0.0250	0.0544	−0.0320	−0.0063	−0.0286	0.0625	0.0191	0.0578	1999	0.1953
2000	−0.0509	−0.0201	0.0967	−0.0308	−0.0219	0.0239	−0.0163	0.0607	−0.0535	−0.0049	−0.0801	0.0041	2000	−0.1014
2001	0.0346	−0.0923	−0.0642	0.0768	0.0051	−0.0250	−0.0108	−0.0641	−0.0817	0.0181	0.0752	0.0076	2001	−0.1304
2002	−0.0156	−0.0208	0.0367	−0.0614	−0.0091	−0.0725	−0.0790	0.0049	−0.1100	0.0865	0.0571	−0.0603	2002	−0.2337

Compound annual return

Table A-4

Small Company Stocks: Total Returns

from January 1926 to December 1970

Year	Jan	Feb	Mar	Apr	May	Jun	Jul	Aug	Sep	Oct	Nov	Dec	Year	Jan–Dec*
1926	0.0699	−0.0639	−0.1073	0.0179	−0.0066	0.0378	0.0112	0.0256	−0.0001	−0.0227	0.0207	0.0332	1926	0.0028
1927	0.0296	0.0547	−0.0548	0.0573	0.0734	−0.0303	0.0516	−0.0178	0.0047	−0.0659	0.0808	0.0316	1927	0.2210
1928	0.0482	−0.0236	0.0531	0.0910	0.0438	−0.0842	0.0059	0.0442	0.0890	0.0276	0.1147	−0.0513	1928	0.3969
1929	0.0035	−0.0026	−0.0200	0.0306	−0.1336	0.0533	0.0114	−0.0164	−0.0922	−0.2768	−0.1500	−0.0501	1929	−0.5136
1930	0.1293	0.0643	0.1007	−0.0698	−0.0542	−0.2168	0.0301	−0.0166	−0.1459	−0.1097	−0.0028	−0.1166	1930	−0.3815
1931	0.2103	0.2566	−0.0708	−0.2164	−0.1379	0.1819	−0.0557	−0.0763	−0.3246	0.0770	−0.1008	−0.2195	1931	−0.4975
1932	0.1019	0.0291	−0.1311	−0.2220	−0.1193	0.0033	0.3523	0.7346	−0.1320	−0.1775	−0.1227	−0.0492	1932	−0.0539
1933	−0.0083	−0.1278	0.1118	0.5038	0.6339	0.2617	−0.0550	0.0924	−0.1595	−0.1236	0.0654	0.0055	1933	1.4287
1934	0.3891	0.0166	−0.0012	0.0240	−0.1275	−0.0024	−0.2259	0.1546	−0.0167	0.0097	0.0948	0.0172	1934	0.2422
1935	−0.0328	−0.0592	−0.1189	0.0791	−0.0024	0.0305	0.0855	0.0545	0.0357	0.0994	0.1412	0.0598	1935	0.4019
1936	0.3009	0.0602	0.0066	−0.1795	0.0272	−0.0231	0.0873	0.0210	0.0542	0.0635	0.1400	0.0160	1936	0.6480
1937	0.1267	0.0658	0.0120	−0.1679	−0.0408	−0.1183	0.1235	−0.0736	−0.2539	−0.1093	−0.1453	−0.1694	1937	−0.5801
1938	0.0534	0.0343	−0.3600	0.2776	−0.0849	0.3498	0.1499	−0.1001	−0.0157	0.2136	−0.0689	0.0487	1938	0.3280
1939	−0.0848	0.0107	−0.2466	0.0142	0.1088	−0.1042	0.2535	−0.1590	0.5145	−0.0397	−0.1053	0.0422	1939	0.0035
1940	0.0009	0.0821	0.0632	0.0654	−0.3674	0.1051	0.0231	0.0255	0.0213	0.0545	0.0245	−0.0447	1940	−0.0516
1941	0.0025	−0.0288	0.0319	−0.0669	0.0044	0.0753	0.2165	−0.0060	−0.0469	−0.0672	−0.0495	−0.1204	1941	−0.0900
1942	0.1894	−0.0073	−0.0709	−0.0353	−0.0032	0.0336	0.0737	0.0325	0.0912	0.1087	−0.0511	0.0413	1942	0.4451
1943	0.2132	0.1931	0.1445	0.0933	0.1156	−0.0083	−0.1083	−0.0002	0.0428	0.0123	−0.1113	0.1241	1943	0.8837
1944	0.0641	0.0295	0.0749	−0.0532	0.0740	0.1384	−0.0299	0.0318	−0.0020	−0.0108	0.0499	0.0869	1944	0.5372
1945	0.0482	0.1009	−0.0861	0.1157	0.0500	0.0855	−0.0556	0.0557	0.0679	0.0701	0.1172	0.0171	1945	0.7361
1946	0.1562	−0.0637	0.0273	0.0696	0.0591	−0.0462	−0.0530	−0.0849	−0.1603	−0.0118	−0.0141	0.0373	1946	−0.1163
1947	0.0421	−0.0041	−0.0336	−0.1031	−0.0534	0.0552	0.0789	−0.0037	0.0115	0.0282	−0.0303	0.0359	1947	0.0092
1948	−0.0154	−0.0783	0.0986	0.0368	0.1059	0.0048	−0.0578	0.0006	−0.0526	0.0647	−0.1116	0.0088	1948	−0.0211
1949	0.0182	−0.0481	0.0629	−0.0336	−0.0564	−0.0096	0.0671	0.0256	0.0489	0.0472	0.0016	0.0690	1949	0.1975
1950	0.0492	0.0221	−0.0037	0.0411	0.0255	−0.0777	0.0591	0.0530	0.0521	−0.0059	0.0322	0.0953	1950	0.3875
1951	0.0830	0.0061	−0.0477	0.0367	−0.0331	−0.0529	0.0373	0.0605	0.0215	−0.0222	−0.0083	0.0044	1951	0.0780
1952	0.0191	−0.0300	0.0175	−0.0519	0.0032	0.0272	0.0112	−0.0006	−0.0161	−0.0103	0.0485	0.0160	1952	0.0303
1953	0.0409	0.0269	−0.0067	−0.0287	0.0141	−0.0486	0.0152	−0.0628	−0.0262	0.0292	0.0126	−0.0266	1953	−0.0649
1954	0.0756	0.0094	0.0183	0.0140	0.0451	0.0086	0.0808	0.0014	0.0410	0.0068	0.0779	0.1112	1954	0.6058
1955	0.0201	0.0479	0.0085	0.0150	0.0078	0.0293	0.0064	−0.0028	0.0109	−0.0170	0.0468	0.0163	1955	0.2044
1956	−0.0047	0.0278	0.0431	0.0047	−0.0398	0.0056	0.0283	−0.0134	−0.0260	0.0104	0.0053	0.0038	1956	0.0428
1957	0.0236	−0.0200	0.0167	0.0248	0.0075	0.0073	−0.0060	−0.0386	−0.0452	−0.0832	0.0113	−0.0481	1957	−0.1457
1958	0.1105	−0.0170	0.0471	0.0376	0.0387	0.0324	0.0492	0.0428	0.0518	0.0407	0.0496	0.0313	1958	0.6489
1959	0.0575	0.0295	0.0027	0.0117	0.0014	−0.0042	0.0327	−0.0088	−0.0431	0.0227	0.0222	0.0322	1959	0.1640
1960	−0.0306	0.0050	−0.0315	−0.0187	0.0204	0.0340	−0.0189	0.0525	−0.0738	−0.0401	0.0437	0.0332	1960	−0.0329
1961	0.0915	0.0589	0.0619	0.0127	0.0427	−0.0543	0.0031	0.0130	−0.0339	0.0262	0.0613	0.0079	1961	0.3209
1962	0.0136	0.0187	0.0057	−0.0777	−0.1009	−0.0785	0.0763	0.0289	−0.0659	−0.0373	0.1248	−0.0089	1962	−0.1190
1963	0.0906	0.0034	0.0149	0.0312	0.0436	−0.0118	0.0033	0.0517	−0.0163	0.0236	−0.0106	−0.0048	1963	0.2357
1964	0.0274	0.0365	0.0219	0.0093	0.0157	0.0163	0.0398	−0.0029	0.0402	0.0205	0.0011	−0.0112	1964	0.2352
1965	0.0529	0.0390	0.0238	0.0509	−0.0078	−0.0901	0.0449	0.0595	0.0347	0.0572	0.0371	0.0622	1965	0.4175
1966	0.0756	0.0311	−0.0192	0.0343	−0.0961	−0.0012	−0.0012	−0.1080	−0.0164	−0.0107	0.0491	0.0065	1966	−0.0701
1967	0.1838	0.0450	0.0615	0.0271	−0.0085	0.1017	0.0951	0.0020	0.0565	−0.0311	0.0117	0.0965	1967	0.8357
1968	0.0154	−0.0709	−0.0109	0.1461	0.0999	0.0030	−0.0345	0.0367	0.0599	0.0030	0.0764	0.0062	1968	0.3597
1969	−0.0166	−0.0990	0.0396	0.0395	0.0173	−0.1165	−0.1070	0.0732	−0.0261	0.0610	−0.0557	−0.0687	1969	−0.2505
1970	−0.0608	0.0387	−0.0285	−0.1728	−0.1031	−0.0929	0.0554	0.0949	0.1086	−0.0706	0.0137	0.0726	1970	−0.1743

* Compound annual return

Table A-4 (continued)

Small Company Stocks: Total Returns

from January 1971 to December 2002

Year	Jan	Feb	Mar	Apr	May	Jun	Jul	Aug	Sep	Oct	Nov	Dec	Year	Jan–Dec*
1971	0.1592	0.0317	0.0564	0.0247	−0.0605	−0.0319	−0.0563	0.0583	−0.0226	−0.0551	−0.0373	0.1144	1971	0.1650
1972	0.1130	0.0296	−0.0143	0.0129	−0.0191	−0.0305	−0.0413	0.0186	−0.0349	−0.0175	0.0592	−0.0214	1972	0.0443
1973	−0.0432	−0.0799	−0.0208	−0.0621	−0.0811	−0.0290	0.1194	−0.0445	0.1064	0.0084	−0.1962	−0.0014	1973	−0.3090
1974	0.1326	−0.0085	−0.0074	−0.0464	−0.0793	−0.0147	−0.0219	−0.0681	−0.0653	0.1063	−0.0438	−0.0788	1974	−0.1995
1975	0.2767	0.0285	0.0618	0.0531	0.0663	0.0750	−0.0254	−0.0574	−0.0182	−0.0050	0.0320	−0.0197	1975	0.5282
1976	0.2684	0.1390	−0.0015	−0.0359	−0.0361	0.0459	0.0045	−0.0290	0.0104	−0.0209	0.0404	0.1180	1976	0.5738
1977	0.0450	−0.0039	0.0131	0.0228	−0.0028	0.0772	0.0030	−0.0107	0.0092	−0.0330	0.1086	0.0081	1977	0.2538
1978	−0.0189	0.0347	0.1032	0.0788	0.0820	−0.0189	0.0684	0.0939	−0.0032	−0.2427	0.0732	0.0168	1978	0.2346
1979	0.1321	−0.0282	0.1120	0.0387	0.0035	0.0472	0.0171	0.0756	−0.0344	−0.1154	0.0858	0.0588	1979	0.4346
1980	0.0836	−0.0284	−0.1778	0.0694	0.0750	0.0452	0.1323	0.0604	0.0418	0.0333	0.0766	−0.0338	1980	0.3988
1981	0.0207	0.0094	0.0943	0.0657	0.0422	0.0076	−0.0316	−0.0684	−0.0733	0.0742	0.0276	−0.0220	1981	0.1388
1982	−0.0196	−0.0296	−0.0086	0.0383	−0.0248	−0.0159	−0.0015	0.0698	0.0327	0.1305	0.0779	0.0132	1982	0.2801
1983	0.0628	0.0712	0.0525	0.0767	0.0870	0.0348	−0.0088	−0.0197	0.0133	−0.0568	0.0516	−0.0145	1983	0.3967
1984	−0.0008	−0.0645	0.0174	−0.0085	−0.0521	0.0300	−0.0420	0.0998	0.0027	−0.0217	−0.0336	0.0150	1984	−0.0667
1985	0.1059	0.0272	−0.0214	−0.0174	0.0276	0.0106	0.0260	−0.0072	−0.0544	0.0261	0.0620	0.0470	1985	0.2466
1986	0.0112	0.0719	0.0477	0.0064	0.0360	0.0026	−0.0710	0.0218	−0.0559	0.0346	−0.0031	−0.0262	1986	0.0685
1987	0.0943	0.0809	0.0233	−0.0313	−0.0039	0.0266	0.0364	0.0287	−0.0081	−0.2919	−0.0397	0.0520	1987	−0.0930
1988	0.0556	0.0760	0.0408	0.0209	−0.0179	0.0612	−0.0025	−0.0246	0.0227	−0.0123	−0.0437	0.0394	1988	0.2287
1989	0.0404	0.0083	0.0358	0.0279	0.0362	−0.0201	0.0407	0.0122	0.0000	−0.0604	−0.0051	−0.0134	1989	0.1018
1990	−0.0764	0.0187	0.0368	−0.0266	0.0561	0.0144	−0.0382	−0.1296	−0.0829	−0.0572	0.0450	0.0194	1990	−0.2156
1991	0.0841	0.1113	0.0680	0.0034	0.0334	−0.0485	0.0407	0.0261	0.0032	0.0317	−0.0276	0.0601	1991	0.4463
1992	0.1128	0.0452	−0.0249	−0.0403	−0.0014	−0.0519	0.0370	−0.0228	0.0131	0.0259	0.0885	0.0441	1992	0.2335
1993	0.0543	−0.0180	0.0289	−0.0306	0.0342	−0.0038	0.0166	0.0339	0.0316	0.0471	−0.0175	0.0194	1993	0.2098
1994	0.0618	−0.0023	−0.0446	0.0060	−0.0012	−0.0262	0.0184	0.0337	0.0105	0.0115	−0.0326	0.0002	1994	0.0311
1995	0.0283	0.0252	0.0145	0.0352	0.0298	0.0568	0.0645	0.0358	0.0195	−0.0487	0.0192	0.0239	1995	0.3446
1996	0.0028	0.0369	0.0228	0.0848	0.0749	−0.0582	−0.0943	0.0476	0.0291	−0.0175	0.0288	0.0204	1996	0.1762
1997	0.0420	−0.0206	−0.0490	−0.0276	0.1022	0.0498	0.0605	0.0509	0.0844	−0.0386	−0.0155	−0.0171	1997	0.2278
1998	−0.0059	0.0649	0.0481	0.0168	−0.0497	−0.0206	−0.0671	−0.2010	0.0369	0.0356	0.0758	0.0252	1998	−0.0731
1999	0.0279	−0.0687	−0.0379	0.0949	0.0387	0.0568	0.0092	−0.0191	−0.0221	−0.0087	0.0971	0.1137	1999	0.2979
2000	0.0595	0.2358	−0.0751	−0.1251	−0.0808	0.1368	−0.0322	0.0925	−0.0217	−0.0706	−0.1110	0.0189	2000	−0.0359
2001	0.1380	−0.0702	−0.0480	0.0731	0.0960	0.0359	−0.0254	−0.0295	−0.1278	0.0645	0.0674	0.0672	2001	0.2277
2002	0.0110	−0.0277	0.0884	0.0243	−0.0273	−0.0356	−0.1448	−0.0057	−0.0674	0.0257	0.0836	−0.0429	2002	−0.1328

*compound annual return

Table A-5

Long–Term Corporate Bonds: Total Returns

from January 1926 to December 1970

Year	Jan	Feb	Mar	Apr	May	Jun	Jul	Aug	Sep	Oct	Nov	Dec	Year	Jan–Dec
1926	0.0072	0.0045	0.0084	0.0097	0.0044	0.0004	0.0057	0.0044	0.0057	0.0097	0.0057	0.0056	1926	0.073
1927	0.0056	0.0069	0.0083	0.0055	-0.0011	0.0043	0.0003	0.0083	0.0149	0.0055	0.0068	0.0068	1927	0.074
1928	0.0027	0.0068	0.0041	0.0014	-0.0078	-0.0024	-0.0010	0.0083	0.0030	0.0083	-0.0036	0.0084	1928	0.028
1929	0.0043	0.0030	-0.0087	0.0019	0.0045	-0.0046	0.0020	0.0020	0.0034	0.0073	-0.0018	0.0192	1929	0.032
1930	0.0059	0.0072	0.0138	0.0084	0.0057	0.0110	0.0056	0.0136	0.0108	0.0054	-0.0012	-0.0090	1930	0.079
1931	0.0203	0.0068	0.0094	0.0067	0.0134	0.0052	0.0052	0.0012	-0.0014	-0.0363	-0.0189	-0.0286	1931	-0.018
1932	-0.0052	-0.0238	0.0356	-0.0176	0.0107	-0.0009	0.0043	0.0436	0.0301	0.0074	0.0073	0.0139	1932	0.108
1933	0.0547	-0.0523	0.0047	-0.0095	0.0588	0.0190	0.0161	0.0093	-0.0014	0.0040	-0.0248	0.0257	1933	0.103
1934	0.0257	0.0146	0.0187	0.0104	0.0090	0.0158	0.0047	0.0047	-0.0061	0.0102	0.0129	0.0101	1934	0.138
1935	0.0211	0.0141	0.0043	0.0112	0.0042	0.0112	0.0111	-0.0042	0.0000	0.0042	0.0069	0.0083	1935	0.096
1936	0.0082	0.0054	0.0082	0.0026	0.0040	0.0082	0.0011	0.0067	0.0067	0.0025	0.0109	0.0010	1936	0.067
1937	0.0024	-0.0046	-0.0114	0.0068	0.0040	0.0053	0.0039	-0.0017	0.0025	0.0067	0.0067	0.0067	1937	0.027
1938	0.0038	0.0010	-0.0087	0.0138	0.0010	0.0095	0.0066	-0.0019	0.0109	0.0080	0.0037	0.0122	1938	0.061
1939	0.0022	0.0064	0.0022	0.0064	0.0049	0.0035	-0.0007	-0.0392	0.0151	0.0237	0.0079	0.0078	1939	0.039
1940	0.0049	0.0021	0.0049	-0.0092	-0.0021	0.0121	0.0021	0.0007	0.0092	0.0049	0.0063	-0.0023	1940	0.033
1941	0.0006	0.0006	-0.0022	0.0078	0.0049	0.0063	0.0063	0.0034	0.0048	0.0034	-0.0094	0.0006	1941	0.027
1942	0.0006	-0.0008	0.0063	0.0006	0.0020	0.0034	0.0020	0.0035	0.0020	0.0006	0.0006	0.0049	1942	0.026
1943	0.0049	0.0006	0.0020	0.0049	0.0048	0.0048	0.0019	0.0019	0.0005	-0.0009	-0.0023	0.0049	1943	0.028
1944	0.0020	0.0034	0.0048	0.0034	0.0005	0.0020	0.0034	0.0034	0.0019	0.0019	0.0048	0.0149	1944	0.047
1945	0.0076	0.0046	0.0018	0.0018	-0.0011	0.0032	-0.0011	0.0004	0.0032	0.0032	0.0032	0.0133	1945	0.040
1946	0.0128	0.0034	0.0034	-0.0043	0.0019	0.0019	-0.0012	-0.0088	-0.0026	0.0020	-0.0025	0.0113	1946	0.017
1947	0.0005	0.0005	0.0067	0.0020	0.0020	0.0004	0.0020	-0.0071	-0.0131	-0.0099	-0.0098	0.0024	1947	-0.023
1948	0.0024	0.0039	0.0115	0.0038	0.0008	-0.0083	-0.0052	0.0055	0.0024	0.0024	0.0085	0.0131	1948	0.041
1949	0.0038	0.0038	0.0007	0.0023	0.0038	0.0084	0.0099	0.0037	0.0021	0.0067	0.0021	-0.0145	1949	0.033
1950	0.0037	0.0007	0.0022	-0.0008	-0.0008	0.0023	0.0069	0.0038	-0.0039	-0.0008	0.0054	0.0023	1950	0.021
1951	0.0019	-0.0044	-0.0237	-0.0009	-0.0015	-0.0093	0.0205	0.0114	-0.0057	-0.0145	-0.0061	0.0058	1951	-0.026
1952	0.0199	-0.0085	0.0076	-0.0004	0.0031	0.0016	0.0016	0.0063	-0.0018	0.0039	0.0108	-0.0091	1952	0.035
1953	-0.0080	-0.0040	-0.0033	-0.0248	-0.0030	0.0109	0.0177	-0.0085	0.0253	0.0227	-0.0073	0.0172	1953	0.034
1954	0.0124	0.0198	0.0039	-0.0034	-0.0042	0.0063	0.0040	0.0018	0.0040	0.0040	0.0025	0.0017	1954	0.053
1955	-0.0097	-0.0063	0.0092	-0.0001	-0.0018	0.0029	-0.0041	-0.0038	0.0076	0.0078	-0.0030	0.0063	1955	0.004
1956	0.0104	0.0026	-0.0146	-0.0115	0.0052	-0.0018	-0.0093	-0.0208	0.0012	-0.0105	-0.0126	-0.0082	1956	-0.068
1957	0.0197	0.0093	0.0050	-0.0066	-0.0075	-0.0322	-0.0110	-0.0009	0.0095	0.0023	0.0311	0.0685	1957	0.087
1958	0.0099	-0.0008	-0.0046	0.0163	0.0031	-0.0038	-0.0153	-0.0320	-0.0096	0.0107	0.0105	-0.0058	1958	-0.022
1959	-0.0028	0.0126	-0.0083	-0.0172	-0.0114	0.0044	0.0089	-0.0068	-0.0088	0.0165	0.0135	-0.0096	1959	-0.009
1960	0.0107	0.0128	0.0191	-0.0022	-0.0021	0.0141	0.0257	0.0117	-0.0063	0.0008	-0.0070	0.0104	1960	0.090
1961	0.0148	0.0210	-0.0029	-0.0116	0.0049	-0.0080	0.0040	-0.0018	0.0144	0.0127	0.0028	-0.0026	1961	0.048
1962	0.0080	0.0052	0.0151	0.0142	0.0000	-0.0026	-0.0015	0.0143	0.0089	0.0068	0.0062	0.0023	1962	0.079
1963	0.0059	0.0023	0.0026	-0.0051	0.0048	0.0043	0.0028	0.0035	-0.0023	0.0049	0.0015	-0.0034	1963	0.021
1964	0.0087	0.0054	-0.0062	0.0040	0.0057	0.0048	0.0052	0.0037	0.0021	0.0050	-0.0004	0.0088	1964	0.047
1965	0.0081	0.0009	0.0012	0.0021	-0.0008	0.0003	0.0019	-0.0006	-0.0015	0.0046	-0.0057	-0.0149	1965	-0.004
1966	0.0022	-0.0113	-0.0059	0.0013	-0.0026	0.0030	-0.0098	-0.0259	0.0078	0.0261	-0.0020	0.0201	1966	0.002
1967	0.0450	-0.0201	0.0117	-0.0071	-0.0254	-0.0223	0.0041	-0.0007	0.0094	-0.0281	-0.0272	0.0127	1967	-0.049
1968	0.0361	0.0037	-0.0197	0.0048	0.0032	0.0122	0.0341	0.0206	-0.0053	-0.0160	-0.0226	-0.0233	1968	0.025
1969	0.0139	-0.0160	-0.0200	0.0335	-0.0227	0.0035	0.0005	-0.0020	-0.0244	0.0127	-0.0471	-0.0134	1969	-0.080
1970	0.0141	0.0401	-0.0045	-0.0250	-0.0163	0.0001	0.0556	0.0100	0.0139	-0.0096	0.0584	0.0372	1970	0.183

* Compound annual return

Table A-5 (continued)

Long–Term Corporate Bonds: Total Returns

From January 1971 to December 2002

Year	Jan	Feb	Mar	Apr	May	Jun	Jul	Aug	Sep	Oct	Nov	Dec	Year	Jan–Dec*
1971	0.0532	–0.0366	0.0258	–0.0236	–0.0161	0.0107	–0.0025	0.0554	–0.0102	0.0282	0.0029	0.0223	1971	0.1101
1972	–0.0033	0.0107	0.0024	0.0035	0.0163	–0.0068	0.0030	0.0072	0.0031	0.0101	0.0249	–0.0004	1972	0.0726
1973	–0.0054	0.0023	0.0045	0.0061	–0.0039	–0.0056	–0.0476	0.0356	0.0356	–0.0066	0.0078	–0.0089	1973	0.0114
1974	–0.0053	0.0009	–0.0307	–0.0341	0.0105	–0.0285	–0.0211	–0.0268	0.0174	0.0885	0.0117	–0.0075	1974	–0.0306
1975	0.0596	0.0137	–0.0247	–0.0052	0.0106	0.0304	–0.0030	–0.0175	–0.0126	0.0553	–0.0088	0.0442	1975	0.1464
1976	0.0188	0.0061	0.0167	–0.0015	–0.0103	0.0150	0.0149	0.0231	0.0167	0.0070	0.0319	0.0347	1976	0.1865
1977	–0.0303	–0.0020	0.0094	0.0100	0.0106	0.0175	–0.0005	0.0136	–0.0022	–0.0038	0.0061	–0.0105	1977	0.0171
1978	–0.0089	0.0051	0.0042	–0.0023	–0.0108	0.0023	0.0101	0.0257	–0.0048	–0.0205	0.0134	–0.0133	1978	–0.0007
1979	0.0184	–0.0128	0.0106	–0.0052	0.0228	0.0269	–0.0031	0.0006	–0.0179	–0.0890	0.0222	–0.0108	1979	–0.0418
1980	–0.0645	–0.0665	–0.0062	0.1376	0.0560	0.0341	–0.0429	–0.0445	–0.0237	–0.0159	0.0017	0.0248	1980	–0.0276
1981	–0.0130	–0.0269	0.0311	–0.0769	0.0595	0.0023	–0.0372	–0.0345	–0.0199	0.0521	0.1267	–0.0580	1981	–0.0124
1982	–0.0129	0.0312	0.0306	0.0338	0.0245	–0.0468	0.0540	0.0837	0.0623	0.0759	0.0201	0.0108	1982	0.4256
1983	–0.0094	0.0428	0.0072	0.0548	–0.0324	–0.0046	–0.0455	0.0051	0.0392	–0.0025	0.0142	–0.0033	1983	0.0626
1984	0.0270	–0.0172	–0.0235	–0.0073	–0.0483	0.0199	0.0586	0.0307	0.0314	0.0572	0.0212	0.0128	1984	0.1686
1985	0.0325	–0.0373	0.0179	0.0296	0.0820	0.0083	–0.0121	0.0260	0.0071	0.0329	0.0370	0.0469	1985	0.3009
1986	0.0045	0.0752	0.0256	0.0016	–0.0164	0.0218	0.0031	0.0275	–0.0114	0.0189	0.0233	0.0117	1986	0.1985
1987	0.0216	0.0058	–0.0087	–0.0502	–0.0052	0.0155	–0.0119	–0.0075	–0.0422	0.0507	0.0125	0.0212	1987	–0.0027
1988	0.0517	0.0138	–0.0188	–0.0149	–0.0057	0.0379	–0.0111	0.0054	0.0326	0.0273	–0.0169	0.0039	1988	0.1070
1989	0.0202	–0.0129	0.0064	0.0213	0.0379	0.0395	0.0178	–0.0163	0.0040	0.0276	0.0070	0.0006	1989	0.1623
1990	–0.0191	–0.0012	–0.0011	–0.0191	0.0385	0.0216	0.0102	–0.0292	0.0091	0.0132	0.0285	0.0167	1990	0.0678
1991	0.0150	0.0121	0.0108	0.0138	0.0039	–0.0018	0.0167	0.0275	0.0271	0.0043	0.0106	0.0436	1991	0.1989
1992	–0.0173	0.0096	–0.0073	0.0016	0.0254	0.0156	0.0308	0.0090	0.0099	–0.0156	0.0069	0.0228	1992	0.0939
1993	0.0250	0.0256	0.0025	0.0052	0.0020	0.0293	0.0100	0.0287	0.0043	0.0051	–0.0188	0.0067	1993	0.1319
1994	0.0202	–0.0286	–0.0383	–0.0097	–0.0062	–0.0081	0.0309	–0.0031	–0.0265	–0.0050	0.0018	0.0157	1994	–0.0576
1995	0.0256	0.0289	0.0095	0.0175	0.0631	0.0079	–0.0101	0.0214	0.0153	0.0185	0.0242	0.0228	1995	0.2720
1996	0.0014	–0.0373	–0.0130	–0.0160	0.0005	0.0172	0.0010	–0.0070	0.0259	0.0361	0.0263	–0.0186	1996	0.0140
1997	–0.0028	0.0028	–0.0221	0.0184	0.0128	0.0187	0.0528	–0.0240	0.0226	0.0191	0.0101	0.0163	1997	0.1295
1998	0.0137	–0.0007	0.0038	0.0053	0.0167	0.0115	–0.0056	0.0089	0.0413	–0.0190	0.0270	0.0010	1998	0.1076
1999	0.0123	–0.0401	0.0002	–0.0024	–0.0176	–0.0160	–0.0113	–0.0026	0.0093	0.0047	–0.0024	–0.0102	1999	–0.0745
2000	–0.0021	0.0092	0.0169	–0.0115	–0.0161	0.0326	0.0179	0.0135	0.0046	0.0045	0.0263	0.0270	2000	0.1287
2001	0.0359	0.0127	–0.0029	–0.0128	0.0132	0.0055	0.0361	0.0156	–0.0152	0.0437	–0.0188	–0.0090	2001	0.1065
2002	0.0175	0.0130	–0.0295	0.0253	0.0113	0.0073	0.0094	0.0452	0.0330	–0.0240	0.0103	0.0361	2002	0.1633

*Compound annual return

Table A-6

Long–Term Government Bonds: Total Returns

from January 1926 to December 1970

Year	Jan	Feb	Mar	Apr	May	Jun	Jul	Aug	Sep	Oct	Nov	Dec	Year	Jan–Dec
1926	0.0138	0.0063	0.0041	0.0076	0.0014	0.0038	0.0004	0.0000	0.0038	0.0102	0.0160	0.0078	1926	0.077
1927	0.0075	0.0088	0.0253	-0.0005	0.0109	-0.0069	0.0050	0.0076	0.0018	0.0099	0.0097	0.0072	1927	0.089
1928	-0.0036	0.0061	0.0045	-0.0004	-0.0077	0.0041	-0.0217	0.0076	-0.0041	0.0158	0.0003	0.0004	1928	0.001
1929	-0.0090	-0.0157	-0.0144	0.0275	-0.0162	0.0110	0.0000	-0.0034	0.0027	0.0382	0.0236	-0.0089	1929	0.034
1930	-0.0057	0.0129	0.0083	-0.0016	0.0139	0.0051	0.0034	0.0013	0.0074	0.0035	0.0042	-0.0070	1930	0.046
1931	-0.0121	0.0085	0.0104	0.0086	0.0145	0.0004	-0.0042	0.0012	-0.0281	-0.0330	0.0027	-0.0220	1931	-0.053
1932	0.0034	0.0413	-0.0018	0.0604	-0.0188	0.0065	0.0481	0.0003	0.0057	-0.0017	0.0032	0.0131	1932	0.168
1933	0.0148	-0.0258	0.0097	-0.0032	0.0303	0.0050	-0.0017	0.0044	0.0023	-0.0091	-0.0149	-0.0113	1933	-0.000
1934	0.0257	0.0081	0.0197	0.0126	0.0131	0.0067	0.0040	-0.0118	-0.0146	0.0182	0.0037	0.0112	1934	0.100
1935	0.0182	0.0092	0.0041	0.0079	-0.0057	0.0092	0.0046	-0.0133	0.0009	0.0061	0.0010	0.0070	1935	0.049
1936	0.0055	0.0081	0.0106	0.0035	0.0040	0.0021	0.0060	0.0111	-0.0031	0.0006	0.0205	0.0038	1936	0.075
1937	-0.0013	0.0086	-0.0411	0.0039	0.0053	-0.0018	0.0138	-0.0104	0.0045	0.0042	0.0096	0.0082	1937	0.002
1938	0.0057	0.0052	-0.0037	0.0210	0.0044	0.0004	0.0043	0.0000	0.0022	0.0087	-0.0022	0.0080	1938	0.055
1939	0.0059	0.0080	0.0125	0.0118	0.0171	-0.0027	0.0113	-0.0201	-0.0545	0.0410	0.0162	0.0145	1939	0.059
1940	-0.0017	0.0027	0.0177	-0.0035	-0.0299	0.0258	0.0052	0.0028	0.0110	0.0031	0.0205	0.0067	1940	0.060
1941	-0.0201	0.0020	0.0096	0.0129	0.0027	0.0066	0.0022	0.0018	-0.0012	0.0140	-0.0029	-0.0177	1941	0.009
1942	0.0069	0.0011	0.0092	-0.0029	0.0075	0.0003	0.0018	0.0038	0.0003	0.0024	-0.0035	0.0049	1942	0.032
1943	0.0033	-0.0005	0.0009	0.0048	0.0050	0.0018	-0.0001	0.0021	0.0011	0.0005	0.0000	0.0018	1943	0.020
1944	0.0021	0.0032	0.0021	0.0013	0.0028	0.0008	0.0036	0.0027	0.0014	0.0012	0.0024	0.0042	1944	0.028
1945	0.0127	0.0077	0.0021	0.0160	0.0056	0.0169	-0.0086	0.0026	0.0054	0.0104	0.0125	0.0194	1945	0.107
1946	0.0025	0.0032	0.0010	-0.0135	-0.0012	0.0070	-0.0040	-0.0111	-0.0009	0.0074	-0.0054	0.0145	1946	-0.001
1947	-0.0006	0.0021	0.0020	-0.0037	0.0033	0.0010	0.0063	0.0081	-0.0044	-0.0037	-0.0174	-0.0192	1947	-0.026
1948	0.0020	0.0046	0.0034	0.0045	0.0141	-0.0084	-0.0021	0.0001	0.0014	0.0007	0.0076	0.0056	1948	0.034
1949	0.0082	0.0049	0.0074	0.0011	0.0019	0.0167	0.0033	0.0111	-0.0011	0.0019	0.0021	0.0052	1949	0.064
1950	-0.0061	0.0021	0.0008	0.0030	0.0033	-0.0025	0.0055	0.0014	-0.0072	-0.0048	0.0035	0.0016	1950	0.000
1951	0.0058	-0.0074	-0.0157	-0.0063	-0.0069	-0.0062	0.0138	0.0099	-0.0080	0.0010	-0.0136	-0.0061	1951	-0.039
1952	0.0028	0.0014	0.0111	0.0171	-0.0033	0.0003	-0.0020	-0.0070	-0.0130	0.0148	-0.0015	-0.0086	1952	0.011
1953	0.0012	-0.0087	-0.0088	-0.0105	-0.0148	0.0223	0.0039	-0.0008	0.0299	0.0074	-0.0049	0.0206	1953	0.036
1954	0.0089	0.0240	0.0058	0.0104	-0.0087	0.0163	0.0134	-0.0036	-0.0010	0.0006	-0.0025	0.0064	1954	0.071
1955	-0.0241	-0.0078	0.0087	0.0001	0.0073	-0.0076	-0.0102	0.0004	0.0073	0.0144	-0.0045	0.0037	1955	-0.012
1956	0.0083	-0.0002	-0.0149	-0.0113	0.0225	0.0027	-0.0209	-0.0187	0.0050	-0.0054	-0.0057	-0.0179	1956	-0.055
1957	0.0346	0.0025	-0.0024	-0.0222	-0.0023	-0.0180	-0.0041	0.0002	0.0076	-0.0050	0.0533	0.0307	1957	0.074
1958	-0.0084	0.0100	0.0102	0.0186	0.0001	-0.0160	-0.0278	-0.0435	-0.0117	0.0138	0.0120	-0.0181	1958	-0.060
1959	-0.0080	0.0117	0.0017	-0.0117	-0.0005	0.0010	0.0060	-0.0041	-0.0057	0.0150	-0.0119	-0.0159	1959	-0.022
1960	0.0112	0.0204	0.0282	-0.0170	0.0152	0.0173	0.0368	-0.0067	0.0075	-0.0028	-0.0066	0.0279	1960	0.137
1961	-0.0107	0.0200	-0.0037	0.0115	-0.0046	-0.0075	0.0035	-0.0038	0.0129	0.0071	-0.0020	-0.0125	1961	0.009
1962	-0.0014	0.0103	0.0253	0.0082	0.0046	-0.0076	-0.0109	0.0187	0.0061	0.0084	0.0021	0.0035	1962	0.068
1963	-0.0001	0.0008	0.0009	-0.0012	0.0023	0.0019	0.0031	0.0021	0.0004	-0.0026	0.0051	-0.0006	1963	0.012
1964	-0.0014	-0.0011	0.0037	0.0047	0.0050	0.0069	0.0008	0.0020	0.0050	0.0043	0.0017	0.0030	1964	0.035
1965	0.0040	0.0014	0.0054	0.0036	0.0018	0.0047	0.0022	-0.0013	-0.0034	0.0027	-0.0062	-0.0078	1965	0.007
1966	-0.0104	-0.0250	0.0296	-0.0063	-0.0059	-0.0016	-0.0037	-0.0206	0.0332	0.0228	-0.0148	0.0413	1966	0.036
1967	0.0154	-0.0221	0.0198	-0.0291	-0.0039	-0.0312	0.0068	-0.0084	-0.0004	-0.0400	-0.0196	0.0192	1967	-0.091
1968	0.0328	-0.0033	-0.0212	0.0227	0.0043	0.0230	0.0289	-0.0003	-0.0102	-0.0132	-0.0269	-0.0363	1968	-0.002
1969	-0.0206	0.0042	0.0010	0.0427	-0.0490	0.0214	0.0079	-0.0069	-0.0531	0.0365	-0.0243	-0.0068	1969	-0.050
1970	-0.0021	0.0587	-0.0068	-0.0413	-0.0468	0.0486	0.0319	-0.0019	0.0228	-0.0109	0.0791	-0.0084	1970	0.121

* Compound annual return

Table A-6 (continued)

Long–Term Government Bonds: Total Returns

from January 1971 to December 2002

Year	Jan	Feb	Mar	Apr	May	Jun	Jul	Aug	Sep	Oct	Nov	Dec	Year	Jan–Dec*
1971	0.0506	−0.0163	0.0526	−0.0283	−0.0006	−0.0159	0.0030	0.0471	0.0204	0.0167	−0.0047	0.0044	1971	0.1323
1972	−0.0063	0.0088	−0.0082	0.0027	0.0270	−0.0065	0.0216	0.0029	−0.0083	0.0234	0.0226	−0.0229	1972	0.0569
1973	−0.0321	0.0014	0.0082	0.0046	−0.0105	−0.0021	−0.0433	0.0391	0.0318	0.0215	−0.0183	−0.0082	1973	−0.0111
1974	−0.0083	−0.0024	−0.0292	−0.0253	0.0123	0.0045	−0.0029	−0.0232	0.0247	0.0489	0.0295	0.0171	1974	0.0435
1975	0.0225	0.0131	−0.0267	−0.0182	0.0212	0.0292	−0.0087	−0.0068	−0.0098	0.0475	−0.0109	0.0390	1975	0.0920
1976	0.0090	0.0062	0.0166	0.0018	−0.0158	0.0208	0.0078	0.0211	0.0145	0.0084	0.0339	0.0327	1976	0.1675
1977	−0.0388	−0.0049	0.0091	0.0071	0.0125	0.0164	−0.0070	0.0198	−0.0029	−0.0093	0.0093	−0.0168	1977	−0.0069
1978	−0.0080	0.0004	−0.0021	−0.0005	−0.0058	−0.0062	0.0143	0.0218	−0.0106	−0.0200	0.0189	−0.0130	1978	−0.0118
1979	0.0191	−0.0135	0.0129	−0.0112	0.0261	0.0311	−0.0085	−0.0035	−0.0122	−0.0841	0.0311	0.0057	1979	−0.0123
1980	−0.0741	−0.0467	−0.0315	0.1523	0.0419	0.0359	−0.0476	−0.0432	−0.0262	−0.0263	0.0100	0.0352	1980	−0.0395
1981	−0.0115	−0.0435	0.0384	−0.0518	0.0622	−0.0179	−0.0353	−0.0386	−0.0145	0.0829	0.1410	−0.0713	1981	0.0186
1982	0.0046	0.0182	0.0231	0.0373	0.0034	−0.0223	0.0501	0.0781	0.0618	0.0634	−0.0002	0.0312	1982	0.4036
1983	−0.0309	0.0492	−0.0094	0.0350	−0.0386	0.0039	−0.0486	0.0020	0.0505	−0.0132	0.0183	−0.0059	1983	0.0065
1984	0.0244	−0.0178	−0.0156	−0.0105	−0.0516	0.0150	0.0693	0.0266	0.0342	0.0561	0.0118	0.0091	1984	0.1548
1985	0.0364	−0.0493	0.0307	0.0242	0.0896	0.0142	−0.0180	0.0259	−0.0021	0.0338	0.0401	0.0541	1985	0.3097
1986	−0.0025	0.1145	0.0770	−0.0080	−0.0505	0.0613	−0.0108	0.0499	−0.0500	0.0289	0.0267	−0.0018	1986	0.2453
1987	0.0161	0.0202	−0.0223	−0.0473	−0.0105	0.0098	−0.0178	−0.0165	−0.0369	0.0623	0.0037	0.0165	1987	−0.0271
1988	0.0666	0.0052	−0.0307	−0.0160	−0.0102	0.0368	−0.0170	0.0058	0.0345	0.0308	−0.0196	0.0110	1988	0.0967
1989	0.0203	−0.0179	0.0122	0.0159	0.0401	0.0550	0.0238	−0.0259	0.0019	0.0379	0.0078	−0.0006	1989	0.1811
1990	−0.0343	−0.0025	−0.0044	−0.0202	0.0415	0.0230	0.0107	−0.0419	0.0117	0.0215	0.0402	0.0187	1990	0.0618
1991	0.0130	0.0030	0.0038	0.0140	0.0000	−0.0063	0.0157	0.0340	0.0303	0.0054	0.0082	0.0581	1991	0.1930
1992	−0.0324	0.0051	−0.0094	0.0016	0.0243	0.0200	0.0398	0.0067	0.0185	−0.0198	0.0010	0.0246	1992	0.0805
1993	0.0280	0.0354	0.0021	0.0072	0.0047	0.0449	0.0191	0.0434	0.0005	0.0096	−0.0259	0.0020	1993	0.1824
1994	0.0257	−0.0450	−0.0395	−0.0150	−0.0082	−0.0100	0.0363	−0.0086	−0.0331	−0.0025	0.0066	0.0161	1994	−0.0777
1995	0.0273	0.0287	0.0091	0.0169	0.0790	0.0139	−0.0168	0.0236	0.0175	0.0294	0.0249	0.0272	1995	0.3167
1996	−0.0011	−0.0483	−0.0210	−0.0165	−0.0054	0.0203	0.0018	−0.0139	0.0290	0.0404	0.0351	−0.0256	1996	−0.0093
1997	−0.0079	0.0005	−0.0252	0.0255	0.0097	0.0195	0.0626	−0.0317	0.0316	0.0341	0.0148	0.0184	1997	0.1585
1998	0.0200	−0.0072	0.0025	0.0026	0.0182	0.0228	−0.0040	0.0465	0.0395	−0.0218	0.0097	−0.0032	1998	0.1306
1999	0.0121	−0.0520	−0.0008	0.0021	−0.0185	−0.0078	−0.0077	−0.0053	0.0084	−0.0012	−0.0061	−0.0155	1999	−0.0896
2000	0.0228	0.0264	0.0367	−0.0076	−0.0054	0.0244	0.0173	0.0240	−0.0157	0.0187	0.0319	0.0243	2000	0.2148
2001	0.0005	0.0191	−0.0074	−0.0313	0.0037	0.0085	0.0376	0.0206	0.0081	0.0464	−0.0471	−0.0183	2001	0.0370
2002	0.0138	0.0115	−0.0436	0.0410	0.0015	0.0187	0.0303	0.0464	0.0417	−0.0294	−0.0122	0.0507	2002	0.1784

* Compound annual return

Table A-7

Long–Term Government Bonds: Income Returns

from January 1926 to December 1970

Year	Jan	Feb	Mar	Apr	May	Jun	Jul	Aug	Sep	Oct	Nov	Dec	Year	Jan–Dec*
1926	0.0031	0.0028	0.0032	0.0030	0.0028	0.0033	0.0031	0.0031	0.0030	0.0030	0.0031	0.0030	1926	0.0373
1927	0.0030	0.0027	0.0029	0.0027	0.0028	0.0027	0.0027	0.0029	0.0027	0.0028	0.0027	0.0027	1927	0.0341
1928	0.0027	0.0025	0.0027	0.0026	0.0027	0.0027	0.0027	0.0029	0.0027	0.0030	0.0027	0.0029	1928	0.0322
1929	0.0029	0.0027	0.0028	0.0034	0.0030	0.0029	0.0032	0.0030	0.0032	0.0031	0.0026	0.0031	1929	0.0347
1930	0.0029	0.0026	0.0029	0.0027	0.0027	0.0029	0.0028	0.0026	0.0029	0.0027	0.0026	0.0028	1930	0.0332
1931	0.0028	0.0026	0.0029	0.0027	0.0026	0.0028	0.0027	0.0027	0.0027	0.0029	0.0031	0.0032	1931	0.0333
1932	0.0032	0.0032	0.0031	0.0030	0.0028	0.0028	0.0028	0.0028	0.0026	0.0027	0.0026	0.0027	1932	0.0369
1933	0.0027	0.0023	0.0027	0.0025	0.0028	0.0025	0.0026	0.0026	0.0025	0.0026	0.0025	0.0028	1933	0.0312
1934	0.0029	0.0024	0.0027	0.0025	0.0025	0.0024	0.0024	0.0024	0.0023	0.0027	0.0025	0.0025	1934	0.0318
1935	0.0025	0.0021	0.0022	0.0023	0.0023	0.0022	0.0024	0.0023	0.0023	0.0023	0.0024	0.0024	1935	0.0281
1936	0.0024	0.0023	0.0024	0.0022	0.0022	0.0024	0.0023	0.0023	0.0021	0.0023	0.0022	0.0022	1936	0.0277
1937	0.0021	0.0020	0.0022	0.0023	0.0022	0.0025	0.0024	0.0023	0.0023	0.0023	0.0024	0.0023	1937	0.0266
1938	0.0023	0.0021	0.0023	0.0022	0.0022	0.0021	0.0021	0.0022	0.0021	0.0022	0.0021	0.0022	1938	0.0264
1939	0.0021	0.0019	0.0021	0.0019	0.0020	0.0018	0.0019	0.0018	0.0019	0.0023	0.0020	0.0019	1939	0.0240
1940	0.0020	0.0018	0.0019	0.0018	0.0019	0.0019	0.0020	0.0019	0.0018	0.0018	0.0018	0.0017	1940	0.0223
1941	0.0016	0.0016	0.0018	0.0017	0.0017	0.0016	0.0016	0.0016	0.0016	0.0016	0.0014	0.0016	1941	0.0194
1942	0.0021	0.0019	0.0021	0.0020	0.0019	0.0021	0.0021	0.0021	0.0020	0.0021	0.0020	0.0021	1942	0.0246
1943	0.0020	0.0019	0.0021	0.0020	0.0019	0.0021	0.0021	0.0021	0.0020	0.0020	0.0021	0.0021	1943	0.0244
1944	0.0021	0.0020	0.0021	0.0020	0.0022	0.0020	0.0021	0.0021	0.0020	0.0021	0.0020	0.0020	1944	0.0246
1945	0.0021	0.0018	0.0020	0.0019	0.0019	0.0019	0.0018	0.0019	0.0018	0.0019	0.0018	0.0018	1945	0.0234
1946	0.0017	0.0015	0.0016	0.0017	0.0018	0.0016	0.0019	0.0017	0.0018	0.0019	0.0018	0.0019	1946	0.0204
1947	0.0018	0.0016	0.0018	0.0017	0.0017	0.0019	0.0018	0.0017	0.0018	0.0018	0.0017	0.0021	1947	0.0213
1948	0.0020	0.0019	0.0022	0.0020	0.0018	0.0021	0.0019	0.0021	0.0020	0.0019	0.0021	0.0020	1948	0.0240
1949	0.0020	0.0018	0.0019	0.0018	0.0020	0.0019	0.0017	0.0019	0.0017	0.0018	0.0017	0.0017	1949	0.0225
1950	0.0018	0.0016	0.0018	0.0016	0.0019	0.0017	0.0018	0.0018	0.0017	0.0019	0.0018	0.0018	1950	0.0212
1951	0.0020	0.0017	0.0019	0.0020	0.0021	0.0020	0.0023	0.0021	0.0019	0.0023	0.0021	0.0022	1951	0.0238
1952	0.0023	0.0021	0.0023	0.0022	0.0020	0.0022	0.0022	0.0021	0.0023	0.0023	0.0021	0.0024	1952	0.0266
1953	0.0023	0.0021	0.0025	0.0024	0.0024	0.0027	0.0025	0.0025	0.0025	0.0023	0.0024	0.0024	1953	0.0284
1954	0.0023	0.0022	0.0025	0.0022	0.0020	0.0025	0.0022	0.0023	0.0022	0.0021	0.0023	0.0023	1954	0.0279
1955	0.0022	0.0022	0.0024	0.0022	0.0025	0.0023	0.0023	0.0027	0.0024	0.0025	0.0024	0.0024	1955	0.0275
1956	0.0025	0.0023	0.0023	0.0026	0.0026	0.0023	0.0026	0.0026	0.0025	0.0029	0.0027	0.0028	1956	0.0299
1957	0.0029	0.0025	0.0026	0.0029	0.0029	0.0025	0.0033	0.0030	0.0031	0.0031	0.0029	0.0029	1957	0.0344
1958	0.0027	0.0025	0.0027	0.0026	0.0024	0.0027	0.0027	0.0027	0.0032	0.0032	0.0028	0.0033	1958	0.0327
1959	0.0031	0.0031	0.0035	0.0033	0.0033	0.0036	0.0035	0.0035	0.0034	0.0035	0.0035	0.0036	1959	0.0401
1960	0.0035	0.0037	0.0036	0.0032	0.0037	0.0034	0.0032	0.0034	0.0032	0.0033	0.0032	0.0033	1960	0.0426
1961	0.0033	0.0030	0.0031	0.0031	0.0034	0.0032	0.0033	0.0033	0.0032	0.0034	0.0032	0.0031	1961	0.0383
1962	0.0037	0.0032	0.0033	0.0033	0.0032	0.0030	0.0034	0.0034	0.0030	0.0035	0.0031	0.0032	1962	0.0400
1963	0.0032	0.0029	0.0031	0.0034	0.0033	0.0030	0.0036	0.0033	0.0034	0.0034	0.0032	0.0036	1963	0.0389
1964	0.0035	0.0032	0.0037	0.0035	0.0032	0.0038	0.0035	0.0035	0.0034	0.0034	0.0035	0.0035	1964	0.0415
1965	0.0033	0.0032	0.0038	0.0033	0.0033	0.0038	0.0034	0.0037	0.0035	0.0034	0.0037	0.0037	1965	0.0419
1966	0.0038	0.0034	0.0040	0.0036	0.0041	0.0039	0.0038	0.0043	0.0041	0.0040	0.0038	0.0039	1966	0.0449
1967	0.0040	0.0034	0.0039	0.0035	0.0043	0.0039	0.0043	0.0042	0.0040	0.0045	0.0045	0.0044	1967	0.0459
1968	0.0050	0.0042	0.0043	0.0049	0.0046	0.0042	0.0048	0.0042	0.0044	0.0045	0.0043	0.0049	1968	0.0550
1969	0.0050	0.0046	0.0047	0.0055	0.0047	0.0055	0.0052	0.0048	0.0055	0.0057	0.0049	0.0060	1969	0.0595
1970	0.0056	0.0052	0.0056	0.0054	0.0055	0.0064	0.0059	0.0057	0.0056	0.0055	0.0058	0.0053	1970	0.0674

* Compound annual return

Table A-7 (continued)

Long–Term Government Bonds: Income Returns

From January 1971 to December 2002

Year	Jan	Feb	Mar	Apr	May	Jun	Jul	Aug	Sep	Oct	Nov	Dec	Year	Jan–Dec*
1971	0.0051	0.0046	0.0056	0.0048	0.0047	0.0056	0.0052	0.0055	0.0049	0.0047	0.0051	0.0050	1971	0.0632
1972	0.0050	0.0047	0.0049	0.0048	0.0055	0.0049	0.0051	0.0049	0.0047	0.0052	0.0048	0.0045	1972	0.0587
1973	0.0054	0.0051	0.0056	0.0057	0.0058	0.0055	0.0061	0.0062	0.0055	0.0063	0.0056	0.0060	1973	0.0651
1974	0.0061	0.0055	0.0058	0.0068	0.0068	0.0061	0.0072	0.0065	0.0071	0.0070	0.0062	0.0067	1974	0.0727
1975	0.0068	0.0060	0.0066	0.0067	0.0067	0.0070	0.0068	0.0065	0.0073	0.0072	0.0061	0.0074	1975	0.0799
1976	0.0065	0.0060	0.0071	0.0064	0.0059	0.0073	0.0065	0.0069	0.0064	0.0061	0.0066	0.0063	1976	0.0789
1977	0.0059	0.0057	0.0065	0.0061	0.0067	0.0062	0.0059	0.0067	0.0061	0.0063	0.0063	0.0062	1977	0.0714
1978	0.0069	0.0060	0.0069	0.0063	0.0075	0.0069	0.0073	0.0070	0.0065	0.0073	0.0071	0.0068	1978	0.0790
1979	0.0079	0.0065	0.0074	0.0076	0.0077	0.0071	0.0076	0.0073	0.0068	0.0082	0.0083	0.0083	1979	0.0886
1980	0.0083	0.0084	0.0099	0.0100	0.0087	0.0086	0.0084	0.0081	0.0097	0.0097	0.0091	0.0108	1980	0.0997
1981	0.0094	0.0088	0.0111	0.0101	0.0104	0.0109	0.0109	0.0110	0.0114	0.0117	0.0113	0.0100	1981	0.1155
1982	0.0108	0.0103	0.0124	0.0112	0.0101	0.0120	0.0114	0.0112	0.0100	0.0091	0.0094	0.0093	1982	0.1350
1983	0.0087	0.0081	0.0089	0.0085	0.0091	0.0090	0.0088	0.0103	0.0096	0.0095	0.0094	0.0094	1983	0.1038
1984	0.0103	0.0092	0.0098	0.0104	0.0103	0.0106	0.0116	0.0106	0.0094	0.0108	0.0091	0.0098	1984	0.1174
1985	0.0096	0.0082	0.0094	0.0102	0.0097	0.0080	0.0094	0.0085	0.0088	0.0089	0.0081	0.0086	1985	0.1125
1986	0.0079	0.0073	0.0071	0.0063	0.0062	0.0070	0.0066	0.0063	0.0065	0.0069	0.0059	0.0070	1986	0.0898
1987	0.0064	0.0059	0.0066	0.0065	0.0066	0.0075	0.0073	0.0075	0.0075	0.0079	0.0075	0.0078	1987	0.0792
1988	0.0072	0.0071	0.0072	0.0070	0.0078	0.0076	0.0071	0.0083	0.0076	0.0076	0.0070	0.0075	1988	0.0897
1989	0.0080	0.0069	0.0079	0.0070	0.0080	0.0070	0.0068	0.0066	0.0065	0.0072	0.0064	0.0064	1989	0.0881
1990	0.0073	0.0066	0.0071	0.0075	0.0075	0.0068	0.0074	0.0071	0.0069	0.0081	0.0071	0.0072	1990	0.0819
1991	0.0071	0.0064	0.0064	0.0076	0.0068	0.0063	0.0076	0.0068	0.0068	0.0065	0.0060	0.0068	1991	0.0822
1992	0.0061	0.0059	0.0067	0.0065	0.0061	0.0067	0.0063	0.0060	0.0058	0.0057	0.0061	0.0063	1992	0.0726
1993	0.0059	0.0055	0.0063	0.0057	0.0052	0.0062	0.0054	0.0056	0.0050	0.0049	0.0053	0.0055	1993	0.0717
1994	0.0055	0.0049	0.0058	0.0057	0.0063	0.0061	0.0060	0.0066	0.0061	0.0066	0.0064	0.0066	1994	0.0659
1995	0.0070	0.0059	0.0064	0.0058	0.0065	0.0054	0.0056	0.0057	0.0052	0.0057	0.0051	0.0049	1995	0.0760
1996	0.0054	0.0048	0.0052	0.0059	0.0058	0.0054	0.0062	0.0057	0.0060	0.0058	0.0052	0.0056	1996	0.0618
1997	0.0056	0.0051	0.0059	0.0059	0.0059	0.0057	0.0058	0.0049	0.0058	0.0054	0.0047	0.0054	1997	0.0664
1998	0.0048	0.0044	0.0052	0.0049	0.0048	0.0052	0.0049	0.0048	0.0044	0.0042	0.0045	0.0045	1998	0.0583
1999	0.0042	0.0040	0.0053	0.0048	0.0045	0.0055	0.0053	0.0053	0.0052	0.0050	0.0056	0.0055	1999	0.0557
2000	0.0057	0.0051	0.0054	0.0047	0.0056	0.0052	0.0052	0.0050	0.0046	0.0053	0.0048	0.0045	2000	0.0650
2001	0.0049	0.0042	0.0045	0.0047	0.0050	0.0047	0.0052	0.0046	0.0041	0.0048	0.0041	0.0046	2001	0.0553
2002	0.0048	0.0043	0.0043	0.0054	0.0049	0.0044	0.0051	0.0044	0.0042	0.0040	0.0040	0.0045	2002	0.0559

*Compound annual return

Table A-8

Long–Term Government Bonds: Capital Appreciation Returns

from January 1926 to December 1970

Year	Jan	Feb	Mar	Apr	May	Jun	Jul	Aug	Sep	Oct	Nov	Dec	Year	Jan–Dec
1926	0.0106	0.0035	0.0009	0.0046	−0.0014	0.0005	−0.0027	−0.0031	0.0007	0.0072	0.0129	0.0048	1926	0.039
1927	0.0045	0.0061	0.0224	−0.0032	0.0081	−0.0096	0.0022	0.0047	−0.0009	0.0071	0.0071	0.0045	1927	0.054
1928	−0.0063	0.0036	0.0019	−0.0029	−0.0104	0.0015	−0.0245	0.0047	−0.0067	0.0128	−0.0024	−0.0024	1928	−0.031
1929	−0.0119	−0.0183	−0.0171	0.0242	−0.0192	0.0081	−0.0032	−0.0064	−0.0004	0.0351	0.0211	−0.0120	1929	−0.002
1930	−0.0086	0.0102	0.0055	−0.0043	0.0113	0.0022	0.0007	−0.0013	0.0045	0.0008	0.0017	−0.0098	1930	0.012
1931	−0.0149	0.0059	0.0076	0.0059	0.0119	−0.0024	−0.0069	−0.0015	−0.0307	−0.0360	−0.0004	−0.0252	1931	−0.084
1932	0.0002	0.0382	−0.0049	0.0574	−0.0216	0.0037	0.0453	−0.0025	0.0031	−0.0044	0.0006	0.0104	1932	0.129
1933	0.0122	−0.0282	0.0070	−0.0057	0.0274	0.0025	−0.0043	0.0018	−0.0002	−0.0117	−0.0174	−0.0140	1933	−0.031
1934	0.0228	0.0057	0.0170	0.0101	0.0106	0.0043	0.0016	−0.0143	−0.0169	0.0155	0.0013	0.0087	1934	0.067
1935	0.0157	0.0070	0.0019	0.0056	−0.0079	0.0070	0.0022	−0.0156	−0.0014	0.0038	−0.0014	0.0047	1935	0.021
1936	0.0031	0.0059	0.0083	0.0013	0.0019	−0.0003	0.0037	0.0088	−0.0053	−0.0017	0.0183	0.0017	1936	0.046
1937	−0.0034	0.0067	−0.0433	0.0016	0.0031	−0.0043	0.0114	−0.0128	0.0022	0.0019	0.0072	0.0059	1937	−0.024
1938	0.0034	0.0031	−0.0059	0.0187	0.0022	−0.0016	0.0022	−0.0022	0.0001	0.0065	−0.0043	0.0059	1938	0.028
1939	0.0038	0.0061	0.0105	0.0099	0.0151	−0.0045	0.0095	−0.0219	−0.0564	0.0386	0.0142	0.0125	1939	0.034
1940	−0.0037	0.0009	0.0158	−0.0053	−0.0318	0.0239	0.0032	0.0009	0.0092	0.0013	0.0187	0.0050	1940	0.037
1941	−0.0217	0.0004	0.0078	0.0112	0.0011	0.0050	0.0005	0.0002	−0.0028	0.0124	−0.0044	−0.0194	1941	−0.010
1942	0.0048	−0.0008	0.0071	−0.0049	0.0056	−0.0018	−0.0003	0.0017	−0.0016	0.0004	−0.0055	0.0028	1942	0.007
1943	0.0013	−0.0024	−0.0012	0.0028	0.0031	−0.0003	−0.0021	0.0000	−0.0009	−0.0015	−0.0021	−0.0003	1943	−0.003
1944	0.0000	0.0012	0.0000	−0.0006	0.0006	−0.0012	0.0015	0.0006	−0.0006	−0.0009	0.0003	0.0022	1944	0.003
1945	0.0105	0.0058	0.0001	0.0141	0.0037	0.0150	−0.0104	0.0007	0.0037	0.0085	0.0108	0.0177	1945	0.082
1946	0.0008	0.0017	−0.0006	−0.0152	−0.0030	0.0054	−0.0058	−0.0129	−0.0028	0.0055	−0.0072	0.0126	1946	−0.021
1947	−0.0024	0.0005	0.0002	−0.0054	0.0016	−0.0009	0.0044	0.0064	−0.0062	−0.0055	−0.0191	−0.0213	1947	−0.047
1948	0.0000	0.0028	0.0013	0.0025	0.0123	−0.0105	−0.0041	−0.0019	−0.0006	−0.0012	0.0055	0.0036	1948	0.009
1949	0.0062	0.0031	0.0055	−0.0006	0.0000	0.0148	0.0016	0.0092	−0.0029	0.0001	0.0004	0.0035	1949	0.041
1950	−0.0080	0.0005	−0.0010	0.0014	0.0014	−0.0042	0.0037	−0.0004	−0.0089	−0.0067	0.0017	−0.0001	1950	−0.020
1951	0.0038	−0.0091	−0.0176	−0.0083	−0.0090	−0.0082	0.0116	0.0077	−0.0098	−0.0012	−0.0157	−0.0083	1951	−0.062
1952	0.0005	−0.0007	0.0088	0.0149	−0.0054	−0.0019	−0.0041	−0.0091	−0.0153	0.0124	−0.0036	−0.0110	1952	−0.014
1953	−0.0011	−0.0108	−0.0113	−0.0129	−0.0171	0.0195	0.0014	−0.0033	0.0275	0.0051	−0.0073	0.0182	1953	0.006
1954	0.0066	0.0218	0.0034	0.0081	−0.0107	0.0138	0.0113	−0.0059	−0.0031	−0.0015	−0.0048	0.0042	1954	0.043
1955	−0.0264	−0.0100	0.0063	−0.0022	0.0048	−0.0099	−0.0125	−0.0022	0.0049	0.0119	−0.0069	0.0013	1955	−0.040
1956	0.0058	−0.0025	−0.0172	−0.0139	0.0199	0.0004	−0.0234	−0.0213	0.0025	−0.0083	−0.0084	−0.0206	1956	−0.084
1957	0.0317	0.0000	−0.0050	−0.0250	−0.0052	−0.0206	−0.0074	−0.0028	0.0045	−0.0081	0.0504	0.0277	1957	0.038
1958	−0.0112	0.0075	0.0075	0.0160	−0.0023	−0.0187	−0.0305	−0.0463	−0.0149	0.0106	0.0092	−0.0213	1958	−0.092
1959	−0.0111	0.0087	−0.0018	−0.0150	−0.0038	−0.0026	0.0025	−0.0076	−0.0091	0.0115	−0.0154	−0.0195	1959	−0.062
1960	0.0077	0.0167	0.0246	−0.0202	0.0115	0.0139	0.0335	−0.0101	0.0043	−0.0061	−0.0098	0.0247	1960	0.092
1961	−0.0140	0.0170	−0.0069	0.0085	−0.0080	−0.0106	0.0001	−0.0071	0.0097	0.0037	−0.0052	−0.0156	1961	−0.028
1962	−0.0051	0.0071	0.0220	0.0049	0.0014	−0.0106	−0.0143	0.0153	0.0031	0.0049	−0.0010	0.0003	1962	0.027
1963	−0.0033	−0.0022	−0.0022	−0.0046	−0.0010	−0.0011	−0.0005	−0.0011	−0.0029	−0.0060	0.0019	−0.0042	1963	−0.027
1964	−0.0048	−0.0043	0.0000	0.0012	0.0018	0.0031	−0.0027	−0.0015	0.0015	0.0009	−0.0018	−0.0005	1964	−0.007
1965	0.0007	−0.0018	0.0016	0.0003	−0.0015	0.0009	−0.0012	−0.0050	−0.0069	−0.0007	−0.0099	−0.0115	1965	−0.034
1966	−0.0142	−0.0284	0.0256	−0.0099	−0.0100	−0.0054	−0.0074	−0.0249	0.0292	0.0188	−0.0187	0.0374	1966	−0.010
1967	0.0115	−0.0255	0.0159	−0.0326	−0.0082	−0.0351	0.0026	−0.0126	−0.0045	−0.0445	−0.0241	0.0148	1967	−0.135
1968	0.0278	−0.0075	−0.0254	0.0178	−0.0003	0.0188	0.0241	−0.0044	−0.0146	−0.0177	−0.0312	−0.0412	1968	−0.055
1969	−0.0256	−0.0004	−0.0036	0.0371	−0.0537	0.0159	0.0027	−0.0117	−0.0586	0.0309	−0.0293	−0.0129	1969	−0.108
1970	−0.0077	0.0535	−0.0124	−0.0467	−0.0523	0.0422	0.0260	−0.0076	0.0172	−0.0164	0.0733	−0.0137	1970	0.048

* Compound annual return

Table A-8 (continued)

Long-Term Government Bonds: Capital Appreciation Returns

from January 1971 to December 2002

Year	Jan	Feb	Mar	Apr	May	Jun	Jul	Aug	Sep	Oct	Nov	Dec	Year	Jan–Dec*
1971	0.0455	−0.0209	0.0470	−0.0331	−0.0053	−0.0214	−0.0022	0.0416	0.0154	0.0120	−0.0098	−0.0006	1971	0.0661
1972	−0.0114	0.0041	−0.0131	−0.0021	0.0215	−0.0113	0.0165	−0.0021	−0.0129	0.0182	0.0178	−0.0275	1972	−0.0035
1973	−0.0375	−0.0037	0.0026	−0.0012	−0.0162	−0.0076	−0.0495	0.0329	0.0263	0.0153	−0.0238	−0.0142	1973	−0.0770
1974	−0.0144	−0.0079	−0.0350	−0.0320	0.0055	−0.0016	−0.0101	−0.0298	0.0176	0.0419	0.0233	0.0105	1974	−0.0345
1975	0.0157	0.0071	−0.0333	−0.0248	0.0145	0.0222	−0.0155	−0.0133	−0.0171	0.0403	−0.0170	0.0316	1975	0.0073
1976	0.0025	0.0001	0.0094	−0.0046	−0.0217	0.0135	0.0013	0.0142	0.0081	0.0023	0.0273	0.0265	1976	0.0807
1977	−0.0447	−0.0106	0.0026	0.0010	0.0058	0.0102	−0.0130	0.0131	−0.0089	−0.0156	0.0031	−0.0230	1977	−0.0786
1978	−0.0149	−0.0056	−0.0090	−0.0068	−0.0133	−0.0132	0.0070	0.0148	−0.0171	−0.0273	0.0117	−0.0198	1978	−0.0905
1979	0.0112	−0.0200	0.0056	−0.0188	0.0184	0.0240	−0.0161	−0.0108	−0.0190	−0.0922	0.0229	−0.0026	1979	−0.0984
1980	−0.0824	−0.0551	−0.0413	0.1424	0.0332	0.0272	−0.0560	−0.0513	−0.0358	−0.0360	0.0009	0.0244	1980	−0.1400
1981	−0.0209	−0.0524	0.0274	−0.0618	0.0518	−0.0288	−0.0462	−0.0496	−0.0259	0.0712	0.1297	−0.0813	1981	−0.1033
1982	−0.0062	0.0079	0.0107	0.0262	−0.0067	−0.0343	0.0387	0.0669	0.0519	0.0543	−0.0097	0.0219	1982	0.2395
1983	−0.0396	0.0410	−0.0183	0.0265	−0.0477	−0.0051	−0.0574	−0.0083	0.0408	−0.0227	0.0089	−0.0152	1983	−0.0982
1984	0.0141	−0.0270	−0.0254	−0.0210	−0.0619	0.0044	0.0577	0.0160	0.0248	0.0453	0.0027	−0.0007	1984	0.0232
1985	0.0268	−0.0575	0.0212	0.0140	0.0798	0.0061	−0.0274	0.0173	−0.0109	0.0248	0.0320	0.0455	1985	0.1784
1986	−0.0105	0.1073	0.0699	−0.0142	−0.0567	0.0543	−0.0173	0.0437	−0.0565	0.0220	0.0208	−0.0087	1986	0.1499
1987	0.0096	0.0143	−0.0289	−0.0538	−0.0171	0.0023	−0.0251	−0.0239	−0.0443	0.0544	−0.0038	0.0088	1987	−0.1069
1988	0.0595	−0.0019	−0.0378	−0.0230	−0.0180	0.0292	−0.0241	−0.0025	0.0269	0.0232	−0.0266	0.0035	1988	0.0036
1989	0.0124	−0.0248	0.0044	0.0088	0.0321	0.0480	0.0170	−0.0325	−0.0046	0.0307	0.0014	−0.0070	1989	0.0862
1990	−0.0416	−0.0090	−0.0115	−0.0277	0.0340	0.0162	0.0033	−0.0490	0.0048	0.0135	0.0331	0.0114	1990	−0.0261
1991	0.0059	−0.0033	−0.0026	0.0065	−0.0068	−0.0126	0.0082	0.0272	0.0236	−0.0011	0.0022	0.0513	1991	0.1010
1992	−0.0385	−0.0008	−0.0161	−0.0049	0.0181	0.0133	0.0334	0.0007	0.0127	−0.0255	−0.0051	0.0183	1992	0.0034
1993	0.0222	0.0299	−0.0042	0.0015	−0.0006	0.0387	0.0138	0.0378	−0.0045	0.0048	−0.0312	−0.0035	1993	0.1071
1994	0.0202	−0.0498	−0.0453	−0.0208	−0.0146	−0.0161	0.0303	−0.0152	−0.0392	−0.0091	0.0002	0.0095	1994	−0.1429
1995	0.0203	0.0227	0.0028	0.0112	0.0725	0.0084	−0.0223	0.0179	0.0122	0.0237	0.0198	0.0223	1995	0.2304
1996	−0.0065	−0.0530	−0.0262	−0.0224	−0.0112	0.0149	−0.0045	−0.0196	0.0230	0.0345	0.0299	−0.0312	1996	−0.0737
1997	−0.0135	−0.0046	−0.0311	0.0196	0.0037	0.0138	0.0567	−0.0367	0.0258	0.0287	0.0101	0.0130	1997	0.0851
1998	0.0152	−0.0116	−0.0028	−0.0023	0.0135	0.0176	−0.0088	0.0416	0.0350	−0.0260	0.0052	−0.0077	1998	0.0689
1999	0.0079	−0.0560	−0.0061	−0.0028	−0.0230	−0.0133	−0.0130	−0.0105	0.0032	−0.0062	−0.0117	−0.0210	1999	−0.1435
2000	0.0171	0.0213	0.0312	−0.0123	−0.0111	0.0192	0.0120	0.0190	−0.0203	0.0135	0.0270	0.0198	2000	0.1436
2001	−0.0044	0.0149	−0.0119	−0.0360	−0.0013	0.0038	0.0324	0.0159	0.0040	0.0416	−0.0512	−0.0229	2001	−0.0189
2002	0.0090	0.0072	−0.0479	0.0355	−0.0034	0.0143	0.0252	0.0420	0.0374	−0.0334	−0.0161	0.0462	2002	0.1169

*Compound annual return

Table A-9

Long-Term Government Bonds: Yields

from January 1926 to December 1970

Year	Jan	Feb	Mar	Apr	May	Jun	Jul	Aug	Sep	Oct	Nov	Dec	Year	Jan–Dec
1926	0.0374	0.0372	0.0371	0.0368	0.0369	0.0368	0.0370	0.0373	0.0372	0.0367	0.0358	0.0354	1926	0.0354
1927	0.0351	0.0347	0.0331	0.0333	0.0327	0.0334	0.0333	0.0329	0.0330	0.0325	0.0320	0.0316	1927	0.0316
1928	0.0321	0.0318	0.0317	0.0319	0.0327	0.0326	0.0344	0.0341	0.0346	0.0336	0.0338	0.0340	1928	0.0340
1929	0.0349	0.0363	0.0377	0.0358	0.0373	0.0367	0.0369	0.0375	0.0375	0.0347	0.0331	0.0340	1929	0.0340
1930	0.0347	0.0339	0.0335	0.0338	0.0329	0.0328	0.0327	0.0328	0.0324	0.0324	0.0322	0.0330	1930	0.0330
1931	0.0343	0.0338	0.0332	0.0327	0.0317	0.0319	0.0325	0.0326	0.0353	0.0385	0.0385	0.0407	1931	0.0407
1932	0.0390	0.0367	0.0370	0.0336	0.0349	0.0347	0.0320	0.0321	0.0319	0.0322	0.0322	0.0315	1932	0.0315
1933	0.0308	0.0325	0.0321	0.0325	0.0308	0.0306	0.0309	0.0308	0.0308	0.0315	0.0327	0.0336	1933	0.0336
1934	0.0321	0.0317	0.0307	0.0300	0.0292	0.0289	0.0288	0.0299	0.0310	0.0300	0.0299	0.0293	1934	0.0293
1935	0.0281	0.0275	0.0274	0.0269	0.0276	0.0270	0.0268	0.0281	0.0282	0.0279	0.0280	0.0276	1935	0.0276
1936	0.0285	0.0281	0.0275	0.0274	0.0273	0.0273	0.0271	0.0264	0.0268	0.0269	0.0257	0.0255	1936	0.0255
1937	0.0258	0.0253	0.0285	0.0284	0.0282	0.0285	0.0277	0.0286	0.0284	0.0283	0.0278	0.0273	1937	0.0273
1938	0.0271	0.0268	0.0273	0.0259	0.0257	0.0259	0.0257	0.0259	0.0259	0.0254	0.0257	0.0252	1938	0.0252
1939	0.0249	0.0245	0.0237	0.0229	0.0217	0.0221	0.0213	0.0231	0.0278	0.0247	0.0236	0.0226	1939	0.0226
1940	0.0229	0.0228	0.0215	0.0220	0.0246	0.0227	0.0224	0.0223	0.0215	0.0214	0.0199	0.0194	1940	0.0194
1941	0.0213	0.0213	0.0206	0.0196	0.0195	0.0191	0.0191	0.0190	0.0193	0.0182	0.0186	0.0204	1941	0.0204
1942	0.0247	0.0247	0.0244	0.0246	0.0243	0.0244	0.0244	0.0244	0.0244	0.0244	0.0247	0.0246	1942	0.0246
1943	0.0245	0.0246	0.0247	0.0246	0.0244	0.0244	0.0245	0.0245	0.0246	0.0247	0.0248	0.0248	1943	0.0248
1944	0.0248	0.0247	0.0247	0.0248	0.0247	0.0248	0.0247	0.0247	0.0247	0.0247	0.0247	0.0246	1944	0.0246
1945	0.0240	0.0236	0.0236	0.0228	0.0226	0.0217	0.0224	0.0223	0.0221	0.0216	0.0210	0.0199	1945	0.0199
1946	0.0199	0.0198	0.0198	0.0207	0.0209	0.0206	0.0209	0.0217	0.0219	0.0216	0.0220	0.0212	1946	0.0212
1947	0.0214	0.0214	0.0213	0.0217	0.0216	0.0216	0.0214	0.0210	0.0213	0.0217	0.0229	0.0243	1947	0.0243
1948	0.0243	0.0241	0.0241	0.0239	0.0231	0.0238	0.0241	0.0242	0.0242	0.0243	0.0239	0.0237	1948	0.0237
1949	0.0233	0.0231	0.0227	0.0227	0.0227	0.0217	0.0216	0.0210	0.0212	0.0212	0.0212	0.0209	1949	0.0209
1950	0.0215	0.0214	0.0215	0.0214	0.0213	0.0216	0.0214	0.0214	0.0220	0.0225	0.0224	0.0224	1950	0.0224
1951	0.0221	0.0228	0.0241	0.0248	0.0254	0.0259	0.0252	0.0246	0.0253	0.0254	0.0264	0.0269	1951	0.0269
1952	0.0268	0.0269	0.0263	0.0254	0.0257	0.0259	0.0261	0.0267	0.0277	0.0269	0.0272	0.0279	1952	0.0279
1953	0.0279	0.0287	0.0294	0.0303	0.0314	0.0301	0.0301	0.0303	0.0284	0.0281	0.0286	0.0274	1953	0.0274
1954	0.0291	0.0279	0.0278	0.0273	0.0279	0.0272	0.0266	0.0269	0.0271	0.0271	0.0274	0.0272	1954	0.0272
1955	0.0286	0.0292	0.0288	0.0290	0.0287	0.0293	0.0300	0.0301	0.0298	0.0292	0.0295	0.0295	1955	0.0295
1956	0.0292	0.0293	0.0303	0.0311	0.0299	0.0299	0.0313	0.0325	0.0324	0.0329	0.0333	0.0345	1956	0.0345
1957	0.0328	0.0328	0.0331	0.0345	0.0348	0.0361	0.0365	0.0367	0.0364	0.0369	0.0340	0.0323	1957	0.0323
1958	0.0330	0.0325	0.0321	0.0311	0.0313	0.0324	0.0343	0.0371	0.0380	0.0374	0.0368	0.0382	1958	0.0382
1959	0.0408	0.0402	0.0403	0.0414	0.0417	0.0419	0.0417	0.0423	0.0429	0.0421	0.0432	0.0447	1959	0.0447
1960	0.0441	0.0429	0.0411	0.0426	0.0417	0.0407	0.0382	0.0390	0.0387	0.0391	0.0399	0.0380	1960	0.0380
1961	0.0404	0.0392	0.0397	0.0391	0.0397	0.0404	0.0404	0.0410	0.0403	0.0400	0.0404	0.0415	1961	0.0415
1962	0.0419	0.0414	0.0398	0.0394	0.0393	0.0401	0.0412	0.0401	0.0398	0.0395	0.0396	0.0395	1962	0.0395
1963	0.0398	0.0400	0.0401	0.0405	0.0406	0.0407	0.0407	0.0408	0.0410	0.0415	0.0414	0.0417	1963	0.0417
1964	0.0421	0.0424	0.0424	0.0423	0.0422	0.0419	0.0421	0.0423	0.0421	0.0421	0.0422	0.0423	1964	0.0423
1965	0.0422	0.0424	0.0422	0.0422	0.0423	0.0423	0.0424	0.0428	0.0433	0.0433	0.0441	0.0450	1965	0.0450
1966	0.0457	0.0477	0.0460	0.0467	0.0473	0.0477	0.0482	0.0499	0.0480	0.0467	0.0480	0.0455	1966	0.0455
1967	0.0448	0.0465	0.0455	0.0477	0.0482	0.0507	0.0505	0.0514	0.0517	0.0549	0.0567	0.0556	1967	0.0556
1968	0.0536	0.0542	0.0560	0.0547	0.0547	0.0534	0.0517	0.0520	0.0531	0.0543	0.0566	0.0598	1968	0.0598
1969	0.0617	0.0618	0.0620	0.0593	0.0635	0.0623	0.0621	0.0630	0.0677	0.0653	0.0676	0.0687	1969	0.0687
1970	0.0693	0.0651	0.0661	0.0699	0.0743	0.0709	0.0687	0.0694	0.0680	0.0693	0.0637	0.0648	1970	0.0648

Table A-9 (continued)

Long-Term Government Bonds: Yields

from January 1971 to December 2002

Year	Jan	Feb	Mar	Apr	May	Jun	Jul	Aug	Sep	Oct	Nov	Dec	Year	Jan–Dec
1971	0.0612	0.0629	0.0593	0.0619	0.0624	0.0641	0.0643	0.0610	0.0598	0.0588	0.0596	0.0597	1971	0.0597
1972	0.0606	0.0602	0.0613	0.0615	0.0597	0.0607	0.0593	0.0595	0.0606	0.0591	0.0577	0.0599	1972	0.0599
1973	0.0685	0.0688	0.0686	0.0687	0.0703	0.0710	0.0760	0.0728	0.0703	0.0689	0.0712	0.0726	1973	0.0726
1974	0.0740	0.0748	0.0783	0.0816	0.0810	0.0812	0.0823	0.0855	0.0837	0.0795	0.0771	0.0760	1974	0.0760
1975	0.0796	0.0788	0.0824	0.0852	0.0836	0.0813	0.0829	0.0844	0.0862	0.0819	0.0838	0.0805	1975	0.0805
1976	0.0802	0.0802	0.0792	0.0797	0.0821	0.0807	0.0805	0.0790	0.0781	0.0779	0.0749	0.0721	1976	0.0721
1977	0.0764	0.0775	0.0772	0.0771	0.0765	0.0754	0.0768	0.0754	0.0764	0.0781	0.0777	0.0803	1977	0.0803
1978	0.0816	0.0822	0.0831	0.0838	0.0852	0.0865	0.0858	0.0843	0.0860	0.0889	0.0877	0.0898	1978	0.0898
1979	0.0886	0.0908	0.0902	0.0922	0.0903	0.0877	0.0895	0.0907	0.0927	0.1034	0.1009	0.1012	1979	0.1012
1980	0.1114	0.1186	0.1239	0.1076	0.1037	0.1006	0.1074	0.1140	0.1185	0.1231	0.1230	0.1199	1980	0.1199
1981	0.1211	0.1283	0.1248	0.1332	0.1265	0.1304	0.1370	0.1445	0.1482	0.1384	0.1220	0.1334	1981	0.1334
1982	0.1415	0.1402	0.1387	0.1348	0.1358	0.1412	0.1352	0.1254	0.1183	0.1112	0.1125	0.1095	1982	0.1095
1983	0.1113	0.1060	0.1083	0.1051	0.1112	0.1119	0.1198	0.1210	0.1157	0.1188	0.1176	0.1197	1983	0.1197
1984	0.1180	0.1217	0.1253	0.1284	0.1381	0.1374	0.1293	0.1270	0.1235	0.1173	0.1169	0.1170	1984	0.1170
1985	0.1127	0.1209	0.1181	0.1162	0.1062	0.1055	0.1091	0.1068	0.1082	0.1051	0.1011	0.0956	1985	0.0956
1986	0.0958	0.0841	0.0766	0.0782	0.0848	0.0790	0.0809	0.0763	0.0827	0.0803	0.0779	0.0789	1986	0.0789
1987	0.0778	0.0763	0.0795	0.0859	0.0880	0.0877	0.0907	0.0936	0.0992	0.0926	0.0931	0.0920	1987	0.0920
1988	0.0852	0.0854	0.0901	0.0929	0.0952	0.0917	0.0947	0.0950	0.0917	0.0889	0.0923	0.0918	1988	0.0918
1989	0.0903	0.0935	0.0929	0.0918	0.0878	0.0821	0.0801	0.0841	0.0847	0.0810	0.0808	0.0816	1989	0.0816
1990	0.0865	0.0876	0.0889	0.0924	0.0883	0.0864	0.0860	0.0920	0.0914	0.0898	0.0858	0.0844	1990	0.0844
1991	0.0837	0.0841	0.0844	0.0837	0.0845	0.0860	0.0850	0.0818	0.0790	0.0791	0.0789	0.0730	1991	0.0730
1992	0.0776	0.0777	0.0797	0.0803	0.0781	0.0765	0.0726	0.0725	0.0710	0.0741	0.0748	0.0726	1992	0.0726
1993	0.0725	0.0698	0.0702	0.0701	0.0701	0.0668	0.0656	0.0623	0.0627	0.0623	0.0651	0.0654	1993	0.0654
1994	0.0637	0.0682	0.0725	0.0745	0.0759	0.0774	0.0746	0.0761	0.0800	0.0809	0.0808	0.0799	1994	0.0799
1995	0.0780	0.0758	0.0755	0.0745	0.0677	0.0670	0.0691	0.0674	0.0663	0.0641	0.0623	0.0603	1995	0.0603
1996	0.0609	0.0659	0.0684	0.0706	0.0717	0.0703	0.0707	0.0726	0.0704	0.0671	0.0643	0.0673	1996	0.0673
1997	0.0689	0.0694	0.0723	0.0705	0.0701	0.0688	0.0637	0.0672	0.0649	0.0623	0.0614	0.0602	1997	0.0602
1998	0.0589	0.0599	0.0602	0.0604	0.0592	0.0576	0.0584	0.0547	0.0517	0.0540	0.0535	0.0542	1998	0.0542
1999	0.0536	0.0587	0.0592	0.0594	0.0615	0.0627	0.0639	0.0649	0.0646	0.0651	0.0662	0.0682	1999	0.0682
2000	0.0666	0.0646	0.0618	0.0630	0.0640	0.0622	0.0611	0.0594	0.0612	0.0600	0.0576	0.0558	2000	0.0558
2001	0.0562	0.0549	0.0559	0.0593	0.0594	0.0590	0.0561	0.0546	0.0542	0.0506	0.0553	0.0575	2001	0.0575
2002	0.0569	0.0563	0.0604	0.0575	0.0578	0.0566	0.0544	0.0510	0.0480	0.0508	0.0521	0.0484	2002	0.0484

Table A-10

Intermediate-Term Government Bonds: Total Returns

from January 1926 to December 1970

Year	Jan	Feb	Mar	Apr	May	Jun	Jul	Aug	Sep	Oct	Nov	Dec	Year	Jan–Dec*
1926	0.0068	0.0032	0.0041	0.0090	0.0008	0.0027	0.0013	0.0009	0.0050	0.0054	0.0045	0.0089	1926	0.0538
1927	0.0057	0.0038	0.0038	0.0016	0.0020	0.0029	0.0043	0.0056	0.0060	−0.0034	0.0083	0.0037	1927	0.0452
1928	0.0046	−0.0004	0.0010	−0.0003	−0.0006	0.0017	−0.0089	0.0050	0.0028	0.0032	0.0019	−0.0007	1928	0.0092
1929	−0.0029	−0.0018	0.0005	0.0089	−0.0061	0.0107	0.0066	0.0052	−0.0014	0.0168	0.0180	0.0044	1929	0.0601
1930	−0.0041	0.0094	0.0161	−0.0071	0.0061	0.0142	0.0054	0.0022	0.0063	0.0076	0.0070	0.0024	1930	0.0672
1931	−0.0071	0.0099	0.0052	0.0083	0.0119	−0.0214	0.0016	0.0017	−0.0113	−0.0105	0.0049	−0.0159	1931	−0.0232
1932	−0.0032	0.0128	0.0078	0.0194	−0.0090	0.0108	0.0120	0.0124	0.0027	0.0045	0.0031	0.0118	1932	0.0881
1933	−0.0016	−0.0001	0.0099	0.0057	0.0199	0.0008	−0.0006	0.0073	0.0026	−0.0025	0.0027	−0.0253	1933	0.0183
1934	0.0130	0.0052	0.0189	0.0182	0.0120	0.0091	−0.0024	−0.0092	−0.0138	0.0190	0.0046	0.0125	1934	0.0900
1935	0.0114	0.0105	0.0125	0.0107	−0.0035	0.0113	0.0037	−0.0071	−0.0057	0.0109	0.0014	0.0120	1935	0.0701
1936	−0.0003	0.0069	0.0031	0.0024	0.0038	0.0012	0.0022	0.0050	0.0010	0.0025	0.0081	−0.0057	1936	0.0306
1937	−0.0031	0.0007	−0.0164	0.0047	0.0080	−0.0012	0.0059	−0.0043	0.0081	0.0032	0.0042	0.0062	1937	0.0156
1938	0.0085	0.0052	−0.0012	0.0230	0.0023	0.0075	0.0010	0.0015	−0.0013	0.0093	−0.0001	0.0052	1938	0.0623
1939	0.0029	0.0082	0.0081	0.0038	0.0095	0.0002	0.0040	−0.0147	−0.0262	0.0315	0.0074	0.0108	1939	0.0452
1940	−0.0014	0.0035	0.0088	0.0002	−0.0214	0.0187	0.0003	0.0043	0.0047	0.0036	0.0056	0.0028	1940	0.0296
1941	0.0001	−0.0047	0.0069	0.0033	0.0012	0.0056	0.0000	0.0011	0.0000	0.0023	−0.0092	−0.0016	1941	0.0050
1942	0.0074	0.0015	0.0023	0.0022	0.0016	0.0013	0.0000	0.0017	−0.0023	0.0017	0.0017	0.0000	1942	0.0194
1943	0.0039	0.0013	0.0021	0.0024	0.0057	0.0033	0.0021	0.0002	0.0014	0.0017	0.0015	0.0021	1943	0.0281
1944	0.0011	0.0016	0.0019	0.0028	0.0005	0.0007	0.0029	0.0024	0.0011	0.0011	0.0009	0.0010	1944	0.0180
1945	0.0052	0.0038	0.0004	0.0014	0.0012	0.0019	0.0000	0.0016	0.0017	0.0016	0.0010	0.0021	1945	0.0222
1946	0.0039	0.0048	−0.0038	−0.0020	0.0006	0.0033	−0.0010	0.0004	−0.0011	0.0026	−0.0008	0.0032	1946	0.0100
1947	0.0023	0.0006	0.0024	−0.0013	0.0008	0.0008	0.0006	0.0026	0.0000	−0.0023	0.0006	0.0021	1947	0.0091
1948	0.0015	0.0018	0.0018	0.0019	0.0053	−0.0008	−0.0002	−0.0004	0.0010	0.0013	0.0021	0.0032	1948	0.0185
1949	0.0028	0.0011	0.0025	0.0015	0.0023	0.0050	0.0020	0.0031	0.0008	0.0006	0.0002	0.0012	1949	0.0232
1950	−0.0005	0.0008	0.0000	0.0008	0.0020	0.0003	0.0020	−0.0007	−0.0004	0.0001	0.0018	0.0008	1950	0.0070
1951	0.0022	0.0007	−0.0127	0.0057	−0.0040	0.0050	0.0058	0.0036	−0.0057	0.0016	0.0032	−0.0016	1951	0.0036
1952	0.0038	−0.0020	0.0067	0.0054	0.0019	−0.0035	−0.0034	−0.0024	0.0019	0.0066	−0.0006	0.0019	1952	0.0163
1953	−0.0002	0.0003	−0.0017	−0.0096	−0.0117	0.0155	0.0056	−0.0008	0.0194	0.0038	0.0014	0.0103	1953	0.0323
1954	0.0065	0.0100	0.0027	0.0043	−0.0073	0.0125	−0.0005	0.0011	−0.0020	−0.0009	−0.0001	0.0005	1954	0.0268
1955	−0.0032	−0.0052	0.0024	0.0004	0.0001	−0.0036	−0.0071	0.0007	0.0082	0.0072	−0.0053	−0.0011	1955	−0.0065
1956	0.0105	0.0003	−0.0100	−0.0001	0.0112	0.0003	−0.0095	−0.0103	0.0092	−0.0019	−0.0047	0.0011	1956	−0.0042
1957	0.0237	−0.0012	0.0018	−0.0101	−0.0017	−0.0106	−0.0015	0.0109	0.0002	0.0043	0.0396	0.0215	1957	0.0784
1958	0.0034	0.0139	0.0053	0.0052	0.0060	−0.0068	−0.0091	−0.0356	−0.0017	0.0002	0.0132	−0.0061	1958	−0.0129
1959	−0.0013	0.0107	−0.0037	−0.0052	−0.0001	−0.0077	0.0034	−0.0078	0.0020	0.0174	−0.0092	−0.0020	1959	−0.0039
1960	0.0154	0.0072	0.0292	−0.0064	0.0031	0.0217	0.0267	−0.0004	0.0029	0.0016	−0.0094	0.0210	1960	0.1176
1961	−0.0059	0.0090	0.0037	0.0054	−0.0028	−0.0025	0.0007	0.0019	0.0079	0.0014	−0.0019	0.0018	1961	0.0185
1962	−0.0045	0.0155	0.0089	0.0025	0.0049	−0.0028	−0.0012	0.0125	0.0021	0.0051	0.0060	0.0056	1962	0.0556
1963	−0.0029	0.0017	0.0027	0.0030	0.0014	0.0014	0.0003	0.0019	0.0014	0.0011	0.0040	0.0003	1963	0.0164
1964	0.0033	0.0012	0.0016	0.0033	0.0081	0.0036	0.0027	0.0027	0.0045	0.0032	−0.0004	0.0058	1964	0.0404
1965	0.0042	0.0018	0.0043	0.0026	0.0035	0.0049	0.0017	0.0019	−0.0005	0.0000	0.0007	−0.0149	1965	0.0102
1966	0.0003	−0.0083	0.0187	−0.0019	0.0011	−0.0024	−0.0025	−0.0125	0.0216	0.0075	0.0027	0.0223	1966	0.0469
1967	0.0118	−0.0013	0.0183	−0.0089	0.0044	−0.0227	0.0133	−0.0036	0.0007	−0.0049	0.0028	0.0007	1967	0.0101
1968	0.0145	0.0040	−0.0026	−0.0016	0.0064	0.0167	0.0176	0.0021	0.0055	0.0009	−0.0013	−0.0173	1968	0.0454
1969	0.0086	−0.0013	0.0097	0.0079	−0.0082	−0.0084	0.0082	−0.0018	−0.0300	0.0333	−0.0047	−0.0193	1969	−0.0074
1970	0.0030	0.0439	0.0087	−0.0207	0.0110	0.0061	0.0152	0.0116	0.0196	0.0095	0.0451	0.0054	1970	0.1686

* Compound annual return

Table A-10 (continued)

Intermediate-Term Government Bonds: Total Returns

From January 1971 to December 2002

Year	Jan	Feb	Mar	Apr	May	Jun	Jul	Aug	Sep	Oct	Nov	Dec	Year	Jan–Dec*
1971	0.0168	0.0224	0.0186	−0.0327	0.0011	−0.0187	0.0027	0.0350	0.0026	0.0220	0.0052	0.0110	1971	0.0872
1972	0.0106	0.0014	0.0015	0.0014	0.0016	0.0045	0.0015	0.0015	0.0014	0.0016	0.0045	0.0192	1972	0.0516
1973	−0.0006	−0.0075	0.0046	0.0064	0.0057	−0.0006	−0.0276	0.0254	0.0250	0.0050	0.0064	0.0040	1973	0.0461
1974	0.0009	0.0035	−0.0212	−0.0152	0.0130	−0.0087	0.0007	−0.0012	0.0319	0.0109	0.0236	0.0185	1974	0.0569
1975	0.0053	0.0148	−0.0059	−0.0186	0.0260	0.0027	−0.0030	−0.0009	0.0010	0.0366	−0.0010	0.0198	1975	0.0783
1976	0.0057	0.0084	0.0075	0.0116	−0.0145	0.0159	0.0119	0.0189	0.0076	0.0147	0.0321	0.0026	1976	0.1287
1977	−0.0190	0.0048	0.0055	0.0051	0.0056	0.0102	0.0001	0.0008	0.0015	−0.0060	0.0079	−0.0023	1977	0.0141
1978	0.0013	0.0017	0.0037	0.0024	−0.0002	−0.0021	0.0098	0.0079	0.0057	−0.0112	0.0092	0.0063	1978	0.0349
1979	0.0055	−0.0059	0.0112	0.0033	0.0193	0.0205	−0.0011	−0.0091	0.0006	−0.0468	0.0363	0.0087	1979	0.0409
1980	−0.0135	−0.0641	0.0143	0.1198	0.0490	−0.0077	−0.0106	−0.0387	−0.0038	−0.0152	0.0029	0.0171	1980	0.0391
1981	0.0032	−0.0235	0.0263	−0.0216	0.0245	0.0060	−0.0270	−0.0178	0.0164	0.0611	0.0624	−0.0142	1981	0.0945
1982	0.0050	0.0148	0.0042	0.0299	0.0146	−0.0135	0.0464	0.0469	0.0325	0.0531	0.0080	0.0185	1982	0.2910
1983	0.0007	0.0252	−0.0049	0.0259	−0.0122	0.0016	−0.0198	0.0081	0.0315	0.0019	0.0103	0.0047	1983	0.0741
1984	0.0177	−0.0064	−0.0035	−0.0003	−0.0250	0.0099	0.0393	0.0101	0.0202	0.0383	0.0192	0.0143	1984	0.1402
1985	0.0206	−0.0179	0.0166	0.0264	0.0485	0.0108	−0.0045	0.0148	0.0113	0.0162	0.0195	0.0257	1985	0.2033
1986	0.0082	0.0275	0.0338	0.0081	−0.0215	0.0276	0.0157	0.0266	−0.0110	0.0162	0.0113	0.0007	1986	0.1514
1987	0.0107	0.0059	−0.0031	−0.0244	−0.0038	0.0122	0.0025	−0.0038	−0.0141	0.0299	0.0083	0.0093	1987	0.0290
1988	0.0316	0.0123	−0.0086	−0.0044	−0.0049	0.0181	−0.0047	−0.0009	0.0196	0.0148	−0.0115	−0.0010	1988	0.0610
1989	0.0121	−0.0051	0.0049	0.0220	0.0212	0.0324	0.0235	−0.0246	0.0069	0.0237	0.0084	0.0012	1989	0.1329
1990	−0.0104	0.0007	0.0002	−0.0077	0.0261	0.0151	0.0174	−0.0092	0.0094	0.0171	0.0193	0.0161	1990	0.0973
1991	0.0107	0.0048	0.0023	0.0117	0.0059	−0.0023	0.0129	0.0247	0.0216	0.0134	0.0128	0.0265	1991	0.1546
1992	−0.0195	0.0022	−0.0079	0.0098	0.0222	0.0177	0.0242	0.0150	0.0194	−0.0182	−0.0084	0.0146	1992	0.0719
1993	0.0270	0.0243	0.0043	0.0088	−0.0009	0.0201	0.0005	0.0223	0.0056	0.0018	−0.0093	0.0032	1993	0.1124
1994	0.0138	−0.0258	−0.0257	−0.0105	−0.0002	−0.0028	0.0169	0.0026	−0.0158	−0.0023	−0.0070	0.0053	1994	−0.0514
1995	0.0182	0.0234	0.0063	0.0143	0.0369	0.0079	−0.0016	0.0086	0.0064	0.0121	0.0149	0.0095	1995	0.1680
1996	0.0006	−0.0138	−0.0118	−0.0050	−0.0032	0.0117	0.0025	−0.0005	0.0155	0.0183	0.0149	−0.0078	1996	0.0210
1997	0.0025	0.0002	−0.0114	0.0148	0.0079	0.0102	0.0264	−0.0098	0.0151	0.0150	−0.0001	0.0106	1997	0.0838
1998	0.0180	−0.0039	0.0026	0.0061	0.0070	0.0079	0.0027	0.0271	0.0330	0.0041	−0.0098	0.0037	1998	0.1021
1999	0.0055	−0.0262	0.0086	0.0021	−0.0147	0.0032	−0.0003	0.0013	0.0097	−0.0008	−0.0008	−0.0048	1999	−0.0177
2000	−0.0053	0.0078	0.0203	−0.0043	0.0052	0.0191	0.0072	0.0134	0.0096	0.0079	0.0174	0.0214	2000	0.1259
2001	0.0098	0.0105	0.0076	−0.0114	−0.0007	0.0066	0.0247	0.0095	0.0253	0.0180	−0.0171	−0.0082	2001	0.0762
2002	0.0036	0.0108	−0.0242	0.0239	0.0118	0.0169	0.0272	0.0167	0.0288	−0.0024	−0.0169	0.0279	2002	0.1293

*Compound annual return

Table A-11

Intermediate-Term Government Bonds: Income Returns

from January 1926 to December 1970

Year	Jan	Feb	Mar	Apr	May	Jun	Jul	Aug	Sep	Oct	Nov	Dec	Year	Jan–De
1926	0.0032	0.0032	0.0032	0.0031	0.0031	0.0031	0.0032	0.0032	0.0032	0.0031	0.0031	0.0030	1926	0.037
1927	0.0029	0.0029	0.0029	0.0029	0.0029	0.0029	0.0029	0.0029	0.0028	0.0029	0.0028	0.0028	1927	0.034
1928	0.0028	0.0028	0.0029	0.0029	0.0030	0.0030	0.0032	0.0032	0.0032	0.0032	0.0032	0.0033	1928	0.036
1929	0.0034	0.0035	0.0036	0.0035	0.0037	0.0035	0.0035	0.0034	0.0035	0.0033	0.0030	0.0030	1929	0.040
1930	0.0031	0.0030	0.0028	0.0030	0.0029	0.0027	0.0026	0.0026	0.0026	0.0025	0.0024	0.0024	1930	0.033
1931	0.0026	0.0025	0.0024	0.0023	0.0021	0.0026	0.0026	0.0026	0.0028	0.0031	0.0031	0.0034	1931	0.031
1932	0.0035	0.0034	0.0033	0.0030	0.0032	0.0031	0.0029	0.0027	0.0027	0.0027	0.0027	0.0025	1932	0.036
1933	0.0026	0.0026	0.0025	0.0025	0.0021	0.0022	0.0022	0.0021	0.0021	0.0022	0.0022	0.0027	1933	0.028
1934	0.0030	0.0024	0.0027	0.0024	0.0023	0.0021	0.0021	0.0021	0.0021	0.0026	0.0022	0.0023	1934	0.029
1935	0.0021	0.0018	0.0018	0.0017	0.0016	0.0015	0.0015	0.0014	0.0015	0.0016	0.0015	0.0016	1935	0.020
1936	0.0014	0.0013	0.0013	0.0012	0.0012	0.0013	0.0012	0.0012	0.0011	0.0011	0.0011	0.0010	1936	0.014
1937	0.0010	0.0010	0.0012	0.0015	0.0013	0.0014	0.0014	0.0013	0.0014	0.0012	0.0012	0.0011	1937	0.014
1938	0.0018	0.0016	0.0017	0.0017	0.0015	0.0014	0.0013	0.0014	0.0013	0.0014	0.0013	0.0013	1938	0.018
1939	0.0013	0.0011	0.0012	0.0010	0.0011	0.0009	0.0009	0.0009	0.0011	0.0015	0.0010	0.0009	1939	0.013
1940	0.0009	0.0008	0.0008	0.0007	0.0007	0.0010	0.0008	0.0008	0.0007	0.0007	0.0006	0.0005	1940	0.009
1941	0.0006	0.0006	0.0008	0.0006	0.0006	0.0006	0.0005	0.0005	0.0005	0.0005	0.0004	0.0007	1941	0.006
1942	0.0008	0.0006	0.0007	0.0006	0.0006	0.0006	0.0006	0.0006	0.0006	0.0006	0.0006	0.0006	1942	0.007
1943	0.0014	0.0013	0.0014	0.0013	0.0013	0.0013	0.0013	0.0012	0.0012	0.0012	0.0012	0.0012	1943	0.015
1944	0.0013	0.0012	0.0013	0.0012	0.0013	0.0012	0.0012	0.0012	0.0011	0.0012	0.0011	0.0011	1944	0.014
1945	0.0012	0.0010	0.0010	0.0010	0.0010	0.0010	0.0010	0.0010	0.0009	0.0010	0.0009	0.0009	1945	0.011
1946	0.0009	0.0008	0.0007	0.0009	0.0009	0.0009	0.0009	0.0009	0.0010	0.0010	0.0009	0.0010	1946	0.010
1947	0.0010	0.0009	0.0010	0.0009	0.0010	0.0011	0.0010	0.0010	0.0010	0.0010	0.0010	0.0012	1947	0.012
1948	0.0013	0.0012	0.0014	0.0013	0.0012	0.0013	0.0012	0.0013	0.0013	0.0013	0.0014	0.0013	1948	0.015
1949	0.0013	0.0012	0.0013	0.0012	0.0013	0.0012	0.0010	0.0011	0.0010	0.0010	0.0010	0.0010	1949	0.013
1950	0.0011	0.0010	0.0011	0.0010	0.0012	0.0011	0.0012	0.0011	0.0011	0.0013	0.0013	0.0013	1950	0.013
1951	0.0016	0.0014	0.0015	0.0018	0.0017	0.0017	0.0018	0.0017	0.0015	0.0019	0.0017	0.0018	1951	0.019
1952	0.0018	0.0017	0.0019	0.0017	0.0016	0.0017	0.0018	0.0018	0.0021	0.0020	0.0017	0.0021	1952	0.021
1953	0.0019	0.0018	0.0021	0.0021	0.0022	0.0027	0.0024	0.0023	0.0023	0.0020	0.0020	0.0020	1953	0.025
1954	0.0016	0.0014	0.0014	0.0013	0.0011	0.0016	0.0011	0.0012	0.0011	0.0012	0.0014	0.0014	1954	0.016
1955	0.0018	0.0017	0.0020	0.0019	0.0021	0.0020	0.0020	0.0025	0.0023	0.0023	0.0021	0.0022	1955	0.024
1956	0.0025	0.0021	0.0022	0.0026	0.0026	0.0023	0.0025	0.0027	0.0026	0.0030	0.0028	0.0030	1956	0.030
1957	0.0030	0.0025	0.0026	0.0029	0.0030	0.0027	0.0036	0.0032	0.0032	0.0033	0.0031	0.0028	1957	0.035
1958	0.0024	0.0021	0.0022	0.0021	0.0019	0.0021	0.0021	0.0022	0.0032	0.0032	0.0029	0.0032	1958	0.029
1959	0.0031	0.0030	0.0033	0.0032	0.0033	0.0037	0.0038	0.0037	0.0039	0.0039	0.0038	0.0041	1959	0.041
1960	0.0039	0.0039	0.0039	0.0032	0.0037	0.0035	0.0031	0.0030	0.0028	0.0029	0.0028	0.0031	1960	0.041
1961	0.0030	0.0028	0.0029	0.0027	0.0030	0.0029	0.0031	0.0031	0.0030	0.0032	0.0030	0.0030	1961	0.035
1962	0.0035	0.0031	0.0031	0.0031	0.0031	0.0029	0.0033	0.0032	0.0028	0.0033	0.0029	0.0030	1962	0.037
1963	0.0030	0.0028	0.0029	0.0032	0.0031	0.0029	0.0034	0.0031	0.0033	0.0033	0.0031	0.0034	1963	0.037
1964	0.0034	0.0030	0.0035	0.0033	0.0031	0.0036	0.0034	0.0033	0.0033	0.0033	0.0034	0.0034	1964	0.040
1965	0.0033	0.0031	0.0037	0.0033	0.0033	0.0037	0.0034	0.0036	0.0034	0.0034	0.0038	0.0037	1965	0.041
1966	0.0040	0.0036	0.0043	0.0038	0.0042	0.0040	0.0040	0.0047	0.0046	0.0044	0.0042	0.0042	1966	0.049
1967	0.0041	0.0035	0.0039	0.0033	0.0042	0.0038	0.0045	0.0042	0.0041	0.0047	0.0046	0.0044	1967	0.048
1968	0.0051	0.0043	0.0043	0.0049	0.0048	0.0043	0.0049	0.0042	0.0044	0.0044	0.0041	0.0047	1968	0.054
1969	0.0054	0.0048	0.0049	0.0057	0.0050	0.0058	0.0059	0.0054	0.0061	0.0067	0.0056	0.0068	1969	0.066
1970	0.0066	0.0061	0.0063	0.0059	0.0062	0.0067	0.0065	0.0062	0.0060	0.0057	0.0058	0.0050	1970	0.074

* Compound annual return

Table A-11 (continued)

Intermediate-Term Government Bonds: Income Returns

from January 1971 to December 2002

Year	Jan	Feb	Mar	Apr	May	Jun	Jul	Aug	Sep	Oct	Nov	Dec	Year	Jan–Dec*
1971	0.0047	0.0043	0.0047	0.0040	0.0044	0.0053	0.0053	0.0056	0.0048	0.0046	0.0047	0.0046	1971	0.0575
1972	0.0048	0.0044	0.0046	0.0044	0.0052	0.0048	0.0049	0.0050	0.0047	0.0053	0.0051	0.0049	1972	0.0575
1973	0.0056	0.0048	0.0054	0.0056	0.0056	0.0053	0.0059	0.0064	0.0055	0.0060	0.0055	0.0056	1973	0.0658
1974	0.0057	0.0051	0.0054	0.0065	0.0067	0.0059	0.0073	0.0067	0.0072	0.0067	0.0061	0.0064	1974	0.0724
1975	0.0061	0.0055	0.0059	0.0060	0.0063	0.0063	0.0063	0.0061	0.0069	0.0068	0.0055	0.0067	1975	0.0735
1976	0.0060	0.0055	0.0066	0.0059	0.0054	0.0069	0.0060	0.0062	0.0056	0.0054	0.0058	0.0050	1976	0.0710
1977	0.0051	0.0050	0.0056	0.0053	0.0058	0.0055	0.0052	0.0059	0.0056	0.0059	0.0059	0.0059	1977	0.0649
1978	0.0066	0.0057	0.0066	0.0060	0.0071	0.0066	0.0070	0.0068	0.0065	0.0072	0.0072	0.0069	1978	0.0783
1979	0.0079	0.0066	0.0075	0.0077	0.0077	0.0070	0.0074	0.0073	0.0070	0.0084	0.0089	0.0086	1979	0.0904
1980	0.0086	0.0083	0.0107	0.0103	0.0081	0.0075	0.0079	0.0076	0.0097	0.0094	0.0096	0.0111	1980	0.1055
1981	0.0101	0.0095	0.0117	0.0106	0.0110	0.0118	0.0116	0.0120	0.0130	0.0129	0.0121	0.0108	1981	0.1297
1982	0.0107	0.0102	0.0122	0.0112	0.0101	0.0118	0.0113	0.0109	0.0097	0.0089	0.0087	0.0085	1982	0.1281
1983	0.0084	0.0079	0.0084	0.0081	0.0086	0.0085	0.0082	0.0103	0.0094	0.0092	0.0091	0.0091	1983	0.1035
1984	0.0096	0.0088	0.0095	0.0101	0.0104	0.0105	0.0113	0.0105	0.0095	0.0110	0.0093	0.0093	1984	0.1168
1985	0.0090	0.0081	0.0089	0.0097	0.0090	0.0073	0.0083	0.0081	0.0082	0.0081	0.0074	0.0078	1985	0.1029
1986	0.0071	0.0066	0.0068	0.0060	0.0060	0.0068	0.0062	0.0057	0.0058	0.0060	0.0052	0.0060	1986	0.0772
1987	0.0055	0.0052	0.0060	0.0058	0.0062	0.0071	0.0066	0.0068	0.0068	0.0073	0.0070	0.0070	1987	0.0747
1988	0.0065	0.0066	0.0064	0.0063	0.0072	0.0070	0.0064	0.0077	0.0072	0.0071	0.0067	0.0071	1988	0.0824
1989	0.0077	0.0066	0.0078	0.0071	0.0080	0.0070	0.0067	0.0061	0.0065	0.0071	0.0063	0.0060	1989	0.0846
1990	0.0071	0.0064	0.0069	0.0071	0.0075	0.0067	0.0072	0.0068	0.0065	0.0074	0.0067	0.0067	1990	0.0815
1991	0.0064	0.0059	0.0059	0.0070	0.0065	0.0059	0.0069	0.0062	0.0061	0.0058	0.0052	0.0056	1991	0.0743
1992	0.0052	0.0052	0.0060	0.0058	0.0056	0.0058	0.0053	0.0050	0.0047	0.0044	0.0050	0.0053	1992	0.0627
1993	0.0049	0.0045	0.0049	0.0045	0.0041	0.0050	0.0041	0.0044	0.0041	0.0038	0.0042	0.0043	1993	0.0553
1994	0.0045	0.0039	0.0048	0.0049	0.0058	0.0055	0.0055	0.0060	0.0055	0.0060	0.0061	0.0063	1994	0.0607
1995	0.0067	0.0056	0.0060	0.0054	0.0062	0.0050	0.0051	0.0051	0.0047	0.0052	0.0047	0.0043	1995	0.0669
1996	0.0046	0.0041	0.0045	0.0053	0.0054	0.0050	0.0058	0.0052	0.0056	0.0053	0.0047	0.0050	1996	0.0582
1997	0.0052	0.0047	0.0054	0.0055	0.0055	0.0053	0.0054	0.0046	0.0054	0.0050	0.0043	0.0052	1997	0.0614
1998	0.0046	0.0041	0.0049	0.0046	0.0045	0.0049	0.0047	0.0046	0.0041	0.0035	0.0036	0.0039	1998	0.0529
1999	0.0037	0.0035	0.0048	0.0043	0.0041	0.0052	0.0049	0.0049	0.0048	0.0046	0.0052	0.0052	1999	0.0530
2000	0.0054	0.0052	0.0056	0.0048	0.0059	0.0054	0.0053	0.0051	0.0047	0.0051	0.0047	0.0043	2000	0.0619
2001	0.0032	0.0026	0.0027	0.0033	0.0042	0.0040	0.0044	0.0039	0.0034	0.0035	0.0030	0.0035	2001	0.0427
2002	0.0038	0.0034	0.0034	0.0045	0.0039	0.0034	0.0037	0.0029	0.0027	0.0022	0.0022	0.0028	2002	0.0398

Compound annual return

Table A-12

Intermediate-Term Government Bonds: Capital Appreciation Returns

from January 1926 to December 1970

Year	Jan	Feb	Mar	Apr	May	Jun	Jul	Aug	Sep	Oct	Nov	Dec	Year	Jan–Dec*
1926	0.0036	0.0000	0.0009	0.0059	−0.0023	−0.0004	−0.0018	−0.0023	0.0018	0.0023	0.0014	0.0059	1926	0.0151
1927	0.0027	0.0009	0.0009	−0.0014	−0.0009	0.0000	0.0014	0.0027	0.0032	−0.0064	0.0055	0.0009	1927	0.0096
1928	0.0018	−0.0032	−0.0018	−0.0032	−0.0036	−0.0014	−0.0122	0.0018	−0.0004	0.0000	−0.0014	−0.0041	1928	−0.0273
1929	−0.0063	−0.0054	−0.0031	0.0054	−0.0098	0.0072	0.0031	0.0018	−0.0049	0.0135	0.0150	0.0014	1929	0.0177
1930	−0.0072	0.0064	0.0133	−0.0100	0.0032	0.0115	0.0028	−0.0005	0.0037	0.0051	0.0046	0.0000	1930	0.0330
1931	−0.0097	0.0074	0.0028	0.0060	0.0098	−0.0240	−0.0009	−0.0009	−0.0142	−0.0136	0.0018	−0.0193	1931	−0.0540
1932	−0.0067	0.0094	0.0045	0.0164	−0.0122	0.0077	0.0091	0.0096	0.0000	0.0018	0.0005	0.0092	1932	0.0502
1933	−0.0041	−0.0028	0.0074	0.0032	0.0178	−0.0014	−0.0028	0.0051	0.0005	−0.0047	0.0005	−0.0280	1933	−0.0099
1934	0.0100	0.0028	0.0162	0.0158	0.0097	0.0070	−0.0044	−0.0113	−0.0160	0.0164	0.0024	0.0102	1934	0.0597
1935	0.0093	0.0088	0.0107	0.0090	−0.0050	0.0098	0.0022	−0.0086	−0.0072	0.0093	−0.0002	0.0105	1935	0.0494
1936	−0.0017	0.0056	0.0018	0.0012	0.0026	−0.0001	0.0010	0.0038	−0.0001	0.0014	0.0070	−0.0067	1936	0.0160
1937	−0.0041	−0.0003	−0.0176	0.0032	0.0067	−0.0027	0.0045	−0.0056	0.0068	0.0020	0.0030	0.0051	1937	0.0005
1938	0.0067	0.0036	−0.0030	0.0214	0.0008	0.0061	−0.0003	0.0000	−0.0026	0.0079	−0.0014	0.0039	1938	0.0437
1939	0.0016	0.0071	0.0069	0.0028	0.0084	−0.0007	0.0030	−0.0155	−0.0273	0.0300	0.0063	0.0098	1939	0.0318
1940	−0.0023	0.0027	0.0080	−0.0005	−0.0221	0.0177	−0.0005	0.0035	0.0040	0.0030	0.0050	0.0023	1940	0.0204
1941	−0.0006	−0.0052	0.0061	0.0027	0.0006	0.0051	−0.0004	0.0006	−0.0004	0.0018	−0.0096	−0.0023	1941	−0.0017
1942	0.0066	0.0009	0.0016	0.0016	0.0010	0.0006	−0.0006	0.0011	−0.0029	0.0011	0.0011	−0.0006	1942	0.0117
1943	0.0025	0.0001	0.0007	0.0010	0.0044	0.0020	0.0008	−0.0010	0.0002	0.0005	0.0002	0.0008	1943	0.0123
1944	−0.0002	0.0004	0.0007	0.0016	−0.0008	−0.0005	0.0016	0.0012	0.0000	−0.0001	−0.0003	−0.0001	1944	0.0035
1945	0.0040	0.0028	−0.0005	0.0005	0.0002	0.0009	−0.0010	0.0006	0.0008	0.0006	0.0001	0.0012	1945	0.0102
1946	0.0030	0.0040	−0.0045	−0.0028	−0.0003	0.0024	−0.0019	−0.0005	−0.0020	0.0015	−0.0018	0.0022	1946	−0.0008
1947	0.0012	−0.0003	0.0014	−0.0022	−0.0002	−0.0003	−0.0004	0.0016	−0.0010	−0.0033	−0.0004	0.0008	1947	−0.0030
1948	0.0002	0.0006	0.0003	0.0006	0.0042	−0.0021	−0.0014	−0.0018	−0.0003	0.0000	0.0006	0.0019	1948	0.0027
1949	0.0015	0.0000	0.0012	0.0003	0.0010	0.0038	0.0010	0.0019	−0.0002	−0.0004	−0.0008	0.0002	1949	0.0095
1950	−0.0016	−0.0002	−0.0011	−0.0003	0.0007	−0.0008	0.0009	−0.0019	−0.0015	−0.0012	0.0005	−0.0004	1950	−0.0069
1951	0.0006	−0.0007	−0.0142	0.0040	−0.0058	0.0033	0.0040	0.0019	−0.0072	−0.0003	0.0015	−0.0033	1951	−0.0163
1952	0.0019	−0.0037	0.0048	0.0037	0.0004	−0.0052	−0.0052	−0.0042	−0.0002	0.0046	−0.0023	−0.0002	1952	−0.0057
1953	−0.0022	−0.0016	−0.0038	−0.0117	−0.0138	0.0129	0.0032	−0.0031	0.0171	0.0018	−0.0006	0.0083	1953	0.0061
1954	0.0049	0.0086	0.0013	0.0031	−0.0084	0.0109	−0.0016	−0.0001	−0.0032	−0.0021	−0.0015	−0.0010	1954	0.0108
1955	−0.0050	−0.0070	0.0004	−0.0014	−0.0019	−0.0057	−0.0091	−0.0018	0.0059	0.0050	−0.0074	−0.0033	1955	−0.0310
1956	0.0080	−0.0018	−0.0122	−0.0027	0.0086	−0.0020	−0.0120	−0.0130	0.0066	−0.0049	−0.0075	−0.0019	1956	−0.0345
1957	0.0207	−0.0037	−0.0009	−0.0130	−0.0047	−0.0133	−0.0051	0.0077	−0.0030	0.0010	0.0365	0.0188	1957	0.0405
1958	0.0010	0.0117	0.0031	0.0031	0.0041	−0.0088	−0.0112	−0.0378	−0.0048	−0.0029	0.0103	−0.0093	1958	−0.0417
1959	−0.0045	0.0078	−0.0070	−0.0084	−0.0033	−0.0113	−0.0004	−0.0116	−0.0019	0.0134	−0.0130	−0.0060	1959	−0.0456
1960	0.0115	0.0032	0.0253	−0.0096	−0.0006	0.0182	0.0236	−0.0034	0.0001	−0.0012	−0.0122	0.0180	1960	0.0742
1961	−0.0089	0.0063	0.0008	0.0026	−0.0058	−0.0054	−0.0024	−0.0012	0.0049	−0.0018	−0.0049	−0.0012	1961	−0.0172
1962	−0.0080	0.0124	0.0058	−0.0006	0.0018	−0.0056	−0.0045	0.0092	−0.0007	0.0018	0.0031	0.0026	1962	0.0173
1963	−0.0059	−0.0011	−0.0002	−0.0002	−0.0017	−0.0015	−0.0030	−0.0012	−0.0019	−0.0022	0.0008	−0.0032	1963	−0.0210
1964	−0.0001	−0.0019	−0.0019	0.0000	0.0049	0.0000	−0.0006	−0.0006	0.0012	0.0000	−0.0037	0.0024	1964	−0.0003
1965	0.0009	−0.0013	0.0006	−0.0007	0.0002	0.0012	−0.0016	−0.0017	−0.0039	−0.0033	−0.0031	−0.0186	1965	−0.0310
1966	−0.0037	−0.0120	0.0145	−0.0056	−0.0032	−0.0064	−0.0065	−0.0171	0.0170	0.0031	−0.0015	0.0180	1966	−0.0041
1967	0.0077	−0.0048	0.0144	−0.0122	0.0002	−0.0265	0.0089	−0.0078	−0.0035	−0.0095	−0.0018	−0.0038	1967	−0.0385
1968	0.0095	−0.0003	−0.0069	−0.0065	0.0015	0.0123	0.0128	−0.0021	0.0011	−0.0034	−0.0054	−0.0220	1968	−0.0099
1969	0.0032	−0.0061	0.0048	0.0021	−0.0131	−0.0142	0.0024	−0.0072	−0.0361	0.0266	−0.0103	−0.0260	1969	−0.0727
1970	−0.0035	0.0378	0.0024	−0.0266	0.0049	−0.0006	0.0087	0.0054	0.0136	0.0037	0.0393	0.0005	1970	0.0871

* Compound annual return

Table A-12 (continued)

Intermediate-Term Government Bonds: Capital Appreciation Returns

from January 1971 to December 2002

Year	Jan	Feb	Mar	Apr	May	Jun	Jul	Aug	Sep	Oct	Nov	Dec	Year	Jan–Dec*
1971	0.0121	0.0181	0.0139	−0.0367	−0.0034	−0.0240	−0.0027	0.0294	−0.0022	0.0173	0.0005	0.0064	1971	0.0272
1972	0.0058	−0.0030	−0.0031	−0.0030	−0.0035	−0.0003	−0.0034	−0.0035	−0.0033	−0.0037	−0.0006	0.0143	1972	−0.0075
1973	−0.0062	−0.0123	−0.0008	0.0007	0.0001	−0.0059	−0.0336	0.0190	0.0195	−0.0010	0.0009	−0.0016	1973	−0.0219
1974	−0.0048	−0.0016	−0.0266	−0.0217	0.0063	−0.0147	−0.0066	−0.0078	0.0247	0.0043	0.0175	0.0120	1974	−0.0199
1975	−0.0008	0.0092	−0.0119	−0.0246	0.0197	−0.0035	−0.0093	−0.0070	−0.0059	0.0298	−0.0065	0.0131	1975	0.0012
1976	−0.0003	0.0028	0.0010	0.0057	−0.0200	0.0090	0.0059	0.0127	0.0019	0.0093	0.0264	−0.0024	1976	0.0525
1977	−0.0241	−0.0002	−0.0001	−0.0001	−0.0002	0.0048	−0.0051	−0.0052	−0.0041	−0.0118	0.0019	−0.0082	1977	−0.0515
1978	−0.0053	−0.0041	−0.0029	−0.0036	−0.0073	−0.0087	0.0028	0.0010	−0.0008	−0.0184	0.0020	−0.0005	1978	−0.0449
1979	−0.0024	−0.0125	0.0038	−0.0044	0.0116	0.0135	−0.0086	−0.0163	−0.0065	−0.0553	0.0274	0.0001	1979	−0.0507
1980	−0.0221	−0.0724	0.0036	0.1095	0.0409	−0.0152	−0.0185	−0.0463	−0.0135	−0.0246	−0.0067	0.0060	1980	−0.0681
1981	−0.0069	−0.0331	0.0146	−0.0322	0.0135	−0.0058	−0.0386	−0.0298	0.0034	0.0482	0.0502	−0.0250	1981	−0.0455
1982	−0.0057	0.0046	−0.0080	0.0186	0.0045	−0.0253	0.0351	0.0359	0.0228	0.0442	−0.0007	0.0100	1982	0.1423
1983	−0.0076	0.0173	−0.0133	0.0177	−0.0208	−0.0069	−0.0280	−0.0022	0.0220	−0.0073	0.0012	−0.0043	1983	−0.0330
1984	0.0081	−0.0153	−0.0129	−0.0104	−0.0353	−0.0007	0.0280	−0.0005	0.0106	0.0274	0.0099	0.0050	1984	0.0122
1985	0.0116	−0.0260	0.0077	0.0167	0.0395	0.0035	−0.0129	0.0067	0.0031	0.0081	0.0121	0.0178	1985	0.0901
1986	0.0011	0.0210	0.0270	0.0021	−0.0274	0.0208	0.0095	0.0209	−0.0168	0.0102	0.0061	−0.0053	1986	0.0699
1987	0.0051	0.0007	−0.0091	−0.0302	−0.0100	0.0051	−0.0040	−0.0105	−0.0209	0.0226	0.0013	0.0023	1987	−0.0475
1988	0.0251	0.0057	−0.0151	−0.0107	−0.0121	0.0111	−0.0111	−0.0086	0.0124	0.0077	−0.0182	−0.0081	1988	−0.0226
1989	0.0044	−0.0117	−0.0029	0.0149	0.0132	0.0254	0.0168	−0.0307	0.0004	0.0166	0.0021	−0.0048	1989	0.0434
1990	−0.0176	−0.0057	−0.0067	−0.0148	0.0186	0.0084	0.0102	−0.0160	0.0030	0.0096	0.0126	0.0095	1990	0.0102
1991	0.0042	−0.0011	−0.0036	0.0046	−0.0006	−0.0081	0.0060	0.0184	0.0155	0.0077	0.0076	0.0209	1991	0.0736
1992	−0.0247	−0.0030	−0.0139	0.0039	0.0166	0.0118	0.0189	0.0100	0.0147	−0.0226	−0.0134	0.0093	1992	0.0064
1993	0.0221	0.0198	−0.0006	0.0043	−0.0051	0.0152	−0.0036	0.0179	0.0015	−0.0020	−0.0135	−0.0011	1993	0.0556
1994	0.0093	−0.0297	−0.0306	−0.0154	−0.0060	−0.0084	0.0115	−0.0034	−0.0213	−0.0084	−0.0131	−0.0010	1994	−0.1114
1995	0.0115	0.0178	0.0003	0.0090	0.0307	0.0030	−0.0066	0.0035	0.0017	0.0069	0.0102	0.0052	1995	0.0966
1996	−0.0040	−0.0178	−0.0164	−0.0103	−0.0086	0.0067	−0.0033	−0.0057	0.0100	0.0129	0.0102	−0.0128	1996	−0.0390
1997	−0.0027	−0.0045	−0.0168	0.0093	0.0024	0.0048	0.0210	−0.0143	0.0098	0.0100	−0.0045	0.0054	1997	0.0194
1998	0.0134	−0.0080	−0.0024	0.0015	0.0025	0.0030	−0.0020	0.0225	0.0289	0.0006	−0.0134	−0.0002	1998	0.0466
1999	0.0018	−0.0297	0.0038	−0.0023	−0.0188	−0.0020	−0.0052	−0.0035	0.0049	−0.0054	−0.0060	−0.0100	1999	−0.0706
2000	−0.0107	0.0026	0.0147	−0.0091	−0.0007	0.0138	0.0019	0.0083	0.0049	0.0028	0.0127	0.0171	2000	0.0594
2001	0.0066	0.0079	0.0049	−0.0146	−0.0049	0.0025	0.0203	0.0056	0.0219	0.0145	−0.0201	−0.0117	2001	0.0323
2002	−0.0003	0.0073	−0.0276	0.0193	0.0079	0.0135	0.0234	0.0138	0.0261	−0.0046	−0.0191	0.0251	2002	0.0865

Compound annual return

Table A-13

Intermediate-Term Government Bonds: Yields

from January 1926 to December 1970

Year	Jan	Feb	Mar	Apr	May	Jun	Jul	Aug	Sep	Oct	Nov	Dec	Year	Jan–Dec
1926	0.0386	0.0386	0.0384	0.0371	0.0376	0.0377	0.0381	0.0386	0.0382	0.0377	0.0374	0.0361	1926	0.0361
1927	0.0355	0.0353	0.0351	0.0354	0.0356	0.0356	0.0353	0.0347	0.0340	0.0354	0.0342	0.0340	1927	0.0340
1928	0.0336	0.0343	0.0347	0.0354	0.0362	0.0365	0.0392	0.0388	0.0389	0.0389	0.0392	0.0401	1928	0.0401
1929	0.0415	0.0427	0.0434	0.0422	0.0444	0.0428	0.0421	0.0417	0.0428	0.0398	0.0365	0.0362	1929	0.0362
1930	0.0378	0.0364	0.0335	0.0357	0.0350	0.0325	0.0319	0.0320	0.0312	0.0301	0.0291	0.0291	1930	0.0291
1931	0.0312	0.0296	0.0290	0.0277	0.0256	0.0308	0.0310	0.0312	0.0343	0.0373	0.0369	0.0412	1931	0.0412
1932	0.0427	0.0406	0.0396	0.0360	0.0387	0.0370	0.0350	0.0329	0.0329	0.0325	0.0324	0.0304	1932	0.0304
1933	0.0313	0.0319	0.0303	0.0296	0.0258	0.0261	0.0267	0.0256	0.0255	0.0265	0.0264	0.0325	1933	0.0325
1934	0.0325	0.0321	0.0296	0.0272	0.0257	0.0246	0.0253	0.0271	0.0298	0.0271	0.0267	0.0249	1934	0.0249
1935	0.0233	0.0218	0.0199	0.0184	0.0193	0.0175	0.0171	0.0187	0.0201	0.0183	0.0183	0.0163	1935	0.0163
1936	0.0166	0.0155	0.0151	0.0149	0.0143	0.0143	0.0141	0.0133	0.0133	0.0130	0.0114	0.0129	1936	0.0129
1937	0.0134	0.0135	0.0184	0.0175	0.0156	0.0164	0.0151	0.0168	0.0147	0.0141	0.0131	0.0114	1937	0.0114
1938	0.0205	0.0200	0.0204	0.0174	0.0173	0.0164	0.0164	0.0164	0.0168	0.0156	0.0158	0.0152	1938	0.0152
1939	0.0149	0.0138	0.0127	0.0122	0.0108	0.0110	0.0105	0.0131	0.0180	0.0127	0.0116	0.0098	1939	0.0098
1940	0.0103	0.0098	0.0083	0.0084	0.0127	0.0092	0.0093	0.0086	0.0078	0.0072	0.0061	0.0057	1940	0.0057
1941	0.0077	0.0089	0.0075	0.0069	0.0067	0.0055	0.0056	0.0055	0.0056	0.0051	0.0076	0.0082	1941	0.0082
1942	0.0083	0.0081	0.0077	0.0074	0.0071	0.0070	0.0071	0.0069	0.0076	0.0073	0.0070	0.0072	1942	0.0072
1943	0.0166	0.0166	0.0164	0.0162	0.0153	0.0149	0.0147	0.0149	0.0149	0.0147	0.0147	0.0145	1943	0.0145
1944	0.0150	0.0150	0.0148	0.0143	0.0146	0.0147	0.0142	0.0139	0.0139	0.0139	0.0140	0.0140	1944	0.0140
1945	0.0127	0.0118	0.0120	0.0118	0.0117	0.0114	0.0118	0.0115	0.0112	0.0109	0.0109	0.0103	1945	0.0103
1946	0.0099	0.0087	0.0101	0.0111	0.0112	0.0103	0.0110	0.0112	0.0120	0.0114	0.0121	0.0112	1946	0.0112
1947	0.0116	0.0117	0.0112	0.0120	0.0121	0.0122	0.0124	0.0117	0.0121	0.0136	0.0138	0.0134	1947	0.0134
1948	0.0160	0.0158	0.0157	0.0155	0.0142	0.0149	0.0154	0.0160	0.0161	0.0161	0.0158	0.0151	1948	0.0151
1949	0.0153	0.0153	0.0148	0.0147	0.0144	0.0129	0.0125	0.0117	0.0118	0.0120	0.0124	0.0123	1949	0.0123
1950	0.0131	0.0132	0.0137	0.0138	0.0134	0.0139	0.0134	0.0145	0.0154	0.0162	0.0159	0.0162	1950	0.0162
1951	0.0179	0.0180	0.0211	0.0202	0.0215	0.0208	0.0199	0.0194	0.0212	0.0212	0.0209	0.0217	1951	0.0217
1952	0.0212	0.0222	0.0209	0.0199	0.0198	0.0213	0.0228	0.0241	0.0242	0.0227	0.0235	0.0235	1952	0.0235
1953	0.0242	0.0245	0.0253	0.0277	0.0307	0.0279	0.0272	0.0279	0.0241	0.0237	0.0238	0.0218	1953	0.0218
1954	0.0187	0.0157	0.0153	0.0142	0.0173	0.0131	0.0138	0.0138	0.0152	0.0161	0.0168	0.0172	1954	0.0172
1955	0.0227	0.0240	0.0240	0.0242	0.0246	0.0257	0.0276	0.0280	0.0267	0.0257	0.0273	0.0280	1955	0.0280
1956	0.0271	0.0275	0.0300	0.0305	0.0287	0.0292	0.0317	0.0346	0.0331	0.0342	0.0359	0.0363	1956	0.0363
1957	0.0326	0.0333	0.0334	0.0357	0.0366	0.0390	0.0399	0.0385	0.0390	0.0388	0.0320	0.0284	1957	0.0284
1958	0.0282	0.0259	0.0253	0.0246	0.0238	0.0250	0.0281	0.0365	0.0376	0.0382	0.0359	0.0381	1958	0.0381
1959	0.0395	0.0378	0.0393	0.0413	0.0420	0.0447	0.0448	0.0477	0.0482	0.0448	0.0482	0.0498	1959	0.0498
1960	0.0471	0.0464	0.0409	0.0431	0.0432	0.0390	0.0334	0.0343	0.0343	0.0346	0.0377	0.0331	1960	0.0331
1961	0.0363	0.0350	0.0348	0.0342	0.0355	0.0368	0.0373	0.0376	0.0365	0.0369	0.0381	0.0384	1961	0.0384
1962	0.0402	0.0377	0.0366	0.0367	0.0363	0.0375	0.0384	0.0365	0.0366	0.0362	0.0355	0.0350	1962	0.0350
1963	0.0368	0.0370	0.0370	0.0371	0.0374	0.0378	0.0385	0.0388	0.0392	0.0398	0.0396	0.0404	1963	0.0404
1964	0.0402	0.0407	0.0411	0.0411	0.0399	0.0399	0.0401	0.0402	0.0399	0.0399	0.0409	0.0403	1964	0.0403
1965	0.0413	0.0416	0.0414	0.0416	0.0415	0.0413	0.0416	0.0420	0.0429	0.0437	0.0444	0.0490	1965	0.0490
1966	0.0482	0.0507	0.0477	0.0489	0.0496	0.0510	0.0525	0.0565	0.0526	0.0519	0.0522	0.0479	1966	0.0479
1967	0.0459	0.0470	0.0437	0.0466	0.0465	0.0530	0.0508	0.0528	0.0537	0.0562	0.0566	0.0577	1967	0.0577
1968	0.0548	0.0549	0.0563	0.0577	0.0574	0.0547	0.0518	0.0523	0.0520	0.0528	0.0541	0.0596	1968	0.0596
1969	0.0637	0.0651	0.0640	0.0636	0.0666	0.0699	0.0693	0.0711	0.0799	0.0735	0.0761	0.0829	1969	0.0829
1970	0.0820	0.0730	0.0724	0.0790	0.0778	0.0780	0.0757	0.0743	0.0707	0.0697	0.0591	0.0590	1970	0.0590

Table A-13 (continued)

Intermediate-Term Government Bonds: Yields

from January 1971 to December 2002

Year	Jan	Feb	Mar	Apr	May	Jun	Jul	Aug	Sep	Oct	Nov	Dec	Year	Jan–Dec
1971	0.0570	0.0526	0.0493	0.0585	0.0593	0.0656	0.0663	0.0585	0.0591	0.0545	0.0543	0.0525	1971	0.0525
1972	0.0556	0.0563	0.0570	0.0577	0.0586	0.0587	0.0595	0.0604	0.0613	0.0623	0.0625	0.0585	1972	0.0585
1973	0.0641	0.0671	0.0673	0.0671	0.0671	0.0686	0.0776	0.0725	0.0674	0.0677	0.0674	0.0679	1973	0.0679
1974	0.0687	0.0691	0.0751	0.0801	0.0786	0.0822	0.0838	0.0857	0.0797	0.0787	0.0743	0.0712	1974	0.0712
1975	0.0730	0.0709	0.0737	0.0798	0.0749	0.0758	0.0782	0.0800	0.0815	0.0736	0.0754	0.0719	1975	0.0719
1976	0.0743	0.0736	0.0733	0.0719	0.0771	0.0747	0.0732	0.0697	0.0692	0.0667	0.0594	0.0600	1976	0.0600
1977	0.0673	0.0673	0.0673	0.0674	0.0674	0.0662	0.0675	0.0689	0.0700	0.0733	0.0727	0.0751	1977	0.0751
1978	0.0773	0.0784	0.0791	0.0800	0.0820	0.0843	0.0836	0.0833	0.0835	0.0887	0.0882	0.0883	1978	0.0883
1979	0.0895	0.0928	0.0918	0.0929	0.0899	0.0864	0.0887	0.0933	0.0951	0.1112	0.1033	0.1033	1979	0.1033
1980	0.1093	0.1294	0.1285	0.1009	0.0903	0.0944	0.0996	0.1133	0.1171	0.1244	0.1264	0.1245	1980	0.1245
1981	0.1275	0.1371	0.1328	0.1427	0.1385	0.1404	0.1533	0.1636	0.1625	0.1472	0.1311	0.1396	1981	0.1396
1982	0.1397	0.1385	0.1406	0.1355	0.1343	0.1417	0.1315	0.1209	0.1144	0.1018	0.1020	0.0990	1982	0.0990
1983	0.1057	0.1010	0.1048	0.0997	0.1059	0.1080	0.1168	0.1175	0.1108	0.1131	0.1127	0.1141	1983	0.1141
1984	0.1137	0.1181	0.1219	0.1251	0.1363	0.1365	0.1274	0.1276	0.1242	0.1154	0.1121	0.1104	1984	0.1104
1985	0.1081	0.1152	0.1131	0.1084	0.0974	0.0963	0.1002	0.0982	0.0973	0.0949	0.0911	0.0855	1985	0.0855
1986	0.0870	0.0815	0.0743	0.0737	0.0816	0.0756	0.0728	0.0668	0.0718	0.0687	0.0669	0.0685	1986	0.0685
1987	0.0685	0.0683	0.0708	0.0793	0.0821	0.0806	0.0818	0.0849	0.0912	0.0844	0.0840	0.0832	1987	0.0832
1988	0.0782	0.0768	0.0807	0.0836	0.0870	0.0839	0.0871	0.0895	0.0859	0.0837	0.0892	0.0917	1988	0.0917
1989	0.0896	0.0927	0.0934	0.0895	0.0860	0.0791	0.0745	0.0834	0.0833	0.0786	0.0779	0.0794	1989	0.0794
1990	0.0842	0.0855	0.0871	0.0907	0.0864	0.0843	0.0819	0.0859	0.0851	0.0826	0.0795	0.0770	1990	0.0770
1991	0.0772	0.0774	0.0783	0.0772	0.0773	0.0793	0.0778	0.0732	0.0693	0.0673	0.0653	0.0597	1991	0.0597
1992	0.0683	0.0690	0.0720	0.0711	0.0674	0.0647	0.0604	0.0581	0.0547	0.0601	0.0634	0.0611	1992	0.0611
1993	0.0588	0.0547	0.0549	0.0540	0.0551	0.0517	0.0526	0.0486	0.0483	0.0488	0.0519	0.0522	1993	0.0522
1994	0.0515	0.0575	0.0638	0.0670	0.0682	0.0699	0.0675	0.0683	0.0730	0.0749	0.0778	0.0780	1994	0.0780
1995	0.0754	0.0708	0.0707	0.0685	0.0606	0.0598	0.0616	0.0606	0.0601	0.0582	0.0553	0.0538	1995	0.0538
1996	0.0528	0.0573	0.0614	0.0640	0.0663	0.0645	0.0654	0.0670	0.0643	0.0607	0.0578	0.0616	1996	0.0616
1997	0.0629	0.0639	0.0677	0.0656	0.0650	0.0639	0.0589	0.0624	0.0601	0.0576	0.0587	0.0573	1997	0.0573
1998	0.0545	0.0562	0.0567	0.0564	0.0558	0.0551	0.0556	0.0503	0.0435	0.0434	0.0467	0.0468	1998	0.0468
1999	0.0467	0.0535	0.0526	0.0532	0.0576	0.0581	0.0593	0.0602	0.0590	0.0604	0.0619	0.0645	1999	0.0645
2000	0.0675	0.0669	0.0636	0.0657	0.0658	0.0626	0.0621	0.0601	0.0589	0.0582	0.0551	0.0507	2000	0.0507
2001	0.0499	0.0482	0.0471	0.0504	0.0515	0.0510	0.0464	0.0450	0.0399	0.0365	0.0413	0.0442	2001	0.0442
2002	0.0459	0.0442	0.0504	0.0461	0.0443	0.0412	0.0358	0.0325	0.0265	0.0276	0.0323	0.0261	2002	0.0261

Table A-14

U.S. Treasury Bills: Total Returns

from January 1926 to December 1970

Year	Jan	Feb	Mar	Apr	May	Jun	Jul	Aug	Sep	Oct	Nov	Dec	Year	Jan–Dec
1926	0.0034	0.0027	0.0030	0.0034	0.0001	0.0035	0.0022	0.0025	0.0023	0.0032	0.0031	0.0028	1926	0.0327
1927	0.0025	0.0026	0.0030	0.0025	0.0030	0.0026	0.0030	0.0028	0.0021	0.0025	0.0021	0.0022	1927	0.0312
1928	0.0025	0.0033	0.0029	0.0022	0.0032	0.0031	0.0032	0.0032	0.0027	0.0041	0.0038	0.0006	1928	0.0356
1929	0.0034	0.0036	0.0034	0.0036	0.0044	0.0052	0.0033	0.0040	0.0035	0.0046	0.0037	0.0037	1929	0.0475
1930	0.0014	0.0030	0.0035	0.0021	0.0026	0.0027	0.0020	0.0009	0.0022	0.0009	0.0013	0.0014	1930	0.0241
1931	0.0015	0.0004	0.0013	0.0008	0.0009	0.0008	0.0006	0.0003	0.0003	0.0010	0.0017	0.0012	1931	0.0107
1932	0.0023	0.0023	0.0016	0.0011	0.0006	0.0002	0.0003	0.0003	0.0003	0.0002	0.0002	0.0001	1932	0.0096
1933	0.0001	−0.0003	0.0004	0.0010	0.0004	0.0002	0.0002	0.0003	0.0002	0.0001	0.0002	0.0002	1933	0.0030
1934	0.0005	0.0002	0.0002	0.0001	0.0001	0.0001	0.0001	0.0001	0.0001	0.0001	0.0001	0.0001	1934	0.0016
1935	0.0001	0.0002	0.0001	0.0001	0.0001	0.0001	0.0001	0.0001	0.0001	0.0001	0.0002	0.0001	1935	0.0017
1936	0.0001	0.0001	0.0002	0.0002	0.0002	0.0003	0.0001	0.0002	0.0001	0.0002	0.0001	0.0000	1936	0.0018
1937	0.0001	0.0002	0.0001	0.0003	0.0006	0.0003	0.0003	0.0002	0.0004	0.0002	0.0002	0.0000	1937	0.0031
1938	0.0000	0.0000	−0.0001	0.0001	0.0000	0.0000	−0.0001	0.0000	0.0002	0.0001	−0.0006	0.0000	1938	−0.0002
1939	−0.0001	0.0001	−0.0001	0.0000	0.0001	0.0001	0.0000	−0.0001	0.0001	0.0000	0.0000	0.0000	1939	0.0002
1940	0.0000	0.0000	0.0000	0.0000	−0.0002	0.0000	0.0001	−0.0001	0.0000	0.0000	0.0000	0.0000	1940	0.0000
1941	−0.0001	−0.0001	0.0001	−0.0001	0.0000	0.0000	0.0003	0.0001	0.0001	0.0000	0.0000	0.0001	1941	0.0006
1942	0.0002	0.0001	0.0001	0.0001	0.0003	0.0002	0.0003	0.0003	0.0003	0.0003	0.0003	0.0003	1942	0.0027
1943	0.0003	0.0003	0.0003	0.0003	0.0003	0.0003	0.0003	0.0003	0.0003	0.0003	0.0003	0.0003	1943	0.0035
1944	0.0003	0.0003	0.0002	0.0003	0.0003	0.0003	0.0003	0.0003	0.0002	0.0003	0.0003	0.0002	1944	0.0033
1945	0.0003	0.0002	0.0002	0.0003	0.0003	0.0002	0.0003	0.0003	0.0003	0.0003	0.0002	0.0003	1945	0.0033
1946	0.0003	0.0003	0.0003	0.0003	0.0003	0.0003	0.0003	0.0003	0.0003	0.0003	0.0003	0.0003	1946	0.0035
1947	0.0003	0.0003	0.0003	0.0003	0.0003	0.0003	0.0003	0.0003	0.0006	0.0006	0.0006	0.0008	1947	0.0050
1948	0.0007	0.0007	0.0009	0.0008	0.0008	0.0009	0.0008	0.0009	0.0004	0.0004	0.0004	0.0004	1948	0.0081
1949	0.0010	0.0009	0.0010	0.0009	0.0010	0.0010	0.0009	0.0009	0.0009	0.0009	0.0008	0.0009	1949	0.0110
1950	0.0009	0.0009	0.0010	0.0009	0.0010	0.0010	0.0010	0.0010	0.0010	0.0012	0.0011	0.0011	1950	0.0120
1951	0.0013	0.0010	0.0011	0.0013	0.0012	0.0012	0.0013	0.0013	0.0012	0.0016	0.0011	0.0012	1951	0.0149
1952	0.0015	0.0012	0.0011	0.0012	0.0013	0.0015	0.0015	0.0015	0.0016	0.0014	0.0010	0.0016	1952	0.0166
1953	0.0016	0.0014	0.0018	0.0016	0.0017	0.0018	0.0015	0.0017	0.0016	0.0013	0.0008	0.0013	1953	0.0182
1954	0.0011	0.0007	0.0008	0.0009	0.0005	0.0006	0.0005	0.0005	0.0009	0.0007	0.0006	0.0008	1954	0.0086
1955	0.0008	0.0009	0.0010	0.0010	0.0014	0.0010	0.0010	0.0016	0.0016	0.0018	0.0017	0.0018	1955	0.0157
1956	0.0022	0.0019	0.0015	0.0019	0.0023	0.0020	0.0022	0.0017	0.0018	0.0025	0.0020	0.0024	1956	0.0246
1957	0.0027	0.0024	0.0023	0.0025	0.0026	0.0024	0.0030	0.0025	0.0026	0.0029	0.0028	0.0024	1957	0.0314
1958	0.0028	0.0012	0.0009	0.0008	0.0011	0.0003	0.0007	0.0004	0.0019	0.0018	0.0011	0.0022	1958	0.0154
1959	0.0021	0.0019	0.0022	0.0020	0.0022	0.0025	0.0025	0.0019	0.0031	0.0030	0.0026	0.0034	1959	0.0295
1960	0.0033	0.0029	0.0035	0.0019	0.0027	0.0024	0.0013	0.0017	0.0016	0.0022	0.0013	0.0016	1960	0.0266
1961	0.0019	0.0014	0.0020	0.0017	0.0018	0.0020	0.0018	0.0014	0.0017	0.0019	0.0015	0.0019	1961	0.0213
1962	0.0024	0.0020	0.0020	0.0022	0.0024	0.0020	0.0027	0.0023	0.0021	0.0026	0.0020	0.0023	1962	0.0273
1963	0.0025	0.0023	0.0023	0.0025	0.0024	0.0023	0.0027	0.0025	0.0027	0.0029	0.0027	0.0029	1963	0.0312
1964	0.0030	0.0026	0.0031	0.0029	0.0026	0.0030	0.0030	0.0028	0.0028	0.0029	0.0029	0.0031	1964	0.0354
1965	0.0028	0.0030	0.0036	0.0031	0.0031	0.0035	0.0031	0.0033	0.0031	0.0031	0.0035	0.0033	1965	0.0393
1966	0.0038	0.0035	0.0038	0.0034	0.0041	0.0038	0.0035	0.0041	0.0040	0.0045	0.0040	0.0040	1966	0.0476
1967	0.0043	0.0036	0.0039	0.0032	0.0033	0.0027	0.0032	0.0031	0.0032	0.0039	0.0036	0.0033	1967	0.0421
1968	0.0040	0.0039	0.0038	0.0043	0.0045	0.0043	0.0048	0.0042	0.0043	0.0044	0.0042	0.0043	1968	0.0521
1969	0.0053	0.0046	0.0046	0.0053	0.0048	0.0051	0.0053	0.0050	0.0062	0.0060	0.0052	0.0064	1969	0.0658
1970	0.0060	0.0062	0.0057	0.0050	0.0053	0.0058	0.0052	0.0053	0.0054	0.0046	0.0046	0.0042	1970	0.0652

* Compound annual return

Table A-14 (continued)

U.S. Treasury Bills: Total Returns

from January 1971 to December 2002

Year	Jan	Feb	Mar	Apr	May	Jun	Jul	Aug	Sep	Oct	Nov	Dec	Year	Jan–Dec*
1971	0.0038	0.0033	0.0030	0.0028	0.0029	0.0037	0.0040	0.0047	0.0037	0.0037	0.0037	0.0037	1971	0.0439
1972	0.0029	0.0025	0.0027	0.0029	0.0030	0.0029	0.0031	0.0029	0.0034	0.0040	0.0037	0.0037	1972	0.0384
1973	0.0044	0.0041	0.0046	0.0052	0.0051	0.0051	0.0064	0.0070	0.0068	0.0065	0.0056	0.0064	1973	0.0693
1974	0.0063	0.0058	0.0056	0.0075	0.0075	0.0060	0.0070	0.0060	0.0081	0.0051	0.0054	0.0070	1974	0.0800
1975	0.0058	0.0043	0.0041	0.0044	0.0044	0.0041	0.0048	0.0048	0.0053	0.0056	0.0041	0.0048	1975	0.0580
1976	0.0047	0.0034	0.0040	0.0042	0.0037	0.0043	0.0047	0.0042	0.0044	0.0041	0.0040	0.0040	1976	0.0508
1977	0.0036	0.0035	0.0038	0.0038	0.0037	0.0040	0.0042	0.0044	0.0043	0.0049	0.0050	0.0049	1977	0.0512
1978	0.0049	0.0046	0.0053	0.0054	0.0051	0.0054	0.0056	0.0055	0.0062	0.0068	0.0070	0.0078	1978	0.0718
1979	0.0077	0.0073	0.0081	0.0080	0.0082	0.0081	0.0077	0.0077	0.0083	0.0087	0.0099	0.0095	1979	0.1038
1980	0.0080	0.0089	0.0121	0.0126	0.0081	0.0061	0.0053	0.0064	0.0075	0.0095	0.0096	0.0131	1980	0.1124
1981	0.0104	0.0107	0.0121	0.0108	0.0115	0.0135	0.0124	0.0128	0.0124	0.0121	0.0107	0.0087	1981	0.1471
1982	0.0080	0.0092	0.0098	0.0113	0.0106	0.0096	0.0105	0.0076	0.0051	0.0059	0.0063	0.0067	1982	0.1054
1983	0.0069	0.0062	0.0063	0.0071	0.0069	0.0067	0.0074	0.0076	0.0076	0.0076	0.0070	0.0073	1983	0.0880
1984	0.0076	0.0071	0.0073	0.0081	0.0078	0.0075	0.0082	0.0083	0.0086	0.0100	0.0073	0.0064	1984	0.0985
1985	0.0065	0.0058	0.0062	0.0072	0.0066	0.0055	0.0062	0.0055	0.0060	0.0065	0.0061	0.0065	1985	0.0772
1986	0.0056	0.0053	0.0060	0.0052	0.0049	0.0052	0.0052	0.0046	0.0045	0.0046	0.0039	0.0049	1986	0.0616
1987	0.0042	0.0043	0.0047	0.0044	0.0038	0.0048	0.0046	0.0047	0.0045	0.0060	0.0035	0.0039	1987	0.0547
1988	0.0029	0.0046	0.0044	0.0046	0.0051	0.0049	0.0051	0.0059	0.0062	0.0061	0.0057	0.0063	1988	0.0635
1989	0.0055	0.0061	0.0067	0.0067	0.0079	0.0071	0.0070	0.0074	0.0065	0.0068	0.0069	0.0061	1989	0.0837
1990	0.0057	0.0057	0.0064	0.0069	0.0068	0.0063	0.0068	0.0066	0.0060	0.0068	0.0057	0.0060	1990	0.0781
1991	0.0052	0.0048	0.0044	0.0053	0.0047	0.0042	0.0049	0.0046	0.0046	0.0042	0.0039	0.0038	1991	0.0560
1992	0.0034	0.0028	0.0034	0.0032	0.0028	0.0032	0.0031	0.0026	0.0026	0.0023	0.0023	0.0028	1992	0.0351
1993	0.0023	0.0022	0.0025	0.0024	0.0022	0.0025	0.0024	0.0025	0.0026	0.0022	0.0025	0.0023	1993	0.0290
1994	0.0025	0.0021	0.0027	0.0027	0.0032	0.0031	0.0028	0.0037	0.0037	0.0038	0.0037	0.0044	1994	0.0390
1995	0.0042	0.0040	0.0046	0.0044	0.0054	0.0047	0.0045	0.0047	0.0043	0.0047	0.0042	0.0049	1995	0.0560
1996	0.0043	0.0039	0.0039	0.0046	0.0042	0.0040	0.0045	0.0041	0.0044	0.0042	0.0041	0.0046	1996	0.0521
1997	0.0045	0.0039	0.0043	0.0043	0.0049	0.0037	0.0043	0.0041	0.0044	0.0042	0.0039	0.0048	1997	0.0526
1998	0.0043	0.0039	0.0039	0.0043	0.0040	0.0041	0.0040	0.0043	0.0046	0.0032	0.0031	0.0038	1998	0.0486
1999	0.0035	0.0035	0.0043	0.0037	0.0034	0.0040	0.0038	0.0039	0.0039	0.0039	0.0036	0.0044	1999	0.0468
2000	0.0041	0.0043	0.0047	0.0046	0.0050	0.0040	0.0048	0.0050	0.0051	0.0056	0.0051	0.0050	2000	0.0589
2001	0.0054	0.0038	0.0042	0.0039	0.0032	0.0028	0.0030	0.0031	0.0028	0.0022	0.0017	0.0015	2001	0.0383
2002	0.0014	0.0013	0.0013	0.0015	0.0014	0.0013	0.0015	0.0014	0.0014	0.0014	0.0012	0.0011	2002	0.0165

Compound annual return

Table A-15

Inflation

from January 1926 to December 1970

Year	Jan	Feb	Mar	Apr	May	Jun	Jul	Aug	Sep	Oct	Nov	Dec	Year	Jan–Dec*
1926	0.0000	−0.0037	−0.0056	0.0094	−0.0056	−0.0075	−0.0094	−0.0057	0.0057	0.0038	0.0038	0.0000	1926	−0.0149
1927	−0.0076	−0.0076	−0.0058	0.0000	0.0077	0.0096	−0.0190	−0.0058	0.0058	0.0058	−0.0019	−0.0019	1927	−0.0208
1928	−0.0019	−0.0097	0.0000	0.0020	0.0058	−0.0078	0.0000	0.0020	0.0078	−0.0019	−0.0019	−0.0039	1928	−0.0097
1929	−0.0019	−0.0020	−0.0039	−0.0039	0.0059	0.0039	0.0098	0.0039	−0.0019	0.0000	−0.0019	−0.0058	1929	0.0020
1930	−0.0039	−0.0039	−0.0059	0.0059	−0.0059	−0.0059	−0.0139	−0.0060	0.0061	−0.0060	−0.0081	−0.0143	1930	−0.0603
1931	−0.0145	−0.0147	−0.0064	−0.0064	−0.0108	−0.0109	−0.0022	−0.0022	−0.0044	−0.0067	−0.0112	−0.0091	1931	−0.0952
1932	−0.0206	−0.0140	−0.0047	−0.0071	−0.0144	−0.0073	0.0000	−0.0123	−0.0050	−0.0075	−0.0050	−0.0101	1932	−0.1030
1933	−0.0153	−0.0155	−0.0079	−0.0027	0.0027	0.0106	0.0289	0.0102	0.0000	0.0000	0.0000	−0.0051	1933	0.0051
1934	0.0051	0.0076	0.0000	−0.0025	0.0025	0.0025	0.0000	0.0025	0.0150	−0.0074	−0.0025	−0.0025	1934	0.0203
1935	0.0149	0.0074	−0.0024	0.0098	−0.0048	−0.0024	−0.0049	0.0000	0.0049	0.0000	0.0049	0.0024	1935	0.0299
1936	0.0000	−0.0048	−0.0049	0.0000	0.0000	0.0098	0.0048	0.0072	0.0024	−0.0024	0.0000	0.0000	1936	0.0121
1937	0.0072	0.0024	0.0071	0.0047	0.0047	0.0023	0.0046	0.0023	0.0092	−0.0046	−0.0069	−0.0023	1937	0.0310
1938	−0.0139	−0.0094	0.0000	0.0047	−0.0047	0.0000	0.0024	−0.0024	0.0000	−0.0047	−0.0024	0.0024	1938	−0.0278
1939	−0.0048	−0.0048	−0.0024	−0.0024	0.0000	0.0000	0.0000	0.0000	0.0193	−0.0047	0.0000	−0.0048	1939	−0.0048
1940	−0.0024	0.0072	−0.0024	0.0000	0.0024	0.0024	−0.0024	−0.0024	0.0024	0.0000	0.0000	0.0048	1940	0.0096
1941	0.0000	0.0000	0.0047	0.0094	0.0070	0.0186	0.0046	0.0091	0.0180	0.0110	0.0087	0.0022	1941	0.0972
1942	0.0130	0.0085	0.0127	0.0063	0.0104	0.0021	0.0041	0.0061	0.0020	0.0101	0.0060	0.0080	1942	0.0929
1943	0.0000	0.0020	0.0158	0.0116	0.0077	−0.0019	−0.0076	−0.0038	0.0039	0.0038	−0.0019	0.0019	1943	0.0316
1944	−0.0019	−0.0019	0.0000	0.0058	0.0038	0.0019	0.0057	0.0038	0.0000	0.0000	0.0000	0.0038	1944	0.0211
1945	0.0000	−0.0019	0.0000	0.0019	0.0075	0.0093	0.0018	0.0000	−0.0037	0.0000	0.0037	0.0037	1945	0.0225
1946	0.0000	−0.0037	0.0074	0.0055	0.0055	0.0109	0.0590	0.0220	0.0116	0.0196	0.0240	0.0078	1946	0.1816
1947	0.0000	−0.0016	0.0218	0.0000	−0.0030	0.0076	0.0091	0.0105	0.0238	0.0000	0.0058	0.0130	1947	0.0901
1948	0.0114	−0.0085	−0.0028	0.0142	0.0070	0.0070	0.0125	0.0041	0.0000	−0.0041	−0.0068	−0.0069	1948	0.0271
1949	−0.0014	−0.0111	0.0028	0.0014	−0.0014	0.0014	−0.0070	0.0028	0.0042	−0.0056	0.0014	−0.0056	1949	−0.0180
1950	−0.0042	−0.0028	0.0043	0.0014	0.0042	0.0056	0.0098	0.0083	0.0069	0.0055	0.0041	0.0135	1950	0.0579
1951	0.0160	0.0118	0.0039	0.0013	0.0039	−0.0013	0.0013	0.0000	0.0064	0.0051	0.0051	0.0038	1951	0.0587
1952	0.0000	−0.0063	0.0000	0.0038	0.0013	0.0025	0.0076	0.0012	−0.0012	0.0012	0.0000	−0.0012	1952	0.0088
1953	−0.0025	−0.0050	0.0025	0.0013	0.0025	0.0038	0.0025	0.0025	0.0012	0.0025	−0.0037	−0.0012	1953	0.0062
1954	0.0025	−0.0012	−0.0012	−0.0025	0.0037	0.0012	0.0000	−0.0012	−0.0025	−0.0025	0.0012	−0.0025	1954	−0.0050
1955	0.0000	0.0000	0.0000	0.0000	0.0000	0.0000	0.0037	−0.0025	0.0037	0.0000	0.0012	−0.0025	1955	0.0037
1956	−0.0012	0.0000	0.0012	0.0012	0.0050	0.0062	0.0074	−0.0012	0.0012	0.0061	0.0000	0.0024	1956	0.0286
1957	0.0012	0.0036	0.0024	0.0036	0.0024	0.0060	0.0047	0.0012	0.0012	0.0000	0.0035	0.0000	1957	0.0302
1958	0.0059	0.0012	0.0070	0.0023	0.0000	0.0012	0.0012	−0.0012	0.0000	0.0000	0.0012	−0.0012	1958	0.0176
1959	0.0012	−0.0012	0.0000	0.0012	0.0012	0.0046	0.0023	−0.0011	0.0034	0.0034	0.0000	0.0000	1959	0.0150
1960	−0.0011	0.0011	0.0000	0.0057	0.0000	0.0023	0.0000	0.0000	0.0011	0.0045	0.0011	0.0000	1960	0.0148
1961	0.0000	0.0000	0.0000	0.0000	0.0000	0.0011	0.0045	−0.0011	0.0022	0.0000	0.0000	0.0000	1961	0.0067
1962	0.0000	0.0022	0.0022	0.0022	0.0000	0.0000	0.0022	0.0000	0.0055	−0.0011	0.0000	−0.0011	1962	0.0122
1963	0.0011	0.0011	0.0011	0.0000	0.0000	0.0044	0.0044	0.0000	0.0000	0.0011	0.0011	0.0022	1963	0.0165
1964	0.0011	−0.0011	0.0011	0.0011	0.0000	0.0022	0.0022	−0.0011	0.0022	0.0011	0.0021	0.0011	1964	0.0119
1965	0.0000	0.0000	0.0011	0.0032	0.0021	0.0053	0.0011	−0.0021	0.0021	0.0011	0.0021	0.0032	1965	0.0192
1966	0.0000	0.0063	0.0031	0.0042	0.0010	0.0031	0.0031	0.0051	0.0020	0.0041	0.0000	0.0010	1966	0.0335
1967	0.0000	0.0010	0.0020	0.0020	0.0030	0.0030	0.0050	0.0030	0.0020	0.0030	0.0030	0.0030	1967	0.0304
1968	0.0039	0.0029	0.0049	0.0029	0.0029	0.0058	0.0048	0.0029	0.0029	0.0057	0.0038	0.0028	1968	0.0472
1969	0.0028	0.0037	0.0084	0.0065	0.0028	0.0064	0.0046	0.0045	0.0045	0.0036	0.0054	0.0062	1969	0.0611
1970	0.0035	0.0053	0.0053	0.0061	0.0043	0.0052	0.0034	0.0017	0.0051	0.0051	0.0034	0.0051	1970	0.0549

* Compound annual return

Table A-15 (continued)

Inflation

From January 1971 to December 2002

Year	Jan	Feb	Mar	Apr	May	Jun	Jul	Aug	Sep	Oct	Nov	Dec	Year	Jan–Dec*
1971	0.0008	0.0017	0.0033	0.0033	0.0050	0.0058	0.0025	0.0025	0.0008	0.0016	0.0016	0.0041	1971	0.0336
1972	0.0008	0.0049	0.0016	0.0024	0.0032	0.0024	0.0040	0.0016	0.0040	0.0032	0.0024	0.0032	1972	0.0341
1973	0.0031	0.0070	0.0093	0.0069	0.0061	0.0068	0.0023	0.0181	0.0030	0.0081	0.0073	0.0065	1973	0.0880
1974	0.0087	0.0129	0.0113	0.0056	0.0111	0.0096	0.0075	0.0128	0.0120	0.0086	0.0085	0.0071	1974	0.1220
1975	0.0045	0.0070	0.0038	0.0051	0.0044	0.0082	0.0106	0.0031	0.0049	0.0061	0.0061	0.0042	1975	0.0701
1976	0.0024	0.0024	0.0024	0.0042	0.0059	0.0053	0.0059	0.0047	0.0041	0.0041	0.0029	0.0029	1976	0.0481
1977	0.0057	0.0103	0.0062	0.0079	0.0056	0.0066	0.0044	0.0038	0.0038	0.0027	0.0049	0.0038	1977	0.0677
1978	0.0054	0.0069	0.0069	0.0090	0.0099	0.0103	0.0072	0.0051	0.0071	0.0080	0.0055	0.0055	1978	0.0903
1979	0.0089	0.0117	0.0097	0.0115	0.0123	0.0093	0.0130	0.0100	0.0104	0.0090	0.0093	0.0105	1979	0.1331
1980	0.0144	0.0137	0.0144	0.0113	0.0099	0.0110	0.0008	0.0065	0.0092	0.0087	0.0091	0.0086	1980	0.1240
1981	0.0081	0.0104	0.0072	0.0064	0.0082	0.0086	0.0114	0.0077	0.0101	0.0021	0.0029	0.0029	1981	0.0894
1982	0.0036	0.0032	−0.0011	0.0042	0.0098	0.0122	0.0055	0.0021	0.0017	0.0027	−0.0017	−0.0041	1982	0.0387
1983	0.0024	0.0003	0.0007	0.0072	0.0054	0.0034	0.0040	0.0033	0.0050	0.0027	0.0017	0.0013	1983	0.0380
1984	0.0056	0.0046	0.0023	0.0049	0.0029	0.0032	0.0032	0.0042	0.0048	0.0025	0.0000	0.0006	1984	0.0395
1985	0.0019	0.0041	0.0044	0.0041	0.0037	0.0031	0.0016	0.0022	0.0031	0.0031	0.0034	0.0025	1985	0.0377
1986	0.0031	−0.0027	−0.0046	−0.0021	0.0031	0.0049	0.0003	0.0018	0.0049	0.0009	0.0009	0.0009	1986	0.0113
1987	0.0060	0.0039	0.0045	0.0054	0.0030	0.0041	0.0021	0.0056	0.0050	0.0026	0.0014	−0.0003	1987	0.0441
1988	0.0026	0.0026	0.0043	0.0052	0.0034	0.0043	0.0042	0.0042	0.0067	0.0033	0.0008	0.0017	1988	0.0442
1989	0.0050	0.0041	0.0058	0.0065	0.0057	0.0024	0.0024	0.0016	0.0032	0.0048	0.0024	0.0016	1989	0.0465
1990	0.0103	0.0047	0.0055	0.0016	0.0023	0.0054	0.0038	0.0092	0.0084	0.0060	0.0022	0.0000	1990	0.0611
1991	0.0060	0.0015	0.0015	0.0015	0.0030	0.0029	0.0015	0.0029	0.0044	0.0015	0.0029	0.0007	1991	0.0306
1992	0.0015	0.0036	0.0051	0.0014	0.0014	0.0036	0.0021	0.0028	0.0028	0.0035	0.0014	−0.0007	1992	0.0290
1993	0.0049	0.0035	0.0035	0.0028	0.0014	0.0014	0.0000	0.0028	0.0021	0.0041	0.0007	0.0000	1993	0.0275
1994	0.0027	0.0034	0.0034	0.0014	0.0007	0.0034	0.0027	0.0040	0.0027	0.0007	0.0013	0.0000	1994	0.0267
1995	0.0040	0.0040	0.0033	0.0033	0.0020	0.0020	0.0000	0.0026	0.0020	0.0033	−0.0007	−0.0007	1995	0.0254
1996	0.0059	0.0032	0.0052	0.0039	0.0019	0.0006	0.0019	0.0019	0.0032	0.0032	0.0019	0.0000	1996	0.0332
1997	0.0032	0.0031	0.0025	0.0013	−0.0006	0.0012	0.0012	0.0019	0.0025	0.0025	−0.0006	−0.0012	1997	0.0170
1998	0.0019	0.0019	0.0019	0.0018	0.0018	0.0012	0.0012	0.0012	0.0012	0.0024	0.0000	−0.0006	1998	0.0161
1999	0.0024	0.0012	0.0030	0.0073	0.0000	0.0000	0.0030	0.0024	0.0048	0.0018	0.0006	0.0000	1999	0.0268
2000	0.0024	0.0059	0.0082	0.0006	0.0006	0.0058	0.0017	0.0012	0.0052	0.0017	0.0006	−0.0006	2000	0.0339
2001	0.0063	0.0040	0.0023	0.0040	0.0045	0.0017	−0.0028	0.0000	0.0045	−0.0034	−0.0017	−0.0039	2001	0.0155
2002	0.0023	0.0040	0.0056	0.0056	0.0000	0.0006	0.0011	0.0033	0.0017	0.0017	0.0000	−0.0022	2002	0.0238

*Compound annual return

Table A-16

Equity Risk Premia

from January 1926 to December 1970

Year	Jan	Feb	Mar	Apr	May	Jun	Jul	Aug	Sep	Oct	Nov	Dec	Year	Jan–Dec
1926	-0.0034	-0.0410	-0.0603	0.0218	0.0178	0.0421	0.0455	0.0223	0.0229	-0.0315	0.0315	0.0168	1926	0.080
1927	-0.0217	0.0510	0.0057	0.0175	0.0575	-0.0093	0.0638	0.0486	0.0429	-0.0526	0.0699	0.0256	1927	0.333
1928	-0.0065	-0.0158	0.1068	0.0322	0.0165	-0.0415	0.0108	0.0768	0.0231	0.0127	0.1248	0.0043	1928	0.386
1929	0.0547	-0.0055	-0.0046	0.0140	-0.0404	0.1082	0.0436	0.0984	-0.0510	-0.2009	-0.1279	0.0245	1929	-0.125
1930	0.0624	0.0229	0.0774	-0.0100	-0.0122	-0.1648	0.0366	0.0132	-0.1301	-0.0863	-0.0101	-0.0719	1930	-0.266
1931	0.0487	0.1189	-0.0687	-0.0942	-0.1287	0.1412	-0.0727	0.0179	-0.2974	0.0885	-0.0813	-0.1411	1931	-0.439
1932	-0.0293	0.0546	-0.1172	-0.2006	-0.2200	-0.0025	0.3811	0.3864	-0.0349	-0.1351	-0.0418	0.0564	1932	-0.090
1933	0.0086	-0.1770	0.0349	0.4242	0.1678	0.1335	-0.0863	0.1203	-0.1119	-0.0855	0.1125	0.0251	1933	0.535
1934	0.1064	-0.0325	-0.0002	-0.0252	-0.0737	0.0228	-0.1132	0.0610	-0.0033	-0.0287	0.0941	-0.0012	1934	-0.016
1935	-0.0412	-0.0342	-0.0287	0.0979	0.0408	0.0698	0.0849	0.0278	0.0255	0.0775	0.0471	0.0392	1935	0.474
1936	0.0669	0.0222	0.0266	-0.0752	0.0543	0.0330	0.0699	0.0150	0.0030	0.0772	0.0133	-0.0029	1936	0.336
1937	0.0389	0.0189	-0.0079	-0.0812	-0.0031	-0.0507	0.1042	-0.0485	-0.1406	-0.0983	-0.0868	-0.0459	1937	-0.352
1938	0.0151	0.0673	-0.2486	0.1446	-0.0330	0.2503	0.0745	-0.0226	0.0164	0.0775	-0.0267	0.0400	1938	0.311
1939	-0.0673	0.0389	-0.1338	-0.0027	0.0732	-0.0613	0.1105	-0.0647	0.1671	-0.0123	-0.0398	0.0270	1939	-0.004
1940	-0.0336	0.0133	0.0124	-0.0025	-0.2288	0.0809	0.0339	0.0350	0.0123	0.0422	-0.0316	0.0009	1940	-0.097
1941	-0.0462	-0.0059	0.0069	-0.0612	0.0182	0.0577	0.0576	0.0009	-0.0069	-0.0657	-0.0285	-0.0407	1941	-0.116
1942	0.0159	-0.0160	-0.0653	-0.0400	0.0794	0.0218	0.0335	0.0161	0.0287	0.0675	-0.0024	0.0546	1942	0.200
1943	0.0734	0.0580	0.0542	0.0032	0.0550	0.0220	-0.0529	0.0168	0.0260	-0.0110	-0.0657	0.0614	1943	0.254
1944	0.0168	0.0039	0.0192	-0.0103	0.0503	0.0539	-0.0195	0.0154	-0.0010	0.0020	0.0130	0.0372	1944	0.193
1945	0.0156	0.0681	-0.0443	0.0899	0.0192	-0.0009	-0.0183	0.0638	0.0436	0.0319	0.0394	0.0113	1945	0.359
1946	0.0711	-0.0643	0.0477	0.0390	0.0285	-0.0373	-0.0242	-0.0676	-0.1000	-0.0063	-0.0030	0.0454	1946	-0.083
1947	0.0252	-0.0079	-0.0152	-0.0365	0.0011	0.0550	0.0378	-0.0206	-0.0117	0.0232	-0.0181	0.0225	1947	0.051
1948	-0.0386	-0.0395	0.0783	0.0283	0.0870	0.0045	-0.0516	0.0149	-0.0279	0.0706	-0.0965	0.0341	1948	0.046
1949	0.0030	-0.0304	0.0318	-0.0188	-0.0268	0.0005	0.0641	0.0210	0.0254	0.0331	0.0166	0.0476	1949	0.175
1950	0.0187	0.0191	0.0060	0.0477	0.0498	-0.0558	0.0109	0.0433	0.0581	0.0081	0.0158	0.0501	1950	0.301
1951	0.0624	0.0146	-0.0166	0.0496	-0.0311	-0.0239	0.0696	0.0464	0.0001	-0.0119	0.0085	0.0411	1951	0.221
1952	0.0165	-0.0293	0.0492	-0.0413	0.0330	0.0475	0.0181	-0.0085	-0.0192	0.0006	0.0560	0.0365	1952	0.164
1953	-0.0065	-0.0120	-0.0230	-0.0253	0.0060	-0.0153	0.0258	-0.0517	0.0018	0.0526	0.0196	0.0040	1953	-0.027
1954	0.0525	0.0104	0.0317	0.0507	0.0412	0.0025	0.0583	-0.0280	0.0842	-0.0174	0.0902	0.0526	1954	0.513
1955	0.0189	0.0090	-0.0040	0.0386	0.0041	0.0830	0.0611	-0.0041	0.0113	-0.0302	0.0808	-0.0003	1955	0.295
1956	-0.0369	0.0393	0.0694	-0.0023	-0.0615	0.0389	0.0507	-0.0344	-0.0457	0.0041	-0.0071	0.0346	1956	0.040
1957	-0.0426	-0.0287	0.0191	0.0362	0.0411	-0.0020	0.0101	-0.0529	-0.0626	-0.0330	0.0203	-0.0418	1957	-0.135
1958	0.0416	-0.0153	0.0318	0.0329	0.0201	0.0276	0.0442	0.0171	0.0481	0.0251	0.0273	0.0512	1958	0.411
1959	0.0032	0.0030	-0.0002	0.0382	0.0217	-0.0047	0.0337	-0.0121	-0.0472	0.0098	0.0160	0.0257	1959	0.087
1960	-0.0730	0.0118	-0.0157	-0.0180	0.0297	0.0187	-0.0247	0.0300	-0.0605	-0.0029	0.0451	0.0463	1960	-0.021
1961	0.0625	0.0304	0.0249	0.0033	0.0221	-0.0294	0.0323	0.0228	-0.0200	0.0279	0.0431	0.0028	1961	0.242
1962	-0.0389	0.0189	-0.0066	-0.0628	-0.0833	-0.0821	0.0624	0.0184	-0.0485	0.0038	0.1064	0.0129	1962	-0.111
1963	0.0479	-0.0261	0.0346	0.0474	0.0169	-0.0210	-0.0048	0.0509	-0.0124	0.0309	-0.0073	0.0232	1963	0.190
1964	0.0252	0.0120	0.0133	0.0045	0.0136	0.0147	0.0164	-0.0146	0.0272	0.0067	-0.0024	0.0024	1964	0.125
1965	0.0315	0.0001	-0.0168	0.0325	-0.0061	-0.0506	0.0116	0.0238	0.0302	0.0257	-0.0066	0.0073	1965	0.082
1966	0.0024	-0.0166	-0.0243	0.0185	-0.0531	-0.0183	-0.0155	-0.0763	-0.0093	0.0446	0.0055	-0.0038	1966	-0.141
1967	0.0752	0.0036	0.0369	0.0403	-0.0508	0.0163	0.0435	-0.0100	0.0309	-0.0314	0.0029	0.0244	1967	0.189
1968	-0.0464	-0.0299	0.0071	0.0787	0.0116	0.0063	-0.0218	0.0121	0.0355	0.0043	0.0486	-0.0443	1968	0.055
1969	-0.0120	-0.0470	0.0311	0.0174	-0.0022	-0.0590	-0.0637	0.0402	-0.0296	0.0397	-0.0347	-0.0240	1969	-0.141
1970	-0.0799	0.0521	-0.0027	-0.0935	-0.0597	-0.0537	0.0696	0.0453	0.0292	-0.0143	0.0488	0.0539	1970	-0.023

* Compound annual return

Table A-16 (continued)

Equity Risk Premia

from January 1971 to December 2002

Year	Jan	Feb	Mar	Apr	May	Jun	Jul	Aug	Sep	Oct	Nov	Dec	Year	Jan–Dec*
1971	0.0379	0.0107	0.0352	0.0348	−0.0396	−0.0016	−0.0438	0.0364	−0.0092	−0.0439	−0.0011	0.0837	1971	0.0951
1972	0.0165	0.0274	0.0045	0.0028	0.0188	−0.0234	0.0005	0.0361	−0.0070	0.0067	0.0466	0.0093	1972	0.1458
1973	−0.0202	−0.0373	−0.0047	−0.0444	−0.0189	−0.0102	0.0328	−0.0385	0.0345	−0.0062	−0.1132	0.0119	1973	−0.2019
1974	−0.0147	−0.0039	−0.0271	−0.0446	−0.0345	−0.0188	−0.0824	−0.0883	−0.1240	0.1599	−0.0499	−0.0245	1974	−0.3192
1975	0.1186	0.0628	0.0194	0.0447	0.0463	0.0419	−0.0704	−0.0191	−0.0379	0.0578	0.0271	−0.0144	1975	0.2968
1976	0.1147	−0.0091	0.0285	−0.0140	−0.0110	0.0382	−0.0114	−0.0028	0.0202	−0.0245	−0.0049	0.0497	1976	0.1785
1977	−0.0523	−0.0186	−0.0156	−0.0024	−0.0186	0.0433	−0.0192	−0.0176	−0.0043	−0.0462	0.0318	−0.0001	1977	−0.1170
1978	−0.0642	−0.0206	0.0222	0.0812	0.0085	−0.0205	0.0501	0.0283	−0.0109	−0.0952	0.0189	0.0093	1978	−0.0058
1979	0.0342	−0.0355	0.0490	−0.0043	−0.0248	0.0326	0.0033	0.0530	−0.0057	−0.0737	0.0411	0.0096	1979	0.0731
1980	0.0526	−0.0057	−0.1094	0.0300	0.0477	0.0233	0.0620	0.0067	0.0204	0.0091	0.0990	−0.0440	1980	0.1904
1981	−0.0536	0.0100	0.0256	−0.0317	−0.0053	−0.0212	−0.0116	−0.0673	−0.0619	0.0403	0.0331	−0.0349	1981	−0.1710
1982	−0.0241	−0.0599	−0.0156	0.0298	−0.0390	−0.0267	−0.0317	0.1182	0.0059	0.1061	0.0372	0.0105	1982	0.0983
1983	0.0277	0.0197	0.0300	0.0682	−0.0120	0.0313	−0.0384	0.0093	0.0059	−0.0209	0.0162	−0.0133	1983	0.1261
1984	−0.0140	−0.0397	0.0097	−0.0012	−0.0608	0.0145	−0.0223	0.1033	−0.0083	−0.0073	−0.0173	0.0188	1984	−0.0326
1985	0.0699	0.0079	−0.0043	−0.0103	0.0545	0.0103	−0.0088	−0.0115	−0.0379	0.0380	0.0651	0.0399	1985	0.2268
1986	−0.0012	0.0704	0.0492	−0.0175	0.0497	0.0113	−0.0618	0.0699	−0.0863	0.0507	0.0216	−0.0311	1986	0.1159
1987	0.1296	0.0368	0.0224	−0.0132	0.0065	0.0449	0.0450	0.0336	−0.0264	−0.2199	−0.0851	0.0696	1987	−0.0022
1988	0.0396	0.0423	−0.0345	0.0062	0.0027	0.0413	−0.0090	−0.0388	0.0360	0.0211	−0.0198	0.0117	1988	0.0984
1989	0.0664	−0.0308	0.0168	0.0446	0.0321	−0.0124	0.0823	0.0118	−0.0104	−0.0299	0.0138	0.0174	1989	0.2133
1990	−0.0724	0.0072	0.0197	−0.0314	0.0901	−0.0132	−0.0099	−0.0962	−0.0549	−0.0104	0.0584	0.0213	1990	−0.1019
1991	0.0388	0.0665	0.0193	−0.0025	0.0379	−0.0497	0.0417	0.0188	−0.0209	0.0091	−0.0441	0.1101	1991	0.2363
1992	−0.0219	0.0099	−0.0229	0.0258	0.0026	−0.0176	0.0371	−0.0227	0.0089	0.0013	0.0313	0.0102	1992	0.0402
1993	0.0050	0.0113	0.0189	−0.0268	0.0248	0.0008	−0.0071	0.0355	−0.0099	0.0181	−0.0119	0.0100	1993	0.0689
1994	0.0309	−0.0291	−0.0461	0.0103	0.0131	−0.0277	0.0303	0.0369	−0.0277	0.0190	−0.0402	0.0101	1994	−0.0250
1995	0.0218	0.0347	0.0249	0.0245	0.0340	0.0187	0.0286	−0.0020	0.0374	−0.0082	0.0396	0.0136	1995	0.3015
1996	0.0300	0.0057	0.0056	0.0101	0.0215	0.0001	−0.0488	0.0170	0.0516	0.0231	0.0715	−0.0241	1996	0.1698
1997	0.0573	0.0042	−0.0457	0.0552	0.0562	0.0408	0.0748	−0.0595	0.0501	−0.0375	0.0422	0.0124	1997	0.2670
1998	0.0068	0.0679	0.0471	0.0057	−0.0211	0.0364	−0.0146	−0.1482	0.0592	0.0778	0.0574	0.0537	1998	0.2263
1999	0.0381	−0.0345	0.0356	0.0349	−0.0269	0.0513	−0.0349	−0.0088	−0.0312	0.0592	0.0166	0.0543	1999	0.1563
2000	−0.0541	−0.0231	0.0927	−0.0345	−0.0254	0.0206	−0.0203	0.0568	−0.0576	−0.0098	−0.0835	−0.0002	2000	−0.1416
2001	0.0299	−0.0946	−0.0672	0.0735	0.0035	−0.0271	−0.0128	−0.0655	−0.0833	0.0168	0.0748	0.0073	2001	−0.1513
2002	−0.0160	−0.0205	0.0362	−0.0621	−0.0088	−0.0724	−0.0794	0.0052	−0.1100	0.0865	0.0576	−0.0599	2002	−0.2337

Compound annual return

Table A-17

Small Stock Premia

from January 1926 to December 1970

Year	Jan	Feb	Mar	Apr	May	Jun	Jul	Aug	Sep	Oct	Nov	Dec	Year	Jan–Dec
1926	0.0699	−0.0265	−0.0529	−0.0072	−0.0241	−0.0076	−0.0350	0.0008	−0.0246	0.0058	−0.0135	0.0133	1926	−0.1017
1927	0.0498	0.0009	−0.0629	0.0365	0.0120	−0.0237	−0.0145	−0.0659	−0.0386	−0.0166	0.0081	0.0037	1927	−0.1119
1928	0.0523	−0.0112	−0.0514	0.0546	0.0236	−0.0476	−0.0081	−0.0334	0.0615	0.0106	−0.0128	−0.0560	1928	−0.0273
1929	−0.0518	−0.0007	−0.0189	0.0128	−0.1011	−0.0545	−0.0341	−0.1081	−0.0468	−0.0991	−0.0290	−0.0761	1929	−0.4689
1930	0.0615	0.0374	0.0180	−0.0623	−0.0450	−0.0648	−0.0082	−0.0304	−0.0203	−0.0264	0.0061	−0.0495	1930	−0.1764
1931	0.1525	0.1226	−0.0035	−0.1356	−0.0114	0.0349	0.0177	−0.0928	−0.0389	−0.0116	−0.0229	−0.0924	1931	−0.1133
1932	0.1326	−0.0265	−0.0173	−0.0278	0.1284	0.0055	−0.0212	0.2507	−0.1009	−0.0493	−0.0846	−0.1000	1932	0.0305
1933	−0.0168	0.0601	0.0738	0.0548	0.3986	0.1128	0.0341	−0.0251	−0.0537	−0.0417	−0.0425	−0.0193	1933	0.5772
1934	0.2549	0.0505	−0.0012	0.0503	−0.0582	−0.0248	−0.1271	0.0882	−0.0134	0.0394	0.0005	0.0183	1934	0.2604
1935	0.0086	−0.0260	−0.0929	−0.0172	−0.0417	−0.0369	0.0004	0.0258	0.0098	0.0201	0.0896	0.0197	1935	−0.0506
1936	0.2192	0.0370	−0.0197	−0.1129	−0.0258	−0.0546	0.0160	0.0058	0.0509	−0.0129	0.1250	0.0190	1936	0.2306
1937	0.0844	0.0458	0.0199	−0.0947	−0.0385	−0.0715	0.0172	−0.0266	−0.1321	−0.0124	−0.0643	−0.1294	1937	−0.3537
1938	0.0377	−0.0310	−0.1482	0.1161	−0.0537	0.0796	0.0703	−0.0793	−0.0318	0.1261	−0.0427	0.0083	1938	0.0128
1939	−0.0187	−0.0273	−0.1302	0.0169	0.0331	−0.0458	0.1288	−0.1007	0.2975	−0.0277	−0.0683	0.0148	1939	0.0076
1940	0.0358	0.0679	0.0502	0.0681	−0.1796	0.0223	−0.0106	−0.0092	0.0088	0.0117	0.0579	−0.0456	1940	0.0513
1941	0.0512	−0.0230	0.0247	−0.0061	−0.0136	0.0166	0.1500	−0.0070	−0.0404	−0.0016	−0.0217	−0.0831	1941	0.0293
1942	0.1706	0.0087	−0.0061	0.0049	−0.0767	0.0112	0.0386	0.0159	0.0605	0.0383	−0.0491	−0.0129	1942	0.2008
1943	0.1299	0.1274	0.0853	0.0895	0.0572	−0.0299	−0.0588	−0.0171	0.0161	0.0233	−0.0490	0.0588	1943	0.4962
1944	0.0461	0.0252	0.0544	−0.0437	0.0223	0.0799	−0.0108	0.0159	−0.0012	−0.0131	0.0361	0.0477	1944	0.2837
1945	0.0319	0.0305	−0.0440	0.0234	0.0299	0.0862	−0.0383	−0.0080	0.0231	0.0367	0.0746	0.0054	1945	0.2725
1946	0.0791	0.0004	−0.0198	0.0292	0.0295	−0.0096	−0.0298	−0.0187	−0.0673	−0.0058	−0.0114	−0.0080	1946	−0.0387
1947	0.0162	0.0036	−0.0190	−0.0694	−0.0547	−0.0002	0.0393	0.0170	0.0229	0.0043	−0.0130	0.0123	1947	−0.0453
1948	0.0234	−0.0411	0.0179	0.0074	0.0166	−0.0006	−0.0074	−0.0149	−0.0257	−0.0059	−0.0172	−0.0250	1948	−0.0722
1949	0.0142	−0.0191	0.0291	−0.0160	−0.0314	−0.0110	0.0020	0.0036	0.0221	0.0128	−0.0156	0.0195	1949	0.0080
1950	0.0289	0.0021	−0.0106	−0.0071	−0.0242	−0.0242	0.0467	0.0083	−0.0067	−0.0150	0.0151	0.0419	1950	0.0534
1951	0.0182	−0.0095	−0.0326	−0.0136	−0.0033	−0.0308	−0.0315	0.0121	0.0202	−0.0120	−0.0177	−0.0365	1951	−0.1307
1952	0.0010	−0.0018	−0.0312	−0.0122	−0.0301	−0.0208	−0.0082	0.0066	0.0015	−0.0123	−0.0082	−0.0214	1952	−0.1296
1953	0.0460	0.0379	0.0149	−0.0051	0.0064	−0.0357	−0.0118	−0.0134	−0.0296	−0.0235	−0.0076	−0.0316	1953	−0.0555
1954	0.0209	−0.0017	−0.0138	−0.0357	0.0033	0.0055	0.0207	0.0298	−0.0407	0.0239	−0.0119	0.0549	1954	0.0521
1955	0.0004	0.0377	0.0115	−0.0237	0.0022	−0.0506	−0.0525	−0.0003	−0.0020	0.0118	−0.0331	0.0147	1955	−0.0845
1956	0.0311	−0.0130	−0.0261	0.0051	0.0208	−0.0340	−0.0235	0.0200	0.0188	0.0038	0.0104	−0.0320	1956	−0.0213
1957	0.0663	0.0066	−0.0047	−0.0134	−0.0347	0.0069	−0.0189	0.0126	0.0159	−0.0547	−0.0115	−0.0089	1957	−0.0425
1958	0.0632	−0.0029	0.0138	0.0037	0.0172	0.0044	0.0041	0.0248	0.0017	0.0134	0.0206	−0.0211	1958	0.1501
1959	0.0519	0.0245	0.0007	−0.0274	−0.0221	−0.0020	−0.0034	0.0015	0.0013	0.0097	0.0036	0.0030	1959	0.0397
1960	0.0423	−0.0096	−0.0194	−0.0026	−0.0117	0.0126	0.0045	0.0201	−0.0158	−0.0394	−0.0026	−0.0140	1960	−0.0374
1961	0.0253	0.0262	0.0340	0.0076	0.0184	−0.0276	−0.0300	−0.0110	−0.0158	−0.0035	0.0159	0.0033	1961	0.0410
1962	0.0522	−0.0021	0.0103	−0.0182	−0.0215	0.0020	0.0104	0.0080	−0.0203	−0.0434	0.0146	−0.0238	1962	−0.0348
1963	0.0381	0.0280	−0.0214	−0.0180	0.0238	0.0071	0.0055	−0.0017	−0.0067	−0.0099	−0.0061	−0.0302	1963	0.0062
1964	−0.0008	0.0215	0.0053	0.0019	−0.0005	−0.0015	0.0200	0.0090	0.0099	0.0108	0.0006	−0.0167	1964	0.0604
1965	0.0178	0.0358	0.0376	0.0147	−0.0048	−0.0449	0.0297	0.0314	0.0013	0.0275	0.0404	0.0511	1965	0.2606
1966	0.0690	0.0448	0.0013	0.0121	−0.0493	0.0136	0.0109	−0.0382	−0.0111	−0.0573	0.0393	0.0063	1966	0.0339
1967	0.0963	0.0375	0.0198	−0.0159	0.0411	0.0812	0.0461	0.0091	0.0216	−0.0036	0.0051	0.0669	1967	0.4807
1968	0.0605	−0.0460	−0.0216	0.0579	0.0825	−0.0074	−0.0177	0.0200	0.0192	−0.0056	0.0221	0.0484	1968	0.2243
1969	−0.0098	−0.0589	0.0036	0.0162	0.0147	−0.0658	−0.0512	0.0266	−0.0026	0.0145	−0.0268	−0.0520	1969	−0.1809
1970	0.0146	−0.0188	−0.0314	−0.0920	−0.0512	−0.0469	−0.0185	0.0419	0.0714	−0.0615	−0.0378	0.0135	1970	−0.2061

* Compound annual return

Table A-17 (continued)

Small Stock Premia

From January 1971 to December 2002

Year	Jan	Feb	Mar	Apr	May	Jun	Jul	Aug	Sep	Oct	Nov	Dec	Year	Jan–Dec*
1971	0.1126	0.0174	0.0175	–0.0125	–0.0247	–0.0340	–0.0171	0.0164	–0.0172	–0.0154	–0.0399	0.0246	1971	0.0191
1972	0.0918	–0.0003	–0.0214	0.0072	–0.0401	–0.0102	–0.0448	–0.0197	–0.0314	–0.0279	0.0084	–0.0340	1972	–0.1222
1973	–0.0277	–0.0482	–0.0206	–0.0236	–0.0681	–0.0240	0.0769	–0.0132	0.0622	0.0082	–0.0987	–0.0193	1973	–0.1903
1974	0.1423	–0.0104	0.0146	–0.0094	–0.0535	–0.0019	0.0585	0.0161	0.0585	–0.0510	0.0011	–0.0622	1974	0.0887
1975	0.1347	–0.0364	0.0373	0.0036	0.0147	0.0275	0.0433	–0.0436	0.0151	–0.0646	0.0006	–0.0101	1975	0.1138
1976	0.1326	0.1456	–0.0330	–0.0262	–0.0290	0.0031	0.0114	–0.0304	–0.0139	–0.0003	0.0413	0.0608	1976	0.2708
1977	0.0987	0.0114	0.0252	0.0214	0.0124	0.0284	0.0184	0.0026	0.0092	0.0089	0.0691	0.0033	1977	0.3508
1978	0.0433	0.0517	0.0736	–0.0076	0.0675	–0.0037	0.0118	0.0579	0.0017	–0.1687	0.0460	–0.0004	1978	0.1586
1979	0.0864	0.0002	0.0515	0.0349	0.0206	0.0060	0.0061	0.0137	–0.0368	–0.0534	0.0327	0.0389	1979	0.2113
1980	0.0213	–0.0313	–0.0878	0.0253	0.0178	0.0152	0.0606	0.0467	0.0134	0.0144	–0.0297	–0.0024	1980	0.0563
1981	0.0675	–0.0112	0.0542	0.0889	0.0358	0.0157	–0.0323	–0.0138	–0.0243	0.0203	–0.0158	0.0046	1981	0.1976
1982	–0.0034	0.0228	–0.0026	–0.0030	0.0041	0.0015	0.0204	–0.0505	0.0215	0.0161	0.0327	–0.0040	1982	0.0543
1983	0.0271	0.0441	0.0154	0.0008	0.0926	–0.0032	0.0232	–0.0361	–0.0003	–0.0440	0.0276	–0.0085	1983	0.1400
1984	0.0057	–0.0328	0.0003	–0.0153	0.0014	0.0077	–0.0281	–0.0114	0.0025	–0.0242	–0.0237	–0.0100	1984	–0.1217
1985	0.0270	0.0133	–0.0232	–0.0142	–0.0319	–0.0052	0.0287	–0.0011	–0.0230	–0.0178	–0.0090	0.0003	1985	–0.0567
1986	0.0068	–0.0039	–0.0073	0.0190	–0.0179	–0.0138	–0.0150	–0.0493	0.0287	–0.0199	–0.0280	0.0002	1986	–0.0981
1987	–0.0353	0.0380	–0.0038	–0.0227	–0.0141	–0.0222	–0.0128	–0.0094	0.0142	–0.0977	0.0460	–0.0203	1987	–0.1381
1988	0.0124	0.0277	0.0732	0.0100	–0.0255	0.0141	0.0015	0.0088	–0.0189	–0.0385	–0.0299	0.0209	1988	0.0519
1989	–0.0297	0.0340	0.0119	–0.0225	–0.0038	–0.0148	–0.0451	–0.0070	0.0039	–0.0380	–0.0254	–0.0361	1989	–0.1621
1990	–0.0100	0.0057	0.0102	–0.0019	–0.0377	0.0216	–0.0351	–0.0432	–0.0354	–0.0537	–0.0182	–0.0078	1990	–0.1899
1991	0.0382	0.0370	0.0432	0.0006	–0.0090	–0.0029	–0.0058	0.0025	0.0199	0.0181	0.0133	–0.0486	1991	0.1079
1992	0.1339	0.0320	–0.0054	–0.0674	–0.0068	–0.0380	–0.0032	–0.0027	0.0016	0.0222	0.0530	0.0306	1992	0.1456
1993	0.0467	–0.0311	0.0072	–0.0063	0.0070	–0.0071	0.0214	–0.0040	0.0393	0.0263	–0.0082	0.0070	1993	0.0999
1994	0.0274	0.0254	–0.0012	–0.0069	–0.0172	–0.0015	–0.0142	–0.0067	0.0355	–0.0111	0.0043	–0.0142	1994	0.0178
1995	0.0022	–0.0131	–0.0147	0.0059	–0.0093	0.0325	0.0302	0.0330	–0.0215	–0.0454	–0.0238	0.0053	1995	–0.0216
1996	–0.0305	0.0270	0.0131	0.0691	0.0479	–0.0620	–0.0521	0.0259	–0.0257	–0.0437	–0.0438	0.0408	1996	–0.0443
1997	–0.0189	–0.0285	–0.0077	–0.0824	0.0384	0.0050	–0.0175	0.1128	0.0281	–0.0054	–0.0591	–0.0337	1997	–0.0794
1998	–0.0168	–0.0067	–0.0030	0.0067	–0.0331	–0.0588	–0.0571	–0.0660	–0.0255	–0.0423	0.0143	–0.0307	1998	–0.2791
1999	–0.0134	–0.0388	–0.0749	0.0541	0.0638	0.0012	0.0417	–0.0142	0.0055	–0.0677	0.0752	0.0518	1999	0.0722
2000	0.1155	0.2596	–0.1575	–0.0980	–0.0615	0.1095	–0.0168	0.0286	0.0328	–0.0667	–0.0349	0.0139	2000	0.0607
2001	0.0990	0.0231	0.0164	–0.0043	0.0887	0.0617	–0.0157	0.0353	–0.0512	0.0446	–0.0086	0.0579	2001	0.3933
2002	0.0260	–0.0086	0.0489	0.0904	–0.0201	0.0384	–0.0725	–0.0122	0.0463	–0.0573	0.0234	0.0169	2002	0.1133

*Compound annual return

Table A-18

Bond Default Premia

from January 1926 to December 1970

Year	Jan	Feb	Mar	Apr	May	Jun	Jul	Aug	Sep	Oct	Nov	Dec	Year	Jan–Dec
1926	−0.0065	−0.0018	0.0043	0.0021	0.0030	−0.0034	0.0053	0.0044	0.0019	−0.0005	−0.0101	−0.0022	1926	−0.0037
1927	−0.0019	−0.0019	−0.0166	0.0060	−0.0118	0.0113	−0.0046	0.0007	0.0131	−0.0043	−0.0029	−0.0003	1927	−0.0136
1928	0.0063	0.0007	−0.0004	0.0018	−0.0001	−0.0065	0.0212	0.0006	0.0071	−0.0073	−0.0039	0.0080	1928	0.0273
1929	0.0134	0.0190	0.0058	−0.0249	0.0210	−0.0154	0.0020	0.0054	0.0006	−0.0298	−0.0249	0.0284	1929	−0.0014
1930	0.0117	−0.0056	0.0054	0.0100	−0.0081	0.0059	0.0021	0.0123	0.0034	0.0018	−0.0054	−0.0020	1930	0.0317
1931	0.0328	−0.0017	−0.0010	−0.0019	−0.0011	0.0048	0.0095	0.0000	0.0274	−0.0034	−0.0216	−0.0068	1931	0.0365
1932	−0.0086	−0.0625	0.0375	−0.0735	0.0301	−0.0074	−0.0418	0.0433	0.0243	0.0091	0.0041	0.0008	1932	−0.0515
1933	0.0393	−0.0272	−0.0049	−0.0063	0.0277	0.0140	0.0178	0.0049	−0.0037	0.0132	−0.0100	0.0374	1933	0.1046
1934	0.0000	0.0064	−0.0010	−0.0021	−0.0041	0.0090	0.0007	0.0167	0.0086	−0.0079	0.0091	−0.0011	1934	0.0347
1935	0.0029	0.0049	0.0002	0.0033	0.0099	0.0020	0.0065	0.0093	−0.0009	−0.0019	0.0059	0.0013	1935	0.0441
1936	0.0027	−0.0027	−0.0024	−0.0009	0.0000	0.0061	−0.0049	−0.0043	0.0098	0.0019	−0.0094	−0.0028	1936	−0.0072
1937	0.0037	−0.0131	0.0310	0.0029	−0.0013	0.0071	−0.0098	0.0088	−0.0020	0.0025	−0.0028	−0.0015	1937	0.0251
1938	−0.0019	−0.0042	−0.0051	−0.0070	−0.0034	0.0090	0.0023	−0.0019	0.0086	−0.0007	0.0059	0.0041	1938	0.0057
1939	−0.0037	−0.0016	−0.0102	−0.0053	−0.0120	0.0062	−0.0119	−0.0195	0.0736	−0.0166	−0.0081	−0.0066	1939	−0.0186
1940	0.0066	−0.0006	−0.0126	−0.0057	0.0287	−0.0134	−0.0031	−0.0021	−0.0018	0.0018	−0.0139	−0.0089	1940	−0.0254
1941	0.0211	−0.0014	−0.0117	−0.0051	0.0022	−0.0003	0.0041	0.0016	0.0060	−0.0105	−0.0065	0.0187	1941	0.0178
1942	−0.0063	−0.0019	−0.0028	0.0035	−0.0055	0.0031	0.0002	−0.0003	0.0017	−0.0018	0.0041	0.0000	1942	−0.0060
1943	0.0016	0.0012	0.0011	0.0001	−0.0002	0.0030	0.0020	−0.0002	−0.0006	−0.0014	−0.0023	0.0031	1943	0.0073
1944	−0.0001	0.0002	0.0027	0.0021	−0.0023	0.0012	−0.0002	0.0007	0.0005	0.0007	0.0024	0.0106	1944	0.0187
1945	−0.0050	−0.0030	−0.0003	−0.0140	−0.0067	−0.0135	0.0076	−0.0022	−0.0022	−0.0072	−0.0092	−0.0060	1945	−0.0601
1946	0.0103	0.0002	0.0024	0.0094	0.0031	−0.0051	0.0028	0.0024	−0.0017	−0.0053	0.0029	−0.0031	1946	0.0183
1947	0.0011	−0.0016	0.0047	0.0057	−0.0013	−0.0006	−0.0042	−0.0151	−0.0088	−0.0062	0.0077	0.0220	1947	0.0029
1948	0.0004	−0.0007	0.0081	−0.0007	−0.0131	0.0001	−0.0031	0.0054	0.0010	0.0017	0.0009	0.0074	1948	0.0071
1949	−0.0043	−0.0011	−0.0067	0.0012	0.0019	−0.0082	0.0065	−0.0073	0.0032	0.0048	0.0000	−0.0196	1949	−0.0298
1950	0.0099	−0.0014	0.0014	−0.0038	−0.0041	0.0048	0.0013	0.0024	0.0034	0.0040	0.0019	0.0007	1950	0.0205
1951	−0.0039	0.0030	−0.0081	0.0054	0.0054	−0.0032	0.0066	0.0015	0.0023	−0.0155	0.0076	0.0120	1951	0.0129
1952	0.0170	−0.0099	−0.0034	−0.0172	0.0065	0.0013	0.0036	0.0134	0.0113	−0.0107	0.0124	−0.0005	1952	0.0233
1953	−0.0092	0.0047	0.0056	−0.0144	0.0119	−0.0111	0.0137	−0.0078	−0.0045	0.0151	−0.0024	−0.0033	1953	−0.0022
1954	0.0034	−0.0041	−0.0019	−0.0136	0.0045	−0.0098	−0.0093	0.0054	0.0050	0.0034	0.0050	−0.0047	1954	−0.0168
1955	0.0148	0.0015	0.0005	−0.0002	−0.0090	0.0106	0.0062	−0.0042	0.0003	−0.0065	0.0015	0.0026	1955	0.0180
1956	0.0021	0.0028	0.0003	−0.0002	−0.0170	−0.0045	0.0118	−0.0022	−0.0037	−0.0051	−0.0069	0.0098	1956	−0.0130
1957	−0.0144	0.0068	0.0074	0.0159	−0.0052	−0.0144	−0.0069	−0.0011	0.0019	0.0074	−0.0211	0.0367	1957	0.0117
1958	0.0185	−0.0107	−0.0147	−0.0023	0.0030	0.0124	0.0129	0.0121	0.0021	−0.0031	−0.0015	0.0125	1958	0.0413
1959	0.0053	0.0009	−0.0099	−0.0056	−0.0109	0.0033	0.0029	−0.0027	−0.0032	0.0014	0.0257	0.0064	1959	0.0132
1960	−0.0005	−0.0074	−0.0089	0.0150	−0.0170	−0.0031	−0.0107	0.0186	−0.0137	0.0036	−0.0004	−0.0170	1960	−0.0414
1961	0.0258	0.0010	0.0009	−0.0228	0.0095	−0.0005	0.0005	0.0020	0.0015	0.0055	0.0048	0.0100	1961	0.0381
1962	0.0094	−0.0050	−0.0100	0.0059	−0.0046	0.0050	0.0095	−0.0043	0.0028	−0.0016	0.0041	−0.0012	1962	0.0099
1963	0.0060	0.0015	0.0017	−0.0039	0.0025	0.0024	−0.0003	0.0014	−0.0027	0.0075	−0.0036	−0.0028	1963	0.0097
1964	0.0101	0.0065	−0.0099	−0.0007	0.0007	−0.0021	0.0044	0.0017	−0.0028	0.0007	−0.0021	0.0058	1964	0.0122
1965	0.0041	−0.0005	−0.0041	−0.0015	−0.0026	−0.0044	−0.0003	0.0007	0.0019	0.0019	0.0005	−0.0072	1965	−0.0116
1966	0.0127	0.0141	−0.0345	0.0076	0.0034	0.0046	−0.0061	−0.0054	−0.0246	0.0032	0.0130	−0.0204	1966	−0.0333
1967	0.0291	0.0020	−0.0079	0.0227	−0.0216	0.0092	−0.0027	0.0078	0.0099	0.0124	−0.0077	−0.0064	1967	0.0466
1968	0.0032	0.0070	0.0015	−0.0175	−0.0011	−0.0106	0.0050	0.0209	0.0050	−0.0028	0.0044	0.0135	1968	0.0284
1969	0.0352	−0.0201	−0.0210	−0.0088	0.0277	−0.0176	−0.0074	0.0049	0.0303	−0.0230	−0.0233	−0.0066	1969	−0.0318
1970	0.0163	−0.0176	0.0023	0.0170	0.0320	−0.0463	0.0229	0.0119	−0.0087	0.0013	−0.0192	0.0460	1970	0.0559

* Compound annual return

able A-18 (continued)

ond Default Premia

om January 1971 to December 2002

ear	Jan	Feb	Mar	Apr	May	Jun	Jul	Aug	Sep	Oct	Nov	Dec	Year	Jan–Dec*
)71	0.0025	–0.0206	–0.0255	0.0048	–0.0155	0.0270	–0.0054	0.0079	–0.0299	0.0113	0.0076	0.0178	1971	–0.0196
)72	0.0031	0.0019	0.0107	0.0008	–0.0105	–0.0003	–0.0182	0.0043	0.0115	–0.0130	0.0022	0.0231	1972	0.0149
)73	0.0276	0.0009	–0.0037	0.0015	0.0066	–0.0035	–0.0045	–0.0034	0.0037	–0.0275	0.0265	–0.0007	1973	0.0227
)74	0.0030	0.0033	–0.0016	–0.0091	–0.0017	–0.0328	–0.0183	–0.0037	–0.0072	0.0377	–0.0173	–0.0242	1974	–0.0711
)75	0.0363	0.0005	0.0021	0.0132	–0.0104	0.0012	0.0057	–0.0108	–0.0028	0.0075	0.0021	0.0050	1975	0.0499
)76	0.0097	–0.0001	0.0001	–0.0033	0.0056	–0.0056	0.0071	0.0019	0.0022	–0.0014	–0.0019	0.0019	1976	0.0162
)77	0.0088	0.0029	0.0003	0.0029	–0.0019	0.0011	0.0066	–0.0061	0.0007	0.0056	–0.0032	0.0064	1977	0.0241
)78	–0.0009	0.0047	0.0063	–0.0018	–0.0050	0.0086	–0.0041	0.0038	0.0058	–0.0005	–0.0054	–0.0003	1978	0.0112
)79	–0.0007	0.0007	–0.0023	0.0061	–0.0032	–0.0041	0.0055	0.0042	–0.0057	–0.0054	–0.0087	–0.0164	1979	–0.0298
)80	0.0104	–0.0208	0.0261	–0.0128	0.0136	–0.0017	0.0049	–0.0014	0.0025	0.0107	–0.0082	–0.0100	1980	0.0124
)81	–0.0015	0.0174	–0.0071	–0.0265	–0.0025	0.0206	–0.0020	0.0043	–0.0055	–0.0284	–0.0125	0.0143	1981	–0.0304
)82	–0.0174	0.0128	0.0073	–0.0034	0.0210	–0.0251	0.0037	0.0052	0.0004	0.0117	0.0203	–0.0198	1982	0.0157
)83	0.0222	–0.0061	0.0167	0.0192	0.0064	–0.0085	0.0033	0.0031	–0.0107	0.0108	–0.0041	0.0026	1983	0.0557
)84	0.0026	0.0006	–0.0080	0.0033	0.0035	0.0049	–0.0100	0.0040	–0.0028	0.0011	0.0093	0.0037	1984	0.0120
)85	–0.0038	0.0126	–0.0124	0.0052	–0.0069	–0.0058	0.0060	0.0001	0.0092	–0.0008	–0.0030	–0.0068	1985	–0.0067
)86	0.0070	–0.0353	–0.0477	0.0097	0.0359	–0.0373	0.0141	–0.0214	0.0406	–0.0097	–0.0033	0.0135	1986	–0.0376
)87	0.0054	–0.0141	0.0139	–0.0030	0.0054	0.0057	0.0060	0.0091	–0.0055	–0.0109	0.0088	0.0046	1987	0.0251
)88	–0.0140	0.0085	0.0122	0.0011	0.0045	0.0010	0.0060	–0.0004	–0.0018	–0.0033	0.0028	–0.0070	1988	0.0094
)89	–0.0001	0.0051	–0.0058	0.0053	–0.0021	–0.0147	–0.0058	0.0098	0.0021	–0.0100	–0.0008	0.0012	1989	–0.0159
)90	0.0157	0.0013	0.0033	0.0011	–0.0029	–0.0014	–0.0005	0.0132	–0.0026	–0.0081	–0.0112	–0.0019	1990	0.0057
)91	0.0019	0.0090	0.0070	–0.0002	0.0039	0.0045	0.0009	–0.0063	–0.0031	–0.0011	0.0024	–0.0137	1991	0.0049
)92	0.0156	0.0045	0.0021	0.0000	0.0011	–0.0043	–0.0086	0.0023	–0.0085	0.0043	0.0059	–0.0018	1992	0.0124
)93	–0.0030	–0.0095	0.0004	–0.0020	–0.0026	–0.0149	–0.0090	–0.0141	0.0038	–0.0045	0.0073	0.0047	1993	–0.0428
)94	–0.0054	0.0171	0.0012	0.0054	0.0021	0.0020	–0.0052	0.0055	0.0068	–0.0026	–0.0048	–0.0004	1994	0.0218
)95	–0.0016	0.0002	0.0004	0.0006	–0.0148	–0.0059	0.0068	–0.0022	–0.0021	–0.0106	–0.0007	–0.0043	1995	–0.0339
)96	0.0025	0.0115	0.0082	0.0005	0.0060	–0.0030	–0.0008	0.0070	–0.0030	–0.0041	–0.0085	0.0072	1996	0.0235
)97	0.0052	0.0023	0.0032	–0.0069	0.0031	–0.0008	–0.0092	0.0080	–0.0087	–0.0145	–0.0046	–0.0021	1997	–0.0251
)98	–0.0062	0.0065	0.0013	0.0027	–0.0015	–0.0111	–0.0016	–0.0359	0.0018	0.0029	0.0172	0.0043	1998	–0.0204
)99	0.0001	0.0126	0.0011	–0.0045	0.0009	–0.0083	–0.0036	0.0026	0.0009	0.0059	0.0037	0.0053	1999	0.0167
)00	–0.0244	–0.0167	–0.0190	–0.0039	–0.0107	0.0080	0.0006	–0.0103	0.0207	–0.0140	–0.0054	0.0027	2000	–0.0709
)01	0.0353	–0.0063	0.0045	0.0191	0.0094	–0.0030	–0.0014	–0.0048	–0.0231	–0.0025	0.0297	0.0095	2001	0.0670
)02	0.0036	0.0015	0.0148	–0.0150	0.0098	–0.0112	–0.0203	–0.0011	–0.0084	0.0056	0.0227	–0.0139	2002	–0.0128

ompound annual return

Table A-19

Bond Horizon Premia

from January 1926 to December 1970

Year	Jan	Feb	Mar	Apr	May	Jun	Jul	Aug	Sep	Oct	Nov	Dec	Year	Jan–De
1926	0.0103	0.0036	0.0011	0.0041	0.0013	0.0004	−0.0018	−0.0025	0.0015	0.0070	0.0129	0.0050	1926	0.043
1927	0.0050	0.0062	0.0223	−0.0030	0.0078	−0.0094	0.0020	0.0048	−0.0003	0.0073	0.0076	0.0049	1927	0.056
1928	−0.0061	0.0028	0.0016	−0.0026	−0.0109	0.0010	−0.0249	0.0044	−0.0067	0.0116	−0.0035	−0.0002	1928	−0.033
1929	−0.0124	−0.0192	−0.0177	0.0239	−0.0205	0.0058	−0.0034	−0.0074	−0.0008	0.0335	0.0198	−0.0125	1929	−0.012
1930	−0.0071	0.0099	0.0048	−0.0037	0.0113	0.0024	0.0015	0.0004	0.0052	0.0027	0.0029	−0.0084	1930	0.022
1931	−0.0136	0.0081	0.0091	0.0078	0.0136	−0.0004	−0.0048	0.0009	−0.0283	−0.0340	0.0010	−0.0232	1931	−0.063
1932	0.0011	0.0389	−0.0035	0.0592	−0.0194	0.0063	0.0479	−0.0001	0.0054	−0.0019	0.0030	0.0130	1932	0.157
1933	0.0147	−0.0256	0.0093	−0.0042	0.0298	0.0047	−0.0019	0.0042	0.0022	−0.0092	−0.0151	−0.0115	1933	−0.003
1934	0.0252	0.0079	0.0195	0.0125	0.0130	0.0066	0.0039	−0.0119	−0.0146	0.0181	0.0036	0.0111	1934	0.098
1935	0.0180	0.0090	0.0040	0.0077	−0.0058	0.0091	0.0044	−0.0135	0.0007	0.0060	0.0007	0.0069	1935	0.048
1936	0.0054	0.0080	0.0105	0.0034	0.0039	0.0018	0.0059	0.0109	−0.0032	0.0004	0.0204	0.0038	1936	0.073
1937	−0.0014	0.0085	−0.0413	0.0035	0.0046	−0.0021	0.0135	−0.0107	0.0041	0.0041	0.0094	0.0082	1937	−0.000
1938	0.0057	0.0051	−0.0036	0.0208	0.0044	0.0004	0.0044	0.0000	0.0021	0.0086	−0.0016	0.0080	1938	0.055
1939	0.0059	0.0079	0.0126	0.0118	0.0170	−0.0028	0.0113	−0.0200	−0.0546	0.0410	0.0162	0.0144	1939	0.059
1940	−0.0017	0.0027	0.0177	−0.0035	−0.0298	0.0258	0.0051	0.0029	0.0110	0.0031	0.0204	0.0067	1940	0.060
1941	−0.0200	0.0021	0.0095	0.0130	0.0027	0.0065	0.0019	0.0017	−0.0012	0.0140	−0.0030	−0.0178	1941	0.008
1942	0.0068	0.0010	0.0091	−0.0030	0.0073	0.0000	0.0015	0.0035	0.0000	0.0021	−0.0038	0.0046	1942	0.029
1943	0.0030	−0.0008	0.0006	0.0045	0.0048	0.0015	−0.0004	0.0018	0.0008	0.0002	−0.0003	0.0015	1943	0.017
1944	0.0018	0.0029	0.0018	0.0011	0.0025	0.0005	0.0033	0.0024	0.0012	0.0009	0.0021	0.0040	1944	0.024
1945	0.0124	0.0074	0.0018	0.0157	0.0053	0.0166	−0.0089	0.0023	0.0051	0.0101	0.0123	0.0191	1945	0.103
1946	0.0022	0.0029	0.0007	−0.0138	−0.0015	0.0067	−0.0043	−0.0114	−0.0012	0.0071	−0.0057	0.0142	1946	−0.004
1947	−0.0009	0.0018	0.0017	−0.0040	0.0031	0.0007	0.0059	0.0079	−0.0050	−0.0044	−0.0180	−0.0200	1947	−0.031
1948	0.0013	0.0039	0.0025	0.0036	0.0133	−0.0093	−0.0029	−0.0007	0.0010	0.0003	0.0072	0.0052	1948	0.025
1949	0.0072	0.0040	0.0065	0.0002	0.0009	0.0157	0.0025	0.0102	−0.0020	0.0010	0.0013	0.0043	1949	0.052
1950	−0.0070	0.0013	−0.0001	0.0021	0.0023	−0.0035	0.0046	0.0004	−0.0083	−0.0059	0.0024	0.0005	1950	−0.011
1951	0.0045	−0.0084	−0.0168	−0.0075	−0.0081	−0.0073	0.0125	0.0085	−0.0092	−0.0005	−0.0147	−0.0073	1951	−0.055
1952	0.0013	0.0002	0.0100	0.0159	−0.0046	−0.0012	−0.0035	−0.0084	−0.0146	0.0134	−0.0026	−0.0102	1952	−0.004
1953	−0.0004	−0.0101	−0.0106	−0.0121	−0.0164	0.0204	0.0025	−0.0024	0.0283	0.0062	−0.0057	0.0193	1953	0.017
1954	0.0078	0.0232	0.0050	0.0095	−0.0092	0.0157	0.0129	−0.0041	−0.0018	−0.0001	−0.0031	0.0056	1954	0.062
1955	−0.0249	−0.0087	0.0077	−0.0010	0.0059	−0.0086	−0.0112	−0.0012	0.0057	0.0126	−0.0062	0.0019	1955	−0.028
1956	0.0061	−0.0021	−0.0164	−0.0131	0.0202	0.0007	−0.0230	−0.0203	0.0031	−0.0079	−0.0078	−0.0202	1956	−0.078
1957	0.0318	0.0001	−0.0047	−0.0246	−0.0048	−0.0204	−0.0070	−0.0023	0.0050	−0.0079	0.0504	0.0282	1957	0.04
1958	−0.0112	0.0088	0.0093	0.0178	−0.0010	−0.0163	−0.0285	−0.0440	−0.0136	0.0120	0.0109	−0.0203	1958	−0.075
1959	−0.0101	0.0098	−0.0005	−0.0136	−0.0027	−0.0014	0.0035	−0.0060	−0.0087	0.0120	−0.0144	−0.0192	1959	−0.050
1960	0.0078	0.0175	0.0247	−0.0189	0.0124	0.0148	0.0354	−0.0084	0.0059	−0.0050	−0.0079	0.0263	1960	0.108
1961	−0.0126	0.0185	−0.0058	0.0097	−0.0064	−0.0095	0.0016	−0.0052	0.0112	0.0052	−0.0036	−0.0143	1961	−0.01
1962	−0.0038	0.0083	0.0232	0.0059	0.0022	−0.0095	−0.0135	0.0163	0.0040	0.0058	0.0001	0.0012	1962	0.040
1963	−0.0026	−0.0015	−0.0014	−0.0037	−0.0002	−0.0003	0.0004	−0.0003	−0.0023	−0.0055	0.0024	−0.0035	1963	−0.018
1964	−0.0043	−0.0037	0.0006	0.0017	0.0025	0.0038	−0.0022	−0.0008	0.0021	0.0014	−0.0012	−0.0001	1964	−0.000
1965	0.0012	−0.0016	0.0018	0.0006	−0.0013	0.0012	−0.0009	−0.0046	−0.0065	−0.0004	−0.0097	−0.0110	1965	−0.03
1966	−0.0141	−0.0284	0.0257	−0.0097	−0.0100	−0.0053	−0.0072	−0.0246	0.0291	0.0182	−0.0188	0.0371	1966	−0.01
1967	0.0111	−0.0256	0.0158	−0.0323	−0.0072	−0.0338	0.0037	−0.0115	−0.0036	−0.0438	−0.0231	0.0158	1967	−0.128
1968	0.0286	−0.0072	−0.0249	0.0183	−0.0002	0.0187	0.0240	−0.0045	−0.0144	−0.0175	−0.0310	−0.0404	1968	−0.052
1969	−0.0257	−0.0004	−0.0036	0.0371	−0.0536	0.0162	0.0026	−0.0119	−0.0590	0.0304	−0.0293	−0.0132	1969	−0.109
1970	−0.0081	0.0522	−0.0124	−0.0461	−0.0518	0.0426	0.0266	−0.0072	0.0173	−0.0154	0.0742	−0.0126	1970	0.05

* Compound annual return

Table A-19 (continued)
Bond Horizon Premia

from January 1971 to December 2002

Year	Jan	Feb	Mar	Apr	May	Jun	Jul	Aug	Sep	Oct	Nov	Dec	Year	Jan–Dec*
1971	0.0466	−0.0196	0.0495	−0.0310	−0.0035	−0.0195	−0.0011	0.0422	0.0166	0.0130	−0.0084	0.0007	1971	0.0847
1972	−0.0092	0.0063	−0.0109	−0.0002	0.0240	−0.0094	0.0184	0.0000	−0.0116	0.0194	0.0188	−0.0266	1972	0.0178
1973	−0.0363	−0.0027	0.0036	−0.0007	−0.0155	−0.0072	−0.0494	0.0319	0.0248	0.0149	−0.0237	−0.0145	1973	−0.0752
1974	−0.0145	−0.0082	−0.0346	−0.0326	0.0047	−0.0016	−0.0099	−0.0290	0.0165	0.0436	0.0240	0.0101	1974	−0.0338
1975	0.0166	0.0088	−0.0307	−0.0225	0.0168	0.0250	−0.0135	−0.0115	−0.0150	0.0417	−0.0149	0.0340	1975	0.0321
1976	0.0043	0.0028	0.0125	−0.0023	−0.0195	0.0163	0.0031	0.0169	0.0101	0.0043	0.0298	0.0286	1976	0.1111
1977	−0.0422	−0.0084	0.0053	0.0033	0.0088	0.0124	−0.0111	0.0153	−0.0072	−0.0142	0.0043	−0.0215	1977	−0.0553
1978	−0.0129	−0.0042	−0.0073	−0.0058	−0.0109	−0.0115	0.0086	0.0161	−0.0167	−0.0266	0.0118	−0.0207	1978	−0.0780
1979	0.0113	−0.0207	0.0048	−0.0190	0.0178	0.0228	−0.0160	−0.0111	−0.0203	−0.0920	0.0211	−0.0038	1979	−0.1052
1980	−0.0814	−0.0551	−0.0430	0.1381	0.0335	0.0296	−0.0526	−0.0492	−0.0334	−0.0355	0.0004	0.0218	1980	−0.1365
1981	−0.0217	−0.0537	0.0260	−0.0618	0.0501	−0.0310	−0.0471	−0.0507	−0.0266	0.0700	0.1290	−0.0793	1981	−0.1120
1982	−0.0034	0.0089	0.0132	0.0258	−0.0071	−0.0316	0.0392	0.0699	0.0564	0.0572	−0.0065	0.0243	1982	0.2697
1983	−0.0375	0.0427	−0.0156	0.0276	−0.0452	−0.0027	−0.0556	−0.0056	0.0425	−0.0206	0.0112	−0.0130	1983	−0.0749
1984	0.0166	−0.0248	−0.0228	−0.0185	−0.0590	0.0074	0.0606	0.0182	0.0254	0.0457	0.0044	0.0026	1984	0.0512
1985	0.0297	−0.0548	0.0244	0.0169	0.0824	0.0086	−0.0241	0.0203	−0.0081	0.0271	0.0338	0.0473	1985	0.2158
1986	−0.0081	0.1087	0.0706	−0.0131	−0.0552	0.0558	−0.0159	0.0451	−0.0543	0.0241	0.0227	−0.0066	1986	0.1730
1987	0.0119	0.0158	−0.0268	−0.0515	−0.0142	0.0050	−0.0223	−0.0211	−0.0412	0.0560	0.0002	0.0126	1987	−0.0776
1988	0.0635	0.0007	−0.0349	−0.0205	−0.0152	0.0318	−0.0219	−0.0002	0.0281	0.0245	−0.0251	0.0046	1988	0.0313
1989	0.0147	−0.0239	0.0055	0.0091	0.0320	0.0476	0.0167	−0.0330	−0.0046	0.0310	0.0009	−0.0067	1989	0.0899
1990	−0.0397	−0.0081	−0.0108	−0.0269	0.0345	0.0167	0.0039	−0.0481	0.0057	0.0146	0.0344	0.0126	1990	−0.0151
1991	0.0078	−0.0017	−0.0006	0.0086	−0.0047	−0.0104	0.0108	0.0293	0.0257	0.0012	0.0043	0.0541	1991	0.1298
1992	−0.0357	0.0023	−0.0127	−0.0017	0.0214	0.0167	0.0366	0.0041	0.0159	−0.0220	−0.0013	0.0217	1992	0.0439
1993	0.0256	0.0331	−0.0004	0.0048	0.0025	0.0422	0.0167	0.0408	−0.0020	0.0074	−0.0283	−0.0003	1993	0.1491
1994	0.0232	−0.0470	−0.0421	−0.0177	−0.0114	−0.0131	0.0335	−0.0122	−0.0366	−0.0063	0.0029	0.0116	1994	−0.1124
1995	0.0230	0.0246	0.0045	0.0124	0.0733	0.0091	−0.0212	0.0189	0.0131	0.0246	0.0206	0.0222	1995	0.2469
1996	−0.0053	−0.0520	−0.0248	−0.0210	−0.0096	0.0162	−0.0027	−0.0180	0.0245	0.0360	0.0309	−0.0301	1996	−0.0583
1997	−0.0124	−0.0033	−0.0294	0.0211	0.0047	0.0157	0.0580	−0.0357	0.0270	0.0297	0.0108	0.0136	1997	0.1007
1998	0.0157	−0.0110	−0.0015	−0.0017	0.0141	0.0186	−0.0079	0.0420	0.0347	−0.0250	0.0066	−0.0069	1998	0.0783
1999	0.0086	−0.0553	−0.0050	−0.0016	−0.0218	−0.0117	−0.0114	−0.0091	0.0045	−0.0050	−0.0097	−0.0197	1999	−0.1304
2000	0.0186	0.0220	0.0318	−0.0121	−0.0104	0.0203	0.0124	0.0189	−0.0207	0.0131	0.0266	0.0191	2000	0.1472
2001	−0.0048	0.0153	−0.0115	−0.0351	0.0005	0.0057	0.0344	0.0174	0.0053	0.0441	−0.0488	−0.0198	2001	−0.0013
2002	0.0124	0.0102	−0.0449	0.0394	0.0000	0.0174	0.0287	0.0449	0.0402	−0.0307	−0.0133	0.0495	2002	0.1593

Compound annual return

Table A-20

Large Company Stocks: Inflation-Adjusted Total Returns

from January 1926 to December 1970

Year	Jan	Feb	Mar	Apr	May	Jun	Jul	Aug	Sep	Oct	Nov	Dec	Year	Jan–Dec
1926	0.0000	−0.0349	−0.0522	0.0158	0.0236	0.0536	0.0579	0.0307	0.0193	−0.0320	0.0308	0.0196	1926	0.1331
1927	−0.0118	0.0618	0.0145	0.0201	0.0526	−0.0161	0.0877	0.0576	0.0390	−0.0557	0.0742	0.0298	1927	0.4041
1928	−0.0020	−0.0029	0.1101	0.0325	0.0138	−0.0310	0.0141	0.0782	0.0179	0.0188	0.1313	0.0089	1928	0.4501
1929	0.0604	0.0000	0.0028	0.0216	−0.0419	0.1096	0.0369	0.0986	−0.0458	−0.1973	−0.1229	0.0342	1929	−0.0859
1930	0.0680	0.0299	0.0876	−0.0138	−0.0038	−0.1575	0.0532	0.0203	−0.1335	−0.0800	−0.0008	−0.0571	1930	−0.2008
1931	0.0656	0.1360	−0.0615	−0.0876	−0.1184	0.1547	−0.0701	0.0205	−0.2941	0.0969	−0.0693	−0.1321	1931	−0.3737
1932	−0.0066	0.0721	−0.1116	−0.1940	−0.2082	0.0051	0.3815	0.4041	−0.0297	−0.1284	−0.0368	0.0673	1932	0.0235
1933	0.0244	−0.1642	0.0436	0.4294	0.1652	0.1219	−0.1118	0.1093	−0.1118	−0.0855	0.1127	0.0305	1933	0.5321
1934	0.1013	−0.0395	0.0000	−0.0227	−0.0759	0.0203	−0.1132	0.0584	−0.0180	−0.0214	0.0969	0.0014	1934	−0.0340
1935	−0.0552	−0.0411	−0.0262	0.0874	0.0460	0.0725	0.0903	0.0280	0.0206	0.0777	0.0423	0.0369	1935	0.4339
1936	0.0670	0.0273	0.0318	−0.0751	0.0545	0.0233	0.0649	0.0079	0.0007	0.0800	0.0134	−0.0029	1936	0.3232
1937	0.0316	0.0167	−0.0147	−0.0852	−0.0071	−0.0526	0.0994	−0.0505	−0.1481	−0.0940	−0.0802	−0.0437	1937	−0.3698
1938	0.0295	0.0775	−0.2487	0.1393	−0.0284	0.2503	0.0719	−0.0203	0.0166	0.0827	−0.0250	0.0376	1938	0.3487
1939	−0.0629	0.0440	−0.1318	−0.0003	0.0733	−0.0612	0.1105	−0.0648	0.1451	−0.0076	−0.0398	0.0320	1939	0.0007
1940	−0.0313	0.0060	0.0148	−0.0024	−0.2307	0.0783	0.0365	0.0375	0.0099	0.0422	−0.0316	−0.0038	1940	−0.1064
1941	−0.0463	−0.0060	0.0023	−0.0700	0.0112	0.0385	0.0531	−0.0080	−0.0243	−0.0759	−0.0368	−0.0427	1941	−0.1942
1942	0.0031	−0.0242	−0.0769	−0.0459	0.0685	0.0200	0.0295	0.0102	0.0269	0.0571	−0.0081	0.0466	1942	0.1011
1943	0.0737	0.0562	0.0382	−0.0081	0.0472	0.0242	−0.0453	0.0210	0.0223	−0.0146	−0.0636	0.0597	1943	0.2204
1944	0.0191	0.0061	0.0195	−0.0157	0.0465	0.0522	−0.0248	0.0119	−0.0008	0.0023	0.0133	0.0335	1944	0.1728
1945	0.0158	0.0703	−0.0441	0.0881	0.0119	−0.0099	−0.0199	0.0641	0.0477	0.0322	0.0358	0.0079	1945	0.3343
1946	0.0714	−0.0606	0.0404	0.0336	0.0232	−0.0474	−0.0783	−0.0874	−0.1100	−0.0251	−0.0261	0.0376	1946	−0.2220
1947	0.0255	−0.0061	−0.0359	−0.0363	0.0044	0.0474	0.0288	−0.0305	−0.0341	0.0238	−0.0232	0.0102	1947	−0.0303
1948	−0.0487	−0.0306	0.0824	0.0147	0.0803	−0.0016	−0.0625	0.0116	−0.0276	0.0754	−0.0899	0.0418	1948	0.0272
1949	0.0053	−0.0187	0.0299	−0.0193	−0.0244	0.0000	0.0725	0.0191	0.0220	0.0398	0.0160	0.0545	1949	0.2097
1950	0.0240	0.0228	0.0027	0.0471	0.0465	−0.0601	0.0020	0.0357	0.0519	0.0038	0.0128	0.0372	1950	0.2450
1951	0.0469	0.0038	−0.0194	0.0496	−0.0336	−0.0215	0.0697	0.0478	−0.0051	−0.0154	0.0045	0.0385	1951	0.1714
1952	0.0181	−0.0220	0.0503	−0.0439	0.0330	0.0464	0.0120	−0.0083	−0.0164	0.0008	0.0571	0.0395	1952	0.1733
1953	−0.0024	−0.0056	−0.0237	−0.0249	0.0052	−0.0171	0.0248	−0.0525	0.0022	0.0514	0.0242	0.0065	1953	−0.0160
1954	0.0510	0.0124	0.0338	0.0542	0.0379	0.0018	0.0589	−0.0263	0.0878	−0.0143	0.0896	0.0561	1954	0.5339
1955	0.0197	0.0098	−0.0030	0.0396	0.0055	0.0841	0.0582	0.0000	0.0092	−0.0284	0.0813	0.0040	1955	0.3107
1956	−0.0335	0.0413	0.0697	−0.0017	−0.0640	0.0345	0.0453	−0.0316	−0.0452	0.0005	−0.0050	0.0345	1956	0.0359
1957	−0.0412	−0.0299	0.0190	0.0350	0.0412	−0.0055	0.0083	−0.0516	−0.0613	−0.0302	0.0195	−0.0395	1957	−0.1340
1958	0.0384	−0.0153	0.0256	0.0313	0.0212	0.0267	0.0437	0.0188	0.0501	0.0270	0.0273	0.0548	1958	0.4088
1959	0.0041	0.0060	0.0020	0.0390	0.0228	−0.0068	0.0339	−0.0091	−0.0476	0.0094	0.0186	0.0292	1959	0.1030
1960	−0.0689	0.0136	−0.0123	−0.0216	0.0326	0.0188	−0.0234	0.0317	−0.0600	−0.0052	0.0453	0.0479	1960	−0.0099
1961	0.0645	0.0319	0.0270	0.0051	0.0239	−0.0286	0.0296	0.0254	−0.0205	0.0298	0.0447	0.0046	1961	0.2604
1962	−0.0366	0.0187	−0.0068	−0.0628	−0.0811	−0.0803	0.0629	0.0208	−0.0517	0.0075	0.1086	0.0164	1962	−0.0983
1963	0.0494	−0.0249	0.0359	0.0500	0.0193	−0.0231	−0.0065	0.0535	−0.0097	0.0328	−0.0057	0.0240	1963	0.2081
1964	0.0271	0.0158	0.0154	0.0064	0.0162	0.0156	0.0173	−0.0107	0.0279	0.0085	−0.0017	0.0045	1964	0.1511
1965	0.0345	0.0031	−0.0143	0.0323	−0.0051	−0.0523	0.0137	0.0294	0.0312	0.0278	−0.0052	0.0074	1965	0.1033
1966	0.0062	−0.0193	−0.0236	0.0177	−0.0502	−0.0177	−0.0151	−0.0772	−0.0073	0.0451	0.0095	−0.0008	1966	−0.1298
1967	0.0798	0.0061	0.0388	0.0416	−0.0505	0.0159	0.0416	−0.0099	0.0321	−0.0305	0.0035	0.0247	1967	0.2032
1968	−0.0463	−0.0290	0.0060	0.0802	0.0131	0.0047	−0.0219	0.0135	0.0370	0.0029	0.0491	−0.0429	1968	0.0608
1969	−0.0096	−0.0462	0.0272	0.0163	−0.0002	−0.0603	−0.0630	0.0407	−0.0279	0.0421	−0.0349	−0.0238	1969	−0.1377
1970	−0.0776	0.0530	−0.0022	−0.0945	−0.0588	−0.0531	0.0715	0.0491	0.0294	−0.0148	0.0500	0.0530	1970	−0.0141

* Compound annual return

Table A-20 (continued)

Large Company Stocks: Inflation-Adjusted Total Returns

from January 1971 to December 2002

Year	Jan	Feb	Mar	Apr	May	Jun	Jul	Aug	Sep	Oct	Nov	Dec	Year	Jan–Dec*
1971	0.0410	0.0124	0.0348	0.0342	−0.0415	−0.0037	−0.0423	0.0387	−0.0064	−0.0419	0.0010	0.0833	1971	0.1060
1972	0.0186	0.0249	0.0056	0.0033	0.0186	−0.0229	−0.0004	0.0375	−0.0075	0.0075	0.0480	0.0099	1972	0.1505
1973	−0.0190	−0.0400	−0.0094	−0.0461	−0.0199	−0.0119	0.0371	−0.0490	0.0385	−0.0078	−0.1147	0.0117	1973	−0.2156
1974	−0.0170	−0.0109	−0.0327	−0.0427	−0.0379	−0.0223	−0.0828	−0.0945	−0.1275	0.1558	−0.0528	−0.0247	1974	−0.3446
1975	0.1201	0.0600	0.0198	0.0440	0.0462	0.0377	−0.0757	−0.0175	−0.0375	0.0572	0.0251	−0.0138	1975	0.2821
1976	0.1172	−0.0082	0.0301	−0.0140	−0.0132	0.0372	−0.0126	−0.0032	0.0205	−0.0245	−0.0038	0.0509	1976	0.1816
1977	−0.0544	−0.0251	−0.0180	−0.0064	−0.0204	0.0406	−0.0194	−0.0170	−0.0038	−0.0441	0.0320	0.0010	1977	−0.1307
1978	−0.0647	−0.0229	0.0206	0.0774	0.0037	−0.0253	0.0484	0.0288	−0.0118	−0.0963	0.0204	0.0117	1978	−0.0226
1979	0.0330	−0.0396	0.0474	−0.0078	−0.0288	0.0314	−0.0020	0.0505	−0.0078	−0.0739	0.0417	0.0086	1979	0.0453
1980	0.0460	−0.0105	−0.1114	0.0313	0.0459	0.0183	0.0667	0.0066	0.0187	0.0098	0.0996	−0.0398	1980	0.1781
1981	−0.0515	0.0103	0.0306	−0.0275	−0.0020	−0.0164	−0.0106	−0.0626	−0.0597	0.0505	0.0411	−0.0293	1981	−0.1271
1982	−0.0198	−0.0542	−0.0049	0.0370	−0.0383	−0.0292	−0.0269	0.1244	0.0093	0.1096	0.0456	0.0215	1982	0.1688
1983	0.0323	0.0257	0.0358	0.0682	−0.0106	0.0347	−0.0352	0.0136	0.0086	−0.0160	0.0216	−0.0074	1983	0.1803
1984	−0.0120	−0.0372	0.0148	0.0020	−0.0562	0.0188	−0.0175	0.1079	−0.0046	0.0001	−0.0101	0.0247	1984	0.0222
1985	0.0748	0.0095	−0.0026	−0.0072	0.0575	0.0128	−0.0041	−0.0083	−0.0351	0.0415	0.0680	0.0441	1985	0.2736
1986	0.0013	0.0791	0.0603	−0.0103	0.0517	0.0116	−0.0572	0.0729	−0.0867	0.0546	0.0247	−0.0273	1986	0.1715
1987	0.1275	0.0373	0.0226	−0.0141	0.0073	0.0456	0.0476	0.0327	−0.0268	−0.2172	−0.0832	0.0741	1987	0.0079
1988	0.0400	0.0443	−0.0344	0.0056	0.0044	0.0420	−0.0082	−0.0372	0.0354	0.0239	−0.0150	0.0164	1988	0.1187
1989	0.0670	−0.0289	0.0177	0.0448	0.0343	−0.0078	0.0872	0.0177	−0.0071	−0.0280	0.0184	0.0220	1989	0.2565
1990	−0.0766	0.0082	0.0207	−0.0262	0.0950	−0.0124	−0.0070	−0.0986	−0.0571	−0.0097	0.0620	0.0274	1990	−0.0874
1991	0.0380	0.0700	0.0223	0.0013	0.0397	−0.0485	0.0453	0.0205	−0.0207	0.0119	−0.0432	0.1135	1991	0.2667
1992	−0.0200	0.0091	−0.0245	0.0276	0.0040	−0.0180	0.0381	−0.0230	0.0086	0.0001	0.0322	0.0138	1992	0.0464
1993	0.0024	0.0100	0.0179	−0.0272	0.0256	0.0019	−0.0047	0.0352	−0.0095	0.0161	−0.0101	0.0123	1993	0.0705
1994	0.0307	−0.0303	−0.0467	0.0116	0.0156	−0.0280	0.0303	0.0365	−0.0267	0.0222	−0.0380	0.0146	1994	−0.0133
1995	0.0219	0.0347	0.0262	0.0257	0.0375	0.0215	0.0333	0.0001	0.0399	−0.0067	0.0447	0.0192	1995	0.3403
1996	0.0284	0.0063	0.0044	0.0108	0.0238	0.0035	−0.0463	0.0193	0.0529	0.0242	0.0739	−0.0196	1996	0.1912
1997	0.0588	0.0049	−0.0440	0.0584	0.0621	0.0433	0.0781	−0.0574	0.0522	−0.0358	0.0469	0.0185	1997	0.3113
1998	0.0092	0.0701	0.0493	0.0082	−0.0190	0.0393	−0.0119	−0.1456	0.0628	0.0787	0.0606	0.0583	1998	0.2654
1999	0.0393	−0.0323	0.0369	0.0312	−0.0236	0.0555	−0.0341	−0.0073	−0.0320	0.0614	0.0197	0.0589	1999	0.1788
2000	−0.0525	−0.0247	0.0888	−0.0307	−0.0211	0.0187	−0.0173	0.0609	−0.0577	−0.0059	−0.0794	0.0055	2000	−0.1208
2001	0.0290	−0.0948	−0.0655	0.0734	0.0022	−0.0260	−0.0071	−0.0626	−0.0849	0.0225	0.0785	0.0128	2001	−0.1323
2002	−0.0168	−0.0231	0.0318	−0.0659	−0.0074	−0.0718	−0.0790	0.0032	−0.1102	0.0862	0.0589	−0.0567	2002	−0.2391

Compound annual return

Table A-21

Small Company Stocks: Inflation-Adjusted Total Returns

from January 1926 to December 1970

Year	Jan	Feb	Mar	Apr	May	Jun	Jul	Aug	Sep	Oct	Nov	Dec	Year	Jan–Dec*
1926	0.0699	−0.0604	−0.1023	0.0084	−0.0010	0.0456	0.0208	0.0315	−0.0058	−0.0264	0.0169	0.0332	1926	0.0179
1927	0.0374	0.0628	−0.0493	0.0573	0.0652	−0.0395	0.0719	−0.0121	−0.0011	−0.0713	0.0829	0.0336	1927	0.2469
1928	0.0502	−0.0141	0.0531	0.0889	0.0377	−0.0771	0.0059	0.0421	0.0806	0.0296	0.1169	−0.0476	1928	0.4106
1929	0.0054	−0.0007	−0.0162	0.0347	−0.1387	0.0492	0.0016	−0.0201	−0.0904	−0.2768	−0.1484	−0.0445	1929	−0.5145
1930	0.1337	0.0685	0.1072	−0.0753	−0.0487	−0.2121	0.0446	−0.0107	−0.1511	−0.1043	0.0054	−0.1038	1930	−0.3418
1931	0.2281	0.2754	−0.0648	−0.2113	−0.1284	0.1950	−0.0536	−0.0742	−0.3216	0.0842	−0.0907	−0.2124	1931	−0.4446
1932	0.1251	0.0437	−0.1270	−0.2164	−0.1065	0.0107	0.3523	0.7561	−0.1277	−0.1713	−0.1183	−0.0395	1932	0.0547
1933	0.0071	−0.1140	0.1206	0.5078	0.6296	0.2484	−0.0816	0.0814	−0.1595	−0.1236	0.0654	0.0106	1933	1.4163
1934	0.3821	0.0090	−0.0012	0.0265	−0.1297	−0.0049	−0.2259	0.1517	−0.0312	0.0172	0.0975	0.0198	1934	0.2175
1935	−0.0470	−0.0661	−0.1167	0.0687	0.0024	0.0330	0.0908	0.0545	0.0306	0.0994	0.1357	0.0573	1935	0.3613
1936	0.3009	0.0654	0.0115	−0.1795	0.0272	−0.0326	0.0820	0.0137	0.0517	0.0661	0.1400	0.0160	1936	0.6283
1937	0.1186	0.0632	0.0048	−0.1718	−0.0453	−0.1203	0.1183	−0.0758	−0.2607	−0.1052	−0.1394	−0.1674	1937	−0.5927
1938	0.0683	0.0441	−0.3600	0.2716	−0.0806	0.3498	0.1472	−0.0980	−0.0157	0.2193	−0.0666	0.0462	1938	0.3659
1939	−0.0805	0.0155	−0.2448	0.0166	0.1088	−0.1042	0.2535	−0.1590	0.4858	−0.0351	−0.1053	0.0472	1939	0.0083
1940	0.0033	0.0743	0.0657	0.0654	−0.3689	0.1024	0.0256	0.0279	0.0188	0.0545	0.0245	−0.0492	1940	−0.0605
1941	0.0025	−0.0288	0.0271	−0.0757	−0.0025	0.0557	0.2110	−0.0150	−0.0638	−0.0774	−0.0577	−0.1223	1941	−0.1706
1942	0.1742	−0.0157	−0.0826	−0.0413	−0.0134	0.0315	0.0693	0.0262	0.0890	0.0976	−0.0567	0.0331	1942	0.3223
1943	0.2132	0.1908	0.1267	0.0807	0.1071	−0.0064	−0.1014	0.0036	0.0388	0.0084	−0.1096	0.1219	1943	0.8260
1944	0.0661	0.0315	0.0749	−0.0587	0.0699	0.1363	−0.0354	0.0280	−0.0020	−0.0108	0.0499	0.0829	1944	0.5055
1945	0.0482	0.1030	−0.0861	0.1136	0.0422	0.0755	−0.0574	0.0557	0.0719	0.0701	0.1131	0.0133	1945	0.6979
1946	0.1562	−0.0602	0.0198	0.0638	0.0534	−0.0565	−0.1057	−0.1045	−0.1699	−0.0308	−0.0373	0.0292	1946	−0.2521
1947	0.0421	−0.0025	−0.0542	−0.1031	−0.0505	0.0472	0.0692	−0.0141	−0.0120	0.0282	−0.0359	0.0227	1947	−0.0742
1948	−0.0264	−0.0704	0.1017	0.0222	0.0982	−0.0022	−0.0694	−0.0035	−0.0526	0.0691	−0.1055	0.0157	1948	−0.0469
1949	0.0196	−0.0374	0.0599	−0.0350	−0.0551	−0.0110	0.0746	0.0228	0.0445	0.0531	0.0002	0.0750	1949	0.2195
1950	0.0536	0.0250	−0.0079	0.0397	0.0212	−0.0829	0.0489	0.0443	0.0449	−0.0113	0.0281	0.0807	1950	0.3115
1951	0.0660	−0.0057	−0.0514	0.0353	−0.0368	−0.0516	0.0360	0.0605	0.0150	−0.0272	−0.0133	0.0006	1951	0.0182
1952	0.0191	−0.0238	0.0175	−0.0555	0.0019	0.0246	0.0036	−0.0018	−0.0149	−0.0115	0.0485	0.0173	1952	0.0213
1953	0.0435	0.0321	−0.0092	−0.0300	0.0116	−0.0522	0.0127	−0.0651	−0.0274	0.0266	0.0164	−0.0253	1953	−0.0707
1954	0.0730	0.0107	0.0196	0.0165	0.0413	0.0073	0.0808	0.0027	0.0436	0.0093	0.0766	0.1140	1954	0.6138
1955	0.0201	0.0479	0.0085	0.0150	0.0078	0.0293	0.0026	−0.0003	0.0072	−0.0170	0.0455	0.0188	1955	0.1999
1956	−0.0035	0.0278	0.0418	0.0034	−0.0445	−0.0006	0.0208	−0.0122	−0.0272	0.0043	0.0053	0.0014	1956	0.0138
1957	0.0224	−0.0235	0.0143	0.0212	0.0051	0.0013	−0.0107	−0.0397	−0.0463	−0.0832	0.0078	−0.0481	1957	−0.1708
1958	0.1040	−0.0181	0.0398	0.0352	0.0387	0.0312	0.0479	0.0440	0.0518	0.0407	0.0484	0.0325	1958	0.6203
1959	0.0562	0.0307	0.0027	0.0105	0.0002	−0.0088	0.0304	−0.0076	−0.0464	0.0192	0.0222	0.0322	1959	0.1468
1960	−0.0295	0.0038	−0.0315	−0.0242	0.0204	0.0317	−0.0189	0.0525	−0.0749	−0.0444	0.0425	0.0332	1960	−0.0470
1961	0.0915	0.0589	0.0619	0.0127	0.0427	−0.0554	−0.0013	0.0142	−0.0360	0.0262	0.0613	0.0079	1961	0.3121
1962	0.0136	0.0165	0.0034	−0.0798	−0.1009	−0.0785	0.0739	0.0289	−0.0710	−0.0363	0.1248	−0.0078	1962	−0.1297
1963	0.0894	0.0023	0.0138	0.0312	0.0436	−0.0162	−0.0011	0.0517	−0.0163	0.0225	−0.0117	−0.0069	1963	0.2156
1964	0.0263	0.0376	0.0208	0.0082	0.0157	0.0141	0.0376	−0.0018	0.0380	0.0194	−0.0011	−0.0122	1964	0.2207
1965	0.0529	0.0390	0.0227	0.0475	−0.0099	−0.0949	0.0437	0.0617	0.0325	0.0561	0.0349	0.0588	1965	0.3908
1966	0.0756	0.0247	−0.0222	0.0301	−0.0971	−0.0043	−0.0043	−0.1125	−0.0184	−0.0147	0.0491	0.0055	1966	−0.1003
1967	0.1838	0.0439	0.0593	0.0250	−0.0115	0.0984	0.0896	−0.0009	0.0544	−0.0340	0.0087	0.0933	1967	0.7815
1968	0.0114	−0.0736	−0.0157	0.1427	0.0967	−0.0028	−0.0392	0.0337	0.0569	−0.0027	0.0724	0.0034	1968	0.2984
1969	−0.0194	−0.1024	0.0309	0.0328	0.0145	−0.1221	−0.1110	0.0684	−0.0305	0.0572	−0.0608	−0.0745	1969	−0.2937
1970	−0.0641	0.0332	−0.0335	−0.1778	−0.1070	−0.0976	0.0517	0.0930	0.1029	−0.0753	0.0103	0.0672	1970	−0.2173

* Compound annual return

Table A-21 (continued)

Small Company Stocks: Inflation-Adjusted Total Returns

from January 1971 to December 2002

Year	Jan	Feb	Mar	Apr	May	Jun	Jul	Aug	Sep	Oct	Nov	Dec	Year	Jan–Dec*
1971	0.1582	0.0299	0.0529	0.0213	−0.0652	−0.0375	−0.0586	0.0557	−0.0234	−0.0567	−0.0389	0.1099	1971	0.1271
1972	0.1121	0.0246	−0.0159	0.0104	−0.0223	−0.0328	−0.0451	0.0170	−0.0387	−0.0206	0.0567	−0.0244	1972	0.0099
1973	−0.0462	−0.0863	−0.0298	−0.0686	−0.0867	−0.0356	0.1169	−0.0615	0.1031	0.0003	−0.2021	−0.0078	1973	−0.3649
1974	0.1229	−0.0211	−0.0185	−0.0517	−0.0894	−0.0241	−0.0291	−0.0799	−0.0764	0.0969	−0.0518	−0.0853	1974	−0.2865
1975	0.2710	0.0213	0.0578	0.0478	0.0616	0.0662	−0.0356	−0.0603	−0.0230	−0.0111	0.0257	−0.0238	1975	0.4280
1976	0.2654	0.1362	−0.0039	−0.0399	−0.0418	0.0404	−0.0014	−0.0336	0.0063	−0.0248	0.0374	0.1148	1976	0.5015
1977	0.0390	−0.0140	0.0068	0.0149	−0.0083	0.0701	−0.0014	−0.0145	0.0054	−0.0357	0.1032	0.0043	1977	0.1743
1978	−0.0241	0.0276	0.0957	0.0692	0.0714	−0.0290	0.0608	0.0883	−0.0102	−0.2488	0.0673	0.0113	1978	0.1324
1979	0.1222	−0.0395	0.1013	0.0269	−0.0087	0.0375	0.0041	0.0649	−0.0443	−0.1233	0.0758	0.0478	1979	0.2662
1980	0.0683	−0.0415	−0.1894	0.0574	0.0645	0.0338	0.1314	0.0536	0.0323	0.0244	0.0670	−0.0420	1980	0.2445
1981	0.0125	−0.0010	0.0865	0.0589	0.0337	−0.0009	−0.0425	−0.0755	−0.0826	0.0719	0.0247	−0.0248	1981	0.0453
1982	−0.0231	−0.0327	−0.0075	0.0339	−0.0343	−0.0278	−0.0070	0.0676	0.0309	0.1274	0.0797	0.0174	1982	0.2323
1983	0.0603	0.0709	0.0518	0.0690	0.0811	0.0314	−0.0128	−0.0229	0.0083	−0.0593	0.0498	−0.0158	1983	0.3456
1984	−0.0064	−0.0688	0.0151	−0.0133	−0.0549	0.0267	−0.0451	0.0952	−0.0021	−0.0242	−0.0336	0.0144	1984	−0.1022
1985	0.1038	0.0230	−0.0257	−0.0214	0.0238	0.0075	0.0244	−0.0093	−0.0573	0.0229	0.0584	0.0444	1985	0.2013
1986	0.0081	0.0748	0.0525	0.0086	0.0328	−0.0023	−0.0713	0.0200	−0.0605	0.0337	−0.0040	−0.0271	1986	0.0566
1987	0.0877	0.0767	0.0187	−0.0365	−0.0068	0.0224	0.0343	0.0230	−0.0130	−0.2937	−0.0411	0.0523	1987	−0.1313
1988	0.0529	0.0732	0.0363	0.0157	−0.0212	0.0567	−0.0067	−0.0287	0.0159	−0.0156	−0.0445	0.0377	1988	0.1767
1989	0.0352	0.0042	0.0299	0.0212	0.0303	−0.0225	0.0382	0.0106	−0.0032	−0.0649	−0.0075	−0.0150	1989	0.0529
1990	−0.0858	0.0139	0.0312	−0.0281	0.0536	0.0089	−0.0419	−0.1375	−0.0905	−0.0629	0.0427	0.0194	1990	−0.2608
1991	0.0777	0.1097	0.0664	0.0019	0.0304	−0.0513	0.0392	0.0231	−0.0012	0.0302	−0.0304	0.0593	1991	0.4033
1992	0.1112	0.0414	−0.0298	−0.0417	−0.0028	−0.0553	0.0348	−0.0256	0.0102	0.0223	0.0870	0.0448	1992	0.1987
1993	0.0491	−0.0214	0.0253	−0.0333	0.0328	−0.0052	0.0166	0.0310	0.0295	0.0428	−0.0182	0.0194	1993	0.1774
1994	0.0589	−0.0057	−0.0478	0.0046	−0.0019	−0.0295	0.0157	0.0295	0.0078	0.0108	−0.0339	0.0002	1994	0.0042
1995	0.0242	0.0211	0.0111	0.0318	0.0278	0.0547	0.0645	0.0331	0.0175	−0.0518	0.0199	0.0246	1995	0.3113
1996	−0.0030	0.0336	0.0175	0.0806	0.0728	−0.0588	−0.0960	0.0456	0.0258	−0.0206	0.0269	0.0204	1996	0.1384
1997	0.0387	−0.0237	−0.0514	−0.0288	0.1029	0.0485	0.0592	0.0489	0.0817	−0.0410	−0.0149	−0.0159	1997	0.2072
1998	−0.0077	0.0629	0.0462	0.0149	−0.0515	−0.0218	−0.0682	−0.2020	0.0356	0.0331	0.0758	0.0258	1998	−0.0878
1999	0.0254	−0.0698	−0.0408	0.0870	0.0387	0.0568	0.0062	−0.0214	−0.0268	−0.0105	0.0964	0.1137	1999	0.2639
2000	0.0570	0.2285	−0.0827	−0.1256	−0.0813	0.1302	−0.0339	0.0912	−0.0268	−0.0722	−0.1115	0.0195	2000	−0.0675
2001	0.1309	−0.0739	−0.0502	0.0689	0.0911	0.0342	−0.0227	−0.0295	−0.1317	0.0681	0.0692	0.0714	2001	0.2089
2002	0.0087	−0.0315	0.0823	0.0186	−0.0273	−0.0361	−0.1457	−0.0090	−0.0689	0.0240	0.0836	−0.0408	2002	−0.1529

Compound annual return

Table A-22

Long–Term Corporate Bonds: Inflation-Adjusted Total Returns

from January 1926 to December 1970

Year	Jan	Feb	Mar	Apr	May	Jun	Jul	Aug	Sep	Oct	Nov	Dec	Year	Jan–Dec*
1926	0.0072	0.0083	0.0141	0.0003	0.0100	0.0080	0.0153	0.0102	0.0000	0.0059	0.0019	0.0056	1926	0.0900
1927	0.0133	0.0146	0.0141	0.0055	−0.0088	−0.0052	0.0196	0.0142	0.0090	−0.0003	0.0087	0.0087	1927	0.0973
1928	0.0046	0.0166	0.0041	−0.0006	−0.0136	0.0054	−0.0010	0.0063	−0.0048	0.0103	−0.0017	0.0123	1928	0.0384
1929	0.0063	0.0050	−0.0048	0.0059	−0.0014	−0.0085	−0.0077	−0.0019	0.0053	0.0073	0.0001	0.0251	1929	0.0307
1930	0.0098	0.0111	0.0198	0.0025	0.0117	0.0170	0.0198	0.0198	0.0047	0.0115	0.0070	0.0054	1930	0.1490
1931	0.0353	0.0218	0.0159	0.0132	0.0245	0.0163	0.0074	0.0034	0.0030	−0.0298	−0.0078	−0.0197	1931	0.0848
1932	0.0157	−0.0099	0.0405	−0.0105	0.0255	0.0064	0.0043	0.0565	0.0352	0.0150	0.0124	0.0242	1932	0.2354
1933	0.0711	−0.0373	0.0127	−0.0069	0.0560	0.0083	−0.0124	−0.0009	−0.0014	0.0040	−0.0248	0.0309	1933	0.0982
1934	0.0205	0.0070	0.0187	0.0129	0.0065	0.0133	0.0047	0.0022	−0.0208	0.0177	0.0154	0.0126	1934	0.1158
1935	0.0061	0.0067	0.0067	0.0014	0.0091	0.0137	0.0160	−0.0042	−0.0049	0.0042	0.0020	0.0059	1935	0.0644
1936	0.0082	0.0103	0.0131	0.0026	0.0040	−0.0015	−0.0037	−0.0005	0.0043	0.0049	0.0109	0.0010	1936	0.0547
1937	−0.0047	−0.0070	−0.0184	0.0021	−0.0007	0.0030	−0.0007	−0.0040	−0.0067	0.0113	0.0137	0.0090	1937	−0.0035
1938	0.0179	0.0105	−0.0087	0.0090	0.0057	0.0095	0.0042	0.0005	0.0109	0.0128	0.0061	0.0098	1938	0.0916
1939	0.0070	0.0112	0.0046	0.0088	0.0049	0.0035	−0.0007	−0.0392	−0.0041	0.0286	0.0079	0.0126	1939	0.0446
1940	0.0073	−0.0051	0.0073	−0.0092	−0.0045	0.0097	0.0045	0.0031	0.0068	0.0049	0.0063	−0.0070	1940	0.0241
1941	0.0006	0.0006	−0.0069	−0.0016	−0.0021	−0.0120	0.0017	−0.0056	−0.0129	−0.0076	−0.0180	−0.0016	1941	−0.0637
1942	−0.0122	−0.0093	−0.0063	−0.0056	−0.0083	0.0013	−0.0021	−0.0026	0.0000	−0.0094	−0.0054	−0.0030	1942	−0.0612
1943	0.0049	−0.0014	−0.0136	−0.0067	−0.0029	0.0067	0.0096	0.0058	−0.0033	−0.0047	−0.0004	0.0030	1943	−0.0032
1944	0.0039	0.0053	0.0048	−0.0024	−0.0033	0.0001	−0.0023	−0.0004	0.0019	0.0019	0.0048	0.0111	1944	0.0257
1945	0.0076	0.0065	0.0018	−0.0001	−0.0085	−0.0061	−0.0029	0.0004	0.0069	0.0032	−0.0005	0.0096	1945	0.0178
1946	0.0128	0.0071	−0.0039	−0.0097	−0.0035	−0.0089	−0.0569	−0.0301	−0.0140	−0.0173	−0.0259	0.0034	1946	−0.1391
1947	0.0005	0.0021	−0.0148	0.0020	0.0051	−0.0072	−0.0070	−0.0174	−0.0360	−0.0099	−0.0155	−0.0105	1947	−0.1041
1948	−0.0089	0.0125	0.0144	−0.0103	−0.0062	−0.0152	−0.0174	0.0014	0.0024	0.0065	0.0154	0.0201	1948	0.0139
1949	0.0052	0.0151	−0.0021	0.0009	0.0052	0.0070	0.0170	0.0009	−0.0021	0.0124	0.0007	−0.0089	1949	0.0521
1950	0.0080	0.0035	−0.0021	−0.0022	−0.0050	−0.0033	−0.0029	−0.0045	−0.0107	−0.0062	0.0013	−0.0111	1950	−0.0347
1951	−0.0139	−0.0160	−0.0275	−0.0022	−0.0054	−0.0080	0.0192	0.0114	−0.0121	−0.0195	−0.0111	0.0020	1951	−0.0809
1952	0.0199	−0.0022	0.0076	−0.0042	0.0018	−0.0009	−0.0059	0.0050	−0.0006	0.0026	0.0108	−0.0079	1952	0.0262
1953	−0.0055	0.0010	−0.0058	−0.0260	−0.0055	0.0071	0.0152	−0.0110	0.0240	0.0202	−0.0036	0.0185	1953	0.0277
1954	0.0099	0.0211	0.0051	−0.0009	−0.0079	0.0051	0.0040	0.0030	0.0065	0.0065	0.0013	0.0042	1954	0.0591
1955	−0.0097	−0.0063	0.0092	−0.0001	−0.0018	0.0029	−0.0078	−0.0013	0.0038	0.0078	−0.0042	0.0088	1955	0.0010
1956	0.0117	0.0026	−0.0158	−0.0127	0.0002	−0.0079	−0.0165	−0.0196	0.0000	−0.0165	−0.0126	−0.0106	1956	−0.0941
1957	0.0185	0.0057	0.0026	−0.0102	−0.0099	−0.0379	−0.0157	−0.0021	0.0083	0.0023	0.0275	0.0685	1957	0.0552
1958	0.0040	−0.0020	−0.0115	0.0140	0.0031	−0.0049	−0.0164	−0.0309	−0.0096	0.0107	0.0093	−0.0047	1958	−0.0391
1959	−0.0039	0.0138	−0.0083	−0.0183	−0.0125	−0.0002	0.0066	−0.0057	−0.0122	0.0130	0.0135	−0.0096	1959	−0.0243
1960	0.0118	0.0116	0.0191	−0.0078	−0.0021	0.0118	0.0257	0.0117	−0.0074	−0.0037	−0.0081	0.0104	1960	0.0748
1961	0.0148	0.0210	−0.0029	−0.0116	0.0049	−0.0091	−0.0005	−0.0007	0.0121	0.0127	0.0028	−0.0026	1961	0.0412
1962	0.0080	0.0030	0.0129	0.0120	0.0000	−0.0026	−0.0037	0.0143	0.0034	0.0079	0.0062	0.0034	1962	0.0664
1963	0.0048	0.0012	0.0015	−0.0051	0.0048	−0.0001	−0.0016	0.0035	−0.0023	0.0038	0.0004	−0.0056	1963	0.0054
1964	0.0076	0.0065	−0.0073	0.0029	0.0057	0.0026	0.0030	0.0048	−0.0001	0.0039	−0.0025	0.0077	1964	0.0354
1965	0.0081	0.0009	0.0001	−0.0011	−0.0029	−0.0050	0.0008	0.0015	−0.0036	0.0035	−0.0078	−0.0180	1965	−0.0233
1966	0.0022	−0.0175	−0.0090	−0.0028	−0.0036	−0.0001	−0.0129	−0.0309	0.0057	0.0219	−0.0020	0.0191	1966	−0.0306
1967	0.0450	−0.0211	0.0097	−0.0091	−0.0283	−0.0252	−0.0009	−0.0037	0.0074	−0.0310	−0.0301	0.0097	1967	−0.0776
1968	0.0320	0.0008	−0.0245	0.0019	0.0003	0.0064	0.0292	0.0177	−0.0081	−0.0216	−0.0263	−0.0261	1968	−0.0205
1969	0.0110	−0.0197	−0.0282	0.0268	−0.0254	−0.0029	−0.0040	−0.0065	−0.0288	0.0091	−0.0522	−0.0195	1969	−0.1338
1970	0.0105	0.0346	−0.0097	−0.0309	−0.0206	−0.0051	0.0520	0.0083	0.0087	−0.0146	0.0548	0.0320	1970	0.1221

* Compound annual return

Table A-22 (continued)

Long–Term Corporate Bonds: Inflation-Adjusted Total Returns

from January 1971 to December 2002

Year	Jan	Feb	Mar	Apr	May	Jun	Jul	Aug	Sep	Oct	Nov	Dec	Year	Jan–Dec*
1971	0.0523	−0.0382	0.0224	−0.0268	−0.0210	0.0049	−0.0050	0.0528	−0.0110	0.0265	0.0013	0.0181	1971	0.0741
1972	−0.0041	0.0058	0.0008	0.0011	0.0130	−0.0092	−0.0010	0.0056	−0.0009	0.0069	0.0225	−0.0035	1972	0.0372
1973	−0.0085	−0.0047	−0.0048	−0.0008	−0.0100	−0.0124	−0.0498	0.0172	0.0325	−0.0146	0.0005	−0.0153	1973	−0.0704
1974	−0.0138	−0.0118	−0.0415	−0.0395	−0.0006	−0.0378	−0.0284	−0.0391	0.0053	0.0793	0.0032	−0.0145	1974	−0.1360
1975	0.0548	0.0066	−0.0284	−0.0102	0.0062	0.0221	−0.0134	−0.0205	−0.0174	0.0489	−0.0148	0.0398	1975	0.0713
1976	0.0164	0.0037	0.0143	−0.0057	−0.0161	0.0096	0.0090	0.0183	0.0126	0.0029	0.0289	0.0317	1976	0.1320
1977	−0.0358	−0.0121	0.0032	0.0021	0.0050	0.0108	−0.0049	0.0097	−0.0060	−0.0065	0.0012	−0.0142	1977	−0.0474
1978	−0.0142	−0.0018	−0.0027	−0.0112	−0.0205	−0.0080	0.0029	0.0205	−0.0118	−0.0283	0.0079	−0.0186	1978	−0.0834
1979	0.0094	−0.0242	0.0010	−0.0164	0.0104	0.0174	−0.0158	−0.0093	−0.0280	−0.0971	0.0127	−0.0211	1979	−0.1543
1980	−0.0777	−0.0791	−0.0203	0.1249	0.0457	0.0228	−0.0437	−0.0506	−0.0326	−0.0244	−0.0073	0.0161	1980	−0.1348
1981	−0.0210	−0.0369	0.0237	−0.0828	0.0508	−0.0062	−0.0481	−0.0418	−0.0297	0.0498	0.1235	−0.0607	1981	−0.0934
1982	−0.0164	0.0279	0.0317	0.0294	0.0145	−0.0583	0.0482	0.0815	0.0605	0.0730	0.0218	0.0150	1982	0.3725
1983	−0.0118	0.0424	0.0065	0.0473	−0.0376	−0.0079	−0.0493	0.0018	0.0340	−0.0051	0.0125	−0.0046	1983	0.0237
1984	0.0213	−0.0217	−0.0257	−0.0121	−0.0511	0.0166	0.0552	0.0264	0.0265	0.0545	0.0212	0.0122	1984	0.1242
1985	0.0305	−0.0412	0.0134	0.0254	0.0780	0.0052	−0.0136	0.0238	0.0040	0.0297	0.0335	0.0443	1985	0.2536
1986	0.0014	0.0782	0.0303	0.0038	−0.0194	0.0168	0.0028	0.0257	−0.0162	0.0180	0.0224	0.0108	1986	0.1851
1987	0.0155	0.0019	−0.0131	−0.0553	−0.0081	0.0113	−0.0139	−0.0130	−0.0469	0.0480	0.0110	0.0215	1987	−0.0448
1988	0.0490	0.0112	−0.0230	−0.0199	−0.0091	0.0335	−0.0153	0.0012	0.0257	0.0239	−0.0177	0.0022	1988	0.0602
1989	0.0151	−0.0170	0.0006	0.0147	0.0320	0.0370	0.0153	−0.0179	0.0008	0.0227	0.0046	−0.0010	1989	0.1107
1990	−0.0291	−0.0059	−0.0065	−0.0206	0.0361	0.0161	0.0063	−0.0381	0.0007	0.0071	0.0262	0.0167	1990	0.0064
1991	0.0090	0.0106	0.0093	0.0123	0.0009	−0.0047	0.0152	0.0245	0.0226	0.0028	0.0077	0.0428	1991	0.1632
1992	−0.0187	0.0060	−0.0123	0.0002	0.0239	0.0120	0.0286	0.0061	0.0070	−0.0191	0.0055	0.0235	1992	0.0631
1993	0.0200	0.0220	−0.0010	0.0024	0.0006	0.0279	0.0100	0.0259	0.0022	0.0010	−0.0195	0.0067	1993	0.1016
1994	0.0174	−0.0319	−0.0416	−0.0110	−0.0069	−0.0115	0.0281	−0.0071	−0.0291	−0.0057	0.0005	0.0157	1994	−0.0822
1995	0.0215	0.0248	0.0062	0.0142	0.0610	0.0059	−0.0101	0.0187	0.0133	0.0152	0.0249	0.0235	1995	0.2406
1996	−0.0044	−0.0404	−0.0181	−0.0198	−0.0014	0.0166	−0.0009	−0.0089	0.0226	0.0328	0.0244	−0.0186	1996	−0.0186
1997	−0.0059	−0.0003	−0.0245	0.0171	0.0134	0.0174	0.0515	−0.0258	0.0201	0.0166	0.0107	0.0176	1997	0.1106
1998	0.0118	−0.0026	0.0019	0.0034	0.0148	0.0103	−0.0068	0.0077	0.0400	−0.0214	0.0270	0.0017	1998	0.0900
1999	0.0098	−0.0412	−0.0028	−0.0096	−0.0176	−0.0160	−0.0143	−0.0050	0.0045	0.0029	−0.0030	−0.0102	1999	−0.0987
2000	−0.0045	0.0033	0.0086	−0.0120	−0.0166	0.0266	0.0161	0.0123	−0.0006	0.0028	0.0257	0.0276	2000	0.0917
2001	0.0294	0.0087	−0.0052	−0.0167	0.0087	0.0038	0.0390	0.0157	−0.0196	0.0473	−0.0171	−0.0051	2001	0.0896
2002	0.0152	0.0091	−0.0349	0.0196	0.0113	0.0067	0.0082	0.0417	0.0313	−0.0256	0.0103	0.0384	2002	0.1363

Compound annual return

Table A-23

Long–Term Government Bonds: Inflation-Adjusted Total Returns

from January 1926 to December 1970

Year	Jan	Feb	Mar	Apr	May	Jun	Jul	Aug	Sep	Oct	Nov	Dec	Year	Jan–Dec*
1926	0.0138	0.0101	0.0098	-0.0018	0.0070	0.0114	0.0100	0.0058	-0.0020	0.0063	0.0122	0.0078	1926	0.0940
1927	0.0151	0.0165	0.0313	-0.0005	0.0031	-0.0163	0.0244	0.0135	-0.0040	0.0040	0.0117	0.0091	1927	0.1124
1928	-0.0017	0.0159	0.0045	-0.0023	-0.0135	0.0120	-0.0217	0.0057	-0.0118	0.0177	0.0023	0.0043	1928	0.0108
1929	-0.0071	-0.0138	-0.0105	0.0316	-0.0220	0.0070	-0.0097	-0.0072	0.0047	0.0382	0.0256	-0.0031	1929	0.0322
1930	-0.0018	0.0169	0.0143	-0.0075	0.0199	0.0111	0.0176	0.0074	0.0013	0.0096	0.0124	0.0074	1930	0.1138
1931	0.0024	0.0236	0.0169	0.0151	0.0256	0.0114	-0.0020	0.0035	-0.0237	-0.0265	0.0141	-0.0130	1931	0.0466
1932	0.0245	0.0561	0.0029	0.0680	-0.0045	0.0139	0.0481	0.0127	0.0107	0.0058	0.0083	0.0234	1932	0.3026
1933	0.0306	-0.0105	0.0177	-0.0006	0.0275	-0.0056	-0.0297	-0.0057	0.0023	-0.0091	-0.0149	-0.0062	1933	-0.0058
1934	0.0205	0.0005	0.0197	0.0151	0.0106	0.0042	0.0040	-0.0143	-0.0291	0.0258	0.0062	0.0138	1934	0.0784
1935	0.0032	0.0018	0.0066	-0.0019	-0.0008	0.0117	0.0095	-0.0133	-0.0040	0.0061	-0.0039	0.0046	1935	0.0194
1936	0.0055	0.0130	0.0156	0.0035	0.0040	-0.0076	0.0012	0.0039	-0.0055	0.0030	0.0205	0.0038	1936	0.0623
1937	-0.0084	0.0063	-0.0479	-0.0008	0.0006	-0.0041	0.0091	-0.0127	-0.0047	0.0088	0.0166	0.0106	1937	-0.0278
1938	0.0199	0.0147	-0.0037	0.0162	0.0092	0.0004	0.0020	0.0024	0.0022	0.0135	0.0002	0.0056	1938	0.0855
1939	0.0107	0.0128	0.0149	0.0142	0.0171	-0.0027	0.0113	-0.0201	-0.0724	0.0459	0.0162	0.0193	1939	0.0645
1940	0.0007	-0.0045	0.0201	-0.0035	-0.0322	0.0234	0.0076	0.0052	0.0086	0.0031	0.0205	0.0019	1940	0.0508
1941	-0.0201	0.0020	0.0048	0.0035	-0.0042	-0.0118	-0.0024	-0.0072	-0.0188	0.0029	-0.0116	-0.0199	1941	-0.0801
1942	-0.0060	-0.0073	-0.0035	-0.0091	-0.0028	-0.0018	-0.0023	-0.0024	-0.0017	-0.0076	-0.0095	-0.0030	1942	-0.0555
1943	0.0033	-0.0025	-0.0146	-0.0068	-0.0026	0.0037	0.0076	0.0059	-0.0028	-0.0033	0.0019	-0.0001	1943	-0.0104
1944	0.0040	0.0051	0.0021	-0.0044	-0.0010	-0.0011	-0.0021	-0.0011	0.0014	0.0012	0.0024	0.0005	1944	0.0069
1945	0.0127	0.0096	0.0021	0.0141	-0.0019	0.0075	-0.0104	0.0026	0.0091	0.0104	0.0088	0.0157	1945	0.0830
1946	0.0025	0.0069	-0.0063	-0.0189	-0.0066	-0.0038	-0.0595	-0.0324	-0.0124	-0.0120	-0.0288	0.0066	1946	-0.1546
1947	-0.0006	0.0037	-0.0194	-0.0037	0.0064	-0.0066	-0.0028	-0.0024	-0.0275	-0.0037	-0.0231	-0.0318	1947	-0.1067
1948	-0.0093	0.0132	0.0063	-0.0096	0.0070	-0.0153	-0.0144	-0.0039	0.0014	0.0048	0.0145	0.0126	1948	0.0067
1949	0.0096	0.0162	0.0046	-0.0003	0.0033	0.0153	0.0104	0.0083	-0.0053	0.0075	0.0007	0.0109	1949	0.0840
1950	-0.0019	0.0050	-0.0034	0.0016	-0.0009	-0.0081	-0.0042	-0.0069	-0.0140	-0.0102	-0.0006	-0.0117	1950	-0.0542
1951	-0.0101	-0.0190	-0.0195	-0.0075	-0.0107	-0.0049	0.0125	0.0099	-0.0143	-0.0041	-0.0186	-0.0098	1951	-0.0926
1952	0.0028	0.0077	0.0111	0.0132	-0.0046	-0.0022	-0.0094	-0.0082	-0.0118	0.0135	-0.0015	-0.0073	1952	0.0027
1953	0.0037	-0.0037	-0.0113	-0.0118	-0.0172	0.0184	0.0014	-0.0032	0.0287	0.0049	-0.0012	0.0219	1953	0.0299
1954	0.0064	0.0252	0.0071	0.0129	-0.0124	0.0150	0.0134	-0.0024	0.0015	0.0031	-0.0037	0.0089	1954	0.0772
1955	-0.0241	-0.0078	0.0087	0.0001	0.0073	-0.0076	-0.0139	0.0029	0.0035	0.0144	-0.0057	0.0062	1955	-0.0166
1956	0.0096	-0.0002	-0.0161	-0.0125	0.0175	-0.0034	-0.0280	-0.0175	0.0037	-0.0115	-0.0057	-0.0202	1956	-0.0821
1957	0.0333	-0.0011	-0.0048	-0.0257	-0.0047	-0.0239	-0.0088	-0.0010	0.0064	-0.0050	0.0496	0.0307	1957	0.0431
1958	-0.0142	0.0089	0.0032	0.0163	0.0001	-0.0171	-0.0289	-0.0424	-0.0117	0.0138	0.0109	-0.0169	1958	-0.0772
1959	-0.0092	0.0129	0.0017	-0.0128	-0.0017	-0.0035	0.0037	-0.0030	-0.0091	0.0116	-0.0119	-0.0159	1959	-0.0370
1960	0.0123	0.0192	0.0282	-0.0225	0.0152	0.0150	0.0368	-0.0067	0.0064	-0.0073	-0.0077	0.0279	1960	0.1212
1961	-0.0107	0.0200	-0.0037	0.0115	-0.0046	-0.0086	-0.0010	-0.0027	0.0107	0.0071	-0.0020	-0.0125	1961	0.0030
1962	-0.0014	0.0081	0.0231	0.0060	0.0046	-0.0076	-0.0131	0.0187	0.0006	0.0095	0.0021	0.0046	1962	0.0559
1963	-0.0012	-0.0003	-0.0002	-0.0012	0.0023	-0.0024	-0.0013	0.0021	0.0004	-0.0037	0.0040	-0.0028	1963	-0.0043
1964	-0.0024	0.0000	0.0026	0.0036	0.0050	0.0047	-0.0014	0.0031	0.0028	0.0032	-0.0005	0.0019	1964	0.0229
1965	0.0040	0.0014	0.0043	0.0004	-0.0004	-0.0006	0.0011	0.0008	-0.0055	0.0017	-0.0083	-0.0109	1965	-0.0119
1966	-0.0104	-0.0311	0.0264	-0.0104	-0.0070	-0.0047	-0.0068	-0.0256	0.0311	0.0187	-0.0148	0.0403	1966	0.0029
1967	0.0154	-0.0231	0.0177	-0.0311	-0.0069	-0.0341	0.0018	-0.0114	-0.0024	-0.0428	-0.0226	0.0162	1967	-0.1186
1968	0.0287	-0.0062	-0.0259	0.0197	0.0014	0.0171	0.0240	-0.0032	-0.0131	-0.0188	-0.0306	-0.0390	1968	-0.0476
1969	-0.0233	0.0004	-0.0073	0.0359	-0.0516	0.0149	0.0034	-0.0114	-0.0574	0.0328	-0.0296	-0.0130	1969	-0.1054
1970	-0.0057	0.0531	-0.0120	-0.0471	-0.0510	0.0432	0.0284	-0.0036	0.0176	-0.0159	0.0755	-0.0134	1970	0.0627

* Compound annual return

Table A-23 (continued)

Long–Term Government Bonds: Inflation-Adjusted Total Returns

from January 1971 to December 2002

Year	Jan	Feb	Mar	Apr	May	Jun	Jul	Aug	Sep	Oct	Nov	Dec	Year	Jan–Dec*
1971	0.0497	−0.0180	0.0491	−0.0315	−0.0056	−0.0215	0.0005	0.0445	0.0195	0.0150	−0.0063	0.0003	1971	0.0955
1972	−0.0072	0.0039	−0.0098	0.0003	0.0237	−0.0088	0.0175	0.0013	−0.0122	0.0202	0.0202	−0.0260	1972	0.0220
1973	−0.0351	−0.0056	−0.0011	−0.0024	−0.0165	−0.0089	−0.0455	0.0207	0.0287	0.0133	−0.0254	−0.0147	1973	−0.0910
1974	−0.0168	−0.0151	−0.0400	−0.0307	0.0011	−0.0051	−0.0103	−0.0356	0.0126	0.0400	0.0209	0.0099	1974	−0.0699
1975	0.0179	0.0061	−0.0304	−0.0231	0.0167	0.0209	−0.0191	−0.0099	−0.0147	0.0411	−0.0169	0.0347	1975	0.0204
1976	0.0066	0.0037	0.0141	−0.0023	−0.0216	0.0154	0.0019	0.0164	0.0104	0.0043	0.0309	0.0298	1976	0.1140
1977	−0.0443	−0.0150	0.0029	−0.0008	0.0069	0.0097	−0.0114	0.0159	−0.0066	−0.0120	0.0044	−0.0205	1977	−0.0699
1978	−0.0133	−0.0065	−0.0089	−0.0094	−0.0156	−0.0164	0.0071	0.0166	−0.0175	−0.0278	0.0133	−0.0184	1978	−0.0936
1979	0.0102	−0.0249	0.0032	−0.0224	0.0137	0.0216	−0.0212	−0.0134	−0.0224	−0.0922	0.0216	−0.0048	1979	−0.1283
1980	−0.0872	−0.0596	−0.0452	0.1395	0.0317	0.0246	−0.0484	−0.0493	−0.0351	−0.0347	0.0009	0.0263	1980	−0.1454
1981	−0.0195	−0.0534	0.0310	−0.0578	0.0535	−0.0263	−0.0462	−0.0459	−0.0244	0.0806	0.1378	−0.0739	1981	−0.0650
1982	0.0010	0.0150	0.0242	0.0330	−0.0064	−0.0341	0.0444	0.0759	0.0600	0.0605	0.0015	0.0354	1982	0.3513
1983	−0.0332	0.0488	−0.0101	0.0276	−0.0438	0.0005	−0.0525	−0.0013	0.0452	−0.0158	0.0167	−0.0072	1983	−0.0303
1984	0.0187	−0.0223	−0.0179	−0.0154	−0.0544	0.0117	0.0659	0.0224	0.0293	0.0534	0.0118	0.0084	1984	0.1108
1985	0.0344	−0.0532	0.0262	0.0201	0.0855	0.0110	−0.0195	0.0237	−0.0052	0.0306	0.0366	0.0515	1985	0.2621
1986	−0.0056	0.1176	0.0819	−0.0059	−0.0534	0.0562	−0.0111	0.0480	−0.0546	0.0280	0.0258	−0.0027	1986	0.2314
1987	0.0100	0.0162	−0.0266	−0.0524	−0.0135	0.0056	−0.0198	−0.0219	−0.0416	0.0595	0.0022	0.0168	1987	−0.0682
1988	0.0639	0.0026	−0.0348	−0.0210	−0.0135	0.0324	−0.0211	0.0016	0.0276	0.0273	−0.0204	0.0093	1988	0.0503
1989	0.0153	−0.0220	0.0064	0.0093	0.0342	0.0525	0.0213	−0.0274	−0.0013	0.0330	0.0054	−0.0022	1989	0.1287
1990	−0.0441	−0.0071	−0.0098	−0.0217	0.0391	0.0175	0.0068	−0.0506	0.0033	0.0154	0.0379	0.0187	1990	0.0007
1991	0.0070	0.0016	0.0023	0.0125	−0.0029	−0.0092	0.0143	0.0310	0.0258	0.0040	0.0053	0.0573	1991	0.1575
1992	−0.0338	0.0015	−0.0143	0.0002	0.0228	0.0164	0.0376	0.0038	0.0157	−0.0233	−0.0004	0.0253	1992	0.0501
1993	0.0230	0.0318	−0.0014	0.0044	0.0033	0.0434	0.0191	0.0405	−0.0015	0.0055	−0.0265	0.0020	1993	0.1508
1994	0.0229	−0.0482	−0.0428	−0.0164	−0.0089	−0.0134	0.0335	−0.0126	−0.0357	−0.0031	0.0053	0.0161	1994	−0.1017
1995	0.0232	0.0246	0.0058	0.0136	0.0769	0.0119	−0.0168	0.0209	0.0155	0.0261	0.0256	0.0279	1995	0.2841
1996	−0.0069	−0.0513	−0.0260	−0.0203	−0.0073	0.0196	−0.0002	−0.0158	0.0257	0.0371	0.0331	−0.0256	1996	−0.0412
1997	−0.0110	−0.0026	−0.0276	0.0242	0.0103	0.0182	0.0612	−0.0336	0.0290	0.0315	0.0154	0.0197	1997	0.1391
1998	0.0181	−0.0090	0.0006	0.0008	0.0164	0.0216	−0.0052	0.0452	0.0382	−0.0242	0.0097	−0.0026	1998	0.1127
1999	0.0097	−0.0531	−0.0038	−0.0052	−0.0185	−0.0078	−0.0107	−0.0076	0.0036	−0.0030	−0.0067	−0.0155	1999	−0.1134
2000	0.0204	0.0203	0.0282	−0.0081	−0.0060	0.0185	0.0155	0.0229	−0.0208	0.0170	0.0313	0.0248	2000	0.1750
2001	−0.0057	0.0150	−0.0097	−0.0351	−0.0008	0.0068	0.0405	0.0206	0.0036	0.0499	−0.0455	−0.0144	2001	0.0211
2002	0.0115	0.0075	−0.0490	0.0352	0.0015	0.0182	0.0292	0.0429	0.0399	−0.0310	−0.0122	0.0530	2002	0.1510

*Compound annual return

Table A-24

Intermediate-Term Government Bonds: Inflation-Adjusted Total Returns

from January 1926 to December 1970

Year	Jan	Feb	Mar	Apr	May	Jun	Jul	Aug	Sep	Oct	Nov	Dec	Year	Jan–Dec
1926	0.0068	0.0069	0.0097	−0.0004	0.0065	0.0102	0.0109	0.0067	−0.0008	0.0016	0.0007	0.0089	1926	0.0697
1927	0.0133	0.0115	0.0096	0.0016	−0.0056	−0.0066	0.0237	0.0115	0.0002	−0.0092	0.0103	0.0057	1927	0.0674
1928	0.0066	0.0094	0.0010	−0.0022	−0.0065	0.0095	−0.0089	0.0031	−0.0050	0.0052	0.0038	0.0032	1928	0.0190
1929	−0.0009	0.0001	0.0044	0.0128	−0.0120	0.0067	−0.0031	0.0014	0.0005	0.0168	0.0200	0.0102	1929	0.0581
1930	−0.0002	0.0133	0.0221	−0.0129	0.0120	0.0202	0.0196	0.0083	0.0002	0.0137	0.0153	0.0169	1930	0.1356
1931	0.0075	0.0249	0.0117	0.0149	0.0230	−0.0106	0.0039	0.0039	−0.0069	−0.0039	0.0163	−0.0069	1931	0.0796
1932	0.0178	0.0272	0.0126	0.0267	0.0055	0.0182	0.0120	0.0249	0.0077	0.0121	0.0082	0.0221	1932	0.2130
1933	0.0140	0.0157	0.0179	0.0084	0.0172	−0.0097	−0.0286	−0.0029	0.0026	−0.0025	0.0027	−0.0204	1933	0.0131
1934	0.0078	−0.0023	0.0189	0.0208	0.0094	0.0065	−0.0024	−0.0117	−0.0283	0.0265	0.0071	0.0150	1934	0.0683
1935	−0.0034	0.0031	0.0150	0.0009	0.0014	0.0138	0.0087	−0.0071	−0.0105	0.0109	−0.0035	0.0096	1935	0.0391
1936	−0.0003	0.0118	0.0080	0.0024	0.0038	−0.0085	−0.0026	−0.0022	−0.0014	0.0049	0.0081	−0.0057	1936	0.0183
1937	−0.0102	−0.0017	−0.0233	0.0000	0.0033	−0.0036	0.0012	−0.0066	−0.0011	0.0078	0.0111	0.0085	1937	−0.0150
1938	0.0227	0.0147	−0.0012	0.0182	0.0070	0.0075	−0.0013	0.0038	−0.0013	0.0142	0.0023	0.0028	1938	0.0927
1939	0.0077	0.0131	0.0105	0.0063	0.0095	0.0002	0.0040	−0.0147	−0.0447	0.0364	0.0074	0.0156	1939	0.0502
1940	0.0010	−0.0036	0.0112	0.0002	−0.0237	0.0162	0.0027	0.0067	0.0024	0.0036	0.0056	−0.0020	1940	0.0199
1941	0.0001	−0.0047	0.0021	−0.0060	−0.0058	−0.0127	−0.0045	−0.0079	−0.0176	−0.0087	−0.0177	−0.0038	1941	−0.0840
1942	−0.0055	−0.0069	−0.0102	−0.0040	−0.0087	−0.0008	−0.0041	−0.0044	−0.0043	−0.0083	−0.0043	−0.0079	1942	−0.0673
1943	0.0039	−0.0006	−0.0134	−0.0092	−0.0020	0.0053	0.0098	0.0041	−0.0024	−0.0021	0.0034	0.0001	1943	−0.0034
1944	0.0030	0.0035	0.0019	−0.0030	−0.0033	−0.0012	−0.0028	−0.0014	0.0011	0.0011	0.0009	−0.0027	1944	−0.0031
1945	0.0052	0.0057	0.0004	−0.0004	−0.0063	−0.0074	−0.0019	0.0016	0.0054	0.0016	−0.0027	−0.0015	1945	−0.0003
1946	0.0039	0.0085	−0.0111	−0.0074	−0.0048	−0.0075	−0.0567	−0.0211	−0.0125	−0.0167	−0.0243	−0.0046	1946	−0.1452
1947	0.0023	0.0021	−0.0190	−0.0013	0.0038	−0.0068	−0.0084	−0.0078	−0.0232	−0.0023	−0.0052	−0.0108	1947	−0.0743
1948	−0.0098	0.0104	0.0046	−0.0122	−0.0017	−0.0078	−0.0125	−0.0045	0.0010	0.0054	0.0090	0.0102	1948	−0.0084
1949	0.0042	0.0124	−0.0003	0.0001	0.0037	0.0036	0.0091	0.0002	−0.0034	0.0062	−0.0012	0.0069	1949	0.0420
1950	0.0038	0.0036	−0.0042	−0.0006	−0.0022	−0.0053	−0.0077	−0.0090	−0.0072	−0.0053	−0.0023	−0.0125	1950	−0.0481
1951	−0.0136	−0.0110	−0.0165	0.0044	−0.0079	0.0063	0.0045	0.0036	−0.0120	−0.0035	−0.0018	−0.0054	1951	−0.0521
1952	0.0038	0.0043	0.0067	0.0016	0.0007	−0.0060	−0.0109	−0.0036	0.0031	0.0054	−0.0006	0.0032	1952	0.0074
1953	0.0023	0.0053	−0.0042	−0.0109	−0.0141	0.0117	0.0030	−0.0033	0.0181	0.0013	0.0051	0.0116	1953	0.0259
1954	0.0040	0.0113	0.0039	0.0068	−0.0110	0.0112	−0.0005	0.0023	0.0005	0.0016	−0.0013	0.0030	1954	0.0320
1955	−0.0032	−0.0052	0.0024	0.0004	0.0001	−0.0036	−0.0108	0.0032	0.0044	0.0072	−0.0066	0.0014	1955	−0.0102
1956	0.0118	0.0003	−0.0113	−0.0014	0.0062	−0.0059	−0.0167	−0.0091	0.0079	−0.0080	−0.0047	−0.0013	1956	−0.0319
1957	0.0225	−0.0049	−0.0006	−0.0137	−0.0041	−0.0165	−0.0062	0.0097	−0.0009	0.0043	0.0359	0.0215	1957	0.0467
1958	−0.0025	0.0127	−0.0017	0.0029	0.0060	−0.0079	−0.0102	−0.0345	−0.0017	0.0002	0.0121	−0.0050	1958	−0.0300
1959	−0.0025	0.0119	−0.0037	−0.0064	−0.0013	−0.0122	0.0011	−0.0067	−0.0015	0.0139	−0.0092	−0.0020	1959	−0.0186
1960	0.0166	0.0060	0.0292	−0.0120	0.0031	0.0194	0.0267	−0.0004	0.0017	−0.0029	−0.0105	0.0210	1960	0.1013
1961	−0.0059	0.0090	0.0037	0.0054	−0.0028	−0.0037	−0.0038	0.0030	0.0056	0.0014	−0.0019	0.0018	1961	0.0117
1962	−0.0045	0.0132	0.0067	0.0002	0.0049	−0.0028	−0.0034	0.0125	−0.0034	0.0062	0.0060	0.0067	1962	0.0429
1963	−0.0040	0.0006	0.0016	0.0030	0.0014	−0.0030	−0.0040	0.0019	0.0014	0.0000	0.0029	−0.0019	1963	−0.0001
1964	0.0022	0.0022	0.0006	0.0022	0.0081	0.0014	0.0006	0.0038	0.0024	0.0022	−0.0025	0.0047	1964	0.0282
1965	0.0042	0.0018	0.0032	−0.0006	0.0014	−0.0004	0.0007	0.0040	−0.0026	−0.0010	−0.0014	−0.0180	1965	−0.0089
1966	0.0003	−0.0145	0.0155	−0.0060	0.0000	−0.0055	−0.0056	−0.0175	0.0195	0.0034	0.0027	0.0212	1966	0.0129
1967	0.0118	−0.0023	0.0163	−0.0109	0.0013	−0.0256	0.0083	−0.0065	−0.0013	−0.0078	−0.0002	−0.0023	1967	−0.0197
1968	0.0106	0.0011	−0.0075	−0.0045	0.0034	0.0108	0.0128	−0.0008	0.0027	−0.0048	−0.0050	−0.0201	1968	−0.0018
1969	0.0058	−0.0051	0.0013	0.0014	−0.0109	−0.0147	0.0037	−0.0063	−0.0344	0.0296	−0.0101	−0.0253	1969	−0.0645
1970	−0.0005	0.0384	0.0035	−0.0267	0.0067	0.0009	0.0117	0.0099	0.0144	0.0043	0.0416	0.0003	1970	0.1078

* Compound annual return

Table A-24 (continued)

Intermediate-Term Government Bonds: Inflation-Adjusted Total Returns

From January 1971 to December 2002

Year	Jan	Feb	Mar	Apr	May	Jun	Jul	Aug	Sep	Oct	Nov	Dec	Year	Jan–Dec*
1971	0.0160	0.0207	0.0152	-0.0359	-0.0039	-0.0244	0.0002	0.0325	0.0017	0.0203	0.0036	0.0069	1971	0.0519
1972	0.0097	-0.0034	-0.0002	-0.0010	-0.0016	0.0020	-0.0025	-0.0001	-0.0026	-0.0016	0.0021	0.0160	1972	0.0169
1973	-0.0038	-0.0145	-0.0047	-0.0006	-0.0004	-0.0074	-0.0298	0.0072	0.0220	-0.0031	-0.0009	-0.0025	1973	-0.0385
1974	-0.0077	-0.0092	-0.0321	-0.0207	0.0019	-0.0182	-0.0067	-0.0138	0.0196	0.0023	0.0150	0.0112	1974	-0.0580
1975	0.0008	0.0077	-0.0097	-0.0235	0.0215	-0.0054	-0.0135	-0.0039	-0.0039	0.0303	-0.0070	0.0155	1975	0.0076
1976	0.0032	0.0059	0.0051	0.0074	-0.0203	0.0105	0.0060	0.0141	0.0035	0.0106	0.0292	-0.0003	1976	0.0769
1977	-0.0246	-0.0054	-0.0007	-0.0027	0.0001	0.0036	-0.0043	-0.0031	-0.0023	-0.0087	0.0030	-0.0061	1977	-0.0502
1978	-0.0041	-0.0052	-0.0032	-0.0065	-0.0100	-0.0123	0.0027	0.0028	-0.0013	-0.0191	0.0037	0.0009	1978	-0.0508
1979	-0.0034	-0.0174	0.0016	-0.0081	0.0069	0.0110	-0.0139	-0.0189	-0.0097	-0.0553	0.0268	-0.0018	1979	-0.0813
1980	-0.0274	-0.0768	-0.0001	0.1074	0.0387	-0.0185	-0.0114	-0.0449	-0.0129	-0.0238	-0.0061	0.0085	1980	-0.0755
1981	-0.0049	-0.0335	0.0190	-0.0278	0.0161	-0.0026	-0.0380	-0.0252	0.0062	0.0588	0.0594	-0.0170	1981	0.0047
1982	0.0014	0.0116	0.0053	0.0255	0.0047	-0.0254	0.0406	0.0447	0.0307	0.0502	0.0097	0.0227	1982	0.2428
1983	-0.0017	0.0249	-0.0055	0.0186	-0.0175	-0.0017	-0.0238	0.0047	0.0263	-0.0008	0.0086	0.0034	1983	0.0348
1984	0.0121	-0.0110	-0.0057	-0.0052	-0.0278	0.0066	0.0359	0.0059	0.0153	0.0357	0.0192	0.0137	1984	0.0968
1985	0.0187	-0.0220	0.0122	0.0222	0.0445	0.0077	-0.0061	0.0126	0.0081	0.0131	0.0161	0.0232	1985	0.1596
1986	0.0052	0.0303	0.0386	0.0103	-0.0245	0.0226	0.0154	0.0247	-0.0158	0.0153	0.0103	-0.0002	1986	0.1385
1987	0.0046	0.0020	-0.0076	-0.0296	-0.0067	0.0081	0.0005	-0.0093	-0.0189	0.0272	0.0068	0.0096	1987	-0.0144
1988	0.0289	0.0096	-0.0129	-0.0095	-0.0083	0.0138	-0.0089	-0.0051	0.0127	0.0115	-0.0123	-0.0026	1988	0.0161
1989	0.0071	-0.0092	-0.0008	0.0154	0.0155	0.0299	0.0210	-0.0261	0.0037	0.0188	0.0060	-0.0004	1989	0.0826
1990	-0.0205	-0.0040	-0.0052	-0.0092	0.0238	0.0096	0.0135	-0.0182	0.0010	0.0110	0.0170	0.0161	1990	0.0342
1991	0.0046	0.0033	0.0008	0.0102	0.0030	-0.0052	0.0115	0.0217	0.0171	0.0119	0.0099	0.0258	1991	0.1203
1992	-0.0209	-0.0014	-0.0129	0.0083	0.0207	0.0140	0.0220	0.0121	0.0165	-0.0216	-0.0098	0.0153	1992	0.0417
1993	0.0220	0.0207	0.0008	0.0060	-0.0023	0.0187	0.0005	0.0194	0.0035	-0.0024	-0.0100	0.0032	1993	0.0826
1994	0.0110	-0.0291	-0.0291	-0.0119	-0.0009	-0.0062	0.0142	-0.0015	-0.0185	-0.0030	-0.0083	0.0053	1994	-0.0762
1995	0.0141	0.0194	0.0029	0.0110	0.0348	0.0060	-0.0016	0.0060	0.0044	0.0088	0.0155	0.0101	1995	0.1391
1996	-0.0052	-0.0169	-0.0169	-0.0088	-0.0051	0.0111	0.0005	-0.0024	0.0123	0.0150	0.0130	-0.0078	1996	-0.0118
1997	-0.0007	-0.0029	-0.0139	0.0135	0.0085	0.0089	0.0251	-0.0116	0.0126	0.0125	0.0005	0.0119	1997	0.0657
1998	0.0161	-0.0057	0.0007	0.0043	0.0051	0.0066	0.0014	0.0258	0.0317	0.0016	-0.0098	0.0043	1998	0.0846
1999	0.0031	-0.0274	0.0056	-0.0052	-0.0147	0.0032	-0.0033	-0.0010	0.0049	-0.0026	-0.0014	-0.0048	1999	-0.0434
2000	-0.0077	0.0019	0.0120	-0.0049	0.0046	0.0132	0.0054	0.0122	0.0044	0.0062	0.0168	0.0219	2000	0.0890
2001	0.0035	0.0065	0.0053	-0.0153	-0.0052	0.0049	0.0276	0.0095	0.0207	0.0214	-0.0154	-0.0043	2001	0.0597
2002	0.0013	0.0068	-0.0296	0.0182	0.0118	0.0163	0.0260	0.0133	0.0271	-0.0041	-0.0169	0.0302	2002	0.1031

*Compound annual return

Table A-25

U.S. Treasury Bills: Inflation-Adjusted Total Returns

from January 1926 to December 1970

Year	Jan	Feb	Mar	Apr	May	Jun	Jul	Aug	Sep	Oct	Nov	Dec	Year	Jan–Dec
1926	0.0034	0.0064	0.0086	−0.0059	0.0057	0.0110	0.0118	0.0083	−0.0035	−0.0006	−0.0007	0.0028	1926	0.048
1927	0.0101	0.0103	0.0088	0.0025	−0.0047	−0.0069	0.0224	0.0086	−0.0037	−0.0033	0.0040	0.0042	1927	0.053
1928	0.0045	0.0131	0.0029	0.0003	−0.0026	0.0110	0.0032	0.0013	−0.0051	0.0060	0.0058	0.0045	1928	0.045
1929	0.0054	0.0055	0.0074	0.0075	−0.0015	0.0013	−0.0064	0.0002	0.0055	0.0046	0.0057	0.0095	1929	0.045
1930	0.0053	0.0069	0.0094	−0.0038	0.0085	0.0087	0.0161	0.0070	−0.0039	0.0069	0.0095	0.0159	1930	0.089
1931	0.0162	0.0153	0.0077	0.0072	0.0118	0.0118	0.0028	0.0026	0.0047	0.0078	0.0130	0.0104	1931	0.117
1932	0.0234	0.0166	0.0064	0.0083	0.0152	0.0076	0.0003	0.0127	0.0053	0.0077	0.0052	0.0103	1932	0.125
1933	0.0157	0.0155	0.0084	0.0036	−0.0022	−0.0103	−0.0279	−0.0098	0.0002	0.0001	0.0002	0.0053	1933	−0.002
1934	−0.0046	−0.0073	0.0002	0.0026	−0.0024	−0.0024	0.0001	−0.0024	−0.0147	0.0075	0.0026	0.0026	1934	−0.018
1935	−0.0146	−0.0071	0.0026	−0.0095	0.0050	0.0026	0.0050	0.0001	−0.0047	0.0001	−0.0046	−0.0023	1935	−0.027
1936	0.0001	0.0050	0.0051	0.0002	0.0002	−0.0094	−0.0047	−0.0070	−0.0023	0.0026	0.0001	0.0000	1936	−0.010
1937	−0.0070	−0.0022	−0.0069	−0.0043	−0.0040	−0.0020	−0.0043	−0.0021	−0.0088	0.0048	0.0071	0.0024	1937	−0.027
1938	0.0141	0.0095	−0.0001	−0.0046	0.0048	0.0000	−0.0024	0.0024	0.0002	0.0049	0.0018	−0.0024	1938	0.028
1939	0.0047	0.0049	0.0023	0.0024	0.0001	0.0001	0.0000	−0.0001	−0.0189	0.0048	0.0000	0.0048	1939	0.005
1940	0.0024	−0.0071	0.0024	0.0000	−0.0025	−0.0023	0.0025	0.0023	−0.0024	0.0000	0.0000	−0.0047	1940	−0.009
1941	−0.0001	−0.0001	−0.0046	−0.0094	−0.0069	−0.0182	−0.0042	−0.0089	−0.0176	−0.0109	−0.0086	−0.0021	1941	−0.088
1942	−0.0126	−0.0083	−0.0124	−0.0062	−0.0100	−0.0018	−0.0038	−0.0058	−0.0017	−0.0097	−0.0057	−0.0076	1942	−0.082
1943	0.0003	−0.0017	−0.0152	−0.0112	−0.0074	0.0022	0.0080	0.0042	−0.0036	−0.0035	0.0022	−0.0016	1943	−0.027
1944	0.0022	0.0022	0.0002	−0.0055	−0.0036	−0.0016	−0.0054	−0.0035	0.0002	0.0003	0.0003	−0.0035	1944	−0.017
1945	0.0003	0.0021	0.0002	−0.0016	−0.0072	−0.0090	−0.0015	0.0003	0.0040	0.0003	−0.0034	−0.0034	1945	−0.018
1946	0.0003	0.0040	−0.0070	−0.0052	−0.0051	−0.0105	−0.0554	−0.0212	−0.0111	−0.0189	−0.0232	−0.0075	1946	−0.150
1947	0.0003	0.0018	−0.0210	0.0003	0.0033	−0.0073	−0.0087	−0.0101	−0.0226	0.0006	−0.0052	−0.0120	1947	−0.078
1948	−0.0105	0.0093	0.0037	−0.0132	−0.0062	−0.0060	−0.0115	−0.0032	0.0004	0.0045	0.0073	0.0074	1948	−0.018
1949	0.0023	0.0121	−0.0018	−0.0005	0.0024	−0.0004	0.0079	−0.0019	−0.0033	0.0065	−0.0006	0.0065	1949	0.029
1950	0.0052	0.0037	−0.0033	−0.0006	−0.0032	−0.0046	−0.0087	−0.0073	−0.0058	−0.0043	−0.0030	−0.0123	1950	−0.043
1951	−0.0145	−0.0107	−0.0028	0.0000	−0.0026	0.0025	0.0001	0.0013	−0.0052	−0.0035	−0.0040	−0.0026	1951	−0.041
1952	0.0015	0.0075	0.0011	−0.0026	0.0000	−0.0010	−0.0060	0.0002	0.0029	0.0001	0.0010	0.0029	1952	0.007
1953	0.0041	0.0064	−0.0007	0.0004	−0.0008	−0.0019	−0.0010	−0.0008	0.0004	−0.0012	0.0045	0.0025	1953	0.011
1954	−0.0014	0.0019	0.0020	0.0034	−0.0032	−0.0007	0.0005	0.0017	0.0034	0.0032	−0.0006	0.0033	1954	0.013
1955	0.0008	0.0009	0.0010	0.0010	0.0014	0.0010	−0.0027	0.0041	−0.0021	0.0018	0.0005	0.0043	1955	0.011
1956	0.0035	0.0019	0.0003	0.0006	−0.0027	−0.0042	−0.0052	0.0029	0.0006	−0.0036	0.0020	0.0000	1956	−0.003
1957	0.0015	−0.0012	−0.0001	−0.0011	0.0002	−0.0035	−0.0018	0.0013	0.0014	0.0029	−0.0008	0.0024	1957	0.001
1958	−0.0031	0.0000	−0.0060	−0.0015	0.0011	−0.0009	−0.0005	0.0016	0.0019	0.0018	−0.0001	0.0034	1958	−0.002
1959	0.0009	0.0030	0.0022	0.0008	0.0010	−0.0021	0.0002	0.0030	−0.0003	−0.0004	0.0026	0.0034	1959	0.014
1960	0.0045	0.0017	0.0035	−0.0037	0.0027	0.0001	0.0013	0.0017	0.0005	−0.0023	0.0002	0.0016	1960	0.011
1961	0.0019	0.0014	0.0020	0.0017	0.0018	0.0009	−0.0026	0.0025	−0.0006	0.0019	0.0015	0.0019	1961	0.014
1962	0.0024	−0.0002	−0.0002	0.0000	0.0024	0.0020	0.0005	0.0023	−0.0034	0.0037	0.0020	0.0034	1962	0.014
1963	0.0014	0.0012	0.0012	0.0025	0.0024	−0.0021	−0.0017	0.0025	0.0027	0.0018	0.0016	0.0008	1963	0.014
1964	0.0019	0.0037	0.0020	0.0018	0.0026	0.0009	0.0008	0.0039	0.0006	0.0019	0.0008	0.0020	1964	0.023
1965	0.0028	0.0030	0.0025	−0.0001	0.0010	−0.0018	0.0020	0.0054	0.0010	0.0021	0.0014	0.0002	1965	0.019
1966	0.0038	−0.0028	0.0007	−0.0007	0.0031	0.0007	0.0005	−0.0010	0.0020	0.0005	0.0040	0.0030	1966	0.013
1967	0.0043	0.0026	0.0019	0.0012	0.0003	−0.0004	−0.0019	0.0001	0.0012	0.0010	0.0006	0.0004	1967	0.011
1968	0.0001	0.0009	−0.0011	0.0014	0.0015	−0.0015	0.0000	0.0013	0.0014	−0.0013	0.0005	0.0014	1968	0.004
1969	0.0024	0.0009	−0.0037	−0.0011	0.0021	−0.0013	0.0008	0.0005	0.0017	0.0024	−0.0002	0.0002	1969	0.004
1970	0.0025	0.0009	0.0004	−0.0011	0.0009	0.0006	0.0018	0.0036	0.0002	−0.0005	0.0012	−0.0008	1970	0.009

* Compound annual return

Table A-25 (continued)

U.S. Treasury Bills: Inflation-Adjusted Total Returns

from January 1971 to December 2002

Year	Jan	Feb	Mar	Apr	May	Jun	Jul	Aug	Sep	Oct	Nov	Dec	Year	Jan–Dec*
1971	0.0030	0.0016	−0.0004	−0.0006	−0.0020	−0.0020	0.0015	0.0022	0.0029	0.0020	0.0021	−0.0004	1971	0.0099
1972	0.0021	−0.0024	0.0011	0.0005	−0.0002	0.0005	−0.0009	0.0013	−0.0006	0.0008	0.0013	0.0006	1972	0.0041
1973	0.0012	−0.0029	−0.0047	−0.0017	−0.0010	−0.0017	0.0041	−0.0109	0.0038	−0.0016	−0.0017	−0.0002	1973	−0.0172
1974	−0.0024	−0.0070	−0.0057	0.0019	−0.0035	−0.0036	−0.0004	−0.0068	−0.0039	−0.0035	−0.0031	−0.0002	1974	−0.0374
1975	0.0013	−0.0027	0.0003	−0.0007	−0.0001	−0.0040	−0.0057	0.0017	0.0004	−0.0006	−0.0020	0.0006	1975	−0.0113
1976	0.0023	0.0010	0.0016	0.0000	−0.0022	−0.0010	−0.0012	−0.0005	0.0003	0.0000	0.0011	0.0012	1976	0.0026
1977	−0.0021	−0.0067	−0.0024	−0.0041	−0.0018	−0.0026	−0.0002	0.0006	0.0005	0.0022	0.0001	0.0011	1977	−0.0155
1978	−0.0005	−0.0023	−0.0016	−0.0036	−0.0048	−0.0049	−0.0016	0.0005	−0.0009	−0.0012	0.0015	0.0024	1978	−0.0169
1979	−0.0011	−0.0043	−0.0015	−0.0035	−0.0041	−0.0012	−0.0052	−0.0024	−0.0021	−0.0002	0.0005	−0.0010	1979	−0.0259
1980	−0.0063	−0.0048	−0.0023	0.0013	−0.0018	−0.0049	0.0045	−0.0001	−0.0017	0.0008	0.0005	0.0044	1980	−0.0103
1981	0.0022	0.0003	0.0048	0.0043	0.0033	0.0049	0.0010	0.0051	0.0023	0.0099	0.0078	0.0059	1981	0.0530
1982	0.0044	0.0060	0.0109	0.0070	0.0007	−0.0026	0.0050	0.0056	0.0034	0.0032	0.0081	0.0109	1982	0.0642
1983	0.0045	0.0058	0.0056	0.0000	0.0015	0.0033	0.0034	0.0043	0.0026	0.0049	0.0054	0.0059	1983	0.0482
1984	0.0020	0.0025	0.0050	0.0032	0.0049	0.0043	0.0050	0.0041	0.0038	0.0074	0.0073	0.0058	1984	0.0567
1985	0.0046	0.0017	0.0017	0.0031	0.0029	0.0024	0.0047	0.0033	0.0029	0.0034	0.0027	0.0040	1985	0.0381
1986	0.0025	0.0081	0.0106	0.0074	0.0019	0.0003	0.0049	0.0028	−0.0004	0.0037	0.0030	0.0040	1986	0.0498
1987	−0.0019	0.0004	0.0002	−0.0009	0.0008	0.0007	0.0025	−0.0009	−0.0004	0.0034	0.0020	0.0042	1987	0.0101
1988	0.0003	0.0020	0.0001	−0.0005	0.0016	0.0006	0.0008	0.0017	−0.0006	0.0028	0.0048	0.0047	1988	0.0185
1989	0.0005	0.0020	0.0009	0.0002	0.0022	0.0047	0.0045	0.0058	0.0033	0.0020	0.0045	0.0045	1989	0.0356
1990	−0.0046	0.0010	0.0010	0.0053	0.0044	0.0008	0.0029	−0.0026	−0.0024	0.0008	0.0034	0.0060	1990	0.0161
1991	−0.0008	0.0033	0.0029	0.0038	0.0018	0.0012	0.0034	0.0017	0.0002	0.0028	0.0010	0.0031	1991	0.0246
1992	0.0019	−0.0008	−0.0017	0.0018	0.0013	−0.0004	0.0009	−0.0002	−0.0003	−0.0012	0.0009	0.0035	1992	0.0059
1993	−0.0026	−0.0013	−0.0010	−0.0004	0.0008	0.0011	0.0024	−0.0003	0.0005	−0.0019	0.0018	0.0023	1993	0.0014
1994	−0.0002	−0.0013	−0.0007	0.0014	0.0025	−0.0003	0.0000	−0.0004	0.0010	0.0032	0.0023	0.0044	1994	0.0120
1995	0.0001	0.0000	0.0013	0.0011	0.0034	0.0027	0.0045	0.0020	0.0023	0.0014	0.0049	0.0055	1995	0.0298
1996	−0.0016	0.0007	−0.0012	0.0007	0.0023	0.0034	0.0026	0.0022	0.0012	0.0011	0.0022	0.0046	1996	0.0182
1997	0.0013	0.0007	0.0018	0.0031	0.0056	0.0024	0.0030	0.0022	0.0019	0.0017	0.0045	0.0060	1997	0.0349
1998	0.0024	0.0020	0.0021	0.0024	0.0022	0.0029	0.0028	0.0031	0.0033	0.0008	0.0031	0.0044	1998	0.0319
1999	0.0011	0.0023	0.0012	−0.0035	0.0034	0.0040	0.0008	0.0015	−0.0009	0.0021	0.0030	0.0044	1999	0.0195
2000	0.0017	−0.0016	−0.0035	0.0040	0.0045	−0.0018	0.0031	0.0039	−0.0001	0.0039	0.0045	0.0056	2000	0.0242
2001	−0.0009	−0.0002	0.0019	0.0000	−0.0013	0.0011	0.0058	0.0031	−0.0017	0.0056	0.0034	0.0054	2001	0.0224
2002	−0.0009	−0.0026	−0.0043	−0.0040	0.0014	0.0007	0.0004	−0.0019	−0.0002	−0.0003	0.0012	0.0033	2002	−0.0071

*Compound annual return

Stocks, Bonds, Bills, and Inflation

1.000	0.962	0.906	0.929	0.946
1.095	1.154	1.164	1.187	1.259
1.529	1.509	1.676	1.733	1.768
2.332	2.328	2.325	2.366	2.280
2.147	2.203	2.382	2.363	2.340
1.592	1.782	1.662	1.506	1.314
0.836	0.883	0.781	0.625	0.488

Appendix B

0.795	0.654	0.678	0.966	1.129
1.344	1.301	1.301	1.268	1.175
1.148	1.109	1.077	1.182	1.231
1.886	1.928	1.980	1.831	1.931
2.459	2.506	2.487	2.286	2.280
1.561	1.666	1.252	1.433	1.386
1.881	1.954	1.692	1.688	1.811
1.941	1.966	1.991	1.986	1.531

IbbotsonAssociates

Appendix B
Cumulative Wealth Indices of Basic Series

Basic Series Indices

Table B-1

Large Company Stocks: Total Return Index

from December 1925 to December 1970

Year	Jan	Feb	Mar	Apr	May	Jun	Jul	Aug	Sep	Oct	Nov	Dec	Yr-end	Index
1925												1.000	1925	1.000
1926	1.000	0.962	0.906	0.929	0.946	0.989	1.036	1.062	1.089	1.058	1.095	1.116	1926	1.116
1927	1.095	1.154	1.164	1.187	1.259	1.251	1.334	1.403	1.466	1.393	1.493	1.535	1927	1.535
1928	1.529	1.509	1.676	1.733	1.768	1.700	1.724	1.862	1.910	1.942	2.193	2.204	1928	2.204
1929	2.332	2.328	2.325	2.366	2.280	2.540	2.660	2.933	2.794	2.243	1.963	2.018	1929	2.018
1930	2.147	2.203	2.382	2.363	2.340	1.960	2.035	2.064	1.800	1.646	1.631	1.516	1930	1.516
1931	1.592	1.782	1.662	1.506	1.314	1.500	1.392	1.418	0.996	1.085	0.999	0.859	1931	0.859
1932	0.836	0.883	0.781	0.625	0.488	0.487	0.672	0.933	0.900	0.779	0.746	0.789	1932	0.789
1933	0.795	0.654	0.678	0.966	1.129	1.280	1.169	1.310	1.164	1.064	1.184	1.214	1933	1.214
1934	1.344	1.301	1.301	1.268	1.175	1.202	1.066	1.131	1.127	1.095	1.198	1.197	1934	1.197
1935	1.148	1.109	1.077	1.182	1.231	1.317	1.429	1.469	1.507	1.624	1.700	1.767	1935	1.767
1936	1.886	1.928	1.980	1.831	1.931	1.995	2.135	2.167	2.174	2.342	2.374	2.367	1936	2.367
1937	2.459	2.506	2.487	2.286	2.280	2.165	2.391	2.276	1.957	1.765	1.612	1.538	1937	1.538
1938	1.561	1.666	1.252	1.433	1.386	1.733	1.862	1.820	1.850	1.993	1.939	2.016	1938	2.016
1939	1.881	1.954	1.692	1.688	1.811	1.701	1.889	1.766	2.062	2.036	1.955	2.008	1939	2.008
1940	1.941	1.966	1.991	1.986	1.531	1.655	1.712	1.772	1.793	1.869	1.810	1.812	1940	1.812
1941	1.728	1.718	1.730	1.624	1.653	1.749	1.850	1.852	1.839	1.718	1.670	1.602	1941	1.602
1942	1.627	1.602	1.497	1.437	1.552	1.586	1.640	1.666	1.715	1.831	1.827	1.927	1942	1.927
1943	2.070	2.190	2.310	2.318	2.446	2.500	2.368	2.409	2.472	2.446	2.286	2.427	1943	2.427
1944	2.468	2.479	2.527	2.502	2.628	2.771	2.717	2.760	2.758	2.764	2.801	2.906	1944	2.906
1945	2.952	3.154	3.015	3.287	3.351	3.349	3.288	3.499	3.652	3.770	3.919	3.965	1945	3.965
1946	4.248	3.976	4.167	4.330	4.455	4.290	4.188	3.906	3.516	3.495	3.486	3.645	1946	3.645
1947	3.738	3.709	3.654	3.521	3.526	3.721	3.863	3.785	3.743	3.832	3.765	3.853	1947	3.853
1948	3.707	3.563	3.846	3.958	4.305	4.329	4.109	4.174	4.059	4.347	3.929	4.065	1948	4.065
1949	4.081	3.960	4.090	4.017	3.913	3.919	4.174	4.265	4.377	4.526	4.605	4.829	1949	4.829
1950	4.924	5.022	5.057	5.303	5.573	5.267	5.330	5.566	5.895	5.949	6.050	6.360	1950	6.360
1951	6.765	6.871	6.764	7.109	6.896	6.739	7.218	7.563	7.573	7.495	7.567	7.888	1951	7.888
1952	8.030	7.804	8.197	7.867	8.137	8.536	8.703	8.642	8.490	8.507	8.993	9.336	1952	9.336
1953	9.291	9.192	8.997	8.783	8.851	8.732	8.971	8.521	8.551	9.012	9.196	9.244	1953	9.244
1954	9.739	9.848	10.168	10.693	11.139	11.173	11.831	11.506	12.485	12.277	13.393	14.108	1954	14.108
1955	14.387	14.528	14.485	15.059	15.142	16.416	17.437	17.393	17.618	17.118	18.533	18.561	1955	18.561
1956	17.917	18.657	19.982	19.973	18.788	19.557	20.594	19.919	19.043	19.169	19.072	19.778	1956	19.778
1957	18.986	18.485	18.882	19.614	20.472	20.481	20.749	19.701	18.516	17.957	18.372	17.646	1957	17.646
1958	18.431	18.170	18.767	19.400	19.810	20.363	21.277	21.651	22.735	23.348	24.012	25.298	1958	25.298
1959	25.430	25.554	25.605	26.635	27.273	27.213	28.199	27.911	26.674	27.017	27.519	28.322	1959	28.322
1960	26.340	26.729	26.400	25.976	26.821	27.388	26.748	27.596	25.968	25.949	27.154	28.455	1960	28.455
1961	30.291	31.257	32.100	32.262	33.033	32.125	33.223	34.029	33.404	34.401	35.940	36.106	1961	36.106
1962	34.784	35.511	35.349	33.204	30.512	28.061	29.891	30.512	29.092	29.279	32.459	32.954	1962	32.954
1963	34.620	33.794	35.045	36.798	37.510	36.805	36.726	38.692	38.318	39.617	39.435	40.469	1963	40.469
1964	41.612	42.222	42.917	43.238	43.940	44.721	45.592	45.055	46.409	46.856	46.878	47.139	1964	47.139
1965	48.763	48.913	48.264	49.984	49.833	47.477	48.177	49.488	51.140	52.618	52.453	53.008	1965	53.008
1966	53.335	52.634	51.555	52.688	50.096	49.363	48.769	45.234	44.993	47.214	47.662	47.674	1966	47.674
1967	51.478	51.846	53.967	56.325	53.641	54.658	57.215	56.817	58.758	57.136	57.507	59.104	1967	59.104
1968	56.592	55.113	55.718	60.363	61.334	61.980	60.916	61.913	64.387	64.945	68.393	65.642	1968	65.642
1969	65.193	62.414	64.653	66.131	66.303	62.708	59.024	61.705	60.251	63.014	61.141	60.059	1969	60.059
1970	55.594	58.850	59.028	53.779	50.837	48.386	52.026	54.672	56.570	56.019	59.020	62.465	1970	62.465

Table B-1 (continued)

Large Company Stocks: Total Return Index

from January 1971 to December 2002

Year	Jan	Feb	Mar	Apr	May	Jun	Jul	Aug	Sep	Oct	Nov	Dec	Yr-end	Index
1971	65.082	65.998	68.522	71.104	68.491	68.636	65.896	68.612	68.231	65.477	65.650	71.406	1971	71.406
1972	72.791	74.969	75.510	75.940	77.605	76.010	76.287	79.271	78.985	79.828	83.856	84.956	1972	84.956
1973	83.603	80.822	80.807	77.619	76.538	76.144	79.146	76.630	79.813	79.835	71.194	72.500	1973	72.500
1974	71.883	72.017	70.453	67.822	65.974	65.127	60.183	55.197	48.740	56.818	54.273	53.311	1974	53.311
1975	59.983	64.027	65.541	68.773	72.270	75.608	70.628	69.610	67.326	71.613	73.857	73.144	1975	73.144
1976	81.916	81.441	84.095	83.262	82.654	86.185	85.596	85.717	87.830	86.025	85.946	90.584	1976	90.584
1977	86.151	84.849	83.841	83.956	82.699	86.626	85.317	84.186	84.187	80.690	83.675	84.077	1977	84.077
1978	79.062	77.786	79.933	86.888	88.072	86.730	91.583	94.696	94.240	85.847	88.078	89.592	1978	89.592
1979	93.368	90.717	95.934	96.280	94.661	98.541	99.620	105.703	105.970	99.022	104.113	106.113	1979	106.113
1980	112.589	112.934	101.792	106.162	112.130	115.445	123.249	124.865	128.369	130.763	145.085	140.514	1980	140.514
1981	134.359	137.154	142.366	139.333	140.197	139.076	139.173	131.463	124.863	131.456	137.253	133.616	1981	133.616
1982	131.438	124.709	123.960	129.092	125.374	123.193	120.544	135.817	137.311	152.772	159.464	162.223	1982	162.223
1983	167.868	172.233	178.519	192.051	191.052	198.350	192.142	195.408	198.066	195.412	199.965	198.745	1983	198.745
1984	197.453	190.977	194.242	195.583	185.139	189.230	186.524	207.508	207.550	208.089	205.988	211.199	1984	211.199
1985	227.419	230.535	230.950	230.211	244.369	248.254	247.609	246.098	238.199	248.846	266.663	279.117	1985	279.117
1986	280.345	301.679	318.392	314.444	331.707	337.213	318.026	341.814	313.717	331.160	339.637	330.671	1986	330.671
1987	375.080	390.571	401.194	397.664	401.760	421.808	442.814	459.862	449.745	352.960	324.052	347.967	1987	347.967
1988	362.826	379.878	368.406	372.385	375.290	392.703	391.132	378.186	394.221	404.983	399.232	406.458	1988	406.458
1989	435.845	424.993	435.023	457.470	475.860	473.290	515.792	525.747	523.696	511.494	522.133	534.455	1989	534.455
1990	498.594	505.025	518.308	505.505	554.792	550.909	549.146	499.558	474.980	473.222	503.698	517.499	1990	517.499
1991	540.372	579.063	592.845	594.505	619.950	591.618	619.306	633.859	623.464	631.818	606.293	675.592	1991	675.592
1992	663.026	671.513	658.351	677.509	681.168	671.291	698.344	684.237	692.106	694.598	718.006	727.412	1992	727.412
1993	732.722	742.613	758.580	739.994	759.974	762.482	758.898	787.812	781.983	797.857	790.357	800.078	1993	800.078
1994	826.881	804.555	769.557	779.561	792.268	772.699	798.276	830.765	810.744	829.310	798.874	810.538	1994	810.538
1995	831.612	863.878	889.449	915.332	951.488	973.848	1006.227	1008.994	1051.271	1047.591	1093.685	1113.918	1995	1113.918
1996	1152.237	1163.299	1174.466	1191.731	1222.478	1227.490	1172.867	1197.731	1265.044	1299.706	1398.354	1370.946	1996	1370.946
1997	1456.082	1467.876	1406.812	1490.799	1582.334	1652.906	1784.147	1684.948	1777.233	1717.873	1797.411	1828.326	1997	1828.326
1998	1848.621	1981.943	2083.439	2104.398	2068.223	2152.235	2129.313	1821.457	1938.140	2095.788	2222.814	2350.892	1998	2350.892
1999	2449.207	2373.085	2468.032	2563.619	2503.092	2642.014	2559.530	2546.861	2477.051	2633.799	2687.344	2845.629	1999	2845.629
2000	2702.664	2651.503	2910.899	2823.310	2765.376	2833.543	2789.254	2962.495	2806.105	2794.235	2573.937	2586.524	2000	2586.524
2001	2678.294	2434.087	2279.888	2457.058	2473.520	2413.315	2389.567	2239.981	2059.102	2098.369	2259.335	2279.127	2001	2279.127
2002	2245.874	2202.574	2285.413	2146.848	2131.026	1979.212	1824.932	1836.922	1637.285	1781.399	1886.252	1775.341	2002	1775.341

Table B-2

Large Company Stocks: Capital Appreciation Index

from December 1925 to December 1970

Year	Jan	Feb	Mar	Apr	May	Jun	Jul	Aug	Sep	Oct	Nov	Dec	Yr-end	Index
1925												1.000	1925	1.000
1926	0.998	0.955	0.898	0.918	0.926	0.966	1.009	1.027	1.050	1.017	1.040	1.057	1926	1.057
1927	1.035	1.085	1.092	1.111	1.168	1.158	1.233	1.288	1.343	1.272	1.350	1.384	1927	1.384
1928	1.377	1.353	1.499	1.548	1.567	1.504	1.523	1.636	1.675	1.699	1.903	1.908	1928	1.908
1929	2.017	2.005	2.001	2.033	1.946	2.165	2.263	2.485	2.364	1.893	1.640	1.681	1929	1.681
1930	1.786	1.824	1.970	1.951	1.919	1.603	1.662	1.675	1.457	1.328	1.299	1.202	1930	1.202
1931	1.261	1.405	1.308	1.183	1.020	1.162	1.076	1.086	0.761	0.825	0.745	0.636	1931	0.636
1932	0.618	0.650	0.573	0.457	0.350	0.347	0.478	0.658	0.633	0.545	0.513	0.540	1932	0.540
1933	0.544	0.444	0.458	0.652	0.755	0.855	0.780	0.869	0.770	0.702	0.774	0.792	1933	0.792
1934	0.875	0.843	0.842	0.820	0.753	0.769	0.680	0.717	0.713	0.690	0.748	0.745	1934	0.745
1935	0.713	0.685	0.664	0.727	0.751	0.802	0.868	0.887	0.908	0.976	1.015	1.053	1935	1.053
1936	1.121	1.140	1.169	1.079	1.129	1.163	1.242	1.253	1.255	1.349	1.354	1.346	1936	1.346
1937	1.397	1.418	1.404	1.288	1.274	1.207	1.331	1.257	1.078	0.969	0.871	0.827	1937	0.827
1938	0.838	0.889	0.666	0.760	0.726	0.906	0.972	0.945	0.959	1.032	0.998	1.035	1938	1.035
1939	0.964	0.995	0.861	0.856	0.909	0.851	0.944	0.876	1.020	1.005	0.956	0.979	1939	0.979
1940	0.944	0.951	0.960	0.955	0.726	0.782	0.806	0.828	0.835	0.868	0.832	0.829	1940	0.829
1941	0.789	0.777	0.781	0.730	0.733	0.772	0.814	0.807	0.799	0.745	0.713	0.681	1941	0.681
1942	0.690	0.673	0.628	0.600	0.639	0.650	0.671	0.676	0.694	0.738	0.728	0.766	1942	0.766
1943	0.821	0.862	0.908	0.908	0.949	0.968	0.915	0.925	0.947	0.934	0.864	0.915	1943	0.915
1944	0.929	0.926	0.942	0.930	0.968	1.017	0.996	1.005	1.002	1.002	1.005	1.041	1944	1.041
1945	1.056	1.121	1.069	1.163	1.176	1.172	1.149	1.216	1.266	1.305	1.347	1.361	1945	1.361
1946	1.455	1.354	1.417	1.470	1.503	1.444	1.408	1.305	1.172	1.163	1.150	1.199	1946	1.199
1947	1.227	1.209	1.189	1.143	1.132	1.192	1.235	1.201	1.184	1.209	1.175	1.199	1947	1.199
1948	1.151	1.097	1.182	1.213	1.308	1.312	1.242	1.252	1.214	1.296	1.156	1.191	1948	1.191
1949	1.193	1.146	1.180	1.155	1.112	1.110	1.179	1.193	1.221	1.257	1.259	1.313	1949	1.313
1950	1.336	1.350	1.355	1.416	1.472	1.386	1.398	1.444	1.524	1.531	1.529	1.600	1950	1.600
1951	1.697	1.708	1.677	1.758	1.687	1.643	1.755	1.824	1.823	1.798	1.793	1.863	1951	1.863
1952	1.892	1.823	1.910	1.828	1.870	1.956	1.991	1.962	1.923	1.922	2.011	2.082	1952	2.082
1953	2.067	2.030	1.982	1.929	1.923	1.892	1.940	1.828	1.830	1.923	1.940	1.944	1953	1.944
1954	2.044	2.049	2.111	2.215	2.288	2.289	2.420	2.338	2.532	2.483	2.683	2.820	1954	2.820
1955	2.871	2.881	2.867	2.975	2.971	3.216	3.411	3.384	3.422	3.318	3.567	3.564	1955	3.564
1956	3.434	3.553	3.799	3.792	3.542	3.681	3.871	3.723	3.554	3.572	3.533	3.658	1956	3.658
1957	3.505	3.390	3.457	3.585	3.717	3.712	3.755	3.544	3.324	3.218	3.270	3.134	1957	3.134
1958	3.268	3.201	3.299	3.404	3.455	3.545	3.698	3.742	3.923	4.023	4.113	4.327	1958	4.327
1959	4.343	4.342	4.345	4.513	4.599	4.582	4.742	4.671	4.458	4.508	4.567	4.694	1959	4.694
1960	4.358	4.398	4.337	4.261	4.375	4.461	4.350	4.464	4.194	4.184	4.353	4.554	1960	4.554
1961	4.842	4.972	5.099	5.118	5.216	5.066	5.232	5.335	5.230	5.378	5.589	5.607	1961	5.607
1962	5.395	5.483	5.451	5.113	4.673	4.291	4.563	4.633	4.410	4.429	4.879	4.945	1962	4.945
1963	5.188	5.038	5.217	5.470	5.549	5.437	5.418	5.682	5.619	5.800	5.739	5.879	1963	5.879
1964	6.038	6.097	6.190	6.227	6.299	6.402	6.519	6.413	6.597	6.650	6.616	6.642	1964	6.642
1965	6.862	6.852	6.752	6.984	6.929	6.592	6.681	6.832	7.050	7.243	7.179	7.244	1965	7.244
1966	7.279	7.149	6.993	7.136	6.750	6.641	6.552	6.042	6.000	6.285	6.305	6.295	1966	6.295
1967	6.788	6.801	7.069	7.368	6.981	7.103	7.426	7.339	7.579	7.359	7.367	7.560	1967	7.560
1968	7.229	7.003	7.069	7.648	7.734	7.804	7.660	7.748	8.046	8.104	8.493	8.139	1968	8.139
1969	8.073	7.690	7.955	8.126	8.108	7.658	7.197	7.485	7.298	7.621	7.352	7.210	1969	7.210
1970	6.663	7.014	7.024	6.389	5.999	5.699	6.117	6.389	6.600	6.524	6.834	7.222	1970	7.222

Table B-2 (continued)

Large Company Stocks: Capital Appreciation Index

from January 1971 to December 2002

Year	Jan	Feb	Mar	Apr	May	Jun	Jul	Aug	Sep	Oct	Nov	Dec	Yr-end	Index
1971	7.514	7.582	7.861	8.147	7.808	7.813	7.491	7.761	7.707	7.385	7.366	8.001	1971	8.001
1972	8.146	8.352	8.401	8.438	8.584	8.397	8.416	8.706	8.664	8.744	9.143	9.252	1972	9.252
1973	9.093	8.752	8.740	8.383	8.225	8.171	8.481	8.170	8.498	8.487	7.520	7.645	1973	7.645
1974	7.568	7.541	7.365	7.078	6.840	6.740	6.215	5.654	4.980	5.792	5.484	5.373	1974	5.373
1975	6.033	6.394	6.533	6.842	7.143	7.460	6.955	6.809	6.573	6.978	7.150	7.068	1975	7.068
1976	7.904	7.814	8.054	7.965	7.851	8.172	8.107	8.065	8.248	8.064	8.002	8.422	1976	8.422
1977	7.996	7.823	7.713	7.715	7.533	7.875	7.747	7.584	7.565	7.237	7.432	7.453	1977	7.453
1978	6.995	6.821	6.991	7.589	7.621	7.487	7.890	8.095	8.036	7.300	7.422	7.532	1978	7.532
1979	7.831	7.545	7.962	7.975	7.765	8.065	8.135	8.567	8.567	7.980	8.320	8.459	1979	8.459
1980	8.947	8.907	8.001	8.330	8.718	8.953	9.535	9.591	9.832	9.989	11.012	10.639	1980	10.639
1981	10.153	10.288	10.658	10.407	10.390	10.285	10.259	9.623	9.105	9.553	9.903	9.605	1981	9.605
1982	9.436	8.865	8.775	9.126	8.769	8.591	8.393	9.367	9.438	10.480	10.858	11.023	1982	11.023
1983	11.388	11.604	11.988	12.886	12.727	13.175	12.741	12.885	13.016	12.818	13.041	12.926	1983	12.926
1984	12.807	12.309	12.475	12.544	11.799	12.005	11.807	13.062	13.017	13.015	12.819	13.106	1984	13.106
1985	14.077	14.198	14.157	14.092	14.854	15.034	14.962	14.783	14.269	14.876	15.844	16.559	1985	16.559
1986	16.598	17.785	18.724	18.460	19.387	19.660	18.506	19.824	18.131	19.123	19.534	18.981	1986	18.981
1987	21.483	22.275	22.864	22.601	22.736	23.825	24.974	25.848	25.222	19.734	18.051	19.366	1987	19.366
1988	20.149	20.991	20.292	20.483	20.548	21.438	21.322	20.499	21.313	21.867	21.454	21.769	1988	21.769
1989	23.317	22.643	23.114	24.272	25.124	24.926	27.129	27.550	27.370	26.680	27.122	27.703	1989	27.703
1990	25.796	26.016	26.648	25.931	28.316	28.065	27.918	25.285	23.991	23.830	25.259	25.886	1990	25.886
1991	26.961	28.774	29.413	29.424	30.559	29.095	30.400	30.998	30.404	30.765	29.413	32.695	1991	32.695
1992	32.045	32.351	31.645	32.528	32.559	31.994	33.254	32.456	32.751	32.820	33.813	34.155	1992	34.155
1993	34.396	34.756	35.406	34.506	35.290	35.317	35.129	36.338	35.975	36.673	36.199	36.565	1993	36.565
1994	37.753	36.619	34.944	35.347	35.785	34.826	35.923	37.273	36.270	37.027	35.565	36.002	1994	36.002
1995	36.876	38.206	39.250	40.348	41.814	42.703	44.060	44.045	45.812	45.583	47.455	48.282	1995	48.282
1996	49.857	50.203	50.600	51.280	52.452	52.570	50.165	51.109	53.878	55.286	59.342	58.066	1996	58.066
1997	61.627	61.992	59.350	62.817	66.496	69.386	74.806	70.509	74.257	71.697	74.893	76.071	1997	76.071
1998	76.844	82.257	86.366	87.149	85.509	88.881	87.849	75.041	79.723	86.124	91.216	96.359	1998	96.359
1999	100.310	97.072	100.838	104.664	102.050	107.606	104.158	103.506	100.551	106.839	108.876	115.174	1999	115.174
2000	109.311	107.113	117.473	113.855	111.360	114.025	112.162	118.970	112.607	112.050	103.078	103.496	2000	103.496
2001	107.081	97.198	90.958	97.944	98.443	95.982	94.948	88.861	81.599	83.076	89.321	89.997	2001	89.997
2002	88.596	86.756	89.943	84.419	83.652	77.591	71.461	71.810	63.909	69.435	73.397	68.969	2002	68.969

Table B-3

Small Company Stocks: Total Return Index

from December 1925 to December 1970

Year	Jan	Feb	Mar	Apr	May	Jun	Jul	Aug	Sep	Oct	Nov	Dec	Yr-end	Index
1925												1.000	1925	1.000
1926	1.070	1.001	0.894	0.910	0.904	0.938	0.949	0.973	0.973	0.951	0.971	1.003	1926	1.003
1927	1.032	1.089	1.029	1.088	1.168	1.133	1.191	1.170	1.176	1.098	1.187	1.224	1927	1.224
1928	1.283	1.253	1.319	1.440	1.503	1.376	1.384	1.445	1.574	1.617	1.803	1.710	1928	1.710
1929	1.716	1.712	1.677	1.729	1.498	1.578	1.596	1.569	1.425	1.030	0.876	0.832	1929	0.832
1930	0.939	1.000	1.101	1.024	0.968	0.758	0.781	0.768	0.656	0.584	0.583	0.515	1930	0.515
1931	0.623	0.783	0.727	0.570	0.491	0.581	0.548	0.507	0.342	0.368	0.331	0.259	1931	0.259
1932	0.285	0.293	0.255	0.198	0.175	0.175	0.237	0.411	0.357	0.293	0.257	0.245	1932	0.245
1933	0.243	0.212	0.235	0.354	0.578	0.729	0.689	0.753	0.633	0.555	0.591	0.594	1933	0.594
1934	0.825	0.839	0.838	0.858	0.749	0.747	0.578	0.667	0.656	0.663	0.726	0.738	1934	0.738
1935	0.714	0.672	0.592	0.639	0.637	0.656	0.713	0.751	0.778	0.855	0.976	1.035	1935	1.035
1936	1.346	1.427	1.436	1.179	1.211	1.183	1.286	1.313	1.384	1.472	1.678	1.705	1936	1.705
1937	1.921	2.047	2.072	1.724	1.654	1.458	1.638	1.517	1.132	1.008	0.862	0.716	1937	0.716
1938	0.754	0.780	0.499	0.638	0.584	0.788	0.906	0.815	0.802	0.974	0.907	0.951	1938	0.951
1939	0.870	0.879	0.663	0.672	0.745	0.667	0.837	0.704	1.066	1.023	0.915	0.954	1939	0.954
1940	0.955	1.033	1.099	1.171	0.741	0.818	0.837	0.859	0.877	0.925	0.947	0.905	1940	0.905
1941	0.907	0.881	0.909	0.848	0.852	0.916	1.115	1.108	1.056	0.985	0.936	0.823	1941	0.823
1942	0.979	0.972	0.903	0.872	0.869	0.898	0.964	0.995	1.086	1.204	1.143	1.190	1942	1.190
1943	1.444	1.723	1.971	2.155	2.404	2.384	2.126	2.126	2.217	2.244	1.994	2.242	1943	2.242
1944	2.385	2.456	2.640	2.499	2.684	3.055	2.964	3.059	3.053	3.020	3.170	3.446	1944	3.446
1945	3.612	3.977	3.634	4.055	4.257	4.621	4.364	4.607	4.920	5.265	5.882	5.983	1945	5.983
1946	6.917	6.476	6.653	7.117	7.537	7.189	6.808	6.230	5.232	5.170	5.097	5.287	1946	5.287
1947	5.509	5.487	5.303	4.756	4.502	4.750	5.125	5.106	5.165	5.311	5.150	5.335	1947	5.335
1948	5.254	4.842	5.320	5.515	6.099	6.128	5.774	5.778	5.474	5.828	5.177	5.223	1948	5.223
1949	5.318	5.062	5.380	5.199	4.906	4.859	5.185	5.318	5.578	5.841	5.851	6.254	1949	6.254
1950	6.562	6.706	6.682	6.956	7.134	6.580	6.969	7.338	7.720	7.675	7.922	8.677	1950	8.677
1951	9.398	9.455	9.004	9.334	9.026	8.548	8.867	9.403	9.606	9.392	9.314	9.355	1951	9.355
1952	9.533	9.248	9.410	8.922	8.950	9.193	9.296	9.291	9.142	9.047	9.486	9.638	1952	9.638
1953	10.032	10.302	10.233	9.939	10.079	9.589	9.735	9.123	8.884	9.143	9.258	9.013	1953	9.013
1954	9.694	9.786	9.965	10.104	10.561	10.651	11.512	11.528	12.000	12.082	13.024	14.473	1954	14.473
1955	14.764	15.471	15.602	15.837	15.960	16.428	16.533	16.487	16.667	16.384	17.152	17.431	1955	17.431
1956	17.348	17.830	18.598	18.685	17.942	18.042	18.552	18.303	17.827	18.013	18.108	18.177	1956	18.177
1957	18.607	18.234	18.540	19.000	19.143	19.283	19.167	18.427	17.595	16.131	16.314	15.529	1957	15.529
1958	17.245	16.952	17.750	18.418	19.131	19.752	20.722	21.610	22.730	23.655	24.828	25.605	1958	25.605
1959	27.076	27.875	27.951	28.277	28.315	28.196	29.118	28.863	27.619	28.245	28.873	29.804	1959	29.804
1960	28.891	29.034	28.120	27.594	28.158	29.116	28.565	30.064	27.844	26.728	27.896	28.823	1960	28.823
1961	31.460	33.314	35.376	35.825	37.355	35.326	35.436	35.898	34.682	35.590	37.772	38.072	1961	38.072
1962	38.591	39.314	39.537	36.464	32.786	30.213	32.518	33.458	31.254	30.087	33.842	33.540	1962	33.540
1963	36.580	36.705	37.251	38.412	40.088	39.613	39.744	41.799	41.118	42.090	41.642	41.444	1963	41.444
1964	42.581	44.134	45.099	45.520	46.234	46.985	48.857	48.715	50.676	51.716	51.772	51.193	1964	51.193
1965	53.902	56.003	57.335	60.252	59.782	54.398	56.837	60.220	62.310	65.876	68.319	72.567	1965	72.567
1966	78.051	80.479	78.935	81.645	73.797	73.709	73.617	65.669	64.595	63.902	67.041	67.479	1966	67.479
1967	79.884	83.475	88.606	91.003	90.232	99.411	108.862	109.085	115.244	111.662	112.965	123.870	1967	123.870
1968	125.779	116.861	115.586	132.468	145.698	146.137	141.088	146.266	155.034	155.505	167.388	168.429	1968	168.429
1969	165.634	149.238	155.142	161.265	164.063	144.954	129.449	138.925	135.301	143.552	135.552	126.233	1969	126.233
1970	118.554	123.145	119.641	98.970	88.762	80.519	84.975	93.037	103.140	95.856	97.170	104.226	1970	104.226

Table B-3 (continued)

Small Company Stocks: Total Return Index

from January 1971 to December 2002

Year	Jan	Feb	Mar	Apr	May	Jun	Jul	Aug	Sep	Oct	Nov	Dec	Yr-end	Index
1971	120.820	124.647	131.676	134.923	126.760	122.710	115.802	122.555	119.780	113.180	108.954	121.423	1971	121.423
1972	135.142	139.141	137.144	138.912	136.257	132.100	126.645	129.005	124.506	122.329	129.576	126.807	1972	126.807
1973	121.329	111.635	109.318	102.527	94.211	91.476	102.398	97.837	108.242	109.155	87.737	87.618	1973	87.618
1974	99.238	98.393	97.661	93.129	85.745	84.485	82.637	77.009	71.978	79.629	76.143	70.142	1974	70.142
1975	89.551	92.105	97.799	102.990	109.821	118.053	115.056	108.456	106.488	105.954	109.341	107.189	1975	107.189
1976	135.960	154.854	154.626	149.081	143.698	150.298	150.976	146.592	148.123	145.028	150.881	168.691	1976	168.691
1977	176.275	175.587	177.880	181.941	181.434	195.445	196.028	193.924	195.715	189.249	209.804	211.500	1977	211.500
1978	207.502	214.707	236.868	255.528	276.484	271.254	289.807	317.010	316.002	239.303	256.811	261.120	1978	261.120
1979	295.623	287.279	319.448	331.805	332.955	348.676	354.642	381.457	368.351	325.827	353.796	374.614	1979	374.614
1980	405.926	394.411	324.303	346.795	372.814	389.666	441.224	467.894	487.473	503.725	542.326	523.992	1980	523.992
1981	534.839	539.866	590.776	629.590	656.158	661.145	640.253	596.460	552.739	593.752	610.140	596.717	1981	596.717
1982	585.021	567.705	562.822	584.378	569.886	560.825	559.983	599.070	618.660	699.395	753.878	763.829	1982	763.829
1983	811.793	869.617	915.267	985.448	1071.150	1108.462	1098.662	1077.054	1091.419	1029.455	1082.532	1066.828	1983	1066.828
1984	1065.974	997.219	1014.571	1005.947	953.537	982.143	940.893	1034.794	1037.588	1015.072	980.966	995.680	1984	995.680
1985	1101.123	1131.074	1106.869	1087.609	1117.627	1129.474	1158.840	1150.497	1087.910	1116.304	1185.515	1241.234	1985	1241.234
1986	1255.136	1345.380	1409.555	1418.576	1469.645	1473.466	1368.850	1398.691	1320.504	1366.193	1361.958	1326.275	1986	1326.275
1987	1451.342	1568.756	1605.308	1555.062	1548.997	1590.201	1648.084	1695.384	1681.651	1190.777	1143.503	1202.966	1987	1202.966
1988	1269.850	1366.359	1422.107	1451.829	1425.841	1513.102	1509.320	1472.190	1505.609	1487.090	1422.104	1478.135	1988	1478.135
1989	1537.852	1550.616	1606.128	1650.939	1710.703	1676.318	1744.544	1765.827	1765.827	1659.171	1650.710	1628.590	1989	1628.590
1990	1504.166	1532.294	1588.682	1546.423	1633.178	1656.695	1593.410	1386.904	1271.929	1199.175	1253.138	1277.449	1990	1277.449
1991	1384.882	1539.020	1643.673	1649.261	1704.347	1621.686	1687.688	1731.737	1737.279	1792.350	1742.882	1847.629	1991	1847.629
1992	2056.041	2148.974	2095.465	2011.018	2008.202	1903.977	1974.424	1929.407	1954.682	2005.308	2182.778	2279.039	1992	2279.039
1993	2402.790	2359.540	2427.731	2353.442	2433.930	2424.681	2464.931	2548.492	2629.024	2752.851	2704.676	2757.147	1993	2757.147
1994	2927.539	2920.806	2790.538	2807.281	2803.912	2730.450	2780.690	2874.399	2904.580	2937.983	2842.205	2842.773	1994	2842.773
1995	2923.224	2996.889	3040.344	3147.364	3241.155	3425.253	3646.182	3776.715	3850.361	3662.848	3733.175	3822.398	1995	3822.398
1996	3833.101	3974.542	4065.162	4409.887	4740.188	4464.309	4043.325	4235.787	4359.048	4282.765	4406.109	4495.993	1996	4495.993
1997	4684.825	4588.318	4363.490	4243.058	4676.698	4909.598	5206.628	5471.646	5933.453	5704.421	5616.003	5519.969	1997	5519.969
1998	5487.401	5843.534	6124.608	6227.501	5917.994	5796.084	5407.166	4320.326	4479.746	4639.225	4990.878	5116.648	1998	5116.648
1999	5259.403	4898.082	4712.445	5159.656	5359.334	5663.744	5715.851	5606.678	5482.771	5435.070	5962.816	6640.788	1999	6640.788
2000	7053.915	8694.984	8041.990	7035.937	6467.434	7352.179	7115.438	7773.616	7604.929	7068.021	6283.471	6402.228	2000	6402.228
2001	7285.736	6774.277	6449.112	6920.542	7584.914	7857.212	7657.639	7431.739	6481.963	6900.049	7365.112	7860.048	2001	7860.048
2002	7946.508	7726.390	8409.403	8613.752	8378.596	8080.318	6910.288	6870.899	6407.801	6572.481	7121.941	6816.409	2002	6816.409

Table B-4

Long-Term Corporate Bonds: Total Return Index

from December 1925 to December 1970

Year	Jan	Feb	Mar	Apr	May	Jun	Jul	Aug	Sep	Oct	Nov	Dec	Yr-end	Index
1925												1.000	1925	1.000
1926	1.007	1.012	1.020	1.030	1.035	1.035	1.041	1.046	1.052	1.062	1.068	1.074	1926	1.074
1927	1.080	1.087	1.096	1.102	1.101	1.106	1.106	1.115	1.132	1.138	1.146	1.154	1927	1.154
1928	1.157	1.165	1.169	1.171	1.162	1.159	1.158	1.168	1.171	1.181	1.177	1.186	1928	1.186
1929	1.192	1.195	1.185	1.187	1.192	1.187	1.189	1.192	1.196	1.204	1.202	1.225	1929	1.225
1930	1.233	1.241	1.259	1.269	1.276	1.290	1.298	1.315	1.329	1.337	1.335	1.323	1930	1.323
1931	1.350	1.359	1.372	1.381	1.400	1.407	1.414	1.416	1.414	1.362	1.337	1.299	1931	1.299
1932	1.292	1.261	1.306	1.283	1.297	1.295	1.301	1.358	1.399	1.409	1.419	1.439	1932	1.439
1933	1.518	1.438	1.445	1.431	1.516	1.544	1.569	1.584	1.582	1.588	1.549	1.588	1933	1.588
1934	1.629	1.653	1.684	1.701	1.717	1.744	1.752	1.760	1.749	1.767	1.790	1.808	1934	1.808
1935	1.846	1.872	1.880	1.901	1.909	1.931	1.952	1.944	1.944	1.952	1.966	1.982	1935	1.982
1936	1.998	2.009	2.026	2.031	2.039	2.056	2.058	2.072	2.086	2.091	2.114	2.116	1936	2.116
1937	2.121	2.111	2.087	2.101	2.110	2.121	2.129	2.125	2.131	2.145	2.159	2.174	1937	2.174
1938	2.182	2.184	2.165	2.195	2.197	2.218	2.233	2.229	2.253	2.271	2.279	2.307	1938	2.307
1939	2.312	2.327	2.332	2.347	2.359	2.367	2.365	2.272	2.307	2.361	2.380	2.399	1939	2.399
1940	2.410	2.415	2.427	2.405	2.400	2.429	2.434	2.436	2.458	2.470	2.486	2.480	1940	2.480
1941	2.482	2.483	2.478	2.497	2.509	2.525	2.541	2.550	2.562	2.570	2.546	2.548	1941	2.548
1942	2.549	2.547	2.563	2.565	2.570	2.579	2.584	2.593	2.598	2.600	2.601	2.614	1942	2.614
1943	2.627	2.628	2.634	2.647	2.659	2.672	2.677	2.682	2.684	2.681	2.675	2.688	1943	2.688
1944	2.693	2.703	2.716	2.725	2.726	2.732	2.741	2.750	2.755	2.761	2.774	2.815	1944	2.815
1945	2.837	2.850	2.855	2.860	2.857	2.866	2.863	2.864	2.873	2.882	2.892	2.930	1945	2.930
1946	2.968	2.978	2.988	2.975	2.981	2.986	2.983	2.956	2.949	2.955	2.947	2.980	1946	2.980
1947	2.982	2.983	3.003	3.009	3.015	3.017	3.023	3.001	2.962	2.933	2.904	2.911	1947	2.911
1948	2.918	2.929	2.963	2.974	2.977	2.952	2.936	2.953	2.960	2.967	2.992	3.031	1948	3.031
1949	3.043	3.054	3.056	3.063	3.075	3.101	3.132	3.143	3.150	3.171	3.178	3.132	1949	3.132
1950	3.143	3.145	3.152	3.150	3.147	3.154	3.176	3.188	3.176	3.173	3.190	3.198	1950	3.198
1951	3.204	3.190	3.114	3.111	3.107	3.078	3.141	3.177	3.159	3.113	3.094	3.112	1951	3.112
1952	3.174	3.147	3.171	3.169	3.179	3.184	3.189	3.209	3.204	3.216	3.251	3.221	1952	3.221
1953	3.196	3.183	3.172	3.094	3.084	3.118	3.173	3.146	3.226	3.299	3.275	3.331	1953	3.331
1954	3.373	3.439	3.453	3.441	3.427	3.448	3.462	3.468	3.482	3.496	3.505	3.511	1954	3.511
1955	3.477	3.455	3.486	3.486	3.480	3.490	3.476	3.462	3.489	3.516	3.505	3.527	1955	3.527
1956	3.564	3.573	3.521	3.481	3.499	3.493	3.460	3.388	3.392	3.357	3.314	3.287	1956	3.287
1957	3.352	3.383	3.400	3.377	3.352	3.244	3.209	3.206	3.236	3.244	3.344	3.573	1957	3.573
1958	3.609	3.606	3.589	3.648	3.659	3.645	3.590	3.475	3.441	3.478	3.515	3.494	1958	3.494
1959	3.484	3.528	3.499	3.439	3.400	3.415	3.445	3.422	3.392	3.447	3.494	3.460	1959	3.460
1960	3.498	3.542	3.610	3.602	3.594	3.645	3.739	3.783	3.759	3.762	3.735	3.774	1960	3.774
1961	3.830	3.911	3.899	3.854	3.873	3.842	3.857	3.850	3.906	3.955	3.966	3.956	1961	3.956
1962	3.988	4.008	4.069	4.127	4.127	4.116	4.110	4.169	4.206	4.234	4.261	4.270	1962	4.270
1963	4.296	4.305	4.317	4.295	4.315	4.334	4.346	4.361	4.351	4.372	4.379	4.364	1963	4.364
1964	4.402	4.426	4.398	4.416	4.441	4.463	4.486	4.502	4.512	4.534	4.533	4.572	1964	4.572
1965	4.609	4.614	4.619	4.629	4.625	4.627	4.635	4.633	4.626	4.647	4.620	4.552	1965	4.552
1966	4.562	4.510	4.483	4.489	4.478	4.491	4.447	4.332	4.366	4.480	4.471	4.560	1966	4.560
1967	4.766	4.670	4.724	4.691	4.572	4.470	4.488	4.485	4.527	4.400	4.280	4.335	1967	4.335
1968	4.491	4.508	4.419	4.440	4.454	4.509	4.662	4.758	4.733	4.658	4.552	4.446	1968	4.446
1969	4.508	4.436	4.347	4.493	4.391	4.406	4.408	4.400	4.292	4.347	4.142	4.086	1969	4.086
1970	4.144	4.310	4.291	4.184	4.115	4.116	4.345	4.388	4.449	4.406	4.664	4.837	1970	4.837

Table B-4 (continued)

Long-Term Corporate Bonds: Total Return Index

from January 1971 to December 2002

Year	Jan	Feb	Mar	Apr	May	Jun	Jul	Aug	Sep	Oct	Nov	Dec	Yr-end	Index
1971	5.095	4.908	5.035	4.916	4.837	4.889	4.876	5.146	5.094	5.238	5.253	5.370	1971	5.370
1972	5.352	5.409	5.422	5.441	5.530	5.493	5.509	5.549	5.566	5.622	5.762	5.760	1972	5.760
1973	5.729	5.742	5.768	5.803	5.780	5.748	5.474	5.669	5.871	5.832	5.878	5.825	1973	5.825
1974	5.795	5.800	5.622	5.430	5.487	5.331	5.218	5.078	5.167	5.624	5.690	5.647	1974	5.647
1975	5.984	6.066	5.916	5.885	5.947	6.128	6.110	6.003	5.927	6.255	6.200	6.474	1975	6.474
1976	6.596	6.636	6.747	6.737	6.667	6.767	6.868	7.027	7.144	7.194	7.424	7.681	1976	7.681
1977	7.448	7.434	7.503	7.579	7.659	7.793	7.789	7.895	7.878	7.848	7.895	7.813	1977	7.813
1978	7.743	7.783	7.815	7.797	7.713	7.731	7.809	8.010	7.971	7.808	7.912	7.807	1978	7.807
1979	7.951	7.849	7.932	7.892	8.072	8.289	8.263	8.269	8.121	7.398	7.563	7.481	1979	7.481
1980	6.998	6.533	6.492	7.386	7.799	8.065	7.719	7.376	7.201	7.086	7.098	7.274	1980	7.274
1981	7.180	6.987	7.204	6.650	7.046	7.062	6.799	6.565	6.434	6.769	7.627	7.185	1981	7.185
1982	7.092	7.313	7.537	7.792	7.983	7.609	8.020	8.691	9.233	9.933	10.133	10.242	1982	10.242
1983	10.146	10.580	10.657	11.241	10.876	10.826	10.334	10.386	10.794	10.767	10.920	10.883	1983	10.883
1984	11.177	10.985	10.727	10.649	10.134	10.336	10.942	11.278	11.632	12.297	12.558	12.718	1984	12.718
1985	13.132	12.642	12.868	13.249	14.336	14.455	14.280	14.651	14.755	15.240	15.804	16.546	1985	16.546
1986	16.620	17.870	18.327	18.357	18.056	18.449	18.506	19.015	18.799	19.154	19.600	19.829	1986	19.829
1987	20.258	20.375	20.198	19.184	19.084	19.380	19.149	19.006	18.204	19.127	19.366	19.776	1987	19.776
1988	20.799	21.086	20.689	20.381	20.265	21.033	20.800	20.912	21.594	22.183	21.808	21.893	1988	21.893
1989	22.335	22.047	22.188	22.661	23.520	24.449	24.884	24.479	24.576	25.255	25.432	25.447	1989	25.447
1990	24.961	24.931	24.903	24.428	25.368	25.916	26.181	25.416	25.647	25.986	26.726	27.173	1990	27.173
1991	27.580	27.914	28.216	28.605	28.717	28.665	29.144	29.945	30.757	30.889	31.216	32.577	1991	32.577
1992	32.014	32.321	32.085	32.136	32.953	33.467	34.497	34.808	35.153	34.604	34.843	35.637	1992	35.637
1993	36.528	37.463	37.557	37.752	37.828	38.936	39.326	40.454	40.628	40.835	40.068	40.336	1993	40.336
1994	41.151	39.974	38.443	38.070	37.834	37.528	38.687	38.567	37.545	37.358	37.425	38.012	1994	38.012
1995	38.985	40.112	40.493	41.202	43.802	44.148	43.702	44.637	45.320	46.158	47.275	48.353	1995	48.353
1996	48.421	46.615	46.009	45.273	45.295	46.074	46.121	45.798	46.984	48.680	49.960	49.031	1996	49.031
1997	48.894	49.031	47.947	48.829	49.454	50.379	53.039	51.766	52.936	53.947	54.492	55.380	1997	55.380
1998	56.139	56.100	56.313	56.611	57.557	58.219	57.893	58.408	60.820	59.664	61.275	61.339	1998	61.339
1999	62.091	59.603	59.617	59.473	58.427	57.493	56.843	56.693	57.221	57.492	57.356	56.772	1999	56.772
2000	56.652	57.174	58.142	57.476	56.552	58.396	59.442	60.245	60.525	60.797	62.394	64.077	2000	64.077
2001	66.377	67.222	67.026	66.166	67.041	67.412	69.844	70.937	69.858	72.913	71.542	70.900	2001	70.900
2002	72.139	73.080	70.925	72.720	73.542	74.079	74.772	78.152	80.729	78.794	79.605	82.480	2002	82.480

Table B-5

Long-Term Government Bonds: Total Return Index

from December 1925 to December 1970

Year	Jan	Feb	Mar	Apr	May	Jun	Jul	Aug	Sep	Oct	Nov	Dec	Yr-end	Index
1925												1.000	1925	1.000
1926	1.014	1.020	1.024	1.032	1.034	1.038	1.038	1.038	1.042	1.053	1.069	1.078	1926	1.078
1927	1.086	1.095	1.123	1.122	1.135	1.127	1.132	1.141	1.143	1.154	1.166	1.174	1927	1.174
1928	1.170	1.177	1.182	1.182	1.173	1.178	1.152	1.161	1.156	1.174	1.175	1.175	1928	1.175
1929	1.165	1.146	1.130	1.161	1.142	1.155	1.155	1.151	1.154	1.198	1.226	1.215	1929	1.215
1930	1.208	1.224	1.234	1.232	1.249	1.256	1.260	1.262	1.271	1.276	1.281	1.272	1930	1.272
1931	1.257	1.267	1.280	1.291	1.310	1.311	1.305	1.307	1.270	1.228	1.231	1.204	1931	1.204
1932	1.208	1.258	1.256	1.332	1.307	1.315	1.379	1.379	1.387	1.385	1.389	1.407	1932	1.407
1933	1.428	1.391	1.405	1.400	1.443	1.450	1.447	1.454	1.457	1.444	1.422	1.406	1933	1.406
1934	1.442	1.454	1.483	1.501	1.521	1.531	1.537	1.519	1.497	1.524	1.530	1.547	1934	1.547
1935	1.575	1.590	1.596	1.609	1.600	1.615	1.622	1.600	1.602	1.611	1.613	1.624	1935	1.624
1936	1.633	1.647	1.664	1.670	1.677	1.680	1.690	1.709	1.704	1.705	1.740	1.746	1936	1.746
1937	1.744	1.759	1.687	1.693	1.702	1.699	1.723	1.705	1.712	1.720	1.736	1.750	1937	1.750
1938	1.760	1.770	1.763	1.800	1.808	1.809	1.817	1.817	1.821	1.837	1.833	1.847	1938	1.847
1939	1.858	1.873	1.896	1.919	1.951	1.946	1.968	1.929	1.824	1.898	1.929	1.957	1939	1.957
1940	1.954	1.959	1.994	1.987	1.927	1.977	1.987	1.993	2.015	2.021	2.062	2.076	1940	2.076
1941	2.034	2.039	2.058	2.085	2.090	2.104	2.109	2.113	2.110	2.140	2.133	2.096	1941	2.096
1942	2.110	2.112	2.132	2.126	2.142	2.142	2.146	2.154	2.155	2.160	2.152	2.163	1942	2.163
1943	2.170	2.169	2.171	2.181	2.192	2.196	2.196	2.201	2.203	2.204	2.204	2.208	1943	2.208
1944	2.213	2.220	2.224	2.227	2.234	2.235	2.243	2.249	2.253	2.255	2.261	2.270	1944	2.270
1945	2.299	2.317	2.321	2.358	2.372	2.412	2.391	2.397	2.410	2.435	2.466	2.514	1945	2.514
1946	2.520	2.528	2.531	2.497	2.493	2.511	2.501	2.473	2.471	2.489	2.475	2.511	1946	2.511
1947	2.510	2.515	2.520	2.511	2.519	2.522	2.537	2.558	2.547	2.537	2.493	2.445	1947	2.445
1948	2.450	2.462	2.470	2.481	2.516	2.495	2.490	2.490	2.494	2.496	2.514	2.529	1948	2.529
1949	2.549	2.562	2.581	2.584	2.589	2.632	2.641	2.670	2.667	2.672	2.678	2.692	1949	2.692
1950	2.675	2.681	2.683	2.691	2.700	2.693	2.708	2.712	2.692	2.679	2.689	2.693	1950	2.693
1951	2.709	2.689	2.646	2.630	2.612	2.596	2.632	2.657	2.636	2.639	2.603	2.587	1951	2.587
1952	2.595	2.598	2.627	2.672	2.663	2.664	2.658	2.640	2.606	2.644	2.640	2.617	1952	2.617
1953	2.620	2.598	2.575	2.548	2.510	2.566	2.576	2.574	2.651	2.671	2.658	2.713	1953	2.713
1954	2.737	2.802	2.819	2.848	2.823	2.869	2.908	2.897	2.894	2.896	2.889	2.907	1954	2.907
1955	2.837	2.815	2.840	2.840	2.861	2.839	2.810	2.811	2.832	2.872	2.859	2.870	1955	2.870
1956	2.894	2.893	2.850	2.818	2.881	2.889	2.829	2.776	2.790	2.775	2.759	2.710	1956	2.710
1957	2.803	2.810	2.804	2.741	2.735	2.686	2.675	2.675	2.696	2.682	2.825	2.912	1957	2.912
1958	2.887	2.916	2.946	3.001	3.001	2.953	2.871	2.746	2.714	2.751	2.785	2.734	1958	2.734
1959	2.712	2.744	2.749	2.717	2.715	2.718	2.734	2.723	2.708	2.748	2.716	2.673	1959	2.673
1960	2.702	2.757	2.835	2.787	2.829	2.878	2.984	2.964	2.986	2.978	2.958	3.041	1960	3.041
1961	3.008	3.068	3.057	3.092	3.078	3.055	3.065	3.054	3.093	3.115	3.109	3.070	1961	3.070
1962	3.066	3.098	3.176	3.202	3.217	3.192	3.158	3.217	3.236	3.263	3.270	3.282	1962	3.282
1963	3.281	3.284	3.287	3.283	3.290	3.297	3.307	3.314	3.315	3.307	3.324	3.322	1963	3.322
1964	3.317	3.313	3.326	3.341	3.358	3.381	3.384	3.390	3.407	3.422	3.428	3.438	1964	3.438
1965	3.452	3.457	3.475	3.488	3.494	3.511	3.518	3.514	3.502	3.511	3.490	3.462	1965	3.462
1966	3.427	3.341	3.440	3.418	3.398	3.393	3.380	3.310	3.420	3.498	3.447	3.589	1966	3.589
1967	3.644	3.564	3.634	3.528	3.515	3.405	3.428	3.399	3.398	3.262	3.198	3.259	1967	3.259
1968	3.366	3.355	3.284	3.359	3.373	3.451	3.550	3.549	3.513	3.466	3.373	3.251	1968	3.251
1969	3.184	3.197	3.201	3.337	3.174	3.242	3.267	3.245	3.073	3.185	3.107	3.086	1969	3.086
1970	3.079	3.260	3.238	3.104	2.959	3.103	3.202	3.196	3.269	3.233	3.489	3.460	1970	3.460

Table B-5 (continued)

Long-Term Government Bonds: Total Return Index

From January 1971 to December 2002

Year	Jan	Feb	Mar	Apr	May	Jun	Jul	Aug	Sep	Oct	Nov	Dec	Yr-end	Index
1971	3.634	3.575	3.763	3.657	3.655	3.597	3.607	3.777	3.854	3.918	3.900	3.917	1971	3.917
1972	3.892	3.927	3.895	3.905	4.011	3.985	4.071	4.082	4.049	4.143	4.237	4.140	1972	4.140
1973	4.007	4.013	4.046	4.064	4.021	4.013	3.839	3.989	4.116	4.205	4.128	4.094	1973	4.094
1974	4.060	4.050	3.932	3.833	3.880	3.897	3.886	3.796	3.890	4.080	4.200	4.272	1974	4.272
1975	4.368	4.426	4.308	4.229	4.319	4.445	4.407	4.377	4.334	4.539	4.490	4.665	1975	4.665
1976	4.707	4.736	4.815	4.824	4.747	4.846	4.884	4.987	5.059	5.102	5.274	5.447	1976	5.447
1977	5.236	5.210	5.257	5.295	5.361	5.449	5.411	5.518	5.502	5.451	5.502	5.410	1977	5.410
1978	5.366	5.368	5.357	5.355	5.323	5.290	5.366	5.483	5.425	5.316	5.416	5.346	1978	5.346
1979	5.448	5.375	5.444	5.383	5.524	5.696	5.647	5.627	5.559	5.091	5.250	5.280	1979	5.280
1980	4.889	4.660	4.514	5.201	5.419	5.613	5.346	5.115	4.982	4.851	4.899	5.071	1980	5.071
1981	5.013	4.795	4.979	4.721	5.015	4.925	4.751	4.568	4.502	4.875	5.562	5.166	1981	5.166
1982	5.189	5.284	5.406	5.608	5.627	5.501	5.777	6.228	6.613	7.033	7.031	7.251	1982	7.251
1983	7.027	7.372	7.303	7.558	7.267	7.295	6.940	6.954	7.305	7.209	7.341	7.298	1983	7.298
1984	7.476	7.343	7.228	7.152	6.782	6.884	7.361	7.557	7.816	8.254	8.352	8.427	1984	8.427
1985	8.734	8.304	8.558	8.766	9.551	9.686	9.512	9.759	9.738	10.067	10.471	11.037	1985	11.037
1986	11.009	12.270	13.215	13.109	12.447	13.210	13.068	13.720	13.034	13.410	13.769	13.745	1986	13.745
1987	13.966	14.247	13.930	13.271	13.132	13.260	13.024	12.810	12.337	13.106	13.154	13.372	1987	13.372
1988	14.263	14.337	13.897	13.675	13.536	14.035	13.797	13.876	14.355	14.796	14.506	14.665	1988	14.665
1989	14.963	14.695	14.875	15.111	15.717	16.582	16.977	16.537	16.569	17.198	17.332	17.322	1989	17.322
1990	16.728	16.686	16.613	16.278	16.954	17.344	17.530	16.796	16.992	17.358	18.056	18.392	1990	18.392
1991	18.632	18.689	18.760	19.023	19.024	18.904	19.202	19.855	20.458	20.569	20.738	21.942	1991	21.942
1992	21.231	21.339	21.140	21.173	21.687	22.121	23.001	23.155	23.584	23.117	23.140	23.709	1992	23.709
1993	24.374	25.237	25.290	25.472	25.591	26.739	27.251	28.433	28.448	28.722	27.979	28.034	1993	28.034
1994	28.755	27.462	26.378	25.981	25.767	25.508	26.435	26.209	25.342	25.280	25.447	25.856	1994	25.856
1995	26.561	27.322	27.572	28.039	30.255	30.675	30.161	30.873	31.413	32.337	33.143	34.044	1995	34.044
1996	34.007	32.366	31.687	31.163	30.994	31.622	31.678	31.237	32.142	33.440	34.612	33.727	1996	33.727
1997	33.459	33.476	32.633	33.465	33.790	34.448	36.603	35.441	36.560	37.807	38.366	39.074	1997	39.074
1998	39.856	39.570	39.668	39.771	40.497	41.421	41.256	43.173	44.876	43.896	44.320	44.178	1998	44.178
1999	44.713	42.390	42.355	42.444	41.660	41.337	41.019	40.803	41.147	41.099	40.849	40.218	1999	40.218
2000	41.135	42.220	43.768	43.437	43.200	44.254	45.018	46.100	45.376	46.227	47.699	48.856	2000	48.856
2001	48.882	49.816	49.447	47.899	48.079	48.488	50.309	51.343	51.758	54.160	51.607	50.662	2001	50.662
2002	51.361	51.951	49.686	51.721	51.798	52.769	54.368	56.888	59.258	57.517	56.817	59.699	2002	59.699

Table B-6

Long-Term Government Bonds: Capital Appreciation Index

from December 1925 to December 1970

Year	Jan	Feb	Mar	Apr	May	Jun	Jul	Aug	Sep	Oct	Nov	Dec	Yr-end	Index
1925												1.000	1925	1.000
1926	1.011	1.014	1.015	1.020	1.018	1.019	1.016	1.013	1.014	1.021	1.034	1.039	1926	1.039
1927	1.044	1.050	1.074	1.070	1.079	1.069	1.071	1.076	1.075	1.083	1.090	1.095	1927	1.095
1928	1.088	1.092	1.094	1.091	1.080	1.081	1.055	1.060	1.053	1.066	1.064	1.061	1928	1.061
1929	1.048	1.029	1.011	1.036	1.016	1.024	1.021	1.014	1.014	1.050	1.072	1.059	1929	1.059
1930	1.050	1.061	1.066	1.062	1.074	1.076	1.077	1.075	1.080	1.081	1.083	1.072	1930	1.072
1931	1.056	1.063	1.071	1.077	1.090	1.087	1.080	1.078	1.045	1.007	1.007	0.982	1931	0.982
1932	0.982	1.019	1.014	1.072	1.049	1.053	1.101	1.098	1.101	1.097	1.097	1.109	1932	1.109
1933	1.122	1.091	1.098	1.092	1.122	1.124	1.120	1.122	1.122	1.108	1.089	1.074	1933	1.074
1934	1.098	1.105	1.123	1.135	1.147	1.152	1.153	1.137	1.118	1.135	1.137	1.146	1934	1.146
1935	1.164	1.173	1.175	1.181	1.172	1.180	1.183	1.164	1.163	1.167	1.166	1.171	1935	1.171
1936	1.175	1.182	1.191	1.193	1.195	1.195	1.199	1.210	1.203	1.201	1.223	1.225	1936	1.225
1937	1.221	1.229	1.176	1.178	1.182	1.176	1.190	1.175	1.177	1.180	1.188	1.195	1937	1.195
1938	1.199	1.203	1.196	1.218	1.221	1.219	1.222	1.219	1.219	1.227	1.222	1.229	1938	1.229
1939	1.233	1.241	1.254	1.266	1.285	1.280	1.292	1.263	1.192	1.238	1.256	1.272	1939	1.272
1940	1.267	1.268	1.288	1.281	1.241	1.270	1.274	1.275	1.287	1.289	1.313	1.319	1940	1.319
1941	1.291	1.291	1.301	1.316	1.317	1.324	1.325	1.325	1.321	1.338	1.332	1.306	1941	1.306
1942	1.312	1.311	1.321	1.314	1.322	1.319	1.319	1.321	1.319	1.319	1.312	1.316	1942	1.316
1943	1.317	1.314	1.313	1.316	1.320	1.320	1.317	1.317	1.316	1.314	1.311	1.311	1943	1.311
1944	1.311	1.312	1.312	1.312	1.312	1.311	1.313	1.314	1.313	1.312	1.312	1.315	1944	1.315
1945	1.329	1.337	1.337	1.356	1.361	1.381	1.367	1.368	1.373	1.384	1.399	1.424	1945	1.424
1946	1.425	1.427	1.427	1.405	1.401	1.408	1.400	1.382	1.378	1.386	1.376	1.393	1946	1.393
1947	1.390	1.390	1.391	1.383	1.385	1.384	1.390	1.399	1.391	1.383	1.357	1.328	1947	1.328
1948	1.328	1.332	1.333	1.337	1.353	1.339	1.333	1.331	1.330	1.328	1.336	1.341	1948	1.341
1949	1.349	1.353	1.360	1.360	1.360	1.380	1.382	1.395	1.391	1.391	1.391	1.396	1949	1.396
1950	1.385	1.386	1.384	1.386	1.388	1.382	1.387	1.387	1.374	1.365	1.367	1.367	1950	1.367
1951	1.372	1.360	1.336	1.325	1.313	1.302	1.317	1.328	1.315	1.313	1.292	1.282	1951	1.282
1952	1.282	1.281	1.293	1.312	1.305	1.302	1.297	1.285	1.266	1.281	1.277	1.263	1952	1.263
1953	1.261	1.248	1.233	1.218	1.197	1.220	1.222	1.218	1.251	1.258	1.248	1.271	1953	1.271
1954	1.280	1.307	1.312	1.322	1.308	1.326	1.341	1.333	1.329	1.327	1.321	1.326	1954	1.326
1955	1.291	1.279	1.287	1.284	1.290	1.277	1.261	1.258	1.265	1.280	1.271	1.272	1955	1.272
1956	1.280	1.277	1.255	1.237	1.262	1.262	1.233	1.207	1.210	1.200	1.189	1.165	1956	1.165
1957	1.202	1.202	1.196	1.166	1.160	1.136	1.127	1.124	1.129	1.120	1.177	1.209	1957	1.209
1958	1.196	1.205	1.214	1.233	1.230	1.207	1.170	1.116	1.100	1.111	1.122	1.098	1958	1.098
1959	1.085	1.095	1.093	1.076	1.072	1.070	1.072	1.064	1.054	1.067	1.050	1.030	1959	1.030
1960	1.038	1.055	1.081	1.059	1.071	1.086	1.122	1.111	1.116	1.109	1.098	1.125	1960	1.125
1961	1.109	1.128	1.121	1.130	1.121	1.109	1.109	1.101	1.112	1.116	1.110	1.093	1961	1.093
1962	1.088	1.095	1.119	1.125	1.126	1.115	1.099	1.115	1.119	1.124	1.123	1.124	1962	1.124
1963	1.120	1.117	1.115	1.110	1.109	1.107	1.107	1.106	1.102	1.096	1.098	1.093	1963	1.093
1964	1.088	1.083	1.083	1.085	1.087	1.090	1.087	1.085	1.087	1.088	1.086	1.085	1964	1.085
1965	1.086	1.084	1.086	1.086	1.085	1.086	1.084	1.079	1.072	1.071	1.060	1.048	1965	1.048
1966	1.033	1.004	1.030	1.019	1.009	1.004	0.996	0.971	1.000	1.019	1.000	1.037	1966	1.037
1967	1.049	1.022	1.038	1.005	0.996	0.961	0.964	0.952	0.947	0.905	0.883	0.896	1967	0.896
1968	0.921	0.914	0.891	0.907	0.907	0.924	0.946	0.942	0.928	0.912	0.883	0.847	1968	0.847
1969	0.825	0.825	0.822	0.853	0.807	0.820	0.822	0.812	0.765	0.788	0.765	0.755	1969	0.755
1970	0.750	0.790	0.780	0.743	0.705	0.734	0.753	0.748	0.761	0.748	0.803	0.792	1970	0.792

Table B-6 (continued)

Long-Term Government Bonds: Capital Appreciation Index

from January 1971 to December 2002

Year	Jan	Feb	Mar	Apr	May	Jun	Jul	Aug	Sep	Oct	Nov	Dec	Yr-end	Index
1971	0.828	0.811	0.849	0.821	0.816	0.799	0.797	0.830	0.843	0.853	0.845	0.844	1971	0.844
1972	0.835	0.838	0.827	0.825	0.843	0.834	0.847	0.846	0.835	0.850	0.865	0.841	1972	0.841
1973	0.810	0.807	0.809	0.808	0.795	0.789	0.750	0.774	0.795	0.807	0.788	0.777	1973	0.777
1974	0.765	0.759	0.733	0.709	0.713	0.712	0.705	0.684	0.696	0.725	0.742	0.750	1974	0.750
1975	0.761	0.767	0.741	0.723	0.733	0.750	0.738	0.728	0.716	0.745	0.732	0.755	1975	0.755
1976	0.757	0.757	0.764	0.761	0.744	0.754	0.755	0.766	0.772	0.774	0.795	0.816	1976	0.816
1977	0.780	0.771	0.773	0.774	0.779	0.787	0.776	0.787	0.780	0.767	0.770	0.752	1977	0.752
1978	0.741	0.737	0.730	0.725	0.715	0.706	0.711	0.721	0.709	0.690	0.698	0.684	1978	0.684
1979	0.692	0.678	0.682	0.669	0.681	0.697	0.686	0.679	0.666	0.604	0.618	0.617	1979	0.617
1980	0.566	0.535	0.512	0.585	0.605	0.621	0.587	0.556	0.537	0.517	0.518	0.530	1980	0.530
1981	0.519	0.492	0.505	0.474	0.499	0.484	0.462	0.439	0.428	0.458	0.518	0.476	1981	0.476
1982	0.473	0.476	0.481	0.494	0.491	0.474	0.492	0.525	0.552	0.582	0.577	0.589	1982	0.589
1983	0.566	0.589	0.578	0.594	0.565	0.563	0.530	0.526	0.547	0.535	0.540	0.532	1983	0.532
1984	0.539	0.524	0.511	0.500	0.469	0.472	0.499	0.507	0.519	0.543	0.544	0.544	1984	0.544
1985	0.558	0.526	0.538	0.545	0.589	0.592	0.576	0.586	0.580	0.594	0.613	0.641	1985	0.641
1986	0.634	0.702	0.751	0.741	0.699	0.737	0.724	0.755	0.713	0.728	0.743	0.737	1986	0.737
1987	0.744	0.755	0.733	0.693	0.682	0.683	0.666	0.650	0.621	0.655	0.652	0.658	1987	0.658
1988	0.697	0.696	0.670	0.654	0.642	0.661	0.645	0.644	0.661	0.676	0.658	0.661	1988	0.661
1989	0.669	0.652	0.655	0.661	0.682	0.715	0.727	0.703	0.700	0.722	0.723	0.718	1989	0.718
1990	0.688	0.681	0.674	0.655	0.677	0.688	0.691	0.657	0.660	0.669	0.691	0.699	1990	0.699
1991	0.703	0.701	0.699	0.703	0.699	0.690	0.695	0.714	0.731	0.730	0.732	0.769	1991	0.769
1992	0.740	0.739	0.727	0.724	0.737	0.747	0.772	0.772	0.782	0.762	0.758	0.772	1992	0.772
1993	0.789	0.813	0.809	0.811	0.810	0.841	0.853	0.885	0.881	0.885	0.858	0.855	1993	0.855
1994	0.872	0.829	0.791	0.775	0.763	0.751	0.774	0.762	0.732	0.726	0.726	0.733	1994	0.733
1995	0.748	0.765	0.767	0.775	0.831	0.838	0.820	0.834	0.845	0.865	0.882	0.901	1995	0.901
1996	0.896	0.848	0.826	0.807	0.798	0.810	0.807	0.791	0.809	0.837	0.862	0.835	1996	0.835
1997	0.824	0.820	0.794	0.810	0.813	0.824	0.871	0.839	0.861	0.885	0.894	0.906	1997	0.906
1998	0.920	0.909	0.907	0.904	0.917	0.933	0.925	0.963	0.997	0.971	0.976	0.968	1998	0.968
1999	0.976	0.921	0.916	0.913	0.892	0.880	0.869	0.860	0.863	0.857	0.847	0.829	1999	0.829
2000	0.844	0.862	0.889	0.878	0.868	0.885	0.895	0.912	0.894	0.906	0.930	0.949	2000	0.949
2001	0.944	0.958	0.947	0.913	0.912	0.915	0.945	0.960	0.964	1.004	0.952	0.931	2001	0.931
2002	0.939	0.946	0.900	0.932	0.929	0.943	0.966	1.007	1.045	1.010	0.993	1.039	2002	1.039

Table B-7

Intermediate-Term Government Bonds: Total Return Index

from December 1925 to December 1970

Year	Jan	Feb	Mar	Apr	May	Jun	Jul	Aug	Sep	Oct	Nov	Dec	Yr-end	Index
1925												1.000	1925	1.000
1926	1.007	1.010	1.014	1.023	1.024	1.027	1.028	1.029	1.034	1.040	1.044	1.054	1926	1.054
1927	1.060	1.064	1.068	1.070	1.072	1.075	1.079	1.086	1.092	1.088	1.097	1.101	1927	1.101
1928	1.107	1.106	1.107	1.107	1.106	1.108	1.098	1.104	1.107	1.110	1.112	1.112	1928	1.112
1929	1.108	1.106	1.107	1.117	1.110	1.122	1.129	1.135	1.133	1.153	1.173	1.178	1929	1.178
1930	1.174	1.185	1.204	1.195	1.202	1.219	1.226	1.229	1.236	1.246	1.255	1.258	1930	1.258
1931	1.249	1.261	1.267	1.278	1.293	1.266	1.268	1.270	1.255	1.242	1.248	1.228	1931	1.228
1932	1.224	1.240	1.250	1.274	1.263	1.276	1.292	1.307	1.311	1.317	1.321	1.337	1932	1.337
1933	1.335	1.334	1.348	1.355	1.382	1.383	1.382	1.393	1.396	1.393	1.396	1.361	1933	1.361
1934	1.379	1.386	1.412	1.438	1.455	1.468	1.465	1.451	1.431	1.458	1.465	1.483	1934	1.483
1935	1.500	1.516	1.535	1.552	1.546	1.564	1.570	1.558	1.550	1.566	1.569	1.587	1935	1.587
1936	1.587	1.598	1.603	1.607	1.613	1.615	1.618	1.626	1.628	1.632	1.645	1.636	1936	1.636
1937	1.631	1.632	1.605	1.613	1.625	1.623	1.633	1.626	1.639	1.644	1.651	1.661	1937	1.661
1938	1.676	1.684	1.682	1.721	1.725	1.738	1.740	1.742	1.740	1.756	1.756	1.765	1938	1.765
1939	1.770	1.785	1.799	1.806	1.823	1.823	1.831	1.804	1.756	1.812	1.825	1.845	1939	1.845
1940	1.842	1.849	1.865	1.865	1.825	1.860	1.860	1.868	1.877	1.884	1.894	1.899	1940	1.899
1941	1.900	1.891	1.904	1.910	1.912	1.923	1.923	1.925	1.925	1.930	1.912	1.909	1941	1.909
1942	1.923	1.926	1.930	1.935	1.938	1.940	1.940	1.944	1.939	1.943	1.946	1.946	1942	1.946
1943	1.953	1.956	1.960	1.965	1.976	1.983	1.987	1.987	1.990	1.993	1.996	2.000	1943	2.000
1944	2.003	2.006	2.010	2.015	2.016	2.017	2.023	2.028	2.030	2.033	2.034	2.036	1944	2.036
1945	2.047	2.055	2.056	2.059	2.061	2.065	2.065	2.068	2.072	2.075	2.077	2.082	1945	2.082
1946	2.090	2.100	2.092	2.088	2.089	2.096	2.094	2.094	2.092	2.098	2.096	2.102	1946	2.102
1947	2.107	2.109	2.114	2.111	2.112	2.114	2.115	2.121	2.121	2.116	2.117	2.122	1947	2.122
1948	2.125	2.129	2.132	2.136	2.148	2.146	2.146	2.145	2.147	2.149	2.154	2.161	1948	2.161
1949	2.167	2.169	2.175	2.178	2.183	2.194	2.198	2.205	2.207	2.208	2.208	2.211	1949	2.211
1950	2.210	2.212	2.212	2.213	2.218	2.218	2.223	2.221	2.220	2.221	2.225	2.227	1950	2.227
1951	2.231	2.233	2.205	2.217	2.208	2.219	2.232	2.240	2.227	2.231	2.238	2.235	1951	2.235
1952	2.243	2.239	2.253	2.266	2.270	2.262	2.254	2.249	2.253	2.268	2.267	2.271	1952	2.271
1953	2.271	2.271	2.267	2.246	2.219	2.254	2.266	2.265	2.309	2.317	2.321	2.345	1953	2.345
1954	2.360	2.383	2.390	2.400	2.382	2.412	2.411	2.414	2.409	2.406	2.406	2.407	1954	2.407
1955	2.400	2.387	2.393	2.394	2.394	2.386	2.369	2.370	2.390	2.407	2.394	2.392	1955	2.392
1956	2.417	2.418	2.393	2.393	2.420	2.421	2.398	2.373	2.395	2.390	2.379	2.382	1956	2.382
1957	2.438	2.435	2.439	2.415	2.411	2.385	2.382	2.408	2.408	2.418	2.514	2.568	1957	2.568
1958	2.577	2.613	2.627	2.640	2.656	2.638	2.614	2.521	2.517	2.518	2.551	2.535	1958	2.535
1959	2.532	2.559	2.550	2.536	2.536	2.517	2.525	2.505	2.510	2.554	2.530	2.525	1959	2.525
1960	2.564	2.583	2.658	2.641	2.649	2.707	2.779	2.778	2.786	2.790	2.764	2.822	1960	2.822
1961	2.805	2.831	2.841	2.856	2.848	2.841	2.843	2.848	2.871	2.875	2.869	2.874	1961	2.874
1962	2.861	2.906	2.932	2.939	2.953	2.945	2.941	2.978	2.984	3.000	3.018	3.034	1962	3.034
1963	3.026	3.031	3.039	3.048	3.053	3.057	3.058	3.064	3.068	3.071	3.083	3.084	1963	3.084
1964	3.094	3.098	3.103	3.113	3.138	3.150	3.158	3.167	3.181	3.191	3.190	3.209	1964	3.209
1965	3.222	3.228	3.242	3.250	3.262	3.278	3.283	3.290	3.288	3.288	3.290	3.242	1965	3.242
1966	3.242	3.215	3.275	3.269	3.273	3.265	3.257	3.216	3.286	3.311	3.320	3.394	1966	3.394
1967	3.434	3.429	3.492	3.461	3.476	3.397	3.443	3.430	3.433	3.416	3.425	3.428	1967	3.428
1968	3.478	3.491	3.482	3.477	3.499	3.557	3.620	3.628	3.648	3.651	3.646	3.583	1968	3.583
1969	3.614	3.609	3.644	3.673	3.643	3.613	3.642	3.636	3.527	3.644	3.627	3.557	1969	3.557
1970	3.568	3.724	3.757	3.679	3.720	3.742	3.799	3.843	3.919	3.956	4.134	4.156	1970	4.156

Table B-7 (continued)

Intermediate-Term Government Bonds: Total Return Index

from January 1971 to December 2002

Year	Jan	Feb	Mar	Apr	May	Jun	Jul	Aug	Sep	Oct	Nov	Dec	Yr-end	Index
1971	4.226	4.321	4.401	4.257	4.262	4.182	4.193	4.340	4.351	4.447	4.470	4.519	1971	4.519
1972	4.567	4.573	4.580	4.586	4.594	4.614	4.621	4.628	4.635	4.642	4.662	4.752	1972	4.752
1973	4.749	4.713	4.735	4.765	4.792	4.790	4.657	4.776	4.895	4.920	4.951	4.971	1973	4.971
1974	4.975	4.993	4.887	4.813	4.876	4.833	4.837	4.831	4.985	5.040	5.159	5.254	1974	5.254
1975	5.282	5.360	5.328	5.229	5.365	5.380	5.363	5.359	5.364	5.561	5.555	5.665	1975	5.665
1976	5.697	5.745	5.788	5.855	5.770	5.862	5.932	6.044	6.089	6.179	6.378	6.394	1976	6.394
1977	6.273	6.303	6.338	6.371	6.407	6.472	6.473	6.478	6.487	6.449	6.499	6.484	1977	6.484
1978	6.492	6.503	6.527	6.543	6.542	6.528	6.592	6.644	6.682	6.608	6.668	6.710	1978	6.710
1979	6.747	6.707	6.783	6.805	6.936	7.079	7.071	7.006	7.010	6.682	6.925	6.985	1979	6.985
1980	6.891	6.449	6.542	7.325	7.684	7.625	7.544	7.252	7.225	7.115	7.136	7.258	1980	7.258
1981	7.281	7.110	7.297	7.140	7.315	7.358	7.160	7.033	7.148	7.585	8.058	7.944	1981	7.944
1982	7.984	8.102	8.137	8.379	8.502	8.387	8.776	9.188	9.486	9.990	10.070	10.256	1982	10.256
1983	10.263	10.522	10.471	10.742	10.611	10.628	10.417	10.501	10.832	10.852	10.964	11.015	1983	11.015
1984	11.211	11.139	11.100	11.097	10.819	10.926	11.355	11.469	11.701	12.149	12.382	12.560	1984	12.560
1985	12.818	12.588	12.798	13.136	13.772	13.922	13.859	14.064	14.222	14.453	14.735	15.113	1985	15.113
1986	15.238	15.657	16.186	16.318	15.968	16.409	16.667	17.109	16.921	17.195	17.389	17.401	1986	17.401
1987	17.587	17.691	17.636	17.205	17.140	17.350	17.394	17.328	17.085	17.596	17.741	17.906	1987	17.906
1988	18.472	18.698	18.537	18.455	18.364	18.698	18.610	18.593	18.957	19.238	19.017	18.999	1988	18.999
1989	19.230	19.133	19.227	19.650	20.067	20.717	21.203	20.682	20.824	21.318	21.497	21.524	1989	21.524
1990	21.299	21.313	21.318	21.154	21.707	22.035	22.418	22.213	22.422	22.804	23.243	23.618	1990	23.618
1991	23.870	23.984	24.039	24.320	24.464	24.409	24.725	25.335	25.881	26.228	26.565	27.270	1991	27.270
1992	26.737	26.796	26.583	26.843	27.438	27.923	28.600	29.029	29.592	29.054	28.810	29.230	1992	29.230
1993	30.021	30.749	30.883	31.156	31.126	31.753	31.769	32.477	32.657	32.714	32.411	32.516	1993	32.516
1994	32.964	32.113	31.286	30.957	30.951	30.863	31.385	31.466	30.968	30.896	30.680	30.843	1994	30.843
1995	31.404	32.140	32.341	32.805	34.014	34.285	34.231	34.525	34.745	35.164	35.687	36.025	1995	36.025
1996	36.048	35.551	35.131	34.955	34.844	35.253	35.340	35.323	35.872	36.527	37.072	36.782	1996	36.782
1997	36.873	36.880	36.460	37.000	37.293	37.671	38.666	38.289	38.867	39.451	39.446	39.864	1997	39.864
1998	40.583	40.426	40.530	40.777	41.062	41.385	41.495	42.619	44.023	44.203	43.772	43.933	1998	43.933
1999	44.175	43.015	43.387	43.476	42.834	42.972	42.958	43.016	43.435	43.401	43.365	43.155	1999	43.155
2000	42.925	43.260	44.140	43.950	44.179	45.024	45.347	45.953	46.394	46.760	47.573	48.589	2000	48.589
2001	49.066	49.583	49.958	49.390	49.356	49.680	50.907	51.391	52.694	53.642	52.725	52.291	2001	52.291
2002	52.477	53.043	51.761	52.997	53.621	54.526	56.007	56.942	58.583	58.442	57.451	59.054	2002	59.054

Table B-8

Intermediate-Term Government Bonds: Capital Appreciation Index

from December 1925 to December 1970

Year	Jan	Feb	Mar	Apr	May	Jun	Jul	Aug	Sep	Oct	Nov	Dec	Yr-end	Index
1925												1.000	1925	1.000
1926	1.004	1.004	1.005	1.010	1.008	1.008	1.006	1.004	1.005	1.008	1.009	1.015	1926	1.015
1927	1.018	1.019	1.020	1.018	1.017	1.017	1.019	1.022	1.025	1.018	1.024	1.025	1927	1.025
1928	1.027	1.023	1.022	1.018	1.015	1.013	1.001	1.003	1.002	1.002	1.001	0.997	1928	0.997
1929	0.991	0.985	0.982	0.987	0.978	0.985	0.988	0.990	0.985	0.998	1.013	1.014	1929	1.014
1930	1.007	1.013	1.027	1.017	1.020	1.032	1.034	1.034	1.038	1.043	1.048	1.048	1930	1.048
1931	1.038	1.045	1.048	1.055	1.065	1.040	1.039	1.038	1.023	1.009	1.011	0.991	1931	0.991
1932	0.985	0.994	0.998	1.015	1.002	1.010	1.019	1.029	1.029	1.031	1.032	1.041	1932	1.041
1933	1.037	1.034	1.042	1.045	1.063	1.062	1.059	1.064	1.065	1.060	1.061	1.031	1933	1.031
1934	1.041	1.044	1.061	1.078	1.088	1.096	1.091	1.079	1.061	1.079	1.081	1.092	1934	1.092
1935	1.103	1.112	1.124	1.134	1.129	1.140	1.142	1.132	1.124	1.135	1.134	1.146	1935	1.146
1936	1.144	1.151	1.153	1.154	1.157	1.157	1.158	1.163	1.163	1.164	1.172	1.165	1936	1.165
1937	1.160	1.159	1.139	1.143	1.150	1.147	1.152	1.146	1.154	1.156	1.159	1.165	1937	1.165
1938	1.173	1.177	1.174	1.199	1.200	1.207	1.207	1.207	1.204	1.213	1.211	1.216	1938	1.216
1939	1.218	1.227	1.235	1.239	1.249	1.248	1.252	1.232	1.199	1.235	1.243	1.255	1939	1.255
1940	1.252	1.255	1.265	1.265	1.237	1.259	1.258	1.262	1.267	1.271	1.278	1.280	1940	1.280
1941	1.280	1.273	1.281	1.284	1.285	1.292	1.291	1.292	1.291	1.294	1.281	1.278	1941	1.278
1942	1.287	1.288	1.290	1.292	1.293	1.294	1.293	1.295	1.291	1.293	1.294	1.293	1942	1.293
1943	1.296	1.297	1.297	1.299	1.304	1.307	1.308	1.307	1.307	1.308	1.308	1.309	1943	1.309
1944	1.309	1.309	1.310	1.312	1.311	1.311	1.313	1.314	1.314	1.314	1.314	1.314	1944	1.314
1945	1.319	1.323	1.322	1.323	1.323	1.324	1.323	1.324	1.325	1.325	1.326	1.327	1945	1.327
1946	1.331	1.336	1.330	1.327	1.326	1.329	1.327	1.326	1.324	1.326	1.323	1.326	1946	1.326
1947	1.328	1.327	1.329	1.326	1.326	1.326	1.325	1.327	1.326	1.322	1.321	1.322	1947	1.322
1948	1.322	1.323	1.323	1.324	1.330	1.327	1.325	1.323	1.322	1.322	1.323	1.326	1948	1.326
1949	1.328	1.328	1.329	1.330	1.331	1.336	1.337	1.340	1.340	1.339	1.338	1.338	1949	1.338
1950	1.336	1.336	1.334	1.334	1.335	1.334	1.335	1.333	1.331	1.329	1.330	1.329	1950	1.329
1951	1.330	1.329	1.310	1.315	1.308	1.312	1.317	1.320	1.310	1.310	1.312	1.307	1951	1.307
1952	1.310	1.305	1.311	1.316	1.317	1.310	1.303	1.297	1.297	1.303	1.300	1.300	1952	1.300
1953	1.297	1.295	1.290	1.275	1.257	1.274	1.278	1.274	1.295	1.298	1.297	1.308	1953	1.308
1954	1.314	1.326	1.327	1.331	1.320	1.334	1.332	1.332	1.328	1.325	1.323	1.322	1954	1.322
1955	1.315	1.306	1.307	1.305	1.302	1.295	1.283	1.281	1.288	1.295	1.285	1.281	1955	1.281
1956	1.291	1.289	1.273	1.270	1.281	1.278	1.263	1.246	1.255	1.248	1.239	1.237	1956	1.237
1957	1.262	1.258	1.257	1.240	1.234	1.218	1.212	1.221	1.217	1.219	1.263	1.287	1957	1.287
1958	1.288	1.303	1.307	1.311	1.317	1.305	1.290	1.242	1.236	1.232	1.245	1.233	1958	1.233
1959	1.228	1.237	1.228	1.218	1.214	1.200	1.200	1.186	1.184	1.200	1.184	1.177	1959	1.177
1960	1.190	1.194	1.224	1.213	1.212	1.234	1.263	1.259	1.259	1.257	1.242	1.264	1960	1.264
1961	1.253	1.261	1.262	1.265	1.258	1.251	1.248	1.246	1.252	1.250	1.244	1.243	1961	1.243
1962	1.233	1.248	1.255	1.254	1.257	1.250	1.244	1.255	1.255	1.257	1.261	1.264	1962	1.264
1963	1.257	1.255	1.255	1.255	1.253	1.251	1.247	1.246	1.243	1.240	1.241	1.237	1963	1.237
1964	1.237	1.235	1.233	1.233	1.239	1.239	1.238	1.237	1.239	1.239	1.234	1.237	1964	1.237
1965	1.238	1.237	1.237	1.236	1.237	1.238	1.236	1.234	1.229	1.225	1.221	1.199	1965	1.199
1966	1.194	1.180	1.197	1.190	1.186	1.179	1.171	1.151	1.171	1.174	1.173	1.194	1966	1.194
1967	1.203	1.197	1.214	1.200	1.200	1.168	1.178	1.169	1.165	1.154	1.152	1.148	1967	1.148
1968	1.159	1.158	1.150	1.143	1.145	1.159	1.173	1.171	1.172	1.168	1.162	1.136	1968	1.136
1969	1.140	1.133	1.139	1.141	1.126	1.110	1.113	1.105	1.065	1.093	1.082	1.054	1969	1.054
1970	1.050	1.090	1.092	1.063	1.068	1.068	1.077	1.083	1.098	1.102	1.145	1.145	1970	1.145

Table B-8 (continued)

Intermediate-Term Government Bonds: Capital Appreciation Index

from January 1971 to December 2002

Year	Jan	Feb	Mar	Apr	May	Jun	Jul	Aug	Sep	Oct	Nov	Dec	Yr-end	Index
1971	1.159	1.180	1.197	1.153	1.149	1.121	1.118	1.151	1.149	1.169	1.169	1.177	1971	1.177
1972	1.183	1.180	1.176	1.173	1.169	1.168	1.164	1.160	1.156	1.152	1.151	1.168	1972	1.168
1973	1.161	1.146	1.145	1.146	1.146	1.140	1.101	1.122	1.144	1.143	1.144	1.142	1973	1.142
1974	1.137	1.135	1.105	1.081	1.088	1.072	1.065	1.056	1.083	1.087	1.106	1.120	1974	1.120
1975	1.119	1.129	1.116	1.088	1.110	1.106	1.095	1.088	1.081	1.114	1.106	1.121	1975	1.121
1976	1.121	1.124	1.125	1.131	1.109	1.119	1.125	1.139	1.142	1.152	1.183	1.180	1976	1.180
1977	1.151	1.151	1.151	1.151	1.151	1.156	1.150	1.144	1.140	1.126	1.128	1.119	1977	1.119
1978	1.113	1.109	1.105	1.101	1.093	1.084	1.087	1.088	1.087	1.067	1.069	1.069	1978	1.069
1979	1.066	1.053	1.057	1.052	1.064	1.079	1.069	1.052	1.045	0.987	1.015	1.015	1979	1.015
1980	0.992	0.920	0.924	1.025	1.067	1.051	1.031	0.983	0.970	0.946	0.940	0.946	1980	0.946
1981	0.939	0.908	0.921	0.892	0.904	0.898	0.864	0.838	0.841	0.881	0.926	0.903	1981	0.903
1982	0.897	0.902	0.894	0.911	0.915	0.892	0.923	0.956	0.978	1.021	1.021	1.031	1982	1.031
1983	1.023	1.041	1.027	1.045	1.023	1.016	0.988	0.986	1.007	1.000	1.001	0.997	1983	0.997
1984	1.005	0.990	0.977	0.967	0.933	0.932	0.958	0.958	0.968	0.994	1.004	1.009	1984	1.009
1985	1.021	0.994	1.002	1.019	1.059	1.063	1.049	1.056	1.059	1.068	1.081	1.100	1985	1.100
1986	1.101	1.124	1.155	1.157	1.125	1.149	1.160	1.184	1.164	1.176	1.183	1.177	1986	1.177
1987	1.183	1.184	1.173	1.138	1.126	1.132	1.127	1.116	1.092	1.117	1.118	1.121	1987	1.121
1988	1.149	1.156	1.138	1.126	1.112	1.125	1.112	1.103	1.116	1.125	1.105	1.096	1988	1.096
1989	1.100	1.088	1.085	1.101	1.115	1.144	1.163	1.127	1.128	1.146	1.149	1.143	1989	1.143
1990	1.123	1.117	1.109	1.093	1.113	1.122	1.134	1.116	1.119	1.130	1.144	1.155	1990	1.155
1991	1.160	1.158	1.154	1.160	1.159	1.150	1.156	1.178	1.196	1.205	1.214	1.240	1991	1.240
1992	1.209	1.206	1.189	1.193	1.213	1.228	1.251	1.263	1.282	1.253	1.236	1.248	1992	1.248
1993	1.275	1.301	1.300	1.305	1.299	1.318	1.314	1.337	1.339	1.336	1.318	1.317	1993	1.317
1994	1.329	1.290	1.250	1.231	1.224	1.213	1.227	1.223	1.197	1.187	1.171	1.170	1994	1.170
1995	1.184	1.205	1.205	1.216	1.253	1.257	1.249	1.253	1.255	1.264	1.277	1.283	1995	1.283
1996	1.278	1.255	1.235	1.222	1.212	1.220	1.216	1.209	1.221	1.237	1.249	1.233	1996	1.233
1997	1.230	1.225	1.204	1.215	1.218	1.224	1.250	1.232	1.244	1.256	1.251	1.257	1997	1.257
1998	1.274	1.264	1.261	1.263	1.266	1.270	1.267	1.296	1.333	1.334	1.316	1.316	1998	1.316
1999	1.318	1.279	1.284	1.281	1.257	1.255	1.248	1.244	1.250	1.243	1.235	1.223	1999	1.223
2000	1.210	1.213	1.231	1.220	1.219	1.236	1.238	1.248	1.254	1.258	1.274	1.296	2000	1.296
2001	1.304	1.315	1.321	1.302	1.295	1.298	1.325	1.332	1.361	1.381	1.353	1.338	2001	1.338
2002	1.337	1.347	1.310	1.335	1.346	1.364	1.396	1.415	1.452	1.445	1.418	1.453	2002	1.453

Table B-9

U.S. Treasury Bills: Total Return Index

from December 1925 to December 1970

Year	Jan	Feb	Mar	Apr	May	Jun	Jul	Aug	Sep	Oct	Nov	Dec	Yr-end	Index
1925												1.000	1925	1.000
1926	1.003	1.006	1.009	1.013	1.013	1.016	1.018	1.021	1.023	1.027	1.030	1.033	1926	1.033
1927	1.035	1.038	1.041	1.044	1.047	1.049	1.053	1.055	1.058	1.060	1.063	1.065	1927	1.065
1928	1.068	1.071	1.074	1.077	1.080	1.084	1.087	1.091	1.093	1.098	1.102	1.103	1928	1.103
1929	1.107	1.111	1.114	1.118	1.123	1.129	1.133	1.137	1.141	1.147	1.151	1.155	1929	1.155
1930	1.157	1.160	1.164	1.167	1.170	1.173	1.175	1.176	1.179	1.180	1.181	1.183	1930	1.183
1931	1.185	1.185	1.187	1.188	1.189	1.190	1.190	1.191	1.191	1.192	1.194	1.196	1931	1.196
1932	1.198	1.201	1.203	1.205	1.205	1.206	1.206	1.206	1.207	1.207	1.207	1.207	1932	1.207
1933	1.207	1.207	1.208	1.209	1.209	1.210	1.210	1.210	1.210	1.210	1.211	1.211	1933	1.211
1934	1.211	1.212	1.212	1.212	1.212	1.212	1.212	1.212	1.212	1.213	1.213	1.213	1934	1.213
1935	1.213	1.213	1.213	1.213	1.214	1.214	1.214	1.214	1.214	1.214	1.215	1.215	1935	1.215
1936	1.215	1.215	1.215	1.216	1.216	1.216	1.216	1.216	1.217	1.217	1.217	1.217	1936	1.217
1937	1.217	1.217	1.218	1.218	1.219	1.219	1.219	1.220	1.220	1.220	1.221	1.221	1937	1.221
1938	1.221	1.221	1.221	1.221	1.221	1.221	1.221	1.221	1.221	1.221	1.221	1.221	1938	1.221
1939	1.220	1.221	1.220	1.220	1.220	1.221	1.221	1.221	1.221	1.221	1.221	1.221	1939	1.221
1940	1.221	1.221	1.221	1.221	1.221	1.221	1.221	1.221	1.221	1.221	1.221	1.221	1940	1.221
1941	1.221	1.221	1.221	1.221	1.221	1.221	1.221	1.221	1.221	1.221	1.221	1.222	1941	1.222
1942	1.222	1.222	1.222	1.222	1.222	1.223	1.223	1.223	1.224	1.224	1.225	1.225	1942	1.225
1943	1.225	1.226	1.226	1.226	1.227	1.227	1.227	1.228	1.228	1.228	1.229	1.229	1943	1.229
1944	1.229	1.230	1.230	1.230	1.231	1.231	1.231	1.232	1.232	1.233	1.233	1.233	1944	1.233
1945	1.233	1.234	1.234	1.234	1.235	1.235	1.235	1.236	1.236	1.237	1.237	1.237	1945	1.237
1946	1.238	1.238	1.238	1.239	1.239	1.239	1.240	1.240	1.240	1.241	1.241	1.242	1946	1.242
1947	1.242	1.242	1.243	1.243	1.243	1.244	1.244	1.244	1.245	1.246	1.247	1.248	1947	1.248
1948	1.249	1.250	1.251	1.252	1.253	1.254	1.255	1.256	1.256	1.257	1.257	1.258	1948	1.258
1949	1.259	1.260	1.262	1.263	1.264	1.265	1.266	1.267	1.269	1.270	1.271	1.272	1949	1.272
1950	1.273	1.274	1.275	1.276	1.278	1.279	1.280	1.281	1.283	1.284	1.286	1.287	1950	1.287
1951	1.289	1.290	1.291	1.293	1.295	1.296	1.298	1.300	1.301	1.303	1.305	1.306	1951	1.306
1952	1.308	1.310	1.311	1.313	1.314	1.316	1.318	1.320	1.322	1.324	1.326	1.328	1952	1.328
1953	1.330	1.332	1.334	1.337	1.339	1.341	1.343	1.345	1.348	1.349	1.350	1.352	1953	1.352
1954	1.354	1.355	1.356	1.357	1.357	1.358	1.359	1.360	1.361	1.362	1.363	1.364	1954	1.364
1955	1.365	1.366	1.367	1.369	1.371	1.372	1.373	1.376	1.378	1.380	1.383	1.385	1955	1.385
1956	1.388	1.391	1.393	1.396	1.399	1.402	1.405	1.407	1.410	1.413	1.416	1.419	1956	1.419
1957	1.423	1.426	1.430	1.433	1.437	1.441	1.445	1.448	1.452	1.456	1.460	1.464	1957	1.464
1958	1.468	1.470	1.471	1.472	1.474	1.474	1.475	1.476	1.479	1.481	1.483	1.486	1958	1.486
1959	1.489	1.492	1.496	1.499	1.502	1.505	1.509	1.512	1.517	1.521	1.525	1.530	1959	1.530
1960	1.535	1.540	1.545	1.548	1.552	1.556	1.558	1.561	1.563	1.567	1.569	1.571	1960	1.571
1961	1.574	1.576	1.579	1.582	1.585	1.588	1.591	1.593	1.596	1.599	1.601	1.604	1961	1.604
1962	1.608	1.612	1.615	1.618	1.622	1.626	1.630	1.634	1.637	1.641	1.645	1.648	1962	1.648
1963	1.652	1.656	1.660	1.664	1.668	1.672	1.677	1.681	1.685	1.690	1.695	1.700	1963	1.700
1964	1.705	1.709	1.715	1.720	1.724	1.729	1.734	1.739	1.744	1.749	1.754	1.760	1964	1.760
1965	1.765	1.770	1.776	1.782	1.787	1.794	1.799	1.805	1.811	1.817	1.823	1.829	1965	1.829
1966	1.836	1.842	1.849	1.856	1.863	1.870	1.877	1.885	1.892	1.901	1.908	1.916	1966	1.916
1967	1.924	1.931	1.939	1.945	1.951	1.957	1.963	1.969	1.975	1.983	1.990	1.997	1967	1.997
1968	2.005	2.012	2.020	2.029	2.038	2.046	2.056	2.065	2.074	2.083	2.092	2.101	1968	2.101
1969	2.112	2.121	2.131	2.143	2.153	2.164	2.175	2.186	2.200	2.213	2.225	2.239	1969	2.239
1970	2.252	2.266	2.279	2.291	2.303	2.316	2.328	2.341	2.353	2.364	2.375	2.385	1970	2.385

Table B-9 (continued)

U.S. Treasury Bills: Total Return Index

from January 1971 to December 2002

Year	Jan	Feb	Mar	Apr	May	Jun	Jul	Aug	Sep	Oct	Nov	Dec	Yr-end	Index
1971	2.394	2.402	2.409	2.416	2.423	2.432	2.442	2.453	2.462	2.471	2.480	2.490	1971	2.490
1972	2.497	2.503	2.510	2.517	2.525	2.532	2.540	2.547	2.556	2.566	2.575	2.585	1972	2.585
1973	2.596	2.607	2.619	2.633	2.646	2.660	2.677	2.695	2.714	2.732	2.747	2.764	1973	2.764
1974	2.782	2.798	2.813	2.835	2.856	2.873	2.893	2.911	2.934	2.949	2.965	2.986	1974	2.986
1975	3.003	3.016	3.028	3.042	3.055	3.067	3.082	3.097	3.113	3.131	3.144	3.159	1975	3.159
1976	3.174	3.184	3.197	3.210	3.222	3.237	3.252	3.265	3.280	3.293	3.306	3.319	1976	3.319
1977	3.331	3.343	3.356	3.368	3.381	3.394	3.408	3.423	3.438	3.455	3.472	3.489	1977	3.489
1978	3.506	3.522	3.541	3.560	3.578	3.597	3.618	3.638	3.660	3.685	3.711	3.740	1978	3.740
1979	3.769	3.796	3.827	3.858	3.889	3.921	3.951	3.981	4.014	4.049	4.089	4.128	1979	4.128
1980	4.161	4.198	4.248	4.302	4.336	4.363	4.386	4.414	4.447	4.489	4.532	4.592	1980	4.592
1981	4.639	4.689	4.746	4.797	4.852	4.917	4.978	5.042	5.105	5.166	5.221	5.267	1981	5.267
1982	5.309	5.358	5.411	5.472	5.530	5.583	5.641	5.684	5.713	5.747	5.783	5.822	1982	5.822
1983	5.862	5.899	5.936	5.978	6.020	6.060	6.105	6.151	6.198	6.245	6.289	6.335	1983	6.335
1984	6.383	6.428	6.475	6.528	6.579	6.629	6.683	6.738	6.796	6.864	6.914	6.959	1984	6.959
1985	7.004	7.044	7.088	7.138	7.186	7.225	7.271	7.311	7.355	7.403	7.448	7.496	1985	7.496
1986	7.538	7.578	7.623	7.663	7.700	7.741	7.781	7.817	7.852	7.889	7.919	7.958	1986	7.958
1987	7.991	8.025	8.063	8.099	8.129	8.169	8.206	8.245	8.282	8.331	8.360	8.393	1987	8.393
1988	8.418	8.456	8.493	8.532	8.576	8.617	8.661	8.712	8.766	8.819	8.869	8.926	1988	8.926
1989	8.975	9.030	9.090	9.152	9.224	9.289	9.354	9.423	9.485	9.549	9.614	9.673	1989	9.673
1990	9.728	9.783	9.846	9.914	9.981	10.043	10.111	10.178	10.238	10.308	10.366	10.429	1990	10.429
1991	10.483	10.533	10.579	10.635	10.685	10.730	10.782	10.832	10.881	10.928	10.970	11.012	1991	11.012
1992	11.049	11.081	11.118	11.154	11.185	11.221	11.255	11.285	11.314	11.340	11.366	11.398	1992	11.398
1993	11.425	11.450	11.479	11.506	11.531	11.561	11.588	11.617	11.647	11.673	11.702	11.728	1993	11.728
1994	11.758	11.783	11.814	11.846	11.884	11.921	11.954	11.998	12.042	12.088	12.132	12.186	1994	12.186
1995	12.237	12.286	12.342	12.397	12.464	12.522	12.579	12.638	12.692	12.752	12.806	12.868	1995	12.868
1996	12.923	12.974	13.025	13.084	13.140	13.192	13.252	13.306	13.365	13.421	13.476	13.538	1996	13.538
1997	13.599	13.652	13.710	13.769	13.837	13.888	13.948	14.005	14.067	14.127	14.182	14.250	1997	14.250
1998	14.311	14.367	14.423	14.485	14.544	14.603	14.662	14.725	14.792	14.840	14.886	14.942	1998	14.942
1999	14.994	15.048	15.112	15.168	15.219	15.280	15.338	15.397	15.457	15.517	15.573	15.641	1999	15.641
2000	15.706	15.774	15.848	15.920	16.001	16.064	16.141	16.223	16.305	16.397	16.480	16.563	2000	16.563
2001	16.652	16.715	16.784	16.850	16.905	16.952	17.004	17.056	17.103	17.142	17.172	17.197	2001	17.197
2002	17.221	17.243	17.266	17.293	17.318	17.340	17.367	17.391	17.416	17.440	17.460	17.480	2002	17.480

Table B-10

Inflation Index

from December 1925 to December 1970

Year	Jan	Feb	Mar	Apr	May	Jun	Jul	Aug	Sep	Oct	Nov	Dec	Yr-end	Index
1925												1.000	1925	1.000
1926	1.000	0.996	0.991	1.000	0.994	0.987	0.978	0.972	0.978	0.981	0.985	0.985	1926	0.985
1927	0.978	0.970	0.965	0.965	0.972	0.981	0.963	0.957	0.963	0.968	0.966	0.965	1927	0.965
1928	0.963	0.953	0.953	0.955	0.961	0.953	0.953	0.955	0.963	0.961	0.959	0.955	1928	0.955
1929	0.953	0.952	0.948	0.944	0.950	0.953	0.963	0.966	0.965	0.965	0.963	0.957	1929	0.957
1930	0.953	0.950	0.944	0.950	0.944	0.939	0.926	0.920	0.926	0.920	0.912	0.899	1930	0.899
1931	0.886	0.873	0.868	0.862	0.853	0.844	0.842	0.840	0.836	0.831	0.821	0.814	1931	0.814
1932	0.797	0.786	0.782	0.777	0.765	0.760	0.760	0.750	0.747	0.741	0.737	0.730	1932	0.730
1933	0.719	0.708	0.702	0.700	0.702	0.709	0.730	0.737	0.737	0.737	0.737	0.734	1933	0.734
1934	0.737	0.743	0.743	0.741	0.743	0.745	0.745	0.747	0.758	0.752	0.750	0.749	1934	0.749
1935	0.760	0.765	0.764	0.771	0.767	0.765	0.762	0.762	0.765	0.765	0.769	0.771	1935	0.771
1936	0.771	0.767	0.764	0.764	0.764	0.771	0.775	0.780	0.782	0.780	0.780	0.780	1936	0.780
1937	0.786	0.788	0.793	0.797	0.801	0.803	0.806	0.808	0.816	0.812	0.806	0.804	1937	0.804
1938	0.793	0.786	0.786	0.790	0.786	0.786	0.788	0.786	0.786	0.782	0.780	0.782	1938	0.782
1939	0.778	0.775	0.773	0.771	0.771	0.771	0.771	0.771	0.786	0.782	0.782	0.778	1939	0.778
1940	0.777	0.782	0.780	0.780	0.782	0.784	0.782	0.780	0.782	0.782	0.782	0.786	1940	0.786
1941	0.786	0.786	0.790	0.797	0.803	0.818	0.821	0.829	0.844	0.853	0.860	0.862	1941	0.862
1942	0.873	0.881	0.892	0.898	0.907	0.909	0.912	0.918	0.920	0.929	0.935	0.942	1942	0.942
1943	0.942	0.944	0.959	0.970	0.978	0.976	0.968	0.965	0.968	0.972	0.970	0.972	1943	0.972
1944	0.970	0.968	0.968	0.974	0.978	0.980	0.985	0.989	0.989	0.989	0.989	0.993	1944	0.993
1945	0.993	0.991	0.991	0.993	1.000	1.009	1.011	1.011	1.007	1.007	1.011	1.015	1945	1.015
1946	1.015	1.011	1.019	1.024	1.030	1.041	1.102	1.127	1.140	1.162	1.190	1.199	1946	1.199
1947	1.199	1.197	1.223	1.223	1.220	1.229	1.240	1.253	1.283	1.283	1.291	1.307	1947	1.307
1948	1.322	1.311	1.307	1.326	1.335	1.345	1.361	1.367	1.367	1.361	1.352	1.343	1948	1.343
1949	1.341	1.326	1.330	1.331	1.330	1.331	1.322	1.326	1.331	1.324	1.326	1.318	1949	1.318
1950	1.313	1.309	1.315	1.317	1.322	1.330	1.343	1.354	1.363	1.371	1.376	1.395	1950	1.395
1951	1.417	1.434	1.439	1.441	1.447	1.445	1.447	1.447	1.456	1.464	1.471	1.477	1951	1.477
1952	1.477	1.467	1.467	1.473	1.475	1.479	1.490	1.492	1.490	1.492	1.492	1.490	1952	1.490
1953	1.486	1.479	1.482	1.484	1.488	1.493	1.497	1.501	1.503	1.507	1.501	1.499	1953	1.499
1954	1.503	1.501	1.499	1.495	1.501	1.503	1.503	1.501	1.497	1.493	1.495	1.492	1954	1.492
1955	1.492	1.492	1.492	1.492	1.492	1.492	1.497	1.493	1.499	1.499	1.501	1.497	1955	1.497
1956	1.495	1.495	1.497	1.499	1.507	1.516	1.527	1.525	1.527	1.536	1.536	1.540	1956	1.540
1957	1.542	1.547	1.551	1.557	1.561	1.570	1.577	1.579	1.581	1.581	1.587	1.587	1957	1.587
1958	1.596	1.598	1.609	1.613	1.613	1.615	1.616	1.615	1.615	1.615	1.616	1.615	1958	1.615
1959	1.616	1.615	1.615	1.616	1.618	1.626	1.629	1.628	1.633	1.639	1.639	1.639	1959	1.639
1960	1.637	1.639	1.639	1.648	1.648	1.652	1.652	1.652	1.654	1.661	1.663	1.663	1960	1.663
1961	1.663	1.663	1.663	1.663	1.663	1.665	1.672	1.670	1.674	1.674	1.674	1.674	1961	1.674
1962	1.674	1.678	1.682	1.685	1.685	1.685	1.689	1.689	1.698	1.696	1.696	1.695	1962	1.695
1963	1.696	1.698	1.700	1.700	1.700	1.708	1.715	1.715	1.715	1.717	1.719	1.723	1963	1.723
1964	1.724	1.723	1.724	1.726	1.726	1.730	1.734	1.732	1.736	1.737	1.741	1.743	1964	1.743
1965	1.743	1.743	1.745	1.750	1.754	1.764	1.765	1.762	1.765	1.767	1.771	1.777	1965	1.777
1966	1.777	1.788	1.793	1.801	1.803	1.808	1.814	1.823	1.827	1.834	1.834	1.836	1966	1.836
1967	1.836	1.838	1.842	1.845	1.851	1.857	1.866	1.872	1.875	1.881	1.886	1.892	1967	1.892
1968	1.899	1.905	1.914	1.920	1.926	1.937	1.946	1.952	1.957	1.968	1.976	1.981	1968	1.981
1969	1.987	1.994	2.011	2.024	2.030	2.043	2.052	2.061	2.071	2.078	2.089	2.102	1969	2.102
1970	2.110	2.121	2.132	2.145	2.155	2.166	2.173	2.177	2.188	2.199	2.207	2.218	1970	2.218

Table B-10 (continued)

Inflation Index

from January 1971 to December 2002

Year	Jan	Feb	Mar	Apr	May	Jun	Jul	Aug	Sep	Oct	Nov	Dec	Yr-end	Index
1971	2.220	2.223	2.231	2.238	2.250	2.263	2.268	2.274	2.276	2.279	2.283	2.292	1971	2.292
1972	2.294	2.305	2.309	2.315	2.322	2.328	2.337	2.341	2.350	2.358	2.363	2.371	1972	2.371
1973	2.378	2.395	2.417	2.434	2.449	2.466	2.471	2.516	2.523	2.544	2.562	2.579	1973	2.579
1974	2.602	2.635	2.665	2.680	2.710	2.736	2.756	2.791	2.825	2.849	2.873	2.894	1974	2.894
1975	2.907	2.927	2.939	2.953	2.967	2.991	3.022	3.032	3.047	3.065	3.084	3.097	1975	3.097
1976	3.104	3.112	3.119	3.132	3.151	3.168	3.186	3.201	3.214	3.227	3.237	3.246	1976	3.246
1977	3.264	3.298	3.318	3.345	3.363	3.386	3.400	3.413	3.426	3.436	3.453	3.466	1977	3.466
1978	3.484	3.508	3.533	3.564	3.600	3.637	3.663	3.682	3.708	3.737	3.758	3.778	1978	3.778
1979	3.812	3.857	3.894	3.939	3.987	4.024	4.076	4.117	4.160	4.197	4.237	4.281	1979	4.281
1980	4.343	4.402	4.466	4.516	4.561	4.611	4.615	4.644	4.687	4.728	4.771	4.812	1980	4.812
1981	4.851	4.901	4.937	4.968	5.009	5.052	5.110	5.149	5.201	5.212	5.227	5.242	1981	5.242
1982	5.261	5.278	5.272	5.294	5.346	5.412	5.441	5.453	5.462	5.477	5.467	5.445	1982	5.445
1983	5.458	5.460	5.464	5.503	5.533	5.551	5.574	5.592	5.620	5.635	5.644	5.652	1983	5.652
1984	5.683	5.710	5.723	5.750	5.767	5.786	5.805	5.829	5.857	5.872	5.872	5.875	1984	5.875
1985	5.886	5.911	5.937	5.961	5.983	6.002	6.011	6.024	6.043	6.061	6.082	6.097	1985	6.097
1986	6.115	6.099	6.071	6.058	6.076	6.106	6.108	6.119	6.149	6.155	6.160	6.166	1986	6.166
1987	6.203	6.227	6.255	6.289	6.307	6.333	6.346	6.382	6.413	6.430	6.439	6.438	1987	6.438
1988	6.454	6.471	6.499	6.532	6.555	6.583	6.610	6.638	6.683	6.705	6.711	6.722	1988	6.722
1989	6.756	6.783	6.822	6.867	6.906	6.923	6.940	6.951	6.973	7.007	7.023	7.034	1989	7.034
1990	7.107	7.140	7.180	7.191	7.207	7.246	7.274	7.341	7.403	7.447	7.464	7.464	1990	7.464
1991	7.509	7.520	7.531	7.542	7.564	7.587	7.598	7.620	7.654	7.665	7.687	7.693	1991	7.693
1992	7.704	7.732	7.771	7.782	7.793	7.821	7.838	7.860	7.882	7.910	7.921	7.916	1992	7.916
1993	7.955	7.983	8.011	8.033	8.044	8.055	8.055	8.078	8.094	8.128	8.133	8.133	1993	8.133
1994	8.156	8.184	8.212	8.223	8.228	8.256	8.278	8.312	8.334	8.340	8.351	8.351	1994	8.351
1995	8.384	8.418	8.446	8.474	8.490	8.507	8.507	8.530	8.546	8.574	8.569	8.563	1995	8.563
1996	8.613	8.641	8.686	8.719	8.736	8.741	8.758	8.775	8.803	8.831	8.847	8.847	1996	8.847
1997	8.875	8.903	8.926	8.937	8.931	8.942	8.953	8.970	8.993	9.015	9.009	8.998	1997	8.998
1998	9.015	9.032	9.048	9.065	9.082	9.093	9.104	9.115	9.126	9.149	9.149	9.143	1998	9.143
1999	9.165	9.177	9.204	9.271	9.271	9.271	9.299	9.322	9.366	9.383	9.389	9.389	1999	9.389
2000	9.411	9.467	9.545	9.550	9.556	9.612	9.628	9.640	9.690	9.707	9.712	9.707	2000	9.707
2001	9.768	9.807	9.829	9.868	9.913	9.930	9.902	9.902	9.946	9.913	9.896	9.857	2001	9.857
2002	9.879	9.919	9.974	10.030	10.030	10.036	10.047	10.080	10.097	10.114	10.114	10.091	2002	10.091

Stocks, Bonds, Bills, and Inflation

−7.2	7.2	−6.7	6.1	−6.4	−7.1
7.2	7.2	6.7	6.1	6.4	7.1
7.3	−7.3	6.8	6.2	−6.5	−7.2
7.1	7.1	6.6	6.0	6.3	7.0
7.3	7.3	−6.9	−6.3	6.6	7.2
7.4	−7.3	6.9	6.3	−6.6	−7.3
−7.2	7.2	−6.7	6.2	−6.5	7.1
7.2	−7.2	6.8	−6.2	−6.5	7.1

Appendix C

7.3	−7.3	−6.9	6.3	6.6	−7.2
−7.2	7.2	6.8	−6.3	−6.6	7.1
7.0	−7.0	−6.6	−6.1	6.4	−6.9
−7.4	7.4	−7.0	−6.5	6.7	−7.3
7.5	−7.5	−7.1	6.6	−6.9	7.4
−7.8	7.8	−7.4	−6.9	−7.2	−7.7
−8.0	8.0	−7.6	7.1	−7.4	7.9
8.1	−8.1	7.7	−7.3	7.5	−8.0
9.2	−9.2	8.7	−8.5	−8.9	9.1

IbbotsonAssociates

Appendix C

Rates of Return for All Yearly Holding Periods: 1926–2002

Basic Series: Total Rates of Return for All Holding Periods

Each table in this section consists of six pages.

Table C-1 (page 1 of 6)

Large Company Stocks Total Returns
Rates of Return for all holding periods
Percent per annum compounded annually

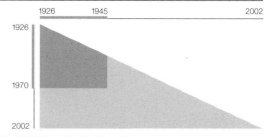

from 1926 to 2002

To the end of	From the beginning of 1926	1927	1928	1929	1930	1931	1932	1933	1934	1935	1936	1937	1938	1939	1940	1941	1942	1943	1944	1945
1926	11.6																			
1927	23.9	37.5																		
1928	30.1	40.5	43.6																	
1929	19.2	21.8	14.7	−8.4																
1930	8.7	8.0	−0.4	−17.1	−24.9															
1931	−2.5	−5.1	−13.5	−27.0	−34.8	−43.3														
1932	−3.3	−5.6	−12.5	−22.7	−26.9	−27.9	−8.2													
1933	2.5	1.2	−3.8	−11.2	−11.9	−7.1	18.9	54.0												
1934	2.0	0.9	−3.5	−9.7	−9.9	−5.7	11.7	23.2	−1.4											
1935	5.9	5.2	1.8	−3.1	−2.2	3.1	19.8	30.9	20.6	47.7										
1936	8.1	7.8	4.9	0.9	2.3	7.7	22.5	31.6	24.9	40.6	33.9									
1937	3.7	3.0	0.0	−3.9	−3.3	0.2	10.2	14.3	6.1	8.7	−6.7	−35.0								
1938	5.5	5.1	2.5	−0.9	0.0	3.6	13.0	16.9	10.7	13.9	4.5	−7.7	31.1							
1939	5.1	4.6	2.3	−0.8	−0.1	3.2	11.2	14.3	8.7	10.9	3.2	−5.3	14.3	−0.4						
1940	4.0	3.5	1.3	−1.6	−1.0	1.8	8.6	11.0	5.9	7.2	0.5	−6.5	5.6	−5.2	−9.8					
1941	3.0	2.4	0.3	−2.4	−1.9	0.5	6.4	8.2	3.5	4.3	−1.6	−7.5	1.0	−7.4	−10.7	−11.6				
1942	3.9	3.5	1.5	−1.0	−0.4	2.0	7.6	9.3	5.3	6.1	1.2	−3.4	4.6	−1.1	−1.4	3.1	20.3			
1943	5.0	4.7	2.9	0.6	1.3	3.7	9.0	10.8	7.2	8.2	4.0	0.4	7.9	3.8	4.8	10.2	23.1	25.9		
1944	5.8	5.5	3.8	1.7	2.5	4.8	9.8	11.5	8.3	9.3	5.7	2.6	9.5	6.3	7.7	12.5	22.0	22.8	19.8	
1945	7.1	6.9	5.4	3.5	4.3	6.6	11.5	13.2	10.4	11.5	8.4	5.9	12.6	10.1	12.0	17.0	25.4	27.2	27.8	36.4
1946	6.4	6.1	4.7	2.8	3.5	5.6	10.1	11.6	8.8	9.7	6.8	4.4	10.1	7.7	8.9	12.4	17.9	17.3	14.5	12.0
1947	6.3	6.1	4.7	3.0	3.7	5.6	9.8	11.2	8.6	9.4	6.7	4.5	9.6	7.5	8.5	11.4	15.8	14.9	12.3	9.9
1948	6.3	6.1	4.7	3.1	3.8	5.6	9.6	10.8	8.4	9.1	6.6	4.6	9.2	7.3	8.2	10.6	14.2	13.2	10.9	8.8
1949	6.8	6.6	5.3	3.8	4.5	6.3	10.1	11.2	9.0	9.7	7.4	5.6	10.0	8.3	9.2	11.5	14.8	14.0	12.2	10.7
1950	7.7	7.5	6.4	4.9	5.6	7.4	11.1	12.3	10.2	11.0	8.9	7.3	11.5	10.0	11.0	13.4	16.6	16.1	14.8	13.9
1951	8.3	8.1	7.1	5.7	6.4	8.2	11.7	12.9	11.0	11.7	9.8	8.4	12.4	11.1	12.1	14.3	17.3	16.9	15.9	15.3
1952	8.6	8.5	7.5	6.2	6.9	8.6	12.0	13.2	11.3	12.1	10.3	9.0	12.8	11.6	12.5	14.6	17.4	17.1	16.1	15.7
1953	8.3	8.1	7.2	5.9	6.5	8.2	11.4	12.4	10.7	11.4	9.6	8.3	11.9	10.7	11.5	13.4	15.7	15.3	14.3	13.7
1954	9.6	9.5	8.6	7.4	8.1	9.7	12.9	14.0	12.4	13.1	11.6	10.4	13.9	12.9	13.9	15.8	18.2	18.0	17.4	17.1
1955	10.2	10.2	9.3	8.2	8.9	10.5	13.7	14.7	13.2	13.9	12.5	11.4	14.8	13.9	14.9	16.8	19.1	19.0	18.5	18.4
1956	10.1	10.1	9.2	8.2	8.8	10.4	13.4	14.4	12.9	13.6	12.2	11.2	14.4	13.5	14.4	16.1	18.2	18.1	17.5	17.3
1957	9.4	9.3	8.5	7.4	8.1	9.5	12.3	13.2	11.8	12.4	11.0	10.0	13.0	12.1	12.8	14.3	16.2	15.9	15.2	14.9
1958	10.3	10.2	9.5	8.5	9.1	10.6	13.3	14.3	12.9	13.6	12.3	11.4	14.3	13.5	14.3	15.8	17.6	17.5	16.9	16.7
1959	10.3	10.3	9.5	8.6	9.2	10.6	13.3	14.2	12.9	13.5	12.3	11.4	14.2	13.4	14.1	15.6	17.3	17.1	16.6	16.4
1960	10.0	10.0	9.3	8.3	8.9	10.3	12.8	13.7	12.4	13.0	11.8	10.9	13.5	12.8	13.5	14.8	16.4	16.1	15.6	15.3
1961	10.5	10.4	9.7	8.8	9.4	10.8	13.3	14.1	12.9	13.4	12.3	11.5	14.1	13.4	14.0	15.3	16.9	16.7	16.2	16.0
1962	9.9	9.9	9.2	8.3	8.8	10.1	12.5	13.2	12.1	12.6	11.4	10.7	13.0	12.3	12.9	14.1	15.5	15.3	14.7	14.4
1963	10.2	10.2	9.5	8.7	9.2	10.5	12.8	13.5	12.4	12.9	11.8	11.1	13.4	12.7	13.3	14.5	15.8	15.6	15.1	14.9
1964	10.4	10.4	9.7	8.9	9.4	10.6	12.9	13.6	12.5	13.0	12.0	11.3	13.5	12.9	13.5	14.5	15.8	15.6	15.2	14.9
1965	10.4	10.4	9.8	9.0	9.5	10.7	12.9	13.6	12.5	13.0	12.0	11.3	13.5	12.9	13.4	14.5	15.7	15.5	15.0	14.8
1966	9.9	9.8	9.2	8.4	8.9	10.1	12.2	12.8	11.8	12.2	11.2	10.5	12.6	12.0	12.4	13.4	14.5	14.3	13.8	13.6
1967	10.2	10.2	9.6	8.8	9.3	10.4	12.5	13.1	12.1	12.5	11.6	10.9	12.9	12.4	12.8	13.8	14.9	14.7	14.2	14.0
1968	10.2	10.2	9.6	8.9	9.3	10.4	12.4	13.1	12.1	12.5	11.6	10.9	12.9	12.3	12.8	13.7	14.7	14.5	14.1	13.9
1969	9.8	9.7	9.1	8.4	8.9	9.9	11.8	12.4	11.4	11.8	10.9	10.3	12.1	11.6	12.0	12.8	13.8	13.6	13.1	12.9
1970	9.6	9.6	9.0	8.3	8.7	9.7	11.6	12.2	11.2	11.6	10.7	10.1	11.9	11.3	11.7	12.5	13.5	13.2	12.8	12.5

Table C-1 (page 2 of 6)

Large Company Stocks Total Returns
Rates of Return for all holding periods
Percent per annum compounded annually

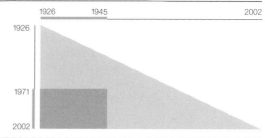

From 1926 to 2002

To the end of	From the beginning of 1926	1927	1928	1929	1930	1931	1932	1933	1934	1935	1936	1937	1938	1939	1940	1941	1942	1943	1944	1945
1971	9.7	9.7	9.1	8.4	8.9	9.9	11.7	12.2	11.3	11.7	10.8	10.2	11.9	11.4	11.8	12.6	13.5	13.3	12.8	12.6
1972	9.9	9.9	9.3	8.7	9.1	10.1	11.9	12.4	11.5	11.9	11.0	10.5	12.1	11.6	12.0	12.8	13.7	13.5	13.0	12.8
1973	9.3	9.3	8.7	8.1	8.5	9.4	11.1	11.7	10.8	11.1	10.3	9.7	11.3	10.8	11.1	11.8	12.7	12.4	12.0	11.7
1974	8.5	8.4	7.8	7.2	7.5	8.4	10.1	10.6	9.7	10.0	9.1	8.5	10.1	9.5	9.8	10.5	11.2	10.9	10.5	10.2
1975	9.0	8.9	8.4	7.7	8.1	9.0	10.6	11.1	10.2	10.6	9.8	9.2	10.7	10.2	10.5	11.1	11.9	11.6	11.2	11.0
1976	9.2	9.2	8.7	8.0	8.4	9.3	10.9	11.4	10.5	10.9	10.1	9.5	11.0	10.5	10.8	11.5	12.2	12.0	11.6	11.3
1977	8.9	8.8	8.3	7.7	8.1	8.9	10.5	10.9	10.1	10.4	9.6	9.1	10.5	10.0	10.3	10.9	11.6	11.4	11.0	10.7
1978	8.9	8.8	8.3	7.7	8.0	8.9	10.4	10.8	10.0	10.3	9.6	9.0	10.4	9.9	10.2	10.8	11.5	11.3	10.9	10.6
1979	9.0	9.0	8.5	7.9	8.2	9.1	10.6	11.0	10.2	10.5	9.8	9.2	10.6	10.1	10.4	11.0	11.7	11.4	11.1	10.8
1980	9.4	9.4	8.9	8.3	8.7	9.5	11.0	11.4	10.6	10.9	10.2	9.7	11.1	10.6	10.9	11.5	12.2	11.9	11.6	11.4
1981	9.1	9.1	8.6	8.1	8.4	9.2	10.6	11.0	10.3	10.6	9.9	9.4	10.7	10.2	10.5	11.1	11.7	11.5	11.1	10.9
1982	9.3	9.3	8.8	8.3	8.6	9.4	10.8	11.2	10.5	10.8	10.1	9.6	10.9	10.5	10.8	11.3	11.9	11.7	11.4	11.2
1983	9.6	9.5	9.1	8.5	8.9	9.6	11.0	11.5	10.7	11.0	10.3	9.9	11.1	10.7	11.0	11.5	12.2	12.0	11.6	11.4
1984	9.5	9.5	9.0	8.5	8.8	9.6	10.9	11.3	10.6	10.9	10.3	9.8	11.0	10.6	10.9	11.4	12.0	11.8	11.5	11.3
1985	9.8	9.8	9.4	8.9	9.2	9.9	11.3	11.7	11.0	11.3	10.7	10.2	11.4	11.1	11.3	11.8	12.4	12.3	12.0	11.8
1986	10.0	9.9	9.5	9.0	9.4	10.1	11.4	11.8	11.2	11.4	10.8	10.4	11.6	11.2	11.5	12.0	12.6	12.4	12.1	11.9
1987	9.9	9.9	9.5	9.0	9.3	10.0	11.3	11.7	11.0	11.3	10.7	10.3	11.5	11.1	11.3	11.8	12.4	12.2	11.9	11.8
1988	10.0	10.0	9.6	9.1	9.4	10.1	11.4	11.8	11.1	11.4	10.8	10.4	11.6	11.2	11.4	11.9	12.5	12.3	12.1	11.9
1989	10.3	10.3	9.9	9.4	9.7	10.5	11.7	12.1	11.5	11.7	11.2	10.8	11.9	11.6	11.8	12.3	12.9	12.7	12.4	12.3
1990	10.1	10.1	9.7	9.2	9.5	10.2	11.5	11.8	11.2	11.4	10.9	10.5	11.6	11.3	11.5	12.0	12.5	12.4	12.1	11.9
1991	10.4	10.4	10.0	9.5	9.8	10.5	11.8	12.1	11.5	11.8	11.2	10.8	11.9	11.6	11.8	12.3	12.9	12.7	12.4	12.3
1992	10.3	10.3	9.9	9.5	9.8	10.5	11.7	12.1	11.4	11.7	11.1	10.8	11.8	11.5	11.8	12.2	12.7	12.6	12.3	12.2
1993	10.3	10.3	9.9	9.5	9.8	10.5	11.7	12.0	11.4	11.7	11.1	10.8	11.8	11.5	11.7	12.2	12.7	12.5	12.3	12.1
1994	10.2	10.2	9.8	9.4	9.7	10.3	11.5	11.8	11.3	11.5	10.9	10.6	11.6	11.3	11.5	12.0	12.5	12.3	12.1	11.9
1995	10.5	10.5	10.2	9.7	10.0	10.7	11.9	12.2	11.6	11.9	11.3	11.0	12.0	11.7	11.9	12.4	12.9	12.7	12.5	12.4
1996	10.7	10.7	10.3	9.9	10.2	10.9	12.0	12.4	11.8	12.0	11.5	11.2	12.2	11.9	12.1	12.6	13.1	12.9	12.7	12.6
1997	11.0	11.0	10.6	10.2	10.5	11.2	12.3	12.7	12.1	12.3	11.8	11.5	12.5	12.2	12.5	12.9	13.4	13.3	13.1	12.9
1998	11.2	11.2	10.9	10.5	10.8	11.4	12.5	12.9	12.3	12.6	12.1	11.8	12.8	12.5	12.7	13.2	13.6	13.5	13.3	13.2
1999	11.3	11.3	11.0	10.6	10.9	11.5	12.7	13.0	12.5	12.7	12.2	11.9	12.9	12.6	12.9	13.3	13.8	13.7	13.5	13.3
2000	11.0	11.0	10.7	10.3	10.6	11.2	12.3	12.6	12.1	12.3	11.9	11.6	12.5	12.2	12.5	12.9	13.3	13.2	13.0	12.9
2001	10.7	10.7	10.4	10.0	10.3	10.9	11.9	12.2	11.7	11.9	11.5	11.1	12.1	11.8	12.0	12.4	12.9	12.7	12.5	12.4
2002	10.2	10.2	9.9	9.5	9.7	10.3	11.4	11.7	11.1	11.3	10.9	10.6	11.5	11.2	11.4	11.7	12.2	12.0	11.8	11.7

Table C-1 (page 3 of 6)

Large Company Stocks Total Returns
Rates of Return for all holding periods
Percent per annum compounded annually

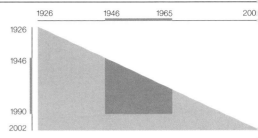

from 1926 to 2002

To the end of	From the beginning of 1946	1947	1948	1949	1950	1951	1952	1953	1954	1955	1956	1957	1958	1959	1960	1961	1962	1963	1964	196
1946	-8.1																			
1947	-1.4	5.7																		
1948	0.8	5.6	5.5																	
1949	5.1	9.8	11.9	18.8																
1950	9.9	14.9	18.2	25.1	31.7															
1951	12.1	16.7	19.6	24.7	27.8	24.0														
1952	13.0	17.0	19.4	23.1	24.6	21.2	18.4													
1953	11.2	14.2	15.7	17.9	17.6	13.3	8.3	-1.0												
1954	15.1	18.4	20.4	23.0	23.9	22.0	21.4	22.9	52.6											
1955	16.7	19.8	21.7	24.2	25.2	23.9	23.9	25.7	41.7	31.6										
1956	15.7	18.4	19.9	21.9	22.3	20.8	20.2	20.6	28.9	18.4	6.6									
1957	13.2	15.4	16.4	17.7	17.6	15.7	14.4	13.6	17.5	7.7	-2.5	-10.8								
1958	15.3	17.5	18.7	20.1	20.2	18.8	18.1	18.1	22.3	15.7	10.9	13.1	43.4							
1959	15.1	17.1	18.1	19.3	19.4	18.1	17.3	17.2	20.5	15.0	11.1	12.7	26.7	12.0						
1960	14.0	15.8	16.6	17.6	17.5	16.2	15.3	14.9	17.4	12.4	8.9	9.5	17.3	6.1	0.5					
1961	14.8	16.5	17.3	18.3	18.3	17.1	16.4	16.2	18.6	14.4	11.7	12.8	19.6	12.6	12.9	26.9				
1962	13.3	14.8	15.4	16.1	15.9	14.7	13.9	13.4	15.2	11.2	8.5	8.9	13.3	6.8	5.2	7.6	-8.7			
1963	13.8	15.2	15.8	16.6	16.4	15.3	14.6	14.3	15.9	12.4	10.2	10.8	14.8	9.9	9.3	12.5	5.9	22.8		
1964	13.9	15.3	15.9	16.6	16.4	15.4	14.7	14.4	16.0	12.8	10.9	11.5	15.1	10.9	10.7	13.5	9.3	19.6	16.5	
1965	13.8	15.1	15.7	16.3	16.2	15.2	14.6	14.3	15.7	12.8	11.1	11.6	14.7	11.1	11.0	13.2	10.1	17.2	14.4	12.
1966	12.6	13.7	14.2	14.7	14.4	13.4	12.7	12.4	13.4	10.7	9.0	9.2	11.7	8.2	7.7	9.0	5.7	9.7	5.6	0.
1967	13.1	14.2	14.6	15.1	14.9	14.0	13.4	13.1	14.2	11.6	10.1	10.5	12.8	9.9	9.6	11.0	8.6	12.4	9.9	7.
1968	13.0	14.0	14.5	14.9	14.7	13.8	13.3	13.0	14.0	11.6	10.2	10.5	12.7	10.0	9.8	11.0	8.9	12.2	10.2	8.
1969	12.0	13.0	13.3	13.7	13.4	12.5	11.9	11.6	12.4	10.1	8.7	8.9	10.7	8.2	7.8	8.7	6.6	9.0	6.8	5.
1970	11.7	12.6	12.9	13.2	13.0	12.1	11.5	11.1	11.9	9.7	8.4	8.6	10.2	7.8	7.5	8.2	6.3	8.3	6.4	4.
1971	11.8	12.6	12.9	13.3	13.0	12.2	11.6	11.3	12.0	10.0	8.8	8.9	10.5	8.3	8.0	8.0	7.1	9.0	7.4	6.
1972	12.0	12.9	13.2	13.5	13.3	12.5	12.0	11.7	12.4	10.5	9.4	9.5	11.0	9.0	8.8	9.5	8.1	9.9	8.6	7.
1973	10.9	11.7	11.9	12.2	11.9	11.2	10.6	10.3	10.8	9.0	7.9	7.9	9.2	7.3	6.9	7.5	6.0	7.4	6.0	4.
1974	9.4	10.1	10.2	10.4	10.1	9.3	8.7	8.2	8.7	6.9	5.7	5.7	6.7	4.8	4.3	4.6	3.0	4.1	2.5	1.
1975	10.2	10.9	11.1	11.3	11.0	10.3	9.7	9.4	9.9	8.2	7.1	7.1	8.2	6.4	6.1	6.5	5.2	6.3	5.1	4.
1976	10.6	11.3	11.5	11.7	11.5	10.8	10.3	9.9	10.4	8.8	7.8	7.9	9.0	7.3	7.1	7.5	6.3	7.5	6.4	5.
1977	10.0	10.7	10.8	11.0	10.7	10.0	9.5	9.2	9.6	8.1	7.1	7.1	8.1	6.5	6.2	6.6	5.4	6.4	5.4	4.
1978	9.9	10.5	10.7	10.9	10.6	9.9	9.4	9.1	9.5	8.0	7.1	7.1	8.0	6.5	6.2	6.6	5.5	6.5	5.4	4.
1979	10.2	10.8	10.9	11.1	10.8	10.2	9.7	9.4	9.8	8.4	7.5	7.6	8.5	7.1	6.8	7.2	6.2	7.1	6.2	5.
1980	10.7	11.3	11.5	11.7	11.5	10.9	10.4	10.2	10.6	9.2	8.4	8.5	9.4	8.1	7.9	8.3	7.4	8.4	7.6	7.
1981	10.3	10.8	11.0	11.2	10.9	10.3	9.9	9.6	10.0	8.7	7.9	7.9	8.8	7.5	7.3	7.6	6.8	7.6	6.9	6.
1982	10.6	11.1	11.3	11.5	11.2	10.7	10.2	10.0	10.4	9.1	8.4	8.4	9.3	8.1	7.9	8.2	7.4	8.3	7.6	7.
1983	10.9	11.4	11.6	11.8	11.6	11.0	10.6	10.4	10.8	9.6	8.8	8.9	9.8	8.6	8.5	8.8	8.1	8.9	8.3	7.
1984	10.7	11.3	11.4	11.6	11.4	10.9	10.5	10.2	10.6	9.4	8.7	8.8	9.6	8.5	8.4	8.7	8.0	8.8	8.2	7.
1985	11.2	11.8	11.9	12.1	11.9	11.4	11.1	10.8	11.2	10.1	9.5	9.6	10.4	9.3	9.2	9.6	8.9	9.7	9.2	8.
1986	11.4	11.9	12.1	12.3	12.1	11.6	11.3	11.1	11.4	10.4	9.7	9.8	10.6	9.6	9.5	9.9	9.3	10.1	9.6	9.
1987	11.2	11.8	11.9	12.1	11.9	11.4	11.1	10.9	11.3	10.2	9.6	9.7	10.4	9.5	9.4	9.7	9.1	9.9	9.4	9.
1988	11.4	11.9	12.0	12.2	12.0	11.6	11.2	11.1	11.4	10.4	9.8	9.9	10.6	9.7	9.6	10.0	9.4	10.1	9.7	9.
1989	11.8	12.3	12.5	12.6	12.5	12.0	11.7	11.6	11.9	10.9	10.4	10.5	11.2	10.3	10.3	10.6	10.1	10.9	10.4	10.
1990	11.4	11.9	12.1	12.2	12.1	11.6	11.3	11.1	11.5	10.5	10.0	10.1	10.8	9.9	9.8	10.2	9.6	10.3	9.9	9.

Table C-1 (page 4 of 6)

Large Company Stocks Total Returns
Rates of Return for all holding periods
Percent per annum compounded annually

From 1926 to 2002

To the end of	From the beginning of																			
	1946	1947	1948	1949	1950	1951	1952	1953	1954	1955	1956	1957	1958	1959	1960	1961	1962	1963	1964	1965
1991	11.8	12.3	12.5	12.6	12.5	12.1	11.8	11.6	12.0	11.0	10.5	10.6	11.3	10.5	10.4	10.8	10.3	11.0	10.6	10.4
1992	11.7	12.2	12.4	12.5	12.4	11.9	11.7	11.5	11.8	10.9	10.4	10.5	11.2	10.4	10.3	10.7	10.2	10.9	10.5	10.3
1993	11.7	12.2	12.3	12.5	12.3	11.9	11.6	11.5	11.8	10.9	10.4	10.5	11.2	10.4	10.3	10.6	10.2	10.8	10.5	10.3
1994	11.5	11.9	12.1	12.2	12.1	11.6	11.4	11.2	11.5	10.7	10.2	10.3	10.9	10.1	10.1	10.4	9.9	10.5	10.2	9.9
1995	11.9	12.4	12.5	12.7	12.6	12.2	11.9	11.8	12.1	11.2	10.8	10.9	11.5	10.8	10.7	11.0	10.6	11.3	10.9	10.7
1996	12.1	12.6	12.7	12.9	12.8	12.4	12.1	12.0	12.3	11.5	11.1	11.2	11.8	11.1	11.1	11.4	10.9	11.6	11.3	11.1
1997	12.5	13.0	13.1	13.3	13.2	12.8	12.6	12.4	12.8	12.0	11.5	11.7	12.3	11.6	11.6	11.9	11.5	12.2	11.9	11.7
1998	12.8	13.2	13.4	13.6	13.5	13.1	12.9	12.8	13.1	12.3	11.9	12.0	12.7	12.0	12.0	12.3	11.9	12.6	12.3	12.2
1999	13.0	13.4	13.5	13.7	13.6	13.3	13.1	12.9	13.3	12.5	12.1	12.2	12.9	12.2	12.2	12.5	12.2	12.8	12.5	12.4
2000	12.5	12.9	13.1	13.2	13.1	12.8	12.5	12.4	12.7	12.0	11.6	11.7	12.3	11.6	11.6	11.9	11.6	12.2	11.9	11.8
2001	12.0	12.4	12.5	12.7	12.6	12.2	12.0	11.9	12.2	11.4	11.0	11.1	11.7	11.0	11.0	11.3	10.9	11.5	11.2	11.1
2002	11.3	11.7	11.8	11.9	11.8	11.4	11.2	11.1	11.3	10.6	10.2	10.3	10.8	10.1	10.1	10.3	10.0	10.5	10.2	10.0

Table C-1 (page 5 of 6)

Large Company Stocks Total Returns
Rates of Return for all holding periods
Percent per annum compounded annually

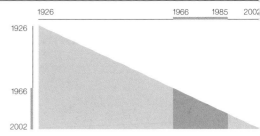

from 1926 to 2002

To the end of	From the beginning of 1966	1967	1968	1969	1970	1971	1972	1973	1974	1975	1976	1977	1978	1979	1980	1981	1982	1983	1984	1985
1966	-10.1																			
1967	5.6	24.0																		
1968	7.4	17.3	11.1																	
1969	3.2	8.0	0.8	-8.5																
1970	3.3	7.0	1.9	-2.4	4.0															
1971	5.1	8.4	4.8	2.8	9.0	14.3														
1972	7.0	10.1	7.5	6.7	12.3	16.6	19.0													
1973	4.0	6.2	3.5	2.0	4.8	5.1	0.8	-14.7												
1974	0.1	1.4	-1.5	-3.4	-2.4	-3.9	-9.3	-20.8	-26.5											
1975	3.3	4.9	2.7	1.6	3.3	3.2	0.6	-4.9	0.4	37.2										
1976	5.0	6.6	4.9	4.1	6.0	6.4	4.9	1.6	7.7	30.4	23.8									
1977	3.9	5.3	3.6	2.8	4.3	4.3	2.8	-0.2	3.8	16.4	7.2	-7.2								
1978	4.1	5.4	3.9	3.2	4.5	4.6	3.3	0.9	4.3	13.9	7.0	-0.5	6.6							
1979	5.1	6.3	5.0	4.5	5.9	6.1	5.1	3.2	6.6	14.8	9.7	5.4	12.3	18.4						
1980	6.7	8.0	6.9	6.5	8.0	8.4	7.8	6.5	9.9	17.5	13.9	11.6	18.7	25.2	32.4					
1981	5.9	7.1	6.0	5.6	6.9	7.2	6.5	5.2	7.9	14.0	10.6	8.1	12.3	14.3	12.2	-4.9				
1982	6.8	8.0	7.0	6.7	7.9	8.3	7.7	6.7	9.4	14.9	12.1	10.2	14.0	16.0	15.2	7.4	21.4			
1983	7.6	8.8	7.9	7.7	8.9	9.3	8.9	8.0	10.6	15.7	13.3	11.9	15.4	17.3	17.0	12.3	22.0	22.5		
1984	7.5	8.6	7.8	7.6	8.7	9.1	8.7	7.9	10.2	14.8	12.5	11.2	14.1	15.4	14.8	10.7	16.5	14.1	6.3	
1985	8.7	9.7	9.0	8.9	10.1	10.5	10.2	9.6	11.9	16.2	14.3	13.3	16.2	17.6	17.5	14.7	20.2	19.8	18.5	32.2
1986	9.1	10.2	9.5	9.4	10.6	11.0	10.8	10.2	12.4	16.4	14.7	13.8	16.4	17.7	17.6	15.3	19.9	19.5	18.5	25.
1987	8.9	9.9	9.3	9.2	10.3	10.6	10.4	9.9	11.9	15.5	13.9	13.0	15.3	16.3	16.0	13.8	17.3	16.5	15.0	18.
1988	9.3	10.2	9.6	9.5	10.6	11.0	10.8	10.3	12.2	15.6	14.1	13.3	15.4	16.3	16.1	14.2	17.2	16.5	15.4	17.8
1989	10.1	11.1	10.5	10.5	11.5	12.0	11.8	11.4	13.3	16.6	15.3	14.6	16.7	17.6	17.5	16.0	18.9	18.6	17.9	20.4
1990	9.5	10.4	9.9	9.8	10.8	11.2	11.0	10.6	12.3	15.3	13.9	13.3	15.0	15.7	15.5	13.9	16.2	15.6	14.6	16.
1991	10.3	11.2	10.7	10.7	11.6	12.0	11.9	11.5	13.2	16.1	14.9	14.3	16.0	16.8	16.7	15.3	17.6	17.2	16.5	18.
1992	10.2	11.1	10.6	10.5	11.5	11.8	11.7	11.3	12.9	15.6	14.5	13.9	15.5	16.1	16.0	14.7	16.7	16.2	15.5	16.
1993	10.2	11.0	10.5	10.5	11.4	11.7	11.6	11.3	12.8	15.3	14.2	13.7	15.1	15.7	15.5	14.3	16.1	15.6	14.9	16.0
1994	9.9	10.6	10.2	10.1	11.0	11.3	11.1	10.8	12.2	14.6	13.5	12.9	14.3	14.8	14.5	13.3	14.9	14.3	13.6	14.4
1995	10.7	11.5	11.1	11.1	11.9	12.2	12.1	11.8	13.2	15.6	14.6	14.1	15.4	16.0	15.8	14.8	16.4	16.0	15.4	16.3
1996	11.1	11.8	11.5	11.5	12.3	12.6	12.5	12.3	13.6	15.9	15.0	14.6	15.8	16.4	16.2	15.3	16.8	16.5	16.0	16.9
1997	11.7	12.5	12.1	12.2	13.0	13.3	13.3	13.1	14.4	16.6	15.8	15.4	16.6	17.2	17.1	16.3	17.8	17.5	17.2	18.
1998	12.2	13.0	12.6	12.7	13.5	13.8	13.8	13.6	14.9	17.1	16.3	16.0	17.2	17.7	17.7	16.9	18.4	18.2	17.9	18.
1999	12.4	13.2	12.9	12.9	13.7	14.1	14.1	13.9	15.2	17.2	16.5	16.2	17.4	17.9	17.9	17.2	18.5	18.4	18.1	18.
2000	11.7	12.5	12.1	12.2	12.9	13.2	13.2	13.0	14.2	16.1	15.3	15.0	16.1	16.5	16.4	15.7	16.9	16.6	16.3	17.
2001	11.0	11.7	11.3	11.3	12.0	12.3	12.2	12.0	13.1	14.9	14.1	13.8	14.7	15.1	15.0	14.2	15.2	14.9	14.5	15.
2002	10.0	10.6	10.2	10.2	10.8	11.0	10.9	10.7	11.7	13.3	12.5	12.1	13.0	13.3	13.0	12.2	13.1	12.7	12.2	12.

Table C-1 (page 6 of 6)

Large Company Stocks Total Returns
Rates of Return for all holding periods
Percent per annum compounded annually

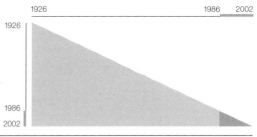

from 1926 to 2002

To the end of	From the beginning of 1986	1987	1988	1989	1990	1991	1992	1993	1994	1995	1996	1997	1998	1999	2000	2001	2002
1986	18.5																
1987	11.7	5.2															
1988	13.3	10.9	16.8														
1989	17.6	17.4	23.9	31.5													
1990	13.1	11.8	14.1	12.8	−3.2												
1991	15.9	15.4	18.0	18.5	12.4	30.5											
1992	14.7	14.0	15.9	15.7	10.8	18.6	7.7										
1993	14.1	13.5	14.9	14.5	10.6	15.6	8.8	10.0									
1994	12.6	11.9	12.8	12.2	8.7	11.9	6.3	5.6	1.3								
1995	14.8	14.4	15.7	15.5	13.0	16.6	13.3	15.3	18.0	37.4							
1996	15.6	15.3	16.5	16.4	14.4	17.6	15.2	17.2	19.7	30.1	23.1						
1997	17.0	16.8	18.0	18.2	16.6	19.8	18.0	20.2	23.0	31.1	28.1	33.4					
1998	17.8	17.8	19.0	19.2	17.9	20.8	19.5	21.6	24.1	30.5	28.3	31.0	28.6				
1999	18.0	18.0	19.1	19.4	18.2	20.9	19.7	21.5	23.5	28.6	26.4	27.6	24.8	21.0			
2000	16.0	15.8	16.7	16.7	15.4	17.5	16.1	17.2	18.2	21.3	18.4	17.2	12.3	4.9	−9.1		
2001	14.0	13.7	14.4	14.2	12.8	14.4	12.9	13.5	14.0	15.9	12.7	10.7	5.7	−1.0	−10.5	−11.9	
2002	11.5	11.1	11.5	11.1	9.7	10.8	9.2	9.3	9.3	10.3	6.9	4.4	−0.6	−6.8	−14.6	−17.2	−22.1

Table C-2 (Page 1 of 6)

Small Company Stocks Total Returns
Rates of Return for all holding periods
Percent per annum compounded annually

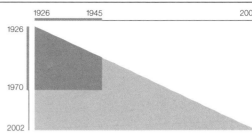

from 1926 to 2002

To the end of	From the beginning of 1926	1927	1928	1929	1930	1931	1932	1933	1934	1935	1936	1937	1938	1939	1940	1941	1942	1943	1944	1945
1926	0.3																			
1927	10.7	22.1																		
1928	19.6	30.6	39.7																	
1929	−4.5	−6.0	−17.6	−51.4																
1930	−12.4	−15.4	−25.1	−45.1	−38.1															
1931	−20.2	−23.7	−32.2	−46.7	−44.3	−49.8														
1932	−18.2	−21.0	−27.5	−38.5	−33.5	−31.1	−5.4													
1933	−6.3	−7.2	−11.4	−19.1	−8.1	4.9	51.6	142.9												
1934	−3.3	−3.8	−7.0	−13.1	−2.4	9.4	41.9	73.7	24.2											
1935	0.3	0.3	−2.1	−6.9	3.7	15.0	41.4	61.7	32.0	40.2										
1936	5.0	5.5	3.7	0.0	10.8	22.1	45.8	62.5	42.1	52.0	64.8									
1937	−2.7	−3.0	−5.2	−9.2	−1.9	4.8	18.5	24.0	4.8	−1.0	−16.8	−58.0								
1938	−0.4	−0.4	−2.3	−5.7	1.5	8.0	20.4	25.4	9.9	6.5	−2.8	−25.3	32.8							
1939	−0.3	−0.4	−2.1	−5.2	1.4	7.1	17.7	21.5	8.2	5.3	−2.0	−17.6	15.4	0.3						
1940	−0.7	−0.7	−2.3	−5.2	0.8	5.8	14.9	17.8	6.2	3.5	−2.6	−14.6	8.1	−2.4	−5.2					
1941	−1.2	−1.3	−2.8	−5.5	−0.1	4.4	12.3	14.4	4.2	1.6	−3.7	−13.5	3.6	−4.7	−7.1	−9.0				
1942	1.0	1.1	−0.2	−2.6	2.8	7.2	14.9	17.1	8.0	6.2	2.0	−5.8	10.7	5.8	7.6	14.7	44.5			
1943	4.6	4.8	3.9	1.8	7.3	12.0	19.7	22.3	14.2	13.1	10.1	4.0	21.0	18.7	23.8	35.3	65.0	88.4		
1944	6.7	7.1	6.3	4.5	9.9	14.5	22.0	24.7	17.3	16.7	14.3	9.2	25.2	23.9	29.3	39.7	61.1	70.2	53.7	
1945	9.4	9.9	9.2	7.6	13.1	17.8	25.2	27.9	21.2	21.0	19.2	15.0	30.4	30.1	35.8	45.9	64.2	71.3	63.4	73.6
1946	8.3	8.7	8.0	6.5	11.5	15.7	22.3	24.5	18.3	17.8	16.0	12.0	24.9	23.9	27.7	34.2	45.0	45.2	33.1	23.9
1947	7.9	8.3	7.6	6.2	10.9	14.7	20.8	22.8	17.0	16.4	14.6	10.9	22.2	21.1	24.0	28.8	36.5	35.0	24.2	15.7
1948	7.5	7.8	7.2	5.7	10.2	13.7	19.3	21.1	15.6	15.0	13.3	9.8	19.8	18.6	20.8	24.5	30.2	28.0	18.4	11.0
1949	7.9	8.3	7.7	6.4	10.6	14.0	19.4	21.0	15.8	15.3	13.7	10.5	19.8	18.7	20.7	24.0	28.8	26.7	18.6	12.7
1950	9.0	9.4	8.9	7.7	11.8	15.2	20.3	21.9	17.1	16.7	15.2	12.3	21.2	20.2	22.2	25.4	29.9	28.2	21.3	16.6
1951	9.0	9.3	8.8	7.7	11.6	14.8	19.7	21.1	16.5	16.1	14.8	12.0	20.1	19.2	21.0	23.7	27.5	25.7	19.6	15.3
1952	8.8	9.1	8.6	7.5	11.2	14.2	18.8	20.2	15.8	15.3	14.0	11.4	18.9	18.0	19.5	21.8	25.1	23.3	17.6	13.7
1953	8.2	8.5	8.0	6.9	10.4	13.3	17.5	18.7	14.6	14.1	12.8	10.3	17.2	16.2	17.4	19.3	22.1	20.2	14.9	11.3
1954	9.7	10.0	9.6	8.6	12.1	14.9	19.1	20.4	16.4	16.0	14.9	12.6	19.3	18.6	19.9	21.9	24.7	23.1	18.5	15.4
1955	10.0	10.3	9.9	9.0	12.4	15.1	19.2	20.4	16.6	16.3	15.2	13.0	19.4	18.7	19.9	21.8	24.4	22.9	18.6	15.9
1956	9.8	10.1	9.7	8.8	12.1	14.7	18.5	19.7	16.0	15.7	14.6	12.6	18.6	17.8	18.9	20.6	22.9	21.5	17.5	14.9
1957	8.9	9.2	8.8	7.9	11.0	13.4	17.1	18.1	14.6	14.2	13.1	11.1	16.6	15.8	16.8	18.2	20.1	18.7	14.8	12.3
1958	10.3	10.7	10.3	9.4	12.5	15.0	18.6	19.6	16.2	15.9	15.0	13.1	18.6	17.9	18.9	20.4	22.4	21.1	17.6	15.4
1959	10.5	10.8	10.5	9.7	12.7	15.0	18.5	19.5	16.3	15.9	15.0	13.2	18.5	17.8	18.8	20.2	22.1	20.9	17.6	15.5
1960	10.1	10.4	10.0	9.2	12.1	14.4	17.7	18.6	15.5	15.1	14.2	12.5	17.4	16.8	17.6	18.9	20.6	19.4	16.2	14.2
1961	10.6	10.9	10.6	9.9	12.7	14.9	18.1	19.0	16.0	15.7	14.9	13.2	18.0	17.4	18.2	19.5	21.1	20.0	17.0	15.2
1962	10.0	10.2	9.9	9.1	11.9	13.9	17.0	17.8	14.9	14.6	13.8	12.1	16.6	16.0	16.7	17.8	19.3	18.2	15.3	13.5
1963	10.3	10.6	10.3	9.5	12.2	14.2	17.2	18.0	15.2	14.9	14.1	12.5	16.9	16.3	17.0	18.1	19.5	18.4	15.7	14.0
1964	10.6	10.9	10.6	9.9	12.5	14.5	17.4	18.2	15.5	15.2	14.4	12.9	17.1	16.6	17.3	18.3	19.7	18.6	16.1	14.4
1965	11.3	11.6	11.3	10.7	13.2	15.2	18.0	18.8	16.2	16.0	15.2	13.8	17.9	17.4	18.1	19.2	20.5	19.6	17.1	15.6
1966	10.8	11.1	10.8	10.2	12.6	14.5	17.2	18.0	15.4	15.2	14.4	13.0	17.0	16.4	17.1	18.0	19.3	18.3	16.0	14.5
1967	12.2	12.5	12.2	11.6	14.1	16.0	18.7	19.5	17.0	16.8	16.1	14.8	18.7	18.3	19.0	20.0	21.3	20.4	18.2	16.9
1968	12.7	13.0	12.8	12.2	14.6	16.5	19.1	19.9	17.5	17.3	16.7	15.4	19.3	18.8	19.5	20.5	21.8	21.0	18.9	17.6
1969	11.6	11.9	11.7	11.1	13.4	15.2	17.7	18.4	16.1	15.8	15.2	13.9	17.5	17.1	17.7	18.6	19.7	18.9	16.8	15.5
1970	10.9	11.1	10.9	10.3	12.5	14.2	16.6	17.3	15.0	14.7	14.1	12.9	16.3	15.8	16.3	17.1	18.2	17.3	15.3	14.0

Table C-2 (Page 2 of 6)

Small Company Stocks Total Returns
Rates of Return for all holding periods
Percent per annum compounded annually

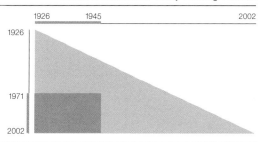

from 1926 to 2002

To the end of	From the beginning of 1926	1927	1928	1929	1930	1931	1932	1933	1934	1935	1936	1937	1938	1939	1940	1941	1942	1943	1944	1945
1971	11.0	11.2	11.0	10.4	12.6	14.3	16.6	17.3	15.0	14.8	14.2	13.0	16.3	15.8	16.4	17.1	18.1	17.3	15.3	14.1
1972	10.9	11.1	10.9	10.3	12.4	14.0	16.3	16.9	14.7	14.5	13.9	12.7	15.9	15.5	16.0	16.7	17.6	16.8	14.9	13.7
1973	9.8	10.0	9.7	9.1	11.2	12.7	14.9	15.4	13.3	13.0	12.4	11.2	14.3	13.8	14.2	14.9	15.7	14.9	13.0	11.8
1974	9.1	9.3	9.0	8.4	10.4	11.8	13.9	14.4	12.3	12.1	11.4	10.3	13.2	12.7	13.1	13.7	14.4	13.6	11.7	10.6
1975	9.8	10.0	9.8	9.2	11.1	12.6	14.7	15.2	13.2	12.9	12.3	11.2	14.1	13.6	14.0	14.6	15.4	14.6	12.8	11.7
1976	10.6	10.8	10.6	10.0	12.0	13.4	15.5	16.0	14.0	13.8	13.2	12.2	15.0	14.6	15.0	15.6	16.4	15.7	14.0	12.9
1977	10.8	11.1	10.9	10.3	12.2	13.7	15.7	16.2	14.3	14.1	13.5	12.5	15.3	14.9	15.3	15.9	16.7	16.0	14.3	13.3
1978	11.1	11.3	11.1	10.6	12.4	13.9	15.9	16.4	14.5	14.3	13.7	12.7	15.5	15.1	15.5	16.1	16.8	16.2	14.6	13.6
1979	11.6	11.8	11.6	11.1	13.0	14.4	16.4	16.9	15.0	14.8	14.3	13.4	16.1	15.7	16.1	16.7	17.5	16.8	15.3	14.3
1980	12.1	12.3	12.1	11.6	13.5	14.9	16.8	17.3	15.5	15.3	14.8	13.9	16.6	16.2	16.6	17.2	18.0	17.4	15.9	15.0
1981	12.1	12.3	12.1	11.7	13.5	14.8	16.8	17.3	15.5	15.3	14.8	13.9	16.5	16.2	16.6	17.2	17.9	17.3	15.8	14.9
1982	12.4	12.6	12.4	12.0	13.7	15.1	17.0	17.5	15.7	15.6	15.1	14.2	16.8	16.4	16.8	17.4	18.1	17.5	16.1	15.3
1983	12.8	13.0	12.9	12.4	14.2	15.5	17.4	17.9	16.2	16.0	15.6	14.7	17.2	16.9	17.3	17.9	18.6	18.0	16.7	15.8
1984	12.4	12.6	12.5	12.0	13.8	15.0	16.9	17.3	15.7	15.5	15.0	14.2	16.6	16.3	16.7	17.3	17.9	17.4	16.0	15.2
1985	12.6	12.8	12.7	12.3	13.9	15.2	17.0	17.5	15.8	15.7	15.2	14.4	16.8	16.5	16.9	17.4	18.1	17.5	16.2	15.4
1986	12.5	12.7	12.6	12.2	13.8	15.1	16.8	17.3	15.7	15.5	15.1	14.2	16.6	16.3	16.6	17.2	17.8	17.3	16.0	15.2
1987	12.1	12.3	12.2	11.8	13.4	14.6	16.3	16.7	15.1	15.0	14.5	13.7	16.0	15.7	16.0	16.5	17.2	16.6	15.4	14.6
1988	12.3	12.5	12.3	11.9	13.5	14.7	16.4	16.8	15.3	15.1	14.7	13.9	16.1	15.8	16.2	16.7	17.3	16.8	15.5	14.8
1989	12.2	12.5	12.3	11.9	13.5	14.6	16.3	16.7	15.2	15.0	14.6	13.8	16.0	15.7	16.0	16.5	17.1	16.6	15.4	14.7
1990	11.6	11.8	11.7	11.3	12.8	13.9	15.5	15.9	14.4	14.2	13.8	13.0	15.2	14.9	15.2	15.6	16.2	15.6	14.5	13.7
1991	12.1	12.3	12.1	11.7	13.2	14.4	15.9	16.3	14.9	14.7	14.3	13.5	15.7	15.4	15.7	16.1	16.7	16.2	15.0	14.3
1992	12.2	12.4	12.3	11.9	13.4	14.5	16.1	16.5	15.0	14.9	14.5	13.7	15.8	15.5	15.8	16.3	16.8	16.3	15.2	14.5
1993	12.4	12.5	12.4	12.0	13.5	14.6	16.1	16.5	15.1	15.0	14.6	13.8	15.9	15.6	15.9	16.3	16.9	16.4	15.3	14.6
1994	12.2	12.4	12.3	11.9	13.3	14.4	15.9	16.3	14.9	14.8	14.4	13.6	15.6	15.4	15.7	16.1	16.6	16.1	15.0	14.4
1995	12.5	12.7	12.6	12.2	13.6	14.7	16.2	16.6	15.2	15.1	14.7	14.0	15.9	15.7	16.0	16.4	16.9	16.5	15.4	14.7
1996	12.6	12.8	12.6	12.3	13.7	14.7	16.2	16.6	15.2	15.1	14.7	14.0	16.0	15.7	16.0	16.4	16.9	16.5	15.4	14.8
1997	12.7	12.9	12.8	12.4	13.8	14.9	16.3	16.7	15.3	15.2	14.8	14.2	16.1	15.8	16.1	16.5	17.0	16.6	15.6	14.9
1998	12.4	12.6	12.5	12.1	13.5	14.5	15.9	16.3	15.0	14.8	14.5	13.8	15.7	15.4	15.7	16.1	16.6	16.1	15.1	14.5
1999	12.6	12.8	12.7	12.3	13.7	14.7	16.1	16.5	15.2	15.0	14.7	14.0	15.9	15.6	15.9	16.3	16.8	16.3	15.3	14.7
2000	12.4	12.6	12.4	12.1	13.4	14.4	15.8	16.1	14.9	14.7	14.4	13.7	15.5	15.3	15.5	15.9	16.4	16.0	15.0	14.4
2001	12.5	12.7	12.6	12.2	13.6	14.5	15.9	16.2	15.0	14.8	14.5	13.9	15.6	15.4	15.7	16.0	16.5	16.1	15.1	14.5
2002	12.1	12.3	12.2	11.9	13.1	14.1	15.4	15.7	14.5	14.4	14.0	13.4	15.1	14.9	15.1	15.5	15.9	15.5	14.6	14.0

Table C-2 (Page 3 of 6)

Small Company Stocks Total Returns
Rates of Return for all holding periods
Percent per annum compounded annually

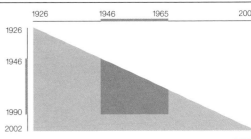

| 1926 | 1946 | 1965 | 2002 |

from 1926 to 2002

To the end of	From the beginning of 1946	1947	1948	1949	1950	1951	1952	1953	1954	1955	1956	1957	1958	1959	1960	1961	1962	1963	1964	1965
1946	−11.6																			
1947	−5.6	0.9																		
1948	−4.4	−0.6	−2.1																	
1949	1.1	5.8	8.3	19.7																
1950	7.7	13.2	17.6	28.9	38.7															
1951	7.7	12.1	15.1	21.4	22.3	7.8														
1952	7.0	10.5	12.6	16.6	15.5	5.4	3.0													
1953	5.3	7.9	9.1	11.5	9.6	1.3	−1.8	−6.5												
1954	10.3	13.4	15.3	18.5	18.3	13.6	15.7	22.5	60.6											
1955	11.3	14.2	15.9	18.8	18.6	15.0	16.8	21.8	39.1	20.4										
1956	10.6	13.1	14.6	16.9	16.5	13.1	14.2	17.2	26.3	12.1	4.3									
1957	8.3	10.3	11.3	12.9	12.0	8.7	8.8	10.0	14.6	2.4	−5.6	−14.6								
1958	11.8	14.0	15.3	17.2	17.0	14.5	15.5	17.7	23.2	15.3	13.7	18.7	64.9							
1959	12.2	14.2	15.4	17.2	16.9	14.7	15.6	17.5	22.1	15.5	14.4	17.9	38.5	16.4						
1960	11.1	12.9	13.9	15.3	14.9	12.8	13.3	14.7	18.1	12.2	10.6	12.2	22.9	6.1	−3.3					
1961	12.3	14.1	15.1	16.5	16.2	14.4	15.1	16.5	19.7	14.8	13.9	15.9	25.1	14.1	13.0	32.1				
1962	10.7	12.2	13.0	14.2	13.8	11.9	12.3	13.3	15.7	11.1	9.8	10.7	16.6	7.0	4.0	7.9	−11.9			
1963	11.4	12.9	13.7	14.8	14.5	12.8	13.2	14.2	16.5	12.4	11.4	12.5	17.8	10.1	8.6	12.9	4.3	23.6		
1964	12.0	13.4	14.2	15.3	15.0	13.5	14.0	14.9	17.1	13.5	12.7	13.8	18.6	12.2	11.4	15.4	10.4	23.5	23.5	
1965	13.3	14.8	15.6	16.7	16.6	15.2	15.8	16.8	19.0	15.8	15.3	16.6	21.3	16.0	16.0	20.3	17.5	29.3	32.3	41.8
1966	12.2	13.6	14.3	15.3	15.0	13.7	14.1	14.9	16.7	13.7	13.1	14.0	17.7	12.9	12.4	15.2	12.1	19.1	17.6	14.8
1967	14.8	16.2	17.0	18.1	18.0	16.9	17.5	18.6	20.6	18.0	17.8	19.1	23.1	19.1	19.5	23.2	21.7	29.9	31.5	34.3
1968	15.6	17.0	17.9	19.0	18.9	17.9	18.5	19.6	21.6	19.2	19.1	20.4	24.2	20.7	21.2	24.7	23.7	30.9	32.4	34.7
1969	13.5	14.8	15.5	16.4	16.2	15.1	15.6	16.3	17.9	15.5	15.2	16.1	19.1	15.6	15.5	17.8	16.2	20.8	20.4	19.8
1970	12.1	13.2	13.8	14.6	14.3	13.2	13.5	14.1	15.5	13.1	12.7	13.3	15.8	12.4	12.1	13.7	11.8	15.2	14.1	12.6
1971	12.3	13.4	13.9	14.7	14.4	13.4	13.7	14.3	15.5	13.3	12.9	13.5	15.8	12.7	12.4	14.0	12.3	15.4	14.4	13.1
1972	12.0	13.0	13.5	14.2	14.0	13.0	13.2	13.8	14.9	12.8	12.4	12.9	15.0	12.1	11.8	13.1	11.6	14.2	13.2	12.0
1973	10.1	11.0	11.4	11.9	11.6	10.6	10.7	11.1	12.0	9.9	9.4	9.7	11.4	8.5	8.0	8.9	7.2	9.1	7.8	6.2
1974	8.9	9.7	10.0	10.5	10.2	9.1	9.2	9.4	10.3	8.2	7.6	7.8	9.3	6.5	5.9	6.6	4.8	6.3	4.9	3.2
1975	10.1	10.9	11.3	11.8	11.5	10.6	10.7	11.0	11.9	10.0	9.5	9.8	11.3	8.8	8.3	9.2	7.7	9.3	8.2	6.9
1976	11.4	12.2	12.6	13.2	13.0	12.1	12.3	12.7	13.6	11.8	11.4	11.8	13.4	11.0	10.7	11.7	10.4	12.2	11.4	10.4
1977	11.8	12.6	13.1	13.6	13.4	12.6	12.7	13.1	14.1	12.4	12.0	12.4	13.9	11.8	11.5	12.4	11.3	13.1	12.3	11.5
1978	12.1	13.0	13.4	13.9	13.7	12.9	13.1	13.5	14.4	12.8	12.5	12.9	14.4	12.3	12.1	13.0	12.0	13.7	13.1	12.3
1979	12.9	13.8	14.2	14.8	14.6	13.9	14.1	14.5	15.4	13.9	13.6	14.1	15.6	13.6	13.5	14.5	13.5	15.3	14.8	14.2
1980	13.6	14.5	14.9	15.5	15.4	14.6	14.9	15.3	16.2	14.8	14.6	15.0	16.5	14.7	14.6	15.6	14.8	16.5	16.1	15.6
1981	13.6	14.5	14.9	15.4	15.3	14.6	14.9	15.3	16.2	14.8	14.6	15.0	16.4	14.7	14.6	15.5	14.8	16.4	16.0	15.5
1982	14.0	14.8	15.2	15.8	15.7	15.0	15.3	15.7	16.5	15.2	15.0	15.5	16.9	15.2	15.1	16.1	15.4	16.9	16.6	16.2
1983	14.6	15.4	15.9	16.4	16.3	15.7	16.0	16.4	17.2	16.0	15.8	16.3	17.7	16.1	16.1	17.0	16.4	17.9	17.6	17.3
1984	14.0	14.8	15.2	15.7	15.6	15.0	15.2	15.6	16.4	15.1	15.0	15.4	16.7	15.1	15.1	15.9	15.2	16.7	16.3	16.0
1985	14.3	15.0	15.4	15.9	15.8	15.2	15.5	15.9	16.6	15.4	15.3	15.7	16.9	15.5	15.4	16.2	15.6	17.0	16.7	16.4
1986	14.1	14.8	15.2	15.7	15.6	15.0	15.2	15.6	16.3	15.2	15.0	15.4	16.6	15.1	15.1	15.9	15.3	16.6	16.3	15.9
1987	13.5	14.2	14.5	15.0	14.8	14.3	14.4	14.8	15.5	14.3	14.1	14.5	15.6	14.2	14.1	14.8	14.2	15.4	15.1	14.7
1988	13.7	14.4	14.7	15.2	15.0	14.5	14.7	15.0	15.7	14.6	14.4	14.7	15.8	14.5	14.4	15.1	14.5	15.7	15.4	15.0
1989	13.6	14.3	14.6	15.0	14.9	14.4	14.5	14.9	15.5	14.4	14.3	14.6	15.7	14.3	14.3	14.9	14.4	15.5	15.2	14.8
1990	12.7	13.3	13.6	14.0	13.9	13.3	13.4	13.7	14.3	13.3	13.1	13.3	14.3	13.0	12.9	13.5	12.9	13.9	13.5	13.2

Table C-2 (Page 4 of 6)

Small Company Stocks Total Returns
Rates of Return for all holding periods
Percent per annum compounded annually

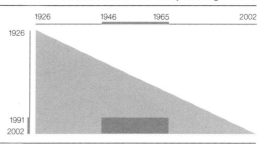

from 1926 to 2002

To the end of	From the beginning of 1946	1947	1948	1949	1950	1951	1952	1953	1954	1955	1956	1957	1958	1959	1960	1961	1962	1963	1964	1965
1991	13.3	13.9	14.2	14.6	14.5	14.0	14.1	14.4	15.0	14.0	13.8	14.1	15.1	13.8	13.8	14.4	13.8	14.8	14.5	14.2
1992	13.5	14.1	14.4	14.8	14.7	14.2	14.3	14.6	15.2	14.2	14.1	14.4	15.3	14.1	14.0	14.6	14.1	15.1	14.8	14.5
1993	13.6	14.2	14.5	14.9	14.8	14.3	14.5	14.8	15.4	14.4	14.3	14.5	15.5	14.3	14.2	14.8	14.3	15.3	15.0	14.7
1994	13.4	14.0	14.3	14.7	14.6	14.1	14.2	14.5	15.1	14.1	14.0	14.2	15.1	14.0	13.9	14.5	14.0	14.9	14.6	14.3
1995	13.8	14.4	14.7	15.1	15.0	14.5	14.6	14.9	15.5	14.6	14.4	14.7	15.6	14.5	14.4	15.0	14.5	15.4	15.2	14.9
1996	13.9	14.4	14.7	15.1	15.0	14.6	14.7	15.0	15.5	14.6	14.5	14.8	15.6	14.6	14.5	15.1	14.6	15.5	15.3	15.0
1997	14.0	14.6	14.9	15.3	15.2	14.7	14.9	15.2	15.7	14.8	14.7	15.0	15.8	14.8	14.7	15.3	14.8	15.7	15.5	15.2
1998	13.6	14.1	14.4	14.8	14.7	14.2	14.4	14.6	15.1	14.3	14.1	14.4	15.2	14.2	14.1	14.6	14.2	15.0	14.8	14.5
1999	13.9	14.4	14.7	15.0	15.0	14.5	14.7	14.9	15.4	14.6	14.5	14.7	15.5	14.5	14.5	15.0	14.5	15.4	15.1	14.9
2000	13.5	14.0	14.3	14.7	14.6	14.1	14.3	14.5	15.0	14.2	14.0	14.3	15.0	14.1	14.0	14.5	14.0	14.8	14.6	14.4
2001	13.7	14.2	14.5	14.8	14.7	14.3	14.4	14.7	15.1	14.3	14.2	14.4	15.2	14.2	14.2	14.7	14.3	15.0	14.8	14.6
2002	13.1	13.6	13.9	14.2	14.1	13.7	13.8	14.0	14.5	13.7	13.5	13.8	14.5	13.5	13.5	13.9	13.5	14.2	14.0	13.7

Table C-2 (Page 5 of 6)

Small Company Stocks Total Returns
Rates of Return for all holding periods
Percent per annum compounded annually

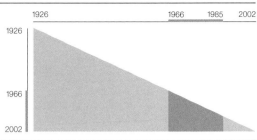

from 1926 to 2002

To the end of	From the beginning of 1966	1967	1968	1969	1970	1971	1972	1973	1974	1975	1976	1977	1978	1979	1980	1981	1982	1983	1984	1985
1966	−7.0																			
1967	30.7	83.6																		
1968	32.4	58.0	36.0																	
1969	14.8	23.2	0.9	−25.1																
1970	7.5	11.5	−5.6	−21.3	−17.4															
1971	9.0	12.5	−0.5	−10.3	−1.9	16.5														
1972	8.3	11.1	0.5	−6.9	0.2	10.3	4.4													
1973	2.4	3.8	−5.6	−12.3	−8.7	−5.6	−15.1	−30.9												
1974	−0.4	0.5	−7.8	−13.6	−11.1	−9.4	−16.7	−25.6	−19.9											
1975	4.0	5.3	−1.8	−6.3	−2.7	0.6	−3.1	−5.4	10.6	52.8										
1976	8.0	9.6	3.5	0.0	4.2	8.4	6.8	7.4	24.4	55.1	57.4									
1977	9.3	10.9	5.5	2.6	6.7	10.6	9.7	10.8	24.6	44.5	40.5	25.4								
1978	10.4	11.9	7.0	4.5	8.4	12.2	11.6	12.8	24.4	38.9	34.6	24.4	23.5							
1979	12.4	14.1	9.7	7.5	11.5	15.3	15.1	16.7	27.4	39.8	36.7	30.5	33.1	43.5						
1980	14.1	15.8	11.7	9.9	13.8	17.5	17.6	19.4	29.1	39.8	37.4	32.8	35.3	41.7	39.9					
1981	14.1	15.6	11.9	10.2	13.8	17.2	17.3	18.8	27.1	35.8	33.1	28.7	29.6	31.7	26.2	13.9				
1982	14.9	16.4	12.9	11.4	14.9	18.1	18.2	19.7	27.2	34.8	32.4	28.6	29.3	30.8	26.8	20.7	28.0			
1983	16.1	17.6	14.4	13.1	16.5	19.6	19.9	21.4	28.4	35.3	33.3	30.1	31.0	32.5	29.9	26.7	33.7	39.7		
1984	14.8	16.1	13.0	11.7	14.8	17.5	17.6	18.7	24.7	30.4	28.1	24.8	24.8	25.0	21.6	17.4	18.6	14.2	−6.7	
1985	15.3	16.6	13.7	12.5	15.4	18.0	18.1	19.2	24.7	29.9	27.8	24.8	24.8	24.9	22.1	18.8	20.1	17.6	7.9	24.7
1986	14.8	16.1	13.3	12.1	14.8	17.2	17.3	18.3	23.2	27.8	25.7	22.9	22.6	22.5	19.8	16.7	17.3	14.8	7.5	15.4
1987	13.6	14.7	12.0	10.9	13.3	15.5	15.4	16.2	20.6	24.4	22.3	19.6	19.0	18.5	15.7	12.6	12.4	9.5	3.0	6.5
1988	14.0	15.1	12.5	11.5	13.8	15.9	15.8	16.6	20.7	24.3	22.4	19.8	19.3	18.9	16.5	13.8	13.8	11.6	6.7	10.4
1989	13.8	14.8	12.4	11.4	13.6	15.6	15.5	16.2	20.0	23.3	21.5	19.1	18.5	18.1	15.8	13.4	13.4	11.4	7.3	10.3
1990	12.2	13.0	10.7	9.6	11.7	13.3	13.2	13.7	17.1	19.9	18.0	15.6	14.8	14.1	11.8	9.3	8.8	6.6	2.6	4.2
1991	13.3	14.2	11.9	11.0	13.0	14.7	14.6	15.1	18.5	21.2	19.5	17.3	16.7	16.2	14.2	12.1	12.0	10.3	7.1	9.2
1992	13.6	14.5	12.4	11.5	13.4	15.1	15.0	15.5	18.7	21.3	19.7	17.7	17.2	16.7	14.9	13.0	13.0	11.6	8.8	10.9
1993	13.9	14.7	12.7	11.8	13.7	15.3	15.3	15.8	18.8	21.3	19.8	17.9	17.4	17.0	15.3	13.6	13.6	12.4	10.0	12.0
1994	13.5	14.3	12.3	11.5	13.3	14.8	14.7	15.2	18.0	20.3	18.8	17.0	16.5	16.1	14.5	12.8	12.8	11.6	9.3	11.1
1995	14.1	14.9	13.0	12.3	14.0	15.5	15.5	16.0	18.7	21.0	19.6	17.8	17.4	17.1	15.6	14.2	14.2	13.2	11.2	13.0
1996	14.2	15.0	13.2	12.4	14.1	15.6	15.5	16.0	18.7	20.8	19.5	17.8	17.5	17.1	15.7	14.4	14.4	13.5	11.7	13.4
1997	14.5	15.3	13.5	12.8	14.4	15.8	15.8	16.3	18.8	20.9	19.6	18.1	17.7	17.4	16.1	14.9	14.9	14.1	12.5	14.1
1998	13.8	14.5	12.8	12.1	13.6	14.9	14.9	15.3	17.7	19.6	18.3	16.8	16.4	16.0	14.8	13.5	13.5	12.6	11.0	12.4
1999	14.2	14.9	13.3	12.6	14.1	15.4	15.4	15.8	18.1	20.0	18.8	17.3	17.0	16.7	15.5	14.3	14.3	13.6	12.1	13.5
2000	13.7	14.3	12.7	12.0	13.5	14.7	14.7	15.0	17.2	19.0	17.8	16.4	16.0	15.7	14.5	13.3	13.3	12.5	11.1	12.3
2001	13.9	14.6	13.0	12.4	13.8	15.0	14.9	15.3	17.4	19.1	18.0	16.6	16.3	16.0	14.8	13.8	13.8	13.1	11.7	12.9
2002	13.1	13.7	12.1	11.5	12.8	14.0	13.9	14.2	16.2	17.8	16.6	15.3	14.9	14.6	13.4	12.4	12.3	11.6	10.3	11.3

Table C-2 (Page 6 of 6)

Small Company Stocks Total Returns
Rates of Return for all holding periods
Percent per annum compounded annually

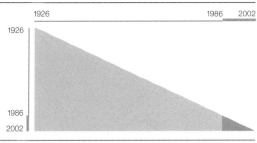

from 1926 to 2002

To the end of	From the beginning of 1986	1987	1988	1989	1990	1991	1992	1993	1994	1995	1996	1997	1998	1999	2000	2001	2002
1986	6.9																
1987	−1.6	−9.3															
1988	6.0	5.6	22.9														
1989	7.0	7.1	16.4	10.2													
1990	0.6	−0.9	2.0	−7.0	−21.6												
1991	6.9	6.9	11.3	7.7	6.5	44.6											
1992	9.1	9.4	13.6	11.4	11.9	33.6	23.3										
1993	10.5	11.0	14.8	13.3	14.1	29.2	22.2	21.0									
1994	9.6	10.0	13.1	11.5	11.8	22.1	15.4	11.7	3.1								
1995	11.9	12.5	15.5	14.5	15.3	24.5	19.9	18.8	17.7	34.5							
1996	12.4	13.0	15.8	14.9	15.6	23.3	19.5	18.5	17.7	25.8	17.6						
1997	13.2	13.8	16.5	15.8	16.5	23.3	20.0	19.4	19.0	24.8	20.2	22.8					
1998	11.5	11.9	14.1	13.2	13.6	18.9	15.7	14.4	13.2	15.8	10.2	6.7	−7.3				
1999	12.7	13.2	15.3	14.6	15.1	20.1	17.3	16.5	15.8	18.5	14.8	13.9	9.7	29.8			
2000	11.6	11.9	13.7	13.0	13.3	17.5	14.8	13.8	12.8	14.5	10.9	9.2	5.1	11.9	−3.6		
2001	12.2	12.6	14.3	13.7	14.0	18.0	15.6	14.7	14.0	15.6	12.8	11.8	9.2	15.4	8.8	22.8	
2002	10.5	10.8	12.3	11.5	11.6	15.0	12.6	11.6	10.6	11.6	8.6	7.2	4.3	7.4	0.9	3.2	−13.3

Table C-3 (Page 1 of 6)

Long-Term Corporate Bonds Total Returns
Rates of Return for all holding periods
Percent per annum compounded annually

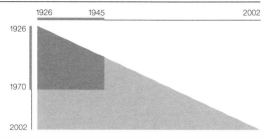

from 1926 to 2002

To the end of	From the beginning of 1926	1927	1928	1929	1930	1931	1932	1933	1934	1935	1936	1937	1938	1939	1940	1941	1942	1943	1944	1945
1926	7.4																			
1927	7.4	7.4																		
1928	5.9	5.1	2.8																	
1929	5.2	4.5	3.1	3.3																
1930	5.8	5.4	4.7	5.6	8.0															
1931	4.4	3.9	3.0	3.1	2.9	−1.9														
1932	5.3	5.0	4.5	4.9	5.5	4.3	10.8													
1933	6.0	5.8	5.5	6.0	6.7	6.3	10.6	10.4												
1934	6.8	6.7	6.6	7.3	8.1	8.1	11.7	12.1	13.8											
1935	7.1	7.0	7.0	7.6	8.3	8.4	11.2	11.3	11.7	9.6										
1936	7.1	7.0	7.0	7.5	8.1	8.1	10.3	10.1	10.0	8.2	6.7									
1937	6.7	6.6	6.5	7.0	7.4	7.4	9.0	8.6	8.2	6.3	4.7	2.7								
1938	6.6	6.6	6.5	6.9	7.3	7.2	8.6	8.2	7.8	6.3	5.2	4.4	6.1							
1939	6.4	6.4	6.3	6.6	6.9	6.8	8.0	7.6	7.1	5.8	4.9	4.3	5.0	4.0						
1940	6.2	6.2	6.1	6.3	6.6	6.5	7.5	7.0	6.6	5.4	4.6	4.1	4.5	3.7	3.4					
1941	6.0	5.9	5.8	6.1	6.3	6.1	7.0	6.6	6.1	5.0	4.3	3.8	4.0	3.4	3.1	2.7				
1942	5.8	5.7	5.6	5.8	6.0	5.8	6.6	6.2	5.7	4.7	4.0	3.6	3.8	3.2	2.9	2.7	2.6			
1943	5.6	5.5	5.4	5.6	5.8	5.6	6.3	5.8	5.4	4.5	3.9	3.5	3.6	3.1	2.9	2.7	2.7	2.8		
1944	5.6	5.5	5.4	5.5	5.7	5.5	6.1	5.8	5.3	4.5	4.0	3.6	3.8	3.4	3.3	3.2	3.4	3.8	4.7	
1945	5.5	5.4	5.3	5.5	5.6	5.4	6.0	5.6	5.2	4.5	4.0	3.7	3.8	3.5	3.4	3.4	3.6	3.9	4.4	4.1
1946	5.3	5.2	5.1	5.3	5.4	5.2	5.7	5.3	5.0	4.3	3.8	3.5	3.6	3.3	3.2	3.1	3.2	3.3	3.5	2.9
1947	5.0	4.9	4.7	4.8	4.9	4.7	5.2	4.8	4.4	3.7	3.3	2.9	3.0	2.6	2.4	2.3	2.2	2.2	2.0	1.1
1948	4.9	4.8	4.7	4.8	4.9	4.7	5.1	4.8	4.4	3.8	3.3	3.0	3.1	2.8	2.6	2.5	2.5	2.5	2.4	1.9
1949	4.9	4.8	4.6	4.7	4.8	4.6	5.0	4.7	4.3	3.7	3.3	3.1	3.1	2.8	2.7	2.6	2.6	2.6	2.6	2.2
1950	4.8	4.7	4.5	4.6	4.7	4.5	4.9	4.5	4.2	3.6	3.2	3.0	3.0	2.8	2.6	2.6	2.6	2.6	2.5	2.1
1951	4.5	4.3	4.2	4.3	4.3	4.2	4.5	4.1	3.8	3.2	2.9	2.6	2.6	2.3	2.2	2.1	2.0	2.0	1.8	1.4
1952	4.4	4.3	4.2	4.2	4.3	4.1	4.4	4.1	3.8	3.3	2.9	2.7	2.7	2.4	2.3	2.2	2.2	2.1	2.0	1.7
1953	4.4	4.3	4.2	4.2	4.3	4.1	4.4	4.1	3.8	3.3	2.9	2.7	2.7	2.5	2.4	2.3	2.3	2.2	2.2	1.9
1954	4.4	4.3	4.2	4.3	4.3	4.2	4.4	4.1	3.8	3.4	3.1	2.9	2.9	2.7	2.6	2.5	2.5	2.5	2.5	2.2
1955	4.3	4.2	4.1	4.1	4.2	4.0	4.3	4.0	3.7	3.2	2.9	2.7	2.7	2.5	2.4	2.4	2.4	2.3	2.3	2.1
1956	3.9	3.8	3.7	3.7	3.7	3.6	3.8	3.5	3.2	2.8	2.4	2.2	2.2	2.0	1.9	1.8	1.7	1.6	1.6	1.3
1957	4.1	4.0	3.8	3.9	3.9	3.7	4.0	3.7	3.4	3.0	2.7	2.5	2.5	2.3	2.2	2.2	2.1	2.1	2.1	1.9
1958	3.9	3.8	3.6	3.7	3.7	3.5	3.7	3.5	3.2	2.8	2.5	2.3	2.3	2.1	2.0	1.9	1.9	1.8	1.8	1.6
1959	3.7	3.6	3.5	3.5	3.5	3.4	3.6	3.3	3.0	2.6	2.3	2.2	2.1	1.9	1.8	1.8	1.7	1.7	1.6	1.4
1960	3.9	3.8	3.7	3.7	3.7	3.6	3.7	3.5	3.3	2.9	2.6	2.4	2.4	2.3	2.2	2.1	2.1	2.1	2.0	1.8
1961	3.9	3.8	3.7	3.7	3.7	3.6	3.8	3.5	3.3	2.9	2.7	2.5	2.5	2.4	2.3	2.2	2.2	2.2	2.2	2.0
1962	4.0	3.9	3.8	3.8	3.9	3.7	3.9	3.7	3.5	3.1	2.9	2.7	2.7	2.6	2.5	2.5	2.5	2.5	2.5	2.3
1963	4.0	3.9	3.8	3.8	3.8	3.7	3.9	3.6	3.4	3.1	2.9	2.7	2.7	2.6	2.5	2.5	2.5	2.5	2.5	2.3
1964	4.0	3.9	3.8	3.8	3.8	3.7	3.9	3.7	3.5	3.1	2.9	2.8	2.8	2.7	2.6	2.6	2.6	2.6	2.6	2.5
1965	3.9	3.8	3.7	3.7	3.7	3.6	3.8	3.6	3.3	3.0	2.8	2.7	2.7	2.5	2.5	2.5	2.4	2.4	2.4	2.3
1966	3.8	3.7	3.6	3.6	3.6	3.5	3.7	3.5	3.2	2.9	2.7	2.6	2.6	2.5	2.4	2.4	2.4	2.3	2.3	2.2
1967	3.6	3.5	3.4	3.4	3.4	3.3	3.4	3.2	3.0	2.7	2.5	2.3	2.3	2.2	2.1	2.1	2.1	2.0	2.0	1.9
1968	3.5	3.4	3.3	3.4	3.4	3.2	3.4	3.2	3.0	2.7	2.5	2.3	2.3	2.2	2.2	2.1	2.1	2.1	2.0	1.9
1969	3.3	3.2	3.1	3.1	3.1	2.9	3.1	2.9	2.7	2.4	2.2	2.0	2.0	1.9	1.8	1.7	1.7	1.7	1.6	1.5
1970	3.6	3.5	3.4	3.4	3.4	3.3	3.4	3.2	3.1	2.8	2.6	2.5	2.5	2.3	2.3	2.3	2.2	2.2	2.2	2.1

Table C-3 (Page 2 of 6)

Long-Term Corporate Bonds Total Returns
Rates of Return for all holding periods
Percent per annum compounded annually

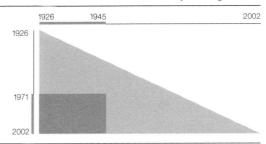

from 1926 to 2002

To the end of	From the beginning of 1926	1927	1928	1929	1930	1931	1932	1933	1934	1935	1936	1937	1938	1939	1940	1941	1942	1943	1944	1945
1971	3.7	3.6	3.6	3.6	3.6	3.5	3.6	3.4	3.3	3.0	2.8	2.7	2.7	2.6	2.6	2.5	2.5	2.5	2.5	2.4
1972	3.8	3.7	3.6	3.7	3.7	3.6	3.7	3.5	3.4	3.1	2.9	2.8	2.8	2.7	2.7	2.7	2.7	2.7	2.7	2.6
1973	3.7	3.7	3.6	3.6	3.6	3.5	3.6	3.5	3.3	3.0	2.9	2.8	2.8	2.7	2.6	2.6	2.6	2.6	2.6	2.5
1974	3.6	3.5	3.4	3.4	3.5	3.4	3.5	3.3	3.1	2.9	2.7	2.6	2.6	2.5	2.5	2.4	2.4	2.4	2.4	2.3
1975	3.8	3.7	3.7	3.7	3.7	3.6	3.7	3.6	3.4	3.2	3.0	2.9	2.9	2.8	2.8	2.8	2.8	2.8	2.8	2.7
1976	4.1	4.0	3.9	4.0	4.0	3.9	4.0	3.9	3.7	3.5	3.4	3.3	3.3	3.2	3.2	3.2	3.2	3.2	3.2	3.2
1977	4.0	4.0	3.9	3.9	3.9	3.9	4.0	3.8	3.7	3.5	3.3	3.2	3.2	3.2	3.2	3.1	3.2	3.2	3.2	3.1
1978	4.0	3.9	3.8	3.8	3.9	3.8	3.9	3.7	3.6	3.4	3.2	3.2	3.2	3.1	3.1	3.1	3.1	3.1	3.1	3.0
1979	3.8	3.7	3.7	3.7	3.7	3.6	3.7	3.6	3.4	3.2	3.1	3.0	3.0	2.9	2.9	2.9	2.9	2.9	2.9	2.8
1980	3.7	3.6	3.5	3.5	3.6	3.5	3.6	3.4	3.3	3.1	2.9	2.8	2.8	2.8	2.7	2.7	2.7	2.7	2.7	2.7
1981	3.6	3.5	3.4	3.5	3.5	3.4	3.5	3.3	3.2	3.0	2.8	2.8	2.8	2.7	2.6	2.6	2.6	2.6	2.6	2.6
1982	4.2	4.1	4.1	4.1	4.1	4.0	4.1	4.0	3.9	3.7	3.6	3.5	3.5	3.4	3.4	3.4	3.5	3.5	3.5	3.5
1983	4.2	4.1	4.1	4.1	4.1	4.1	4.2	4.0	3.9	3.7	3.6	3.5	3.6	3.5	3.5	3.5	3.5	3.5	3.6	3.5
1984	4.4	4.4	4.3	4.3	4.3	4.3	4.4	4.3	4.2	4.0	3.9	3.8	3.8	3.8	3.8	3.8	3.8	3.8	3.9	3.8
1985	4.8	4.7	4.7	4.7	4.8	4.7	4.8	4.7	4.6	4.4	4.3	4.3	4.3	4.3	4.3	4.3	4.3	4.4	4.4	4.4
1986	5.0	5.0	4.9	5.0	5.0	5.0	5.1	5.0	4.9	4.7	4.6	4.6	4.6	4.6	4.6	4.6	4.7	4.7	4.8	4.8
1987	4.9	4.9	4.8	4.9	4.9	4.9	5.0	4.9	4.8	4.6	4.5	4.5	4.5	4.5	4.5	4.5	4.6	4.6	4.6	4.6
1988	5.0	5.0	4.9	5.0	5.0	5.0	5.1	5.0	4.9	4.7	4.6	4.6	4.6	4.6	4.6	4.6	4.7	4.7	4.8	4.8
1989	5.2	5.2	5.1	5.2	5.2	5.1	5.3	5.2	5.1	4.9	4.8	4.8	4.8	4.8	4.8	4.9	4.9	5.0	5.0	5.0
1990	5.2	5.2	5.1	5.2	5.2	5.2	5.3	5.2	5.1	5.0	4.9	4.8	4.9	4.9	4.9	4.9	4.9	5.0	5.0	5.1
1991	5.4	5.4	5.4	5.4	5.4	5.4	5.5	5.4	5.3	5.2	5.1	5.1	5.1	5.1	5.1	5.2	5.2	5.3	5.3	5.3
1992	5.5	5.4	5.4	5.5	5.5	5.5	5.6	5.5	5.4	5.3	5.2	5.2	5.2	5.2	5.2	5.3	5.3	5.4	5.4	5.4
1993	5.6	5.6	5.5	5.6	5.6	5.6	5.7	5.6	5.5	5.4	5.3	5.3	5.4	5.3	5.4	5.4	5.5	5.5	5.6	5.6
1994	5.4	5.4	5.4	5.4	5.4	5.4	5.5	5.4	5.3	5.2	5.1	5.1	5.1	5.1	5.2	5.2	5.2	5.3	5.3	5.3
1995	5.7	5.7	5.6	5.7	5.7	5.7	5.8	5.7	5.7	5.5	5.5	5.4	5.5	5.5	5.5	5.5	5.6	5.7	5.7	5.7
1996	5.6	5.6	5.6	5.6	5.7	5.6	5.7	5.7	5.6	5.5	5.4	5.4	5.4	5.4	5.4	5.5	5.5	5.6	5.6	5.6
1997	5.7	5.7	5.7	5.7	5.8	5.7	5.9	5.8	5.7	5.6	5.5	5.5	5.5	5.5	5.6	5.6	5.7	5.7	5.8	5.8
1998	5.8	5.8	5.8	5.8	5.8	5.8	5.9	5.9	5.8	5.7	5.6	5.6	5.6	5.6	5.6	5.7	5.7	5.8	5.9	5.9
1999	5.6	5.6	5.6	5.6	5.6	5.6	5.7	5.6	5.6	5.4	5.4	5.4	5.4	5.4	5.4	5.4	5.5	5.5	5.6	5.6
2000	5.7	5.7	5.7	5.7	5.7	5.7	5.8	5.7	5.7	5.6	5.5	5.5	5.5	5.5	5.5	5.6	5.6	5.7	5.7	5.7
2001	5.8	5.7	5.7	5.8	5.8	5.8	5.9	5.8	5.7	5.6	5.6	5.6	5.6	5.6	5.6	5.7	5.7	5.8	5.8	5.8
2002	5.9	5.9	5.9	5.9	5.9	5.9	6.0	6.0	5.9	5.8	5.7	5.7	5.8	5.7	5.8	5.8	5.9	5.9	6.0	6.0

Table C-3 (Page 3 of 6)

Long-Term Corporate Bonds Total Returns
Rates of Return for all holding periods
Percent per annum compounded annually

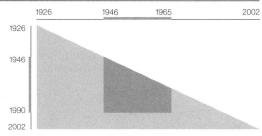

from 1926 to 2002

To the end of	From the beginning of 1946	1947	1948	1949	1950	1951	1952	1953	1954	1955	1956	1957	1958	1959	1960	1961	1962	1963	1964	1965
1946	1.7																			
1947	-0.3	-2.3																		
1948	1.1	0.8	4.1																	
1949	1.7	1.7	3.7	3.3																
1950	1.8	1.8	3.2	2.7	2.1															
1951	1.0	0.9	1.7	0.9	-0.3	-2.7														
1952	1.4	1.3	2.0	1.5	0.9	0.4	3.5													
1953	1.6	1.6	2.3	1.9	1.6	1.4	3.5	3.4												
1954	2.0	2.1	2.7	2.5	2.3	2.4	4.1	4.4	5.4											
1955	1.9	1.9	2.4	2.2	2.0	2.0	3.2	3.1	2.9	0.5										
1956	1.1	1.0	1.4	1.0	0.7	0.5	1.1	0.5	-0.4	-3.2	-6.8									
1957	1.7	1.7	2.1	1.8	1.7	1.6	2.3	2.1	1.8	0.6	0.7	8.7								
1958	1.4	1.3	1.7	1.4	1.2	1.1	1.7	1.4	1.0	-0.1	-0.3	3.1	-2.2							
1959	1.2	1.2	1.5	1.2	1.0	0.9	1.3	1.0	0.6	-0.3	-0.5	1.7	-1.6	-1.0						
1960	1.7	1.7	2.0	1.8	1.7	1.7	2.2	2.0	1.8	1.2	1.4	3.5	1.8	3.9	9.1					
1961	1.9	1.9	2.2	2.1	2.0	2.0	2.4	2.3	2.2	1.7	1.9	3.8	2.6	4.2	6.9	4.8				
1962	2.2	2.3	2.6	2.5	2.4	2.4	2.9	2.9	2.8	2.5	2.8	4.5	3.6	5.1	7.3	6.4	7.9			
1963	2.2	2.3	2.6	2.5	2.4	2.4	2.9	2.8	2.7	2.4	2.7	4.1	3.4	4.5	6.0	5.0	5.0	2.2		
1964	2.4	2.4	2.7	2.6	2.6	2.6	3.0	3.0	2.9	2.7	2.9	4.2	3.6	4.6	5.7	4.9	4.9	3.5	4.8	
1965	2.2	2.3	2.5	2.4	2.4	2.4	2.8	2.7	2.6	2.4	2.6	3.7	3.1	3.8	4.7	3.8	3.6	2.1	2.1	-0.5
1966	2.1	2.1	2.4	2.3	2.2	2.2	2.6	2.5	2.4	2.2	2.4	3.3	2.7	3.4	4.0	3.2	2.9	1.7	1.5	-0.1
1967	1.8	1.8	2.0	1.9	1.8	1.8	2.1	2.0	1.9	1.6	1.7	2.5	1.9	2.4	2.9	2.0	1.5	0.3	-0.2	-1.8
1968	1.8	1.8	2.0	1.9	1.9	1.8	2.1	2.0	1.9	1.7	1.8	2.5	2.0	2.4	2.8	2.1	1.7	0.7	0.4	-0.7
1969	1.4	1.4	1.6	1.4	1.3	1.3	1.5	1.4	1.3	1.0	1.1	1.7	1.1	1.4	1.7	0.9	0.4	-0.6	-1.1	-2.2
1970	2.0	2.0	2.2	2.1	2.1	2.1	2.3	2.3	2.2	2.0	2.1	2.8	2.4	2.7	3.1	2.5	2.3	1.6	1.5	0.9
1971	2.4	2.4	2.6	2.5	2.5	2.5	2.8	2.7	2.7	2.5	2.7	3.3	3.0	3.4	3.7	3.3	3.1	2.6	2.6	2.3
1972	2.5	2.6	2.8	2.7	2.7	2.7	3.0	2.9	2.9	2.8	2.9	3.6	3.2	3.6	4.0	3.6	3.5	3.0	3.1	2.9
1973	2.5	2.5	2.7	2.6	2.6	2.6	2.9	2.9	2.8	2.7	2.8	3.4	3.1	3.5	3.8	3.4	3.3	2.9	2.9	2.7
1974	2.3	2.3	2.5	2.4	2.4	2.4	2.6	2.6	2.5	2.4	2.5	3.1	2.7	3.0	3.3	2.9	2.8	2.4	2.4	2.1
1975	2.7	2.7	2.9	2.9	2.8	2.9	3.1	3.1	3.1	3.0	3.1	3.6	3.4	3.7	4.0	3.7	3.6	3.3	3.3	3.2
1976	3.2	3.2	3.4	3.4	3.4	3.4	3.7	3.7	3.7	3.6	3.8	4.3	4.1	4.5	4.8	4.5	4.5	4.3	4.4	4.4
1977	3.1	3.2	3.3	3.3	3.3	3.4	3.6	3.6	3.6	3.5	3.7	4.2	4.0	4.3	4.6	4.4	4.3	4.1	4.2	4.2
1978	3.0	3.1	3.2	3.2	3.2	3.2	3.5	3.5	3.5	3.4	3.5	4.0	3.8	4.1	4.4	4.1	4.1	3.8	4.0	3.9
1979	2.8	2.8	3.0	3.0	2.9	3.0	3.2	3.2	3.2	3.1	3.2	3.6	3.4	3.7	3.9	3.7	3.6	3.4	3.4	3.3
1980	2.6	2.7	2.8	2.8	2.8	2.8	3.0	3.0	2.9	2.8	2.9	3.4	3.1	3.4	3.6	3.3	3.3	3.0	3.1	2.9
1981	2.5	2.5	2.7	2.6	2.6	2.6	2.8	2.8	2.8	2.7	2.8	3.2	3.0	3.2	3.4	3.1	3.0	2.8	2.8	2.7
1982	3.4	3.5	3.7	3.6	3.7	3.7	3.9	3.9	3.9	3.9	4.0	4.5	4.3	4.6	4.8	4.6	4.6	4.5	4.6	4.6
1983	3.5	3.6	3.7	3.7	3.7	3.8	4.0	4.0	4.0	4.0	4.1	4.5	4.4	4.6	4.9	4.7	4.7	4.6	4.7	4.7
1984	3.8	3.9	4.1	4.1	4.1	4.1	4.4	4.4	4.4	4.4	4.5	5.0	4.8	5.1	5.3	5.2	5.2	5.1	5.2	5.2
1985	4.4	4.5	4.7	4.7	4.7	4.8	5.0	5.1	5.1	5.1	5.3	5.7	5.6	5.9	6.2	6.1	6.1	6.1	6.2	6.3
1986	4.8	4.9	5.0	5.1	5.1	5.2	5.4	5.5	5.6	5.6	5.7	6.2	6.1	6.4	6.7	6.6	6.7	6.6	6.8	6.9
1987	4.7	4.7	4.9	4.9	5.0	5.0	5.3	5.3	5.4	5.4	5.5	6.0	5.9	6.2	6.4	6.3	6.4	6.3	6.5	6.6
1988	4.8	4.9	5.0	5.1	5.1	5.2	5.4	5.5	5.5	5.5	5.7	6.1	6.0	6.3	6.6	6.5	6.5	6.5	6.7	6.7
1989	5.0	5.1	5.3	5.3	5.4	5.5	5.7	5.7	5.8	5.8	6.0	6.4	6.3	6.6	6.9	6.8	6.9	6.8	7.0	7.1
1990	5.1	5.2	5.3	5.4	5.4	5.5	5.7	5.8	5.8	5.8	6.0	6.4	6.3	6.6	6.9	6.8	6.9	6.8	7.0	7.1

Table C-3 (Page 4 of 6)

Long-Term Corporate Bonds Total Returns
Rates of Return for all holding periods
Percent per annum compounded annually

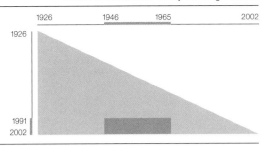

from 1926 to 2002

To the end of	From the beginning of																			
	1946	1947	1948	1949	1950	1951	1952	1953	1954	1955	1956	1957	1958	1959	1960	1961	1962	1963	1964	1965
1991	5.4	5.5	5.6	5.7	5.7	5.8	6.0	6.1	6.2	6.2	6.4	6.8	6.7	7.0	7.3	7.2	7.3	7.3	7.4	7.5
1992	5.5	5.5	5.7	5.8	5.8	5.9	6.1	6.2	6.3	6.3	6.5	6.8	6.8	7.1	7.3	7.3	7.3	7.3	7.5	7.6
1993	5.6	5.7	5.9	5.9	6.0	6.1	6.3	6.4	6.4	6.5	6.6	7.0	7.0	7.2	7.5	7.4	7.5	7.5	7.7	7.8
1994	5.4	5.4	5.6	5.7	5.7	5.8	6.0	6.1	6.1	6.1	6.3	6.7	6.6	6.9	7.1	7.0	7.1	7.1	7.2	7.3
1995	5.8	5.9	6.0	6.1	6.1	6.2	6.4	6.5	6.6	6.6	6.8	7.1	7.1	7.4	7.6	7.6	7.6	7.6	7.8	7.9
1996	5.7	5.8	5.9	6.0	6.0	6.1	6.3	6.4	6.5	6.5	6.6	7.0	6.9	7.2	7.4	7.4	7.5	7.4	7.6	7.7
1997	5.8	5.9	6.1	6.1	6.2	6.3	6.5	6.5	6.6	6.6	6.8	7.1	7.1	7.3	7.6	7.5	7.6	7.6	7.8	7.9
1998	5.9	6.0	6.2	6.2	6.3	6.3	6.5	6.6	6.7	6.7	6.9	7.2	7.2	7.4	7.7	7.6	7.7	7.7	7.8	7.9
1999	5.6	5.7	5.9	5.9	6.0	6.0	6.2	6.3	6.4	6.4	6.5	6.9	6.8	7.0	7.2	7.2	7.3	7.2	7.4	7.5
2000	5.8	5.8	6.0	6.0	6.1	6.2	6.4	6.4	6.5	6.5	6.7	7.0	6.9	7.2	7.4	7.3	7.4	7.4	7.5	7.6
2001	5.9	5.9	6.1	6.1	6.2	6.3	6.5	6.5	6.6	6.6	6.7	7.1	7.0	7.3	7.5	7.4	7.5	7.5	7.6	7.7
2002	6.0	6.1	6.3	6.3	6.4	6.4	6.6	6.7	6.8	6.8	6.9	7.3	7.2	7.4	7.7	7.6	7.7	7.7	7.8	7.9

Table C-3 (Page 5 of 6)

Long-Term Corporate Bonds Total Returns
Rates of Return for all holding periods
Percent per annum compounded annually

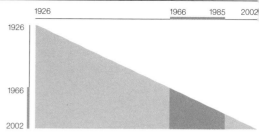

from 1926 to 2002

To the end of	From the beginning of 1966	1967	1968	1969	1970	1971	1972	1973	1974	1975	1976	1977	1978	1979	1980	1981	1982	1983	1984	1985
1966	0.2																			
1967	-2.4	-5.0																		
1968	-0.8	-1.3	2.6																	
1969	-2.7	-3.6	-2.9	-8.1																
1970	1.2	1.5	3.7	4.3	18.4															
1971	2.8	3.3	5.5	6.5	14.6	11.0														
1972	3.4	4.0	5.8	6.7	12.1	9.1	7.3													
1973	3.1	3.6	5.0	5.6	9.3	6.4	4.2	1.1												
1974	2.4	2.7	3.9	4.1	6.7	3.9	1.7	-1.0	-3.1											
1975	3.6	4.0	5.1	5.5	8.0	6.0	4.8	4.0	5.4	14.6										
1976	4.9	5.4	6.6	7.1	9.4	8.0	7.4	7.5	9.7	16.6	18.6									
1977	4.6	5.0	6.1	6.5	8.4	7.1	6.4	6.3	7.6	11.4	9.9	1.7								
1978	4.2	4.6	5.5	5.8	7.5	6.2	5.5	5.2	6.0	8.4	6.4	0.8	-0.1							
1979	3.6	3.9	4.7	4.8	6.2	5.0	4.2	3.8	4.3	5.8	3.7	-0.9	-2.1	-4.2						
1980	3.2	3.4	4.1	4.2	5.4	4.2	3.4	3.0	3.2	4.3	2.4	-1.4	-2.4	-3.5	-2.8					
1981	2.9	3.1	3.7	3.8	4.8	3.7	3.0	2.5	2.7	3.5	1.8	-1.3	-2.1	-2.7	-2.0	-1.2				
1982	4.9	5.2	5.9	6.1	7.3	6.5	6.0	5.9	6.5	7.7	6.8	4.9	5.6	7.0	11.0	18.7	42.6			
1983	5.0	5.2	5.9	6.1	7.2	6.4	6.1	6.0	6.4	7.6	6.7	5.1	5.7	6.9	9.8	14.4	23.1	6.3		
1984	5.6	5.9	6.5	6.8	7.9	7.1	6.9	6.8	7.4	8.5	7.8	6.5	7.2	8.5	11.2	15.0	21.0	11.4	16.9	
1985	6.7	7.0	7.7	8.0	9.1	8.5	8.4	8.5	9.1	10.3	9.8	8.9	9.8	11.3	14.1	17.9	23.2	17.3	23.3	30.1
1986	7.3	7.6	8.3	8.7	9.7	9.2	9.1	9.2	9.9	11.0	10.7	9.9	10.9	12.4	14.9	18.2	22.5	18.0	22.1	24.9
1987	6.9	7.2	7.9	8.2	9.2	8.6	8.5	8.6	9.1	10.1	9.8	9.0	9.7	10.9	12.9	15.4	18.4	14.1	16.1	15.9
1988	7.1	7.4	8.0	8.3	9.2	8.7	8.6	8.7	9.2	10.2	9.8	9.1	9.8	10.9	12.7	14.8	17.3	13.5	15.0	14.5
1989	7.4	7.8	8.4	8.7	9.6	9.1	9.0	9.1	9.7	10.6	10.3	9.7	10.3	11.3	13.0	14.9	17.1	13.9	15.2	14.9
1990	7.4	7.7	8.3	8.6	9.4	9.0	8.9	9.0	9.5	10.3	10.0	9.4	10.1	11.0	12.4	14.1	15.9	13.0	14.0	13.5
1991	7.9	8.2	8.8	9.0	9.9	9.5	9.4	9.5	10.0	10.9	10.6	10.1	10.7	11.6	13.0	14.6	16.3	13.7	14.7	14.4
1992	7.9	8.2	8.8	9.1	9.9	9.5	9.4	9.5	10.0	10.8	10.6	10.1	10.6	11.5	12.8	14.2	15.7	13.3	14.1	13.7
1993	8.1	8.4	9.0	9.2	10.0	9.7	9.6	9.7	10.2	10.9	10.7	10.2	10.8	11.6	12.8	14.1	15.5	13.3	14.0	13.7
1994	7.6	7.9	8.4	8.6	9.3	9.0	8.9	9.0	9.3	10.0	9.8	9.3	9.8	10.4	11.4	12.5	13.7	11.5	12.0	11.6
1995	8.2	8.5	9.0	9.2	10.0	9.6	9.6	9.7	10.1	10.8	10.6	10.2	10.7	11.3	12.4	13.5	14.6	12.7	13.2	12.9
1996	8.0	8.2	8.7	9.0	9.6	9.3	9.2	9.3	9.7	10.3	10.1	9.7	10.1	10.7	11.7	12.7	13.7	11.8	12.3	11.9
1997	8.1	8.4	8.9	9.1	9.8	9.4	9.4	9.5	9.8	10.4	10.2	9.9	10.3	10.9	11.8	12.7	13.6	11.9	12.3	12.0
1998	8.2	8.5	8.9	9.1	9.8	9.5	9.4	9.5	9.9	10.4	10.3	9.9	10.3	10.9	11.7	12.6	13.4	11.8	12.2	11.9
1999	7.7	7.9	8.4	8.6	9.2	8.9	8.8	8.8	9.2	9.7	9.5	9.1	9.4	9.9	10.7	11.4	12.2	10.6	10.9	10.5
2000	7.8	8.1	8.5	8.7	9.3	9.0	8.9	9.0	9.3	9.8	9.6	9.2	9.6	10.0	10.8	11.5	12.2	10.7	11.0	10.6
2001	7.9	8.2	8.6	8.8	9.3	9.0	9.0	9.0	9.3	9.8	9.6	9.3	9.6	10.1	10.8	11.5	12.1	10.7	11.0	10.6
2002	8.1	8.4	8.8	9.0	9.5	9.3	9.2	9.3	9.6	10.1	9.9	9.6	9.9	10.3	11.0	11.7	12.3	11.0	11.2	10.9

Table C-3 (Page 6 of 6)

Long-Term Corporate Bonds Total Returns
Rates of Return for all holding periods
Percent per annum compounded annually

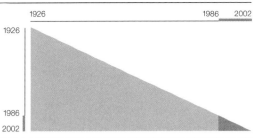

from 1926 to 2002

To the end of	From the beginning of																
	1986	1987	1988	1989	1990	1991	1992	1993	1994	1995	1996	1997	1998	1999	2000	2001	2002
1986	19.8																
1987	9.3	−0.3															
1988	9.8	5.1	10.7														
1989	11.4	8.7	13.4	16.2													
1990	10.4	8.2	11.2	11.4	6.8												
1991	12.0	10.4	13.3	14.2	13.1	19.9											
1992	11.6	10.3	12.5	13.0	11.9	14.5	9.4										
1993	11.8	10.7	12.6	13.0	12.2	14.1	11.3	13.2									
1994	9.7	8.5	9.8	9.6	8.4	8.8	5.3	3.3	−5.8								
1995	11.3	10.4	11.8	12.0	11.3	12.2	10.4	10.7	9.5	27.2							
1996	10.4	9.5	10.6	10.6	9.8	10.3	8.5	8.3	6.7	13.6	1.4						
1997	10.6	9.8	10.8	10.9	10.2	10.7	9.2	9.2	8.2	13.4	7.0	12.9					
1998	10.6	9.9	10.8	10.9	10.3	10.7	9.5	9.5	8.7	12.7	8.3	11.8	10.8				
1999	9.2	8.4	9.2	9.0	8.4	8.5	7.2	6.9	5.9	8.4	4.1	5.0	1.2	−7.4			
2000	9.4	8.7	9.5	9.4	8.8	9.0	7.8	7.6	6.8	9.1	5.8	6.9	5.0	2.2	12.9		
2001	9.5	8.9	9.5	9.5	8.9	9.1	8.1	7.9	7.3	9.3	6.6	7.7	6.4	4.9	11.8	10.6	
2002	9.9	9.3	10.0	9.9	9.5	9.7	8.8	8.8	8.3	10.2	7.9	9.1	8.3	7.7	13.3	13.5	16.3

Table C-4 (Page 1 of 6)

Long-Term Government Bonds Total Returns
Rates of Return for all holding periods
Percent per annum compounded annually

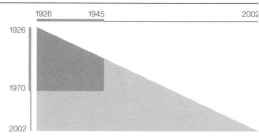

from 1926 to 2002

To the end of	From the beginning of 1926	1927	1928	1929	1930	1931	1932	1933	1934	1935	1936	1937	1938	1939	1940	1941	1942	1943	1944	1945
1926	7.8																			
1927	8.3	8.9																		
1928	5.5	4.4	0.1																	
1929	5.0	4.1	1.7	3.4																
1930	4.9	4.2	2.7	4.0	4.7															
1931	3.1	2.2	0.6	0.8	-0.5	-5.3														
1932	5.0	4.5	3.7	4.6	5.0	5.2	16.8													
1933	4.4	3.9	3.1	3.7	3.7	3.4	8.1	-0.1												
1934	5.0	4.6	4.0	4.7	4.9	5.0	8.7	4.9	10.0											
1935	5.0	4.7	4.1	4.7	5.0	5.0	7.8	4.9	7.5	5.0										
1936	5.2	4.9	4.5	5.1	5.3	5.4	7.7	5.5	7.5	6.2	7.5									
1937	4.8	4.5	4.1	4.5	4.7	4.7	6.4	4.5	5.6	4.2	3.8	0.2								
1938	4.8	4.6	4.2	4.6	4.8	4.8	6.3	4.6	5.6	4.5	4.4	2.8	5.5							
1939	4.9	4.7	4.4	4.7	4.9	4.9	6.3	4.8	5.7	4.8	4.8	3.9	5.7	5.9						
1940	5.0	4.8	4.5	4.9	5.0	5.0	6.2	5.0	5.7	5.0	5.0	4.4	5.9	6.0	6.1					
1941	4.7	4.5	4.2	4.5	4.6	4.6	5.7	4.5	5.1	4.4	4.3	3.7	4.6	4.3	3.5	0.9				
1942	4.6	4.5	4.2	4.5	4.5	4.5	5.5	4.4	4.9	4.3	4.2	3.6	4.3	4.0	3.4	2.1	3.2			
1943	4.5	4.3	4.0	4.3	4.4	4.3	5.2	4.2	4.6	4.0	3.9	3.4	3.9	3.6	3.1	2.1	2.6	2.1		
1944	4.4	4.2	4.0	4.2	4.3	4.2	5.0	4.1	4.5	3.9	3.8	3.3	3.8	3.5	3.0	2.3	2.7	2.4	2.8	
1945	4.7	4.6	4.3	4.6	4.6	4.6	5.4	4.6	5.0	4.5	4.5	4.1	4.6	4.5	4.3	3.9	4.7	5.1	6.7	10.7
1946	4.5	4.3	4.1	4.3	4.4	4.3	5.0	4.2	4.6	4.1	4.0	3.7	4.1	3.9	3.6	3.2	3.7	3.8	4.4	5.2
1947	4.1	4.0	3.7	3.9	4.0	3.9	4.5	3.8	4.0	3.6	3.5	3.1	3.4	3.2	2.8	2.4	2.6	2.5	2.6	2.5
1948	4.1	4.0	3.7	3.9	3.9	3.9	4.5	3.7	4.0	3.6	3.5	3.1	3.4	3.2	2.9	2.5	2.7	2.6	2.7	2.7
1949	4.2	4.1	3.8	4.0	4.1	4.0	4.6	3.9	4.1	3.8	3.7	3.4	3.7	3.5	3.2	2.9	3.2	3.2	3.4	3.5
1950	4.0	3.9	3.7	3.8	3.9	3.8	4.3	3.7	3.9	3.5	3.4	3.1	3.4	3.2	2.9	2.6	2.8	2.8	2.9	2.9
1951	3.7	3.6	3.3	3.5	3.5	3.4	3.9	3.3	3.4	3.1	3.0	2.7	2.8	2.6	2.4	2.0	2.1	2.0	2.0	1.9
1952	3.6	3.5	3.3	3.4	3.4	3.3	3.8	3.2	3.3	3.0	2.8	2.6	2.7	2.5	2.3	1.9	2.0	1.9	1.9	1.8
1953	3.6	3.5	3.3	3.4	3.4	3.3	3.8	3.2	3.3	3.0	2.9	2.6	2.8	2.6	2.4	2.1	2.2	2.1	2.1	2.0
1954	3.7	3.6	3.4	3.5	3.6	3.5	3.9	3.4	3.5	3.2	3.1	2.9	3.0	2.9	2.7	2.4	2.6	2.5	2.5	2.5
1955	3.6	3.4	3.2	3.4	3.4	3.3	3.7	3.1	3.3	3.0	2.9	2.6	2.8	2.6	2.4	2.2	2.3	2.2	2.2	2.2
1956	3.3	3.1	2.9	3.0	3.0	3.0	3.3	2.8	2.9	2.6	2.5	2.2	2.3	2.2	1.9	1.7	1.7	1.6	1.6	1.5
1957	3.4	3.3	3.1	3.2	3.2	3.1	3.5	3.0	3.1	2.8	2.7	2.5	2.6	2.4	2.2	2.0	2.1	2.0	2.0	1.9
1958	3.1	3.0	2.8	2.9	2.8	2.8	3.1	2.6	2.7	2.4	2.3	2.1	2.1	2.0	1.8	1.5	1.6	1.5	1.4	1.3
1959	2.9	2.8	2.6	2.7	2.7	2.6	2.9	2.4	2.5	2.2	2.1	1.9	1.9	1.8	1.6	1.3	1.4	1.3	1.2	1.1
1960	3.2	3.1	2.9	3.0	3.0	2.9	3.2	2.8	2.9	2.6	2.5	2.3	2.4	2.3	2.1	1.9	2.0	1.9	1.9	1.8
1961	3.2	3.0	2.9	3.0	2.9	2.9	3.2	2.7	2.8	2.6	2.5	2.3	2.4	2.2	2.1	1.9	1.9	1.9	1.8	1.8
1962	3.3	3.1	3.0	3.1	3.1	3.0	3.3	2.9	3.0	2.7	2.6	2.5	2.5	2.4	2.3	2.1	2.2	2.1	2.1	2.1
1963	3.2	3.1	2.9	3.0	3.0	3.0	3.2	2.8	2.9	2.7	2.6	2.4	2.5	2.4	2.2	2.1	2.1	2.1	2.1	2.0
1964	3.2	3.1	2.9	3.0	3.0	3.0	3.2	2.8	2.9	2.7	2.6	2.4	2.5	2.4	2.3	2.1	2.2	2.1	2.1	2.1
1965	3.2	3.0	2.9	3.0	3.0	2.9	3.2	2.8	2.9	2.6	2.6	2.4	2.5	2.4	2.2	2.1	2.1	2.1	2.1	2.0
1966	3.2	3.1	2.9	3.0	3.0	2.9	3.2	2.8	2.9	2.7	2.6	2.4	2.5	2.4	2.3	2.1	2.2	2.1	2.1	2.1
1967	2.9	2.7	2.6	2.7	2.6	2.6	2.8	2.4	2.5	2.3	2.2	2.0	2.1	2.0	1.8	1.7	1.7	1.7	1.6	1.6
1968	2.8	2.7	2.5	2.6	2.6	2.5	2.7	2.4	2.4	2.2	2.1	2.0	2.0	1.9	1.8	1.6	1.6	1.6	1.6	1.5
1969	2.6	2.5	2.3	2.4	2.4	2.3	2.5	2.1	2.2	2.0	1.9	1.7	1.8	1.7	1.5	1.4	1.4	1.3	1.3	1.2
1970	2.8	2.7	2.5	2.6	2.6	2.5	2.7	2.4	2.5	2.3	2.2	2.0	2.1	2.0	1.9	1.7	1.7	1.7	1.7	1.6

Table C-4 (Page 2 of 6)

Long-Term Government Bonds Total Returns
Rates of Return for all holding periods
Percent per annum compounded annually

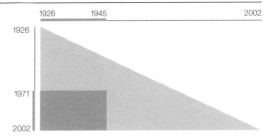

from 1926 to 2002

To the end of	From the beginning of 1926	1927	1928	1929	1930	1931	1932	1933	1934	1935	1936	1937	1938	1939	1940	1941	1942	1943	1944	1945
1971	3.0	2.9	2.8	2.8	2.8	2.8	3.0	2.7	2.7	2.5	2.5	2.3	2.4	2.3	2.2	2.1	2.1	2.1	2.1	2.0
1972	3.1	3.0	2.8	2.9	2.9	2.8	3.1	2.7	2.8	2.6	2.6	2.4	2.5	2.4	2.3	2.2	2.2	2.2	2.2	2.2
1973	3.0	2.9	2.8	2.8	2.8	2.8	3.0	2.6	2.7	2.5	2.5	2.3	2.4	2.3	2.2	2.1	2.1	2.1	2.1	2.1
1974	3.0	2.9	2.8	2.8	2.8	2.8	3.0	2.7	2.7	2.6	2.5	2.4	2.4	2.4	2.3	2.1	2.2	2.2	2.2	2.1
1975	3.1	3.0	2.9	3.0	3.0	2.9	3.1	2.8	2.9	2.7	2.7	2.6	2.6	2.5	2.4	2.3	2.4	2.4	2.4	2.4
1976	3.4	3.3	3.2	3.2	3.2	3.2	3.4	3.1	3.2	3.0	3.0	2.9	3.0	2.9	2.8	2.7	2.8	2.8	2.8	2.8
1977	3.3	3.2	3.1	3.2	3.2	3.1	3.3	3.0	3.1	3.0	2.9	2.8	2.9	2.8	2.7	2.6	2.7	2.7	2.7	2.7
1978	3.2	3.1	3.0	3.1	3.1	3.0	3.2	2.9	3.0	2.9	2.8	2.7	2.8	2.7	2.6	2.5	2.6	2.5	2.6	2.6
1979	3.1	3.0	2.9	3.0	3.0	2.9	3.1	2.9	2.9	2.8	2.7	2.6	2.7	2.6	2.5	2.4	2.5	2.4	2.5	2.4
1980	3.0	2.9	2.8	2.9	2.8	2.8	3.0	2.7	2.8	2.6	2.6	2.5	2.5	2.4	2.3	2.3	2.3	2.3	2.3	2.3
1981	3.0	2.9	2.8	2.8	2.8	2.8	3.0	2.7	2.7	2.6	2.5	2.4	2.5	2.4	2.3	2.2	2.3	2.3	2.3	2.2
1982	3.5	3.5	3.4	3.4	3.4	3.4	3.6	3.3	3.4	3.3	3.2	3.1	3.2	3.2	3.1	3.0	3.1	3.1	3.1	3.1
1983	3.5	3.4	3.3	3.4	3.4	3.4	3.5	3.3	3.3	3.2	3.2	3.1	3.2	3.1	3.0	3.0	3.0	3.0	3.0	3.0
1984	3.7	3.6	3.5	3.6	3.6	3.6	3.7	3.5	3.6	3.4	3.4	3.3	3.4	3.4	3.3	3.2	3.3	3.3	3.3	3.3
1985	4.1	4.0	3.9	4.0	4.0	4.0	4.2	4.0	4.0	3.9	3.9	3.8	3.9	3.9	3.8	3.8	3.8	3.9	3.9	3.9
1986	4.4	4.3	4.3	4.3	4.3	4.3	4.5	4.3	4.4	4.3	4.3	4.2	4.3	4.3	4.2	4.2	4.3	4.3	4.3	4.4
1987	4.3	4.2	4.1	4.2	4.2	4.2	4.4	4.2	4.3	4.2	4.1	4.1	4.2	4.1	4.1	4.0	4.1	4.1	4.2	4.2
1988	4.4	4.3	4.2	4.3	4.3	4.3	4.5	4.3	4.4	4.3	4.2	4.2	4.3	4.2	4.2	4.2	4.2	4.2	4.3	4.3
1989	4.6	4.5	4.4	4.5	4.5	4.5	4.7	4.5	4.6	4.5	4.5	4.4	4.5	4.5	4.5	4.4	4.5	4.5	4.6	4.6
1990	4.6	4.5	4.5	4.5	4.6	4.6	4.7	4.5	4.6	4.5	4.5	4.5	4.5	4.5	4.5	4.5	4.5	4.6	4.6	4.7
1991	4.8	4.7	4.7	4.8	4.8	4.8	5.0	4.8	4.9	4.8	4.8	4.7	4.8	4.8	4.8	4.7	4.8	4.8	4.9	4.9
1992	4.8	4.8	4.7	4.8	4.8	4.8	5.0	4.8	4.9	4.8	4.8	4.8	4.9	4.8	4.8	4.8	4.9	4.9	5.0	5.0
1993	5.0	5.0	4.9	5.0	5.0	5.0	5.2	5.0	5.1	5.0	5.0	5.0	5.1	5.1	5.1	5.0	5.1	5.2	5.2	5.3
1994	4.8	4.8	4.7	4.8	4.8	4.8	5.0	4.8	4.9	4.8	4.8	4.8	4.8	4.8	4.8	4.8	4.9	4.9	4.9	5.0
1995	5.2	5.1	5.1	5.2	5.2	5.2	5.4	5.2	5.3	5.2	5.2	5.2	5.3	5.2	5.2	5.2	5.3	5.3	5.4	5.5
1996	5.1	5.0	5.0	5.1	5.1	5.1	5.3	5.1	5.2	5.1	5.1	5.1	5.1	5.1	5.1	5.1	5.2	5.2	5.3	5.3
1997	5.2	5.2	5.1	5.2	5.2	5.2	5.4	5.2	5.3	5.3	5.3	5.2	5.3	5.3	5.3	5.3	5.4	5.4	5.5	5.5
1998	5.3	5.3	5.2	5.3	5.3	5.4	5.5	5.4	5.4	5.4	5.4	5.3	5.4	5.4	5.4	5.4	5.5	5.5	5.6	5.7
1999	5.1	5.1	5.0	5.1	5.1	5.1	5.3	5.1	5.2	5.1	5.1	5.1	5.2	5.2	5.2	5.2	5.2	5.3	5.3	5.4
2000	5.3	5.3	5.2	5.3	5.3	5.4	5.5	5.4	5.4	5.4	5.4	5.3	5.4	5.4	5.4	5.4	5.5	5.5	5.6	5.6
2001	5.3	5.3	5.2	5.3	5.3	5.3	5.5	5.3	5.4	5.3	5.4	5.3	5.4	5.4	5.4	5.4	5.5	5.5	5.6	5.6
2002	5.5	5.4	5.4	5.5	5.5	5.5	5.7	5.5	5.6	5.5	5.5	5.5	5.6	5.6	5.6	5.6	5.6	5.7	5.7	5.8

Table C-4 (Page 3 of 6)

Long-Term Government Bonds Total Returns
Rates of Return for all holding periods
Percent per annum compounded annually

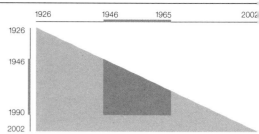

from 1926 to 2002

To the end of	From the beginning of 1946	1947	1948	1949	1950	1951	1952	1953	1954	1955	1956	1957	1958	1959	1960	1961	1962	1963	1964	1965
1946	-0.1																			
1947	-1.4	-2.6																		
1948	0.2	0.3	3.4																	
1949	1.7	2.3	4.9	6.4																
1950	1.4	1.8	3.3	3.2	0.1															
1951	0.5	0.6	1.4	0.8	-2.0	-3.9														
1952	0.6	0.7	1.4	0.9	-0.9	-1.4	1.2													
1953	1.0	1.1	1.7	1.4	0.2	0.2	2.4	3.6												
1954	1.6	1.8	2.5	2.4	1.6	1.9	4.0	5.4	7.2											
1955	1.3	1.5	2.0	1.8	1.1	1.3	2.6	3.1	2.9	-1.3										
1956	0.7	0.8	1.1	0.9	0.1	0.1	0.9	0.9	0.0	-3.5	-5.6									
1957	1.2	1.4	1.8	1.6	1.0	1.1	2.0	2.2	1.8	0.0	0.7	7.5								
1958	0.6	0.7	1.0	0.8	0.2	0.2	0.8	0.7	0.2	-1.5	-1.6	0.5	-6.1							
1959	0.4	0.5	0.7	0.5	-0.1	-0.1	0.4	0.3	-0.2	-1.7	-1.8	-0.5	-4.2	-2.3						
1960	1.3	1.4	1.7	1.5	1.1	1.2	1.8	1.9	1.6	0.7	1.2	2.9	1.5	5.5	13.8					
1961	1.3	1.3	1.6	1.5	1.1	1.2	1.7	1.8	1.6	0.8	1.1	2.5	1.3	3.9	7.2	1.0				
1962	1.6	1.7	2.0	1.9	1.5	1.7	2.2	2.3	2.1	1.5	1.9	3.2	2.4	4.7	7.1	3.9	6.9			
1963	1.6	1.7	1.9	1.8	1.5	1.6	2.1	2.2	2.0	1.5	1.8	3.0	2.2	4.0	5.6	3.0	4.0	1.2		
1964	1.7	1.8	2.0	1.9	1.6	1.8	2.2	2.3	2.2	1.7	2.0	3.0	2.4	3.9	5.2	3.1	3.8	2.4	3.5	
1965	1.6	1.7	2.0	1.9	1.6	1.7	2.1	2.2	2.1	1.6	1.9	2.8	2.2	3.4	4.4	2.6	3.1	1.8	2.1	0.7
1966	1.7	1.8	2.0	2.0	1.7	1.8	2.2	2.3	2.2	1.8	2.1	2.9	2.4	3.5	4.3	2.8	3.2	2.3	2.6	2.2
1967	1.2	1.2	1.4	1.3	1.1	1.1	1.5	1.5	1.3	0.9	1.1	1.7	1.1	2.0	2.5	1.0	1.0	-0.1	-0.5	-1.8
1968	1.1	1.2	1.4	1.3	1.0	1.1	1.4	1.4	1.2	0.8	1.0	1.5	1.0	1.7	2.2	0.8	0.8	-0.2	-0.4	-1.4
1969	0.9	0.9	1.1	1.0	0.7	0.7	1.0	1.0	0.8	0.4	0.5	1.0	0.5	1.1	1.4	0.2	0.1	-0.9	-1.2	-2.1
1970	1.3	1.3	1.5	1.4	1.2	1.3	1.5	1.6	1.4	1.1	1.3	1.8	1.3	2.0	2.4	1.3	1.3	0.7	0.6	0.1
1971	1.7	1.8	2.0	1.9	1.7	1.8	2.1	2.1	2.1	1.8	2.0	2.5	2.1	2.8	3.2	2.3	2.5	2.0	2.1	1.9
1972	1.9	1.9	2.1	2.1	1.9	2.0	2.3	2.3	2.3	2.0	2.2	2.7	2.4	3.0	3.4	2.6	2.8	2.4	2.5	2.3
1973	1.8	1.8	2.0	1.9	1.8	1.8	2.1	2.2	2.1	1.8	2.0	2.5	2.2	2.7	3.1	2.3	2.4	2.0	2.1	2.0
1974	1.8	1.9	2.1	2.0	1.9	1.9	2.2	2.3	2.2	1.9	2.1	2.6	2.3	2.8	3.2	2.5	2.6	2.2	2.3	2.2
1975	2.1	2.2	2.3	2.3	2.1	2.2	2.5	2.5	2.5	2.3	2.5	2.9	2.7	3.2	3.5	2.9	3.0	2.7	2.9	2.8
1976	2.5	2.6	2.8	2.8	2.6	2.7	3.0	3.1	3.1	2.9	3.1	3.6	3.4	3.9	4.3	3.7	3.9	3.7	3.9	3.9
1977	2.4	2.5	2.7	2.7	2.5	2.6	2.9	2.9	2.9	2.7	2.9	3.3	3.1	3.7	4.0	3.4	3.6	3.4	3.5	3.5
1978	2.3	2.4	2.6	2.5	2.4	2.5	2.7	2.8	2.8	2.6	2.7	3.1	2.9	3.4	3.7	3.2	3.3	3.1	3.2	3.2
1979	2.2	2.3	2.4	2.4	2.3	2.3	2.6	2.6	2.6	2.4	2.6	2.9	2.7	3.2	3.5	2.9	3.1	2.8	2.9	2.9
1980	2.0	2.1	2.2	2.2	2.1	2.1	2.3	2.4	2.3	2.2	2.3	2.6	2.4	2.8	3.1	2.6	2.7	2.4	2.5	2.5
1981	2.0	2.1	2.2	2.2	2.1	2.1	2.3	2.4	2.3	2.2	2.3	2.6	2.4	2.8	3.0	2.6	2.6	2.4	2.5	2.4
1982	2.9	3.0	3.2	3.1	3.0	3.1	3.4	3.5	3.4	3.3	3.5	3.9	3.7	4.1	4.4	4.0	4.2	4.0	4.2	4.2
1983	2.8	2.9	3.1	3.1	3.0	3.1	3.3	3.4	3.4	3.2	3.4	3.7	3.6	4.0	4.3	3.9	4.0	3.9	4.0	4.0
1984	3.2	3.2	3.4	3.4	3.3	3.4	3.6	3.7	3.7	3.6	3.8	4.1	4.0	4.4	4.7	4.3	4.5	4.4	4.5	4.6
1985	3.8	3.9	4.0	4.1	4.0	4.1	4.4	4.5	4.5	4.4	4.6	5.0	4.9	5.3	5.6	5.3	5.5	5.4	5.6	5.7
1986	4.2	4.3	4.5	4.6	4.5	4.6	4.9	5.0	5.0	5.0	5.2	5.6	5.5	5.9	6.3	6.0	6.2	6.1	6.4	6.5
1987	4.1	4.2	4.3	4.4	4.3	4.4	4.7	4.8	4.8	4.7	4.9	5.3	5.2	5.6	5.9	5.6	5.8	5.8	6.0	6.1
1988	4.2	4.3	4.5	4.5	4.4	4.6	4.8	4.9	4.9	4.9	5.1	5.4	5.4	5.8	6.0	5.8	6.0	5.9	6.1	6.2
1989	4.5	4.6	4.8	4.8	4.8	4.9	5.1	5.2	5.3	5.2	5.4	5.8	5.7	6.1	6.4	6.2	6.4	6.4	6.6	6.7
1990	4.5	4.6	4.8	4.8	4.8	4.9	5.2	5.3	5.3	5.3	5.5	5.8	5.7	6.1	6.4	6.2	6.4	6.3	6.5	6.7

Table C-4 (Page 4 of 6)

Long-Term Government Bonds Total Returns
Rates of Return for all holding periods
Percent per annum compounded annually

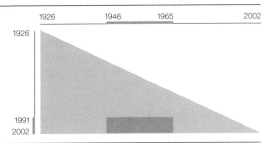

From 1926 to 2002

To the end of	From the beginning of																			
	1946	1947	1948	1949	1950	1951	1952	1953	1954	1955	1956	1957	1958	1959	1960	1961	1962	1963	1964	1965
1991	4.8	4.9	5.1	5.2	5.1	5.2	5.5	5.6	5.7	5.6	5.8	6.2	6.1	6.5	6.8	6.6	6.8	6.8	7.0	7.1
1992	4.9	5.0	5.2	5.2	5.2	5.3	5.6	5.7	5.7	5.7	5.9	6.2	6.2	6.6	6.8	6.6	6.8	6.8	7.0	7.1
1993	5.2	5.3	5.4	5.5	5.5	5.6	5.8	6.0	6.0	6.0	6.2	6.5	6.5	6.9	7.2	7.0	7.2	7.2	7.4	7.5
1994	4.9	5.0	5.1	5.2	5.2	5.3	5.5	5.6	5.7	5.6	5.8	6.1	6.1	6.4	6.7	6.5	6.7	6.7	6.8	7.0
1995	5.3	5.5	5.6	5.7	5.7	5.8	6.0	6.1	6.2	6.2	6.4	6.7	6.7	7.1	7.3	7.1	7.3	7.3	7.5	7.7
1996	5.2	5.3	5.5	5.5	5.5	5.6	5.9	6.0	6.0	6.0	6.2	6.5	6.5	6.8	7.1	6.9	7.1	7.1	7.3	7.4
1997	5.4	5.5	5.7	5.7	5.7	5.9	6.1	6.2	6.3	6.2	6.4	6.7	6.7	7.1	7.3	7.1	7.3	7.3	7.5	7.6
1998	5.6	5.7	5.8	5.9	5.9	6.0	6.2	6.3	6.4	6.4	6.6	6.9	6.9	7.2	7.5	7.3	7.5	7.5	7.7	7.8
1999	5.3	5.4	5.5	5.6	5.6	5.7	5.9	6.0	6.0	6.0	6.2	6.5	6.5	6.8	7.0	6.8	7.0	7.0	7.2	7.3
2000	5.5	5.7	5.8	5.9	5.8	6.0	6.2	6.3	6.3	6.3	6.5	6.8	6.8	7.1	7.3	7.2	7.4	7.4	7.5	7.7
2001	5.5	5.6	5.8	5.8	5.8	5.9	6.1	6.2	6.3	6.3	6.4	6.7	6.7	7.0	7.3	7.1	7.3	7.3	7.4	7.5
2002	5.7	5.8	6.0	6.0	6.0	6.1	6.3	6.5	6.5	6.5	6.7	7.0	6.9	7.3	7.5	7.3	7.5	7.5	7.7	7.8

Table C-4 (Page 5 of 6)

Long-Term Government Bonds Total Returns
Rates of Return for all holding periods
Percent per annum compounded annually

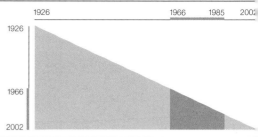

from 1926 to 2002

To the end of	From the beginning of 1966	1967	1968	1969	1970	1971	1972	1973	1974	1975	1976	1977	1978	1979	1980	1981	1982	1983	1984	1985
1966	3.7																			
1967	−3.0	−9.2																		
1968	−2.1	−4.8	−0.3																	
1969	−2.8	−4.9	−2.7	−5.1																
1970	0.0	−0.9	2.0	3.2	12.1															
1971	2.1	1.8	4.7	6.4	12.7	13.2														
1972	2.6	2.4	4.9	6.2	10.3	9.4	5.7													
1973	2.1	1.9	3.9	4.7	7.3	5.8	2.2	−1.1												
1974	2.4	2.2	3.9	4.7	6.7	5.4	2.9	1.6	4.4											
1975	3.0	3.0	4.6	5.3	7.1	6.2	4.5	4.1	6.7	9.2										
1976	4.2	4.3	5.9	6.7	8.5	7.9	6.8	7.1	10.0	12.9	16.8									
1977	3.8	3.8	5.2	5.8	7.3	6.6	5.5	5.5	7.2	8.2	7.7	−0.7								
1978	3.4	3.4	4.6	5.1	6.3	5.6	4.5	4.4	5.5	5.8	4.6	−0.9	−1.2							
1979	3.1	3.0	4.1	4.5	5.5	4.8	3.8	3.5	4.3	4.3	3.1	−1.0	−1.2	−1.2						
1980	2.6	2.5	3.5	3.8	4.6	3.9	2.9	2.6	3.1	2.9	1.7	−1.8	−2.1	−2.6	−3.9					
1981	2.5	2.5	3.3	3.6	4.4	3.7	2.8	2.5	2.9	2.7	1.7	−1.1	−1.1	−1.1	−1.1	1.9				
1982	4.4	4.5	5.5	5.9	6.8	6.4	5.8	5.8	6.6	6.8	6.5	4.9	6.0	7.9	11.2	19.6	40.4			
1983	4.2	4.3	5.2	5.5	6.3	5.9	5.3	5.3	6.0	6.1	5.8	4.3	5.1	6.4	8.4	12.9	18.9	0.7		
1984	4.8	4.9	5.7	6.1	6.9	6.6	6.1	6.1	6.8	7.0	6.8	5.6	6.5	7.9	9.8	13.5	17.7	7.8	15.5	
1985	6.0	6.1	7.0	7.5	8.3	8.0	7.7	7.8	8.6	9.0	9.0	8.2	9.3	10.9	13.1	16.8	20.9	15.0	23.0	31.0
1986	6.8	6.9	7.9	8.3	9.2	9.0	8.7	8.9	9.8	10.2	10.3	9.7	10.9	12.5	14.6	18.1	21.6	17.3	23.5	27.7
1987	6.3	6.5	7.3	7.7	8.5	8.3	8.0	8.1	8.8	9.2	9.2	8.5	9.5	10.7	12.3	14.9	17.2	13.0	16.3	16.6
1988	6.5	6.6	7.4	7.8	8.5	8.4	8.1	8.2	8.9	9.2	9.2	8.6	9.5	10.6	12.0	14.2	16.1	12.5	15.0	14.9
1989	6.9	7.1	7.9	8.3	9.0	8.8	8.6	8.8	9.4	9.8	9.8	9.3	10.2	11.3	12.6	14.6	16.3	13.2	15.5	15.5
1990	6.9	7.0	7.8	8.2	8.9	8.7	8.5	8.6	9.2	9.6	9.6	9.1	9.9	10.8	12.0	13.7	15.2	12.3	14.1	13.9
1991	7.4	7.5	8.3	8.7	9.3	9.2	9.0	9.2	9.8	10.1	10.2	9.7	10.5	11.5	12.6	14.2	15.6	13.1	14.8	14.6
1992	7.4	7.5	8.3	8.6	9.3	9.1	9.0	9.1	9.7	10.0	10.0	9.6	10.4	11.2	12.2	13.7	14.9	12.6	14.0	13.8
1993	7.8	7.9	8.6	9.0	9.6	9.5	9.4	9.5	10.1	10.4	10.5	10.1	10.8	11.7	12.7	14.1	15.1	13.1	14.4	14.3
1994	7.2	7.3	8.0	8.3	8.9	8.7	8.6	8.7	9.2	9.4	9.4	9.0	9.6	10.4	11.2	12.3	13.2	11.2	12.2	11.9
1995	7.9	8.1	8.7	9.1	9.7	9.6	9.4	9.6	10.1	10.4	10.4	10.1	10.8	11.5	12.4	13.5	14.4	12.6	13.7	13.5
1996	7.6	7.8	8.4	8.7	9.3	9.2	9.0	9.1	9.6	9.8	9.9	9.5	10.1	10.8	11.5	12.6	13.3	11.6	12.5	12.3
1997	7.9	8.0	8.6	9.0	9.5	9.4	9.2	9.4	9.9	10.1	10.1	9.8	10.4	11.0	11.8	12.8	13.5	11.9	12.7	12.5
1998	8.0	8.2	8.8	9.1	9.6	9.5	9.4	9.5	10.0	10.2	10.3	10.0	10.5	11.1	11.8	12.8	13.5	12.0	12.8	12.6
1999	7.5	7.6	8.2	8.5	8.9	8.8	8.7	8.8	9.2	9.4	9.4	9.1	9.5	10.1	10.7	11.5	12.1	10.6	11.3	11.0
2000	7.9	8.0	8.5	8.8	9.3	9.2	9.1	9.2	9.6	9.8	9.9	9.6	10.0	10.6	11.2	12.0	12.6	11.2	11.8	11.6
2001	7.7	7.9	8.4	8.7	9.1	9.0	8.9	9.0	9.4	9.6	9.6	9.3	9.8	10.3	10.8	11.6	12.1	10.8	11.4	11.1
2002	8.0	8.1	8.7	8.9	9.4	9.3	9.2	9.3	9.7	9.9	9.9	9.6	10.1	10.6	11.1	11.9	12.4	11.1	11.7	11.5

Table C-4 (Page 6 of 6)

Long-Term Government Bonds Total Returns
Rates of Return for all holding periods
Percent per annum compounded annually

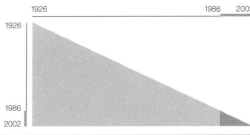

from 1926 to 2002

To the end of	From the beginning of 1986	1987	1988	1989	1990	1991	1992	1993	1994	1995	1996	1997	1998	1999	2000	2001	2002
1986	24.5																
1987	10.1	-2.7															
1988	9.9	3.3	9.7														
1989	11.9	8.0	13.8	18.1													
1990	10.8	7.6	11.2	12.0	6.2												
1991	12.1	9.8	13.2	14.4	12.6	19.3											
1992	11.5	9.5	12.1	12.8	11.0	13.5	8.1										
1993	12.4	10.7	13.1	13.8	12.8	15.1	13.0	18.2									
1994	9.9	8.2	9.9	9.9	8.3	8.9	5.6	4.4	-7.8								
1995	11.9	10.6	12.4	12.8	11.9	13.1	11.6	12.8	10.2	31.7							
1996	10.7	9.4	10.8	11.0	10.0	10.6	9.0	9.2	6.4	14.2	-0.9						
1997	11.1	10.0	11.3	11.5	10.7	11.4	10.1	10.5	8.7	14.8	7.1	15.9					
1998	11.3	10.2	11.5	11.7	11.0	11.6	10.5	10.9	9.5	14.3	9.1	14.4	13.1				
1999	9.7	8.6	9.6	9.6	8.8	9.1	7.9	7.8	6.2	9.2	4.3	6.0	1.5	-9.0			
2000	10.4	9.5	10.5	10.5	9.9	10.3	9.3	9.5	8.3	11.2	7.5	9.7	7.7	5.2	21.5		
2001	10.0	9.1	10.0	10.0	9.4	9.6	8.7	8.8	7.7	10.1	6.8	8.5	6.7	4.7	12.2	3.7	
2002	10.4	9.6	10.5	10.5	10.0	10.3	9.5	9.7	8.8	11.0	8.4	10.0	8.8	7.8	14.1	10.5	17.8

Table C-5 (Page 1 of 6)

Intermediate-Term Government Bonds Total Returns
Rates of Return for all holding periods
Percent per annum compounded annually

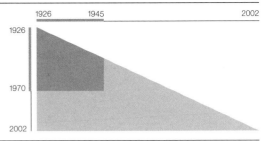

from 1926 to 2002

To the end of	From the beginning of 1926	1927	1928	1929	1930	1931	1932	1933	1934	1935	1936	1937	1938	1939	1940	1941	1942	1943	1944	1945
1926	5.4																			
1927	4.9	4.5																		
1928	3.6	2.7	0.9																	
1929	4.2	3.8	3.4	6.0																
1930	4.7	4.5	4.5	6.4	6.7															
1931	3.5	3.1	2.8	3.4	2.1	-2.3														
1932	4.2	4.0	3.9	4.7	4.3	3.1	8.8													
1933	3.9	3.7	3.6	4.1	3.7	2.7	5.3	1.8												
1934	4.5	4.4	4.3	4.9	4.7	4.2	6.5	5.4	9.0											
1935	4.7	4.7	4.7	5.2	5.1	4.8	6.6	5.9	8.0	7.0										
1936	4.6	4.5	4.5	4.9	4.8	4.5	5.9	5.2	6.3	5.0	3.1									
1937	4.3	4.2	4.2	4.6	4.4	4.1	5.2	4.4	5.1	3.8	2.3	1.6								
1938	4.5	4.4	4.4	4.7	4.6	4.3	5.3	4.7	5.3	4.4	3.6	3.9	6.2							
1939	4.5	4.4	4.4	4.7	4.6	4.3	5.2	4.7	5.2	4.5	3.8	4.1	5.4	4.5						
1940	4.4	4.3	4.3	4.6	4.4	4.2	5.0	4.5	4.9	4.2	3.7	3.8	4.6	3.7	3.0					
1941	4.1	4.0	4.0	4.2	4.1	3.9	4.5	4.0	4.3	3.7	3.1	3.1	3.5	2.6	1.7	0.5				
1942	4.0	3.9	3.9	4.1	3.9	3.7	4.3	3.8	4.1	3.4	3.0	2.9	3.2	2.5	1.8	1.2	1.9			
1943	3.9	3.8	3.8	4.0	3.9	3.6	4.1	3.7	3.9	3.4	2.9	2.9	3.1	2.5	2.0	1.7	2.4	2.8		
1944	3.8	3.7	3.7	3.9	3.7	3.5	4.0	3.6	3.7	3.2	2.8	2.8	2.9	2.4	2.0	1.8	2.2	2.3	1.8	
1945	3.7	3.6	3.6	3.8	3.6	3.4	3.8	3.5	3.6	3.1	2.7	2.7	2.9	2.4	2.0	1.8	2.2	2.3	2.0	2.2
1946	3.6	3.5	3.5	3.6	3.5	3.3	3.6	3.3	3.4	2.9	2.6	2.5	2.7	2.2	1.9	1.7	2.0	2.0	1.7	1.6
1947	3.5	3.4	3.3	3.5	3.3	3.1	3.5	3.1	3.2	2.8	2.4	2.4	2.5	2.1	1.8	1.6	1.8	1.7	1.5	1.4
1948	3.4	3.3	3.3	3.4	3.2	3.1	3.4	3.0	3.1	2.7	2.4	2.3	2.4	2.0	1.8	1.6	1.8	1.8	1.6	1.5
1949	3.4	3.3	3.2	3.3	3.2	3.0	3.3	3.0	3.1	2.7	2.4	2.3	2.4	2.1	1.8	1.7	1.9	1.8	1.7	1.7
1950	3.3	3.2	3.1	3.2	3.1	2.9	3.2	2.9	2.9	2.6	2.3	2.2	2.3	2.0	1.7	1.6	1.7	1.7	1.5	1.5
1951	3.1	3.1	3.0	3.1	3.0	2.8	3.0	2.7	2.8	2.4	2.2	2.1	2.1	1.8	1.6	1.5	1.6	1.5	1.4	1.3
1952	3.1	3.0	2.9	3.0	2.9	2.7	3.0	2.7	2.7	2.4	2.1	2.1	2.1	1.8	1.6	1.5	1.6	1.6	1.4	1.4
1953	3.1	3.0	2.9	3.0	2.9	2.7	3.0	2.7	2.8	2.4	2.2	2.1	2.2	1.9	1.7	1.6	1.7	1.7	1.6	1.6
1954	3.1	3.0	2.9	3.0	2.9	2.7	3.0	2.7	2.8	2.5	2.2	2.2	2.2	2.0	1.8	1.7	1.8	1.8	1.7	1.7
1955	2.9	2.9	2.8	2.9	2.8	2.6	2.8	2.6	2.6	2.3	2.1	2.0	2.0	1.8	1.6	1.5	1.6	1.6	1.5	1.5
1956	2.8	2.8	2.7	2.8	2.6	2.5	2.7	2.4	2.5	2.2	2.0	1.9	1.9	1.7	1.5	1.4	1.5	1.5	1.4	1.3
1957	3.0	2.9	2.9	2.9	2.8	2.7	2.9	2.6	2.7	2.4	2.2	2.2	2.2	2.0	1.9	1.8	1.9	1.9	1.8	1.8
1958	2.9	2.8	2.7	2.8	2.7	2.5	2.7	2.5	2.5	2.3	2.1	2.0	2.0	1.8	1.7	1.6	1.7	1.7	1.6	1.6
1959	2.8	2.7	2.6	2.7	2.6	2.4	2.6	2.4	2.4	2.2	2.0	1.9	1.9	1.7	1.6	1.5	1.6	1.5	1.5	1.4
1960	3.0	2.9	2.9	3.0	2.9	2.7	2.9	2.7	2.7	2.5	2.3	2.3	2.3	2.2	2.0	2.0	2.1	2.1	2.0	2.1
1961	3.0	2.9	2.9	2.9	2.8	2.7	2.9	2.7	2.7	2.5	2.3	2.3	2.3	2.1	2.0	2.0	2.1	2.1	2.0	2.0
1962	3.0	3.0	2.9	3.0	2.9	2.8	3.0	2.8	2.8	2.6	2.4	2.4	2.4	2.3	2.2	2.2	2.2	2.2	2.2	2.2
1963	3.0	2.9	2.9	3.0	2.9	2.8	2.9	2.7	2.8	2.6	2.4	2.4	2.4	2.3	2.2	2.1	2.2	2.2	2.2	2.2
1964	3.0	3.0	2.9	3.0	2.9	2.8	3.0	2.8	2.8	2.6	2.5	2.4	2.5	2.3	2.2	2.2	2.3	2.3	2.3	2.3
1965	3.0	2.9	2.9	2.9	2.9	2.7	2.9	2.7	2.7	2.6	2.4	2.4	2.4	2.3	2.2	2.2	2.2	2.2	2.2	2.2
1966	3.0	3.0	2.9	3.0	2.9	2.8	2.9	2.8	2.8	2.6	2.5	2.5	2.5	2.4	2.3	2.3	2.3	2.3	2.3	2.3
1967	3.0	2.9	2.9	2.9	2.8	2.7	2.9	2.7	2.8	2.6	2.4	2.4	2.4	2.3	2.2	2.2	2.3	2.3	2.3	2.3
1968	3.0	3.0	2.9	3.0	2.9	2.8	2.9	2.8	2.8	2.6	2.5	2.5	2.5	2.4	2.3	2.3	2.4	2.4	2.4	2.4
1969	2.9	2.9	2.8	2.9	2.8	2.7	2.8	2.7	2.7	2.5	2.4	2.4	2.4	2.3	2.2	2.2	2.2	2.3	2.2	2.3
1970	3.2	3.2	3.1	3.2	3.1	3.0	3.2	3.0	3.1	2.9	2.8	2.8	2.8	2.7	2.7	2.6	2.7	2.7	2.7	2.8

Table C-5 (Page 2 of 6)

Intermediate-Term Government Bonds Total Returns
Rates of Return for all holding periods
Percent per annum compounded annually

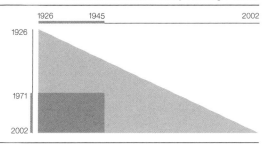

from 1926 to 2002

To the end of	From the beginning of 1926	1927	1928	1929	1930	1931	1932	1933	1934	1935	1936	1937	1938	1939	1940	1941	1942	1943	1944	1945
1971	3.3	3.3	3.3	3.3	3.3	3.2	3.3	3.2	3.2	3.1	2.9	2.9	3.0	2.9	2.8	2.8	2.9	2.9	3.0	3.0
1972	3.4	3.3	3.3	3.4	3.3	3.2	3.4	3.2	3.3	3.1	3.0	3.0	3.0	3.0	2.9	2.9	3.0	3.0	3.0	3.1
1973	3.4	3.4	3.3	3.4	3.3	3.2	3.4	3.3	3.3	3.1	3.0	3.0	3.1	3.0	3.0	3.0	3.0	3.1	3.1	3.1
1974	3.4	3.4	3.4	3.4	3.4	3.3	3.4	3.3	3.3	3.2	3.1	3.1	3.2	3.1	3.0	3.0	3.1	3.2	3.2	3.2
1975	3.5	3.5	3.5	3.5	3.5	3.4	3.5	3.4	3.5	3.3	3.2	3.2	3.3	3.2	3.2	3.2	3.3	3.3	3.3	3.4
1976	3.7	3.7	3.7	3.7	3.7	3.6	3.7	3.6	3.7	3.5	3.5	3.5	3.5	3.4	3.4	3.4	3.5	3.6	3.6	3.6
1977	3.7	3.6	3.6	3.7	3.6	3.6	3.7	3.6	3.6	3.5	3.4	3.4	3.5	3.4	3.4	3.4	3.5	3.5	3.5	3.6
1978	3.7	3.6	3.6	3.7	3.6	3.6	3.7	3.6	3.6	3.5	3.4	3.4	3.5	3.4	3.4	3.4	3.5	3.5	3.5	3.6
1979	3.7	3.6	3.6	3.7	3.6	3.6	3.7	3.6	3.6	3.5	3.4	3.4	3.5	3.4	3.4	3.4	3.5	3.5	3.5	3.6
1980	3.7	3.6	3.6	3.7	3.6	3.6	3.7	3.6	3.6	3.5	3.4	3.4	3.5	3.4	3.4	3.4	3.5	3.5	3.5	3.6
1981	3.8	3.7	3.7	3.8	3.7	3.7	3.8	3.7	3.7	3.6	3.6	3.6	3.6	3.6	3.5	3.6	3.6	3.7	3.7	3.7
1982	4.2	4.1	4.1	4.2	4.2	4.1	4.2	4.2	4.2	4.1	4.0	4.1	4.1	4.1	4.1	4.1	4.2	4.2	4.3	4.3
1983	4.2	4.2	4.2	4.3	4.2	4.2	4.3	4.2	4.3	4.2	4.1	4.1	4.2	4.2	4.1	4.2	4.3	4.3	4.4	4.4
1984	4.4	4.4	4.4	4.4	4.4	4.4	4.5	4.4	4.5	4.4	4.3	4.3	4.4	4.4	4.4	4.4	4.5	4.5	4.6	4.7
1985	4.6	4.6	4.6	4.7	4.7	4.6	4.8	4.7	4.7	4.7	4.6	4.6	4.7	4.7	4.7	4.7	4.8	4.9	4.9	5.0
1986	4.8	4.8	4.8	4.9	4.8	4.8	4.9	4.9	4.9	4.8	4.8	4.8	4.9	4.9	4.9	4.9	5.0	5.1	5.2	5.2
1987	4.8	4.8	4.8	4.8	4.8	4.8	4.9	4.8	4.9	4.8	4.8	4.8	4.9	4.8	4.8	4.9	5.0	5.1	5.1	5.2
1988	4.8	4.8	4.8	4.8	4.8	4.8	4.9	4.9	4.9	4.8	4.8	4.8	4.9	4.9	4.9	4.9	5.0	5.1	5.1	5.2
1989	4.9	4.9	4.9	5.0	5.0	4.9	5.1	5.0	5.1	5.0	4.9	5.0	5.0	5.0	5.0	5.1	5.2	5.2	5.3	5.4
1990	5.0	5.0	5.0	5.1	5.0	5.0	5.1	5.1	5.1	5.1	5.0	5.1	5.1	5.1	5.1	5.2	5.3	5.3	5.4	5.5
1991	5.1	5.1	5.1	5.2	5.2	5.2	5.3	5.2	5.3	5.2	5.2	5.2	5.3	5.3	5.3	5.4	5.5	5.5	5.6	5.7
1992	5.2	5.2	5.2	5.2	5.2	5.2	5.3	5.3	5.3	5.3	5.2	5.3	5.4	5.3	5.4	5.4	5.5	5.6	5.6	5.7
1993	5.3	5.3	5.3	5.3	5.3	5.3	5.4	5.4	5.4	5.4	5.3	5.4	5.5	5.4	5.5	5.5	5.6	5.7	5.7	5.8
1994	5.1	5.1	5.1	5.2	5.2	5.1	5.2	5.2	5.2	5.2	5.2	5.2	5.3	5.2	5.3	5.3	5.4	5.5	5.5	5.6
1995	5.3	5.3	5.3	5.3	5.3	5.3	5.4	5.4	5.4	5.4	5.3	5.4	5.4	5.4	5.5	5.5	5.6	5.7	5.7	5.8
1996	5.2	5.2	5.2	5.3	5.3	5.2	5.4	5.3	5.4	5.3	5.3	5.3	5.4	5.4	5.4	5.4	5.5	5.6	5.6	5.7
1997	5.3	5.3	5.3	5.3	5.3	5.3	5.4	5.4	5.4	5.4	5.3	5.4	5.4	5.4	5.4	5.5	5.6	5.6	5.7	5.8
1998	5.3	5.3	5.3	5.4	5.4	5.4	5.5	5.4	5.5	5.4	5.4	5.5	5.5	5.5	5.5	5.6	5.7	5.7	5.8	5.9
1999	5.2	5.2	5.2	5.3	5.3	5.3	5.4	5.3	5.4	5.3	5.3	5.3	5.4	5.4	5.4	5.4	5.5	5.6	5.6	5.7
2000	5.3	5.3	5.3	5.4	5.4	5.4	5.5	5.4	5.5	5.4	5.4	5.4	5.5	5.5	5.5	5.6	5.6	5.7	5.8	5.8
2001	5.3	5.3	5.4	5.4	5.4	5.4	5.5	5.5	5.5	5.5	5.4	5.5	5.5	5.5	5.5	5.6	5.7	5.7	5.8	5.9
2002	5.4	5.4	5.5	5.5	5.5	5.5	5.6	5.6	5.6	5.6	5.5	5.6	5.6	5.6	5.7	5.7	5.8	5.9	5.9	6.0

Table C-5 (Page 3 of 6)

Intermediate-Term Government Bonds Total Returns
Rates of Return for all holding periods
Percent per annum compounded annually

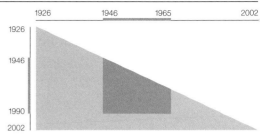

from 1926 to 2002

To the end of	From the beginning of 1946	1947	1948	1949	1950	1951	1952	1953	1954	1955	1956	1957	1958	1959	1960	1961	1962	1963	1964	1965
1946	1.0																			
1947	1.0	0.9																		
1948	1.3	1.4	1.8																	
1949	1.5	1.7	2.1	2.3																
1950	1.4	1.4	1.6	1.5	0.7															
1951	1.2	1.2	1.3	1.1	0.5	0.4														
1952	1.3	1.3	1.4	1.3	0.9	1.0	1.6													
1953	1.5	1.6	1.7	1.6	1.5	1.7	2.4	3.2												
1954	1.6	1.7	1.8	1.8	1.7	2.0	2.5	3.0	2.7											
1955	1.4	1.4	1.5	1.5	1.3	1.4	1.7	1.7	1.0	-0.7										
1956	1.2	1.3	1.3	1.2	1.1	1.1	1.3	1.2	0.5	-0.5	-0.4									
1957	1.8	1.8	1.9	1.9	1.9	2.1	2.3	2.5	2.3	2.2	3.6	7.8								
1958	1.5	1.6	1.6	1.6	1.5	1.6	1.8	1.9	1.6	1.3	2.0	3.2	-1.3							
1959	1.4	1.4	1.5	1.4	1.3	1.4	1.5	1.5	1.2	1.0	1.4	2.0	-0.8	-0.4						
1960	2.1	2.1	2.2	2.3	2.2	2.4	2.6	2.8	2.7	2.7	3.4	4.3	3.2	5.5	11.8					
1961	2.0	2.1	2.2	2.2	2.2	2.3	2.5	2.7	2.6	2.6	3.1	3.8	2.9	4.3	6.7	1.8				
1962	2.2	2.3	2.4	2.5	2.5	2.6	2.8	2.9	2.9	2.9	3.5	4.1	3.4	4.6	6.3	3.7	5.6			
1963	2.2	2.3	2.4	2.4	2.4	2.5	2.7	2.8	2.8	2.8	3.2	3.8	3.1	4.0	5.1	3.0	3.6	1.6		
1964	2.3	2.4	2.5	2.5	2.5	2.6	2.8	2.9	2.9	2.9	3.3	3.8	3.2	4.0	4.9	3.3	3.7	2.8	4.0	
1965	2.2	2.3	2.4	2.4	2.4	2.5	2.7	2.8	2.7	2.7	3.1	3.5	3.0	3.6	4.2	2.8	3.1	2.2	2.5	1.0
1966	2.4	2.4	2.5	2.5	2.6	2.7	2.8	2.9	2.9	2.9	3.2	3.6	3.1	3.7	4.3	3.1	3.4	2.8	3.2	2.8
1967	2.3	2.4	2.4	2.5	2.5	2.6	2.7	2.8	2.8	2.8	3.0	3.4	2.9	3.4	3.9	2.8	3.0	2.5	2.7	2.2
1968	2.4	2.5	2.5	2.6	2.6	2.7	2.8	2.9	2.9	2.9	3.2	3.5	3.1	3.5	4.0	3.0	3.2	2.8	3.0	2.8
1969	2.3	2.3	2.4	2.4	2.4	2.5	2.6	2.7	2.6	2.6	2.9	3.1	2.8	3.1	3.5	2.6	2.7	2.3	2.4	2.1
1970	2.8	2.9	3.0	3.0	3.1	3.2	3.3	3.4	3.4	3.5	3.8	4.1	3.8	4.2	4.6	3.9	4.2	4.0	4.4	4.4
1971	3.0	3.1	3.2	3.3	3.3	3.4	3.6	3.7	3.7	3.8	4.1	4.4	4.1	4.5	5.0	4.4	4.6	4.5	4.9	5.0
1972	3.1	3.2	3.3	3.3	3.4	3.5	3.7	3.8	3.8	3.9	4.1	4.4	4.2	4.6	5.0	4.4	4.7	4.6	4.9	5.0
1973	3.2	3.2	3.3	3.4	3.4	3.6	3.7	3.8	3.8	3.9	4.1	4.4	4.2	4.6	5.0	4.5	4.7	4.6	4.9	5.0
1974	3.2	3.3	3.4	3.5	3.5	3.6	3.8	3.9	3.9	4.0	4.2	4.5	4.3	4.7	5.0	4.5	4.7	4.7	5.0	5.1
1975	3.4	3.5	3.6	3.6	3.7	3.8	4.0	4.1	4.1	4.2	4.4	4.7	4.5	4.8	5.2	4.8	5.0	4.9	5.2	5.3
1976	3.7	3.8	3.9	4.0	4.0	4.1	4.3	4.4	4.5	4.5	4.8	5.1	4.9	5.3	5.6	5.2	5.5	5.5	5.8	5.9
1977	3.6	3.7	3.8	3.9	3.9	4.0	4.2	4.3	4.3	4.4	4.6	4.9	4.7	5.1	5.4	5.0	5.2	5.2	5.5	5.6
1978	3.6	3.7	3.8	3.8	3.9	4.0	4.2	4.3	4.3	4.4	4.6	4.8	4.7	5.0	5.3	4.9	5.1	5.1	5.3	5.4
1979	3.6	3.7	3.8	3.9	3.9	4.0	4.2	4.2	4.3	4.4	4.6	4.8	4.7	4.9	5.2	4.9	5.1	5.0	5.2	5.3
1980	3.6	3.7	3.8	3.9	3.9	4.0	4.1	4.2	4.3	4.3	4.5	4.8	4.6	4.9	5.2	4.8	5.0	5.0	5.2	5.2
1981	3.8	3.9	4.0	4.0	4.1	4.2	4.3	4.4	4.5	4.5	4.7	4.9	4.8	5.1	5.3	5.1	5.2	5.2	5.4	5.5
1982	4.4	4.5	4.6	4.7	4.8	4.9	5.0	5.2	5.2	5.3	5.5	5.8	5.7	6.0	6.3	6.0	6.2	6.3	6.5	6.7
1983	4.5	4.6	4.7	4.8	4.8	5.0	5.1	5.2	5.3	5.4	5.6	5.8	5.8	6.1	6.3	6.1	6.3	6.3	6.6	6.7
1984	4.7	4.8	4.9	5.0	5.1	5.2	5.4	5.5	5.6	5.7	5.9	6.1	6.1	6.3	6.6	6.4	6.6	6.7	6.9	7.1
1985	5.1	5.2	5.3	5.4	5.5	5.6	5.8	5.9	6.0	6.1	6.3	6.6	6.5	6.8	7.1	6.9	7.2	7.2	7.5	7.7
1986	5.3	5.4	5.5	5.6	5.7	5.9	6.0	6.2	6.3	6.4	6.6	6.9	6.8	7.1	7.4	7.2	7.5	7.5	7.8	8.0
1987	5.3	5.4	5.5	5.6	5.7	5.8	6.0	6.1	6.2	6.3	6.5	6.7	6.7	7.0	7.2	7.1	7.3	7.4	7.6	7.8
1988	5.3	5.4	5.5	5.6	5.7	5.8	6.0	6.1	6.2	6.3	6.5	6.7	6.7	6.9	7.2	7.0	7.2	7.3	7.5	7.7
1989	5.5	5.6	5.7	5.8	5.9	6.0	6.1	6.3	6.4	6.5	6.7	6.9	6.9	7.1	7.4	7.3	7.5	7.5	7.8	7.9
1990	5.5	5.7	5.8	5.9	5.9	6.1	6.2	6.4	6.4	6.5	6.8	7.0	7.0	7.2	7.5	7.3	7.5	7.6	7.8	8.0

Table C-5 (Page 4 of 6)

Intermediate-Term Government Bonds Total Returns
Rates of Return for all holding periods
Percent per annum compounded annually

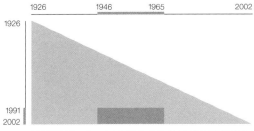

from 1926 to 2002

To the end of	From the beginning of 1946	1947	1948	1949	1950	1951	1952	1953	1954	1955	1956	1957	1958	1959	1960	1961	1962	1963	1964	1965
1991	5.8	5.9	6.0	6.1	6.2	6.3	6.5	6.6	6.7	6.8	7.0	7.2	7.2	7.5	7.7	7.6	7.8	7.9	8.1	8.2
1992	5.8	5.9	6.0	6.1	6.2	6.3	6.5	6.6	6.7	6.8	7.0	7.2	7.2	7.5	7.7	7.6	7.8	7.8	8.1	8.2
1993	5.9	6.0	6.1	6.2	6.3	6.4	6.6	6.7	6.8	6.9	7.1	7.3	7.3	7.6	7.8	7.7	7.9	8.0	8.2	8.3
1994	5.7	5.8	5.9	5.9	6.0	6.2	6.3	6.4	6.5	6.6	6.8	7.0	6.9	7.2	7.4	7.3	7.5	7.5	7.7	7.8
1995	5.9	6.0	6.1	6.2	6.3	6.4	6.5	6.6	6.7	6.8	7.0	7.2	7.2	7.4	7.7	7.5	7.7	7.8	8.0	8.1
1996	5.8	5.9	6.0	6.1	6.2	6.3	6.4	6.5	6.6	6.7	6.9	7.1	7.1	7.3	7.5	7.4	7.6	7.6	7.8	7.9
1997	5.8	5.9	6.0	6.1	6.2	6.3	6.5	6.6	6.7	6.7	6.9	7.1	7.1	7.3	7.5	7.4	7.6	7.6	7.8	7.9
1998	5.9	6.0	6.1	6.2	6.3	6.4	6.5	6.7	6.7	6.8	7.0	7.2	7.2	7.4	7.6	7.5	7.6	7.7	7.9	8.0
1999	5.8	5.9	6.0	6.0	6.1	6.2	6.4	6.5	6.5	6.6	6.8	7.0	6.9	7.2	7.4	7.2	7.4	7.4	7.6	7.7
2000	5.9	6.0	6.1	6.2	6.2	6.4	6.5	6.6	6.7	6.8	6.9	7.1	7.1	7.3	7.5	7.4	7.5	7.6	7.7	7.8
2001	5.9	6.0	6.1	6.2	6.3	6.4	6.5	6.6	6.7	6.8	6.9	7.1	7.1	7.3	7.5	7.4	7.5	7.6	7.7	7.8
2002	6.0	6.1	6.2	6.3	6.4	6.5	6.6	6.7	6.8	6.9	7.1	7.2	7.2	7.4	7.6	7.5	7.7	7.7	7.9	8.0

Table C-5 (Page 5 of 6)

Intermediate-Term Government Bonds Total Returns
Rates of Return for all holding periods.
Percent per annum compounded annually

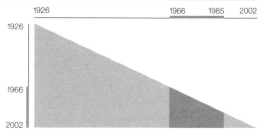

from 1926 to 2002

To the end of	From the beginning of 1966	1967	1968	1969	1970	1971	1972	1973	1974	1975	1976	1977	1978	1979	1980	1981	1982	1983	1984	1985
1966	4.7																			
1967	2.8	1.0																		
1968	3.4	2.8	4.5																	
1969	2.3	1.6	1.9	-0.7																
1970	5.1	5.2	6.6	7.7	16.9															
1971	5.7	5.9	7.2	8.0	12.7	8.7														
1972	5.6	5.8	6.8	7.3	10.1	6.9	5.2													
1973	5.5	5.6	6.4	6.8	8.7	6.1	4.9	4.6												
1974	5.5	5.6	6.3	6.6	8.1	6.0	5.2	5.1	5.7											
1975	5.7	5.9	6.5	6.8	8.1	6.4	5.8	6.0	6.8	7.8										
1976	6.4	6.5	7.2	7.5	8.7	7.4	7.2	7.7	8.8	10.3	12.9									
1977	5.9	6.1	6.6	6.8	7.8	6.6	6.2	6.4	6.9	7.3	7.0	1.4								
1978	5.8	5.8	6.3	6.5	7.3	6.2	5.8	5.9	6.2	6.3	5.8	2.4	3.5							
1979	5.6	5.7	6.1	6.3	7.0	5.9	5.6	5.7	5.8	5.9	5.4	3.0	3.8	4.1						
1980	5.5	5.6	5.9	6.1	6.7	5.7	5.4	5.4	5.6	5.5	5.1	3.2	3.8	4.0	3.9					
1981	5.8	5.8	6.2	6.3	6.9	6.1	5.8	5.9	6.0	6.1	5.8	4.4	5.2	5.8	6.6	9.5				
1982	7.0	7.2	7.6	7.8	8.5	7.8	7.7	8.0	8.4	8.7	8.8	8.2	9.6	11.2	13.7	18.9	29.1			
1983	7.0	7.2	7.6	7.8	8.4	7.8	7.7	7.9	8.3	8.6	8.7	8.1	9.2	10.4	12.1	14.9	17.8	7.4		
1984	7.4	7.5	7.9	8.2	8.8	8.2	8.2	8.4	8.8	9.1	9.2	8.8	9.9	11.0	12.5	14.7	16.5	10.7	14.0	
1985	8.0	8.2	8.6	8.8	9.5	9.0	9.0	9.3	9.7	10.1	10.3	10.0	11.2	12.3	13.7	15.8	17.4	13.8	17.1	20.3
1986	8.3	8.5	8.9	9.2	9.8	9.4	9.4	9.7	10.1	10.5	10.7	10.5	11.6	12.6	13.9	15.7	17.0	14.1	16.5	17.7
1987	8.1	8.2	8.6	8.8	9.4	9.0	9.0	9.2	9.6	9.9	10.1	9.8	10.7	11.5	12.5	13.8	14.5	11.8	12.9	12.5
1988	8.0	8.1	8.5	8.7	9.2	8.8	8.8	9.0	9.4	9.6	9.8	9.5	10.3	11.0	11.8	12.8	13.3	10.8	11.5	10.9
1989	8.2	8.4	8.7	8.9	9.4	9.0	9.1	9.3	9.6	9.9	10.0	9.8	10.5	11.2	11.9	12.8	13.3	11.2	11.8	11.4
1990	8.3	8.4	8.8	8.9	9.4	9.1	9.1	9.3	9.6	9.8	10.0	9.8	10.5	11.1	11.7	12.5	12.9	11.0	11.5	11.1
1991	8.5	8.7	9.0	9.2	9.7	9.4	9.4	9.6	9.9	10.2	10.3	10.2	10.8	11.4	12.0	12.8	13.1	11.5	12.0	11.7
1992	8.5	8.6	9.0	9.1	9.6	9.3	9.3	9.5	9.8	10.0	10.1	10.0	10.6	11.1	11.6	12.3	12.6	11.0	11.5	11.1
1993	8.6	8.7	9.0	9.2	9.7	9.4	9.4	9.6	9.8	10.1	10.2	10.0	10.6	11.1	11.6	12.2	12.5	11.1	11.4	11.1
1994	8.1	8.2	8.5	8.6	9.0	8.7	8.7	8.9	9.1	9.3	9.3	9.1	9.6	10.0	10.4	10.9	11.0	9.6	9.8	9.4
1995	8.4	8.5	8.8	8.9	9.3	9.0	9.0	9.2	9.4	9.6	9.7	9.5	10.0	10.4	10.8	11.3	11.4	10.1	10.4	10.1
1996	8.2	8.3	8.5	8.7	9.0	8.7	8.7	8.9	9.1	9.2	9.3	9.1	9.6	9.9	10.3	10.7	10.8	9.6	9.7	9.4
1997	8.2	8.3	8.5	8.7	9.0	8.7	8.7	8.9	9.1	9.2	9.3	9.1	9.5	9.8	10.2	10.5	10.6	9.5	9.6	9.3
1998	8.2	8.3	8.6	8.7	9.1	8.8	8.8	8.9	9.1	9.3	9.3	9.2	9.5	9.9	10.2	10.5	10.6	9.5	9.7	9.4
1999	7.9	8.0	8.2	8.4	8.7	8.4	8.4	8.5	8.7	8.8	8.8	8.7	9.0	9.3	9.5	9.8	9.9	8.8	8.9	8.6
2000	8.0	8.1	8.4	8.5	8.8	8.5	8.5	8.7	8.8	8.9	9.0	8.8	9.2	9.4	9.7	10.0	10.0	9.0	9.1	8.8
2001	8.0	8.1	8.3	8.5	8.8	8.5	8.5	8.6	8.8	8.9	8.9	8.8	9.1	9.3	9.6	9.9	9.9	9.0	9.0	8.8
2002	8.2	8.3	8.5	8.6	8.9	8.6	8.6	8.8	8.9	9.0	9.1	8.9	9.2	9.5	9.7	10.0	10.0	9.1	9.2	9.0

Table C-5 (Page 6 of 6)

Intermediate-Term Government Bonds Total Returns
Rates of Return for all holding periods.
Percent per annum compounded annually

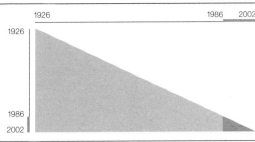

from 1926 to 2002

To the end of	From the beginning of 1986	1987	1988	1989	1990	1991	1992	1993	1994	1995	1996	1997	1998	1999	2000	2001	2002
1986	15.1																
1987	8.8	2.9															
1988	7.9	4.5	6.1														
1989	9.2	7.3	9.6	13.3													
1990	9.3	7.9	9.7	11.5	9.7												
1991	10.3	9.4	11.1	12.8	12.6	15.5											
1992	9.9	9.0	10.3	11.4	10.7	11.2	7.2										
1993	10.1	9.3	10.5	11.3	10.9	11.2	9.2	11.2									
1994	8.2	7.4	8.1	8.4	7.5	6.9	4.2	2.7	−5.1								
1995	9.1	8.4	9.1	9.6	9.0	8.8	7.2	7.2	5.3	16.8							
1996	8.4	7.8	8.3	8.6	8.0	7.7	6.2	5.9	4.2	9.2	2.1						
1997	8.4	7.8	8.3	8.6	8.0	7.8	6.5	6.4	5.2	8.9	5.2	8.4					
1998	8.6	8.0	8.5	8.7	8.3	8.1	7.1	7.0	6.2	9.2	6.8	9.3	10.2				
1999	7.8	7.2	7.6	7.7	7.2	6.9	5.9	5.7	4.8	6.9	4.6	5.5	4.0	−1.8			
2000	8.1	7.6	8.0	8.1	7.7	7.5	6.6	6.6	5.9	7.9	6.2	7.2	6.8	5.2	12.6		
2001	8.1	7.6	8.0	8.1	7.7	7.5	6.7	6.7	6.1	7.8	6.4	7.3	7.0	6.0	10.1	7.6	
2002	8.3	7.9	8.3	8.4	8.1	7.9	7.3	7.3	6.9	8.5	7.3	8.2	8.2	7.7	11.0	10.2	12.9

Table C-6 (Page 1 of 6)

U.S. Treasury Bills Total Returns
Rates of Return for all holding periods.
Percent per annum compounded annually

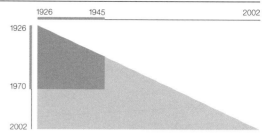

from 1926 to 2002

To the end of	From the beginning of 1926	1927	1928	1929	1930	1931	1932	1933	1934	1935	1936	1937	1938	1939	1940	1941	1942	1943	1944	1945
1926	3.3																			
1927	3.2	3.1																		
1928	3.3	3.3	3.6																	
1929	3.7	3.8	4.2	4.7																
1930	3.4	3.5	3.6	3.6	2.4															
1931	3.0	3.0	2.9	2.7	1.7	1.1														
1932	2.7	2.6	2.5	2.3	1.5	1.0	1.0													
1933	2.4	2.3	2.2	1.9	1.2	0.8	0.6	0.3												
1934	2.2	2.0	1.9	1.6	1.0	0.6	0.5	0.2	0.2											
1935	2.0	1.8	1.7	1.4	0.8	0.5	0.4	0.2	0.2	0.2										
1936	1.8	1.7	1.5	1.2	0.7	0.5	0.4	0.2	0.2	0.2	0.2									
1937	1.7	1.5	1.4	1.1	0.7	0.4	0.3	0.2	0.2	0.2	0.2	0.3								
1938	1.5	1.4	1.2	1.0	0.6	0.4	0.3	0.2	0.2	0.2	0.2	0.1	0.0							
1939	1.4	1.3	1.1	0.9	0.6	0.3	0.3	0.2	0.1	0.1	0.1	0.1	0.0	0.0						
1940	1.3	1.2	1.1	0.9	0.5	0.3	0.2	0.1	0.1	0.1	0.1	0.1	0.0	0.0	0.0					
1941	1.3	1.1	1.0	0.8	0.5	0.3	0.2	0.1	0.1	0.1	0.1	0.1	0.0	0.0	0.0	0.1				
1942	1.2	1.1	0.9	0.8	0.5	0.3	0.2	0.1	0.1	0.1	0.1	0.1	0.1	0.1	0.1	0.2	0.3			
1943	1.2	1.0	0.9	0.7	0.4	0.3	0.2	0.2	0.2	0.1	0.1	0.1	0.1	0.1	0.2	0.2	0.3	0.3		
1944	1.1	1.0	0.9	0.7	0.4	0.3	0.2	0.2	0.2	0.2	0.2	0.2	0.1	0.2	0.2	0.3	0.3	0.3	0.3	
1945	1.1	1.0	0.8	0.7	0.4	0.3	0.2	0.2	0.2	0.2	0.2	0.2	0.2	0.2	0.2	0.3	0.3	0.3	0.3	0.3
1946	1.0	0.9	0.8	0.7	0.4	0.3	0.3	0.2	0.2	0.2	0.2	0.2	0.2	0.2	0.2	0.3	0.3	0.3	0.3	0.3
1947	1.0	0.9	0.8	0.7	0.4	0.3	0.3	0.2	0.2	0.2	0.2	0.2	0.2	0.2	0.3	0.3	0.4	0.4	0.4	0.4
1948	1.0	0.9	0.8	0.7	0.4	0.3	0.3	0.3	0.3	0.3	0.3	0.3	0.3	0.3	0.3	0.4	0.4	0.4	0.5	0.5
1949	1.0	0.9	0.8	0.7	0.5	0.4	0.3	0.3	0.3	0.3	0.3	0.3	0.3	0.4	0.4	0.5	0.5	0.5	0.6	0.6
1950	1.0	0.9	0.8	0.7	0.5	0.4	0.4	0.4	0.4	0.4	0.4	0.4	0.4	0.4	0.5	0.5	0.6	0.6	0.7	0.7
1951	1.0	0.9	0.9	0.7	0.6	0.5	0.4	0.4	0.4	0.4	0.5	0.5	0.5	0.5	0.6	0.6	0.7	0.7	0.8	0.8
1952	1.1	1.0	0.9	0.8	0.6	0.5	0.5	0.5	0.5	0.5	0.5	0.5	0.6	0.6	0.6	0.7	0.8	0.8	0.9	0.9
1953	1.1	1.0	0.9	0.8	0.7	0.6	0.6	0.5	0.6	0.6	0.6	0.6	0.6	0.7	0.7	0.8	0.8	0.9	1.0	1.0
1954	1.1	1.0	0.9	0.8	0.7	0.6	0.6	0.6	0.6	0.6	0.6	0.6	0.7	0.7	0.7	0.8	0.9	0.9	0.9	1.0
1955	1.1	1.0	0.9	0.8	0.7	0.6	0.6	0.6	0.6	0.6	0.7	0.7	0.7	0.7	0.8	0.8	0.9	1.0	1.0	1.1
1956	1.1	1.1	1.0	0.9	0.8	0.7	0.7	0.7	0.7	0.7	0.7	0.8	0.8	0.8	0.9	0.9	1.0	1.1	1.1	1.2
1957	1.2	1.1	1.1	1.0	0.8	0.8	0.8	0.8	0.8	0.8	0.9	0.9	0.9	1.0	1.0	1.1	1.1	1.2	1.3	1.3
1958	1.2	1.1	1.1	1.0	0.9	0.8	0.8	0.8	0.8	0.9	0.9	0.9	0.9	1.0	1.0	1.1	1.2	1.2	1.3	1.3
1959	1.3	1.2	1.1	1.1	0.9	0.9	0.9	0.9	0.9	0.9	1.0	1.0	1.0	1.1	1.1	1.2	1.3	1.3	1.4	1.4
1960	1.3	1.2	1.2	1.1	1.0	1.0	0.9	0.9	1.0	1.0	1.0	1.1	1.1	1.2	1.2	1.3	1.3	1.4	1.5	1.5
1961	1.3	1.3	1.2	1.1	1.0	1.0	1.0	1.0	1.0	1.0	1.1	1.1	1.1	1.2	1.3	1.3	1.4	1.4	1.5	1.6
1962	1.4	1.3	1.3	1.2	1.1	1.0	1.0	1.0	1.1	1.1	1.1	1.2	1.2	1.3	1.3	1.4	1.4	1.5	1.6	1.6
1963	1.4	1.4	1.3	1.2	1.1	1.1	1.1	1.1	1.1	1.2	1.2	1.2	1.3	1.3	1.4	1.4	1.5	1.6	1.6	1.7
1964	1.5	1.4	1.4	1.3	1.2	1.2	1.2	1.2	1.2	1.2	1.3	1.3	1.4	1.4	1.5	1.5	1.6	1.7	1.7	1.8
1965	1.5	1.5	1.4	1.4	1.3	1.3	1.3	1.3	1.3	1.3	1.4	1.4	1.5	1.5	1.6	1.6	1.7	1.8	1.8	1.9
1966	1.6	1.6	1.5	1.5	1.4	1.3	1.4	1.4	1.4	1.4	1.5	1.5	1.6	1.6	1.7	1.7	1.8	1.9	1.9	2.0
1967	1.7	1.6	1.6	1.5	1.5	1.4	1.4	1.4	1.5	1.5	1.6	1.6	1.7	1.7	1.8	1.8	1.9	2.0	2.0	2.1
1968	1.7	1.7	1.7	1.6	1.5	1.5	1.5	1.6	1.6	1.6	1.7	1.7	1.8	1.8	1.9	2.0	2.0	2.1	2.2	2.2
1969	1.8	1.8	1.8	1.7	1.7	1.6	1.7	1.7	1.7	1.8	1.8	1.9	1.9	2.0	2.0	2.1	2.2	2.3	2.3	2.4
1970	2.0	1.9	1.9	1.9	1.8	1.8	1.8	1.8	1.8	1.9	1.9	2.0	2.1	2.1	2.2	2.3	2.3	2.4	2.5	2.6

Table C-6 (Page 2 of 6)

U.S. Treasury Bills Total Returns
Rates of Return for all holding periods
Percent per annum compounded annually

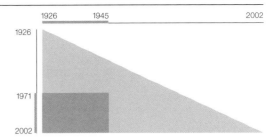

from 1926 to 2002

To the end of	From the beginning of 1926	1927	1928	1929	1930	1931	1932	1933	1934	1935	1936	1937	1938	1939	1940	1941	1942	1943	1944	1945
1971	2.0	2.0	1.9	1.9	1.8	1.8	1.9	1.9	1.9	2.0	2.0	2.1	2.1	2.2	2.3	2.3	2.4	2.5	2.6	2.6
1972	2.0	2.0	2.0	2.0	1.9	1.9	1.9	1.9	2.0	2.0	2.1	2.1	2.2	2.2	2.3	2.4	2.4	2.5	2.6	2.7
1973	2.1	2.1	2.1	2.1	2.0	2.0	2.0	2.0	2.1	2.1	2.2	2.2	2.3	2.4	2.4	2.5	2.6	2.7	2.7	2.8
1974	2.3	2.2	2.2	2.2	2.1	2.1	2.2	2.2	2.2	2.3	2.3	2.4	2.4	2.5	2.6	2.7	2.7	2.8	2.9	3.0
1975	2.3	2.3	2.3	2.3	2.2	2.2	2.2	2.3	2.3	2.4	2.4	2.5	2.5	2.6	2.7	2.8	2.8	2.9	3.0	3.1
1976	2.4	2.4	2.3	2.3	2.3	2.3	2.3	2.3	2.4	2.4	2.5	2.5	2.6	2.7	2.7	2.8	2.9	3.0	3.1	3.1
1977	2.4	2.4	2.4	2.4	2.3	2.3	2.4	2.4	2.4	2.5	2.5	2.6	2.7	2.7	2.8	2.9	3.0	3.0	3.1	3.2
1978	2.5	2.5	2.5	2.5	2.4	2.4	2.5	2.5	2.5	2.6	2.6	2.7	2.8	2.8	2.9	3.0	3.1	3.1	3.2	3.3
1979	2.7	2.6	2.6	2.6	2.6	2.6	2.6	2.7	2.7	2.8	2.8	2.9	2.9	3.0	3.1	3.2	3.3	3.3	3.4	3.5
1980	2.8	2.8	2.8	2.8	2.7	2.7	2.8	2.8	2.9	2.9	3.0	3.1	3.1	3.2	3.3	3.4	3.5	3.5	3.6	3.7
1981	3.0	3.0	3.0	3.0	3.0	3.0	3.0	3.1	3.1	3.2	3.2	3.3	3.4	3.5	3.5	3.6	3.7	3.8	3.9	4.0
1982	3.1	3.1	3.1	3.1	3.1	3.1	3.2	3.2	3.3	3.3	3.4	3.5	3.5	3.6	3.7	3.8	3.9	4.0	4.1	4.2
1983	3.2	3.2	3.2	3.2	3.2	3.2	3.3	3.3	3.4	3.4	3.5	3.6	3.6	3.7	3.8	3.9	4.0	4.1	4.2	4.3
1984	3.3	3.3	3.3	3.3	3.3	3.3	3.4	3.4	3.5	3.6	3.6	3.7	3.8	3.9	3.9	4.0	4.1	4.2	4.3	4.4
1985	3.4	3.4	3.4	3.4	3.4	3.4	3.5	3.5	3.6	3.6	3.7	3.8	3.9	3.9	4.0	4.1	4.2	4.3	4.4	4.5
1986	3.5	3.5	3.5	3.5	3.4	3.5	3.5	3.6	3.6	3.7	3.8	3.8	3.9	4.0	4.1	4.2	4.3	4.3	4.4	4.5
1987	3.5	3.5	3.5	3.5	3.5	3.5	3.5	3.6	3.7	3.7	3.8	3.9	3.9	4.0	4.1	4.2	4.3	4.4	4.5	4.6
1988	3.5	3.5	3.5	3.5	3.5	3.5	3.6	3.6	3.7	3.8	3.8	3.9	4.0	4.1	4.1	4.2	4.3	4.4	4.5	4.6
1989	3.6	3.6	3.6	3.6	3.6	3.6	3.7	3.7	3.8	3.8	3.9	4.0	4.1	4.1	4.2	4.3	4.4	4.5	4.6	4.7
1990	3.7	3.7	3.7	3.7	3.7	3.7	3.7	3.8	3.8	3.9	4.0	4.1	4.1	4.2	4.3	4.4	4.5	4.6	4.7	4.8
1991	3.7	3.7	3.7	3.7	3.7	3.7	3.8	3.8	3.9	3.9	4.0	4.1	4.2	4.2	4.3	4.4	4.5	4.6	4.7	4.8
1992	3.7	3.7	3.7	3.7	3.7	3.7	3.8	3.8	3.9	3.9	4.0	4.1	4.1	4.2	4.3	4.4	4.5	4.6	4.7	4.7
1993	3.7	3.7	3.7	3.7	3.7	3.7	3.8	3.8	3.9	3.9	4.0	4.1	4.1	4.2	4.3	4.4	4.4	4.5	4.6	4.7
1994	3.7	3.7	3.7	3.7	3.7	3.7	3.8	3.8	3.9	3.9	4.0	4.1	4.1	4.2	4.3	4.4	4.4	4.5	4.6	4.7
1995	3.7	3.7	3.7	3.7	3.7	3.7	3.8	3.8	3.9	3.9	4.0	4.1	4.1	4.2	4.3	4.4	4.5	4.5	4.6	4.7
1996	3.7	3.7	3.8	3.8	3.7	3.8	3.8	3.8	3.9	4.0	4.0	4.1	4.2	4.2	4.3	4.4	4.5	4.5	4.6	4.7
1997	3.8	3.8	3.8	3.8	3.8	3.8	3.8	3.9	3.9	4.0	4.1	4.1	4.2	4.3	4.3	4.4	4.5	4.6	4.6	4.7
1998	3.8	3.8	3.8	3.8	3.8	3.8	3.8	3.9	3.9	4.0	4.1	4.1	4.2	4.3	4.3	4.4	4.5	4.6	4.6	4.7
1999	3.8	3.8	3.8	3.8	3.8	3.8	3.9	3.9	4.0	4.0	4.1	4.1	4.2	4.3	4.3	4.4	4.5	4.6	4.6	4.7
2000	3.8	3.8	3.8	3.8	3.8	3.8	3.9	3.9	4.0	4.0	4.1	4.2	4.2	4.3	4.4	4.4	4.5	4.6	4.7	4.7
2001	3.8	3.8	3.8	3.8	3.8	3.8	3.9	3.9	4.0	4.0	4.1	4.2	4.2	4.3	4.4	4.4	4.5	4.6	4.7	4.7
2002	3.8	3.8	3.8	3.8	3.8	3.8	3.9	3.9	3.9	4.0	4.1	4.1	4.2	4.2	4.3	4.4	4.5	4.5	4.6	4.7

Table C-6 (Page 3 of 6)

U.S. Treasury Bills Total Returns
Rates of Return for all holding periods
Percent per annum compounded annually

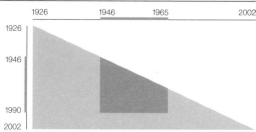

from 1926 to 2002

To the end of	From the beginning of 1946	1947	1948	1949	1950	1951	1952	1953	1954	1955	1956	1957	1958	1959	1960	1961	1962	1963	1964	1965
1946	0.4																			
1947	0.4	0.5																		
1948	0.6	0.7	0.8																	
1949	0.7	0.8	1.0	1.1																
1950	0.8	0.9	1.0	1.1	1.2															
1951	0.9	1.0	1.2	1.3	1.3	1.5														
1952	1.0	1.1	1.3	1.4	1.4	1.6	1.7													
1953	1.1	1.2	1.3	1.5	1.5	1.7	1.7	1.8												
1954	1.1	1.2	1.3	1.4	1.4	1.5	1.4	1.3	0.9											
1955	1.1	1.2	1.3	1.4	1.4	1.5	1.5	1.4	1.2	1.6										
1956	1.3	1.3	1.4	1.5	1.6	1.6	1.7	1.7	1.6	2.0	2.5									
1957	1.4	1.5	1.6	1.7	1.8	1.9	1.9	2.0	2.0	2.4	2.8	3.1								
1958	1.4	1.5	1.6	1.7	1.7	1.8	1.9	1.9	1.9	2.2	2.4	2.3	1.5							
1959	1.5	1.6	1.7	1.8	1.9	1.9	2.0	2.0	2.1	2.3	2.5	2.5	2.2	3.0						
1960	1.6	1.7	1.8	1.9	1.9	2.0	2.1	2.1	2.2	2.4	2.5	2.6	2.4	2.8	2.7					
1961	1.6	1.7	1.8	1.9	2.0	2.0	2.1	2.1	2.2	2.3	2.5	2.5	2.3	2.6	2.4	2.1				
1962	1.7	1.8	1.9	1.9	2.0	2.1	2.1	2.2	2.2	2.4	2.5	2.5	2.4	2.6	2.5	2.4	2.7			
1963	1.8	1.9	2.0	2.0	2.1	2.2	2.2	2.3	2.3	2.5	2.6	2.6	2.5	2.7	2.7	2.7	2.9	3.1		
1964	1.9	2.0	2.0	2.1	2.2	2.3	2.3	2.4	2.4	2.6	2.7	2.7	2.7	2.9	2.8	2.9	3.1	3.3	3.5	
1965	2.0	2.1	2.1	2.2	2.3	2.4	2.4	2.5	2.5	2.7	2.8	2.9	2.8	3.0	3.0	3.1	3.3	3.5	3.7	3.9
1966	2.1	2.2	2.3	2.4	2.4	2.5	2.6	2.7	2.7	2.9	3.0	3.0	3.0	3.2	3.3	3.4	3.6	3.8	4.1	4.3
1967	2.2	2.3	2.4	2.5	2.5	2.6	2.7	2.8	2.8	3.0	3.1	3.2	3.2	3.3	3.4	3.5	3.7	3.9	4.1	4.3
1968	2.3	2.4	2.5	2.6	2.7	2.8	2.8	2.9	3.0	3.1	3.3	3.3	3.3	3.5	3.6	3.7	3.9	4.1	4.3	4.5
1969	2.5	2.6	2.7	2.8	2.9	3.0	3.0	3.1	3.2	3.4	3.5	3.6	3.6	3.8	3.9	4.0	4.3	4.5	4.7	4.9
1970	2.7	2.8	2.9	3.0	3.0	3.1	3.2	3.3	3.4	3.6	3.7	3.8	3.8	4.0	4.1	4.3	4.5	4.7	5.0	5.2
1971	2.7	2.8	2.9	3.0	3.1	3.2	3.3	3.4	3.4	3.6	3.7	3.8	3.9	4.0	4.1	4.3	4.5	4.7	4.9	5.1
1972	2.8	2.9	3.0	3.0	3.1	3.2	3.3	3.4	3.5	3.6	3.7	3.8	3.9	4.0	4.1	4.2	4.4	4.6	4.8	4.9
1973	2.9	3.0	3.1	3.2	3.3	3.4	3.5	3.6	3.6	3.8	3.9	4.0	4.1	4.2	4.3	4.4	4.6	4.8	5.0	5.1
1974	3.1	3.2	3.3	3.4	3.5	3.6	3.7	3.8	3.8	4.0	4.1	4.2	4.3	4.5	4.6	4.7	4.9	5.1	5.3	5.4
1975	3.2	3.3	3.4	3.5	3.6	3.7	3.7	3.8	3.9	4.1	4.2	4.3	4.4	4.5	4.6	4.8	5.0	5.1	5.3	5.5
1976	3.2	3.3	3.4	3.5	3.6	3.7	3.8	3.9	4.0	4.1	4.2	4.3	4.4	4.6	4.7	4.8	5.0	5.1	5.3	5.4
1977	3.3	3.4	3.5	3.6	3.7	3.8	3.9	3.9	4.0	4.2	4.3	4.4	4.4	4.6	4.7	4.8	5.0	5.1	5.3	5.4
1978	3.4	3.5	3.6	3.7	3.8	3.9	4.0	4.1	4.2	4.3	4.4	4.5	4.6	4.7	4.8	4.9	5.1	5.3	5.4	5.5
1979	3.6	3.7	3.8	3.9	4.0	4.1	4.2	4.3	4.4	4.5	4.7	4.8	4.8	5.0	5.1	5.2	5.4	5.5	5.7	5.8
1980	3.8	3.9	4.0	4.1	4.2	4.3	4.4	4.5	4.6	4.8	4.9	5.0	5.1	5.3	5.4	5.5	5.7	5.9	6.0	6.2
1981	4.1	4.2	4.3	4.4	4.5	4.7	4.8	4.9	5.0	5.1	5.3	5.4	5.5	5.7	5.8	5.9	6.1	6.3	6.5	6.7
1982	4.3	4.4	4.5	4.6	4.7	4.8	4.9	5.1	5.2	5.3	5.5	5.6	5.7	5.9	6.0	6.1	6.3	6.5	6.7	6.9
1983	4.4	4.5	4.6	4.7	4.8	4.9	5.1	5.2	5.3	5.4	5.6	5.7	5.8	6.0	6.1	6.2	6.4	6.6	6.8	7.0
1984	4.5	4.6	4.8	4.9	5.0	5.1	5.2	5.3	5.4	5.6	5.7	5.8	5.9	6.1	6.2	6.4	6.6	6.8	6.9	7.1
1985	4.6	4.7	4.8	4.9	5.1	5.2	5.3	5.4	5.5	5.7	5.8	5.9	6.0	6.2	6.3	6.4	6.6	6.8	7.0	7.1
1986	4.6	4.8	4.9	5.0	5.1	5.2	5.3	5.4	5.5	5.7	5.8	5.9	6.0	6.2	6.3	6.4	6.6	6.8	6.9	7.1
1987	4.7	4.8	4.9	5.0	5.1	5.2	5.3	5.4	5.5	5.7	5.8	5.9	6.0	6.2	6.3	6.4	6.6	6.7	6.9	7.0
1988	4.7	4.8	4.9	5.0	5.1	5.2	5.3	5.4	5.5	5.7	5.8	5.9	6.0	6.2	6.3	6.4	6.6	6.7	6.9	7.0
1989	4.8	4.9	5.0	5.1	5.2	5.3	5.4	5.5	5.6	5.8	5.9	6.0	6.1	6.2	6.3	6.5	6.6	6.8	6.9	7.1
1990	4.9	5.0	5.1	5.2	5.3	5.4	5.5	5.6	5.7	5.8	5.9	6.0	6.1	6.3	6.4	6.5	6.7	6.8	6.9	7.1

Table C-6 (Page 4 of 6)

U.S. Treasury Bills Total Returns
Rates of Return for all holding periods
Percent per annum compounded annually

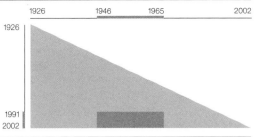

from 1926 to 2002

To the end of	From the beginning of																			
	1946	1947	1948	1949	1950	1951	1952	1953	1954	1955	1956	1957	1958	1959	1960	1961	1962	1963	1964	1965
1991	4.9	5.0	5.1	5.2	5.3	5.4	5.5	5.6	5.7	5.8	5.9	6.0	6.1	6.3	6.4	6.5	6.6	6.8	6.9	7.0
1992	4.8	4.9	5.0	5.1	5.2	5.3	5.4	5.5	5.6	5.7	5.9	6.0	6.0	6.2	6.3	6.4	6.5	6.7	6.8	6.9
1993	4.8	4.9	5.0	5.1	5.2	5.3	5.4	5.5	5.5	5.7	5.8	5.9	6.0	6.1	6.2	6.3	6.4	6.5	6.7	6.8
1994	4.8	4.9	5.0	5.1	5.2	5.2	5.3	5.4	5.5	5.6	5.7	5.8	5.9	6.0	6.1	6.2	6.3	6.4	6.5	6.6
1995	4.8	4.9	5.0	5.1	5.2	5.2	5.3	5.4	5.5	5.6	5.7	5.8	5.9	6.0	6.1	6.2	6.3	6.4	6.5	6.6
1996	4.8	4.9	5.0	5.1	5.2	5.2	5.3	5.4	5.5	5.6	5.7	5.8	5.9	6.0	6.1	6.2	6.3	6.4	6.5	6.6
1997	4.8	4.9	5.0	5.1	5.2	`5.2	5.3	5.4	5.5	5.6	5.7	5.8	5.9	6.0	6.0	6.1	6.3	6.4	6.5	6.5
1998	4.8	4.9	5.0	5.1	5.2	5.2	5.3	5.4	5.5	5.6	5.7	5.8	5.8	5.9	6.0	6.1	6.2	6.3	6.4	6.5
1999	4.8	4.9	5.0	5.1	5.1	5.2	5.3	5.4	5.5	5.6	5.7	5.7	5.8	5.9	6.0	6.1	6.2	6.3	6.4	6.4
2000	4.8	4.9	5.0	5.1	5.2	5.2	5.3	5.4	5.5	5.6	5.7	5.7	5.8	5.9	6.0	6.1	6.2	6.3	6.3	6.4
2001	4.8	4.9	5.0	5.1	5.1	5.2	5.3	5.4	5.4	5.5	5.6	5.7	5.8	5.9	5.9	6.0	6.1	6.2	6.3	6.4
2002	4.8	4.8	4.9	5.0	5.1	5.1	5.2	5.3	5.4	5.5	5.5	5.6	5.7	5.8	5.8	5.9	6.0	6.1	6.2	6.2

Table C-6 (Page 5 of 6)

U.S. Treasury Bills Total Returns
Rates of Return for all holding periods
Percent per annum compounded annually

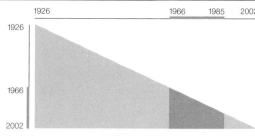

from 1926 to 2002

To the end of	From the beginning of 1966	1967	1968	1969	1970	1971	1972	1973	1974	1975	1976	1977	1978	1979	1980	1981	1982	1983	1984	1985
1966	4.8																			
1967	4.5	4.2																		
1968	4.7	4.7	5.2																	
1969	5.2	5.3	5.9	6.6																
1970	5.5	5.6	6.1	6.6	6.5															
1971	5.3	5.4	5.7	5.8	5.5	4.4														
1972	5.1	5.1	5.3	5.3	4.9	4.1	3.8													
1973	5.3	5.4	5.6	5.6	5.4	5.0	5.4	6.9												
1974	5.6	5.7	5.9	6.0	5.9	5.8	6.2	7.5	8.0											
1975	5.6	5.7	5.9	6.0	5.9	5.8	6.1	6.9	6.9	5.8										
1976	5.6	5.6	5.8	5.9	5.8	5.7	5.9	6.4	6.3	5.4	5.1									
1977	5.5	5.6	5.7	5.8	5.7	5.6	5.8	6.2	6.0	5.3	5.1	5.1								
1978	5.7	5.7	5.9	5.9	5.9	5.8	6.0	6.3	6.2	5.8	5.8	6.1	7.2							
1979	6.0	6.1	6.2	6.3	6.3	6.3	6.5	6.9	6.9	6.7	6.9	7.5	8.8	10.4						
1980	6.3	6.4	6.6	6.7	6.7	6.8	7.0	7.4	7.5	7.4	7.8	8.5	9.6	10.8	11.2					
1981	6.8	7.0	7.2	7.3	7.4	7.5	7.8	8.2	8.4	8.4	8.9	9.7	10.8	12.1	13.0	14.7				
1982	7.0	7.2	7.4	7.6	7.6	7.7	8.0	8.5	8.6	8.7	9.1	9.8	10.8	11.7	12.1	12.6	10.5			
1983	7.1	7.3	7.5	7.6	7.7	7.8	8.1	8.5	8.6	8.7	9.1	9.7	10.4	11.1	11.3	11.3	9.7	8.8		
1984	7.3	7.4	7.6	7.8	7.9	7.9	8.2	8.6	8.8	8.8	9.2	9.7	10.4	10.9	11.0	11.0	9.7	9.3	9.8	
1985	7.3	7.4	7.6	7.8	7.8	7.9	8.2	8.5	8.7	8.7	9.0	9.5	10.0	10.4	10.5	10.3	9.2	8.8	8.8	7.7
1986	7.3	7.4	7.5	7.7	7.7	7.8	8.1	8.4	8.5	8.5	8.8	9.1	9.6	9.9	9.8	9.6	8.6	8.1	7.9	6.9
1987	7.2	7.3	7.4	7.6	7.6	7.7	7.9	8.2	8.3	8.3	8.5	8.8	9.2	9.4	9.3	9.0	8.1	7.6	7.3	6.4
1988	7.1	7.2	7.4	7.5	7.6	7.6	7.8	8.1	8.1	8.1	8.3	8.6	8.9	9.1	8.9	8.7	7.8	7.4	7.1	6.4
1989	7.2	7.3	7.4	7.5	7.6	7.6	7.8	8.1	8.1	8.2	8.3	8.6	8.9	9.0	8.9	8.6	7.9	7.5	7.3	6.8
1990	7.2	7.3	7.5	7.6	7.6	7.7	7.8	8.1	8.1	8.1	8.3	8.5	8.8	8.9	8.8	8.5	7.9	7.6	7.4	7.0
1991	7.1	7.2	7.4	7.5	7.5	7.6	7.7	7.9	8.0	8.0	8.1	8.3	8.6	8.7	8.5	8.3	7.7	7.3	7.2	6.8
1992	7.0	7.1	7.2	7.3	7.3	7.4	7.5	7.7	7.7	7.7	7.8	8.0	8.2	8.3	8.1	7.9	7.3	6.9	6.7	6.4
1993	6.9	6.9	7.0	7.1	7.1	7.2	7.3	7.5	7.5	7.5	7.6	7.7	7.9	7.9	7.7	7.5	6.9	6.6	6.4	6.0
1994	6.8	6.8	6.9	7.0	7.0	7.0	7.1	7.3	7.3	7.3	7.4	7.5	7.6	7.7	7.5	7.2	6.7	6.3	6.1	5.8
1995	6.7	6.8	6.9	6.9	7.0	7.0	7.1	7.2	7.2	7.2	7.3	7.4	7.5	7.5	7.4	7.1	6.6	6.3	6.1	5.7
1996	6.7	6.7	6.8	6.9	6.9	6.9	7.0	7.1	7.2	7.1	7.2	7.3	7.4	7.4	7.2	7.0	6.5	6.2	6.0	5.7
1997	6.6	6.7	6.8	6.8	6.8	6.8	6.9	7.1	7.1	7.0	7.1	7.2	7.3	7.3	7.1	6.9	6.4	6.1	6.0	5.7
1998	6.6	6.6	6.7	6.8	6.8	6.8	6.9	7.0	7.0	6.9	7.0	7.1	7.2	7.2	7.0	6.8	6.3	6.1	5.9	5.6
1999	6.5	6.6	6.6	6.7	6.7	6.7	6.8	6.9	6.9	6.8	6.9	7.0	7.1	7.1	6.9	6.7	6.2	6.0	5.8	5.5
2000	6.5	6.5	6.6	6.7	6.7	6.7	6.8	6.9	6.9	6.8	6.9	6.9	7.0	7.0	6.8	6.6	6.2	6.0	5.8	5.6
2001	6.4	6.5	6.5	6.6	6.6	6.6	6.7	6.8	6.7	6.7	6.7	6.8	6.9	6.9	6.7	6.5	6.1	5.9	5.7	5.5
2002	6.3	6.3	6.4	6.4	6.4	6.4	6.5	6.6	6.6	6.5	6.5	6.6	6.7	6.6	6.5	6.3	5.9	5.7	5.5	5.3

Table C-6 (Page 6 of 6)

U.S. Treasury Bills Total Returns
Rates of Return for all holding periods
Percent per annum compounded annually

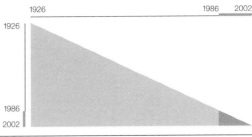

from 1926 to 2002

To the end of	From the beginning of 1986	1987	1988	1989	1990	1991	1992	1993	1994	1995	1996	1997	1998	1999	2000	2001	2002
1986	6.2																
1987	5.8	5.5															
1988	6.0	5.9	6.3														
1989	6.6	6.7	7.4	8.4													
1990	6.8	7.0	7.5	8.1	7.8												
1991	6.6	6.7	7.0	7.3	6.7	5.6											
1992	6.2	6.2	6.3	6.3	5.6	4.5	3.5										
1993	5.8	5.7	5.7	5.6	4.9	4.0	3.2	2.9									
1994	5.5	5.5	5.5	5.3	4.7	4.0	3.4	3.4	3.9								
1995	5.6	5.5	5.5	5.4	4.9	4.3	4.0	4.1	4.7	5.6							
1996	5.5	5.5	5.5	5.3	4.9	4.4	4.2	4.4	4.9	5.4	5.2						
1997	5.5	5.4	5.4	5.3	5.0	4.6	4.4	4.6	5.0	5.4	5.2	5.3					
1998	5.4	5.4	5.4	5.3	5.0	4.6	4.5	4.6	5.0	5.2	5.1	5.1	4.9				
1999	5.4	5.3	5.3	5.2	4.9	4.6	4.5	4.6	4.9	5.1	5.0	4.9	4.8	4.7			
2000	5.4	5.4	5.4	5.3	5.0	4.7	4.6	4.8	5.1	5.2	5.2	5.2	5.1	5.3	5.9		
2001	5.3	5.3	5.3	5.2	4.9	4.7	4.6	4.7	4.9	5.0	5.0	4.9	4.8	4.8	4.9	3.8	
2002	5.1	5.0	5.0	4.9	4.7	4.4	4.3	4.4	4.5	4.6	4.5	4.4	4.2	4.0	3.8	2.7	1.6

Table C-7 (Page 1 of 6)

Inflation
Rates of Return for all holding periods
Percent per annum compounded annually

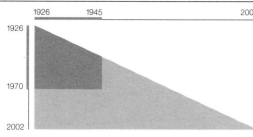

from 1926 to 2002

To the end of	From the beginning of 1926	1927	1928	1929	1930	1931	1932	1933	1934	1935	1936	1937	1938	1939	1940	1941	1942	1943	1944	1945
1926	-1.5																			
1927	-1.8	-2.1																		
1928	-1.5	-1.5	-1.0																	
1929	-1.1	-1.0	-0.4	0.2																
1930	-2.1	-2.2	-2.3	-3.0	-6.0															
1931	-3.4	-3.7	-4.2	-5.2	-7.8	-9.5														
1932	-4.4	-4.9	-5.4	-6.5	-8.6	-9.9	-10.3													
1933	-3.8	-4.1	-4.5	-5.1	-6.4	-6.6	-5.0	0.5												
1934	-3.2	-3.4	-3.6	-4.0	-4.8	-4.5	-2.7	1.3	2.0											
1935	-2.6	-2.7	-2.8	-3.0	-3.5	-3.0	-1.3	1.8	2.5	3.0										
1936	-2.2	-2.3	-2.3	-2.5	-2.9	-2.3	-0.8	1.7	2.1	2.1	1.2									
1937	-1.8	-1.8	-1.8	-1.9	-2.1	-1.6	-0.2	2.0	2.3	2.4	2.2	3.1								
1938	-1.9	-1.9	-1.9	-2.0	-2.2	-1.7	-0.6	1.2	1.3	1.1	0.5	0.1	-2.8							
1939	-1.8	-1.8	-1.8	-1.8	-2.0	-1.6	-0.6	0.9	1.0	0.8	0.2	-0.1	-1.6	-0.5						
1940	-1.6	-1.6	-1.6	-1.6	-1.8	-1.3	-0.4	0.9	1.0	0.8	0.4	0.2	-0.8	0.2	1.0					
1941	-0.9	-0.9	-0.8	-0.8	-0.9	-0.4	0.6	1.9	2.0	2.0	1.9	2.0	1.7	3.3	5.2	9.7				
1942	-0.3	-0.3	-0.2	-0.1	-0.1	0.4	1.3	2.6	2.8	2.9	2.9	3.2	3.2	4.8	6.6	9.5	9.3			
1943	-0.2	-0.1	0.0	0.1	0.1	0.6	1.5	2.6	2.9	2.9	2.9	3.2	3.2	4.4	5.7	7.3	6.2	3.2		
1944	0.0	0.0	0.2	0.2	0.2	0.7	1.5	2.6	2.8	2.9	2.8	3.1	3.0	4.1	5.0	6.0	4.8	2.6	2.1	
1945	0.1	0.2	0.3	0.4	0.4	0.8	1.6	2.6	2.7	2.8	2.8	3.0	2.9	3.8	4.5	5.2	4.2	2.5	2.2	2.3
1946	0.9	1.0	1.2	1.3	1.3	1.8	2.6	3.6	3.9	4.0	4.1	4.4	4.5	5.5	6.4	7.3	6.8	6.2	7.3	9.9
1947	1.2	1.4	1.5	1.7	1.7	2.2	3.0	4.0	4.2	4.4	4.5	4.8	5.0	5.9	6.7	7.5	7.2	6.8	7.7	9.6
1948	1.3	1.4	1.6	1.7	1.8	2.3	3.0	3.9	4.1	4.3	4.4	4.6	4.8	5.6	6.2	6.9	6.5	6.1	6.7	7.8
1949	1.2	1.3	1.4	1.5	1.6	2.0	2.7	3.5	3.7	3.8	3.9	4.1	4.2	4.9	5.4	5.9	5.5	4.9	5.2	5.8
1950	1.3	1.5	1.6	1.7	1.8	2.2	2.9	3.7	3.9	4.0	4.0	4.2	4.3	4.9	5.4	5.9	5.5	5.0	5.3	5.8
1951	1.5	1.6	1.8	1.9	2.0	2.4	3.0	3.8	4.0	4.1	4.1	4.3	4.4	5.0	5.5	5.9	5.5	5.1	5.4	5.8
1952	1.5	1.6	1.8	1.9	1.9	2.3	2.9	3.6	3.8	3.9	4.0	4.1	4.2	4.7	5.1	5.5	5.1	4.7	4.9	5.2
1953	1.5	1.6	1.7	1.8	1.9	2.2	2.8	3.5	3.6	3.7	3.8	3.9	4.0	4.4	4.8	5.1	4.7	4.3	4.4	4.7
1954	1.4	1.5	1.6	1.7	1.8	2.1	2.7	3.3	3.4	3.5	3.5	3.7	3.7	4.1	4.4	4.7	4.3	3.9	4.0	4.2
1955	1.4	1.5	1.6	1.7	1.7	2.1	2.6	3.2	3.3	3.4	3.4	3.5	3.5	3.9	4.2	4.4	4.0	3.6	3.7	3.8
1956	1.4	1.5	1.6	1.7	1.8	2.1	2.6	3.2	3.3	3.3	3.3	3.5	3.5	3.8	4.1	4.3	3.9	3.6	3.6	3.7
1957	1.5	1.5	1.7	1.8	1.8	2.1	2.6	3.2	3.3	3.3	3.3	3.4	3.5	3.8	4.0	4.2	3.9	3.5	3.6	3.7
1958	1.5	1.6	1.7	1.8	1.8	2.1	2.6	3.1	3.2	3.3	3.3	3.4	3.4	3.7	3.9	4.1	3.8	3.4	3.4	3.5
1959	1.5	1.6	1.7	1.8	1.8	2.1	2.5	3.0	3.1	3.2	3.2	3.3	3.3	3.6	3.8	3.9	3.6	3.3	3.3	3.4
1960	1.5	1.6	1.7	1.7	1.8	2.1	2.5	3.0	3.1	3.1	3.1	3.2	3.2	3.5	3.7	3.8	3.5	3.2	3.2	3.3
1961	1.4	1.5	1.6	1.7	1.8	2.0	2.4	2.9	3.0	3.0	3.0	3.1	3.1	3.4	3.5	3.7	3.4	3.1	3.1	3.1
1962	1.4	1.5	1.6	1.7	1.7	2.0	2.4	2.8	2.9	3.0	3.0	3.0	3.0	3.3	3.4	3.6	3.3	3.0	3.0	3.0
1963	1.4	1.5	1.6	1.7	1.7	2.0	2.4	2.8	2.9	2.9	2.9	3.0	3.0	3.2	3.4	3.5	3.2	2.9	2.9	2.9
1964	1.4	1.5	1.6	1.7	1.7	2.0	2.3	2.8	2.8	2.9	2.9	2.9	2.9	3.1	3.3	3.4	3.1	2.8	2.8	2.9
1965	1.4	1.5	1.6	1.7	1.7	2.0	2.3	2.7	2.8	2.8	2.8	2.9	2.9	3.1	3.2	3.3	3.1	2.8	2.8	2.8
1966	1.5	1.6	1.7	1.7	1.8	2.0	2.4	2.8	2.8	2.8	2.8	2.9	2.9	3.1	3.2	3.3	3.1	2.8	2.8	2.8
1967	1.5	1.6	1.7	1.8	1.8	2.0	2.4	2.8	2.8	2.8	2.8	2.9	2.9	3.1	3.2	3.3	3.1	2.8	2.8	2.8
1968	1.6	1.7	1.8	1.8	1.9	2.1	2.4	2.8	2.9	2.9	2.9	3.0	3.0	3.1	3.3	3.4	3.1	2.9	2.9	2.9
1969	1.7	1.8	1.9	1.9	2.0	2.2	2.5	2.9	3.0	3.0	3.0	3.0	3.0	3.2	3.4	3.5	3.2	3.0	3.0	3.0
1970	1.8	1.9	2.0	2.0	2.1	2.3	2.6	3.0	3.0	3.1	3.1	3.1	3.1	3.3	3.4	3.5	3.3	3.1	3.1	3.1

Table C-7 (Page 2 of 6)

Inflation
Rates of Return for all holding periods
Percent per annum compounded annually

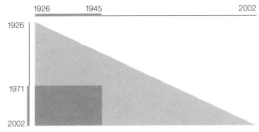

from 1926 to 2002

To the end of	From the beginning of																			
	1926	1927	1928	1929	1930	1931	1932	1933	1934	1935	1936	1937	1938	1939	1940	1941	1942	1943	1944	1945
1971	1.8	1.9	2.0	2.1	2.1	2.3	2.6	3.0	3.0	3.1	3.1	3.1	3.1	3.3	3.4	3.5	3.3	3.1	3.1	3.1
1972	1.9	1.9	2.0	2.1	2.1	2.3	2.6	3.0	3.1	3.1	3.1	3.1	3.1	3.3	3.4	3.5	3.3	3.1	3.1	3.2
1973	2.0	2.1	2.2	2.2	2.3	2.5	2.8	3.1	3.2	3.2	3.2	3.3	3.3	3.5	3.6	3.7	3.5	3.3	3.3	3.3
1974	2.2	2.3	2.4	2.4	2.5	2.7	3.0	3.3	3.4	3.4	3.4	3.5	3.5	3.7	3.8	3.9	3.7	3.6	3.6	3.6
1975	2.3	2.4	2.5	2.5	2.6	2.8	3.1	3.4	3.5	3.5	3.5	3.6	3.6	3.8	3.9	4.0	3.8	3.7	3.7	3.7
1976	2.3	2.4	2.5	2.6	2.6	2.8	3.1	3.4	3.5	3.6	3.6	3.6	3.6	3.8	3.9	4.0	3.9	3.7	3.7	3.8
1977	2.4	2.5	2.6	2.7	2.7	2.9	3.2	3.5	3.6	3.6	3.6	3.7	3.7	3.9	4.0	4.1	3.9	3.8	3.8	3.9
1978	2.5	2.6	2.7	2.8	2.8	3.0	3.3	3.6	3.7	3.7	3.8	3.8	3.8	4.0	4.1	4.2	4.1	3.9	4.0	4.0
1979	2.7	2.8	2.9	3.0	3.0	3.2	3.5	3.8	3.9	4.0	4.0	4.0	4.1	4.2	4.4	4.4	4.3	4.2	4.2	4.3
1980	2.9	3.0	3.1	3.2	3.2	3.4	3.7	4.0	4.1	4.1	4.2	4.2	4.2	4.4	4.5	4.6	4.5	4.4	4.4	4.5
1981	3.0	3.1	3.2	3.3	3.3	3.5	3.8	4.1	4.2	4.2	4.3	4.3	4.4	4.5	4.6	4.7	4.6	4.5	4.5	4.6
1982	3.0	3.1	3.2	3.3	3.3	3.5	3.8	4.1	4.2	4.2	4.2	4.3	4.3	4.5	4.6	4.7	4.6	4.5	4.5	4.6
1983	3.0	3.1	3.2	3.3	3.3	3.5	3.8	4.1	4.2	4.2	4.2	4.3	4.3	4.5	4.6	4.7	4.6	4.5	4.5	4.6
1984	3.0	3.1	3.2	3.3	3.4	3.5	3.8	4.1	4.2	4.2	4.2	4.3	4.3	4.5	4.6	4.7	4.6	4.5	4.5	4.5
1985	3.1	3.1	3.2	3.3	3.4	3.5	3.8	4.1	4.2	4.2	4.2	4.3	4.3	4.5	4.6	4.7	4.5	4.4	4.5	4.5
1986	3.0	3.1	3.2	3.3	3.3	3.5	3.8	4.0	4.1	4.1	4.2	4.2	4.2	4.4	4.5	4.6	4.5	4.4	4.4	4.4
1987	3.0	3.1	3.2	3.3	3.3	3.5	3.8	4.0	4.1	4.1	4.2	4.2	4.2	4.4	4.5	4.6	4.5	4.4	4.4	4.4
1988	3.1	3.1	3.2	3.3	3.4	3.5	3.8	4.0	4.1	4.1	4.2	4.2	4.3	4.4	4.5	4.6	4.5	4.4	4.4	4.4
1989	3.1	3.2	3.3	3.3	3.4	3.5	3.8	4.1	4.1	4.2	4.2	4.2	4.3	4.4	4.5	4.6	4.5	4.4	4.4	4.4
1990	3.1	3.2	3.3	3.4	3.4	3.6	3.8	4.1	4.2	4.2	4.2	4.3	4.3	4.4	4.5	4.6	4.5	4.4	4.4	4.5
1991	3.1	3.2	3.3	3.4	3.4	3.6	3.8	4.1	4.1	4.2	4.2	4.2	4.3	4.4	4.5	4.6	4.5	4.4	4.4	4.5
1992	3.1	3.2	3.3	3.4	3.4	3.6	3.8	4.1	4.1	4.2	4.2	4.2	4.2	4.4	4.5	4.5	4.4	4.3	4.4	4.4
1993	3.1	3.2	3.3	3.3	3.4	3.6	3.8	4.0	4.1	4.1	4.1	4.2	4.2	4.3	4.4	4.5	4.4	4.3	4.3	4.4
1994	3.1	3.2	3.3	3.3	3.4	3.5	3.8	4.0	4.1	4.1	4.1	4.2	4.2	4.3	4.4	4.5	4.4	4.3	4.3	4.4
1995	3.1	3.2	3.3	3.3	3.4	3.5	3.7	4.0	4.0	4.1	4.1	4.1	4.2	4.3	4.4	4.4	4.3	4.3	4.3	4.3
1996	3.1	3.2	3.3	3.3	3.4	3.5	3.7	4.0	4.0	4.1	4.1	4.1	4.1	4.3	4.4	4.4	4.2	4.2	4.3	4.3
1997	3.1	3.2	3.2	3.3	3.4	3.5	3.7	3.9	4.0	4.0	4.0	4.1	4.1	4.2	4.3	4.4	4.3	4.2	4.2	4.2
1998	3.1	3.1	3.2	3.3	3.3	3.5	3.7	3.9	4.0	4.0	4.0	4.0	4.1	4.2	4.3	4.3	4.2	4.1	4.2	4.2
1999	3.1	3.1	3.2	3.3	3.3	3.5	3.7	3.9	3.9	4.0	4.0	4.0	4.0	4.2	4.2	4.3	4.2	4.1	4.1	4.2
2000	3.1	3.1	3.2	3.3	3.3	3.5	3.7	3.9	3.9	4.0	4.0	4.0	4.0	4.1	4.2	4.3	4.2	4.1	4.1	4.2
2001	3.1	3.1	3.2	3.2	3.3	3.4	3.6	3.8	3.9	3.9	3.9	4.0	4.0	4.1	4.2	4.2	4.1	4.1	4.1	4.1
2002	3.0	3.1	3.2	3.2	3.3	3.4	3.6	3.8	3.9	3.9	3.9	4.0	4.0	4.1	4.2	4.2	4.1	4.0	4.0	4.1

Table C-7 (Page 3 of 6)

Inflation
Rates of Return for all holding periods
Percent per annum compounded annually

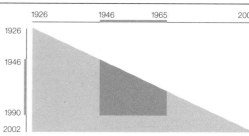

from 1926 to 2002

To the end of	From the beginning of 1946	1947	1948	1949	1950	1951	1952	1953	1954	1955	1956	1957	1958	1959	1960	1961	1962	1963	1964	1965
1946	18.2																			
1947	13.5	9.0																		
1948	9.8	5.8	2.7																	
1949	6.8	3.2	0.4	-1.8																
1950	6.6	3.8	2.2	1.9	5.8															
1951	6.5	4.3	3.1	3.2	5.8	5.9														
1952	5.6	3.7	2.6	2.6	4.2	3.3	0.9													
1953	5.0	3.2	2.3	2.2	3.3	2.4	0.8	0.6												
1954	4.4	2.8	1.9	1.8	2.5	1.7	0.3	0.1	-0.5											
1955	4.0	2.5	1.7	1.6	2.1	1.4	0.3	0.2	-0.1	0.4										
1956	3.9	2.5	1.8	1.7	2.2	1.7	0.8	0.8	0.9	1.6	2.9									
1957	3.8	2.6	2.0	1.9	2.3	1.9	1.2	1.3	1.4	2.1	2.9	3.0								
1958	3.6	2.5	1.9	1.9	2.3	1.8	1.3	1.3	1.5	2.0	2.5	2.4	1.8							
1959	3.5	2.4	1.9	1.8	2.2	1.8	1.3	1.4	1.5	1.9	2.3	2.1	1.6	1.5						
1960	3.3	2.4	1.9	1.8	2.1	1.8	1.3	1.4	1.5	1.8	2.1	1.9	1.6	1.5	1.5					
1961	3.2	2.2	1.8	1.7	2.0	1.7	1.3	1.3	1.4	1.7	1.9	1.7	1.4	1.2	1.1	0.7				
1962	3.1	2.2	1.7	1.7	1.9	1.6	1.3	1.3	1.4	1.6	1.8	1.6	1.3	1.2	1.1	0.9	1.2			
1963	3.0	2.2	1.7	1.7	1.9	1.6	1.3	1.3	1.4	1.6	1.8	1.6	1.4	1.3	1.3	1.2	1.4	1.6		
1964	2.9	2.1	1.7	1.6	1.9	1.6	1.3	1.3	1.4	1.6	1.7	1.6	1.4	1.3	1.2	1.2	1.4	1.4	1.2	
1965	2.8	2.1	1.7	1.7	1.9	1.6	1.3	1.4	1.4	1.6	1.7	1.6	1.4	1.4	1.4	1.3	1.5	1.6	1.6	1.9
1966	2.9	2.2	1.8	1.8	2.0	1.7	1.5	1.5	1.6	1.7	1.9	1.8	1.6	1.6	1.6	1.7	1.9	2.0	2.2	2.6
1967	2.9	2.2	1.9	1.8	2.0	1.8	1.6	1.6	1.7	1.8	2.0	1.9	1.8	1.8	1.8	1.9	2.1	2.2	2.4	2.8
1968	3.0	2.3	2.0	2.0	2.2	2.0	1.7	1.8	1.9	2.0	2.2	2.1	2.0	2.1	2.1	2.2	2.4	2.6	2.8	3.3
1969	3.1	2.5	2.2	2.2	2.4	2.2	2.0	2.0	2.1	2.3	2.5	2.4	2.4	2.4	2.5	2.6	2.9	3.1	3.4	3.8
1970	3.2	2.6	2.3	2.3	2.5	2.3	2.2	2.2	2.3	2.5	2.7	2.6	2.6	2.7	2.8	2.9	3.2	3.4	3.7	4.1
1971	3.2	2.6	2.4	2.4	2.5	2.4	2.2	2.3	2.4	2.6	2.7	2.7	2.7	2.7	2.8	3.0	3.2	3.4	3.6	4.0
1972	3.2	2.7	2.4	2.4	2.6	2.4	2.3	2.3	2.4	2.6	2.7	2.7	2.7	2.8	2.9	3.0	3.2	3.4	3.6	3.9
1973	3.4	2.9	2.6	2.6	2.8	2.7	2.6	2.6	2.8	2.9	3.1	3.1	3.1	3.2	3.3	3.4	3.7	3.9	4.1	4.4
1974	3.7	3.2	3.0	3.0	3.2	3.1	3.0	3.1	3.2	3.4	3.5	3.6	3.6	3.7	3.9	4.0	4.3	4.6	4.8	5.2
1975	3.8	3.3	3.1	3.1	3.3	3.2	3.1	3.2	3.4	3.5	3.7	3.7	3.8	3.9	4.1	4.2	4.5	4.7	5.0	5.4
1976	3.8	3.4	3.2	3.2	3.4	3.3	3.2	3.3	3.4	3.6	3.8	3.8	3.8	4.0	4.1	4.3	4.5	4.8	5.0	5.3
1977	3.9	3.5	3.3	3.3	3.5	3.4	3.3	3.4	3.6	3.7	3.9	3.9	4.0	4.1	4.2	4.4	4.7	4.9	5.1	5.4
1978	4.1	3.7	3.5	3.5	3.7	3.6	3.5	3.6	3.8	3.9	4.1	4.2	4.2	4.3	4.5	4.7	4.9	5.1	5.4	5.7
1979	4.3	3.9	3.8	3.8	4.0	3.9	3.9	4.0	4.1	4.3	4.5	4.5	4.6	4.8	4.9	5.1	5.4	5.6	5.9	6.2
1980	4.5	4.2	4.0	4.1	4.3	4.2	4.2	4.3	4.4	4.6	4.8	4.9	4.9	5.1	5.3	5.5	5.7	6.0	6.2	6.6
1981	4.7	4.3	4.2	4.2	4.4	4.4	4.3	4.4	4.6	4.8	4.9	5.0	5.1	5.3	5.4	5.6	5.9	6.1	6.4	6.7
1982	4.6	4.3	4.2	4.2	4.4	4.3	4.3	4.4	4.5	4.7	4.9	5.0	5.1	5.2	5.4	5.5	5.8	6.0	6.2	6.5
1983	4.6	4.3	4.2	4.2	4.4	4.3	4.3	4.4	4.5	4.7	4.9	4.9	5.0	5.1	5.3	5.5	5.7	5.9	6.1	6.4
1984	4.6	4.3	4.1	4.2	4.4	4.3	4.3	4.4	4.5	4.7	4.8	4.9	5.0	5.1	5.2	5.4	5.6	5.8	6.0	6.3
1985	4.6	4.3	4.1	4.2	4.3	4.3	4.3	4.4	4.5	4.6	4.8	4.9	4.9	5.0	5.2	5.3	5.5	5.7	5.9	6.1
1986	4.5	4.2	4.1	4.1	4.3	4.2	4.2	4.3	4.4	4.5	4.7	4.7	4.8	4.9	5.0	5.2	5.4	5.5	5.7	5.9
1987	4.5	4.2	4.1	4.1	4.3	4.2	4.2	4.3	4.4	4.5	4.7	4.7	4.8	4.9	5.0	5.1	5.3	5.5	5.6	5.8
1988	4.5	4.2	4.1	4.1	4.3	4.2	4.2	4.3	4.4	4.5	4.7	4.7	4.8	4.9	5.0	5.1	5.3	5.4	5.6	5.8
1989	4.5	4.2	4.1	4.1	4.3	4.2	4.2	4.3	4.4	4.5	4.7	4.7	4.8	4.9	5.0	5.1	5.3	5.4	5.6	5.7
1990	4.5	4.2	4.1	4.2	4.3	4.3	4.2	4.3	4.4	4.6	4.7	4.8	4.8	4.9	5.0	5.1	5.3	5.4	5.6	5.8

Table C-7 (Page 4 of 6)

Inflation
Rates of Return for all holding periods
Percent per annum compounded annually

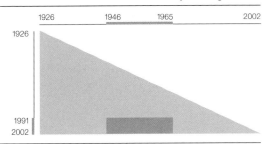

From 1926 to 2002

To the end of	From the beginning of																			
	1946	1947	1948	1949	1950	1951	1952	1953	1954	1955	1956	1957	1958	1959	1960	1961	1962	1963	1964	1965
1991	4.5	4.2	4.1	4.1	4.3	4.3	4.2	4.3	4.4	4.5	4.7	4.7	4.8	4.8	5.0	5.1	5.2	5.4	5.5	5.7
1992	4.5	4.2	4.1	4.1	4.3	4.2	4.2	4.3	4.4	4.5	4.6	4.7	4.7	4.8	4.9	5.0	5.1	5.3	5.4	5.6
1993	4.4	4.2	4.1	4.1	4.2	4.2	4.1	4.2	4.3	4.4	4.6	4.6	4.6	4.7	4.8	4.9	5.1	5.2	5.3	5.5
1994	4.4	4.1	4.0	4.1	4.2	4.2	4.1	4.2	4.3	4.4	4.5	4.5	4.6	4.7	4.8	4.9	5.0	5.1	5.2	5.4
1995	4.4	4.1	4.0	4.0	4.2	4.1	4.1	4.2	4.2	4.4	4.5	4.5	4.5	4.6	4.7	4.8	4.9	5.0	5.1	5.3
1996	4.3	4.1	4.0	4.0	4.1	4.1	4.1	4.1	4.2	4.3	4.4	4.5	4.5	4.6	4.7	4.8	4.9	5.0	5.1	5.2
1997	4.3	4.0	3.9	4.0	4.1	4.0	4.0	4.1	4.2	4.3	4.4	4.4	4.4	4.5	4.6	4.7	4.8	4.9	5.0	5.1
1998	4.2	4.0	3.9	3.9	4.0	4.0	4.0	4.0	4.1	4.2	4.3	4.3	4.4	4.4	4.5	4.6	4.7	4.8	4.9	5.0
1999	4.2	4.0	3.9	3.9	4.0	4.0	3.9	4.0	4.1	4.2	4.3	4.3	4.3	4.4	4.5	4.5	4.6	4.7	4.8	4.9
2000	4.2	3.9	3.9	3.9	4.0	4.0	3.9	4.0	4.1	4.2	4.2	4.3	4.3	4.4	4.4	4.5	4.6	4.7	4.8	4.9
2001	4.1	3.9	3.8	3.8	3.9	3.9	3.9	3.9	4.0	4.1	4.2	4.2	4.2	4.3	4.4	4.4	4.5	4.6	4.7	4.8
2002	4.1	3.9	3.8	3.8	3.9	3.9	3.8	3.9	4.0	4.1	4.1	4.2	4.2	4.3	4.3	4.4	4.5	4.6	4.6	4.7

Table C-7 (Page 5 of 6)

Inflation
Rates of Return for all holding periods
Percent per annum compounded annually

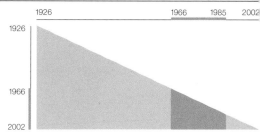

from 1926 to 2002

To the end of	1966	1967	1968	1969	1970	1971	1972	1973	1974	1975	1976	1977	1978	1979	1980	1981	1982	1983	1984	1985
1966	3.4																			
1967	3.2	3.0																		
1968	3.7	3.9	4.7																	
1969	4.3	4.6	5.4	6.1																
1970	4.5	4.8	5.4	5.8	5.5															
1971	4.3	4.5	4.9	5.0	4.4	3.4														
1972	4.2	4.3	4.6	4.6	4.1	3.4	3.4													
1973	4.8	5.0	5.3	5.4	5.2	5.2	6.1	8.8												
1974	5.6	5.9	6.3	6.5	6.6	6.9	8.1	10.5	12.2											
1975	5.7	6.0	6.4	6.6	6.7	6.9	7.8	9.3	9.6	7.0										
1976	5.6	5.9	6.2	6.4	6.4	6.6	7.2	8.2	8.0	5.9	4.8									
1977	5.7	5.9	6.2	6.4	6.4	6.6	7.1	7.9	7.7	6.2	5.8	6.8								
1978	6.0	6.2	6.5	6.7	6.7	6.9	7.4	8.1	7.9	6.9	6.9	7.9	9.0							
1979	6.5	6.7	7.0	7.3	7.4	7.6	8.1	8.8	8.8	8.1	8.4	9.7	11.1	13.3						
1980	6.9	7.1	7.4	7.7	7.8	8.1	8.6	9.3	9.3	8.8	9.2	10.3	11.6	12.9	12.4					
1981	7.0	7.2	7.6	7.8	7.9	8.1	8.6	9.2	9.3	8.9	9.2	10.1	10.9	11.5	10.7	8.9				
1982	6.8	7.0	7.3	7.5	7.6	7.8	8.2	8.7	8.7	8.2	8.4	9.0	9.5	9.6	8.3	6.4	3.9			
1983	6.6	6.8	7.1	7.2	7.3	7.5	7.8	8.2	8.2	7.7	7.8	8.2	8.5	8.4	7.2	5.5	3.8	3.8		
1984	6.5	6.7	6.9	7.0	7.1	7.2	7.5	7.9	7.8	7.3	7.4	7.7	7.8	7.6	6.5	5.1	3.9	3.9	4.0	
1985	6.4	6.5	6.7	6.8	6.9	7.0	7.2	7.5	7.4	7.0	7.0	7.3	7.3	7.1	6.1	4.8	3.8	3.8	3.9	3.8
1986	6.1	6.2	6.4	6.5	6.5	6.6	6.8	7.1	6.9	6.5	6.5	6.6	6.6	6.3	5.3	4.2	3.3	3.2	2.9	2.4
1987	6.0	6.2	6.3	6.4	6.4	6.5	6.7	6.9	6.8	6.3	6.3	6.4	6.4	6.1	5.2	4.2	3.5	3.4	3.3	3.1
1988	6.0	6.1	6.2	6.3	6.3	6.4	6.5	6.7	6.6	6.2	6.1	6.3	6.2	5.9	5.1	4.3	3.6	3.6	3.5	3.4
1989	5.9	6.0	6.2	6.2	6.2	6.3	6.4	6.6	6.5	6.1	6.0	6.1	6.1	5.8	5.1	4.3	3.7	3.7	3.7	3.7
1990	5.9	6.0	6.1	6.2	6.2	6.3	6.4	6.6	6.5	6.1	6.0	6.1	6.1	5.8	5.2	4.5	4.0	4.0	4.1	4.1
1991	5.8	5.9	6.0	6.1	6.1	6.1	6.2	6.4	6.3	5.9	5.9	5.9	5.9	5.6	5.0	4.4	3.9	3.9	3.9	3.9
1992	5.7	5.8	5.9	5.9	5.9	6.0	6.1	6.2	6.1	5.7	5.7	5.7	5.7	5.4	4.8	4.2	3.8	3.8	3.8	3.8
1993	5.6	5.7	5.8	5.8	5.8	5.8	5.9	6.0	5.9	5.6	5.5	5.6	5.5	5.2	4.7	4.1	3.7	3.7	3.7	3.7
1994	5.5	5.6	5.7	5.7	5.7	5.7	5.8	5.9	5.8	5.4	5.4	5.4	5.3	5.1	4.6	4.0	3.6	3.6	3.6	3.6
1995	5.4	5.5	5.5	5.6	5.5	5.6	5.6	5.7	5.6	5.3	5.2	5.2	5.2	4.9	4.4	3.9	3.6	3.5	3.5	3.5
1996	5.3	5.4	5.5	5.5	5.5	5.5	5.6	5.6	5.5	5.2	5.1	5.1	5.1	4.8	4.4	3.9	3.6	3.5	3.5	3.5
1997	5.2	5.3	5.3	5.4	5.3	5.3	5.4	5.5	5.3	5.1	5.0	5.0	4.9	4.7	4.2	3.8	3.4	3.4	3.4	3.3
1998	5.1	5.1	5.2	5.2	5.2	5.2	5.3	5.3	5.2	4.9	4.8	4.8	4.7	4.5	4.1	3.6	3.3	3.3	3.3	3.2
1999	5.0	5.1	5.1	5.1	5.1	5.1	5.2	5.2	5.1	4.8	4.7	4.7	4.6	4.4	4.0	3.6	3.3	3.3	3.2	3.2
2000	5.0	5.0	5.1	5.1	5.1	5.0	5.1	5.2	5.0	4.8	4.7	4.7	4.6	4.4	4.0	3.6	3.3	3.3	3.2	3.2
2001	4.9	4.9	5.0	5.0	4.9	4.9	5.0	5.0	4.9	4.6	4.6	4.5	4.5	4.3	3.9	3.5	3.2	3.2	3.1	3.1
2002	4.8	4.8	4.9	4.9	4.9	4.8	4.9	4.9	4.8	4.6	4.5	4.5	4.4	4.2	3.8	3.4	3.2	3.1	3.1	3.1

Table C-7 (Page 6 of 6)

Inflation
Rates of Return for all holding periods
Percent per annum compounded annually

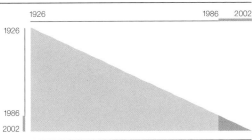

from 1926 to 2002

To the end of	From the beginning of 1986	1987	1988	1989	1990	1991	1992	1993	1994	1995	1996	1997	1998	1999	2000	2001	2002
1986	1.1																
1987	2.8	4.4															
1988	3.3	4.4	4.4														
1989	3.6	4.5	4.5	4.6													
1990	4.1	4.9	5.1	5.4	6.1												
1991	4.0	4.5	4.6	4.6	4.6	3.1											
1992	3.8	4.3	4.2	4.2	4.0	3.0	2.9										
1993	3.7	4.0	4.0	3.9	3.7	2.9	2.8	2.7									
1994	3.6	3.9	3.8	3.7	3.5	2.8	2.8	2.7	2.7								
1995	3.5	3.7	3.6	3.5	3.3	2.8	2.7	2.7	2.6	2.5							
1996	3.4	3.7	3.6	3.5	3.3	2.9	2.8	2.8	2.8	2.9	3.3						
1997	3.3	3.5	3.4	3.3	3.1	2.7	2.6	2.6	2.6	2.5	2.5	1.7					
1998	3.2	3.3	3.2	3.1	3.0	2.6	2.5	2.4	2.4	2.3	2.2	1.7	1.6				
1999	3.1	3.3	3.2	3.1	2.9	2.6	2.5	2.5	2.4	2.4	2.3	2.0	2.1	2.7			
2000	3.1	3.3	3.2	3.1	3.0	2.7	2.6	2.6	2.6	2.5	2.5	2.3	2.6	3.0	3.4		
2001	3.0	3.2	3.1	3.0	2.9	2.6	2.5	2.5	2.4	2.4	2.4	2.2	2.3	2.5	2.5	1.6	
2002	3.0	3.1	3.0	2.9	2.8	2.5	2.5	2.5	2.4	2.4	2.4	2.2	2.3	2.5	2.4	2.0	2.4

Volatility\ˌvä-lə-'ti-lə-tē\
1: The extent to which an asset's
returns fluctuate from period to
period.

Glossary

IbbotsonAssociates

Glossary

American Stock Exchange (AMEX)

One of the largest stock exchanges in the U.S. Securities traded on this exchange are generally of small to medium-size companies.

Arbitrage Pricing Theory (APT)

A model in which multiple betas and multiple risk premia are used to generate the expected return of a security.

Arithmetic Mean Return

A simple average of a series of returns.

Asset Class

A grouping of securities with similar characteristics and properties. As a group, these securities will tend to react in a specific way to economic factors (e.g., stocks, bonds, and real estate are all asset classes).

Balanced Mutual Fund

Fund that seeks both income and capital appreciation by investing in a generally fixed combination of stocks and bonds.

Basic Series

The seven primary time series representing Stocks, Bonds, Bills and Inflation: large company stocks, small company stocks, long-term corporate bonds, long-term government bonds, intermediate-term government bonds, U.S. Treasury bills, and inflation.

Beta

The systematic risk of a security as estimated by regressing the security's returns against the market portfolio's returns. The slope of the regression is beta.

Book-to-Market Ratio

The ratio of total book value to total market capitalization. Value companies have a high book-to-market ratio, while growth companies have a low book-to-market ratio.

Callable Bonds

Bonds that the issuer has the right to redeem (or call) prior to maturity at a specified price.

Capital Appreciation Return

The component of total return which results from the price change of an asset class over a given period.

Capital Asset Pricing Model (CAPM)

A model in which the cost of capital for any security or portfolio of securities equals the riskless rate plus a risk premium that is proportionate to the amount of systematic risk of the security or portfolio.

Convexity

The property of a bond that its price does not change in proportion to changes in its yield. A bond with positive convexity will rise in price faster than the rate at which yields decline, and will fall in price slower than the rate at which yields rise.

Correlation Coefficient

The degree of association or strength between two variables. A value of +1 indicates a perfectly positive relationship, –1 indicates a perfectly inverse relationship, and 0 indicates no relationship between the variables.

Cost of Capital

The discount rate which should be used to derive the present value of an asset's future cash flows.

Coupon

The periodic interest payment on a bond.

Currency Risk

The risk of losing money when gains and losses are exchanged from foreign currencies into U.S. dollars. Also known as exchange rate risk.

Decile

One of 10 portfolios formed by ranking a set of securities by some criteria and dividing them into 10 equally populated subsets. The New York Stock Exchange market capitalization deciles are formed by ranking the stocks traded on the Exchange by their market capitalization.

Derived Series

The components or elemental parts of the returns of the seven primary Stocks, Bonds, Bills, and Inflation asset classes. The two categories of derived series are: risk premia, or payoffs for taking various types of risk, and inflation-adjusted asset returns.

Discount Rate

The rate used to convert a series of future cash flows to a single present value.

Dow Jones Industrial Average

The oldest stock price index beginning in 1884 with 11 stocks currently consisting of 30 representative large stocks.

Duration (Macauley Duration)

The weighted average term-to-maturity of a security's cash flows. The weights are the present values of each cash flow as a percentage of the present value of all cash flows.

Economic Modeling

A type of Monte Carlo simulation that involves modeling the movements of the yield curve through time and then layering on various equity and fixed income risk premia to derive returns.

Efficient Frontier

The set of portfolios that provides the highest expected returns for their respective risk levels. The efficient frontier is calculated for a given set of assets with estimates of expected return and standard deviation for each asset, and a correlation coefficient for each pair of asset returns.

Europe Stocks

Morgan Stanley Capital International Europe Index.

FF All Growth Stocks

A portfolio of stocks constructed by setting a book-to-market ratio cutoff at the bottom 30 percent of NYSE stocks and selecting all NYSE, AMEX, and NASDAQ stocks with a book-to-market ratio lower than the cutoff. Data supplied by Eugene Fama and Ken French.

FF All Value Stocks

A portfolio of stocks constructed by setting a book-to-market ratio cutoff at the top 30 percent of NYSE stocks and selecting all NYSE, AMEX, and NASDAQ stocks with a book-to-market ratio higher than the cutoff. Data supplied by Eugene Fama and Ken French.

FF Large Growth Stocks

A portfolio of stocks constructed by setting a book-to-market ratio cutoff at the bottom 30 percent of NYSE stocks and a market capitalization cutoff at the median of NYSE stocks and selecting all NYSE, AMEX, and NASDAQ stocks with a book-to-market ratio lower than the book-to-market cutoff and a market capitalization greater than the market capitalization cutoff. Data supplied by Eugene Fama and Ken French.

FF Large Value Stocks

A portfolio of stocks constructed by setting a book-to-market ratio cutoff at the top 30 percent of NYSE stocks and a market capitalization cutoff at the median of NYSE stocks and selecting all NYSE, AMEX, and NASDAQ stocks with a book-to-market ratio higher than the book-to-market cutoff and a market capitalization greater than the market capitalization cutoff. Data supplied by Eugene Fama and Ken French.

FF Small Growth Stocks

A portfolio of stocks constructed by setting a book-to-market ratio cutoff at the bottom 30 percent of NYSE stocks and a market capitalization cutoff at the median of NYSE stocks and selecting all NYSE, AMEX, and NASDAQ stocks with a book-to-market ratio lower than the book-to-market cutoff and a market capitalization smaller than the market capitalization cutoff. Data supplied by Eugene Fama and Ken French.

FF Small Value Stocks

A portfolio of stocks constructed by setting a book-to-market ratio cutoff at the top 30 percent of NYSE stocks and a market capitalization cutoff at the median of NYSE stocks and selecting all NYSE, AMEX, and NASDAQ stocks with a book-to-market ratio higher than the book-to-market cutoff and a market capitalization smaller than the market capitalization cutoff. Data supplied by Eugene Fama and Ken French.

Geometric Mean Return

The compound rate of return. The geometric mean of a return series is a measure of the actual average performance of a portfolio over a given time period.

Histogram

A bar graph in which the frequency of occurrence for each class of data is represented by the relative height of the bars.

IA All Growth Stocks

A portfolio of stocks constructed using the lagged market capitalization-weighted returns of the large-, mid-, small-, and micro-cap growth series.

IA All Value Stocks

A portfolio of stocks constructed using the lagged market capitalization-weighted returns of the large-, mid-, small-, and micro-cap value series.

IA Large-cap Growth Stocks

A portfolio of stocks constructed by first selecting deciles 1-2 of the NYSE universe. Once these breakpoints are established, similar-sized AMEX and NASDAQ companies are assigned to the corresponding portfolios. The companies are then ranked by book-to-market, creating a growth portfolio (low B/M) where the total market capitalization of the growth and value indices are equal within each portfolio.

IA Large-cap Value Stocks

A portfolio of stocks constructed by first selecting deciles 1-2 of the NYSE universe. Once these breakpoints are established, similar-sized AMEX and NASDAQ companies are assigned to the corresponding portfolios. The companies are then ranked by book-to-market, creating a value portfolio (high B/M) where the total market capitalization of the growth and value indices are equal within each portfolio.

IA Micro-cap Growth Stocks

A portfolio of stocks constructed by first selecting deciles 9-10 of the NYSE universe. Once these breakpoints are established, similar-sized AMEX and NASDAQ companies are assigned to the corresponding portfolios. The companies are then ranked by book-to-market, creating a growth portfolio (low B/M) where the total market capitalization of the growth and value indices are equal within each portfolio.

IA Micro-cap Value Stocks

A portfolio of stocks constructed by first selecting deciles 9-10 of the NYSE universe. Once these breakpoints are established, similar-sized AMEX and NASDAQ companies are assigned to the corresponding portfolios. The companies are then ranked by book-to-market, creating a value portfolio (high B/M) where the total market capitalization of the growth and value indices are equal within each portfolio.

IA Mid-cap Growth Stocks

A portfolio of stocks constructed by first selecting deciles 3-5 of the NYSE universe. Once these breakpoints are established, similar-sized AMEX and NASDAQ companies are assigned to the corresponding portfolios. The companies are then ranked by book-to-market, creating a growth portfolio (low B/M) where the total market capitalization of the growth and value indices are equal within each portfolio.

IA Mid-cap Value Stocks

A portfolio of stocks constructed by first selecting deciles 3-5 of the NYSE universe. Once these breakpoints are established, similar-sized AMEX and NASDAQ companies are assigned to the corresponding portfolios. The companies are then ranked by book-to-market, creating a value portfolio (high B/M) where the total market capitalization of the growth and value indices are equal within each portfolio.

IA Small-cap Growth Stocks

A portfolio of stocks constructed by first selecting deciles 6-8 of the NYSE universe. Once these breakpoints are established, similar-sized AMEX and NASDAQ companies are assigned to the corresponding portfolios. The companies are then ranked by book-to-market, creating a growth portfolio (low B/M) where the total market capitalization of the growth and value indices are equal within each portfolio.

IA Small-cap Value Stocks

A portfolio of stocks constructed by first selecting deciles 6-8 of the NYSE universe. Once these breakpoints are established, similar-sized AMEX and NASDAQ companies are assigned to the corresponding portfolios. The companies are then ranked by book-to-market, creating a value portfolio (high B/M) where the total market capitalization of the growth and value indices are equal within each portfolio.

Income Return

The component of total return which results from a periodic cash flow, such as dividends.

Index Value

The cumulative value of returns on a dollar amount invested. It is used when measuring investment performance and computing returns over non-calendar periods.

Inflation

The rate of change in consumer prices. The Consumer Price Index for All Urban Consumers (CPI-U), not seasonally adjusted, is used to measure inflation. Prior to January 1978, the CPI (as compared with CPI-U) was used. Both inflation measures are constructed by the U.S. Department of Labor, Bureau of Labor Statistics, Washington.

Inflation-Adjusted Returns

Asset class returns in real terms. The inflation-adjusted return of an asset is calculated by geometrically subtracting inflation from the asset's nominal return.

Intermediate-Term Government Bonds

A one-bond portfolio with a maturity near 5 years.

International Stocks

Morgan Stanley Capital International EAFE® (Europe, Australasia, Far East) Index. Represents 21 developed equity markets outside of North America.

Large Company Stocks

The Standard and Poor's 500 Stock Composite Index® (S&P 500).

Liquidity Risk

The risk that an asset will be difficult to buy or sell quickly and in large volume without substantially affecting the asset's price.

Logarithmic Scale

A scale in which equal percentage changes are represented by equal distances.

Lognormal Distribution

The distribution of a random variable whose natural logarithm is normally distributed. A lognormal distribution is skewed so that a higher proportion of possible returns exceed the expected value versus falling short of the expected value. In the lognormal forecasting model, one plus the total return has a lognormal distribution.

Long-Term Corporate Bonds

Salomon Brothers long-term, high-grade corporate bond total return index.

Long-Term Government Bonds

A one-bond portfolio with a maturity near 20 years.

Low-cap Stocks

The portfolio of stocks comprised of the 6-8th deciles of the New York Stock Exchange.

Market Capitalization

The current market price of a security determined by the most recently recorded trade multiplied by the number of issues outstanding of that security. For equities, market capitalization is computed by taking the share price of a stock times the number of shares outstanding.

Mean-Variance Optimization (MVO)

The process of identifying portfolios that have the highest possible return for a given level of risk or the lowest possible risk for a given return. The inputs for MVO are return, standard deviation, and the correlation coefficients of returns for each pair of asset classes.

Micro-cap Stocks

The portfolio of stocks comprised of the 9-10th deciles of the New York Stock Exchange.

Mid-cap Stocks

The portfolio of stocks comprised of the 3-5th deciles of the New York Stock Exchange.

Monte Carlo Simulation

A technique that starts with a set of assumptions about the estimated mean, standard deviation, and correlations for a set of asset classes or investments. These assumptions are used to randomly generate hundreds of possible future return scenarios. These returns can then be used in conjunction with a client's year-by-year cash flows, taxes, asset allocation, and financial product selections. A large number of possible "financial lives" for the client are produced.

National Association of Securities Dealers Automated Quotation System (NASDAQ)

A computerized system showing current bid and asked prices for stocks traded on the Over-the-Counter market, as well as some New York Stock Exchange listed stocks.

New York Stock Exchange (NYSE)

The largest and oldest stock exchange in the United States, founded in 1792.

Non-Parametric

A type of Monte Carlo simulation that uses purely historical data.

Over-the-Counter Market (OTC)

A market in which assets are not traded on an organized exchange like the New York Stock Exchange, but rather through various dealers or market makers who are linked electronically.

Pacific Stocks

Morgan Stanley Capital International Pacific Index.

Parametric

A type of Monte Carlo simulation that is based on the mean, standard deviation, and correlations for the assets being forecast. These are the parameters that give this method its name. Once these parameters are set, a computer program is used to generate random samples from the bell curve that these parameters define.

Price-Weighted Index

An index in which component stocks are weighted by their price. Thus, higher-priced stocks have a greater percentage impact on the index than lower-priced stocks.

Quintile

One of 5 portfolios formed by ranking a set of securities by some criteria and dividing them into 5 equally populated subsets. The micro-cap stocks are a market capitalization quintile.

R-squared

Measures the "goodness of fit" of the regression line and describes the percentage of variation in the dependent variable that is explained by the independent variable. The R-squared measure may vary from zero to one.

Return

see Total Return

Risk

The extent to which an investment is subject to uncertainty. Risk may be measured by standard deviation.

Riskless Rate of Return

The return on a riskless investment; it is the rate of return an investor can obtain without taking market risk.

Risk Premium

The reward which investors require to accept the uncertain outcomes associated with securities. The size of the risk premium will depend upon the type and extent of the risk.

Rolling Period Returns

A series of overlapping contiguous periods of returns defined by the frequency of the data

under examination. In examining 5-year rolling periods of returns for annual data that starts in 1970, the first rolling period would be 1970–1974, the second rolling period would be 1971–1975, the third rolling period would be 1972–1976, etc.

Rolling Period Standard Deviation

A series of overlapping contiguous periods of standard deviations defined by the frequency of the data under examination. In examining 5-year rolling periods of standard deviation for annual data that starts in 1970, the first rolling period would be 1970–1974, the second rolling period would be 1971–1975, the third rolling period would be 1972–1976, etc.

Serial Correlation (Autocorrelation)

The degree to which the return of a given series is related from period to period. A serial correlation near +1 or -1 indicates that returns are predictable from one period to the next; a serial correlation near zero indicates returns are random or unpredictable.

Small Company Stocks

A portfolio of stocks represented by the fifth capitalization quintile of stocks on the NYSE for 1926–1981. For 1982 to March 2001, the series is represented by the Dimensional Fund Advisors (DFA) Small Company 9/10 Fund and the DFA Micro Cap Fund thereafter.

S&P 500®

Stock index including 500 of the largest stocks (in terms of stock market value) in the United States representing 88 separate industries. Prior to 1957, it consisted of 90 of the largest stocks.

Standard Deviation

A measure of the dispersion of returns of an asset, or the extent to which returns vary from the arithmetic mean. It represents the volatility or risk of an asset. The greater the degree of dispersion, the greater the risk associated with the asset.

Systematic Risk

The risk that is unavoidable according to CAPM. It is the risk that is common to all risky securities and cannot be eliminated through diversification. The amount of an asset's systematic risk is measured by its beta.

Total Return

A measure of performance of an asset class over a designated time period. It is comprised of income return, reinvestment of income return and capital appreciation return components.

Treasury Bills

A one-bill portfolio containing, at the beginning of each month, the bill having the shortest maturity not less than one month.

Unsystematic Risk

The portion of total risk specific to an individual security that can be avoided through diversification.

Volatility

The extent to which an asset's returns fluctuate from period to period.

World Stocks

Morgan Stanley Capital International World Index.

Yield

The yield to maturity is the internal rate of return that equates the bond's price with the stream of cash flows promised to the bondholder. The yield on a stock is the percentage rate of return paid in dividends.

Stocks, Bonds, Bills,
and Inflation

G
A
L
C
M
D
R

Index

IbbotsonAssociates

Index

M

IBBOTSON INVESTMENT TOOLS + RESOURCES

SBBI® Report Subscriptions

Receive the most up-to-date data available when you subscribe to our SBBI reports on a monthly, quarterly or semi-annual basis. The SBBI reports contain year-to-date data on a calendar year basis. These reports feature:

- Updated returns and index values available on a monthly basis for six U.S. asset classes plus inflation.
- Inflation-adjusted returns and index values plus other derived series.
- Quarterly updates to the Stocks, Bonds, Bills, and Inflation index graph.
- Market commentary on a semi-annual basis.
- Prompt delivery of time-sensitive market data via fax.
- All report subscriptions include a 2003 Classic Edition Yearbook and can begin at any time throughout the year.

SBBI Classic Edition Yearbook with Monthly Reports* $695
SBBI Classic Edition Yearbook with Quarterly Reports** $280
SBBI Classic Edition Yearbook with Semi-Annual Report*** $160

The Cost of Capital Center Web Site

Visit Ibbotson's enhanced valuation web site, The Cost of Capital Center, where you can conveniently purchase cost of capital information online. Located at **http://www.ibbotson.com**, the site enables you to purchase Cost of Capital Quarterly analysis on over 300 industries, purchase individual company betas from the Beta Book database of over 5,000 companies, and purchase risk premia and company tax rate reports.

2003 Cost of Capital Yearbook

Providing data on over 300 industries, the Cost of Capital Yearbook is an invaluable reference for anyone performing discounted cash flow analysis. The yearbook contains critical statistics you need to analyze corporations and industries and includes:

- Five separate measures of cost of equity.
- Weighted average cost of capital.
- Detailed statistics for sales, profitability, capitalization, beta, multiples, ratios, equity returns and capital structure.

Published annually, the Cost of Capital Yearbook is updated with data through March 2003. For the most frequent data available, subscribe to the Cost of Capital Yearbook with Cost of Capital Quarterly™ updates.

Cost of Capital Yearbook with 3 Quarterly Updates $995
Cost of Capital Yearbook $395 (Shipped in June)

* Last report ships in December with data through November.
** Last report ships in October with data through September.
*** Report ships in July with data through June.

Ibbotson Presentation Materials

Ibbotson Sales Presentations features Ibbotson charts and presentations packaged three ways—in Microsoft PowerPoint as a complete Asset Allocation Library or as individual Sales Presentation Modules, or individually as 8½" x 11" laminated prints of our 15 most popular graphs.

Asset Allocation Library $800
Sales Presentation Module $100 each
Ibbotson Select Charts $25 each

2003 Stocks, Bonds, Bills, and Inflation® Valuation Edition Yearbook

Since its introduction in 1999, the SBBI Valuation Edition has earned a reputation as the industry standard in valuation reference materials. Filled with real world examples and useful graphs to illustrate the analyses, the SBBI Valuation Edition will help you make the most informed decisions in your cost of capital estimation.

The Valuation Edition covers the topics that come up most often when performing valuation analysis, including:

- Tables that enable you to calculate equity risk premia and size premia for any time period.
- Evidence of size premia by industry.
- Alternative methods of calculating equity risk premia, size premia and beta.
- New developments in the field of cost of capital estimation.
- Problems and possible solutions in estimating the cost of capital for international markets.

The Valuation Edition also contains an easy-to-understand overview and comparison of the build-up method, CAPM (Capital Asset Pricing Model), Fama-French 3-factor model, and the DCF (discounted cash flow) approach.

2003 SBBI Valuation Edition Yearbook $110

Ibbotson Beta Book

The Beta Book is an invaluable resource for modeling stock performance and accurately pricing securities. With data on over 5,000 companies, the book provides statistics critical for calculating cost of equity with the CAPM and the Fama-French 3-factor model. Employing the most current methods, the Beta Book contains traditional 60-month levered beta calculations, unlevered betas, betas adjusted for thinly traded securities and betas adjusted toward peer group averages. Published semi-annually, the First Edition provides data through December 2002 and the Second Edition provides data through June 2003.

2003 First Edition $625 (Shipped in February)
2003 Second Edition $625 (Shipped in August)
Both Editions $1,000

Ibbotson Software + Data

We have developed a line of software that allows you to discover, understand and present the tradeoffs that must be considered when working toward the right balance between risk and reward for your clients.

Ibbotson Analyst™

Ibbotson Analyst is designed to help you look at the historical behavior of a variety of asset classes. Create graphs, charts and tables of statistical data from as early as 1926 to explore fundamental investment concepts and alternatives, communicate these concepts to clients and present diversified investment choices to clients. Choose from a wide selection of Ibbotson data or import your own. Series are updated monthly via our web site, **www.ibbotson.com.**

First year subscription $1,500

Ibbotson Portfolio Strategist®

Changing client needs and objectives, unique constraints, and a variety of risk tolerances—all these factors must be considered when you are designing, implementing and monitoring asset allocation strategies for your clients. Portfolio Strategist can help you build better portfolios for your clients and help determine the asset mix that offers the best chance of achieving the highest return for a given level of risk.

Portfolio Strategist also integrates seamlessly with Ibbotson Fund Strategist to move from classifying security holdings to recommending an asset allocation to implementing the plan with mutual funds, using the exclusive Ibbotson Security Classifier and Ibbotson Fund Optimizer applications.

First year subscription $1,100

Ibbotson Fund Strategist®

Selecting funds to implement an asset allocation policy can be difficult, especially when you encounter outdated or abbreviated holdings, changing managers and objectives, and most importantly, drifting, shifting or mislabeled styles. Fund Strategist simplifies the process and helps you strengthen your approach to mutual fund selection with the returns-based style analysis in this easy-to-use software tool.

Fund Strategist analysis results are presented in a concise, fact sheet-style format. The full color, one-page fund profiles include descriptive tables and graphs highlighting the fund's style and performance over time. Financial advisors can use the sheets with clients, while mutual fund companies can use them as fund fact sheets with distributors.

Fund Strategist also integrates seamlessly with Ibbotson Portfolio Strategist to move from classifying security holdings to recommending an asset allocation to implementing the plan with mutual funds, using the exclusive Ibbotson Security Classifier and Ibbotson Fund Optimizer.

First year subscription $600

Ibbotson Portfolio Strategist and Ibbotson Fund Strategist

Includes Security Classifier and Fund Optimizer.

First year subscription $1,445

Ibbotson EnCorr™

Designed for money managers, plan sponsors and consultants, the EnCorr software system embodies sophisticated investment concepts within an easy-to-use framework. EnCorr is a modular system that integrates historical data analysis, strategic asset allocation, forecasting, style analysis, performance measurement, portfolio attribution and a wide array of statistical and graphical analyses into one family.

Prices begin at $1,500

For more information or to request a product catalog, call 800 758 3557 or visit our web site at **www.ibbotson.com.**

2004 Yearbook ORDER Form

To Order

Call:	800 758 3557
Fax:	312 616 0404
Web:	**www.ibbotson.com**
Mail:	Ibbotson Associates

225 North Michigan Avenue
Suite 700
Chicago, Illinois 60601-7676
Attn: Order Processing

Item	Price	Quantity	Total
SBBI 2004 Yearbook (PB001-04)	$110		
SBBI 2004 Yearbook and Semi-Annual Report	$160		
SBBI 2004 Yearbook and Quarterly Reports	$280		
SBBI 2004 Yearbook and Monthly Reports	$695		
	Merchandise Total		
	Add applicable sales tax (IL, NY, TX, AZ, CA, OH, Canada)		
	Shipping and Handling		$12.50
	Special delivery surcharge (see table at left)		
	Total Amount		

For delivery outside the United States and Canada, please add $27.50.
For an extra charge, we can expedite delivery to most U.S. and Canadian destinations.
Overnight delivery add $22.50 Express delivery (2-day) add $12.50

code=B3380

Name

Company

Street Address   Suite/Floor

City   State   Zip

Phone Number

Payment Method

○ Check enclosed, payable to:
Ibbotson Associates (in U.S. dollars)
○ American Express   ○ MasterCard
                            ○ Visa

Card Number

Expiration Date

Signature of Authorized Buyer

IbbotsonAssociates